C0-AVV-060

DAVID H. CLARKE
University of Maryland

AND

H. HARRISON CLARKE
University of Oregon

RESEARCH PROCESSES IN PHYSICAL EDUCATION, RECREATION, AND HEALTH

PRENTICE-HALL, INC.

Englewood Cliffs, New Jersey

To

Louise Terani Clarke

Library of Congress Catalog Number: 76-95759

Printed in the United States of America

13-774463-3

Current Printing (last number):

10 9 8 7 6 5 4 3

PRENTICE-HALL INTERNATIONAL, INC., *London*
PRENTICE-HALL OF AUSTRALIA, PTY. LTD., *Sydney*
PRENTICE-HALL OF CANADA, LTD., *Toronto*
PRENTICE-HALL OF INDIA PRIVATE LIMITED, *New Delhi*
PRENTICE-HALL OF JAPAN, INC., *Tokyo*

PREFACE

Although intended for the beginner investigator, *Research Processes in Physical Education, Recreation, and Health* should provide some suggestions for experienced researchers. The various research methods are presented in sufficient detail so that they can be applied by the scientist. Selected completed studies are described throughout in order to illustrate the various research processes considered. The content is sufficient to provide a graduate course in research methods; in addition, an adequate coverage of elementary statistics as related to essential research applications is included.

The book is divided into five parts. Part I, Initial Considerations in Research, contains materials common to all research. Chapter 1, The Importance and Meaning of Research, considers the place of research in our society and in graduate education and the influences that have developed and shaped research in physical education, recreation, and health. Chapter 2, The Problem, deals with locating and defining the research problem, including criteria in selecting the problem, limiting and delimiting the problem, and evolving the problem statement. Chapter 3, Literature Search, presents the need for surveying related literature, major sources of literature, and methods of library reading and note taking.

In Part II, Nonlaboratory Studies, investigations in physical education, recreation, and health that do not require laboratory sources are presented. These studies do not usually require the testing of subjects, the conducting of experiments, and the analysis of quantitative data. The subdivisions of Part II are: Chapter 4, Historical Method; Chapter 5, Philosophical Studies; and Chapter 6, Surveys and Case Studies.

Part III, Statistical Applications, is devoted to statistical computations—interpretations and applications to studies in physical education, recreation, and health. In any scientific research, test data must be analyzed in ways proper to the research design; to do so, a knowledge of statistics is absolutely essential. In this part, the statistical methods are those that can be presented in a beginning course of a term or a semester; some projection is also made into more advanced concepts as mention of them cannot be avoided in considering laboratory research. The chapters are: Chapter 7, Tabulation, Central Tendency, Percentiles; Chapter 8, Measures of Variability; Chapter 9, The Normal Curve; Chapter 10, Reliability and Tests of Significance; Chapter 11, Product-Moment Correlation.

In Part IV, Scientific Laboratory Research, laboratory resources are considered as a formally established laboratory but also as a gymnasium, athletic field, track, or swimming pool when utilized for conducting scientific investigations. Such studies involve the adoption of a study design with appropriate hypotheses, the use of proper tests to measure the essential elements under investigation, and the statistical analyses of these data in appropriate ways. The first chapter in this part, Chapter 12, presents Laboratory and Experimental Research. Methods given are common to the various types of studies considered in subsequent chapters. This practice was adopted in order to avoid unnecessary duplication of methodology. The chapters are devoted to five broad areas of investigation: Chapter 13, Physiology of Exercise; Chapter 14, Motor Learning; Chapter 15, Psychological Studies; Chapter 16, Kinesiological Research; Chapter 17, Growth and Development. In each chapter, the testing instruments unique to the area are evaluated. Illustrated studies are presented, although a review of the literature in each area is not intended; these examples of research studies should help the novice researcher by showing how successful investigators have formulated hypotheses, established experimental designs, applied evaluation procedures, analyzed data, and drawn appropriate conclusions.

Part V, The Research Report, has only one subdivision, Chapter 18, Preparation of the Research Report. This chapter is written primarily for the graduate student undertaking his first research writing. The main topics consider the organization of the thesis, the use of written and oral sources, the construction and use of tables and graphs, forms for footnotes and bibliography, and publication based on the thesis.

D. H. C.
H. H. C.

CONTENTS

CHAPTER 11

Product-moment Correlation **221**

PART IV

LABORATORY RESEARCH 241

CHAPTER 12

Laboratory and Experimental Research **243**

CHAPTER 13

Physiology of Exercise **267**

CHAPTER 14

Motor Learning **304**

CHAPTER 15

Psychological Studies **330**

CHAPTER 16

Kinesiological Research **364**

PART I

INITIAL CONSIDERATIONS IN RESEARCH

In Part I, the initial considerations that are common to all research are presented in three chapters. The importance and meaning of research are presented, including historical and current developments and the influences shaping investigations in physical education, recreation, and health. Criteria to apply in selecting problems for study and processes for evolving the problem statement are included. The need to survey literature germane to the problem area and methods of doing so are indicated. The chapters are: 1, The Importance and Meaning of Research; 2, The Problem; and 3, Literature Search.

CHAPTER 1

The Importance and Meaning of Research

RESEARCH IN OUR CIVILIZATION

Our life is permeated, saturated, and may be even surfeited with research. At Hiroshima, the atomic age was blasted into existence. Now, we have the atomic powered submarine that has sailed under the Arctic polar cap. We have sputniks and satellites, systems-guided aircraft and missiles, and a spaceship is in prospect. Space officials envision establishing communities on the moon in the near future. Society today respects science and readily accepts its findings; but this was not always so.

An Overview

Historically, research in our civilization has been profoundly influenced by the early discoveries. They have exerted tremendous influences upon the way man has lived. It goes without saying that the discovery of fire, the wheel, numbers and the alphabet, paper and the process of printing, the development of metals, agriculture, and the use of steam and electricity have all been milestones in the development and refinement of civilization. More recently has come the use of atomic power and the penetration of outer space, which in a very real sense is the culmination of long years of research and development.

Dr. Frank Porter Graham, President of the University of North Carolina, speaking on "Machines and Ideas in World Cooperation" before an annual meeting of the Department of Higher Education, NEA, stated that close to the center of three great economic transitions of modern times are three mechanisms:

1. Compass. The compass released trade from the narrow confines of navigation routes established and used for thousands of years and made world-wide the great Commercial Revolution. It was two simple but basic ideas that entered into both the substance and the value of the compass: the idea that the earth was round and the idea that the earth was a great magnet.

2. Steam Engine. The steam engine was the dynamic element of the Industrial Revolution, which has changed the way men have worked and lived in the last 175 years more than they had changed before in the preceding 3,000 years. It was based upon the expansive power of latent heat, developed by Professor Joseph Black of the University of Glasgow. "When James Watt took the pure theory from the mind of Joseph Black and rearranged the ideas of the steam engine in his own mind, he rearranged the whole structure of the modern world."

3. Atomic Mechanism. The long-accepted idea that the atom was the irreducible substance of the universe gave way in the last 50 years to the idea that the atom itself was a little universe of whirling bodies of tremendous energy and power. The Atomic Revolution received its revolutionary meaning and source of power from the minds of men and women working quietly in university laboratories.

To the great transitions listed above could be added the development of Space Exploration, which has given a new horizon for man's environment, and, while still in its infancy, has provided insight into the future course of man's accomplishments. Properly designed, the impetus given to space flights could signal the application of a new dimension to old problems. Already such problems are being solved in various laboratories around the world.

The twentieth century has also seen industrial progress of startling proportions with new developments occurring simultaneously along a variety of research fronts.[1] The automobile industry has achieved the status of being the largest manufacturing industry in the country; and it has grown from an estimated one car for every 10,000 people in 1910 to the present ratio of one for every three people. The airplane has progressed from the simple flying machine of World War I to the present high speed, high altitude jets for commercial and military use. Plastics of all kinds have been developed for use in such home and industrial products as packaging, pipes and fittings, and insulation. The widespread acceptance of such synthetic fibers as rayon, nylon, orlon, dacron, and others has transformed the marketing of fabrics. Also, the communications industry has progressed remarkably since World War I, with such innovations as radio, motion pictures, television, radar, and the communications satellites.

It is difficult to place the progress of science in its proper perspective. This is especially the case when one considers the development of the universe

---

[1] Harry A. Kuljian, *Man and the World of Science* (New York: A. S. Barnes and Company, Inc., 1964), p. 99.

and of this planet; the daily contributions of scientists seem small. Yet the following statement takes on special significance relative to the "knowledge spiral" that we are witnessing today.

> Physical changes such as the elevation of a range of mountains take a matter of a million years. Changes of climate are measured in terms of 5,000 years. Technological change, such as from fire to domesticated animals to metallurgy, are 500-year steps . . . . Since the turn of the century, however, we have seen a rate of change unlike anything the world has seen before. Knowledge has doubled each decade. Some 90 percent of all the scientists who have ever lived on this planet are still alive. Within the span of one lifetime we have witnessed the development of electricity, air travel, radio, the automobile, television, antibiotics, atomic energy, and space flight. This is a far cry from 500-year steps.[2]

These observations forcefully emphasize the contention that gigantic technological advances that are being made daily must have profound influences on our lives. Whereas for early man they were few and far between, for modern man they have come with an overwhelming rush. It has been estimated that the advances of 100,000 stone age years is surpassed in a single year now. The upward spiral must indeed be exponential with no end in sight.

Historical Concepts

In the beginning such study as might be termed research was in reality trial and error, perhaps only the astute observation of nature, that resulted in discoveries of far-reaching significance, although a most personal and practical need was the primary stimulus. The details of much of early civilization are lost with the exact accounting being speculative and inconclusive and the subject of interesting legend. Nevertheless, the modern development of science was helped immeasurably by the early ideas expressed, especially in such fields as mathematics, astronomy, physics, and biology. In such social and humanistic sciences as literature, art, and philosophy, the study of the Greek and Roman classics—paintings, poetry, and philosophy—became essential and integral parts of the newer era.

The scientific method was difficult to establish and was hampered by the pronounced lack of interest in natural phenomena in the Middle Ages. The reliance upon the supernatural, the dependence upon the mystical, and

---

[2] William P. Tolley, "What Does it Mean to be Educated?" *Journal of Health, Physical Education and Recreation*, 33, No. 7 (October 1962), 26. Reprinted by permission of the author, and *JOHPER*.

the dominance of religious dogma prevented the full development of a free-thinking society. Medieval practice of witchcraft attested to the non-scientific reliance upon magic and miracles rather than the encouragement of naturalism and experimentation. From this atmosphere, modern science emerged, stimulated in part by two great forces. The most important force perhaps was the intelligence level of the individuals at the time; their insight and perception of reality plus the environment provided a powerful impetus. The second force was the heritage of knowledge and writings left from pagan antiquity, which gave real evidence that scientific activity was not without precedent and that it was possible to have free and independent thinking along many intellectual fronts. These forces, together with the apparent rejection of the medieval outlook and dissatisfaction with that antiquated way of life, gave birth in the sixteenth and seventeenth centuries to the modern period in science.

To suggest that the emergence of free scientific thought was met with universal enthusiasm is to belie the facts. Medieval Christendom usually managed to suppress attempts of scholars whose findings were at variance with the beliefs of the Church or who challenged existing religious doctrine. To experiment was to reject the Divine Being; consequently, such attempts at scientific inquiry were often met with persecution. For instance, Roger Bacon, a thirteenth-century philosopher who stressed the importance of experience as a source of man's knowledge was credited by many as being the first European to emphasize the value of the experiment. Writing on such topics as anatomy, medieval chemistry, and literature, he spent the last years of his life in jail as a "reward" for offering the fruits of his experiments.

Paracelsus (1493–1541), a Swiss alchemist and physician, taught that the activities of the human body were chemical, that health depended upon the proper chemical composition of the organs and fluids, and that the purpose of chemistry was to prepare medicine. He introduced the use of many drugs and was the first to point out the relation between parental goiter deficiencies and resulting cretinism in the child. He was persecuted for his revolutionary ideas.

Copernicus (1473–1543) challenged the teachings of Ptolemy who said that the earth existed as a fixed body in the center of the universe and that the planets and the sun revolved around it every 24 hours. He believed in the heliocentric theory that the sun was the center of the solar system; because of the opposition to his views, he refrained from publishing his findings until on his death bed. His discoveries were so profound that they became the foundation of what is known as the Copernican Revolution; he laid the theoretical framework for the later works of Galileo, Brahe, and Newton.

Galileo (1564–1642) became a follower of the Copernican theory and was the first to use the telescope as a scientific instrument. He found four moons revolving around Jupiter; he discovered that Venus had phases like the Moon; he identified the nature of the Milky Way and first observed the sunspots. He also contradicted the Aristotelian belief that if two bodies of the same substance fell from the same height the heavier body would reach the ground first; that a body twice as heavy as another must reach the earth in half the time. His advocacy of the Copernican theory gained for him an accusation of heresy from the Church.

Subsequently, scientific advances followed in rapid succession. Astronomy led the way followed by physics, chemistry, and the biological sciences. Early research was largely an individual effort, a fact that contrasts markedly with the trend today in all fields. Modern research is more a group effort that is spawned by the tremendous development of scientific talent and fanned by the availability of financial support. It has cultivated a new skill, sometimes called "grantsmanship," which functions not only in industry and government but in the universities as well. Full-time administrative positions have been created with the major responsibility of providing advice and counsel to scientists as they make applications for extramural grants.

Governmental and industrial agencies or private institutes may be funded by more or less primary sources. Universities, on the other hand, provide very little of the total research money spent on campuses from the general operating fund, but they depend upon the faculty to attract grants and be rewarded with research contracts. This practice has increasingly become an important phase of university operation because of the overhead allowances gained from the grants. In fact, many operations of universities today would be drastically affected if a wholesale withdrawal of such fiscal sources were to occur. As a consequence, contracts seem to be for notably larger and larger amounts that all but subsidize some institutions.

No longer is it possible under such conditions for one individual to work alone on his projects, as was formerly the case; rather, he must gather together a number of his colleagues, perhaps a sizable group of graduate students, and very likely he may cut across departmental lines to bring in ancillary disciplines. The principal investigator may then become the administrator of the project, directing the efforts of others, controlling the disbursement of funds, recruiting technicians, and supervising data collection and analysis. He is the "idea man" with the theoretical knowledge and ingenuity to identify the problem and to see that it is attacked properly; he has major responsibility for preparing technical reports and submitting manuscripts for publication, both of which tasks are crucial to the renewal of the grant or the procurement of yet another.

War Effects

Another occurrence of importance that has affected the development of research in our civilization has been the world wars of this century, during which national defense brought forth a wide variety of mechanisms that eventually were put to peaceful civilian use. One can see a blending of the applied and basic research here and quite often the immediate need of the finished product providing a high priority to the completion of the project. Frequently, the results were dramatic and far-reaching.

Gunpowder. Used by the ancient Chinese, the precise composition of gunpowder was not known to the Western world until Roger Bacon discovered it in the thirteenth century. For many centuries, it was used to fire bullets from guns; by the time of World War I, it was utilized as a base for many bombs and torpedoes. Since that time, more powerful explosives have been used, so its direct use in fire power has become limited. Today, gunpowder is used occasionally in industrial and construction projects requiring explosives, although more powerful agents are now available.

Airplane. The history of air travel is long and distinguished. It is difficult to place exactly the date when the possibility of flying first occurred to man, but legends and pictures reveal early concern with such a venture. Roger Bacon suggested the principle of balloon flights with hot air, and Leonardo de Vinci in the fifteenth century made drawings of parachutes, propellers, and helicopters. Since the Wright brothers' flight in 1903, developments have come very rapidly. However, it was not until World War I that airplanes were improved to any considerable extent. What began as crude, open bodies became closed, maneuverable crafts. The valuable use of airplanes for warfare spurred further research and development into aerodynamics that resulted in a number of technological improvements. World War II encouraged research to increase speed and range of flight, and the period saw the construction of some 300,000 airplanes from 1940 to 1945. Now, jet aircraft have moved to the research frontier, and a whole range of developments for civilian and military use are apparent, including the penetration of outer space.

Radar. Early radio discoveries made in the late nineteenth century preceded the actual development of radar, but it became an important military device during World War II. The reflection of radio waves from distant objects permitted the detection of ships and planes, and radar became extremely effective in aiming antiaircraft guns. Research since that time has adapted radar for such uses as detecting channel markers or ice fields in navigation of ships, for highway speed control, and for forecasting the intensity of tornadoes, hurricanes, or other storms.

Atomic Energy. The power of atomic energy was forcefully demonstrated at the close of World War II; since that time, major efforts have been made to convert the ideas developed for destruction to peaceful uses. Such prospects as use for the generation of electricity or for various uses in medicine, industry, and agriculture signal the potentially widespread peaceful employment of atomic energy.

Medicine. The recent world wars have spurred advances in medicine, particularly in physical medicine and rehabilitation of war victims. Battle casualties produced numerous disabilities and provided the impetus for physical therapy following World War I and corrective therapy following World War II. The concept of treatment of orthopedic and neurological conditions underwent radical revision. Recently, the findings of research in space exploration have indicated that certain techniques will be effective in future patient care—monitoring devices to track and record certain physical functions, electronic pacemakers for cardiac patients, and lasers utilized in surgery, to mention a few.

An important lesson can be learned from the beginnings of many research products. They were crude, almost impossible contraptions, but they developed over the years to marvels of intricate and effective mechanisms. In your mind's eye, contrast the first automobiles with today's cars; do the same for airplanes, ships, locomotives, radio, television, and the like.

In *The Doctors Mayo*, Clapsattle described an early form of aseptic surgery thus:

> Walls of the room were lined with large jars full of many kinds of antiseptic solution, each a different color. The operating table was covered with rubber and flanked all around with drain pans to catch pail-fulls of boiled water that were sloshed generously over everything in sight. The surgical staff wore rubber boots.

When the budding scientist in physical education becomes discouraged with the crudity of his instruments, with the ineptness of experimental procedure, with the tentativeness of his generalizations, let him remember what it once was and take heart.

RESEARCH AND GRADUATE EDUCATION

Gradually, Europe emerged from the Middle Ages with a deep and enduring appreciation for the role of the scholar. Universities became true centers of learning with the professor at the center of attention. The European tradition involved more direct contact between professor and student; the student had to satisfy the professor in charge that he had mastered the appropriate subject matter before being granted his degree. Graduate work became research oriented, and the primary concern was the student's competency in the chosen research area; when he had established himself in his specialty he was considered worthy of the degree. Rigorous examinations were the usual test of his competence in the field of knowledge as exhibited by his research. Research in graduate education has, therefore, a long and distinguished history.

Although today in this country graduate education retains some of the traditional aspects of European programs, typically there are too many students for the student-professor ratio to be so favorable. Instead, the student is exposed to a variable sequence of courses that often give more breadth than depth, and a number of credits are reserved for the thesis. In its most favorable light, therefore, it could be argued that research is still the center of graduate work, supported by certain courses that would lead to competence in the subject matter.

The major change to be noted today is the growth in subsidization of research. For the physical sciences, one can see a return to the traditional concept—the professor with the research grant attracting students who wish to concentrate in his field. This concept is contrasted with the present status of the social sciences, which are not subsidized to nearly the same extent as the physical sciences. Physical education, moreover, may very well be at the stage of development today as the physical sciences were at the time of World War I.

RESEARCH AND THE UNIVERSITY

The long established role of the university has been to foster research and scholarly activity as well as to disseminate knowledge. Research can be carried on in other types of institutions, centers, or laboratories, but the university alone blends the two in a partnership that is at once more highly creative and intellectually stimulating than would be possible if they were separate. An opportunity is provided for the student to be on the inside of new developments, to watch new knowledge being obtained and new theories examined, and, more important, to watch the frontiers of knowledge pushed forward. Further, the professor involved will be intellectually stimulated by the inquiring minds of his students; not infrequently, he will be challenged by new and fresh insights into problems that research has spawned. This is the function of the university; it is what characterizes graduate study.

Other institutions and centers conduct research as well. One of the most dramatic new developments in recent years has been the rise of the industrial research laboratory sponsored by manufacturers for the development of specific retail products. Many industries that at one time were solely concerned with the invention of a new sales item, which was almost entirely applied research, now have basic research laboratories with corresponding freedom of activity for the scientist to study current problems without the necessity of providing immediate practical application. Ultimately, industry must realize that the broad base of factual knowledge will culminate in far more sales products than would the restricted, applied research. What is missing in large measure here, however, is the dissemination of knowledge to students of the research worker, who could in turn carry his work forward. This continuation of projects is performed primarily in colleges and universities at the graduate level.

It has sometimes been said that teaching and research are not compatible, that the researcher is far more interested in his research than in his students or his teaching to the extent that his teaching suffers. Such statements seem to have been made more often in the fields of education than in other physical or social sciences, a fact that alone should be worth a closer examination. Unfortunately, however, the fact remains that an undercurrent of mistrust exists relative to the marriage of these two purposes. Possibly such comments should be relegated to the role of a cliché; certainly, the evidence in support of this belief is flimsy and inconclusive. The overwhelming opinion in higher education on university campuses today holds that the most effective and stimulating teacher is the one who is continuously active in research; he is the one who is most prone to have a thorough knowledge of and insight into his field.

A rather practical problem, which concerns the manner in which faculty research is to be evaluated, may be raised at this point. This evaluation is especially difficult in the various fields of education where perfectly straightforward experimental studies in the classical sense are not always undertaken. As will be seen, the measurement of several parameters or the administration of a variety of procedures must often be given to a rather substantial number of subjects. When these subjects are humans, perhaps students, whose lives cannot always be ordered to suit the convenience of the investigator, a number of months may elapse between inauguration and end of data collection. Even the most rigorous time table involving data reduction, analysis, and writing of the paper may require many more months. Thus, the report may not appear in publication for yet another year after data have been collected.

In physical education, this situation is realistic; the evaluation of scholarship should not necessarily be based upon the same criterion as for other sciences. Numbers of reprints of worthy papers, for instance, are certainly indicative of productivity, but for an estimate of true scholarship the extent of activity and involvement in scholarly efforts should also be appraised. When such is not done, serious injustice may result, or, even worse, poor scholarship may actually be encouraged. There is no abundance of long-term studies that review aspects of longevity, training, detraining, growth and development, retention of learning, and other areas of basic concern. The urgency of publication tends to destroy efforts in these directions, particularly on the part of the younger research worker or faculty member, and it encourages a reliance upon the more short-term studies. Pressures of time might justly be placed on the graduate student; however, the professor should be free to make his contribution in the manner of his choice.

If one were to adopt the point of view that research is any activity that broadens or deepens the base of man's knowledge through independent scholarly means, then he must be willing to accept as research any form that is truly creative—that is, it must be new, and it must strive to enhance the future activity of the field. For physical education, much of modern research employs the experimental method, but also pertinent are historical and philosophical techniques. Moreover, a special need exists to consider "creative expression" as an art form in the dance, in much the way it is accepted in departments of art and music. Just how such efforts are to be evaluated may well rest upon the interpretation given to research from one institution to another.

RESEARCH IN PHYSICAL EDUCATION

Graduate Study

The production and dissemination of scholarly knowledge are efforts essential to the field of physical education. This field includes professional content particular to the utilization of its activities, mostly in educational institutions but by no means so confined. Further, this field must include certain portions of such diverse traditional disciplines as anatomy, physiology, physics, chemistry, anthropology, psychology, nutrition, growth and development, and sociology. The focus of attention is on the study of man as an individual engaging in motor performances. Physical education is also inextricably associated with the well-being of man's total organism, his physical fitness, mental alertness, personal-social adjustment, and emotional stability.

A person could be well-educated by ordinary standards in the traditional disciplines and yet be quite ignorant with respect to comprehensive and integrated knowledge of the motor behavior and capabilities of man and to the application of physical activity for organismic effectiveness. The areas of knowledge that are vital to physical education receive haphazard and peripheral treatment, rather than systematic development, since the focus of attention is directed toward the traditional curriculum. Furthermore, physical education over the past century has developed a body of knowledge of its own, which would be largely, if not totally, disregarded if its graduate study and research were allocated and dispersed to other disciplines.

The study of physical education does not consist of the application of the disciplines of anatomy, physiology, psychology, sociology, and the like to the study of physical activity. On the contrary, physical education, as a discipline in its own right, utilizes appropriate aspects of these associated disciplines. The graduate student in physical education will not become a physiologist or an anatomist or a psychologist. Moreover, the emphasis must frequently be placed on special areas within each of these fields, areas that receive little or no attention otherwise.

One may well raise the question: Where is the borderline between physical education and associated disciplines? No simple definitive statement is possible, but examples may be given to illustrate the region of demarcation. For example: What causes oxygen debt is physiology; the role of oxygen debt in various physical performances is physical education. The study of skeletal maturity is anthropology; a consideration of the nature, extent, and significance of skeletal and bodily maturity for physical activity of boys and girls of the same sex and age is physical education. The origin and attachments of muscles are functions of anatomy; the identification of the muscles involved in various physical performances is physical education. How the individual learns is a function of psychology; how this knowledge can be applied to complex motor performances is physical education. Physical fitness is more than freedom from disease and handicap; the physical educator is vitally concerned with strength and stamina and how they may be properly and effectively developed. Cultural anthropologists have long been aware of the role of physical games and sports in all cultures; however, comprehensive treatment of this topic, so intimately related to physical education, does not appear in anthropology textbooks.

It would be unfair to say that scholars in various traditional disciplines feel that it is unimportant to study man as an individual engaging in physical activity. Rather, the neglect is because this aspect is of peripheral rather than of central interest to the scholars in those other fields. Further, the physiologist, the anatomist, and the psychologist do not adequately understand man as an individual engaging in motor performances; in general, they have not studied the relationship of man's muscular and physiological status to his physical fitness, mental alertness, personal-social adjustment, and emotional stability. *They are not scholars of physical education.*

Present Status

Emphasis on research is a definite characteristic of graduate study in physical education. Certainly, evidence exists that most research in this field is done by graduate students. Adequate training in research methods, experimental design, utilization of quantitative methods of treating data, and understanding and evaluation of laboratory testing and research processes are required of doctoral candidates in the more stringent graduate programs in physical education. Adequate resources both of faculty and facilities are available for proper research in physical education at a number of universities. There is no reason to believe that these institutions consider research to be less important for physical education than for other disciplines.

Probably the best way to assess the quality of graduate work in physical education is to determine how effectively its purposes are accomplished. From the standpoint of preparing college teachers and administrators the record is impressive. Many of those who have received doctorates in physical education are serving with distinction in colleges and universities. Hundreds have been called upon by federal, state, and local governments, by the armed services, by industry, business and medicine, by various youth-serving agencies, and by the Veterans Administration for consultation services in the field of their specialization. An appreciable number have achieved eminence as scholars by any definition of that term.

Evidence is available of the acceptance and contribution of graduate research in physical education; many studies have made significant scientific contributions. The following data are presented in support of this contention:

1. Scientific studies in physical education have been conducted in institutions of higher learning since 1861, when the first chair in this field was established at Amherst College. Early scholars were Edward Hitchcock, Amherst College; Dudley A. Sargent, Harvard University; William G. Anderson, Yale University; R. Tait McKenzie, University of Pennsylvania; James H. McCurdy, Springfield College; and others.

2. The *Research Quarterly* has been supported since 1930 by the fields of health, physical education, and recreation. A research council currently with nearly 150 physical education researchers as members has existed since 1942. In the field of publishing, an international scientific monograph series in physical education has been initiated; the first monograph has been written and others are in progress, mostly authored by physical educators; and, physical education scientists compose the editorial board for this series.

3. Many graduate departments of physical education now have well-established, comprehensive research laboratories. Associated with these laboratories are well-prepared and experienced professors with local, national, and international reputations as scientists in this field.

4. As a nonprofit service to the professional fields of health, physical education, and recreation, the University of Oregon has published in microcard form master's degree and doctoral studies completed at many universities and scholarly works out-of-print. The current bulletin contains nearly 2000 titles; over 100 university libraries throughout the United States subscribe to this service, and many others purchase selected titles.

5. Physical education scientists have published in many journals outside their particular field, including those in medicine, rehabilitation,

physiology, psychology, child growth and development, and the like. Such publications are respected throughout the world.

6. A number of physical education scientists have received grants from federal agencies, including the Department of Defense, National Institutes of Health, and the U.S. Office of Education.

7. Physical educators in the United States have played prominent roles in international scientific conferences. This was especially true at the Olympic Games Symposia held in Helsinki (1952), Rome (1960), Tokyo (1964), and Mexico City (1968).

8. Physical education scientists have served jointly with the scientists of other disciplines in the application of research to the solution of human problems. An apt example is the formation of the American College of Sports Medicine, a national branch of an international organization. Many physical educators are fellows who are associated in membership and professional efforts with fellows from medicine and physiology. Physical educators have also worked jointly with orthopedic physicians and other medical specialists in the solution of vital problems pertaining to the prevention and care of athletic injuries.

9. In recent years, athletic performances have been transformed. Skilled techniques and training regimens have been vastly improved; performance standards and records are being constantly improved. Although a number of outstanding coaches and trainers have been effective innovators, physical education scientists have contributed most significantly to these developments.

10. Knowledge developed by physical education scientists has been applied effectively in many ways outside education. For example, physical educators have served as human performance consultants to industry. Physical educators were engaged extensively by the armed forces medical services in the physical reconditioning of battle casualties during World War II; since then, they have been utilized as corrective therapists in Veterans Administration hospitals. For many years, physical educators have been associated with the psychiatric care of patients in mental hospitals. Physical educators have served on the President's Council on Physical Fitness. In connection with their efforts in these and other ways, they have contributed significant research.

NEED FOR RESEARCH TRAINING

The basic premise on which research rests is that through the scholarly investigation of specific subject matter areas the body of knowledge of the various disciplines will be revealed and developed. This is particularly true for physical education, where the extent of the academic discipline is not so widely known outside the field. The subject matter will be defined according to the direction provided by the published research studies. This should not be permitted to occur in a haphazard manner; however, there is serious doubt that any priority for the subjects to be published could be successfully proposed.

The most significant development in research today is the engagement of the university professor in scholarly study. Such participation will have upgrading effects upon his teaching. It will serve to assure that proper research methods will be employed and that subject matter will be developed systematically, at least within the abilities and interests of the faculty member. But perhaps the greatest asset will be the progressive and logical development of the field. Certainly, the reverse can be argued, for with increasing competition in the academic market place, the concern of the thoughtful individual is to support and define his subject matter. The graduate approach today must be through the avenue of scholarly investigation.

This text, therefore, is dedicated to the assumptions that research areas in physical education have been identified, that means available for the solution of many of the problems have been developed, and that training and academic backgrounds of the researchers are adequate for solution of these problems. The preparatory training of laboratory and scientific personnel can be made available for conducting sophisticated research in this field. Such preparation requires the careful blending of major and minor subject matter for the graduate student so that his preparation supports his research problem. This is more vital to the doctoral candidate than to the master's degree student, primarily because of the nature, extent, and scope of the dissertation but also because doctoral degree study provides basic preparatory training for the college and university professor. The doctoral student should be prepared not only for university teaching but also for university research.

At many colleges and universities, too, academic promotions depend largely upon how soon and how well the physical educator is able to blend his teaching and research. This situation is not so crucial for master's degree candidates; for many of them, this degree will be terminal. In such cases, the thesis is frequently not required for the degree, and additional courses and examinations may be substituted. Placed in proper perspective, the master's thesis prepares the graduate student for the doctoral dissertation, and it points toward a greater understanding of the science and discipline of his field.

Related to the graduate program is the less scientific approach to physical education for the students who do not contemplate research careers but who anticipate teaching and administration in public schools or in the service programs of colleges and universities. Even so, a substantial number of these graduate students will still be required to complete an independent research study. Two justifications for this course of action seem valid.

First, the progress of any discipline is dependent in part at least upon the ability of its graduates to be knowledgeable in the current developments of its subject matter. As knowledge is created and theories are developed, not only must a means for dissemination be available but a receptive audience that can read and evaluate the current developments is essential. Inasmuch as all academic fields are becoming more technical and detailed, the need for informed practitioners is readily apparent. The ability to read and to evaluate critically the literature of the field is a primary requisite in physical education.

The second justification stems from observation of the academic trend of our times, which sees more and more younger men and women pursuing graduate work, stimulated perhaps by a desire to improve themselves, either for promotional reasons or for financial gain or both. The short-range view for the young student might be to finish his graduate study as quickly and as easily as possible, but this may be a very hasty decision. With maturity may come a desire to go further in the academic world; a premature determination not to do research might very well place him at a disadvantage later should he desire to undertake further graduate work or contemplate a research or university teaching career.

Thus, the scope of this text must of necessity be directed primarily to the graduate or advanced undergraduate student who is to learn the techniques of research in order to formulate a problem, collect data, analyze data, and, finally, to write the report. In so doing, certain basic elements that permeate most categories of research will be noted, but perhaps more striking will be the realization that a properly formulated problem is a very specific undertaking. The formats may look very familiar when one scans a number of studies, but upon careful inspection the similarities are more apparent than real. This situation is entirely proper because each problem should be mostly original. Certainly, the problems presented are many and varied.

Hopefully, the attainment of a degree will not terminate research; rather, for any field to be a functioning one, the reverse must be true. An exposure to all forms of research may well stimulate a genuine interest in or at least a wide appreciation of the many problems facing physical education.

SUMMARY

This chapter has considered the importance and meaning of research. Discovery and research have profoundly influenced the emergence and development of our civilization from the earliest discoveries to the present utilization of nuclear power. Although the process has been continuous for many centuries, it now occurs with tremendous speed. Science is a dynamic force in today's society.

The long-established role of the university has been to foster research and scholarly activity as well as the dissemination of knowledge. Other institutions and centers conduct research, especially industrial research sponsored by manufacturers for the development of their products. However, the university is unique in the training of research workers. Further, in the fields of health, physical education, and recreation, nearly all research is being conducted at the graduate level of colleges and universities.

The production and the dissemination of scholarly knowledge are essential to the effectiveness of health, physical education, and recreation. These fields contain professional content unique to the utilization of their activities, but they also include elements of such related disciplines as anatomy, physiology, physics, chemistry, anthropology, psychology, nutrition, growth and development, and sociology. Evidence of the acceptance and contributions of graduate research in physical education has been presented plus the enumeration of many studies that have made significant contributions and that have been recognized by scholars in other fields.

CHAPTER 2

The Problem

The delineation of the problem to be solved by research is the first theoretical hurdle to be met by the researcher, and it must be dealt with successfully before outlining research procedure. This chapter provides suggestions that will help the research worker in locating and defining the problem. It is a temptation to suggest that the process of problem formulation can be standardized, but such is not the case. Often it has been said that the experienced research worker has no difficulty finding problems. Indeed, his problem is finding time to pursue all the things that interest him. Fortunately, for the development of scientists in any discipline, problems beget problems. Almost invariably, the solution of one research problem points to numerous side issues that require additional work. This pattern of sustained activity, perhaps followed over a number of years, marks the career of the true researcher.

In the beginning, however, most researchers follow a similar pattern at the graduate level. They are required to develop a research plan, submit it for approval, and then pursue it to completion. All the various steps have to be followed in a sequence—under the guidance of a professor—in accordance with a carefully prepared timetable. Therefore, the premium for many graduate students is the identification of a suitable problem as early as possible in the program. At best this is difficult, and at the master's level it is especially precarious, principally because the degree program covers such a short period of time. If a knowledge of the subject matter is essential, and there is little doubt that this is so, then the thesis topic may require development before the discipline itself is mastered. For the doctoral dissertation, this is not such a severe problem, for the program of study is longer, the subject matter has greater depth, and the student himself is apt to be more mature. In addition, he may already have completed a master's thesis that has provided him with knowledge of the essential ingredients of research and scholarly study. In turn, his research problem will have greater depth, and thus reflect advanced training and theoretical development.

It is a mistake to think of the master's thesis as some sort of substandard problem. Although it may be the student's first research effort, this may mean simply that a more scientifically valid report requires greater attention to detail and closer supervision rather than that the study is a compromise on scientific standards. As a matter of fact, any lessening of essential procedural controls will remove the effort from the category of research altogether. The primary difference between the master's thesis and the doctoral dissertation is in the scope of the study. Typically, the dissertation has greater breadth and/or depth than the thesis; as a result, it takes longer to complete, and is more thorough in the selection of parameters. However, both must be scientifically sound.

LOCATING THE PROBLEM

A number of suggestions are offered that will help the student make an appropriate choice of a research topic. A variety of areas are available where investigation is needed, but it would be at once hopeless, biased, and promptly out-of-date to give a list of specific research topics. The suggestions, then, are given as guides for effective study. They are not intended to be exhaustive, but it is hoped that there is sufficient breadth in the choice that a wide variety of research topics would emerge.

The following suggestions are designed to provide direction in the search for a research problem.

1. Systematically record unsolved problems. This suggestion is intended to be nonspecific, for as the student pursues his study, his professional reading may point out several unsolved problems that could serve as research projects. These should be noted systematically with the source, a few notes of explanation, and perhaps suggestions for solution; add any circumstances that make a particular problem unique, particularly with reference to the type of sample or data obtained.

Class discussion often yields ideas for unsolved problems. The attuned student should make note of any such propositions and immediately prepare brief notes of explanation. If the whole problem is not amenable to solution, perhaps part of it can become a side issue for study. At any rate, a professor will occasionally indicate an area that has not been thoroughly studied. To the conscientious student, these leads are like nuggets of gold, to be seized upon and developed.

Critical thinking is another valuable asset to the researcher; it permeates all the work the scientist does (as will be discussed later when dealing with philosophical research). However, in the earliest stages of problem development, it will be one of the most important assets for the researcher. The ability to analyze critically any field of knowledge and to assess accurately the gaps in theory marks the true scientist. Careful reflection may bring to light research ideas that are worthy of pursuit. Whenever this occurs, these ideas should be noted and briefly developed while still fresh. Too often good ideas are lost when not immediately recorded.

2. Analyze literature in an area or subject field. An analysis of the literature in a particular field is a most important source for research problems, and it is perhaps the one that is most difficult for the beginning student to master. Some of the specific techniques of library work will be discussed in a subsequent chapter, but effective scholarship is accomplished by thoroughly knowing the literature. Obviously, no one person can know everything; therefore, as the student plans his academic course of study, he should emphasize those areas that have the greatest interest for him. In so doing, he can make a series of decisions that will direct his attention to certain portions of the published literature. Important suggestions that can be made here are as follows:

(a) Note the distribution of research completed in the area. Do all facets of the problem seem to be well covered? What gaps exist? Where is the greatest interest?
(b) Discover any trends that may become evident. Have all aspects been investigated? Do deficiencies exist in any of the research completed? Do new avenues of interest appear as possible sources of research?
(c) Examine critiques of a given field. Often key areas of neglect can be ascertained either explicitly or implicitly in critiques of various facets of the field. It may be possible to note deficiencies and strengths in this way.
(d) Analyze statements of needed investigations. Occasionally authors indicate areas or specific studies that are currently needed. If their review is comprehensive, this may be an excellent lead. Quite frequently the writers of theses or dissertations include such a section as a parting gesture to indicate related studies that they feel should be undertaken.

3. Analyze thoroughly an area of special interest. Very closely related to the previous category, the intent here is to recommend that the student select an area of special interest and pursue it diligently to determine the items that require further study. He may intuitively sense that certain aspects are not completely understood, and so his first task is to list the problems that he sees. Next, it is necessary to review completed research to discover gaps in knowledge. This, in all likelihood, will cause the list of problems to grow and will require that a priority be established. When this has been accomplished successfully the last step is to become thoroughly familiar with the research concerning the topic. One literally becomes a scholar in a specialty, and suddenly the problems become all too obvious. This usually requires that a number of revisions be made in the original selection of a topic in light of the more thorough understanding that has occurred from the literature review. The student must be flexible at this point and actually seek out alterations that will make his study sounder. At the same time, he must be prepared to accept the fact that his original idea may not be appropriate for investigation or that it is not an acceptable problem.

4. Study research already completed. The essence of graduate study is in the research literature; the thesis and dissertation reflect the skill of research in graduate programs. The student who is intent on pursuing a basic research problem will find that ideas fostered without at least a working knowledge of the supporting literature frequently are immature and lack sufficient sophistication.

The review of other studies may point to the need for new or slightly different studies or perhaps to other problems of a similar nature. The requirements for student research vary from one institution to another, but one of the characteristics that seems basic to many is the requirement that the study be original. Although not intentioned to abolish this requirement, many scientists feel that this imposes rather unnecessary restrictions on the establishment of theory. There are times when corroboration is necessary in order to have confidence in the state of knowledge; unless additional data are brought to bear upon a particular phenomenon, often the hypotheses must remain unsubstantiated. When independent research efforts agree, this assurety is established. Consequently, a theoretical issue may be approached from several points of view, which, in a sense, reinvestigates the problem. Unless particularly difficult or laborious, the conscientious student will add a new variable or a new approach so that additional information can be obtained at the same time.

5. Examine controversial issues. Controversy may be seen in any number of professional and academic areas; many controversies have proven of interest to the researcher. If the central issue can be clearly defined, it might be attacked in a number of ways so that over a period of time the issue can be resolved. Recently, such issues as competitive athletics for young boys, the Kraus-Weber report, the Hettinger-Müller findings concerning muscular strength improvement, the role of exercise in the reduction of serum cholesterol in the arteries, and the relationship of both to cardiovascular disease have undergone rather extensive investigation. Whether or not all facets of each issue have been adequately solved cannot be determined here, but the reader will recognize a number of studies in each.

Probably, many controversial issues cannot be solved experimentally, for not all such problems can be reduced to specific items. Occasionally, when so reduced, the missing ingredient may be the very one that has been eliminated—namely, the combined effect of all factors. Consider the difficulties encountered in studying the effect of desegregation on educational achievement or the establishment of standards for teacher preparation. It should be recognized that to solve the major complex issues of the day is at best a multidimensional problem; the student in this case needs to make the primary decision on the most appropriate approach for him to take at the time. Such delimitations of research problems will be considered later in this chapter.

6. Become informed of research going on at the university. It is a wise practical suggestion to mention that the student should inform himself of the research currently being undertaken at his university or in his department. With the increasing availability of funds, large-scale research projects may frequently be sponsored and conducted in physical education or in conjunction with other departments. Quite often, graduate students can gain valuable research experience by becoming part of the enterprise, sometimes aiding as a member of the testing or laboratory team or assisting in data reduction and statistical treatment. Even in such situations the student should exercise his initiative and propose a topic that is in line with the objectives of the overall project. This would be of help to both parties, as the project director is committed to completion of the study, and in many instances he would welcome the help of graduate students in developing certain aspects. The student also benefits, as it gives him an opportunity to observe a large and integrated research study and to appreciate the depths of knowledge that are being explored; as a member of the team, he can learn more advanced techniques of measurement and gather data that would otherwise be impossible if he were to function alone. The result of such an approach has much to be commended as a learning research experience.

The graduate student's search of pertinent literature and other processes connected with thesis or dissertation provide him with a unique background from which his own future activity can grow. Much the same can be said for participation in research institutes, where a group of scholars from several disciplines come together to work on multidimensional research studies that are supported by a common thread but held together by rather diverse interests. Quite often facilities, equipment, and funds can be made available to qualified graduate students to work on problems of interest to their field. Financial support of this type is important, for it sometimes makes possible the pursuit of projects too costly for a single department.

7. Consult with members of the faculty. To suggest that students consult with faculty members may be to state the obvious, for it is usually expected that the student will be assigned to an advisor. However, lest this be misinterpreted, the concern is not with the student who follows normal advisory procedures, which at the beginning may only involve course work designations. When the student does not have an approved topic, there is often difficulty; strained relations may develop when a student expects a faculty member to provide the research problem. Although graduate advisors are not noted for their agreement on the approach to advising, the fact remains that the student should exercise caution in approaching a faculty member when he has not given prior consideration to a topic.

It is perfectly legitimate to discuss a specific research proposal provided that some of the background reading has been done and the problem has been outlined in some detail. The key to success lies in whether or not the project can be justified in light of current knowledge. If the student can properly defend his ideas, the advisor can react more definitively and can offer suggestions for improvement, or he can direct the student to pertinent literature that he may have missed. Approval is not necessarily ensured, but without such preparation, no meaningful basis for discussion is present.

The "shotgun" approach is also poor, whereby the student hastily jots down a number of ideas and asks the professor to react to each or perhaps to select the one he feels is best. Frequently, the list is quickly prepared and poorly researched, and often the student is hopelessly unbiased in his own preference. The best result possible is that the student will be asked to narrow down his choices, pursue a few selected topics, then finally develop the one that emerges as most acceptable.

Graduate faculty members in physical education often have rather wide interests and capabilities, but almost invariably they have certain areas that are considered crucial and that probably have formed a major part of their own research. The student may wish to study the literature in his advisor's area of specialization and determine whether appropriate topics can be chosen. An advantage of this approach is the likelihood that necessary equipment is readily available for immediate use or can be adapted, so that the study may be operable.

8. Discover interests of associations or societies. Frequently, various professional groups have expressed interests in furthering specific kinds of research. Therefore, such groups may provide a source of ideas for the student, as each represents current concern for certain studies It should not be expected, though, that because an association encourages a certain type of project that it will provide an immediate grant of approval to a college or university. Such arrangements must be worked out separately and within the framework established for graduate research. Examples of such efforts in the past have been the following:

(a) The Research Council in 1954–56 urged research on the effects of athletics on young children.

(b) The Research Council in 1964–65 encouraged research on specific sports in an effort to assist coaches of various sports.

(c) The Oregon State Education Department stressed the need for a motor fitness test with norms.

(d) The California State Department of Education cited the necessity of acquiring a physical performance test.

(e) The New York State Standards Project is another example of state involvement in physical fitness efforts.

(f) The School District at Coos Bay, Oregon, desired a fitness survey of all boys and girls in the system.

(g) The President's Council on Physical Fitness has urged research efforts in the area of physical fitness for a number of years and has generally indicated the problems that need solution.

(h) The American Association for Health, Physical Education and Recreation has sponsored a physical fitness testing project and has encouraged research in some related areas.

CRITERIA IN SELECTING A PROBLEM

A number of factors should be considered in deciding whether or not to proceed with a particular study The following criteria are given:

1. Is the problem of interest to you? Very likely, in the chronology of events, interest in the problem is the first consideration of the student. He naturally is drawn toward questions that interest him and that he feels should be done and will not be as enthusiastic about subjects that hold no interest for him. Certainly, if the research subject is clearly distasteful, there seems to be little point in continuing with the project.

For example, some individuals would find working on animal studies less than enjoyable, especially if dissection was required. Others would find the library study required for historical research too boring or the repetitious testing necessary for experimental research distasteful, particularly if it were to involve a great deal of statistical analysis. On the other hand, the advice to novice researchers at the graduate level would be to adopt a permissive attitude—assume that interest is not an overriding factor and consider any worthwhile project to be acceptable. As long as the research area is not completely repulsive, experience has shown that most students become enthusiastic about their work once they are involved with it. To spend an inordinate amount of time in search of some magical combination of factors would seem ill-advised if progress in a positive direction could be made with a second order of priority. The accent must still be on the topic being acceptable, because no amount of interest can supplant scientific validity.

2. Is it possible to obtain data appropriate to the solution of the problem? This is a question of major concern to the researcher, as it is obvious that if the question cannot be answered affirmatively, there is little value in proceeding with research. No amount of skill can save the project if the data are inappropriate. In many cases, especially in the psychological or sociological areas, certain assumptions, which are roughly equivalent to establishing validity of the testing instrument, must be made. Thus, for example, in assessing the emotional health of junior high school students, Lawrence[1] not only found it necessary to define emotional health as the state of adjustment of the individual as related to himself, others, and his environment, but the validity of a prepared questionnaire as indicator of emotional health had to be established. Similar procedures were also used by Kenyon[2] to assess certain psychosocial and cultural traits of prospective physical education teachers.

In these instances, the issues were not completely straightforward but required careful definition and selection of measuring instruments. Contrast this with the assessment by Pacheco[3] of improvement in jumping performances resulting from preliminary exercise where the essential ingredients were rather precisely stated and measured. It is not intended to encourage or discourage the student with regard to any particular form of research by these examples, as a wide variety is needed if progress is to be made.

3. Are techniques available for the solution of the problem? Akin to the previous question is the additional one of the techniques available for solving a problem. Examples of inadequate means for research abound in the area of laboratory experimentation where scientists had to wait for the development of precise instruments. Every discipline has experienced this difficulty. With the advent of new devices has come a resurgence of interest in various phenomena heretofore left unexamined. The electron microscope permitted more detailed analysis of muscular contraction; the cable tensiometer permitted readily usable techniques for gross strength assessment; the electromyograph provided quantitative data on muscular activity; and the electrogoniometer gave greater validity to range of joint movement studies. These examples and others illustrate the development of measurement techniques that have advanced the research possibilities in physical education. It is a truism that the absence of accurate, precise instruments retards research efforts. If the techniques are unavailable for solution of the student's problem, then the project must be revised or abandoned.

A secondary consideration involves the perplexing situation whereby the techniques required by the research design are known and have been adequately documented, yet the instruments themselves are not available to the student at his institution. Assuming that they cannot be purchased immediately, the solution may be found in either borrowing the equipment from another university or perhaps going to another department on campus

---

[1] Trudys Lawrence, "Appraisal of Emotional Health at the Secondary School Level," *Research Quarterly*, 37, No. 2 (May 1966), 252.

[2] Gerald S. Kenyon, "Certain Psychosocial and Cultural Characteristics Unique to Prospective Teachers of Physical Education," *Research Quarterly*, 36, No. 1 (March 1965), 105.

[3] Betty A. Pacheco, "Improvement in Jumping Performance Due to Preliminary Exercise," *Research Quarterly*, 28, No. 1 (March 1957), 55.

where help may be obtained. This latter course of action has proven quite successful, particularly when blood analysis, animal tissue analysis, or other technical procedures not only require special equipment, but trained assistance is needed. Such interdepartmental cooperation is usually encouraged in universities, for it enlarges the research possibilities of a single department.

4. Is the research feasible? The feasibility of a research study is generally linked to the dual problems of time and cost. If the researcher has no particular deadline to meet—as would be true with the full-time research worker or the professor engaged in his own scholarly pursuits—then time may not be a crucial factor to consider. On the other hand, the student ordinarily has a deadline to meet, which means that he must give some consideration to the length of time it will take to complete the study. Those with research experience who direct graduate work will recognize the futility of trying to equate all studies on the factor of time. No meaningful standards can be set in this regard, except, possibly, for the longer period of time it usually takes for completion of the doctoral study as against the master's thesis. Even in this case the reason for more time is generally dictated by the scope of the study rather than by any arbitrary decision.

Some studies simply take longer to complete. This is particularly true of certain types of research where the investment of time is the key factor. For example, it has been known for years that more longitudinal data need to be obtained on factors of growth and development; yet, few such long-range studies exist in physical education. The Medford Boys' Growth Study, inaugurated in 1956 and continued for 12 years, is an example of such sustained research.[4] When such a continuous project is sponsored by the university, it does have the built-in advantage that the time factor can be condensed; the student need not necessarily have collected data himself for each year or each age group, although he should have been a participant in the project for one or more years.

Conditioning or training studies over a long period of time have also been lacking, and yet physical fitness has always been a primary objective in physical education. Studies designed to progress for several weeks, whether the subjects are human[5] or animal,[6] should be encouraged. Often the studies on conditioning follow a basic 10-week plan and thereby fit into university calendars for activity classes, or they utilize members of athletic teams, in which case the studies may be more seasonal. Another area of importance

---

[4] H. Harrison Clarke, "Contributions and Implications of the Medford Boys' Growth Study," 4th ed. Eugene, Oregon: The Author, University of Oregon, 1968 (mimeographed).

[5] David H. Clarke and Franklin M. Henry, "Neuromotor Specificity and Increased Speed from Strength Development," *Research Quarterly*, 32, No. 3 (October 1961), 315.

[6] Dale Hanson, Wayne Van Huss, and Gundars Strautneik, "Effects of Forced Exercise upon the Amount and Intensity of the Spontaneous Activity of Young Rats," *Research Quarterly*, 37, No. 2 (May 1966), 221.

that requires extended time is the study of retention of learning. Sometimes requiring several months[7] for completion (perhaps even years), these investigations on motor learning are receiving more attention as the field becomes better understood.

The question of cost is also a major factor for any researcher. When the investigator must personally finance his study to any great extent, an insuperable barrier may be imposed. It is the rare student who is able to underwrite large expenses for the completion of his study; in fact, he should neither be expected nor required to do so. A function of the department should be to supply the necessary equipment and supplies to carry on research at the graduate level. If the necessary tools are not available and cannot be borrowed or purchased in time, then the problem that has been selected must be revised or discarded.

Occasionally students will become involved in studies where the true expenses are hidden, as in those that involve large surveys where considerable paper and postage costs may accrue, or if on-the-spot interviews are to be held individually, then traveling and lodging expenses may be rather large.[8]

The precedent established in physical education has been to obtain volunteer subjects for research studies. This is still by far the most prevalent practice, as quite often male or female students in required activity classes are interested in the research undertaken in physical education. If the investigator is endorsed by the activity instructor, sufficient subjects can be obtained for almost any project. A difficulty may arise in obtaining subjects who are on the one hand volunteers and yet not known personally by the investigator. With the advent of research grants, many departments or project leaders are able to remunerate the subjects for their time and effort spent on the research project. At many institutions, the time has apparently come when subjects are sophisticated enough to expect to be paid for their involvement. If the graduate student must do this alone, the cost may be rather substantial. If there must be some sort of monetary reward, then perhaps the researcher should give some thought to providing an incentive for participation and try to ensure full cooperation and completion of all assignments.[9]

Advance attention should be given in the research design to possible use of computers in data analysis. Quite often the amount of data obtained is substantial; with the availability of computers to assist in statistical analysis,

---

[7] E. Dean Ryan, "Retention of Stabilometer Performance over Extended Periods of Time," *Research Quarterly*, 36, No. 1 (March 1965), 46.

[8] John W. Fox, "Practices and Trends in Physical Education Programs for Boys in Selected Oregon Schools," microcard Doctoral Dissertation, University of Oregon, 1958.

[9] William J. Tomik, "The Effects of Speed, Load, and Repetition of Interval Training Bouts on Endurance Performance," unpublished Doctoral Dissertation, University of Maryland, 1968.

the wise student will investigate all facets of this facility. In many cases, no charge is made to the student; in others, he may have to pay for such items as computer operating time or card-punching time.

5. *Do you have adequate training and experience to interpret results?* A hierarchy of laboratory skills in research does exist; some skills require extensive training, whereas others need relatively little experience. This observation is not to be confused with the validity of the study, for the sole criterion here is based upon whether the tool or technique provides adequate data. Whether it is a simple chronoscope or a complicated gas analyzer is irrelevant so long as the appropriate device is used for the problem at hand. The more difficult the procedure, proportionally more time and training will be required for its use in research.

Other techniques may require an extensive theoretical background and perhaps demand that the student have courses of advanced study. The subject of intergroup relations[10] is not approached without proper academic preparation nor are studies involving advanced psychological techniques.[11] If the student has not planned well in advance for this exigency, it would seem ill-advised to propose them for research purposes. Thus, some kinds of research are closed to him until adequate preparation is achieved. At the doctoral level such preparation should be expected and, in fact, encouraged.

From time to time among historians in education and physical education, the advisability of encouraging historical or philosophical research at the master's degree level has been questioned. Not only are too few students academically readied for this task, but the difficulty of the subject matter puts the student who is not adequately prepared at a serious disadvantage. Certainly, such studies have been satisfactorily accomplished by master's degree students,[12] but frequently the student must be prepared to study the subject matter in some depth. On the positive side, however, those students whose backgrounds and interests qualify should be encouraged to follow such depth research, as physical education must be developed more fully in the historical and philosophical areas.

A somewhat similar situation exists concerning adequate training and experience for utilization and interpretation of statistics in experimental studies. The concensus of opinion is that formal training in statistics at the graduate level should be required for anyone using an experimental design.

---

[10] Martin Bloom, "Types of Action Used in Resolving Inter-group Problems in Physical Education: Experiences of the Springfield College Physical Education Faculty Members," microcard Master's Thesis, Springfield College, 1947.

[11] Warren R. Johnson, Benjamin H. Massey, and George F. Kramer, "Effect of Posthypnotic Suggestions on All-Out Effort of Short Duration," *Research Quarterly*, 31, No. 2 (May 1960), 142.

[12] David Samuel Crockett, "Sports and Recreational Practices of Union and Confederate Soldiers," *Research Quarterly*, 32, No. 3 (October 1961), 335.

Without this competency, an undue burden is placed upon the advisor, the student, or even some outside party to oversee every computational step in the analysis of data. Thus, not only must the researcher know the appropriate statistics to use and be able to calculate the correct answer, but he must also have the ability to interpret the results.

6. Will the problem make a significant contribution? This question may be approached in two ways. First, does it add significantly to the field of knowledge, and second, does it make a significant professional contribution? In some respects, these may not be separate issues, but some differentiation may be apparent. In any case, studies contributing to both are needed, and certainly no attempt is made here to set up a hierarchy of research. Perhaps, the differentiation is best observed if the basic research problem contributes primarily to the field of knowledge and if the applied research supports the professional literature.

The question of whether or not the research problem is significant is difficult to assess at the time; certainly, the investigator is in a poor position to evaluate the future and ultimate value of his work. To decide on the value of a research problem, a number of factors can be given: How well does it fit into the current state of knowledge? How timely is it? Does it make a significant improvement over studies of a similar nature? Does it fit into existing gaps in current knowledge? Does it open new avenues of investigation? These and other questions are important, but perhaps one of the universal criteria can be mentioned: Is it likely that the study will meet the standards required for publication? For anyone seriously engaged in research, this is a key consideration. If the graduate student would use the publication standards as his criteria, little objection would be found to his study.

DEFINING AND DELIMITING PROBLEMS

Once the problem has been selected and found to be generally acceptable, the next step is to establish the proper limits and extent of the study. The problem must be defined and delimited so that it is not too broad or unmanageable. This is frequently a problem encountered in the initial research efforts; the tendency to want to do too much must be resisted, although each problem will have its own separate limits that will defy generalization. Each research study is a highly individualistic enterprise, and broad statements must be regarded entirely within the framework of the study itself.

As a matter of fact, many of the simpler topics have been treated so that in order to progress the student occasionally must propose a larger problem to be able to obtain sufficient data. Sometimes this can be done by narrowing the scope of the study to allow more intensive investigation in one limited area. The main problem is to keep the study within the limits established by the prevailing criteria selected. In some way a balance of factors must be achieved so that the student is not burdened with an impossible task that would involve an extraordinary effort to complete alone. On the other hand, the problem should not be so narrow or trivial that it amounts to nothing more than an interesting little project lacking in real substance.

The delimitations of a study should be clearly stated so that the reader understands the nature of the topic. Quite often this is done formally in a section labeled "scope" or "limitations" or "delimitations"; they may also be shown in the title, although there are restrictions on length, as will be discussed below. Perhaps a clarification is in order concerning the terms limitations and delimitations in a research study. They are often confused, and frequently used interchangeably in theses.

Limitations. Limitations of studies are usually those items that impinge on the study in some substantive way. As applied to the thesis, a section of limitations should reflect in an honest way any drawbacks to the study that should be known to the reader at the outset. Very frequently, a problem of instrumentation or procedure may be present that bears on interpretation of the data. For example, the study of specific gravity from underwater weighing—key to the measurement of lean body mass—raises the question of residual air determination.[13] It is essential to indicate whether residual air was measured or estimated; if estimated, it is helpful to state the extent that this is likely to influence the data. Physiological maturity can be estimated from bone growth, by pubic hair assessment, or by both.[14] Whichever is used, it is helpful once again to make this clear to the reader.

The limitations section is probably one of the most abused parts of the thesis study. Examples can be found where nearly every problem encountered was mentioned, whether or not it had a direct bearing on the study. The general rule should be to give only those items that indeed limit the acceptability of the data or impinge on the applicability of the findings. In the planning of the research, the investigator should make every effort to eliminate any serious limitations before beginning. Certainly, if there are major shortcomings in procedure, it is unwise to continue. Merely stating the limitations later does not absolve the investigator from responsibility, and it certainly does nothing to improve the validity of the study. Occasionally, however, things come to light very late in the study or occur suddenly during

---

[13] David H. Nielsen, "Body Composition and its Relationship to Selected Measures of Muscular Strength," unpublished Master's Thesis, University of Maryland, 1967.

[14] H. Harrison Clarke and Ernest W. Degutis, "Comparison of Skeletal Age and Various Physical and Motor Factors with the Pubescent Development of 10, 13, and 16 Year-Old Boys," *Research Quarterly*, 33, No. 3 (October 1962), 356.

data collection, or a new finding is published after the study has begun. Perhaps the solution here is to indicate the extent that this affects the present study and enter it in the limitations section.

Delimitations. Delimitations should be interpreted to mean the boundaries of the study. This is a section, often called the scope of the study, that gives the reader a brief idea of the restrictions imposed on such items as the number and kind of variables to be used, the number and type of subjects employed, or other important features that place the study in the proper frame of reference. In a brief space, the essential ramifications of the data can be made clear in order to avoid any misunderstandings created by the title. For example, it is not a limitation to the study for the subjects to be college-age males (necessarily); in fact, the type of subject may be an asset. It may be a limiting factor if there are too few subjects, but when extraordinarily difficult data are obtained on few individuals, this may be a strong point. As will be made clear in later chapters, the size of the sample is important; but, if it can be assumed that an insufficient number of subjects is employed for adequate statistical treatment, this then becomes a delimitation. What will be done with the subjects and what variables will be examined are also delimitations and may or may not need to be placed in a special section.

The first place where the scope of the study appears is in the title. This is a very important part of the study, as it must accurately reflect the nature of the work, but it cannot be excessively long. Occasionally a compromise must be made with the hope that the title will lead the reader to a section, preferably in the first chapter, that sets forth the delimitations more exactly. No general consensus of opinion exists as to just how long the title should be nor what it should contain, but it is clear that every feature of the data cannot be mentioned. Perhaps the best guideline is that it should be long enough to cover the subject, yet short enough to be interesting. It should not be misleading or so vague and general that it is not helpful to the individual searching for literature of related topics.

Thus, great care should be taken to formulate the title so that it does reflect adequately and concisely the topic to be studied. Such phrases as "an investigation of" or "the measurement of" are usually superfluous in the title, and naming the specific variable used in the data collection probably should be used only when it is crucial to the understanding of the content. Certainly, when multiple variables are used—or one that is not well known—a general category can be given, such as "strength measures" or "anthropometric variables." The reader can be expected to look further in the study to determine just which ones were employed. Much the same technique is utilized in the published article. Examples of titles are given in Chapter 18.

EVOLVING THE PROBLEM STATEMENT

Suppose the graduate student is interested in studying "coaching of athletics." This statement is hopelessly vague, although it does tell two things: The study will be concerned with coaching and with athletics. However, athletics can cover many sports, so a delimitation could be "coaching of football." But football is coached at many levels: in school and out-of-school, professional and Pop Warner, and so on. The student must again restate: "coaching of interscholastic high school football." Two delimitations have now been added: interscholastic football and high school football. The delimitation may well continue with profit. For example, note the additional delimitations in the following title: "Coaching of Football in Class A High Schools of Massachusetts."

The title can tell a great deal. However, limitations may also be listed or, the converse, the items to be covered. Thus, clarification should be made relative to the inclusion or omission of duties performed by the coach—the kinds of drills he uses, the emphasis he places on various aspects of the game, numerous details of equipment and facilities, and a host of other related facets. All such details, of course, cannot be carried in the title, although a qualifying word or phrase to "coaching" may be included: "On-the-Field Coaching of Football in Class A High Schools in Massachusetts."

THE BASIC PURPOSE AND METHOD OF SCIENCE[15]

The basic aim of science is the achievement of understanding. In the final analysis, scientifically speaking, knowledge is the equivalent of confirmed theories. Research provides information as to why and how certain things affect other things and explains how it works, what are its properties, and so on. Facts, as such, do not represent knowledge; rather, they are the raw material that can lead to knowledge. Thus, the accumulation of facts is one step in research, an important contribution to the total picture but only a means to the main purpose—the formulation and confirmation of theory.

The use of the term *theory* is generally misunderstood by the layman. To him it is a term of derision (it is only a theory, not a fact), but to the scientist the test of the maturity and vitality of a division of knowledge is how much

---

[15] Modified with permission from a statement prepared by Franklin M. Henry, *Physiology of Work*, University of California, Berkeley, 1968.

confirmed theory is available. Thus, the hierarchy of scientific knowledge is as follows:

1. Hypothesis. An hypothesis is a preliminary, tentative organization of facts in a meaningful way, to be tested and accepted or discarded on the basis of crucial observation or experiment.

2. Theory. In general, a theory is more comprehensive and less tentative than the hypothesis. It must be testable. A body of verified theories constitutes a field of knowledge.

3. Law. A particularly well-verified theory may be called a law. Since knowledge is not static, most so-called laws soon become laws by courtesy only.

When a field of knowledge is adequately established, practical problems can be solved in a straightforward, economical, accurate, and profitable manner. The successful, practical man has, although perhaps informally, made use of the scientific method. The basic method of science is not limited to or characteristic of a particular branch of science, but it is used in anthropology and history as well as in physiology, physics, or physical education.

BASIC VS. APPLIED RESEARCH

This text does not promote one form of research at the expense of another, for there is a place for all types. It is essential, though, that whatever is done be done well; excellence in research should be the utmost consideration. A controversy prevails today, particularly in physical education, however, that may affect the direction that discipline will take in the future. Although not unique to this field, the question centers around the merits of basic vs. applied research. The trend today is toward basic research in most academic disciplines and should probably be the case in physical education as well.

Applied research seeks some immediate practical outcome; the student typically wishes to "solve a problem." His interest is stimulated as a result of his teaching or athletic background in which "problems" are altogether numerous and real. The result of his study, he would hope, would be to end this difficulty once and for all. It is suspected that this is the genesis of the many studies dealing with the methodology of teaching skills or the best techniques for strength development that have been so popular over the years.

On the other hand is basic research, which in the purest sense seeks no immediate practical outcome. It seeks to increase man's understanding of his environment—to provide new insights into the way men live. Obviously, new knowledge can result from both forms of research, but it is not always so obvious that ultimately basic research can also be practical. Examples may be found wherever man's search for knowledge has laid the foundation for our very way of life and literally made it possible to exist in a modern society.

Perhaps the difficulty in a field such as physical education is that the differentiation between the two forms of endeavor is not easily recognized or not emphasized early enough in the student's undergraduate preparation. Consequently, he begins a graduate program without a full understanding of the depth of knowledge that is available. Also, the curriculum of most undergraduate programs is education centered; the preparation of teachers is a primary obligation and the driving motivation of prospective candidates. The focus of attention, therefore, may be on the solution of problems related to teaching of activities, development of a curricula, or the administration of programs. In addition, the avid enthusiasm of most male physical education students for coaching is often apt to reveal a number of practical problems in the area of their sports specialty.

Unfortunately, the solution of such problems is beyond the ability of most individuals at the early stages of their research careers. A common misconception is that the problems solved "in the field" can be done more easily than the so-called more sophisticated laboratory experiment. What is not anticipated so frequently is that the field approach may neglect the necessary control and standardization that are required to draw sufficient generalizations from the data. Not only is there danger that the immediate question may not be solved properly but that the evidence may not impart the fundamental nature of the point in question.

The impression is not intended that all research should be done in the confines of a formal laboratory, although many problems can only be solved there; rather, the site of research must be entirely appropriate to the specific nature of the study. Those experiments undertaken on the track or in the swimming pool may be just as basic as those in the laboratory. What is common to the basic research plan is that rather than being specific to one skill or technique of teaching, it seeks to broaden the base of knowledge common to all skills or techniques, or it seeks to obtain information about some unknown phenomena relative to man and his environment. It is the acceptance of the doctrine "knowledge for its own sake," without recourse to the question "Is it practical?" It should be seen, then, that when the basic problems are solved the practical applications will come along naturally. When enough is known about learning of skills or performing complex coordinative acts, the utilization of these results should be obvious.

The decision to undertake the more practical study or to follow a basic research design will ultimately be conditioned by a number of factors. It is not the intent here to favor either form but to present the emerging picture with respect to physical education. Whether historical or experimental, the field is aligning itself and patterning its activities more and more along the lines of other physical, social, or biological sciences. More particularly, the aim of physical education is to study all pertinent aspects of man in action, whether it be the study of basic movement patterns, physiological adaptations to exercise, psychological manifestations related to performance, or the historical or sociological analysis of contemporary sports and the dance. The exact definition of this form of research can be made once the various fields of knowledge within physical education are made clear.

THE FIELDS OF KNOWLEDGE

By identifying the various areas where research efforts would seem most fruitful, the scholar may identify those around which a graduate program would most logically proceed. The research techniques accompanying the various areas will be presented in future chapters. Briefly, then, the following research fields in physical education are indicated.

1. Physiology of Exercise. The cellular organization and the theory of muscular contraction as well as the functional study of the human organism is classed as physiology and would typically be studied in departments of physiology. The study of the role of these factors as they relate to human movement, performance, or training is within the pervue of physical education and would come under the more specific heading of physiology of exercise.

2. Motor Learning. The area of motor learning generally encompasses neuromotor coordination, kinesthesis, learning of motor acts, retention, and transfer. The emphasis is on the use of gross motor activity rather than fine motor skills; the terms *motor learning* or *psychological basis of physical activity* designate this research area.

3. Sports Psychology. More concerned with the personality, emotional, or motivational aspects of sports and physical activity, sports psychology employs many of the techniques used in psychology, but it is a research area developed to serve physical education.

4. Kinesiology. The field of kinesiology has been developed to analyze movement and skill performance, particularly with respect to laws of motion and anatomical capabilities. Also included are pertinent aspects of body mechanics.

5. History. The role of sports, games, and the dance is of special interest both on an historical and a contemporary basis; not only history but sociology and cultural anthropology are included under this heading.

6. *Measurement and Evaluation.* This field, which overlaps with many of the fields mentioned above, is a common denominator that involves instrumentation, techniques of measurement, and statistical applications.

7. *Growth and Development.* The study of physical growth and development emphasizes aspects of maturity, physique, and musculature, as well as the development of strength and endurance, most particularly from childhood to maturity.

8. *Rehabilitation and Medicine.* The development of knowledge in rehabilitation or adapted physical education is reflected in career fields of physical therapy, corrective therapy, and recreation therapy; it is also related to abnormal psychology, motor development, and sports medicine.

It should now be possible to see more clearly the relationship of basic research to the various fields of physical education. Although the definitions expressed above will not be accepted by all, they will serve as a point of departure for subsequent discussion; graduate course offerings in these and related fields exist on most colleges and universities. Certainly, then, research activity should endeavor to further the pools of common knowledge within these special fields. As Henry has expressed it:

> The focus of attention is on the study of man as an individual, engaging in the motor performance required by his daily life and in other motor performances yielding aesthetic values or serving as expressions of his physical and competitive nature, accepting challenges of his capability in pitting himself against a hostile environment and participating in the leisure time activities that have become of increasing importance in our culture.[16]

If the above discourse expresses the basic intent of the field, a wide latitude for research activity is present. This is immediately evident when one studies the *Research Quarterly* or the volumes of completed theses and dissertations prepared by the American Association for Health, Physical Education and Recreation. Fortified by appropriate background courses in the specific field of his interest, the student decides upon his area of interest and then pursues it to a conclusion. The conclusion in this case would be the research project.

SUMMARY

This chapter has indicated the process of locating and defining the research problem, including criteria in selecting the problem, limiting and

---

[16] Franklin M. Henry, "Physical Education: An Academic Discipline," *Journal of Health, Physical Education and Recreation*, 35, No. 7 (September 1964), 32. Reprinted by permission of the author and *JOHPER*.

delimiting the problem after the problem area is located, and evolving the formal problem statement. Most problems emerge from a systematic recording of unresolved issues, an analysis of the literature in a subject area, studies of research already completed, the examination of controversial issues, and an inquiry into continuous research at the graduate student's institution. Criteria in the selection of a problem for study include the specific interests of the student, the availability of appropriate testing techniques and data, the feasibility of the proposed research, and the training and experience of the investigator. Once the problem is selected and found to be generally acceptable, it must be defined and delimited so as not to be too broad and unmanageable.

The basic purposes and methods of science were considered in this chapter. The heirarchy of scientific knowledge exists as hypothesis, theory, and law. Differentiation was made between basic and applied research. The investigative fields were identified as exercise physiology, motor learning, sports psychology, kinesiology, history, measurement and evaluation, growth and development, and rehabilitation and medicine.

CHAPTER 3

Literature Search

As stated previously, knowledge of the literature of the field will readily reveal problems. The beginner scholar, however, will not have a broad or a deep understanding of the published research in his field. To acquire this knowledge is the aim of the graduate program itself; the culminating study of some phenomenon in detail should bring to focus the need of current research in some area.

Once the problem has been outlined, the next step is to examine the literature to identify properly the extent of the problem, to make certain that the study has not been done before, to develop an understanding of the various techniques available for such a study, and to develop ideas that contribute to the overall rationale and interpretation of the data. These purposes can only be accomplished by a systematic and thorough study of the research literature with every effort made to seek out all available sources. If the study was properly conceived in the first place, the result will most likely be a more refined and scholarly work. Improperly selected topics can not be saved by merely citing more studies in reference. The alert student will recognize signs of weakness and take steps to make the problem more acceptable.

No simple way exists to become knowledgeable of the literature in the chosen field of interest, except by dint of hard work and diligent attention to detail. The student must demonstrate a willingness to pursue obscure leads and to read far more studies than may ever appear in the completed research report. In this process, the student develops a sophistication and an awareness of the peripheral issues and can place his study in the proper frame of scientific reference. In addition to becoming thoroughly capable in the pertinent subject matter, he can see the implications of his study to the furtherance of knowledge.

The survey of literature must be accomplished before the data have been collected. The obvious reason, of course, is to make certain that the study is properly formulated—that major considerations have not been overlooked—or simply to prevent unwarranted duplication. This should not be interpreted to mean that once the collection of data has begun there is no longer any need to pursue further studies. This process is seldom over until all available sources have been exhausted; it is not unusual even then to discover other references that were previously overlooked.

Moreover, during the months of data collection, analysis, and writing, other research of a similar nature or related to the problem may be published and must be acknowledged. Those who have sent manuscripts to various research journals may recall the discovery of pertinent work that was published while the material was "in press." Even then, it may be possible to acknowledge such efforts in the galley proofs. This practice should be restricted to the most crucial articles, however, to those that bear so directly on the results of the study that to ignore them may be a sign of poor scholarship.

NEED TO SURVEY RELATED LITERATURE

It should be clear, then, that before proceeding formally with data collection, the survey of related literature should be completed. The following rationale is given to stress the importance that is generally attributed to this research function. A perusal of the literature should do several things:

1. Determine if a study has already been completed and published. The most valid consideration for making a search of the literature is to determine whether or not a comparable study has already been completed; this consideration should be foremost in the mind of the investigator as he reads and analyzes the research literature. As mentioned before, quite frequently the student will develop an idea that is the outgrowth of some practical problem that has been encountered in teaching, in classroom lecture, or participating in sports. In such instances, a perusal of the literature may suggest a means of solution. This method of problem delineation has some merit, except that the likelihood exists that such a thought may have occurred to others before him; if the study is readily amenable to solution, it may have been done already. Examples from the realm of weight-training methods can be cited to illustrate this point; a search of the literature would reveal a plethora of studies to determine the relative effectiveness of various combinations and permutations of procedures to increase muscular strength. The student would quickly discover that this field is widely covered. On the other hand, if the study can be justified on logical grounds, the absence of duplication in the literature is undoubtedly a most valuable justification for the study at hand. However, on occasion, the duplication of a study—especially in a controversial area—has value as further validation of the first study. If all other criteria have been met, nothing is more satisfying than the knowledge that no other research can be found that has examined an issue in the same way.

The emphasis so far is upon the published literature, but unpublished studies, such as theses and dissertations, are not to be ignored in the review of literature. The feeling is extant in various quarters, though, that if a study is properly conceived and carried out, it should be published. No doubt, the acceptance of a paper by a board of editors of a scholarly journal gives an aura of respect to the report, and it naturally commands greater attention. The point of view adopted here, however, is for *evaluation* of the research literature to be made wherever it is found. Quite acceptable unpublished studies exist, and quite unacceptable published studies can also be found. Frequently, too, unpublished theses have been completed so recently that time has not been sufficient to consumate publication.

2. Determine if a study of a similar nature is in progress. Much more difficulty is experienced in finding related research that has not been completed and published—that is, the study is still in progress. Technically, the point may be valid that a student's current project can still be undertaken even if some work of a similar nature is underway. Theoretically, no problem is the sole right of an investigator, and the chances of exact duplication of effort would seem extremely remote. However, if such a study is found, the wisest choice of action would be to try to add significantly to the problem in some area or perhaps modify the methodology in some valid way. On the other hand, examples from scientific literature can be found where studies of a similar nature were being conducted simultaneously in laboratories separated widely by geographic location. Where scientists are concerned with certain fundamental phenomena such duplication is inevitable and even welcomed. Consider the advancement in theory that is made when the data are in agreement.

Several means are available for locating similar studies that may be in progress. As like studies tend to attract similar projects, a check on the ongoing research at the investigator's institution should be made. Because the interests of faculty members are reflected in their research, if the project seems allied to these interests, it may be that such a study is already underway either by the professor or one of his students. A discussion with the appropriate individual should elicit this information.

In the event that the local situation is clarified, then a similar search of other laboratories would be in order. Once again, the literature should indicate the most likely insitution, or individual, most closely associated with such a study; more careful checking should bring to light any projects that bear directly on the investigation at hand. One of the values inherent in attending research meetings at annual conventions is the ability to keep abreast of the trends and developments in the field. The research presentations permit one to obtain an advance prospectus of the current activities of workers in the field. Such a forum seeks out the active researchers so that their most recent projects can be presented for critical appraisal. Such strategy should provide the graduate student not only with fresh material but with an idea as to where overlapping might occur.

3. Discover research allied to the problem. Frequently, the investigator will find it essential to examine published accounts of research that are allied to the problem, although these may be somewhat peripheral in nature. More will be said about this later, but the search for literature must entail a wide variety of articles that give the student more breadth of understanding. In this way, he is able to place his own study in a proper frame of reference. For example, the study of certain personality traits must inevitably lead to perusal of the literature on mental health. Likewise, the concern with problems of circulatory endurance would be incomplete without an understanding of other cardiovascular variables.

Many examples can be given of the beginner researcher who views his problem as narrow and thereby unduly restricts his survey of literature. For instance, the student who wishes to examine various means of providing movement through the water must keep in mind that the basic phenomenon under investigation is propulsion. The review of completed research might very well entail a wide variety of studies that shed light upon this concept, whether or not they meet the exact specifications of the current study. In this way, the individual develops greater sophistication in the subject matter itself.

4. Provide ideas, theories, explanations, or hypotheses valuable in understanding and formulating the problem. In addition to understanding the results of other studies, the investigator must depend upon the interpretation and discussion of the data provided by other authors in an effort to formulate adequately the problem and to place exactly the right frame of reference on the theory involved. This is the precise point where reliance upon textbook analysis for development of theory comes to an end. Although textbooks are acceptable as background reading for comprehension of elementary theory, it is essential for the graduate student to progress beyond this level as quickly as possible and depend upon the published research literature for hypothesis formulation and theoretical background for problem development. If the studies reviewed have been carefully prepared, considerable theoretical discussion should be contained in the publication so that an adequate expression of the author's concept of his results is provided. Ordinarily, the discussion section of the paper will contain this information, and a careful reading of this section is essential for a thorough appreciation of the problem.

5. Locate comparable material useful in interpreting the results. The review of the literature may serve as an important adjunct to the investigator in assisting him in the interpretation of his own study. Often possible interpretations of his findings will be suggested so that his results are placed in proper perspective in light of the published body of knowledge. His own discussion section is enhanced by knowing the available theory relevant to his findings; the researcher should be prepared to restudy the pertinent references following his analysis of the data. A properly conceived study, then, would require that the researcher refer to the other literature in an effort to show either support or refutation of his results. It is incumbent that he discuss the pertinent theory involved—not in an effort to justify his results so much as to point out the logic. If, in fact, the data are in agreement with the expected outcome, then this should be shown with appropriate references. On the other hand, if there seems to be a conflict between what has occurred and what theoretically should have happened, the disagreement should be pointed out as well. Also, some idea as to the reasons for such disagreement should be indicated. If, in fact, no logical answer can be found, this also should be stated.

6. Understand the significance of the research. The investigator may be able to develop sufficient insight to understand the significance of his research; in any event, such would only be possible if the results obtained by other researchers on the same problem were known. Timeliness and appropriateness are helpful factors to know, especially if the problem is of current interest. Quite often, those studies that help to settle a controversial point are welcome. Also, those research endeavors that open up new areas of study hold a particular distinction, as they may foster a number of studies to follow. The extent of this reaction may be dependent upon how much theory is involved. When an important theoretical concept is exposed, it often permits attack or investigation from many sides, and the ramifications may be felt for years. However, the extent and significance of the challenges will very likely be dependent upon how well done the research is in the first place. Although there are examples of studies that have achieved considerable notoriety because they were not carefully conducted, it is safe to say that a research effort merely for the sake of attacking a writer should be avoided assiduously; reasons to justify such an effort should be well justified.

It is a prevalent tendency for theses to contain a section on the significance of the study; in this section, the author states his views on the importance of his work or, at least, on the importance of the topic. It may seem a bit presumptuous of the author to state his views of the significance of his study, for in the final analysis it will not be his decision to make. The ultimate acceptance and appraisal of a study will depend upon a number of factors, chief of which is the extent that a theory has been further explicated. In turn, this will be reflected in the care and precision of testing and adequacy of problem development. Years may elapse before the true significance of a study can be known, and then the evaluation will be made by a "jury" of the author's peers.

7. Be included as a background of the written research report. Eventually, the research will culminate in a written report, whether it is in thesis form or in article form, and the results of the review of literature will be made apparent at this time. Most of this material will appear in the thesis in the section on review of the literature, but it should not be felt that this is the only place where research studies may be cited. The major substantiation of the state of knowledge should be reviewed carefully and completely, but many times key studies should be cited early in the report in order to justify the problem or to formulate the hypothesis or hypotheses. Thus, for the thesis, reference to some of the literature will appear in introductory material where the problem is stated; the bulk of it, however, will be presented in the formal review section.

The author may also need to give reference to other related studies using similar procedures or instruments in his description of method and perhaps to justify the inclusion of specific techniques or variables in his study. Not only does this indicate just why he proceeded as he did but it serves to supplement his report. Quite often, lengthy descriptions of instruments or techniques may be bypassed by referring to published accounts where additional material can be found. Beyond this, the author may wish to return to the literature after presenting his own results in order to place them in the appropriate frame of reference and to discuss his findings.

The preparation of a manuscipt for publication is usually approached in a slightly different manner from that of a thesis. As a matter of fact, research journals do not publish theses but only research articles; therefore, any study done in partial fulfillment of the requirements for a higher degree must be rewritten to conform to the editorial policies of a particular journal. The manner of organization should be sufficiently flexible to permit a high degree of individuality in presentation; it is seldom possible to present a complete review of the literature in an article. The author must reduce his review to the basic essentials that give an appropriate and clear account of the study under investigation. He may begin with an introduction of other studies that have reviewed past work and then base his review on studies that have been completed since his investigation. At any rate, it seems inappropriate to formalize a review of the literature in a research journal, for it tends to segregate or separate a portion of the work that seems to require complete integration into the written report. Perhaps this should be the writer's choice.

MAJOR SOURCES OF LITERATURE

It is impossible to present here a discussion of all the pertinent sources of information available to researchers in health, physical education, and recreation, as the scope is as broad as the type of problems undertaken. However, there are certain sources that are uniquely appropriate to these fields, and these will be discussed.

The first important decision the investigator must make in deciding what to survey is how to differentiate between critical and allied sources. To the beginner, this is often bewildering, as the ramifications of his study may still be hazy and the choices of studies to be cited nebulous. Quite frequently, he views his own research very narrowly, and at first he is apt to look only for studies that are directly related—that is, that have been done on exactly the same topic. In this situation, the researcher is oriented to his experimental *variables* rather than to the theory that is involved. Thus, he is likely to search for studies done on bowling, for example, rather than on the theoretical concepts of learning that are involved in the activity. Wider reading helps to form a theoretical framework for the construction of the study. The mere fact that bowling is the activity involved is important to the literature only so far as it contributes to the theoretical concepts of learning. Other studies using bowling may be found, but there is no guarantee that they will be pertinent to the present research. The same might be said of muscular strength variables or other studies that could be mentioned; their relevancy to the research problem must be established on grounds other than their mere similarity of use.

1. Critical Literature. As the name would suggest, there are certain published studies that relate directly to the topic under investigation and so are critical to the subject. These studies must be cited for the review of literature to be complete. For example, if the study involves the effect of decreased environmental temperature on muscular endurance for college-aged males,[1] the literature critical to the problem would involve similar studies that have investigated the effects of cold on performance, those that have been concerned with muscular endurance (whether or not temperature has been a variable), and those pertinent studies that have utilized adult males.

2. Allied Literature. Allied literature involves those studies that are related to the investigation but are more peripheral than central in nature. They form an important part of the study because they provide the background upon which it rests. In the example given above, the literature allied to the problem might include those studies that have investigated other temperatures (i.e., hot), those concerned with muscular strength or other variables, and perhaps those utilizing other age levels. In essence, each research proposal will require separate analysis to determine just which articles in the literature are critical and which are allied. No formula can be

---

[1] Richard A. Wojciechowicz, "The Effect of Low Environmental Temperatures on Fatigue Parameters of the Forearm Flexor Muscles," unpublished Master's Thesis, University of Maryland, 1967.

given for this, and opinions might differ on the precise delineation. Obviously, many opportunities for overlapping occur, so at some point a decision must be made as to what to include and what not to include.

Just how far afield one should go in reviewing research for a problem is open to discussion; some feel that only the very critical studies should be cited, whereas others would permit wide latitude. Most research studies, however, probably involve a rather small but select group of articles that really form the nucleus for the current undertaking. When the investigator has completed his thorough search of the literature, he will probably have identified a certain number of citations that provides the best means for development of his study and statement of the problem. Obviously, the identification of these citations must wait for the review to be completed; when the writing begins they will be mentioned prominently. At the same time, he may decide to eliminate certain of the articles reviewed, as they may be neither critical nor allied. There seems to be little justification for giving space to those studies that cannot fit into either classification; such efforts are admirable but are not signs of good scholarship. They may be essential to the student who needs the background reading, but direct inclusion in the study may result in excessive padding.

3. Justification and Understanding of Tests Used. Sometimes, a familiarity with the literature concerning the particular test items to be employed in the study is necessary. This is particularly true for those that are new or unfamiliar to most readers. Tests that are in continuous use and are well-known or that are inherently valid in description may not require much justification. Tests of muscular strength, measurement of reaction time, and many others are employed so often that for most ordinary purposes they can be considered satisfactorily justified. However, if extraordinary use is to be made of the test, such as utilizing grip strength to represent total body strength or reaction time to represent intelligence, then the tests are not satisfactorily justified. Thus, it would appear that the variables, coupled with their use, are the prime determinates of whether or not extensive justification is needed. The best advice might be to include such items in the review of the literature if there is any doubt.

The major point to be made here is that the researcher should know the background of the tools with which he is working. The reason is simply that such knowledge gives him the theoretical bases and the assumptions underlying the tests he plans to use. If the experiment is well conceived, then, no difficulty will be experienced; occasionally, however, the review of the literature will reveal inadequacies not anticipated at the outset. The first research effort by a student often results in blind acceptance of any test that has been used previously, especially if it has been published. If there is a basic defect in the original test, the student's results will add another defective study to the literature. Such problems associated with test construction and instrumentation will be discussed in detail in a later chapter, but it should be obvious that two wrongs do not make a right. The inappropriate use of a technique, no matter how much supporting evidence it offered, cannot be condoned.

LIBRARY SOURCES

The source material to be sought is scattered throughout the various library divisions; the range of topics in the fields of health, physical education, and recreation is wide as well. Therefore, a discussion here must be somewhat limited; the researcher will soon discover, from the sources given, those that are most likely to be fruitful to his topic. The physical educator interested in problems in exercise physiology is likely to see reference material from a quite different point of view from the health educator interested in health knowledge or from the recreation major studying municipal planning. The student will soon discover what are the most likely research journals and where to find the appropriate indexes. He will also learn very quickly how to use his library, the card-index file, the location of study rooms, and other details of library management when he is interested in undertaking a research project. As he develops his leads and begins to itemize his bibliography, he will very likely find that the reference listing will send him to various parts of the library. Perhaps if the particular library is new to the student, this experience will serve as a short course in orientation.

The plight of the student pursuing an historical study is somewhat more involved than one doing experimental research, as his needs for source material far exceed the ordinary demands. Historical research is centered almost entirely on library sources or similar repositories for documents, and the demands for literature are far more pronounced. This will be discussed in detail in a subsequent chapter.

Quite often the student—and faculty as well—will find that his own library is inadequate for all studies needed. In fact, the growth of the graduate/faculty population often is greater than the increase in library financial support, so that a lag exists between the need for research literature and the facilities to provide it. Small schools are notably less endowed than the large universities, and some large institutions are far ahead of others of comparable size. If reference is found to material unavailable in the local library, it is incumbent for the investigator to obtain it. This can usually be done by securing the appropriate reference through interlibrary loan, or sometimes a reproduction or copy of an article can be obtained in the event a journal cannot be sent by mail. In metropolitan areas, however, several libraries within reasonable distance may be available; these avenues should be investigated. The saving of time may be considerable, and the advantage in maintaining continuity of effort is well worth the pursuit to secure references locally, if at all possible. The plight of the small, isolated college is unfortunate, as very often sufficient references are unavailable on campus; thus, great difficulty may be experienced in completing adequately the literature review. Perseverance and willingness to travel can usually solve most of these problems.

The following listing is offered to assist the researcher in his organization and search of the literature.

Bibliographies and Indexes

A number of specific sources are available in health, physical education, and recreation to assist in obtaining references that are apt to be found in the literature of the field. These are mentioned specifically because of their acclaimed usefulness and unique contributions to these areas.

1. Research Quarterly Indexes. Because the *Research Quarterly* itself is probably the most widely used source of articles in health, physical education, and recreation, it is essential to survey these volumes. The reader should be aware of three types of indexes available for locating by subject and author references in the *Research Quarterly.*

Volume Index. Each year in the December issue of the *Research Quarterly*, an index for the current volume appears with author names and important topics given.

10–Year Indexes. The same information has been assembled for 3 10–year periods from 1930 through 1959 and appear as publications of the *Research Quarterly*, as follows:

1930–39, December, 1952 Supplement
1940–49, December, 1951 Supplement
1950–59, December, 1960 Part 2

30–Year Index. Prepared by George B. Pearson and Jacqueline K. Whalin (San Diego: All American Productions and Publishers, 1964), the 30–year period from 1930 through 1959 has been completely indexed by author and subject.

2. Abstracts. A number of journals provide an abstracting service that can be very helpful in searching for relevant literature. Chief among these are the abstracts that appeared for a number of years in issues of the *Research Quarterly*. Prepared by members of the Research Council of the American Association for Health, Physical Education and Recreation, a large number of journals were examined for appropriate articles of interest to research workers in these fields. The project was abandoned after May 1965, however, because of the difficulty in sustaining an adequate continuity through the use of volunteer committee activity. Other abstracts appear in *Child Development* abstracts and other journals such as the *Archives of Physical Medicine and Rehabilitation.*

Since 1953, abstracts of graduate theses in health, physical education, and recreation completed at the University of Illinois have been compiled and edited by Thomas K. Cureton. These abstracts were made available to others at a nominal price. Allen V. Sapora and Mary A. Vance prepared an *Index to the Literature of Leisure, Recreation, Parks, and Other Recreation Sources*; this volume of 252 pages is available through the National Recreation and Park Association. *Synthesis of Research in Selected Areas of Health Instruction* (1962) has been published by the American Association for Health, Physical Education and Recreation. A Canadian Documentation Center for Fitness and Sport has been established at the University of Ottawa and is supported by a federal grant from the Department of National Health and Welfare; Doris W. Plewes was the first director.

3. Published Bibliographies. Aside from the general research bibliographies and indexes mentioned previously, there are a number of bibliographies that are particularly concerned with health, physical education, recreation, and related areas. For example, George B. Affleck's "bibliographies" appeared annually in the *American Physical Education Review*[2] from March 10, 1910 to June 1929 and then appeared in the *Research Quarterly* in October 1930, May 1931, October 1932, December 1932, and every December thereafter through 1941. Affleck also published a bibliography of Springfield College theses, 1929–1934, in the May 1935 Supplement of the *Research Quarterly*. Also included this quarterly: T. K. Cureton presented a list of doctoral theses completed from 1930–1946 in March 1949; A. D. Browne provided a list of masters theses in October 1931; C. H. McCloy entered a bibliography in health and physical education, October 1932, and McCloy and Greene on the same topic in December 1936. A number of other bibliographies appear in various issues of the *Research Quarterly* on a wide variety of special subjects, particularly in the earlier years of publication. In recent years, the editorial policy of the *Research Quarterly* has discouraged the presentation of bibliographies as regular articles.

Of special note are the efforts of such individuals as A. W. Hubbard, Raymond A. Weiss, and Robert N. Singer to present in some regular and continuous manner the results of many of the theses and dissertations that are completed each year. Started in mimeographed form, the project was adopted by the American Association for Health, Physical Education and

---

[2] All issues of the *American Physical Education Review* (1896–1929), as well as the *Research Quarterly* from 1930–1949 inclusive, are available on microcards.

Recreation in 1959; as a consequence, a volume of *Completed Research in Health, Physical Education and Recreation* is published each year. Far from presenting only abstracts of several hundred theses and dissertations, current volumes describe and index research published in more than 1000 periodicals as well. Betty van der Smissen, State University of Iowa, in 1960 prepared "Compilation of Research Related to Recreation, Part I Theses and Dissertations: A Collection of 547 Titles." *The Research Letter* is published ten times yearly by the National Institute of Recreation Research of the National Recreation Association.

In the late 1940s, several bibliographies were compiled as master's projects at Springfield College, including the following:

Bruce, Robert M. "An Annotated and Indexed Bibliography of Basketball Publications," 1946.

Conyne, A. M. "Bibliography for Aquatic Courses at Springfield College," 1949.

LoMoglio, A. P. "An Annotated Bibliography of Soccer Publications," 1948.

Robertson, R. R. "An Annotated and Cross-Indexed Bibliography of Physical Reconditioning Material Published in the United States Between January 1941 and June 1947," 1949.

Stewart, M. W. "An Indexed Bibliography of Selected Football References," 1948.

The Springfield College bibliographies are not confined to research references, although these are included. Further, of course, they are only complete at the times listed for completion of the projects.

4. Foreign Literature. Abstracts of articles appearing in a variety of foreign publications are presented in *The Physical Educator*, a publication of the Physical Education fraternity, Phi Epsilon Kappa.

Microcards

The growth of microcard publications in recent years has duplicated many studies in the fields of health, physical education, and recreation. Originating in 1944, the development of microcards fell under the direction of the Microcard Committee, a national governing body that was to coordinate the publishing of microcards by various organizations and institutions.[3] In January 1949, Springfield College was authorized to publish microcards of areas related to health, physical education, and recreation. A committee in the Research Council of AAHPER was appointed to an advisory role;

---

[3] H. Harrison Clarke, "Microcard Publication," *Journal of the American Association for Health, Physical Education and Recreation*, 20, No. 7 (September 1949), 440.

efforts to proceed with microcarding of materials was begun.[4] The emphasis has been on obtaining books out-of-print and on unpublished materials, especially doctoral dissertations and master's theses. The success of this project is indicated by the wide selection of reference material that is available.

Presently, nearly 2,000 complete references can be obtained for a reasonable cost or are available in many libraries, and they bring to the researcher a valuable source of information. A complete listing of titles and a subject index is available—Volume I of the *Microcard Bulletin* covering the period October 1949 to March 1965—from the School of Health, Physical Education, and Recreation, University of Oregon, Eugene, Oregon. New titles issued from October 1965 are contained cumulatively in a growing Volume II that incorporates annual supplements.

Periodicals

The following list of journals is representative of the type of reference that would be utilized by students in the fields of health, physical education, and recreation. This list is adapted from those periodicals considered especially relevant by the Committee on Abstracting of the Research Council when the committee was functioning as an abstracting service for the *Research Quarterly*. The list is not considered complete for all substantive material, both foreign and domestic, that might be helpful to a review of the literature; the investigator will locate articles in sources ranging from the *Journal of Physics* to the *Australian Journal of Psychology*, as dictated by the nature of his study. However, an examination of several recent volumes of the *Research Quarterly* reveals that these journals are indeed well representative of those considered most important:

Acta Physiologica Scandinavica
American Anthropologist
American Heart Journal
American Journal of Anatomy
American Journal of Cardiology
American Journal of Hygiene
American Journal of Physical Anthropology
American Journal of Physical Medicine
American Journal of Physiology
American Journal of Psychiatry

---

[4] H. Harrison Clarke, "Microcards," *Journal of the American Association for Health, Physical Education and Recreation*, 22, No. 5 (May 1951), 34.

American Journal of Public Health
American Journal of Sociology
American Physical Therapy Association Journal (*Physical Therapy Review*)
Arbeitsphysiologie (*Int. Z. angeiv. Physiol. einschl. Arbeitsphysiol*)
Archives of Physical Medicine and Rehabilitation
British Journal of Psychology
British Journal of Statistical Psychology
Camping
Child Development
Circulation
Circulation Research
Dairy Council Digest
Electrical and Clinical Neurophysiology
Employee Recreation
Endocrinology
Ergonomics
Growth
Health Education Journal
Human Biology
Human Factors
Industrial Sports and Recreation
International Journal of Health Education
Journal of Abnormal and Social Psychology
Journal of American Medical Association
Journal of American Statistical Association
Journal of Anatomy
Journal of Applied Physiology
Journal of Applied Psychology
Journal of Association for Physical and Mental Rehabilitation
Journal of Aviation Medicine
Journal of Biological Chemistry
Journal of Bone and Joint Surgery
Journal of Chemical Investigation
Journal of Educational Psychology
Journal of Educational Research
Journal of Educational Sociology
Journal of Experimental Education

Journal of Experimental Medicine
Journal of Experimental Psychology
Journal of Experimental Zoology
Journal of General Physiology
Journal of General Psychology
Journal of Health and Human Behavior
Journal of Heredity
Journal of Hygiene
Journal of Motor Behavior
Journal of Nutrition
Journal of Personal and Social Psychology
Journal of Personality
Journal of Physiology
Journal of Psychology
Journal of School Health
Journal of Sports Medicine and Physical Fitness
Lancet
Mental Hygiene
Modern Medicine
Monographs of Society for Research in Child Development
Nature
Perceptual and Motor Skills
Phi Delta Kappa
Physical Educator
Physiological Reviews
Progressive Physical Educator
Psychological Abstracts
Psychological Bulletin
Psychological Monographs
Psychometrica
Psychosomatic Medicine
Public Health Bulletin
Public Health Reports
Quarterly Bulletin of American Recreational Society
Quarterly Journal of Experimental Physiology
Quarterly Journal of Experimental Psychology
Recreation

Research Bulletin, NEA
Research Quarterly
Review of Educational Research
Russian Journal of Physiology
Safety Education
School and Society
Science
Scientific American
Today's Health (Hygeia)

Indexes and Abstracts

Many indexes and abstracts are available for the investigator's use in searching the literature. The local librarian and his staff will aid the graduate student in identifying and locating them. Only a limited number of the more important ones for health, physical education, and recreation will be mentioned here.

Bibliography Index
Book Review Index
Child Development Abstracts and Bibliography
Cumulative Book Index
Current List of Medical Literature
Dissertation Abstracts
Education Index
Encyclopedia of Educational Research
International Index of Periodical Literature
Library of Congress Catalogue
Mental Measurements Yearbook
Microfilm Abstracts
Nutrition Abstracts and Review
Physiological Reviews
Psychological Abstracts
Quarterly Cumulative Index Medicus
Reader's Guide to Periodical Literature
Review of Educational Research
Social Science Abstracts
Wistar Institute of Anatomy and Biology Abstracts

LIBRARY READING

A number of suggestions can be made to assist the researcher in making the most effective use of his time in library reading. Sources exist in the form of indexes and bibliographies that cover topically any number of subjects, and they should be used whenever possible. It is a temptation to suggest that one proceed from the general references to the specific article, and indeed this advice is acceptable. Yet, at the very beginning, a far better method is to search for recent literature in the most likely places. For example, the researcher may already be aware of specific sources or studies that bear directly on his research; in fact, the formulation of the study could hardly have been made without knowing of at least several such articles, These sources should be examined first for content and then for the bibliography where additional references can be found. As this procedure is continued, the bibliographical entries will begin to grow.

Working Bibliography

An appropriate way to proceed initially, then, is to begin with the most recent known studies, abstract them, make entries of the studies mentioned, and then trace backward by date. In this way, the researcher will pick up references that gradually lead to the end of the search. Keeping in mind the decision he has made with respect to critical and allied literature, he should proceed first to those studies that by title would seem to be most crucial and then to all others. It may be possible to delay critical reading until the *primary list* has been completed, but eventually the detailed reading will have to be undertaken.

The researcher should realize at this point that his efforts have passed the initial stage only and that certainly the first task is to uncover the most obvious and most easily obtained references. However, when these have been exhausted, the *secondary list* should be developed by consulting the appropriate indexes and bibliographies under headings that are appropriate to his problem. This in no way implies that references obtained here are secondary in importance or in any way inferior or substandard; actually, the studies uncovered from a multitude of publications may be just as appropriate as are those more easily obtained. The most obvious reason is that the abstracting services can observe more journals than any one person could possibly be able to manage; the exposure by carefully combing the indexes is greatly enhanced. In other words, the references obtained for the secondary list may be both critical and allied; the decision of where to place them can be made later after they have been read and analyzed by the investigator.

A research bibliography is therefore compiled by title with as many sources cited as are applicable. As indicated previously—and this cannot be stressed too often—the entire process is not complete until the manuscript goes to the typist for the final draft. It would seem reasonable to suggest that other papers published after this point do not have to be included in the current study, as some decision has to be made to terminate the review of literature.

Card System

The investigator should adopt some system whereby he can make appropriate notations. Actually, any method will be acceptable, as long as it contains the necessary information that will be needed at a later time. The listing of references on paper is not satisfactory, as they cannot be manipulated in the appropriate manner; they tend to become lost, multilated, or misplaced, and no entries of content can be made. A useful practice is to use 3″ × 5″ or 5″ × 8″ cards with a single reference on each card. Occasionally, cards with certain prepared headings and places for pertinent information can be purchased commercially and are very useful, but more often the user will wish to devise his own style that will suit his specific needs. Whatever the form, certain factual information that can be used when the writing phase begins must be recorded.

The first concern is completeness of bibliographical data. Frequently, the initial efforts by students in their search of literature is haphazard and inconsistent, and often little regard is given to care and completeness of notation. Those experienced readers may remember times when they were bothered by the lack of attention to small details and will recall the hours involved in trying to trace page or volume numbers in references that were read weeks or months earlier.

Several acceptable styles for bibliographical entries exist. The student should find out which ones are favored by his institution and then adopt that style in making his entries. This procedure will assure consistency and will thoroughly acquaint him with the technicalities of notation so that no alterations will have to be made when the bibliography is finalized; all pertinent information will have been recorded. Bibliographical and footnote forms are presented in Chapter 18.

The key, of course, is to obtain *all* pertinent information including all nuances of punctuation; if the style adopted somehow results in excessive brevity, a place on the card should be provided for other details. This latter procedure is helpful should additional information be needed for publication at a later time. Notice should also be taken of possible differences between bibliographical entries and footnote entries so that the requirements for both are met; frequently, they are different. The following specific information should be recorded in accordance with the style adopted:

1. Book. Author's name (last name first, followed by first name and initial), title, city, publisher, copyright date, and total number of pages. It is also helpful for future reference to give the library call number.

2. Article. Author's name as above (given exactly as it appears on the article), title, periodical, volume number, issue number, month and year, and inclusive page numbers for the article.

Classification

The next task is to classify the references from the titles into various categories, as suggested by the nature of the study and by the references themselves. Quite often, the literature can be divided into more or less discrete entities by titles, although this decision cannot always be made arbitrarily, but must await a more careful reading. Other references sometimes fit more than one category; in such cases, a cross-reference should be made and multiple index cards prepared. As this classification is made primarily on the basis of title, some errors will probably occur as titles are often misleading. With the card system suggested, however, adjustments can be simply made later as needed.

Skimming

The primary need in reading the literature is an ability to bring out the salient features of the material under perusal. At first, the decision must be made as to whether or not the material is actually pertinent and usable. For a book, the table of contents is helpful in giving a rapid overview of the material covered and will point out the most likely sources where specific information is to be found. Ordinarily, the reader would then scan a chapter to be more specific in his search for pertinent information and then make appropriate notes. Other key areas yielding information on the type of material to be found are the preface or forward, the index, and the bibliography. If the information sought is more for the research ideas than for the research results, which would probably be more likely when examining a book, then the reader will quickly skim the selected areas and headings found to be most suggestive and proceed from there. Quite often, introductory and final chapters are helpful in acquainting the reader with the forecast of material to be covered, and thus aid in the summary of results.

A similar process is suggested for articles, although they are organized quite differently, and the material is greatly condensed. If an abstract is available, the reader should peruse it carefully to decide on the applicability of the findings. When doubts still persist or further detail is needed at this point, they should be cleared up by reading further. When no abstract accompanies the article, the investigator must search for appropriate portions that describe the study: introductory statements, including a statement of the problem (if one exists), summary and conclusions, methodology, results, discussion sections, etc. In this way, the decision can be made as to the pertinence of the data.

These decision-making processes are important, and as more experience is gained, they are relatively easy. The book or article can be scanned rather quickly to see whether it should be part of the review of literature, whether there is meaningful material presented, or whether ideas are pertinent to the problem. This process is not as quickly accomplished when examining microcards or microfilm. Due to the mechanical relationship between the material and the reader, more care must be exercised in planning the search. It is suggested for microcards that the table of contents (for theses and dissertations) be consulted first, and then perhaps proceed to the abstract or summary and conclusions sections.

Abstracting

The processes of skimming and abstracting should not be arbitrarily separated into discrete categories, as frequently they will proceed together. This process is largely a matter of convenience, for once the work is located it is perhaps easier to read it carefully then rather than look it up again. However, the mere listing of references does not need to await the reading. There comes a time, though, when the investigator must critically examine the references he has found.

Inasmuch as the review will take some time to complete, the researcher cannot afford to trust his memory for the details of his reading. He should rely upon his abstracting ability to provide the best information that will be absolutely clear to him later when he begins to collate his material. A number of decisions will have to be made as the writing is anticipated so that the notes will supply enough of the correct information. In general, the more critical the study the more material will need to be recorded; those articles that are allied to the study may only require a brief note.

No simplified technique in gleaning the pertinent information from a study is available. Examination of the abstract and the summary gives an overview of what the author has considered pertinent, but this is seldom sufficient; in fact, it is usually so brief as to be almost totally lacking in real substance. Pertinent results are so often entirely neglected here that the reader must pursue further in order to understand the study adequately.

It is not good scholarship to merely copy down the abstract and then perhaps the conclusions without first examining the content to determine if other important facts are necessary. The same can be said of material located in various abstracting services; these abstracts are not sufficient for the researcher to use in lieu of actually reading the primary source.

Thus, good note taking is an essential ingredient to the process of reviewing the literature. Keeping in mind the possibilities for later incorporation into the written portion of the thesis, the researcher will make as extensive notes as deemed necessary. One of the most important considerations is the extent of the use of quotations. If the author's exact words are being copied onto the note card, it is wise to place them in quotes and then make a record of the page number. In no way should this imply that they be used as quotes in the manuscript, for it is not considered particularly good form to use them too liberally. Occasionally, when the author's words seem the best way to express a thought, quotes can be used, but paraphrasing is usually desirable. In any event, it is imperative to know if the notes are quotations or are paraphrasing, so this should be made absolutely clear in the notes that are taken. Moreover, direct quotations must be entirely accurate—a fact that cannot be stressed too strongly, as any errors made at this stage in note taking are made throughout.

A special problem exists when one source quotes another or paraphrases the results of another study. Reliance can not be placed upon such secondary accounts, as other authors will bring out findings that are pertinent to their studies; in such reviews, seldom is the information sufficient. Every effort should be made to find the primary source before accepting the findings. One of the most difficult problems for the researcher in this respect is in literature published in foreign languages. It is suspected that translations are not always performed or obtained and that a secondary source is occasionally used. Actually, the same situation exists here: The researcher must assure himself of the accuracy of the results before utilizing the reference. In the event that it is not possible to find the article or obtain a translation (which is becoming more and more an unacceptable condition), material may be utilized by giving credit to both sources. In this way, it is clear that the investigator did not actually see the original paper.

SUMMARY

Before any research is undertaken, the literature related to the problem area must be searched. The reasons for such a search are to determine if the study has already been completed or is in progress, to discover research allied to the problem, to provide ideas, explanations, or hypotheses valuable in understanding and formulating the problem, to locate comparable material useful in interpreting the results, and to understand the significance of the research.

A discussion of all pertinent sources of information available to researchers in physical education, recreation, and health is tremendously broad and was not undertaken in this chapter. Rather, those sources uniquely appropriate to these fields were discussed. Library sources considered were bibliographies and indexes, microcards, periodicals, and abstracts. Suggestions related to library reading were included with emphasis on working bibliographies, card systems for recording essential materials, reference classifications, and skimming and abstracting.

PART II

NONLABORATORY STUDIES

In Part II, studies in health, physical education, and recreation that do not require laboratory resources are presented. These studies do not usually require the testing of subjects, the conducting of experiments, and the analysis of quantitative data.* A separate chapter is devoted to each of the following research methods: Chapter 4, Historical Method; Chapter 5, Philosophical Studies; and Chapter 6, Surveys and Case Studies.

---

* Exceptions will be found in the normative type of survey, in case studies, and in the construction of profiles.

CHAPTER 4

Historical Method

History serves to bring together information about and to tell an accurate, continuous story of past events. It aims at a complete understanding of some phase of former periods. The historian employs historical documents, accounts, relics, and the like with scholarly care and evaluates them against the criteria available to him. He is not just a storyteller who fills in historical gaps from his imagination, although today's historian does attempt to make his account interesting. He strives for accuracy and validity with the same conscientiousness as does the experimental scientist.

The product of history has undergone significant changes in meaning. Woody has expressed this concept well:

> To pre-literate man, history is remembered tradition; in literate societies it may come to be thought of as the written record of things past. To the politically conscious, history is past politics, and politics is history in the making. To philosophers, history is philosophy teaching by example. None of these notions is sufficiently inclusive: things change and have histories as do men. Were there no change, there would be no history. History, the Book of Changes, is the totality of what has transpired: environment, and what it has done to man; man, and what he has done and sought to do with himself and his environment. Whether the totality be known, or knowable, and how precisely, are mooted matters; but historical study aims at the fullest possible knowledge of the past.[1]

Historical research should be encouraged because it relates to the heritage of any field. No established profession has depth, traditions, customs, or a present without a history. This heritage should be recorded and preserved for future generations. The origins, growth, and development of the field; the problems faced and solved; the cultural forces exerted; the movements that have waned and persisted; the changes in implements, facilities, and costumes; the thoughts and deeds of the pioneers and leaders who shaped the

---

[1] Thomas Woody, "Of History and Its Method," *Journal of Experimental Education* (March 1947), p. 175.

profession over the years; and many other factors are subjects for historical research.

HISTORY IS FUNCTIONAL

History can be functional inasmuch as man can profit by past experiences in the solution of present-day problems. Even nations so profit. For example, following World War I, the United States refused to join the League of Nations believing that great oceans provided sufficient protection against potentially powerful enemies; this country no longer wanted to become involved with international tensions and frictions. World War II demonstrated convincingly that such isolationism of a world power was impossible. Consequently, the United States became a leading exponent and forceful participant in the United Nations; it has worked energetically and aggressively to solve international problems in the interests of world peace.

Between world wars, several nations attempted to appease Hitler's Germany in order to "obtain peace in our time." The results were a black mark on the history of nations. The United States is now wary of a policy of appeasement with aggressor powers. In fact, the lesson may have been overlearned as the United States has been accused of attempts to police the world. Certainly, new national lessons will be learned from the vicissitudes of Korea and Vietnam.

A fascinating example of the use of historical materials in a very real, functional sense is contained in the description of the Sorge spy ring by Major General Charles A. Willoughby, General MacArthur's Chief of Intelligence from 1941 to 1951.[2] Probably never in history has there been a spy ring more bold or more successful. Dr. Richard Sorge and his companions were a daring and skillful band of spies who for nine years worked in Japan for their fatherland, Russia. Sorge, a German Communist and correspondent for several distinguished German newspapers, lived on intimate terms with the German ambassador; Ozaki Hozumi, his lieutenant, had a similar, close relationship with Prince Konoye, thrice premier of Japan. From these sources of information, they were able to transmit intelligence to the U.S.S.R. by concealed radio, by courier, and through the Soviet embassy. After June 1941, their primary intelligence targets were Japanese plans and intentions for attack on the Soviet Union. As the German armies raced into western Russia, as great Soviet military formations were smashed and destroyed, reinforcement from the Siberian border became vital. But, the Red Army could not weaken Siberian defenses if the Japanese army

---

[2] Charles A. Willoughby, *The Shanghai Conspiracy: The Sorge Spy Ring* (New York: E. P. Dutton and Co., Inc., 1952).

intended to attack. Sorge was able to assure his superiors that no attack would be made; the Siberian divisions were entrained and appeared on the Western Front in time for the successful defense of Moscow.

What about history? At the time of Sorge's arrest, the discovery of 800 to 1,000 books at his home proved a source of considerable annoyance to the police. In building up his library, he had collected every foreign edition of any original Japanese work that could be obtained, the best books that foreigners had written on Japan, and the best translations of basic Japanese works. He took particular pains with the study of ancient Japanese history, ancient political history, and ancient social and economic history. The voluminous and excellent translations on Japan's ancient economy and politics proved invaluable.

With this background as a point of departure, it was a simple matter for Sorge to grasp Japanese economic and political problems: the agrarian question, industry, social position of farmer and worker, culture, and art. The passing political scene told the observant Sorge, versed in ancient history, far more than the alien police suspected; with this information, Japan's current foreign policy was easy to understand. For example, none of the border disputes between Japan and the U.S.S.R. worried Sorge because he quickly recognized them as innocuous, but he regarded the various China incidents, and particularly the one in 1937, as the prelude to a great war that would engulf all China. In his words: "My research also permitted me to evaluate correctly the reliability of information and rumors of vital importance to my secret activities since intelligence in the Far East contains far more rumors and conjectures than in Europe."[3]

The following quotation from the August 1958 *Royal Bank of Canada Monthly Letter*[4] summarizes the functional value of history:

> The vital beliefs and good practices of our western world rest on the fulcrum of historic knowledge. There is no basis of our society save its past. There is no guide to business decisions except that given by business experience. There is no personal maturity that is not built upon reflection of events of yesterday . . . . When we can pluck an example from the past and use it to help us today that is a very practical use of history.

Can it be said that physical education has used history in a functional manner? Without being exhaustive, but very general indeed, the historical treatment of physical fitness may be cited. Formal physical education was founded in the United States by refugees from other countries, especially Germany; the Jahn system, so prevalent at the beginning, had the purpose of

[3] *Ibid.*, p. 226.

[4] "What Use is History?" *The Royal Bank of Canada Monthly Letter*, 39, No. 8 (August 1958).

developing the capabilities and fitness of the body. From 1860 to World War I, physical fitness was the major, and essentially only, objective of physical training as then designated; the doctors of medicine who pioneered physical education during this period employed exercise for its value in preventive medicine. Following World War I, a new urgency to improve the nation's physical fitness became evident, and state laws requiring physical education in the schools became commonplace as a result. Then, in the 1930s, physical education generally repudiated physical fitness, considering it as a concomitant of any activity program conducted with other objectives in mind. The error of this practice was dramatically demonstrated by continued high draft rejections in World War II and by the deplorable physical condition of many draftees reporting for military duty.

Many conscientious physical educators vowed—in retrospect—that this experience would not be repeated. Dynamic support came from a totally unexpected source, the President of the United States, who recognized this situation and intervened by establishing in 1955 the President's Council on Youth Fitness. No longer is a physical educator ridiculed because he uses strength tests to assess his pupils, utilizes weight training to strengthen muscles, and employs jogging to develop circulatory endurance. The lessons of history become explicit.

THE SCIENCE OF HISTORY

The question of whether or not the historical method is scientific has been debated. Generally, early historians wrote history more as an instrument of propaganda; their purpose was to glorify the cause espoused, whether it be the State, the Church, a given organization or institution, or the perpetuation of the memory of a public servant or professional pioneer. Certainly, the historical method so employed was far from scientific. Before the nineteenth century, history as a science was generally unknown.

The contention is made, however, that modern historians are basically scientific in that they critically and objectively investigate their source materials; they formulate and evaluate hypotheses; they make explanations, tentatively at least, of the occurrence of events or conditions. But unlike scientists, historians cannot test their hypotheses by direct experimentation; they cannot employ controlled observation. Original conditions cannot be repeated; history cannot be re-enacted. The primary function of science is to reconstruct the human scene and judge its meaning—to get at the true facts, or probabilities, as precisely as possible by weighing all the available evidence. Historical evidence can be evaluated. Cause and effect relationships and the prediction of outcome, after the manner of other sciences, however, are not so readily realized by historical method.

Actually, the scholar in physical education, recreation, and health need not be unduly concerned as to whether the historical method is or is not scientific. It is sufficient to know that certain sources of evidence are available for historical study, that these sources can be appropriately evaluated, that generalizations regarding the past can be made, and that hypotheses relative to the future can be proposed. The method of history must be understood and rigidly followed if historical studies are to be undertaken.

SOURCES OF HISTORICAL MATERIALS

As for any investigation, the historian must define his problem and indicate any limitations to be imposed. Hypotheses to be evaluated, issues to be specifically investigated, or special questions to be answered should be included. Such a statement at the start of the project is essential as it defines the scope of the materials to be assembled. This process was considered generally in Chapter 2 and will not be repeated here.

Two sources of historical materials exist—primary sources and secondary sources. Some materials will be from one or the other of these sources; other materials may be derived from both.

Primary Sources

Primary sources are original materials. As differentiated by some: For a primary source, only one mind comes between the event and the user of the source. The importance of primary sources cannot be overestimated. They compose the solid basis for historical writing and should be utilized whenever possible; in fact, the student should make every effort to study original documents or exhibits no matter how much has been written about them by others.

A number of primary sources can be identified. The most common of these are given here.

1. Official records. Official records are multitudinous. State, district, and national professional associations have minutes of meetings, reports of committees, annual reports, official documents of various kinds, budgets, honors and awards made, attendance records, papers presented, administrative edicts, and the like. State departments have syllabuses, reports of committees and meetings, published materials, laws, court proceedings and decisions, etc. Local institutions or schools have courses of study, participation statistics, and many other primary documents.

2. Personal records. Especially valuable for biographies are letters, diaries, autobiographies, contracts, lecture notes, honors, diplomas, honorary degrees, and original drafts of speeches, articles, and books.

3. Oral statements. Included here are oral traditions, such as myths, family stories, superstitions, ceremonies, and the like. (At times, these are secondary sources.) Eyewitness accounts of events as told by the beholder are also pertinent. Interviews may be recorded. Speeches may be made.

4. Pictorial records. Obvious pictorial records are photographs, movies, drawings, paintings, sculpture, and recorded creative expressions.

5. Published material. Some published materials, such as syllabuses and courses of study have been mentioned. Other such sources are newspaper accounts, pamphlets, yearbooks, magazine stories, and journal articles.

6. Physical remains. Classified as physical remains are buildings, facilities, apparatus, equipment, awards, costumes, and various implements.

7. Printed materials. Printed materials—other than those mentioned—are textbooks, record blanks, certificates, report cards, newspaper advertisements, and contracts.

8. Mechanical records. In today's age of electronics, primary source materials may include tape or video recordings of interviews, meetings, and speeches.

As can be seen, the above categories of primary sources are not mutually exclusive; certain overlaps were pointed out and there are others. Further, the same source material may be either a document or a relic depending on its use. For example, a basketball score book is a relic; but, if the score book is used to report the record of a team's season of play, it is a document.

Secondary Sources

Secondary sources are descriptions of primary sources. They are not first-hand reports. They are written by persons who did not live in the period under study or who were not in direct contact with the events reported. More than one mind came between the original happening and its description.

Examples of secondary sources are textbooks, newspaper articles written from interviews with on-the-spot observers, and historical accounts. A source may be secondary or primary depending on its use. For example, a tests and measurements textbook is a secondary source, but it is a primary source for a scholar who is reviewing the contents of such textbooks over a period of years. A citation made to a professional leader is a primary source; its content is very likely a secondary source. Further, in some documents, both primary and secondary materials may appear: A reporter's account of a street riot may describe incidents he actually saw as well as those described to him by other people.

Secondary source materials have definite value for the novice historian. They acquaint him with work that has already been done in the study area; they provide initial background information relative to the investigation; they usually include a number of key primary sources to be examined. Secondary sources will be especially useful for investigators who cannot obtain the original sources because of their unavailability or who cannot read them because of a language barrier.

However, a secondary source is only as good as the person who produced it; its value is proportional to the competency of the author and the extent to which he used primary sources. Even so, the author of a secondary source has had to select materials he considered germane to his purpose from primary documents, and he made his own interpretations of their contents. This situation is compounded when the author of a secondary source himself has used secondary sources in his account; actually, some secondary source materials are based on third-, fourth-, and fifth-hand information. If at all possible, an historian should not be dependent upon others for such selections and interpretations; he should make them himself from primary sources.

EVALUATION OF HISTORICAL MATERIALS

The actual existence of either primary or secondary historical sources does not guarantee their authenticity, accuracy, or validity. The historian must be consistently critical of the historical materials he obtains and examines. A remain may not be genuine, a record may not be correct, a photograph may be faked or "doctored," a speech may have been written by a ghost writer, or a newspaper story may be slanted in support of a cause. Thus, historical materials must be rigorously evaluated. Such evaluations are made by applying two types of criticism: external and internal. These forms of criticism are not mutually exclusive, but they do serve to explain the types of evaluation that should be applied to historical sources.

External Criticism

Through external criticism, the historian determines whether or not a given source is genuine and admissable as evidence. What is its origin and legality? The answers to a number of questions must be sought.

1. Who is the author? Establishing authorship is a common practice performed by historians. Many times—and especially with professional people—authorship is readily determined. Some documents, however, do not carry the name of the writer. The authorship of committee and other reports, no matter by whom they are given, may be uncertain. A writer may use a pseudonym, which could make his identification especially difficult. For example, what reader can identify the physical educator who wrote the following: Count Sissicran Etoxinod, "How to Checkmate Certain Vicious Consequences of True-False Examinations," *Education* (December 1940)? This may (or may not) help: The same writer has personally published books and other materials under the publisher's name, The Pleiades Company.

2. Was the document written by a ghost writer or by another person? Particularly in political life, the question of who actually wrote a speech may frequently be perplexing. Of course, too, many people in public life employ writers to help with the preparation of the numerous speeches they are called upon to give. Occasionally, the name of a senior professor at a university will be included as a joint author of a research paper or book with one of his graduate students, when actually he may have done little or none of the writing.

3. What were the qualifications of the author? For an author to write with authority on a subject, he must be well-informed on the subject. For example, for a foreign physical education leader to describe American football after seeing his first game would be an inept performance; an understanding of the intricacies of this sport requires a great deal of technical knowledge and appreciation of strategy. An American going abroad for a short time and posing as an authority on foreign physical education upon his return is another illustration of unqualified reporting. The common man could describe the mushroom-shaped cloud created by an atomic explosion, but it requires an atomic scientist to describe its composition and physical dimensions—and he would rely on many testing instruments strategically arranged before the blast. Occasionally, authorities in one field pose as authorities on the same level in other fields where their qualifications do not apply.

4. Is a particular item of equipment, piece of apparatus, costume, or other professional artifact authentic? Physical education remains should be established as to validity, date of origin, changes and development, and uses to which they were put. This historical effort should be extended to the evolution of games and game rules. At times, initial errors of fact have been perpetuated because subsequent historians accepted original findings without checking. For example, Cooperstown's Baseball Hall of Fame has projected the "fact" that General Abner Doubleday as a young man invented the name and the game of baseball at a single stroke one afternoon in 1839: Henderson[5] has shown that baseball came from the English game of rounders, which came from stool-ball and other old English forms of "baseball." Further, he demonstrates that all these as well as other ball games came from the French medieval game-ritual of *la soule*, which in turn was adapted by the Christian religion from Islamic rites that traced back through pagan rites to the worship of Osiris in Egypt. Any historian want to challenge this research?

Internal Criticism

Internal criticism is concerned with the meaning and accuracy of statements. Evaluation is transferred from the authenticity of the document to the trustworthiness of its contents. A number of questions will serve to clarify this form of criticism.

1. Is the meaning of words the same? The meaning of words may change with time or the same word may have different nuances of meaning for different people. The word "football" is an example: Depending on the country, this sport may be American football, soccer, rugby, or Australian rules football. These games have great differences in playing rules. The word "gymnastics" has had various meanings since early times.

2. Is the author writing seriously? At times, an author may not be writing in a serious vein but, rather, in a humorous, ironic, or symbolic manner. Occasionally, satire is used to emphasize meaning through ridicule and sarcasm. The historian must be able and ready to recognize the difference between serious, straightforward statements of fact and meaning and other forms of expression and to treat them accordingly.

3. Is the author expressing his real beliefs? For the most part, beliefs are expressed succinctly and forcefully. On occasion, however, an author may express ideas that his audience wants to hear whether they accord with his actual beliefs or not. Political speeches are notorious for this fault.

4. How soon after the event was the document written? Of course, the nearer to an event it is recorded, the more reliable is the account. To ask a person to reminisce back five, ten, fifteen, or more years is to seek the impossible as far as details are concerned. On the other hand, in retrospect the meaning and significance of the happening may be enhanced, as only time can validate these values.

---

[5] Robert W. Henderson, *Ball, Bat, and Bishop* (New York: Rockport Press, 1947).

5. Was the author biased in any way? Both primary and secondary sources may be biased in numerous ways, almost too many to mention. However, influences stemming from the following may result in prejudice and bias: race, religion, nationality, political party, social or economic group, professional body, period in history, educational philosophy, ideology, special or limited interests within a profession, malice, self-aggrandizement, and need for defensive action. Bias is not always easy to detect, but the historian should be alert to its presence in documents that he reviews.

6. Are written sources evaluated with an understanding of the times and conditions under which they were produced? Such data need to be interpreted from an historical rather than a contemporary point of view. For example, health education in the 1920s was subject to the strong influences of the temperance union and was not the broad, practical field it is today. Mores and codes of conduct change with time; therefore, the historian needs to be steeped in the culture of the time when the historical events that he is examining occurred.

General Principles of Criticism

As can be seen from the above, the historian must make judgments relative to his source materials. Woody[6] briefly stated the following principles to be observed in judging and reading historical sources:

1. Do not read into earlier documents the conceptions of later times.
2. Do not judge an author ignorant of certain events necessarily because he fails to mention them (the argument *ex silentio*) or that they did not occur, for the same reason.
3. Underestimating a source is no less an error than overestimating it in the same degree, and there is no more virtue in placing an event too late than in dating it too early by the same number of years or centuries.
4. A single true source may establish the existence of an idea, but other direct, competent, independent witnesses are required to prove the reality of events or objective facts.
5. Identical errors prove the dependence of sources on each other or a common source.
6. If witnesses contradict each other on a certain point, one or the other may be true, but both may be in error.
7. Direct, competent, independent witnesses who report the same central fact and also many peripheral matters in a casual way may be accepted for the points of their agreement.

---

[6] Woody, *op. cit.*, p. 190.

8. Official testimony, oral or written, must be compared with unofficial testimony whenever possible, for neither one nor the other is alone sufficient.

9. A document may provide competent and dependable evidence on certain points, yet carry no weight in respect to others it mentions.

HISTORICAL HYPOTHESES

Historians do not simply collect primary and secondary sources, subject them to external and internal criticisms, and present this mass of facts in some orderly way. To be sure, such procedures add to knowledge about the history of a movement, association, or person being studied. However, scholars of history go beyond the mere massing of facts. Rather, they formulate hypotheses to explain the occurrence of events and conditions and then search and apply data to determine whether or not they are tenable.

As in all research, hypotheses are proposed for testing, not for defending. The hypothesis is a tentative assumption that is based on the available facts and best judgments at the time; some elements may be known while others are conceptual. The conceptual elements go beyond known facts to the realm of plausible explanation. Van Dalen[7] states that hypotheses logically relate known facts to intelligent guesses about unknown conditions in an effort to extend and enlarge knowledge. Through conceptualization, investigators can go beyond the known data relating to a problem and suggest possible, theoretical solutions.

The tyro historian may have, and usually does have, difficulty in locating and clearly defining hypotheses. Possibly, too, hypotheses may not occur or be appropriate in some historical studies. However, the investigator should read widely while considering the meanings and implications derived from his sources; through such critical reading, hypotheses may develop.

PITFALLS IN HISTORICAL WRITING

The investigator should guard against various pitfalls—error areas—that are present in historical research. Several of these pitfalls are listed.

1. Complete misunderstanding of the meaning of historical sources and the ways to evaluate them. To succumb to this pitfall is to ignore what has been written in this chapter about primary and secondary sources and the external and internal criticisms that should be applied to them. However, the graduate student, especially at the doctoral level, who contemplates an

---

[7] D. B. Van Dalen, "The Function of Hypotheses in Research," *Physical Educator*, 26, No. 1 (March 1957), 21.

historical dissertation or who wishes to pursue historical research as a scholarly endeavor in the future should study the historical method intensively. He would be well-advised to take one or more graduate courses on historical methodology, and he should read extensively on this subject in the available literature.

2. Attempt to fill historic gaps with little or no basic evidence and to color narration for the sake of interest, thus sacrificing accuracy and fidelity. The good historian will recognize and make every effort to obtain facts that are missing and causing gaps in his account; if unable to do so, he will admit to this situation rather than attempt to cover up by use of his imagination. If he wishes to speculate, he may certainly do so, but it should be made clear that this is what he is doing. An interesting presentation of history is certainly legitimate but not at the expense of accuracy and validity.

3. Use of poor logic in handling historical materials and in drawing conclusions from them. The historian, as has been repeatedly emphasized, is more than a chronicler of dates and happenings. His real skill and insight are demonstrated by weighing the evidence, characterizing the results, generalizing on his findings, and even predicting future events. The ability to formulate and test historical hypotheses is the epitome of scholarly historical writing.

4. Bias. Bias is one of the greatest dangers in historical writing; it is a dangerous pitfall to be avoided. Bias may rear its ugly head either consciously or unconsciously; its source may be prejudice, self-interest, long-held preconceived notions, or desire to promote a cause or to commemorate an individual. Some years ago there was an historical report on "rehabilitation in World War II" published, in which the author's chief intent was to commend all those who played a leading role in this worthwhile effort. In another instance, a graduate student wrote a biography of his college coach, but, knowing that the coach would read it, he was loath to make even mildly negative comments about him. The historian must strive for the same sort of objectivity that the scientist in a laboratory employs in evaluating his data and drawing his conclusions.

5. Carelessness in reporting. Very obviously, the historian must employ extreme care in making records of his readings, interviews, and other investigative efforts.

ILLUSTRATED STUDIES

In order to illustrate the use of the historical method in health, physical education, and recreation, a number of studies that use this method are described in this section.

Research Section, AAHPER

A limited historical study of the Research Section of the American Association for Health, Physical Education and Recreation was reported in 1938 by Clarke.[8] At the time this study was conducted, the Research Section was 10 years old, having been officially accepted as a section of the association in 1928. However, the origins were actually traced back to an organization known as the Athletic Research Society, which held its initial meeting in December 1907. This meeting was attended by men concerned with athletics for boys in elementary schools, secondary schools, colleges, the Young Men's Christian Association, and boys' clubs. In 1911, a Federated Committee was formed to enlarge the research function and effectiveness of the society. With the great expansion of physical education following World War I, the usefulness of the Athletic Research Society waned; it sought affiliation with the American Physical Education Association, as the AAHPER was then known. Affiliation did not take place immediately; a transition period followed, which culminated in 1928 by formation of the Research Section.

The main historical sources for this study were the following:

1. Reports and minutes of meetings of the Legislative Council of the American Physical Education Association, 1885–1938.

2. Historical articles, official announcements, and news notes that appeared in:

(a) *Proceedings of the Association for the Advancement of Physical Education*, 1885–1895.

(b) *American Physical Education Review*, 1896–1929.

(c) *Proceedings of the Athletic Research Society*, 1907–1921. (Many of these were published in the *American Physical Education Review*.)

(d) *Journal of Health and Physical Education* and *Research Quarterly*, 1930–1938.

3. Correspondence with past secretaries of the Athletic Research Society, national and district chairmen of the Research Section, and the national office of the American Association for Health and Physical Education (as it was then known).

A difficult problem in completing this historical study was to reconstruct the period from 1920 to 1928, during which the transition occurred from the Athletic Research Society to the Research Section of the American Physical Education Association; considerable correspondence was conducted with the leaders involved during this period. Definite affiliation of the society with the association did not occur until 1925, although its place in the association was not defined at that date. The last meeting of the society was held on

---

[8] H. Harrison Clarke, "History of the Research Section of the American Association for Health and Physical Education," *Research Quarterly*, 9, No. 3 (October 1968), 25.

December 28, 1927; the year 1928 marked the beginning of the Research Section. The growth of the section was rapid; by 1938, five of the association's districts had each formed a Research Section.

NCAA and AAU

The purpose of a doctoral dissertation at the University of Michigan by Flath[9] was to present a history of the relations between the National Collegiate Athletic Association and the Amateur Athletic Union of the United States from 1905 to 1963. The following questions were posed as a guide for the study: (1) What was the early history of amateur athletics in the United States? (2) How was control of amateur athletics in the United States accomplished by the Amateur Athletic Union and the National Collegiate Athletic Association? (3) What has been the nature of cooperative efforts in the administration of amateur athletics by the National Collegiate Athletic Association and the Amateur Athletic Union? (4) What have been the sources of controversy between the National Collegiate Athletic Association and the Amateur Athletic Union? (5) What is the nature of present relations between the National Collegiate Athletic Association and the Amateur Athletic Union?

The need for the study emerged from the controversy that existed between the NCAA and the AAU over the control of amateur sports in the United States, especially as related to international competition. As with any controversial issue, a vast amount of material has been written in newspapers, magazines, and books relative to some phase of NCAA-AAU relations. Much of what has been written has been so biased that it was nearly impossible to be objective in arriving at any decision concerning amateur athletics in this country. The author believed that an historical account of the relations between these two organizations would contribute toward clarifying their respective roles.

The process used in applying the historical method to this study included the collection of data from primary and secondary sources, criticism of the collected data, and presentation of the facts concerning the relations between the NCAA and the AAU. Secondary sources were used in tracing the historical development of amateur athletics for the time period up to 1879; the main body of the study that dealt with the establishment of amateur athletic control and NCAA-AAU relations was based mostly on primary

[9] Arnold W. Flath, *A History of Relations Between the National Collegiate Athletic Association and the Amateur Athletic Union of the United States* (1905–1963) (Champaign, Ill.: Stipes Publishing Co., 1964). Excerpts reprinted by permission of the author and publisher.

sources. The sources of data include:

1. Secondary sources: histories of American society, dictionaries, and encyclopedia.

2. Proceedings of sports bodies: National Collegiate Athletic Association, Amateur Athletic Union, and Inter-Collegiate Association of Amateur Athletes of America.

3. Reports, surveys, investigations, and observations made by official bodies.

4. Newspapers, periodicals, articles: popular, professional, and trade publications.

5. Personal visits: visits to the offices of the National Collegiate Athletic Association and the Amateur Athletic Union.

Public Health in Oregon

As a doctoral dissertation at the University of Oregon, Smolensky[10] studied the history of the public health movement in Oregon from the time the Territory of Oregon was created by an act of Congress on August 14, 1848, to 1953. The author's intentions were to depict early health problems that existed in Oregon cities and towns and to determine how through the years these problems were first recognized, then faced, and finally solved.

When the Oregon legislature created the State Board of Health in 1903, epidemics of bubonic plague, smallpox, and other contagious diseases threatened Oregon. Today, plague is an extremely rare disease; smallpox has all but disappeared from the state, with only one case reported between 1949 and 1953. In addition, significant reductions have occurred in the frequency of both cases and deaths from typhoid fever, diphtheria, tuberculosis, whooping cough, influenza, pneumonia, the dysentaries, and the tick-borne diseases. An Oregonian born in 1900 had a life expectancy of fifty years; by 1950, the expectancy was sixty-seven years.

The major divisions of this historical account dealt with the Office of Dairy and Food Commissioner, the Portland Bureau of Health, the Oregon State Board of Health, and water supplies and sewage disposal. Following is an overview of the sources utilized:

1. Oregon Laws, Portland City Ordinances, Oregon Senate and House Journals, and *Oregon Messages and Documents* from 1851 to 1955 read.

2. Visits made to Oregon State Board of Health, Portland Bureau of Health, and Multnomah County Department; staff members interviewed and annuals, records, bulletins, and other materials reviewed.

---

[10] Jack Smolensky, "A History of Public Health in Oregon," microcard Doctoral Dissertation, University of Oregon, 1957. Excerpts printed by permission of the author.

3. Letters of inquiry regarding public health information sent to each of thirty-one health departments in Oregon; scrap books, early annual reports, records, news clippings, and documents received and reviewed; visits made to fifteen of the county health departments.

4. Oregon newspapers searched from 1851 to 1930.

5. Other sources were: Oregon collection at University of Oregon, University of Oregon Library, State Board of Health Library, Portland Bureau of Health, Oregon Historical Society Library, State Supreme Court Library, University of Oregon Medical School Library, Portland and Eugene Public Libraries, University of Oregon Law School Library, Oregon State University Library, Oregon State Library, Portland and Eugene City Halls, State Department of Agriculture, and Eugene Water and Electric Board.

At all times, the author strove for conclusive facts that pertained to the public health movement in Oregon; to do so, he constantly searched for corroborative evidence. His primary and secondary sources were subjected to rigorous external and internal criticisms.

Biography of Edward Hitchcock

The biography of Edward Hitchcock, professor of hygiene and physical education at Amherst College from 1861 until his death in 1911, was written by Welch as a doctoral dissertation at George Peabody College for Teachers.[11] As director of the first successful program of physical education in any American college, Hitchcock was in fact the "founder of physical education in the college curriculum." Health instruction was also a vital phase of the Amherst plan; Hitchcock gave regular lectures in "hygiene" to the freshman class.

Hitchcock was a pioneer in research; he applied the science of anthropometry to problems of the emerging profession. He wrote only one textbook, which was in anatomy and physiology; however, a list of his published articles, manuals, and reports covered eight pages in the *American Physical Education Review*. Hitchcock was the first president of the American Association for the Advancement of Physical Education and was chairman *pro tem.* at the founding meeting of the Society for College Gymnasium Directors. He received many honors and recognitions. Hitchcock Memorial Field and Hitchcock Memorial Room at Amherst College were dedicated in his memory.

---

[11] J. Edmund Welch, "Edward Hitchcock, M.D., Founder of Physical Education in the College Curriculum," microcard Doctoral Dissertation, George Peabody College for Teachers, 1962. Copyright 1962 by J. Edmund Welch. Excerpts reprinted by permission of the author.

The Memorial Room not only preserves Hitchcock's historical materials but contains memorabilia of Amherst College.

In preparing this bibliography, Welch consulted such primary and secondary sources as the following:

1. Hitchcock Memorial Room, Amherst College: contains several thousand books, bound volumes, articles, pamphlets, tracts, clippings, certificates, pictures, files, scrapbooks, and letters.

2. Amherst College campus: Barrett Hall and Pratt Hall, now serving as language and geology buildings, were the college gymnasiums where Hitchcock did his work; Pratt Hall is still in use; his desk and mementos of his career are preserved.

3. Other primary sources: Official procedures, minutes, papers, comments and speeches are found in *Proceedings of the American Association for the Advancement of Physical Education*, *American Physical Education Review*, *Mind and Body*, *Posse Gymnasium Journal*, and *Physical Education*.

4. Secondary sources: Numerous books contain items about Hitchcock, including histories of physical education and biographies of Hitchcock's contemporaries; booklets, pamphlets, and articles written by others, publications of government and learned societies, and encyclopedia articles are available.

In Welch's study, verification of facts was consistently sought. Where doubt still existed as to the accuracy of any source, this doubt was stated in the biography.

Contributions of James Huff McCurdy

As a doctoral study at Springfield College, Kidess[12] historically studied the contributions of James Huff McCurdy. The author placed McCurdy's work in the professional perspective of the period—nearly a half century—during which he was active. Only in this way can the true value of his principles and ideals be measured, not only in light of contemporary society but in light of the foundations he helped build for present-day achievements in physical education.

McCurdy started his professional career as physical director at the 23rd Street YMCA in New York City. He joined the physical education staff at Springfield College in 1895, became director in 1907, and continued in this capacity until his retirement. McCurdy was editor of the *American Physical*

---

[12] Attalah A. Kidess, "A study of the Work and Contributions of Dr. James Huff McCurdy to Physical Education," microcard Doctoral Dissertation, Springfield College, 1958. Excerpts reprinted by permission of the author.

Education Review from 1906 until its demise in 1929; he was secretary-treasurer of the American Physical Education Association for all but the first of these years. He was a pioneer in research, especially in exercise physiology and wrote the first book on this subject in 1924; he was in the forefront in the construction of tests typical of his period. Over the years, he developed the curriculum of physical education at Springfield College to a position of national and international stature, which has continued to this day.

The sources utilized by Kidess in preparing this biography were as follows:

1. Springfield College Library: books, bound volumes, articles, pamphlets, and the like.

2. Letters: by McCurdy, from his contemporaries, and letters evaluating McCurdy's contributions by present leaders.

3. Interviews: with his son, Hugh McCurdy, and with his former associates on the Springfield College faculty.

4. Records: publications of the American Physical Education Association.

WRITING THE REPORT

The writing of an historical account has many of the same characteristics as the writing of any research report. A statement of the problem and any limitations imposed should be made. Questions to be answered may be posed, as in the NCAA-AAU illustration above, or hypotheses may be stated. Special care should be exercised in identifying the primary and secondary sources found and utilized. The ways by which events are double-checked, contradictions resolved, and facts sifted from rumor or conjecture should be clear to the reader.

Considerable thought should be given to the organization of the historical report. Such reports are usually lengthy and need to conform to a definite plan to avoid duplication and confusion. Still, they should be concise and to the point; they should be accurate and cohesive. If questions have been asked or hypotheses have been formulated, the organization can center around them. Otherwise, the historian should pattern his material in some systematic order, such as chronological, geographical, topical, or a combination of these. Judgments need to be made relative to the amount of emphasis or space given to each phase of the history. Minor points or trivia should be treated as such. Such accounts should be as interesting as the material will permit without sacrificing accuracy or meaning; historians must refrain from embellishing their narrations with dramatic statements that distort the truth. "Their objective is to write lucid, lively, logical accounts that are honest and scholarly."[13]

SUMMARY

As has been mentioned in this chapter, the history of any field is its heritage. Not only is the past recorded for posterity, but many lessons can be learned that may be applied as a guide for and a prediction of the future. Historical research can also be fascinating. Professional vistas unfold before the historian's consciousness; the unexpected is encountered, evaluated, and resolved; doubtful facets of history may be clarified; new acquaintance is gained with great leaders of the past; new respect and understanding of the profession and its pioneers are engendered.

In this chapter, the processes of historical writing were explained. The nature of primary and secondary sources and the means of evaluating them by external and internal criticisms were presented. The use of hypotheses was considered. Some pitfalls of historical writing were discussed. Illustrations of completed historical studies were provided. More and more, historical studies are being made by scholars in health, physical education, and recreation. Some professionals in these fields are now turning to historical writing as their contributions to scholarship.

---

[13] D. B. Van Dalen, "The Historical Method," in *Research Methods in Health Physical Education, and Recreation* (2nd ed.), ed. M. Gladys Scott (Washington, D.C.: American Association for Health, Physical Education, and Recreation, 1959), p. 480.

CHAPTER 5

Philosophical Studies

JUSTIFICATION OF A PHILOSOPHICAL METHOD

It is the purpose of this book to propose various methods for solving research problems. Each method is appropriate to the nature of a particular problem. If the background of a professional association is to be traced in order to establish guidelines for the future, the historical method is employed; if the values of two regimens of exercise for the development of strength are to be compared, experimentation is the appropriate method; if the status of health, physical education, or recreation in a state is to be determined, a survey by questionnaire or visitation is the procedure. In these research methods, as well as others, data are collected, analyzed, and interpreted; in each instance, explicit procedures for research have been developed.

Of what use is the philosophical method? Certainly, it is utilized for resolving problems, especially problems that currently cannot be solved by other means or that cannot wait on other means for an answer. The philosophical method can be applied to a problem at once without protracted experimentation. Therefore, the philosophical solution is timely; but such a solution is more prone to be wrong than are solutions gleaned by other methods, as subsequent experimentation may reveal.

The most vital and far-reaching decisions made in education are philosophically based. Objectives of education, the organization of the curriculum, the content of courses, and the selection of methodology are established more prevalently by philosophical considerations than through scientific means although the latter are not ignored in reaching decisions. Even before objectives are set, the ideology of a society is determined on a philosophical basis, since education systems planned for democratic and totalitarian states are vastly different. The same considerations apply to religions and the choice of denominations within religions. Today, how are such great human challenges as intergroup and racial relations, poverty, war, and crime being met? Certainly, the decisions made have profound influences upon man's way of being and living.

In this time of science, man is prone to rely upon material resources; and, certainly, these have been developed in overwhelming abundance. To meld these resources for the common good is more vital today than increasing them. But with what means will man accomplish this task? The concepts and methods of instrumental thinking—a result of unbridled science—cannot enable man to grasp absolute ends that are capable of directing him to use those instruments. "Instrumental thinking will rather be tempted to misrepresent all absolute ends as sheer useful fictions or imaginary satisfactions of human desires."[1]

Philosophical studies are needed in education, which, of course, includes physical education, recreation, and health, and they should be dedicated to the task of establishing the vision of ultimate ends. Philosophical solutions should be considered tentative and subject to constant reappraisal. But, then, is this not true of science as well—where today's firmly held truth is modified by tomorrow's fresh discovery? The growing and menacing gap between man's technical and scientific capacity and his apparent inability to deal with his own affairs on a rational basis must be narrowed.

NATURE OF THE PHILOSOPHICAL METHOD

Although the philosophical method by itself is not scientific, this method is needed to resolve certain kinds of problems. The philosophical method is largely subjective, since the solution of the problem is accomplished through critical thinking. However, this thinking is based upon whatever evidence that may be available. Reason is applied to this evidence and is supplemented by astute observation of the passing scene and the historical forces that brought it into being.

In its broadest sense, philosophy is the study of processes that govern thought and conduct, of the principles of laws that regulate the universe and underlie all knowledge and reality. Included in the study of philosophy are aesthetics, logic, ethics, and metaphysics. Philosophy projects the meanings derived from experience and from knowledge in terms of purposes appropriate for the guidance of man's choices and conduct.

Philosophical research involves critical thinking on levels of extensive generalization beyond the realm of fact-finding science. Philosophy takes the conclusions of science, uses these facts as raw materials for further reflection, and thereby develops larger and more inclusive points of view. Philosophy constructively criticizes experience as it exists at a given time and thus renders experience as more unified, stable, and progressive. The conflicts

---

[1] Maximillian Beck, "A Plea for Philosophical Research," *School and Society*, 62, No. 1610 (November 3, 1945), 293.

of experience demand a thorough, critical appraisal of contents and procedures. However, criticism does not end with mere intellectual discrimination; it provides a basis for the projection of values as yet unrealized—values that may be translated into ends that move men to action. Philosophy, thus conceived, makes the greatest possible use of experience resulting from both empirical and scientific observations.

THE METHOD OF PHILOSOPHY

When confronted with a problem, man frequently tries to recall a personal experience that will help lead to a solution. For example, the football coach may remember a play that worked well against a particular team the previous year and use it again against the same opponent. Although reference to personal experience is a useful and common method of reaching decisions on problems, its uncritical use can lead to erroneous conclusions. Thus, an individual's experience may have been too limited to justify reliance on it; evidence may be omitted that does not agree with his opinion; significant factors related to a specific situation may be overlooked; only evidence that supports his bias or prejudices may be selected; the situation may be sufficiently different so that previous experience does not apply (as in the football illustration, the opponents may also realize the possibility and be ready for it). To avoid these general pitfalls, the philosophical method must be applied with the same care in weighing the evidence as the scientist applies in weighing his results. He must consider the pros and cons as objectively as possible, raising objections to all suggested solutions until the proper one seems to emerge.

Various steps in critical thinking have been proposed by eminent authorities. Some years ago, John Dewey[2] proposed five such steps, as follows:

1. The occurrence of a felt difficulty:

(a) In the lack of adoption of means to end.
(b) In identifying the character of an object.
(c) In explaining an unexpected event.

2. Definition of the difficulty in terms of a problem statement.

3. Occurrence of a suggested explanation or possible solution: a guess, hypothesis, inference, or theory.

4. The rational elaboration of an idea through the development of its implications, by means of the collection of data (evidence).

5. Corroboration of the idea and formation of a concluding belief through experimental verification of the hypothesis.

---

[2] John Dewey, *How We Think* (Boston: D. C. Heath and Company, 1933), p. 12.

As can be seen, the steps proposed by Dewey exceed the purely philosophical, since they provide for experimentation. This observation indicates the close association between philosophy and science. Actually, no scientific work can be undertaken without critical thinking, as will be demonstrated below.

The first three of Dewey's steps are common to all research. Certainly, the investigator has a "felt difficulty," as from it comes his research topic. The difficulty is formulated into a problem with appropriate delimitations that permit solution, and the method of solution is determined, which includes the statement of an hypothesis. If a differentiation may be proposed in the fourth step, the philosopher basically gathers existing evidence to use in appraising his hypothesis whereas the scientist resorts to experimental procedures to produce his evidence. Thus, for philosophical studies, Dewey's steps stop short of scientific evaluation.

Philosophical research rests heavily on the formulation of an hypothesis and the application of critical reasoning in its appraisal. The hypothesis is a statement tentatively accepted in light of what is known about a phenomenon at the time; it is employed as a basis for action in the search for new truth. The hypothesis should be in agreement with observed facts; it should not conflict with known truths but may challenge them in light of new evidence or reasoning.

The hypothesis is stated for the purpose of evaluating its tenability. At no time should it be considered a statement that must be defended at all costs in order "not to lose face." Actually, rejected hypotheses contribute to knowledge in a negative sort of way; the investigator may not have arrived at a solution to his problem, but he does know some possibilities that are not correct. Many highly respected sciences are strewn with rejected hypotheses that lead to the one final solution that was found to be valid.

Thus, in philosophical research, the investigator follows certain specific steps, as follows:

1. Identifies the problem area; the problem is defined and delimited to manageable proportions.

2. Collects available facts related to the problem.

3. Synthesizes and analyzes the facts, working them into patterns that identify relationships among them.

4. From these patterns, derives general principles that describe the relationships inherent in the principles.

5. States these principles in the form of hypotheses or tentative assumptions.

6. Tests the hypotheses for acceptance, rejection, or modification.

THE CRITICAL-THINKING CONTINUUM

As mentioned above, a close association exists between philosophy and science; no sharp line of demarcation between the two is identifiable. In actuality, the most scientific study imaginable requires critical thinking—the primary feature of the philosophical method. Thus, in such a scientific study, the problem must be identified, hypotheses must be stated, results must be analyzed and integrated, and conclusions must be drawn.

On the other hand, philosophical studies per se depend more on critical thinking. Instead of the deliberately acquired experimental evidence in the scientific study, existing knowledge is assembled and applied with a heightened utilization of reflective process. Some philosophical studies may have an abundance of available evidence whereas others may need to obtain additional evidence to guide thinking. Thus, the degree of reliance upon critical appraisal applied to studies may be considered on a continuum, extending from the minimal amount in scientific studies to the maximal amount where astute observation is dominant, as in proposing a philosophy for health, physical education, or recreation. Examples of these extremes—minimal and maximal poles—may help clarify the meaning of this critical-thinking continuum, as well as the definition and concept of philosophical research intended here.

Minimal Pole

The minimal pole of the critical-thinking continuum—the pole with the minimal amount of critical thinking upon which to base results—is illustrated by an investigation of the "memory drum" theory of neuromotor reaction by Henry and Rogers.[3] The theory proposes a nonconscious mechanism that uses stored information (motor memory) to channel existing nervous impulses from brain waves and general afferent stimuli into the appropriate neuromuscular coordination centers, subcenters, and efferent nerves and thus causes the desired movement.

Hypothesis formulation. The authors first indicated that the time for the simplest voluntary response to a stimulus (*RT*) is .15 seconds under the most favorable circumstances, although longer times of .20 to .25 seconds are more typical. When complications are present, such as discrimination between several stimuli and/or choice between several possible movements, the *RT* increases and may be twice as long as these times.

---

[3] Franklin M. Henry and Donald E. Rogers, "Increased Response Latency for Complicated Movements and a 'Memory Drum' Theory of Neuromotor Reaction," *Research Quarterly*, 31, No. 3 (October 1960), 448. Reprinted by permission.

Based on current knowledge of the neuromuscular system and its control by cephalic nervous centers, the investigators modified the traditional reflex theories of voluntary response time. The facts cited in the formulation of their theory were: (1) No reflex exists in the modern physiological use of the term, since a reflex must be nonwillful and not voluntary. (2) Not more than a minimal involvement of the cerebral cortex is involved in the *RT* response, because the neuromuscular coordination centers and pathways are chiefly cerebral or subcortical without cortical termination. (3) As a consequence, perhaps neuroanatomy, neuromotor perception is extremely poor, although neuromotor coordination or kinesthetic adjustment is well-developed in humans.

Next, it was observed that performance of acts of skill may involve neuromuscular memory. Such memory was operationally defined as "improved neuromotor coordination and more effective response, the improvement being the result of experience and practice, possibly accumulated over a period of many years." The implication was made that this neuromotor memory is different from ideational or perceptual memory, since conscious imagery is indefinite and largely excluded.

However, a rich store of unconscious motor memory is available for the performance of neuromotor skill. Added to this are innate motor coordinations that are important in motor acts. The use of this store of motor responses was thought of broadly by the authors as a "memory drum" phenomenon, using an analogy from the electronic computer. "The neural pattern for a specific and well-coordinated motor act is controlled by a stored program that is used to direct the neuromotor details of its performance. In the absence of an available stored program, an unlearned complicated task is carried out under conscious control in an awkward, step-by-step, poorly coordinated manner."

The authors indicated that the concepts discussed can lead to a number of testable predictions. One of the implications becomes the hypothesis for this study. This hypothesis was that simple reaction time becomes longer when the response movement required is of greater complexity. It was contended that a longer latent time for the more complicated circulation of neural impulses through the coordination centers is inevitable when more complicated patterns are involved.

Experimentation. Without going into detail concerning the methodology of this sample study, as that is not the purpose of this presentation, the hypothesis that simple reaction time becomes lengthened with increased movement complexity was tested. Data were obtained on 120 subjects—college men and women and 12- and 8-year-old boys. Sixty of the subjects were tested with two experimental procedures in order to improve the adequacy of the control conditions. Three types of movement varying in complexity were used; both reaction time and movement time were measured.

The results were in agreement with the hypothesis. By substituting a very simple finger movement with an arm movement of moderate complexity, the reaction was slowed by about 20 per cent; additional complexity produced a furthering slowing of reaction of 7 per cent. Other aspects of this study, each of which represented another hypothesis which was investigated in this study, were reported as follows: (1) The speed of an arm movement is considerably faster in college men than in college women or younger boys. (2) The correlation between reaction time and speed of movement is approximately zero. (3) Individual differences in ability to make a fast arm movement are about 70 per cent specific to the particular movement being made; "general ability for arm speed" occurs only to the extent of 30 per cent.

Comments. The study by Henry and Rogers was presented to show the reliance upon critical thinking required even in a highly scientific study. Evidence was marshalled from several sources, especially knowledge of the neuromuscular systems. A "memory drum" theory of neuromotor reaction was evolved. From this theory, a number of hypotheses were stated. Up to this point, the investigators had confined their efforts to the critical evaluation of existing facts and the formulation of implications from them. Obviously, the philosopher does likewise. However, the point of departure between science and philosophy was reached when the scientist began experimentation.

Maximal Pole

The maximal pole of the critical-thinking continuum requires the maximal amount of critical thinking and the minimal amount of scientific evidence available to guide that thinking. This pole is illustrated by the charts of "The Aims and Anathemata of Education" developed by Frederick Rand Rogers[4] and shown in Figures 1A for males and 1B for females. The aims of this study were prepared with the assistance of scores of men and women in all walks of life and after exhaustive analyses of the aims and objectives of some sixty educational leaders, including state commissioners, college presidents, and deans of schools of education. The charts are briefly described in the reference and more briefly here.

---

[4] Frederick Rand Rogers, "An Educational Mariner's Portfolio of Basic Charts," 221 Cambon Avenue, St. James, Long Island, New York, 1960. Copyright 1960 by F.R.R.; charts reproduced here with his permission. An earlier form of these charts appears in: Frederick Rand Rogers, ed., *Dance: A Basic Educational Technique* (New York: The Macmillan Company, 1941), pp. 7–17.

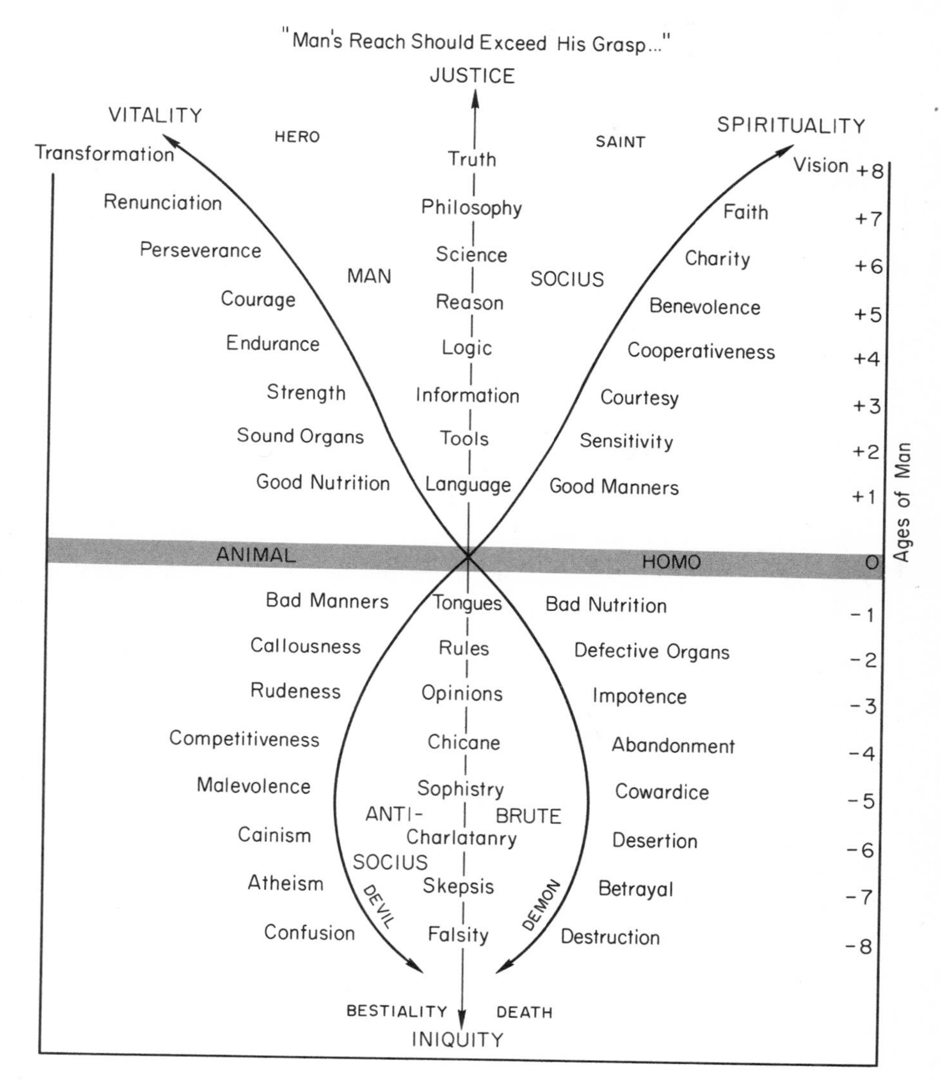

Figure 1A. The ♂ Objectives and Anathemata of Education

A complete exposition of this formalized hierarchy of aims, objectives, and their anathemas would require considerable space, including particular definitions of each word that appears and the logical, psychological, and social justification for its inclusion. In philosophically establishing the charts of aims, such explanations must be made. The investigator draws on his observations of the passing scene and interprets them in the light of current

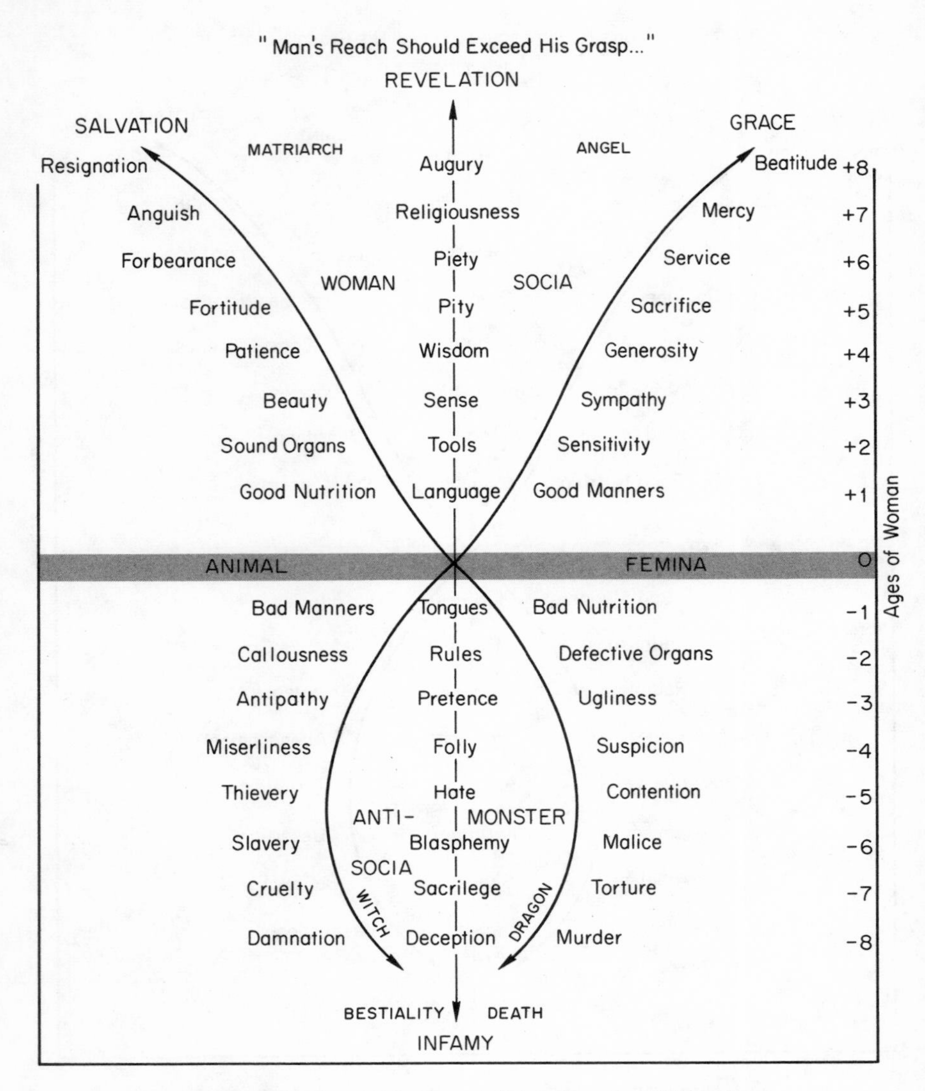

Figure 1B. The ♀ Objectives and Anathemata of Education

knowledge and the pioneering aims of leading educational philosophers. Obviously, the logic must be sound and be supported by an objective approach to the truth where pros and cons for each concept are carefully weighed before being accepted. The following interpretations are made as an aid to understanding the charts.

1. The aims and objectives of boys and girls are separate and different.

The logic is: Nature made men and women differently, including different constructions of their bodies and different manifestations of emotions of their spirits; boys were intended to grow into men and girls into women; and the continuance of life itself depends on nurturing the unique qualities of male and female.

2. The aims are listed in heavy print at the top of each chart: Vitality, Justice, and Spirituality for boys; Salvation, Revelation, and Grace for girls. These aims are admittedly above mortal man's grasp; they are spiritual rather than secular, indefinitely extended into the future, as expressed by "man's reach should exceed his grasp." However, these aims are only logical extensions of mundane striving for health, culture, and social efficiency. Their religious terminology is appropriate, since one appeals to religion for spiritual terms.

3. Each sex has three kinds of growth represented by three scales that extend upward from the midpoint of its own base. These indicate physical, mental, and social development leading toward ultimate goals. Teachers must be equally concerned with all three kinds of growth. A strong man who is antisocial can be a menace to society. A beautiful girl who lacks sympathy is a perpetual source of anxiety.

4. The qualities, virtues, or kinds of behavior named on each scale are to represent objectives to be achieved during each stage of growth. Eight stages are indicated by the objectives on the chart; they are considered to be approximations and are subject to changes in order.

5. The author did not intend that the order must be maintained in the effort to reach higher levels. For example, boys can persevere before they are strong and courageous, and girls can serve before they are sympathetic, generous, and sacrificial; but they are not as likely to do so. On the other hand, the placing of each virtue gives a clue to its proper definition. Thus, perseverence placed above endurance and courage means the capacity to persevere significantly for the benefit of society. Further, the separation of men's and women's qualities is not intended to convey that boys should have no feminine traits and that girls should have no masculine traits. For example, women must have strength to fulfill their life's functions, and men need some courtesy to be bearable. Nor is it possible for most men and women to move equally up all scales.

6. Knowledge of the anathematic of aims and objectives is almost as necessary as is appreciation of virtues and ultimate goals. This concept recognizes that education can have undesirable as well as desirable results, depending on the educational process. Eight negative stages are indicated from the midpoints on the charts, leading to "iniquity" for men and "infamy" for women.

7. The curvings of the scales away from each midpoint illustrate growing and expanding life. As a boy becomes strong, informed, and courteous, his

horizons and influence widen and increase. As a girl becomes beautiful, sensible, and sympathetic, so does her life expand.

8. To illustrate applications of the traits, "strength" *presupposes* sound organs and good nutrition; it *indicates* ability to work, play, and study for long hours without fatigue; it *implies* not great absolute strength (a Sampson) but abundant strength in proportion to sex, age, and weight. Likewise, "beauty" *presupposes* sound organs and good nutrition for girls; it *indicates* clear complexion, general cleanliness, regularity of feature and figure, grace, and poise of body, graciousness of bearing; it *implies* not a pretty face but a sympathetic spirit shining through a healthy body.

The author intimated:

> A whimsical reader might imagine each chart to represent a "cup of life"—a holy grail—into which is poured, from on high, the human spirit. It comes to rest at the midpoint—as Life—at the instant of conception. The Spirit then *climbs*, aided by nurture, education, and inspiration, growing and expanding toward the Infinite. Failing to strive, poorly nurtured, misguided, or lacking inspiration, this human Spirit slips down through bad manners, bad nutrition, confused language, and, successively, other anathemas, toward the bottom of the chalice, where are found the very dregs of life.[5]

Comments. The charts of aims of education developed by Rogers show the results of a philosophical approach in which maximal reliance is placed on critical thinking. The process by which Rogers arrived at his charts of aims is not described in this statement other than to say that assistance was obtained from many laymen and educators. The author had a broad background of education and experience upon which to draw information; he was familiar with allied professional and scientific literature, which helped to guide his thinking. This process is typical of the establishment of educational aims and objectives whether they be prepared by individuals or by committees or commissions. Their impact on education is great, so they should be approached with true critical appraisal, free of bias, prejudice, or self-interest.

SELECTED EXAMPLES OF PHILOSOPHICAL STUDIES

In order to indicate various approaches to the conduct of philosophical studies, several examples of such studies actually completed will be given. In selecting the studies for review, unique features in each were sought.

---

[5] *Ibid.*, *Dance*, p. 14.

Principles of Physical Education

In 1938, as a doctoral dissertation at the State University of Iowa, Arthur A. Esslinger[6] submitted a philosophical study of principles for selecting activities in physical education. The need expressed for the study and the proposals that resulted should be judged in view of the situation facing physical education in the mid-1930s rather than the present day. However, much of what he wrote then is still germane now.

Esslinger justified the need for the study on the chaotic condition of physical education in the United States at the time. Courses of study lagged behind current physical education philosophy; considerable divergence of opinion existed as to the activities that best attained the aims and objectives of physical education; advocates of different activities contended in favor of their particular programs. Needed were underlying principles upon which the selection of all physical education subject matter can be based. Such fundamental principles, while allowing for local adaptations, were considered necessary to give some semblance of uniformity to the physical education program and to eliminate the confused condition that existed.

Purposes. The purposes of this study were: (1) To establish principles upon which the selection of subject matter could be based. (2) To develop implications for the physical education program based on the principles established. A principle was conceived of as being a fundamental belief based upon facts available. Drawn from the facts that developed and substantiated the principle, implications were offered as practical suggestions for selecting and adapting the content of the program.

Procedures. The principles and their implications were developed from facts regarding the child and his present and future environment. The specific steps in this process were:

1. Discovering the facts.
(a) Facts related to the growth and development and the capacities and interests of the child that are of significance for the physical educator were derived from a study of anatomy, physiology, psychology, and education. (b) Facts related to the needs of the child and the adult were found by the study of present-day society and social trends.

2. Evolving the principles from the facts.
(a) From a study of the facts that had been collected, the chief characteristics of the facts were determined. Those that appeared to have some

---

[6] Arthur A. Esslinger, "A Philosophical Study of Principles for Selecting Activities in Physical Education," microcard Doctoral Dissertation, State University of Iowa, 1938. Excerpts reprinted by permission of the author.

characteristics in common or seemed to be of the same general type were organized under an appropriate head stated in the form of a generalized statement. (b) After a generalized statement or principle had been evolved, it was substantiated with all the facts that were applicable to it.

3. Development of the implications. By a careful study of each principle and the facts used to substantiate it, practical implications for the program were suggested. Although it was not the purpose of the investigation to construct a course of study, these implications offered concrete suggestions in regard to the definite activities or types of activities that should be included in the program.

Principles Established. As an indication of the results of this philosophical study, the principles evolved are given:

1. The physical education program should provide opportunities for a wide range of muscular movements involving the large-muscle groups.
2. The activities of the physical education program should be selected and adapted in light of the known facts regarding the biological growth and development of children.
3. The activities should be selected in the light of the psychological age characteristics of the child.
4. The individual differences that exist among children should be considered in the selection of the activities.
5. Only activities that are physiologically wholesome should be selected for the physical education program.
6. The physical education program should consist predominantly of activities organized and developed from the racial activities.
7. In the selection of the activities, some provision should be made for progression.
8. The curriculum should stress those activities that are recreative in nature.
9. Activities should be selected for their contribution to the youth's training for citizenship in a democracy.
10. Activities that are valuable in providing opportunities for training and expressing the emotions should receive much emphasis in the physical education curriculum.

Implications of a Principal Aim. To illustrate the implications of a principle in this study, the second principle above is chosen: "The activities of the physical education program should be selected and adapted in light of the known facts regarding the biological growth and development of children." The implications developed are:

1. The activities should be selected for the child upon the basis of the physiological rather than the chronological age.

2. The facts related to the growth and development of the skeleton indicate the need for an early selection of postural activities.

3. The elementary school program should consist of a variety of activities rather than just a few.

4. The elementary school child has a great need for physical education activities that are valuable in developing neuromuscular coordination. The junior high school boy and girl also need coordinating activities.

5. The physical education time allotment in the elementary school is far from being adequate to meet the needs of children for large-muscle exercise.

6. No differentiation in the program of activities is necessary for boys and girls until the seventh grade.

7. The facts suggest the inadvisability of strenuous exercise during the junior high school period.

8. The lack of arm and shoulder girdle strength of junior and senior high school boys requires the special attention of the physical educator.

9. Activities emphasizing the development of the upper body should be selected for the physical education program for girls in senior high school and college.

10. Various activities should be modified for the girls' physical education program in junior and senior high schools and college.

11. It is generally conceded that active, vigorous sports and games are valuable for girls and that participation in them does not interfere with the special biological functions of women.

Comments. Esslinger's study conforms closely to the classical approach to a philosophical study; his methodology is located toward the maximal pole of the critical-thinking continuum. He utilized a vast resource of available facts and current pioneer thinking to formulate and justify his principles. Then, he followed through by making numerous implications for physical education for boys and girls from elementary school through college. New scientific facts were not sought; rather, the resource was a synthesis of existing knowledge.

An interesting observation that the thoughtful, informed reader would make is that some of the implications are no longer valid or not nearly so valid.[7] Such a consequence is inevitable in any such philosophical study completed years ago, for human knowledge continues to increase and at an accelerated rate in recent years. The appropriateness of the proposals made

[7] For example, the sixth and seventh implications above would now be challenged in light of present research. A recent application of growth and development knowledge to elementary school physical education is contained in: H. Harrison Clarke and Franklin B. Haar, *Health and Physical Education for the Elementary School Classroom Teacher* (Englewood Cliffs, N.J.: Prentice-Hall, Inc., 1963), Ch. 2.

in this study must be judged in relation to the time when they were made and the level of knowledge and thought available then.

Another exhaustive philosophical study to establish the principles that are essential for the realization of the objectives of physical education was completed by Hartley d'O. Price[8] in 1946 as a doctoral dissertation at New York University. In 1949, this study received a Research Citation from the American Academy of Physical Education.

Intergroup Problems

In 1947, Martin Bloom[9] studied types of action taken in resolving intergroup relations in physical education as a master's thesis at Springfield College. This study dealt primarily with Caucasian-Negro racial situations, although some other minority groups were involved. As for Esslinger's study, the proposals made must be viewed from the 1940s and before rather than today; certainly racial concepts have undergone changes in our society since then; these changes are undergoing great acceleration in this decade.

In this philosophical study, the investigator relied heavily on the experiences of coaches and physical educators who had been exposed to, were involved in, or had observed intergroup incidents in sports and physical education. Thus, this study illustrates a philosophical approach in which the investigator deliberately sought certain types of information to guide the thinking process.

Purposes. The purposes of this study were: (1) to collect experiences in intergroup relations of the Springfield College physical education faculty members in order to discover some of the factors incident to the participation of Negroes and other minority groups in sports and intercollegiate athletic competition; (2) to categorize types of action that were used in resolving these intergroup incidents; (3) to propose ways by which physical education and athletics can foster improved intergroup relations.

Procedures. The basic procedures for this study were to collect anecdotal accounts of the intergroup experiences of the college's physical education faculty members and to analyze these critically in order to categorize types of action taken. The steps in this process were:

---

[8] Hartley d'O. Price, "The Establishment of the Principles Which Are Essential for the Realization of the Objectives of Physical Education," microcard Doctoral Dissertation, New York University, 1946.

[9] Martin Bloom, "Types of Action Used in Resolving Intergroup Problems in Physical Education," microcard Master's Thesis, Springfield College, 1947.

1. Conduct of interviews. After obtaining endorsement and support of the college's Committee on Intergroup Relations, individual interviews were held with each physical education faculty member. The members were asked to describe all intergroup problems they had observed or participated in during their professional careers whether at Springfield College or elsewhere. A phonographic recording was made of each interview.

2. Categorization. The recordings of the interviews were replayed as often as necessary to obtain a complete and accurate statement of each intergroup incident and its resolution. The types of action taken in the various incidents were identified in broad categories.

3. Implications. Implications for the improvement of intergroup relations through the conduct of sports and collegiate athletics were made.

Types of Action. The categories developed, which indicate the types of action taken in resolving the intergroup problems encountered in sports and intercollegiate athletics by the faculty members, were:

1. Learning through personal participation in intergroup activities: persons with prejudices voluntarily or through compulsion taking part in some common intergroup endeavor with the result that they learn about each other.
2. Fait accompli: putting into practice with few words one's belief in democratic human relations after realizing that very little would be accomplished by discussing the question.
3. No compromise: refusing to make any concessions where the question of democratic human rights is concerned.
4. Clearing the problem through channels: anticipating possible objections to the participation in an intercollegiate competition of a team member who belongs to a minority group, obtaining prior consent from the opposing team for the players participation.
5. Compromise: conceding on some points to make some progress toward the furtherance of democratic human relations.
6. Appeasement: submitting to the will of those who do not practice democratic human relations.
7. Suppression: using one's authority to prevent an untoward act from developing further.

Implications. Fifteen ways were proposed for the improvement of intergroup relations through the conduct of sports and athletic programs. Space does not permit their inclusion here, although some summary will be made. The starting point is the conviction of the coaches and physical educators that all human beings are fundamentally alike biologically, socially, and spiritually and of their dedication to the furtherance of this concept. Other procedures for effectively building better human relationships: engagement of Negroes on coaching and physical education staffs; refusal to compete with teams that condone racial discrimination; inclusion of Negroes in professional organizations; and consciously using intergroup incidents that occur on the athletic field or in the gymnasium to develop sound and healthy democratic attitudes.

Comments. Bloom's study illustrates a philosophical approach to a vital problem in today's society that could be researched at the master's degree level. This study is well along toward the maximal pole of the critical-thinking continuum. Scientific facts were not developed in this study. However great reliance was placed on the intergroup incidents recounted by the coaches and physical educators, which he deliberately acquired as the basis for his study. The investigator needed a good general background in intergroup relations in order to categorize, evaluate, and place his material in the proper frame of reference in the light of current knowledge and thought in this field.

As will be readily recognized, certain of the intergroup problems encountered in 1947 by Bloom have largely disappeared from the scene today or are not so severe an issue now as then. Again, as for the Esslinger study above, this type of philosophical research, which relies heavily upon the facts and thought of the time, can be outmoded or partially invalidated at a later date.

Leaders in American Physical Education

In 1958, Richard B. Morland[10] examined the philosophical views held by selected leaders in American physical education as a doctoral dissertation at New York University. This philosophical study is quite different from the ones previously described. The views of the selected leaders were identified from their writings and then related to systematic schools of educational philosophy. Seven leaders were selected who were influential in determining the direction of physical education during the period following World War I when the field was striving for educational status and recognition. These leaders were Thomas D. Wood, Clark W. Hetherington, Jesse Feiring Williams, Jay B. Nash, Charles H. McCloy, Mabel Lee, and Elmer D. Mitchell.

A comparative approach to philosophy was adopted. After reviewing several different classifications, four schools of thought were selected as the

---

[10] Richard B. Morland, "A Philosophical Interpretation of the Educational Views Held by Leaders in American Physical Education," microcard Doctoral Dissertation, New York University, 1958. Excerpts reprinted by permission of the author.

proposals included: conscious attempts on the part of staffs to develop bases for interpretation: progressivism, reconstructionism, essentialism, and perennialism. A broad frame of reference consisting of twenty subareas was constructed as a basis for the comparative analysis. These areas centered on specific aspects of the educational process and its theoretical foundations. Included were the general philosophical orientation, the nature and factors involved in learning, the curriculum and the role of the teacher, administration and administrative practices, school and community relations, and educational aims. Quotations were gathered from the works of 96 different educators and philosophers who were chosen as exponents of the four schools of thought. A basic approach toward each of the subareas of the general frame of reference was formulated from the themes of each of these competing philosophies.

Using the same topical headings, quotations were collected from the writings of the seven physical education leaders; a synopsis of their beliefs about each of these four philosophies, whether expressed explicitly or implicitly, was set forth. By comparing the views expressed by the physical educators with the general position as determined from the expositions of the representatives of the four schools of educational philosophy, the physical educators were classified in accordance with the consistency with which they followed the line of thought in one of the four schools. Upon this basis, Wood, Hetherington, Williams, Nash, and Mitchell were classified primarily as progressivists; McCloy and Lee supported essentialism.

Donn E. Bair[11] also completed a study of the philosophical beliefs of American physical education leaders and submitted it in 1956 as a doctoral dissertation at the University of Southern California. This investigator, however, employed a much different approach than did Morland. He surveyed by checklist 51 contemporary leaders in the field. The purpose of the study was to determine with what eminent philosophies these leaders were identified and from such identification to consider the philosophical directions that seemed to be indicated for American physical education.

The checklist was comprised of twelve categories selected from background reading that indicated these to be areas where philosophical beliefs were manifest. The following categories were included: the universe, the nature of man, values, education, program building, program content, the administrator, the teacher, the learner, learning, teaching methods, and evaluation. Each category contained statements representative of four eminent philosophical positions—idealism, realism, pragmatism, and aritomism.

---

[11] Donn E. Bair, "An Identification of Some Philosophical Beliefs Held by Influential Professional Leaders in American Physical Education," microcard Doctoral Dissertation, University of Southern California, 1956. Excerpts reprinted by permission of the author.

The study was approached through an examination of numerous publications that describe the philosophical systems underlying present-day education and the forces that have shaped American physical education. The philosophical comparisons were with naturalism and spiritualism. The investigator's definitions of these philosophies were: Naturalistic philosophy includes realism and holds that the universe requires no supernatural explanation; the universe is self-directing and constitutes the whole of reality; nature is dynamic and characterized by change. The spiritualistic philosophy is a general doctrine that includes idealism and aritomism; the ultimate reality in the universe is spirit; the universe is changeless and is comprised of primary, stable factors that stem from a supernatural source.

On the basis of the beliefs revealed, most of the physical education leaders appeared to be providing a predominantly naturalistic direction to American physical education. However, the study revealed some evidences of strong spiritualistic beliefs, which suggest a dual influence and lack of general agreement in some areas.

Comments. The studies reported in this section are not philosophical per se, as envisaged in this chapter. Thus, a philosophy was not developed, aims and objectives were not proposed, and principles were not formulated through critical thinking based on existing evidence, forefront thinking, and astute observation. Rather, they dealt with comparative philosophies, in which the philosophical beliefs of physical education leaders were compared with eminent philosophies broadly developed and accepted by educators on the frontier of educational thought.

The study by Morland has historical connotations, as he studied the philosophical views of a small group of seven leaders who dynamically influenced physical education during the critical period following World War I. The author, himself, suggested that additional research is needed to determine if the favorable ratio to progressivism, which he found, holds as well for other leaders in the profession and whether or not the philosophy of progressivism is the most representative of practicing teachers. The study by Bair provides a statement of current beliefs, as beliefs change with time as do the leaders. In time, too, this study will have historical value.

SUMMARY

In this chapter, the philosophical approach to the resolution of educational problems has been presented. Although the philosophical method by itself is not scientific, it is needed for dealing with certain kinds of problems. The method of philosophy is the application of critical thinking, but the thought processes are guided by available facts and current pioneer thinking. A critical-thinking continuum was proposed, extending from a minimal amount in scientific studies to the maximal amount where astute observation is dominant. Examples of these extremes were provided. The chapter concluded with selected examples of philosophical studies, each selected to illustrate different and unique approaches.

CHAPTER 6

Surveys and Case Studies

In this chapter, surveys by questionnaire and by interview are considered; normative surveys are described; and case studies and profiles are discussed.

BROAD SURVEY BY QUESTIONNAIRE

The purpose of the broad survey is to obtain responses and reactions from a large number of individuals who could not be interviewed personally within a short period of time and without considerable expense. By this means, a wide segment of the population can be sampled with regard to a variety of specific topics. The instrument of the broad survey is the questionnaire.

The questionnaire should be used sparingly in research and then only after very careful preparation so that the responses reflect with integrity the information sought. In general, the primary justification for its use rests on the need for information that cannot be reasonably obtained in any other way. If careful planning precedes administration of the questionnaire and the details of data collection are given ample thought, this approach may be employed; however, the use of questionnaires has received strong criticism. Poor questions, improper procedures, a sample that is too large or too small or inappropriate for the responses needed, or that the problem itself is too trivial are all reasons that have contributed to their rejection. Thus, the indictment of the questionnaire or the broad survey may be less of method itself than of the way it is applied.

Types of Information

Several types of information may be secured by the questionnaire and may be categorized generally as follows:

Status studies. The most frequent use of the questionnaire is to secure information of status or of the current practice of individuals, groups, or institutions. Status studies seek to determine events or practices as they are, which in health and physical education have often meant the status of the curriculum, the facilities, or some other aspect of operation. This type of questionnaire may be the simplest to construct; it relies heavily on factual information rather than on opinion and seeks information about events that are often a matter of operational records.

Status studies of the attitudes and beliefs of individuals may also be part of the research design and may be incorporated as items in the questionnaire. Questions such as those concerning the advisability of athletics for children, for example, call for the opinion of the respondent, and they must be very carefully phrased for appropriate answers to be obtained. The term "opinionnaire" has been used to designate such instruments; in format, they may resemble those tests used in some psychological studies.

A further use of status studies may be found in those testing knowledge. Used extensively in health education, they seek to sample the extent of factual information on the part of some population or group. For example, the knowledge of nutrition, sex education, or health misconceptions may be of interest to those concerned with curricular matters. Such devices resemble typical examinations of subject matter but are more difficult to construct since they are intended to reach a group with varied background, experience, and education.

Expert opinion. The second major type of information that may be obtained by the broad survey is the opinion of experts. In the present context, experts are those who qualify as authorities by virtue of their specific training, position, or some other fact that gives them unique status. For example, deans and department heads, presidents of associations, emeritus professors, head coaches, and others possess certain backgrounds that give their responses added weight when opinions are sought on some question within their range of expertise.

Construction of the Questionnaire

The most important ingredient to be found in the survey is the questionnaire itself. A criticism frequently made of this type of research involves the design and handling of the instrument. The study will only be as good as the questionnaire. A hastily and poorly contrived questionnaire will very likely result in that kind of response, *if it is completed at all.* Therefore, the investigator should take great care in developing an instrument that will assure an adequate reply and will result in meaningful data. The following suggestions are offered to help in constructing the questionnaire:

1. The researcher must have the training and experience necessary to conduct such a study in a competent manner. Unfortunately, many look upon the survey as an easy research method and fail to realize that skill and background are necessary, that it is not a matter of asking a few simple questions, mailing out the questionnaire, and then sitting back and awaiting the replies. If a serious study is to be undertaken, the substantive portion of the questionnaire must reflect a well-informed and knowledgeable investigator who has studied the subject matter thoroughly.

2. The investigator must have a clear purpose for his study and must then pursue his objectives in the most appropriate manner. A common misconception is to believe that a survey may easily include peripheral matters, that extraneous questions can be asked "just to see what will happen" in the faint hope that some meaningful relationships will emerge. The respondent will quickly sense this ruse; and his entire approach to the task may be distorted as a result.

3. The researcher should also be cognizant of the limitations of the questionnaire approach and weigh very carefully the various factors before proceeding further. The most important problem concerns the accuracy of response: Will the subject give truthful and complete answers to questions? If questions involve controversial or sensitive matters, will he be honest? The tendency for self-protection is strong, and often individuals will color their responses in order to produce a favorable impression. Furthermore, a very real danger is that subjects whose educational practices are contrary to current standards in the field may not return the questionnaire, which, consequently, results in biased returns.

4. The investigator should begin by outlining the field of study systematically. Broad categories of information should be identified so that overlapping may be avoided, and the questions should be developed in an orderly fashion. A hierarchy of interrogatives should be established based upon categories of questions. In this manner, the investigator will gain insight into the task of writing questions, and it will also assure that nothing of importance is omitted. Without first organizing the task, the omission of essential information is likely, the sequence of questions will appear disjointed, and the reader may justly conclude that the study has been ill-conceived.

5. The questions should be arranged in a logical order. Once the decision is made on the organizational pattern, the questions themselves should be presented. They should follow the theme of the study, adhering to some adopted pattern—such as proceeding from the simple to the complex, the easy to the difficult or building each succeeding question upon the one that came before. The respondent, particularly if he has received the instrument in the mail and does not know the investigator personally, must be made to feel that the study has been carefully prepared. Otherwise his attitude and care in answering the questions may be affected.

6. Each question in the survey must be absolutely clear. This is a difficult task and is the most exacting portion of the study. In fact, the success or failure of the whole project may rest upon the care and precision that is taken in stating the questions so that no statement contains ambiguities or grammatical errors or is misleading. The use of words must be clear. For example, such words as "extracurricular," "intramural," "recreation," and many others must be defined so that all respondents know exactly how they are being used. If the respondent does not understand what is being asked, he cannot respond validly. Unfortunately, the investigator may never know if this has occurred; he must be able to assume that the response is accurate.

7. The questions should be stated in such a manner that short answers can be given. If the questions require extensive answers, respondents may become discouraged and rightly feel that they do not have the time to write essay responses to a number of questions. Further, understanding the meaning of questions becomes difficult. The best questions are those that are well stated, clear, and require short answers.

8. Associated with the previous statements is the need for responses that can be easily and completely summarized. When long essay responses are obtained, it is very difficult for the investigator to group the data in convenient form for analysis; thus, some scheme should be worked out that will yield objective answers, preferably, countable answers. If possible, simply checking a category is best for the respondent's reply.

9. When questions call for opinions, some form of the Likert[1] scale is found helpful in estimating the strength of feeling. Thus, the statement "interscholastic athletics are harmful to children in elementary school" may be followed by five degrees of agreement or disagreement, such as (a) strongly approve, (b) approve, (c) undecided, (d) disapprove, and (e) strongly disapprove. If the investigator assigns a score of 5 to strongly approve, 1 for strongly disapprove, and the remaining values for the intervening responses, then he has a basis for later statistical analysis. In such attitude studies, care must be taken in phrasing the questions and assigning the numerical values so that the high score always reflects the best attitude. Thus, a score of 5 may accompany strongly approve in some cases and strongly disapprove in others.

10. The possibility of precoding the items for future data processing should be considered. An examination, such as used in knowledge studies, may have responses keyed in such a manner that the scoring is accomplished by automatic methods. If this is feasible in surveys with a questionnaire, the investigator should explore procedures that would implement this technique. Evaluative questions may also be coded for computer tabulation and

---

[1] R. Likert, "A Technique for the Measurement of Attitudes," *Archives of Psychology*, No. 140, 1932.

statistical treatment, especially if the answers can be given a quantitative value. For instance, the question given above on interscholastic athletics for children can be easily coded for data processing, so that extensive analysis can later be made by computer. The time saved by this process may permit a far more detailed statistical treatment than might be feasible if the investigator must proceed with hand scoring and tabulation.

Appearance of Questionnaire

A most important consideration in survey research is the appearance of the questionnaire. Although not involved with content per se and not affecting the quality of research, it may be a determining factor in the overall acceptance of the study by the respondent. Anything that deters a prompt and accurate response will influence the research results by default. Other things being equal, the more attractive the format the more likely will be the return of the questionnaire.

Several features of the questionnaire may be mentioned to illustrate the items that must be considered for effective presentation:

1. The selection of paper size is ordinarily the typical $8\frac{1}{2} \times 11$ inches, a size that conveniently fits into standard-size envelopes. The paper need not be white, as attractive colors are available. One device that has been successfully employed is to code different groups of subjects by color so that upon receipt of the completed questionnaire they may be quickly separated simply by noting the colors. Considerable time will be saved, for, unless some other scheme is used, the investigator must search through various mailing lists to determine the correct category of each questionnaire.

2. Consideration should be given to the neatness and proper spatial arrangement of the questionnaire. A questionnaire that is hastily constructed shows it. Special care is required to arrange the headings symmetrically, to make major headings larger than subheadings, to assure proper alignment, and a host of other details that may not bear on the subject matter itself but that may affect the number of returns. If the investigator can afford the expense, a printed questionnaire is preferable; it usually gets more returns than other kinds and so may be more profitable in the long run. The ditto questionnaire should be avoided; mimeographing is more satisfactory; and, better yet, lithographing is an excellent possibility. The use of cheap paper, ineptness in typing, crowding, and other factors serve to detract from the appearance of a study that otherwise may be entirely satisfactory.

3. Provide adequate space for answers. A common error that is made on many questionnaires is providing too little space for answers. Nothing is more exasperating than being asked to respond to a question only to find that the space for the answer is inadequate. The requirement of adequate

space begins with the heading where the name and address of the respondent will go, and extends to all questions thereafter. If open-ended questions are included on the questionnaire, sufficient space should be allowed for each answer.

4. The place for all answers should be clear. Failure to offer some easy-to-follow scheme invites inaccurate replies. For an objective response, parenthesis ( ), a block □, or other scheme may be used. When factual information is requested, such as the number of children in physical education classes, a short dotted or solid line may be provided. Questions should not be split between two pages in order to insure its continuity.

5. At the top of the first page, the questionnaire should contain the following items:

(a) Complete name and address of the investigator, so that the respondent knows where the questionnaire originated.
(b) A statement concerning the purpose of the questionnaire and asking for support. If a covering letter is used, to be considered below, this statement can be shorter than would otherwise be the case.
(c) Complete instructions must be given for filling out the questionnaire. These instructions should be clear, concise, and explicit. Do not assume that the respondent will understand simply by looking at the format. Experienced surveyors have discovered that even with the best of instructions some individuals will make errors. For example, if it is necessary for the best single answer to be selected in all cases, this must be explicitly stated in the instructions. Even then, several unanswered questions may remain, which must be dealt with in some manner in tabulating or scoring. No response does not necessarily constitute an incorrect answer; such responses must be coded in a separate category. Occasionally, a category may be offered on the questionnaire for a "no opinion" or "do not know" in order to care for situations in which the respondent has no basis for an answer.
(d) Instructions for returning the questionnaire to its source must be included. This usually consists of giving the name and address of the investigator, although occasionally it may be sent to another individual or to a processing firm.
(e) A place for the name, address, and position of the person replying should appear on the questionnaire. Other data relative to this individual may be considered essential, but only those items should be requested that actually bear directly on the study. Very little is gained by requesting superfluous information that will not be used. This is particularly true of sensitive matters concerning race, religion, salary, and other things that may be considered personal. If such items are necessary, it should be so stated; and then it may also be helpful to make assurances that the information will be kept confidential.

Questionnaire Development

The development of the questionnaire will take the greatest amount of preparatory time and will probably be the most difficult portion of the study. It is not a simple matter to phrase questions properly so that no ambiguities exist and so that the terminology is precise and to the point. Yet, if this is not accomplished, the responses may be inadequate or incorrect. The following procedures apply to questionnaire development:

Initial writing. The first attempt at writing the questions and organizing the progression will require several revisions before the final draft is ready. The writer must be prepared to change and rephrase statements when desirable so that the meaning is clear to the reader, the sequence is proper, and the directions are appropriate. As a general rule, the directions should be simply stated, clear, and concise so that the reader will not misunderstand the manner in which he is to respond. Occasionally, the sequence of questions will depend upon the answer to one main question (e.g., "If you conduct an interscholastic athletic program for either grades 4, 5, or 6, please answer the following questions"); this must be clarified and at the same time the ones who do not have such a program must be instructed to move on to another section.

In writing questionnaire items, some problems occur that serve to make questions unacceptable, which, if corrected, may assure valid responses. Some of the more prominent difficulties will be mentioned:

1. Using specialized terminology. Graduate students are expected to examine the literature of their subject matter and in doing so will come upon terms that may not be generally known to teachers or administrators in the field. The answer to such a question as "all schools should employ tests of aerobic capacity in examining the physical fitness of their students" may well depend upon the respondent's understanding of the term "aerobic capacity"; such terms should be defined or simpler ones used.

2. Questions obviously biased. Occasionally, questions are phrased in such a way that the bias involved precludes subdivision into categories. For example, the question "athletics are always harmful to children" would leave little room for argument, and it would be unusual for a respondent to answer in any way but "strongly disagree." He might feel different if he knew what type of athletics, what was considered as harmful (including psychological as well as physical aspects), and what category of children was involved.

3. Questions not complete. When a question such as "isometric exercises contribute most" is used, the reader is completely at a loss as to what to answer (contribute most to what or compared with what?).

4. *Question too long.* Sometimes a lengthy question is necessary so that the meaning is clear and the terms are carefully described. The danger in employing long and complicated questions, however, is that the reader may miss a key phrase, or if it is too complex, he may give up entirely. Worse yet, he may just guess at the answer. If the question is essential, it would be best to break it up into more than one question or state the meaning in other ways.

5. *Question too difficult or time consuming.* In questionnaire surveys, the respondent may be reluctant to reply if he is asked to locate information that is unusual. Asking him to calculate the percentage of freshmen girls that play tennis in intramurals may be quite time consuming if the information is not already available. However, it may not be too difficult to check categories such as "not offered," "below 25%," "25–49%," "50–74%," "75–99%," or "100%."

Trial run. After the questionnaire has been written to the satisfaction of the researcher—when it includes all items considered essential and the sequence has been organized in a logical and orderly manner—the next step is to submit it to a trial run. The purpose of the trail run is to discover if the meanings of all statements on the questionnaire are clear and if the questions are adequate to obtain the information desired. Preliminary to the trial run, of course, graduate students will seek reviews of their instrument from their respective advisers and from other staff members and fellow graduate students who are knowledgeable in the study area. For the trial run, send the initial questionnaire, as revised, to a number of individuals corresponding in category to those who will receive the final instrument. These individuals should answer the questionnaire in the same manner as will be required when it is actually used for data collection. In addition, ask them to criticize it, especially as to the clarity and adequacy of the questions.

Tabulation. Also as a trial, tabulate the results of the trial run. Quite possibly, some additional modification of the question or rearrangement of the answer locations may be found that will permit easier tabulation when the final questionnaire responses are analyzed.

Rewriting. Based upon the information obtained from the trial run, again revise the questionnaire.

The Sample

The population that is to be sampled for the questionnaire survey will depend upon the nature and design of the study. A discussion of sampling techniques is not included here; however, some consideration of sampling theory and process is included in Chapter 10. In some cases of a limited population, all members may be utilized (e.g., state directors of physical education), but in most instances the investigator will wish to utilize a random sample from a known population (e.g., secondary school principals in the nation, or in a state or region). Or a sample from a more restricted population, such as the freshmen at a given university, may be desired.

If randomizing is needed for purposes of mailing, some thought should be given to the possibility of utilizing computer facilities. For example, if names and addresses can be put on data processing cards, the computer can be programmed to select a randomized sample, print out the list, and at the same time print out several sets of address labels that can be placed on envelopes without additional moistening. This process will save a great deal of time that otherwise might be spent in typing separate envelopes for the initial mailing and any follow-up procedures that are used. In addition, the labels themselves may be used as the check list for returns; thus, at the time of the follow-up, only those lables are used that have not been canceled.

Aids to Responses

The primary difficulty in questionnaire surveys is to obtain an adequate response. Obviously, if the investigator could personally administer the questionnaire to the respondent or enlist the support of colleagues for personal approach, then he could be assured of a complete return. However, for those surveys relying upon mailing the investigator should adopt procedures that will encourage the greatest possible return. The following aids are presented for this purpose:

1. Enclose in the mailing a self-addressed and stamped envelope. This provides a tangible means whereby the respondent may get the questionnaire off his desk and at no cost to him. Further, this procedure insures that the correct return address is used. For those employing a large sample, the appropriate return address can be printed on the envelopes when they are ordered, or a rubber stamp may be made to facilitate this process. Some feel that a psychological advantage is evident in using a stamp on the return envelope rather than employing a franked envelope, the impression being that there is greater reluctance to discard the stamp.

2. The initial appeal in the form of a covering letter to the recipient will be an important procedure in securing a good return of the questionnaire. This letter should not be an emotional appeal or a "hat-in-the-hand" approach, but it should be a carefully worded and thoughtful statement that presents the reasons and purposes of the study and a compelling picture of the contribution to knowledge anticipated. If the respondent can be made to feel that he is an important part of a worthwhile project, he will be more inclined to participate wholeheartedly. On the other hand, a poorly worded

statement or one that relies primarily on the plea that "it is in partial fulfillment of the degree" may not personally involve the reader; as a result, he may feel that his time is too valuable to spend in answering the questionnaire. Other things being equal, the timeliness and scholarship exhibited by the study will do more to gain its acceptance than any other single factor. If the study is properly conceived in the first place, then this should be conveyed to the recipient in the most effective manner possible.

3. Frequently, support of the survey by a sponsor aids materially in securing a greater return of questionnaires. Such a sponsor may be an individual or an organization that has status in the population to be sampled. For example, the state superintendent of schools might influence teachers in the state; the commissioner of athletics could well affect the response of coaches; the executive secretary of an association would be expected to carry weight among the membership. The investigator may indicate the sponsor's interest in the survey in his covering letter; better yet, the sponsor may be persuaded to provide the covering letter setting forth his strong endorsement of the project and urging all recipients of the questionnaire to reply.

4. Another aid to increase the number of responses is to agree to send respondents a summary of the results. If the project is timely and appropriate, the recipients of the questionnaire may be eager to know the results. However, if this plan is adopted, it is best to provide a space for the respondent to check whether or not he wants such a copy; this procedure may increase the number of returns, as certainly the respondent would not check "yes" unless he filled out the rest of the questionnaire. The investigator should recognize, of course, that this agreement constitutes an obligation to provide the summaries when the survey is completed.

5. Occasionally, survey research deals with subject matter or asks questions that are personal or sensitive in nature, such as amounts of salaries, personnel practices, rating of teachers, and other matters. In such instances, it may be best to indicate that the replies will be kept confidential, that the questionnaires will be secured, and that there will be no identification of the individual or school in the final report. Thus, apprehensions may be allayed that the information may be used against the respondent or his institution and may help in obtaining a greater number of returns. It is incumbent that the investigator keep the information confidential if he has so stated. The broad survey distributed by mail that attempts to delve into highly personal matters is almost certainly doomed to failure. If recipients reply at all, quite likely the information may be inaccurate, incomplete, or biased. Under this circumstance the interview technique is best, as it provides time to develop rapport with the respondent and to establish confidence in the integrity of the research.

6. Anonymous questionnaires are utilized in an attempt to secure a greater return; it is based upon the premise that if the respondent cannot be

identified he will be more likely to cooperate. No doubt, situations exist in which this is helpful as a technique, but there is no guarantee that the responses will be more accurate, that greater care will be taken, or that fidelity of response will result. One could argue that the reverse may occur on occasion, simply because the respondent assumes that anonymity gives impunity. From the point of view of the recipient, he may be disappointed in realizing that he will not be identified after spending some time in answering the questionnaire; and, of course, the investigator loses any opportunity to follow-up the study or to ask the subject for additional information in case he would like to do so. In using the anonymous questionnaire, however, the following considerations are pertinent:

(a) Do not use it unless it is absolutely necessary. The use of anonymity may cause certain suspicions on the part of the recipient so that he may be more guarded than might otherwise be the case. Many times merely assuring that the results will be kept confidential is enough.
(b) If it is decided to keep the questionnaire responses anonymous, then this procedure must be followed. It would seem ill-advised to claim that no one will know who has completed the instrument and then to set up an elaborate scheme to do just that, even though there are techniques that could be followed to gain this sort of intelligence.[2]
(c) Sometimes, little can be done to conceal the identity of the respondent, especially when he is "one of a few selected national leaders." The postmark on the return envelope is certain to reflect the source of the sender, and thus the anonymity is destroyed.
(d) The more appropriate method of handling such a situation is simply to state that the identity of the respondent is not essential, but should the researcher learn his name, it will be kept in the strictest confidence.

7. The questionnaire should be sent at an appropriate time, when it will have the best chance of being answered. Educators are frequently especially busy or may be absent at certain times of the year, so it may be helpful to consider the academic calendar and avoid such times as holidays, vacations, registration and examination periods, and the like. Questionnaires sent to coaches during their sports season may get short shift.

8. A technique that has been successful on occasion is that of sending out an advance letter and self-addressed card and asking for a willingness to participate in the study. This practice has the advantage of providing a willing group of respondents. A similar device is simply to send out an advance notice announcing that in a few days the individual will receive a questionnaire and appealing for support. This tends to soften the impact of a questionnaire being received without prior knowledge.

---

[2] J. Francis Rummel, *An Introduction to Research Procedures in Education*, (2nd ed.) (New York: Harper & Row, Publishers, 1964), pp. 145–46.

9. The most valuable device that may be used to obtain the maximum number of responses is the follow-up. It is anticipated that a questionnaire mailed to a random selection of the population will yield from 10 to 50 per cent return, although returns from professional physical educators have frequently been higher.[3] The return may be improved if the investigator takes advantage of the devices mentioned above and if he is sufficiently aggressive in his follow-up procedures. A limit need not be imposed on the number of times that a recipient may be contacted asking for return of the questionnaire. However, each mailing requires an expenditure of money for stationery and postage. The greatest number of returns will result from the initial mailing; a steady decline will occur thereafter. Unless the population is a very select one, all questionnaires will not be retrieved even after the most vigorous efforts. The following suggested protocol involves five follow-up notices spaced at intervals of two weeks after mailing of the original questionnaire; if five follow-ups prove too many and too time consuming for some, the ones listed that seem most appropriate for a given survey may be utilized.

(a) *First follow-up.* A postcard, mailed two weeks after the original mailing, is sent to all individuals in the study, regardless of whether or not they have returned their questionnaires. This could be prepared at the time of the original materials and held in abeyance for the proper time. Obviously, a large number of questionnaires will have been received by this time, but unless they can be checked in quickly it will not pay to sort through the cards and pull out those that have responded. If an individual who receives this follow-up notice has already complied, it will be a simple matter to discard the reminder.
(b) *Second follow-up.* At the end of the fourth week, a copy of the original covering letter is sent to those who have not responded to the original mailing and first follow-up appeal with a note attached indicating the importance of receiving their response. Another copy of the questionnaire is enclosed.
(c) *Third follow-up.* A separate letter, indicating delight in the response to date and appealing to the unresponsive to complete their questionnaires, is sent to the individuals who have not replied by the end of the sixth week. A statement may also be included suggesting that if they have misplaced the questionnaire to so indicate so that another may be sent.
(d) *Fourth follow-up.* A personalized letter, indicating a desire to receive the response of all persons in the study may be written as the fourth follow-up by the end of eight weeks. A copy of the questionnaire and, if desired, a

---

[3] Claire Selltig, Marie Jahoda, Morton Deutsch, and Stuart W. Cook, *Research Methods in Social Research*, rev. ed. (New York: Holt, Rinehart and Winston, Inc., 1959), p. 241.

self-addressed, stamped envelope may be enclosed to facilitate the response. (e) *Fifth follow-up.* Finally, the fifth follow-up, consisting of a personalized letter with or without another questionnaire, may be sent after another two weeks. This would be the final appeal and should result in the maximum number of returns. Those that do not respond probably will not do so under any circumstances and will constitute the inevitable "no replies" that usually accompany this type of broad survey.

INTERVIEW SURVEY

The interview, or visit, is a better method of obtaining survey information than the broad survey in which a mailed questionnaire is utilized. Rather than rely on the impersonal approach inherent in the latter technique, the interviewer gathers data directly from individuals in face-to-face contact. The interview has been likened to an oral questionnaire. It has the obvious advantage of insuring a greater return. Occasionally, the investigator will be unable to interview an individual for one reason or another, but this will occur far less frequently than with the survey by mail.

Characteristics of the Interview

The interview survey is marked by several unique characteristics that make it a useful adjunct to the researcher. These are as follows:

1. The interview may permit obtaining confidential information. Whereas the recipient of a questionnaire by mail may be reluctant to divulge information that is classified as confidential or that he may think reflects adversely on his policies or practices, the interview may make it possible to obtain such data. The investigator must show insight and gain rapport with the interviewee and give him assurance that the information will be kept confidential. This procedure has been notably successful in medicine and health education where personal health information or sexual practices have been under investigation.

2. The personal contact has the advantage of drawing out the informant by on-the-spot follow-up questions, which is not possible through a formal questionnaire. For example, methods of administration, operation of the budget, practices in athletics, and so forth frequently are handled in different ways; the interview allows considerable adaptation to different situations.

3. The interview permits the interpretation of the meaning of questions. No matter how carefully phrased is the questionnaire, the likelihood is present that some questions may be misunderstood or certain concepts misinterpreted; in the interview, the investigator can make sure that the intent is clear and thereby obtain more adequate responses.

4. The interview permits the follow-up of leads. In a relatively unstructured situation provided by the interview, leads that are uncovered can be followed-up by a series of questions designed to obtain additional information. It is obvious that this advantage is not permitted in the usual survey, which is rigidly bound by the questions asked. The manner in which this information is to be used later may pose a problem of a different nature, and the researcher who feels more comfortable in being bound to objective questions and answers may find this sort of data a little more difficult to work with. However, in terms of investigating a problem, the more insight that is obtained the better will be the study.

5. The investigator can form some judgment of the adequacy of replies. One of the most difficult problems in surveys is to obtain data that are accurate or, to be more to the point, truthful. This is not to suggest that dishonesty prevails in survey research, but it must be admitted that occasionally the truth may be strained in the interest of self enhancement; frequently, such biases are caused simply by a misunderstanding of the question and, so, are unintentional. For example, a positive response to the question "do you have an intramural program" may be based wholly on the fact that in physical education class the students frequently compete against each other. The interview would provide a means for obtaining this information by more direct questioning.

6. The interview survey would afford an opportunity for the interviewer to *give* information and to develop rapport with the respondent. This aspect of the interview is seen to permeate the whole atmosphere, where the respondent can make clear the intent of the research, perhaps bring out the salient facts that precede the study, and develop the confidence of the interviewee. If this is done properly, the response will be much better, and therefore the information that is needed will be given more readily. Obviously, if the interviewer antagonizes the respondent, the reverse would hold true.

The Interview

The investigator should carefully prepare for the interview. It is a mistake to think that this survey method consists merely of making an appointment and sitting down and asking a series of questions; this could be done by mail. If the study warrants an interview, then the researcher must develop his method of presentation as precisely as possible. This does not mean that he must make the same statement to each person in exactly the same manner, as this may provide very little flexibility. Informality in the interview may well enhance the rapport between interviewer and interviewee.

The well-prepared investigator who has carefully researched his study should have no trouble in the interview. He should expect to conduct it in the same manner that he would any business meeting—striving to be courteous and friendly yet attempting to direct the questions along the lines that have been prepared. Not all interviewees will have an unlimited amount of time available, so it is important not to waste it with extended small talk or to permit the discussion to digress for long periods, even if this seems acceptable at the time. The successful interviewer will adroitly maneuver the conversation so that the areas of the study are covered. Because time is a factor, the respondent should be told approximately how long the interview would be expected to last.

The questioning must be performed in such a manner as not to introduce an aspect of bias; thus, an impersonal but professional attitude should be maintained. The examiner should avoid leading the respondent. Questions beginning with "you don't . . ." would imply that "you shouldn't," and this would very likely put the individual on the defensive. After all, if he thinks he should not, very likely he will agree that he does not. Also, voice inflection may imply the direction an answer should go, which, of course, would bias the response. It is human nature to wish to agree with someone, and if a note of disapproval can be sensed, the response may be influenced in that direction.

In planning for the interview, attention should be given to the classification of responses which should be similar to those employed in the broad survey. Once again, open-ended questions are difficult to handle objectively, and, because the type of response may vary from very short replies to lengthy and detailed commentaries, it may be difficult to make proper notations. The investigator should not hesitate to make whatever record is necessary at the time, even though it may detract somewhat from the interview; if he waits until later, he must rely on memory, which may introduce inaccuracies into the interview record. An example of the interview procedure employed in conjunction with a questionnaire survey may be found in a study by Fox.[4]

The use of a tape recorder may be permissible, provided the respondent agrees to this and if it can be situated unobtrusively. The taping of interviews, even video taping, is growing in popularity so that it can no longer be considered a novelty. However, some individuals have difficulty in speaking freely under these conditions; if this occurs, such attempts would be abandoned. It would certainly be inappropriate to use a recorder of some sort without the knowledge of the interviewee.

Immediately, after the interview, the investigator should review all materials, organize his notes, and fill in any details while they are still fresh in mind. All notes and data should be kept with the interview questionnaire for future reference.

---

[4] John W. Fox, "Practices and Trends in Physical Education Programs for Boys in Selected Oregon Schools," microcard Doctoral Dissertation, University of Oregon, 1958.

NORMATIVE SURVEY

Normative surveys refer to those studies that are made primarily with the use of established or objective tests. They have been used extensively in education to make comparisons of students with available norms on a variety of achievement tests. They have been used in physical education less frequently, partly because recognized tests are fewer in number and comparable data are difficult to obtain.

One of the well-known normative surveys related to physical education was conducted by Kraus and Hirschland[5] who compared eastern United States school children with Swiss, Austrian, and Italian children utilizing the Kraus-Weber tests of minimum muscular fitness. Subsequently, similar surveys were conducted in Iowa,[6] Indiana,[7] Oregon,[8] and elsewhere around the world. Similar types of comparisons have also been made with the AAHPER Youth Fitness Test.

Sampling process. Any sample approximates only the total population from which it is drawn, and repeated samples from the same population will differ from each other within the limits of normal probability. However, if randomly drawn, the differences between these samples will not differ significantly when statistical tests of such variances are applied.[9] Thus, if two samples, wherever drawn, differ significantly, at least two reasons could account for it: Either the populations are definitely different or the samples are not comparable—that is, not drawn in a comparable manner. It is this latter situation that could account, unconsciously or carelessly, for a difference in test scores between two groups under comparison.

In any event, samples are only justified when drawn entirely at random, where every child in the population has an equal chance of being chosen. Extreme care should be exercised in all normative surveys to describe precisely how samples are drawn. If comparisons are to be made, all samples must be drawn in an identical manner.

---

[5] Hans Kraus and Ruth P. Hirschland, "Minimum Muscular Fitness Tests in School Children," *Research Quarterly*, 25, No. 2 (May 1954), 178.

[6] Margaret Fox and Janet Atwood, "Results of Testing Iowa School Children for Health and Fitness," *Journal of Health, Physical Education, and Recreation*, 26, No. 7 (September 1955), 20.

[7] Marjorie Phillips and associates, "Analysis of Results from the Kraus-Weber Test of Minimum Muscular Fitness in Children," *Research Quarterly*, 26, No. 3 (October 1955), 314.

[8] Glenn Kirchner and Don Glines, "Comparative Analysis of Eugene, Oregon, Elementary School Children Using the Kraus-Weber Test of Minimum Muscular Fitness," *Research Quarterly*, 28, No. 1 (March 1957), 16.

[9] See Chapter 10.

Testing Techniques. If comparisons on the basis of test scores are to be made between groups, states, or nations, the testing techniques must be precisely the same in all instances. It can be demonstrated easily that a test as simple as chinning oneself can be given differently with considerable variance in results. Such things as placement of the hands, permitting body sway or kipping movements, or not requiring that the elbows straighten completely may permit spurious scores to occur. Comparable differences in testing techniques could easily be found in giving many of the tests commonly used in physical education. In any research project, whether it be a normative survey or a laboratory experiment, extreme care should be taken to qualify testers before data are obtained.

Subject motivation. The concept of motivation is dealt with in Chapter 16, where it was noted that differential motive-incentive conditions play an important role in the performance of certain types of physical activities. In experimental situations, researchers routinely attempt to invoke a common motivational pattern in test administration in order to equalize this factor. In applying subject motivation to the normative surveys, the necessity for using a common motivational approach can be seen. However, it will always be possible for boys and girls of other countries to compete against American standards. Just how much motivation this provides cannot be calculated, but it could conceivably contribute significantly to increased test performances. Only when both groups are knowingly or not knowingly competing against each other should international comparisons be made.

Analysis of data. Various statistical applications can be made to normative survey data. In the Kraus-Weber and AAHPER test comparisons, percentages for passing or reaching certain standards were commonly employed. The comparison of test results with norms has been done by use of chi square.

CASE STUDIES AND PROFILES

The limitation of studies to single individuals, or at most to a very limited number in research, has received rather wide condemnation in physical education, although the practice is still employed in medicine and in physiology. Single cases, of course, can claim little validity as a sample representing a population; more and more, as a greater understanding of sampling procedures and probability is obtained, the need for samples of some size is recognized.

However, certain kinds of problems do not lend themselves to the usual statistical treatment, where a population as such cannot be defined, where the number of individuals is limited, or where the interrelation of several factors in the same individual is derived. For example, the study of cerebral palsy children with varying degrees of involvement, of the mentally retarded, of champion athletes, or of physically unfit boys and girls may require an individual approach. Such studies permit analysis of the total individual.

Case Studies

The case-study approach has been successfully employed in developmental physical education classes for those students who are subpar in basic physical fitness elements, especially those who do not improve through exercise.[10] The causes of poor physical fitness are many and vary from individual to individual; case studies reveal a variety of patterns to account for this condition. The following three objectives typify the extent to which case studies may be employed.

1. To conduct intensive studies of individuals within a defined group. This is the most obvious objective of the case-study procedure; the primary justification rests on the assumption that the individuals are unique in some way and that an examination of them as individuals should be carried out in some depth. Cursory testing or trivial examination procedures would not suffice to make this process acceptable research. The number of such subjects that must be employed cannot be stated, as it would depend upon a number of factors; conceivably, a small number might be studied if the data gathered were extensive and quite unique. The student who desires to use this procedure for fulfillment of the thesis requirement should weigh such factors as time and availability of subjects. One thing seems clear: The case study approach is not a substitute for a small sample size if, in fact, a larger sample could be obtained and the appropriate statistical treatment applied.

2. To attempt to generalize from a synthesis of the individuals in the group. The ultimate aim of most research is to be able to draw generalizations from an examination of the members of a particular population. For example, from a study of certain champion athletes has come a greater understanding of a number of essential qualities that help make championship performances possible. At the other end of the scale, with the assessment of the individual with exceptionally inadequate physical ability has come an appreciation of some of the causes of poor fitness. In the latter instance, case studies have led to the identification of a medical rather than a physical genesis for the difficulty, and they point up the possibility for the use of case

---

[10] H. Harrison Clarke and David H. Clarke, *Developmental and Adapted Physical Education* (Englewood Cliffs, N.J.: Prentice-Hall, Inc., 1963), Ch. 6.

study techniques in adapted physical education. One would suppose that a synthesis of enough subjects within a group would eventually lead to satisfactory generalizations.

3. To contrast groups. The objective of most experimental research is to contrast groups on various traits; a similar possibility exists with case studies. A synthesis of information from one group may be contrasted with similar data from another group. Although the comparison may not be statistical, other descriptive methods may be employed.

Applications. The student who wishes to employ the case-study approach may get suggestions and guidance from the following collections of case studies of boys with low physical fitness indices:

Coefield, John R., and Robert H. McCollum, "A Case Study Report of 78 University Freshmen with Low Physical Fitness Indices," microcard Master's Thesis, University of Oregon, 1955.

Page, C. Getty, "Case Studies of College Men with Low Physical Fitness Indices," Master's Thesis, Syracuse University, 1940.

Popp, James C., "Comparison of Sophomore High School Boys Who Have High and Low Physical Fitness Indices through Case Study Procedures," microcard Master's Thesis, University of Oregon, 1959.

Wilson, Peter G., "Personality Traits, Academic Achievement, and Health Status of University Freshman Men with Low and High Physical Fitness Scores," microcard Master's Thesis, University of Oregon, 1967.

Profiles

Profile studies have been employed in order to show various trait patterns. Essentially, they involve placement of the individual on test scales for a number of characteristics. Thus, the individual's strengths and weaknesses may be noted from his position on a common scale for all traits. The scale may be from norms already available or may be constructed from a sample of the population to which the subjects belong. The *T* scale, described in Chapter 9, is a convenient scale for this purpose, although other scales have also been used.

Three examples of the use of profiles are cited as references to this procedure. Behnke[11] employed profiles based upon a number of anthropometric variables so that the relative size and proportions of the body could be assessed. Shelley[12] presented Hull scale profiles of 38 outstanding elementary

---

[11] Albert R. Behnke, "Anthropometric Estimate of Body Size, Shape and Fat Content," *Postgraduate Medicine*, 34, No. 2 (August 1963), 190.

[12] Morgan E. Shelley, "Maturity, Structure, Strength, Motor Ability, and Intelligence Test Profiles of Outstanding Elementary School and Junior High School Athletes," microcard Master's Thesis, University of Oregon, 1960.

and junior high school athletes on 22 maturity, structural, strength, motor ability, and intelligence tests. Howe[13] contrasted *T* scale profiles of 20 outstanding 12- and 15-year-old athletes on maturity, body size, strength, motor ability, and scholastic aptitude and achievement when they were 9, 12, and 15 years of age.

SUMMARY

A method of research that entails the gathering of data from a large number of individuals is termed the broad survey and it employs the questionnaire as the investigative tool. Although use of the questionnaire has certain limitations, it may be justified in situations where data that would otherwise be impossible in a reasonable length of time and expense must be obtained. Through these means, status studies and the assessment of expert opinion may be obtained.

The questionnaire must be constructed with great precision, for it must be made as acceptable as possible to the recipients. The investigator should have a clear purpose of his study in mind and then set about outlining the field to be covered carefully and systematically, arranging the questions in a logical order so that each one is clear and correct. The best questions are usually those that seek a short answer so that the responses may be effectively summarized and coded for statistical treatment. The questionnaire should be neat in appearance and have instructions precisely written; a cover letter should accompany it, which may be from the investigator or a sponsor, setting forth the aims of the study and urging completion by the recipient.

The sequence that should be followed in development of the questionnaire would include the initial writing, a trial run, tabulation of the preliminary results, and the rewriting of any questions that seem ambiguous or unclear. A number of factors contribute to the greater acceptability of a survey by the respondents, among which is a vigorous follow-up campaign designed to obtain as many responses as possible.

Another type of survey is by interview, in which the investigator visits the subject in person rather than through a questionnaire. The personal contact helps to insure a more adequate and thorough response. Even though the interview is more informal, it is nevertheless rather highly structured. This survey method insures that no information is omitted and permits greater study in depth.

---

[13] Bruce L. Howe, "Test Profiles of Outstanding Twelve-Year-Old Elementary School Athletes at Nine, Twelve, and Fifteen Years of Age," microcard Master's Thesis, University of Oregon, 1966.

Normative surveys have been employed in research in physical education to compare subjects on various tests with established norms. In such instances, certain precautions that include attention to the sampling process, the testing techniques, and subject motivation, are indicated. In addition, the study of individual subjects may occasionally be desirable through case study and profile techniques.

PART III

STATISTICAL APPLICATIONS

A knowledge of statistics is essential for any kind of scientific laboratory research. In such research, the investigator administers tests in order to measure various elements that are essential to his study. These test data must be analyzed in ways appropriate to the research design. Such analyses can only be accomplished through the application of pertinent statistics. Part III is devoted to statistical computations and their interpretations and applications. This presentation precedes descriptions of laboratory research methods, as such methods cannot be understood and applied without the necessary statistics.

The amount of statistical applications that may be presented is very great. In this book, the statistical methods included are those that could well be contained in a beginning course of a term or a semester; some projection is also made into more advanced concepts, as mention of them cannot be avoided in considering laboratory research. The material includes: Chapter 7, Distribution, Central Tendency, Percentiles; Chapter 8, Measures of Variability; Chapter 9, The Normal Curve; Chapter 10, Reliability and Tests of Significance; and Chapter 11, Product-Moment Correlation.

CHAPTER 7

Distribution, Central Tendency, Percentiles

Since this part is devoted to an explanation of statistics and their application to research problems, the statistics included are those needed in the treatment of quantitative data for scientific studies in education and psychology with special emphasis on the concepts found in physical education, recreation, and health research. A statistic is the same no matter in what field it is used, whether in psychology, general education, physical education, health education, sociology, agriculture, or medicine. Quite naturally, the test data treated will differ from field to field, but these should in no way interfere with the basic understanding of the nature of statistics.

NATURE OF STATISTICS

Statistical procedures constitute the means by which quantitative data—such as test scores from many individuals—are organized, analyzed, and interpreted. No educator may be considered to possess even minimal scientific competency without some background in statistics, for only through statistical applications may scientific data be treated and made meaningful. As Walker expressed this concept:

> Statistical method is one of the devices by which men try to understand the generality of life. Out of the welter of single events, human beings seek endlessly for general trends; out of the vast and confusing variety of individual characters, they continually search for underlying group characters, for some picture of the group to which the individual belongs.[1]

Scientific research involves measurement, which thus produces quantitative data. Statistical methods are applied in order to gain a summarized

---

[1] Helen M. Walker, *Elementary Statistical Methods* (New York: Holt, Rinehart and Winston, Inc., 1943), p. 1.

description or analysis of the findings. In order to realize this function, it is essential to know what kind of description is wanted, what statistic or statistics will provide the most valid description, and whether or not the assumptions underlying each selected statistic are satisfied by the data being treated.

Five types of statistical processes may be generally recognized: descriptive, comparative, relationship, inferential, and predictive. In descriptive statistics, the characteristics of a single group are described in various ways. In comparative statistics, the characteristics of two or more groups are contrasted. In relationship statistics, the correlations between numerous human traits as possessed by the same population are determined. In inferential statistics, observed data from a sample are used as a basis for generalizing to the total population from which the sample was drawn. In predictive statistics, unknown facts about the individual are predicted or inferred from known measurable qualities.

NEED FOR UNDERSTANDING STATISTICS

As indicated above, the need for understanding statistics is vital for the scientifically trained educator. Although the purpose of this text is to prepare professional students to conduct research, other values may be cited for the study of statistics. These values are discussed briefly here.

1. To understand and interpret scientific literature. This value alone justifies the study of statistics, since the use of statistical terms is commonplace in research journals. For example, seldom has the *Research Quarterly* of the American Association for Health, Physical Education and Recreation published an article in which quantitative data are not analyzed statistically in some way. To illustrate, the October 1966 *Research Quarterly* was examined: All 16 articles and all but 1 of the 7 "Notes" contained statistics; 18 different statistical processes were employed, and most articles utilized more than one statistic; the statistics used ranged from the elementary mean, standard deviation, and correlation to the advanced multiple correlation, factor analysis, analysis of variance and of covariance, and Duncan's multiple-range test. To understand these articles and to evaluate these researches are impossible without a statistical background.

2. To determine the scientific worth of tests. Although the construction of tests is a phase of research, the evaluation of tests should be a concern of all educators who use them. Statistical procedures are utilized widely in this process: to validate, to establish reliability, and to prepare norms and standards. The ability, therefore, to determine the scientific worth of tests is dependent upon a knowledge of statistics.

3. To prepare reports based on test results. The preparation of annual or more frequent reports of progress made in school programs is a common responsibility of educators. An effective aspect of such reports is the inclusion of test results that show progress made by pupils. The utilization of graphs and some of the common, easily understood statistics—such as frequency distributions, percentages, medians, and quartiles—are of value for this purpose.

4. To conduct research. The primary purpose of this book is to prepare students to conduct research. Some research methods—such as historical, philosophical, case study, and survey—do not require the use of statistics. However, the same cannot be said for instrument construction, growth, experimental, comparative, relationship, and predictive investigations. These types of studies require a great variety and complexity of statistics which the student must master before he can undertake them. Even though the student, especially the doctoral candidate, does not intend to lead a life of research, he may eventually become the advisor of graduate theses and will need a strong background in statistics in order to fulfill this responsibility properly.

5. To discriminate between satisfactory and unsatisfactory evidence in reports containing statistical analyses. In today's society, man is bombarded from every side with statistical reports, ranging from some nauseating TV and radio commercials to dignified and searching presentations by respected investigators. A knowledge of statistics makes the student critical of these reports and prone to evaluate them, to look behind the figures to the manner in which they were derived. All too frequently, statistics have been misused to misrepresent; to recognize when this occurs is one mark of an educated man.

QUANTITATIVE DATA

The term *quantitative data* refers to a collection of numerical values that are usually expressed in education and psychology as scores on a test. The number of scores may be as small as a half dozen or so or as large as compilations running into the hundreds. It is with quantitative data that statistics are involved. In general, quantitative data consist of two types—attributes and variables.

Attributes. An attribute has a nongradient classification, that is, there is no numerical basis of grouping. Attributes may be in two or more classes. Examples of two-class attributes are teachers as men and women, curricula as college preparatory and noncollege preparatory, and pupils as boys and girls. Illustrations of more than two-class attributes are color of hair or eyes, various nationalities or races, and different major fields of study.

Variables. A variable has a gradient classification, that is, there is a numerical basis of grouping. Variables are of two types—continuous and discontinuous (or discrete). A *continuous variable* is capable of any degree of subdivision. The only limitation of possible subdivision is the ability to measure infinitesimal subdivisions. However, in education, the fineness of measurement is usually limited to some convenient number. Most of the quantitative data used in education and psychology are of a continuous nature. Examples of continuous variables are muscular strength, anthropometric dimensions, intelligence, personality traits, and motor ability elements.

A *discontinuous variable* cannot be, or is not generally, subdivided by less than whole numbers or units. Illustrations are basketball scores, number of pupils in a classroom or children in a family, school buildings, and salary scales. Thus, a basketball team could not score $47\frac{1}{2}$ points; the number of children in a family cannot be $2\frac{1}{3}$; school buildings are not counted until completely built; and, although salary scales can be theoretically reduced to dollars and cents, in practice, they are not. However, although fractions of such scores are unrealistic, discontinuous data are frequently treated statistically as though they were continuous in order to provide significant differentiations. For example, to state that the average numbers of children in families of two nationalities are 2.5 and 3.4 is to state the impossible; yet, no other comparison would indicate the difference of nearly one child, since to recognize only whole numbers would round off the number of children to 3.0 for both nationalities.

FREQUENCY DISTRIBUTION

In today's age of the computer, statistical computations are frequently done directly from the raw data (i.e., from individual test scores) by use of these electronic marvels. However, if the data are to be treated by hand, with or without the aid of a desk calculator, grouping the scores into a frequency distribution will be found advantageous. However, in the computation of the statistics to follow, both raw-score and frequency-distribution methods will be presented.

A frequency distribution consists of grouping the scores into step intervals, frequently called just steps or intervals. A frequency table consists of a number of intervals each of the same size over the entire range of scores. The process of constructing a frequency table does not consist of an exact, mathematical application. Rather, some judgments are permitted by the investigator; the judgments, though, are made by application of general rules. As a consequence of this leniency, different frequency tables may be constructed from the same test scores by various investigators and, yet, all be within the rules. The subsequent answers for statistics computed from the different distributions will vary somewhat. However, the differences would not be appreciable if a large number of test scores were used; it would not be desirable or advisable to utilize the frequency table for a small number of scores—say, below 30.

Raw Data

The data utilized to illustrate the construction of a frequency table are the skeletal ages of 67 boys 13 years of age in the Medford, Oregon, Boy's Growth Study. Skeletal age is a measure of physiological maturity. It is obtained from an X-ray of the wrist and hand as assessed by use of the Greulich-Pyle atlas.[2] Normally, skeletal age corresponds to chronological age until maturity (age 19 years) is reached. Thus, a skeletal age of 13 years means that a boy has the maturity of a boy who is 13 years old. In obtaining the data used here, each boy was tested within two months of his birthday; thus, the chronological ages of the subjects did not vary in any instance by more than four months. The skeletal ages of the 67 boys are given below in months.

149	162	158	144	154	161	177	132
150	146	155	147	148	151	156	169
157	149	148	168	135	154	154	136
153	144	154	163	154	156	162	140
136	164	168	144	134	136	162	157
168	139	140	158	128*	154	148	151
144	182*	151	168	156	135	156	171
158	147	140	154	171	169	153	138
154	162	156					

In looking at these data, little sense can be made of them, as just a hodgepodge of scores appears. As will be shown, once they are organized into a frequency table, Table 1, a definite pattern will emerge.

Meaning of a Single Score

Before constructing a frequency table, the meaning of a single score in a continuous series must be understood. Although the above 67 skeletal ages are given in whole months, this does not mean that each boy's skeletal age fell exactly on a whole month. These ages could be given in fractions of a month if the investigator so desired and the test so refined as to permit it.

---

[2] W. W. Greulich and S. I. Pyle, *Radiographic Atlas of Skeletal Development of the Hand and Wrist*, (2nd ed.) (Palo Alto, Calif.: Stanford University Press, 1959).

So, a rounding-off process has been in effect. Subsequently, the data should be treated in accordance with the rounding-off procedure employed.

The usual method of recording test scores is to round them to the nearest whole number, which was the case for the skeletal ages. Thus, the first score of 149 months could actually be anywhere between 148.50 and 149.49 months. Thus, this number actually starts at 148.50, although not so recorded.

Another, but seldom used, method of rounding off scores is to keep the same whole number until the next highest whole number is reached. In this instance, the range of a score of 149 would be 149.00 to 149.99. If this method is utilized by the investigator, future calculations would need to be adjusted accordingly. However, in the computations to follow, the first means of recording a score—rounding off to the nearest whole number—will be assumed.

Frequency Table

1. Range of scores. The range of scores is found in order to determine the distance over which the scores are spread. To determine the range, the low and high scores must be located. For the skeletal ages, these scores are 128* and 182*, as identified in the table by asterisks. The range is the difference between these scores. Thus:

$$\begin{aligned} \text{Range} &= X_H - X_L \\ &= 182 - 128 = 54 \end{aligned} \tag{7.1}$$

In this formula and all formulas to follow, X will indicate raw scores. Thus, X_H represents the highest score in the distribution; and X_L, the lowest score. Therefore, the range is 54 months.

Technically, the range of scores is one month more in order to include both high and low scores within the range. Therefore, the formula would be:

$$\begin{aligned} \text{Range} &= X_H - X_L + 1 \\ &= 182 - 128 + 1 = 55 \end{aligned} \tag{7.2}$$

to illustrate, simply, given the scores of 25, 26, 27, 28, 29, 30. By formula 7.1, the range is $30 - 25 = 5$. Yet, there is a range of 6 when the inclusive scores are included: $30 - 25 + 1 = 6$.

Unless the range is small, as for times in a short run, formula 7.1 is generally used, as will be the case here.

2. *Number of intervals.* The decision as to the number of step intervals to include in the frequency distribution is guided by a general rule. Although the rule has been variously stated, the following will serve: The number of steps should be between 10 and 20, the selection depending upon the number of scores and their range. With a relatively small number of cases, the number of intervals should be nearer 10; whereas with many cases, the number should be nearer 20. A limited range, however, would set this guideline aside. For example, the range of heights of young girls might be 9 inches; if so, 9 intervals would be an automatic choice regardless of the number of subjects tested. Thus, the general 10-to-20 rule applies to the number of scores with the rule being modified if a short range is encountered.

For the skeletal ages in this problem, the number of 67 is certainly not large, although smaller numbers are possible. A preliminary decision could be that the number of intervals will be somewhere between 10 and 15 but probably nearer 10. The final decision will rest on the grouping convenience of interval size to be considered next.

3. *Interval size.* Some step-interval sizes are preferable as they are more convenient for the tabulation of scores. These sizes are 1, 2, 3, 4, 5, 10, 20, and 25. These intervals will take care of most sets of data. Where greater intervals are necessary, as sometimes happens in physical education with strength scores from large muscle groups, 50, 100, 200, and so forth are usually more desirable than numbers between.

For the 67 skeletal age scores with a range of 54 months and a decision to use somewhere near 10 intervals, the size of each step could conveniently be 5. This selection was made; as shown in Table 1, the number of step intervals became 12, which corresponds satisfactorily with the application of the rule. If an interval size of 4 had been adopted, the number of intervals would have been 15; for an interval size of 6, 10 intervals would have resulted. In both instances, the interval sizes are not as convenient as 5, so 5 was the choice. It should be noted that the adoption of 4 or 6 as the interval size would not necessarily be wrong; it is just that neither is quite as convenient in constructing the frequency table.

4. *Tabulation.* The step intervals should next be arranged in tabular form with the largest scores at the top and the smallest at the bottom. The reasons for this arrangement are that it is customarily followed in practice and that it is a more convenient order for calculation. The limits of the top interval, obviously, should be such as to include the highest score. Instead of using the highest score as the upper limit of this step, however, it is simpler and just as satisfactory to make each lower limit a multiple of the size of the interval selected, which is 5 in this problem.

For the 67 skeletal ages, the highest score is 182. Thus, the top interval should be 180–184. Each of the following five scores is included: 180, 181,

182, 183, and 184. In accordance with an earlier explanation, scores of 179.5 to 180.4 are considered 180; scores of 183.5 to 184.4 are recorded 184. Thus, this interval actually extends from 179.5 to 184.4, as the whole scores were obtained by rounding off to the nearest whole number.

All step intervals should then be arranged from top to bottom, beginning with the step 180–184 and continuing down until the lowest step includes the smallest score, 128 months, as shown in Table 1. Each of the 67 skeletal ages is then placed in its proper step interval. For example, the first score of 149 in the tabulation goes in the step 145–149; the second, 150, in 150–154, and so on until all the scores are placed, and each is indicated by a check mark opposite the proper step interval. The number of scores in each step is then designated with the appropriate figure. This column is known as the "frequency column" and is designated by the letter *f*. The total of the frequency column, indicated by N, should equal 67—the original number of skeletal ages.

Table 1

Frequency Distribution for Skeletal Ages of Boys 13 Years of Age

Step intervals	Tallies	f
180–184	/	1
175–179	/	1
170–174	//	2
165–169	𝍸 /	6
160–164	𝍸 //	7
155–159	𝍸 𝍸 /	11
150–154	𝍸 𝍸 ////	14
145–149	𝍸 ///	8
140–144	𝍸 //	7
135–139	𝍸 //	7
130–134	//	2
125–129	/	1
		$N = 67$

Assumptions

Two assumptions are made when statistics are calculated from a frequency table.

1. The scores are evenly distributed within the interval. This assumption is made when computing the median, other percentiles, and quartile deviation. In these instances, as will be shown later, the calculations are made by interpolating within the step intervals, that is, taking a definite proportion of the size of the interval. Thus, the process demands a linear scale.

2. The average of the scores within each interval is equal to the midpoint of the interval. This assumption is necessary when calculating the mean and standard deviation, as it is necessary to represent the scores within an interval by a single score. The individual scores within the various intervals are not identifiable from the frequency table, so the only consistent way to represent them is to utilize the midpoints of the intervals. Further, although the midpoints may not average out when the actual scores in the intervals are averaged, they balance out quite well throughout the distribution. The greatest violation of this assumption may occur at the tails of the distribution, where the *f*'s are small. In symmetrical distributions, which generally occur with a very large number of randomly selected subjects, all midpoints represent their respective intervals with considerable fidelity.

A slight grouping error is present in even the most symmetrical of distributions, such as the normal curve, when midpoints are utilized to represent the scores in the intervals. The build-up in the center with scores diminishing symmetrically toward the high and low extremes of the distribution—as in Table 1—causes a natural tendency for scores in the intervals to crowd toward the center of the distribution. Thus, the averages of scores in the upper intervals of the distribution tend to be slightly lower than their midpoints; and the averages for the lower intervals tend to be slightly higher. This grouping error is so slight that it is generally disregarded in making computations. Further, the upper and lower errors cancel out, especially when the mean is computed. For the standard deviation, however, the grouping error persists; a correction for it is possible, as will be explained later.

GRAPHING THE FREQUENCY DISTRIBUTION

As indicated earlier, an advantage of understanding statistics is being able to use them in the preparation of reports based on test results for presentation to school authorities and the public or for illustrating research findings. Instead of using tables of figures for this purpose, graphs of the data will provide a superior pictorial image of the results obtained. It has been said that one good picture is more effective in presenting an idea than are many words—graphs "picture" results. From time to time, the construction of appropriate graphs in the presentation of statistical results will be presented in this book.

An inspection of the frequency distribution of skeletal ages of the 67 boys in Table 1 gives a much better idea of the data in this problem than was obtained from the hodgepodge of individual scores on which the tabulation was based. The frequencies show the shape of the distribution: a concentration of scores in the center and a sloping away above and below the center.

This symmetrical distribution is typical of most random samples of subjects tested with a variety of measures.

Two graphs, known as the *frequency polygon* and the *histogram*, can be drawn from the frequency table. Procedures for constructing each of these graphs follow, utilizing the skeletal age data in Table 1. All graphs have two coordinate axes: a horizontal, or *X*, axis—the *abscissa*; the vertial, or *Y*, axis—the *ordinate*.

In plotting both the frequency polygon and the histogram, the "75 per cent" rule should be followed. The height of the graph should be 75 per cent of its width. The rule should be considered an approximation, as some variance from it is permissible. The purpose of the rule is to provide good balance and a pleasing effect for the graph. Also, different graphs can be compared visually if the proportions conform. Changing the proportions can drastically change the appearance of a graph and, thus, give faulty impressions of the data. For the same frequency distribution, a graph with a height 40 per cent of its width will have a flat, drawn-out shape; a graph with a height greater than its width will be peaked, highly concentrated in the center.

Frequency Polygon

The frequency polygon for the 67 skeletal age scores of 13-year-old boys is shown in Figure 2; the frequency distribution plotted is from Table 1. The steps in constructing this graph are as follows:

1. The score values, as represented by the step intervals, are placed on the abscissa—base line. There are different ways of identifying these values. The exact lower limits of each interval could be used, as 124.5, 129.5, and so forth. By this arrangement, an unnecessary and confusing number of numerals would be necessary. Another method would be to give the midpoints of each interval. However, the method selected here is to use the same interval designations as expressed in the frequency table, as 125, 130, and so on.

2. An extra interval at the lower end and at the upper end of the distribution is necessary in order to start and end the curve on the base line. Otherwise, the entire polygon would be separated from the abscissa by at least one frequency (only one in the illustration). The break in the *X* axis (∫∫) indicates the separation of the values from 0; that is, the vertical axis has been moved in for convenience.

3. The frequencies are plotted from the ordinate. In the problem, the maximum frequency is 14, so the ordinate must accommodate this number. Instead of listing each frequency as 1, 2, 3, and so forth, every second one in the example was taken. The reason is to avoid crowding the axis with numbers, resulting in an unpleasant appearance. Similar adjustments should be made depending on the amount of the maximum frequency. For example,

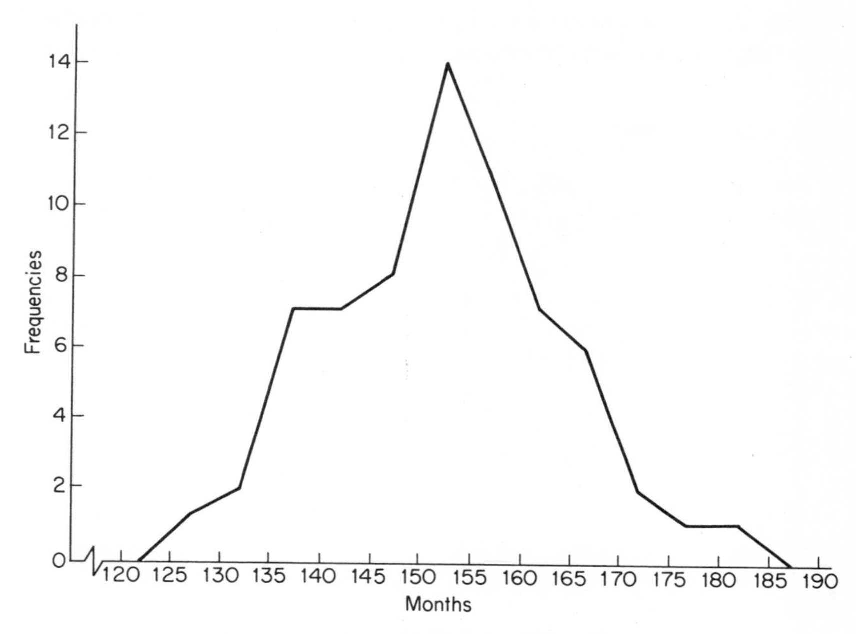

Figure 2. Frequency Polygon: Skeletal Ages

if this frequency were 50 (instead of 14), every fifth numeral would be given—5, 10, 15, and so on.

4. The frequencies for each interval are plotted with a dot above the midpoints of the intervals given on the abscissa. The first interval given on the graph (120–125) has no scores, so the graph starts on the base line at the midpoint of this interval, which is 122. The next interval (125–130) has a frequency of 1; the dot is placed opposite the frequency of 1 and above the midpoint of 127. This procedure is followed for all frequencies. The final plot will be on the base line again at 187 months—the midpoint of the upper interval (185–190), which contains no score. The dots throughout the graph are finally connected with a series of straight lines to form the frequency polygon.

5. Occasionally, when the sample is small and the distribution is irregular, the polygon will be jagged in outline. To reduce chance, or sampling irregularities and to get a better picture of how the figure might look if the sample were larger, the frequency table may be *smoothed.* Each frequency may be smoothed by averaging it with the frequencies above and below it. Thus, the smoothed f for interval 150–154 is $(11 + 14 + 8)/3 = 11.0$; for interval 135–139, $(2 + 7 + 7)/3 = 5.3$. The smoothed f for 125–129 is $(0 + 1 + 2)/3 = 1.0$; and for 180–184, $(1 + 1 + 0)/3 = .7$. In graphing,

the smoothed frequencies are joined by the straight lines; however, the actual frequencies should be shown on the polygon by small, open dots.

Histogram

Another way of graphing the frequency distribution is by means of a histogram or column diagram, as shown in Figure 3, again utilizing the

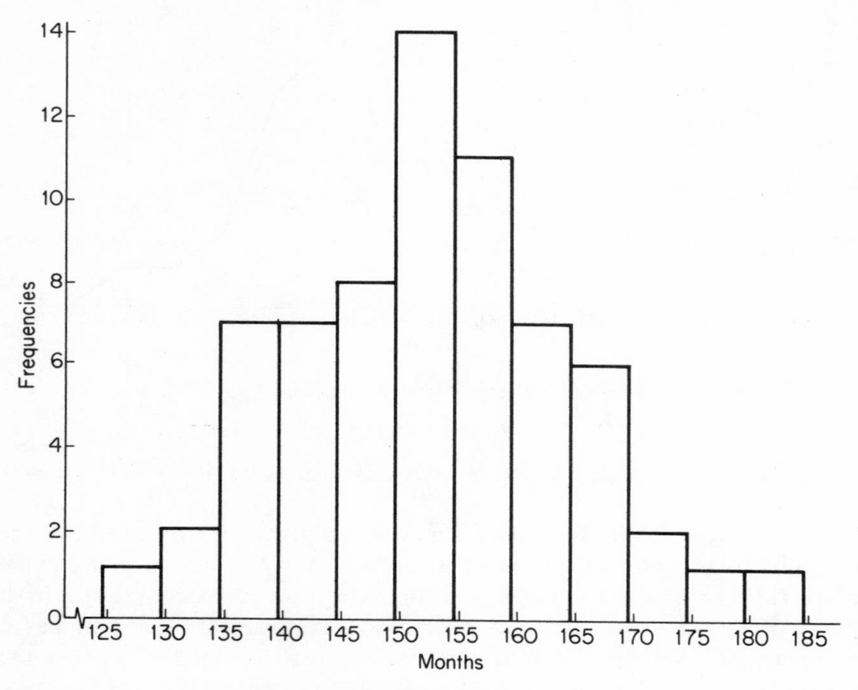

Figure 3. Histogram: Skeletal Ages

skeletal age scores for the distribution (Table 1). The abscissa and ordinate are set up in the same way as for the frequency polygon, except that the zero intervals are not needed. In plotting, instead of bringing the graph line to the midpoint of each interval, the line encompasses the entire breadth of the interval. However, this line for each interval starts and stops .5 months below the value shown on the base line. Thus, the first interval in the histogram begins at 124.5, the exact lower limit of the interval, and ends at 129.5, the exact upper limit of the interval. Each interval may be represented by a separate rectangular, as is done in Figure 3, or just a columnar outline may be used.

MEASURES OF CENTRAL TENDENCY

A measure of central tendency is a single score that represents all the scores in a distribution. If one asked the accomplishment of a class on an examination, the answer would not be that David received 85; Nancy, 75; Louise, 90; Stanley, 71; and so on until all the individual scores had been enumerated. Such a response would be both meaningless and confusing; one would still wonder how well the class had performed. Instead, the answer would probably be: "The average of the class was 75," or whatever the average may have been. The answer, thus, is in terms of central tendency —a single score that represents all the scores.

The three measures of central tendency most frequently encountered in educational research are the median, mean, and mode. Each of these measures describes the massing of scores in a particular manner.

Median

The median is the midpoint in a distribution, that point above which and below which lie 50 per cent of the scores; it may or may not be an actual score, as central tendency is considered to be a central position.

Ungrouped data. When scores are ungrouped but arranged in order from high to low, it is quite easy to find the center, or middle score by counting. To know how far to count, the following formula may be used:

$$Mdn = \frac{N + 1}{2}$$

To illustrate: Given five scores, 18, 17, 15, 12, 9

$$Mdn = \frac{5 + 1}{2} = 3$$

Thus, the third score is the middle score whether counting from the top or bottom. If an even number of scores are given: 18, 17, 15, 11, 9, 8

$$Mdn = \frac{6 + 1}{2} = 3.5$$

By counting 3.5 scores from either end, the median falls between 11 and 15. The median is halfway between these scores, or 13, even though a score of 13 does not appear; 13 is the center position.

Grouped data. With grouped data, or scores in a frequency table, the computation of the median is not so simple. In this situation, the median is found by counting frequencies to the interval that contains the middle point and interpolating to determine its location. The mechanics of this computation may be easier for some and will be described first; then, a formula will be provided. This process is illustrated in Table 2, which contains the frequency distribution of the 67 skeletal ages of 13-year-old boys tabulated earlier.

Table 2

Calculation of the Median, Mean, and Mode from Skeletal Age Data Grouped into a Frequency Table

Step intervals Scores in months	f	d	fd	
180–184	1	6	6	
175–179	1	5	5	
170–174	2	4	8	
165–169	6	3	18	
160–164	7	2	14	
155–159	11 (28)	1	11	+62
150–154	14	0	0	
145–149	8 (25)	−1	−8	
140–144	7	−2	−14	
135–139	7	−3	−21	
130–134	2	−4	−8	
125–129	1	−5	−5	−56
	$N = 67$			+6

(1) $$Median = l + \left(\frac{\frac{N}{2} - F}{f_m} i\right)$$

$$= 149.5 + \frac{\frac{67}{2} - 25}{14} 5 = 152.54$$

(2) $$Mean = AM + \left(\frac{\Sigma fd}{N} i\right)$$

$$= 152.0 + \left(\tfrac{6}{67}\right) 5 = 152.45$$

(3) *Crude Mode:* Falls in step interval 150–154, or at 152.0 (the midpoint).

With 67 scores, the middle score is at 33.5. Counting up from the lower end of the frequency (f) column, there are 25 scores below the interval

150–154. Thus, the point 149.5, the lower limit of the step, is reached; remember all scores have been rounded off to the nearest whole number, so 150 actually starts at 149.5.[3] The 33.5 score, then, is somewhere in this interval, so the approximate proportion of it is added to the lower limit. With 25 scores counted out, 8.5 more are needed to reach the middle: $33.5 - 25 = 8.5$. As there are 14 scores in the step interval, 8.5/14 of it should be taken, or 8.5/14 of 5, the size of the interval. This amount is 3.04, obtained by:[4,5]

$$\frac{8.5}{14} \times 5 \quad \text{or} \quad \frac{8.5 \times 5}{14} = 3.04$$

Adding this amount to the lower limit gives the median:

$$149.5 + 3.04 = 152.54 \text{ months}$$

The formula for computing the median is as follows:

$$Mdn = 1 + \left(\frac{\frac{N}{2} - F}{f_m}\right)i \quad \text{or} \quad 1 + \left(\frac{.5N - F}{f_m}\right)i \qquad (7.3)$$

To use this formula, start with $N/2$, and proceed as before. The calculation process is shown under Table 2.

The median may also be obtained by counting down from the top of the frequency distribution. The count down is 28 through the interval 155–159; 5.5 scores are needed to reach 33.5. Lower limits must always be used, so the computation is:

$$154.5 - \left(\frac{5.5}{14}\right)5 = 154.5 - 1.96 = 152.54$$

It may be worthwhile to mention special situations that may occur in calculating the median from a frequency table; the same situations apply to

---

[3] If the rounding off had been to the next whole number, the lower limit of the interval would have been 150.

[4] This method of computation is used to reduce rounding error. If the division 8.5/14 was done first, the amount added or dropped in the rounding process is multplied, in effect, by the size of the interval, thus increasing the amount of the error.

[5] In making computations, the general rule followed is to round off to two decimal places. This procedure will apply throughout the book, except for correlations where the answers nearly always start with a decimal.

computing percentiles explained later in this chapter. These situations are as follows:

1. The median falls between intervals. In this situation, the count to the median comes out even on a step interval, with no additional scores to add. The lower limit of the interval above the last interval with frequencies counted would be the median. If this had occurred in the skeletal age problem (although impossible because of the odd number of subjects), 149.5 would have been the median.

2. The median falls at an interval with no frequencies. When this occurs, the count to the median comes out even at the end of a step interval, and the interval above it is devoid of frequencies. Instead of jumping over this interval to the lower limit of an interval with frequencies in it, the midpoint of the interval with no frequencies is designated as the median. If more than one interval has no frequencies, the midpoint of the combined intervals constitutes the median. It is highly unlikely that this situation will be encountered in computing the median due to the typically high concentration of scores in the center of frequency distributions. However, it could happen in calculating high and low percentiles where scores in frequency distributions are relatively meager.

Mean

The mean expresses the central massing of scores according to the distance of the scores that fall from the center of the distribution. Therefore, each score in the distribution is weighted by its distance from central tendency.

The terms *mean* and *average* may be used interchangeably. The average, of course, is universally known and used. In common utilization, it is calculated by the arithmetic method of adding the scores and dividing by the number. Thus:

$$Ave \text{ (or } M) = \frac{\sum X}{N} \tag{7.4}$$

in which Σ means the summation, or addition, of scores, and N is the number of scores. In statistics, this method is also used to compute the mean from raw data, that is, from ungrouped scores.

The mean may also be computed from the frequency distribution. A longer than necessary method of doing this is to multiply the midpoint of each interval by the number of scores in the interval, add the results, and divide by N. This method, as does the short method to be described next, assumes that the midpoints adequately represent the scores in the intervals. This assumption was discussed earlier in the chapter.

The short method of determining the mean is to select a midpoint, to be called an assumed mean (AM), and then to apply a correction. Any midpoint in the distribution may be selected and will produce the same answer. However, the amount of arithmetic involved is less when the assumed mean is a midpoint near the center of the distribution.

Once the assumed mean is selected, the correction is in terms of the deviations of the scores from this midpoint. Initially, the deviations are in terms of the number of intervals from the assumed mean to be designated as d. The formula is developed as follows:

$$M = AM + C$$

$$C = c \times i$$

$$c = \frac{\sum fd}{N} \tag{7.5}$$

or

$$M = AM + \left(\frac{\sum fd}{N}\right) i$$

In the sample problem of the 67 skeletal ages of 13-year-old boys given in Table 2, the assumed mean is selected at the 150–154 interval; as the midpoint of the interval is used, the AM is 152.0.[6] The step interval deviations of the scores from AM are shown in the column, d. Each interval above the AM interval is 1 point farther removed, so the deviations are 1, 2, 3, 4, 5, and 6. These are positive deviations, as they represent numerically higher values than the assumed mean. Below the assumed mean, the same situation exists, except that the deviations are negative, as the values are numerically lower than the assumed mean. If the assumed mean selected is low in the distribution, a predominance of positive values will result; if high, the predominance will be negative. This situation is the reason the same answer will result no matter which assumed mean is selected, so long as only the midpoints are utilized. By selecting the midpoint of the lowest interval as the AM, all positive values would appear in the computation.

Since the number of subjects varies from interval to interval, this fact must be taken into consideration. To do so, the number of scores in each interval (f column) is multiplied by the step-interval deviation (d column). Thus, $f \times d = fd$. The scores in this final column are then added. As there

[6] The midpoint is obtained by adding one-half the size of the interval to the lower limit of the interval. In this problem one-half of 5 is 2.5; adding 2.5 to 149.5 gives a midpoint of 152.0.

are positive and negative values in the column, they must be added separately and their difference determined. In the problem, the sum of the positive values is 62 and the sum of the negative values is -56. Thus, the sum of the columns is 6. Substitution in the formula may now be completed:

$$M = AM + \left(\frac{\sum fd}{N}\right) i$$

$$= 152.0 + (\tfrac{6}{67})5 = 152.45$$

By experimenting with other assumed means, the student will find that the same answer is obtained each time. For example, if 157.0 were selected as the assumed mean, the sum of *fd* would be -4.55. The answer: $157.0 - 4.55 = 152.45$.

Mode

The mode is the score that appears most frequently. It may also be defined as the point of maximum frequency or the point of maximum concentration. When scores are ungrouped but arranged in order from high to low, the score that appears the greatest number of times is easily seen. For example, in the 67 skeletal ages as listed for the sample problem, 154 months appears 8 times—the largest number for any single score; consequently, it is the mode by raw-data method of determination.

From grouped scores, however, the most frequent score cannot be seen. A crude mode, however, may be designated as the midpoint of the step interval in which there are the largest number of scores. For the data contained in Table 2, 14 scores—the largest number in any one step—are found in the interval 150–154. The crude mode, therefore, is 152.0, the midpoint of this interval.

If adjacent intervals both contain the highest number of scores or one of them contains the highest and the other nearly as high, the crude mode would be the midpoint of the combined intervals. When in doubt or when confinement of the mode to a midpoint forces the crude mode too far from the central concentration, as reflected by the mean and median, the computed mode obtained from the following formula may be utilized:

$$\text{Computed mode} = 3\ (\text{Median}) - 2\ (\text{Mean}) \tag{7.6}$$

Characteristics and Uses

In the sample problem, the three measures of central tendency vary only slightly: median, 152.54 months; mean, 152.45 months; mode, 152.0 months

When these scores are individually added and divided by the number of scores (formula 7.4), the average is also close, 152.82 months. These results are typical of symmetrical distributions that peak in the center and taper off about equally on either side. In an exactly symmetrical distribution, these three measures of central tendency are identical. In this instance, obviously, any one of the measures will represent central tendency equally well.

However, for various reasons to be considered, frequency distributions are not always so symmetrical as this one. Therefore, further explanation of the characteristics and uses of the three measures of central tendency will be made.

Mode. The mode is generally a rough measure of central tendency and has little value in statistical work. However, the mode is useful in such circumstances as the following:

1. When the phenomenon or situation that happens most frequently is wanted. For example, when teaching skills, the skill that is missed most often is the mode.

2. When the central concentration is especially pronounced. For example, the modal age of children in a single grade in school would adequately represent central tendency.

3. When high concentrations are especially significant. For example, the modal shoe size or suit would be needed for stocking physical education uniforms.

In rare instances, a frequency distribution may have more than one peak. When this occurs, the description of typical performance as having two or more modes is preferable to a single measure of central tendency. To illustrate, a frequency distribution of the number of hits by 102 major-league baseball players during a single competitive season is contained in Table 3.

Table 3

Distribution of Hits by Major-League Baseball Players

Hits	f
Above 190	6
180–189	6
170–179	9
160–169	10
150–159	18
140–149	10
130–139	7
120–129	7
110–119	16
100–109	10
99 and Below	3
	$N = 102$

This distribution contains two concentrations; thus, it is bi-modal with the modes designated as 115 and 155.[7] In deciding upon the bi-modal nature of a distribution, the reason for the occurrence should be sought. In the illustration, the ball players making up the lower concentration around 115 hits are those who did not play daily, such as pitchers, relief pitchers, and pinch hitters, and those who were out of play because of injuries or who had moved up to the majors after the season was underway.

Median. The median may be computed quickly and easily. It is not affected by extreme scores or when the equality of a measurement unit is uncertain. The following uses are indicated for this measure of central tendency:

1. When the influence of extremely high or extremely low scores on the measure of central tendency is to be avoided. The actual size of scores within the distribution does not affect the median, as the scores are merely counted in making the calculation. For example, in Table 2, all 25 scores below the interval containing the median could have been in the interval 145–149 without changing the answer; they could also be spread out for any distance below. The mean would be drastically affected by these changes but not the median.

2. When the distribution is truncated—cut off at the top or bottom. A truncated distribution would occur as a result of using a strength-testing instrument with a capacity less than the strongest subjects. Truncation would also occur in some physical education tests, especially when zeros are possible or even probable, as in chinning. In this situation, a zero score does not mean that the pupil has no arm strength; rather, the test does not measure the amount. Further, one pupil with a zero score for chinning may differ significantly in arm strength from another pupil with a zero score; the test does not differentiate at these low levels of performance.

3. When the equality of the unit of measurement is uncertain. The uncertainty of measurement equality occurs when the performers are arranged in rank order; the actual difference between those with high and low ranks may well be greater than between those with middle ranks. Judges' ratings may sometimes have a truncation effect at the top and bottom of the scale used by them. Also, the median is useful when numerical measurement is impossible, as in an arrangement of silhouettes depicting poor to good posture.

Mean. The mean is the most reliable of the measures of central tendency; there is less fluctuation from sample to sample from the same population than is true for the mode and the median, as explained in Chapter 10. The mean should be used when distributions are reasonably symmetrical,

---

[7] These data are treated as discrete scores, that is, fractions of scores (hits) are impossible, so a score of 115 remains 115 until another hit is made and the score becomes 116.

when they are not skewed, or when they do not contain extremes at one end of the distribution; extremes at both ends balance each other. Actually, the mean should be used unless the mode or median is more appropriate, as indicated above. Further, the mean should be the measure of central tendency when advanced statistics are to be employed in analyses.

Each score in the distribution carries a weight equal to its distance from the mean when the mean is calculated. This distance from the mean for each score is sometimes called a *moment*, although it is more commonly indicated as *distance from the mean*, designated by the symbol, x.

Thus,

$$x = X - M \qquad \text{and} \qquad \sum x = \sum (X - M)$$

The arithmetic mean is the only measure of central tendency for which the deviations from central tendency always add algebraically to zero. This situation is illustrated in Table 4. The sum of the deviations of the 8 scores

Table 4

Illustrations of Some Properties of the Mean and Median

	(1) Individual scores (X)	(2) Deviations from M ($X - M$)	(3) Deviations from Mdn ($X - Mdn$)	(4) Deviations squared from M $(X - M)^2$	(5) Deviations squared from Mdn $(X - Mdn)^2$
	20	11	12.5	121	156.25
	15	6	7.5	36	56.25
	10	1	2.5	1	6.25
	8	−1	.5	1	.25
	7	−2	−.5	4	.25
	6	−3	−1.5	9	2.25
	4	−5	−3.5	25	12.25
	2	−7	−5.5	49	30.25
Σ	72	0	12.0	246	264.00
M	9	0.0	1.5		
Mdn	7.5				

from the mean (column 2) is 0; thus, the mean of these deviations is also zero. On the other hand, the sum of the deviations from the median (column 3) is 12.0; the mean of this column is 1.5.

In some statistical calculations, deviations of the scores from central tendency must be squared; therefore the moments are squared. An important property of the mean is that the sum of the squared deviations around it is smaller than the sum of the squared deviations around the median. A demonstration of this characteristic appears in Table 4. The sum of the squared deviations from the mean (column 4) is 246, whereas the sum for the median (column 5) is 264.

PERCENTILES

The use of percentiles is valuable in making test scores meaningful; a table of percentiles is one way of presenting norms for a given test. It is impossible to know how well one has done on a test unless his score is shown in relationship to others taking or having taken the same test. For example, merely giving a score of 150 on an examination is meaningless. However, if the 30th percentile score is 150, it is immediately known that the pupil has exceeded 30 per cent of those taking the test but is below scores achieved by 70 per cent. Percentiles may also be used in comparing the standing of different individuals in a number of tests. To illustrate, how does a score of 11 seconds in the 100-yard dash compare with a score of 16 feet in the long jump. If 11 seconds is at the 75th percentile and 16 feet is at the 65th percentile, the comparison becomes clear.

A given percentile indicates the percentage of scores below that point in the distribution. Thus, 30 per cent of the scores are below the 30th percentile, 87 per cent are below the 87th percentile, and so forth. The 25th and 75th percentiles have special significance because they are also known as the first and third quartiles (each 25th percentile); they are used in computing the quartile deviation, as shown in the next chapter.

A percentile scale extends from P_0 to P_{100}. Although all 100 percentiles appear in a percentile scale or table, only computations of the deciles and quartiles will be presented here in order to reduce the magnitude of the work involved. The method of calculating the percentiles is similar to that used for finding the median except different points are sought; in fact, the median is a percentile, the 50th. For example, the 10th percentile is found by counting off one-tenth; the 20th is found by counting off two-tenths (one-fifth) from the low end of the distribution, rather than one-half, as was true for the median.

Table 5 illustrates the method used in computing the deciles (each 10th percentile) and the quartiles in the distribution of 67 skeletal ages utilized in the calculation of the measures of central tendency. A cumulative frequency column (*cf*) appears in the table; those scores were obtained by adding the frequencies cumulatively, beginning with the lowest interval and continuing to the highest. This column is of assistance in locating the desired interval when counting for any particular percentile.

To explain the procedure, the 10th percentile (P_{10}) is located by finding $\frac{1}{10}$ of 67 (.1 N), or 6.7. From the *cf* column, 3 scores are below the interval 135–139, so the lower limit of this interval, 134.5, has been reached; 3.7 more scores are needed ($6.7 - 3 = 3.7$). Interpolating into the interval, as was done for the median, P_{10} is computed as 137.14 skeletal age months. The percentiles between the decile points are obtained in a similar manner. Thus, for P_{37}:

$$P_{37} = .37N = .37 \times 67 = 24.79$$

$$144.5 + \frac{7.79 \times 5}{8} = 149.37$$

The 0 and 100th percentiles may be designated in different ways. The method adopted for Table 5 is to designate the lowest score in the distribution as P_0 and the highest score as P_{100}. In the problem, these scores were

Table 5

Calculation of Deciles and Quartiles from Skeletal Age Data Grouped into a Frequency Table

Scores (Months)	f	cf	
			Quartiles
180–184	1	67	$Q_1 = 144$
175–179	1	66	$Q_3 = 160$
170–174	2	65	Percentiles at
165–169	6	63	decile points
160–164	7	57	P_{100} 182
155–159	11	50	P_{90} 167
150–154	14	39	P_{80} 162
145–149	8	25	P_{70} 158
140–144	7	17	P_{60} 155
135–139	7	10	P_{50} 153
130–134	2	3	P_{40} 150
125–129	1	1	P_{30} 146
	$N = 67$		P_{20} 142
			P_{10} 137
			P_0 128

Calculation of deciles

$P_{10} = .1N = 6.7 \quad 134.5 + \frac{3.7 \times 5}{7} = 137.14$

$P_{20} = .2N = 13.4 \quad 139.5 + \frac{3.4 \times 5}{7} = 141.93$

$P_{30} = .3N = 20.1 \quad 144.5 + \frac{3.1 \times 5}{8} = 146.44$

$P_{40} = .4N = 26.8 \quad 149.5 + \frac{1.8 \times 5}{14} = 150.14$

$P_{50} = .5N = 33.5 \quad 149.5 + \frac{8.5 \times 5}{14} = 152.54$ (*Mdn*)

$P_{60} = .6N = 40.2 \quad 154.5 + \frac{1.2 \times 5}{11} = 155.05$

$P_{70} = .7N = 46.9 \quad 154.5 + \frac{7.9 \times 5}{11} = 158.09$

$P_{80} = .8N = 53.6 \quad 159.5 + \frac{3.6 \times 5}{7} = 162.07$

$P_{90} = .9N = 60.3 \quad 164.5 + \frac{3.3 \times 5}{6} = 167.25$

Calculation of quartiles

$Q_1 = .25N = 16.75$

$139.5 + \frac{6.75 \times 5}{7} = 144.32$

$Q_3 = .75N = 50.25$

$159.5 + \frac{.25 \times 5}{7} = 159.68$

128 and 182 months, respectively. Another method is simply to use the lower and upper limits of the frequency distribution. Had this been done in the problem, P_0 would equal 125, and P_{100} would be 185. These two values indicate the boundaries of the percentile scale; they are regulated by two single individuals tested in the sample from which the scale was developed, so are subject to considerable chance in their random selection. Consequently, the latter method of designating P_0 and P_{100} would usually provide some leeway in future testing should more extreme scores be encountered than in the original sample; thus, there is less likelihood that individuals who fell either above or below the values provided on the percentile scale would be subsequenty tested.

In test construction, when a percentile scale is presented, the percentile values are frequently given in whole numbers, as in the upper right part of Table 5. The decision as to whether or not this should be done is dependent upon the range of scores and the importance of fractions. For example, in the problem, a fraction of a month would probably not be important for practical purposes in scoring a boy's skeletal age. However, if a percentile scale were constructed for standing height, where the range of scores is small for any given age, fractions of an inch should be used.

The percentile scale favors mediocre or "average" performance. As seen in Table 5, the values cluster closely in the center of the scale and spread out at the ends. The differences between deciles in the central area is small, only 2 points—for example, between P_{50} and P_{60} (153 to 155 months); at the extremes, the differences are much larger—15 points between P_{90} and P_{100} (167 to 182 months). For this reason, it is comparatively easy for an individual to improve his percentile position in the middle of the distribution but very difficult at the ends. To equal the 15 months required to go from P_{90} to P_{100}, a boy could go from P_{30} almost to P_{80} (162 to 146 = 16), which is one-half the scale. Further, due to the inequalities in scale values, percentiles may not be properly summed and averaged. Because of these characteristics of the percentile scale, other scaling methods have been sought, as will be explained in the next chapter.

CUMULATIVE CURVES

Two cumulative curves are in general use: the cumulative frequency curve and the cumulative percentage, or ogive, curve. These graphs show the effect of cumulatively adding frequencies in the distribution from low to high intervals. These graphs reflect the progressive development of a trait in a sample. Also, the percentiles may be obtained from them without computation. A single graph will be presented here, Figure 4, which combines these curves. The data consist of the 67 skeletal ages of 13-year-old boys. The

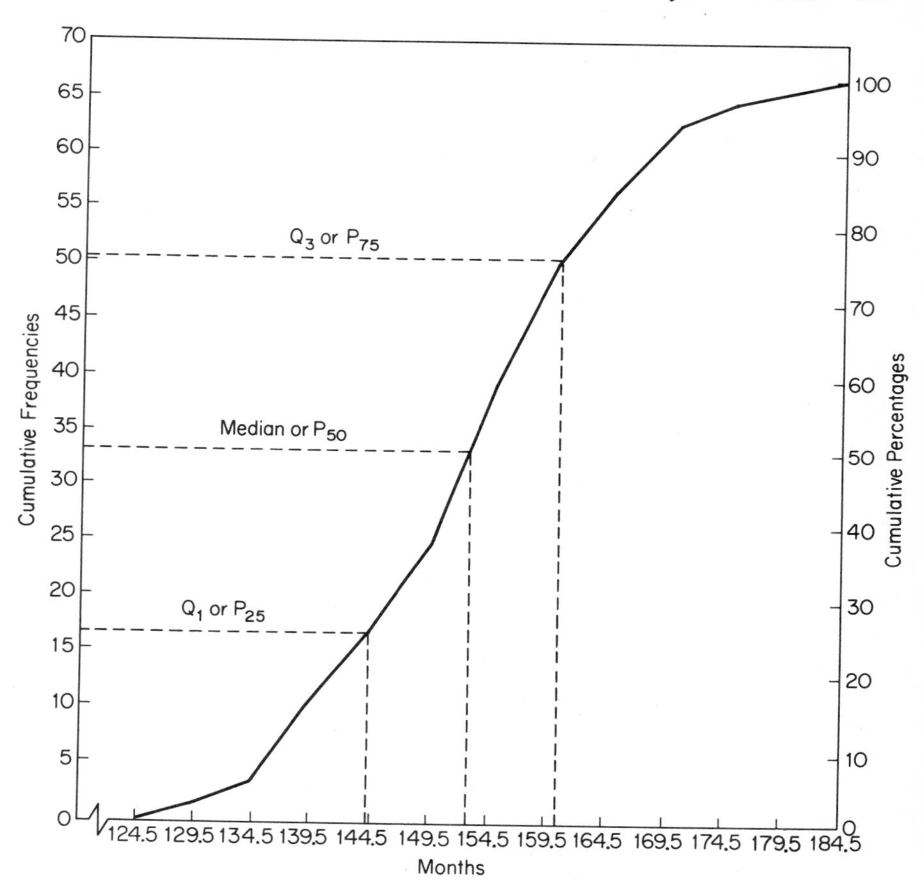

Figure 4. Cumulative Frequencies and Percentages: Skeletal Ages

basic process is to construct the cumulative frequency graph, as follows:

1. Place the step-interval values along the absicissa in the same manner as for the frequency polygon, less the intervals with 0 frequencies. For the ordinate, however, the cumulative frequencies are given. The *cf* column in Table 5 is plotted; this column extends to a *cf* of 67.

2. Plotting throughout the graph is done at the upper limits of the interval; thus, the graph lines cross the intervals. To illustrate:

125–129: from 0 *cf* at 124.5 to 1 *cf* at 129.5

150–154: from 25 *cf* at 149.5 to 39 *cf* at 154.5

180–184: from 66 *cf* at 179.5 to 67 *cf* at 184.5

3. The plots are connected by lines in the usual manner. The *S*-shaped curve in Figure 4 is typical in shape to cumulative frequency curves constructed from normal and other symmetrical distributions.

Percentiles may be readily determined from the cumulative frequency curve, either by taking the proper proportion of the number or by measurement with a ruler. Illustrations on the graph are for the median and quartiles. In explanation of the proportionate-number method:

$$Mdn = .5N = .5 \times 67 = 33.5$$

From 33.5 on the left margin ordinate, cross horizontally to the cumulative frequency line, then drop vertically to the abscissa. The value on the base line is 153, which corresponds to the computation in Table 5. Similar procedures are followed for the quartiles:

$$Q_1 = .25N = .25 \times 67 = 16.75 \qquad Q_1 = 144$$

$$Q_3 = .75N = .75 \times 67 = 50.25 \qquad Q_3 = 160$$

With a ruler, measure the distance from the abscissa to the *cf* of 67. One-half the distance falls at 33.5, the same *cf* as for the median. One-fourth and three-fourths distances will give positions for Q_1 and Q_3.

The cumulative frequency curve can be converted into a cumulative percentage curve by merely placing the corresponding percentiles as measured with the ruler along the right marginal ordinate, as in Figure 4. From this ordinate, the percentiles can be obtained directly. The ogive may also be constructed from cumulative percentages. To do this from Table 5, convert the cumulative frequency column to a cumulative percentage column by multiplying each *cf* by a rate. The rate is the percentage value of 1 score. Thus:

$$\frac{1}{N} \times 100 \qquad \text{or} \qquad \frac{1}{67} \times 100 = 1.49$$

To check: $67 \times 1.49 = 99.83$ (approximately 100 per cent).

The ogive has an additional convenience in that the percentile for a given score may be readily obtained. For example, if a subject has a score of 146 months, from 146 on the base line, erect a line perpendicular to the curve; then cross horizontally to the right scale; the percentile is 30.

PERCENTILE BAR DIAGRAM

Another useful graph that may be constructed from percentiles is the percentile bar diagram. For this graph, a scale that will accommodate the range of values in the distribution is placed vertically on the left side. The following percentiles are designated: P_0, P_{10}, P_{25}, P_{50}, P_{75}, P_{90}, and P_{100}. The arrangement of these values can be seen in Figure 5.

Figure 5 portrays the results of testing approximately 100 sophomore high school girls in each of five Oregon schools with Rogers' Physical Fitness Index (PFI) test; the 6th percentile bar diagram represents the median values for eleven schools that participated in the state project. These tests were retests with the initial tests having been given three months earlier; in some schools, the women physical education teachers had stressed physical fitness activities for their girls during the interim period. By way of information,

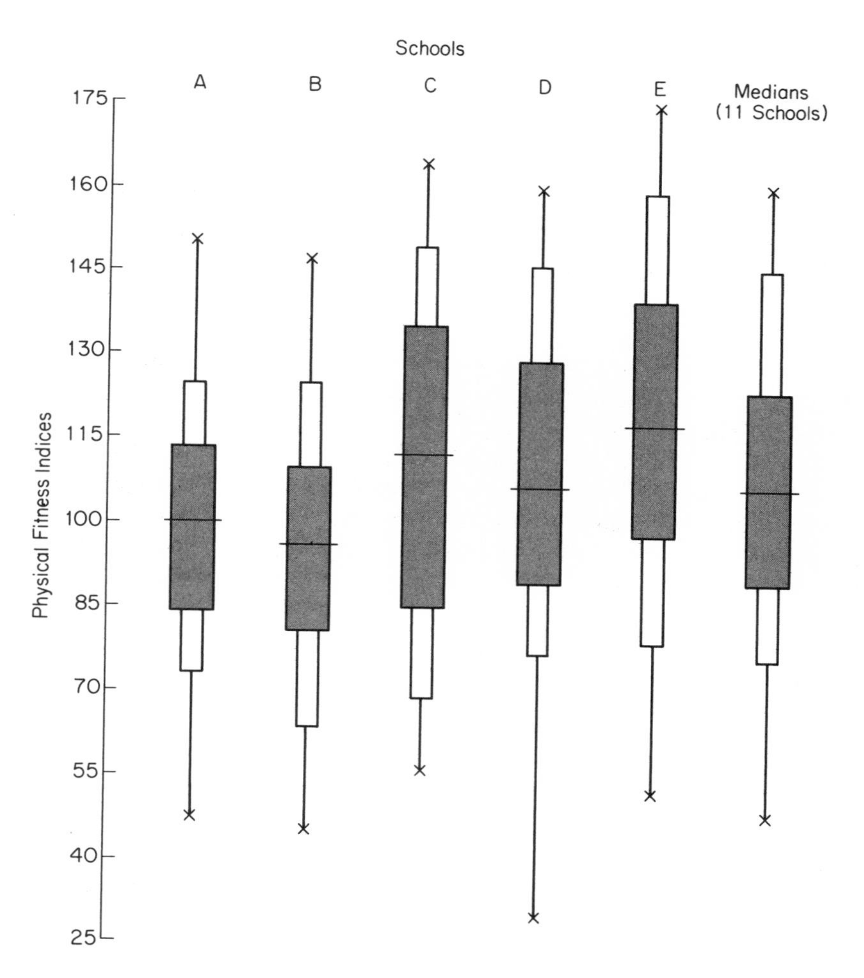

Figure 5. Percentile Bar Diagrams: Girls' Physical Fitness Indices

normal PFI expectations are 100 for the median and 85 and 115 for the first and third quartiles, respectively.

In each percentile bar diagram, the middle horizontal line represents P_{50}; the solid middle block, the middle 50 per cent, with P_{25} and P_{75} at the lower and upper ends; the lower and upper ends of the narrower open blocks, P_{10} and P_{90}; and lower and upper X's at the ends of the single lines, P_0 and P_{100}.

An examination of the percentile bar diagrams will reveal several interesting features, such as: (1) The girls in only one school (*B*) had a median PFI below the national expectation of 100. (2) The highest median PFI (School *E*) exceeded the national P_{75}; the median for this school exceeded the P_{75} of Schools *A* and *B*. (3) The P_{25} of School *E* nearly reached the normal median of 100. (4) All but one school had first quartiles near the expected 85, thus indicating that a sizable number of these girls needed physical fitness attention. This observation is supported by the low P_{10} values and the lowest scores. Overall, these results also indicated that developmental programs for girls can be effective. For the eleven schools participating in the project, the initial median was 93; the median three months later was 106.

SUMMARY

Inasmuch as the statistics chapters in this book assumed that the student had no prior knowledge of this subject, this chapter began with a consideration of the nature of statistics and types of statistical data. The development of the frequency table was explained and the table was graphed through use of the frequency polygon and the histogram. The computations of three measures of central tendency—mode, median, and mean—were described utilizing both grouped and ungrouped data; their characteristics and uses in research were considered. Finally, the calculation of percentiles and quartiles were presented; the construction of a percentile was described and its strength and weaknesses as a scoring scale were indicated. Additional graphs based on cumulative frequencies and percentages and percentile positions were constructed.

CHAPTER 8

Measures of Variability

Measures of central tendency were presented in the preceding chapter. Test scores were described in terms of typical performance; the point of greatest concentration of scores was indicated. In many studies and in any presentation of test results for whatever purpose, some form of central tendency will be essential.

However, central tendency alone does not adequately give the total picture of the sample measured. For example, two groups of sophomore high school girls (Groups *A* and *B*) have the same Physical Fitness Index mean of 100. From this information, the two groups seem alike in so far as the quality being measured is concerned. Suppose, however, that the highest PFI in Group *A* is 150, and the lowest is 50; in Group *B*, the highest is 125, and the lowest is 75. The two groups are no longer alike: Group *A* has a range of 100, and Group *B* has a range of 50. The Group *A* range is twice the Group *B* range. Although central tendency is the same, the internal arrangement of the scores is not.

In the above illustration, a measure of variability—the range—was applied. For a definition: A measure of variability indicates the spread of the scores in a distribution, usually around a measure of central tendency. In this instance, a distance on a scale is expressed by a single measure, as a range of 100 and a range of 50 in the illustration. This measure is never a point on a scale, as was true for measures of central tendency. The following five measures of variability will be described in this chapter: range, quartile deviation, mean deviation, standard deviation, and probable error. Special attention will be given to the computation and use of the quartile and standard deviations.

RANGE

The range indicates the spread of all the scores in the distribution; in use here, it is not related to a measure of central tendency. As explained and illustrated in the preceding chapter (formulas 7.1 and 7.2), the range is obtained by finding the difference between the highest and lowest scores. Its use as a measure of variability is unreliable when extreme scores occur in the distribution, for it takes into account only the two scores at the ends of the distribution. In order to avoid this situation, the other measures of variability consider only the spread of scores in the center of the distribution.

QUARTILE DEVIATION

The quartile deviation, or Q, indicates the spread of the middle 50 per cent of the scores taken from the median. Thus, in an effort to eliminate the effect of extreme scores on the measure of variability, this measure cuts 25 per cent from each end. The formula for calculating Q is as follows:

$$Q = \frac{Q_3 - Q_1}{2} \tag{8.1}$$

As both Q_3 and Q_1 were calculated in the preceding chapter, the additional mathematical process is quite simple. This calculation is shown in Table 7 for the 67 skeletal ages of 13-year-old boys. The third and first quartiles, 159.68 and 144.32 months, are taken from Table 5. The distance between the two quartiles is 15.36 months, a distance referred to as the *interquartile range.* One-half of this distance, or Q, is 7.68 months.

The meaning of Q is illustrated in Figure 6, using the quartiles, median,

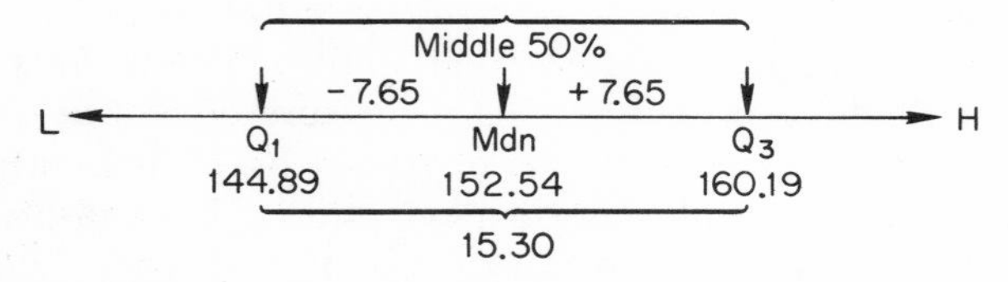

Figure 6. Quartile Deviation Relationships: Skeletal Ages in Months

and quartile deviation found in the problem presented. In interpreting Q, this value is marked off in plus and minus distances from the median. In a completely symmetrical distribution, adding and subtracting Q from the median will equal the calculated Q_3 and Q_1. In the illustrated problem, the results are nearly so. Thus, 152.54 months, the median, plus and minus 7.68 months equal 160.19 and 144.89 months, while the calculated Q_3 and Q_1 are 159.68 and 144.32 months.

MEAN DEVIATION

If the distribution conforms to a normal curve, the mean deviation indicates the spread of the middle 57.5 per cent of the scores taken from any measure of central tendency. This measure of variability is infrequently found in research, as its calculation does not conform to proper algebraic procedure; plus and minus values are added in the calculation without regard to the negative signs.

STANDARD DEVIATION

The standard deviation, or sigma, is the most important of the measures of variability. It is designated either by *SD* or the Greek sigma sign, σ. This variability measure indicates the spread of the middle 68.26 per cent of the scores taken from the mean. The percentage value of 68.26 per cent will not be seen from the calculation, as the middle 50 per cent for the quartile deviation was seen. The percentage applies when distributions are normal, and it is obtained from the properties of the normal probability curve, as explained in Chapter 9.

Ungrouped Data

Basically, the standard deviation is calculated as the square root of the average of the squared deviations from the mean. As expressed in formula:

$$\sigma = \sqrt{\frac{\sum x^2}{N}} \tag{8.2}$$

The calculation of *SD* by this formula is illustrated in Table 6, Method A. The column headed X contains 10 scores from which the computation is made; the mean of these scores is 13.2. The second column, x, gives the deviations of the scores from the mean. Thus: $x = X - M$. To illustrate with the first two x scores of 13 and 17:

$$13 - 13.2 = -.2$$

$$17 - 13.2 = 3.8$$

In the third column, each of the x values is squared. This column is added, and the amount is 51.60. The formula is then applied; the *SD* equals 2.27.

Another method of calculating *SD* from ungrouped data will be presented. For this method, the calculations are directly from the raw scores. As a consequence, the formula has special usefulness in this day of the electronic computer, as it can be programmed for this purpose. The formula is as follows:

$$\sigma = \frac{\sqrt{N \sum X^2 - (\sum X)^2}}{N} \tag{8.3}$$

The calculation of sigma by this formula is illustrated in Table 6, Method B. The same ten scores utilized in the first method are given in the first column; the sum of this column ($\sum X$) equals 132. In the second column, the first

Table 6

Calculation of the Standard Deviation from Raw Data

Method A: From the mean				Method B: From raw scores directly		
X	x	x^2		X	X^2	
13	−.2	.04	$M = \frac{132}{10} = 13.2$	13	169	$\sigma = \frac{\sqrt{N \sum X^2 - (\sum X)^2}}{N}$
17	3.8	14.44	$\sigma = \sqrt{\frac{\sum x^2}{N}}$	17	289	
15	1.8	3.24		15	225	$= \frac{\sqrt{10(1794) - (132)^2}}{10}$
11	−2.2	4.84		11	121	
13	−.2	.04	$= \sqrt{\frac{51.60}{10}}$	13	169	$= \frac{\sqrt{17{,}940 - 17{,}424}}{10}$
17	3.8	14.44		17	289	$= \frac{\sqrt{516}}{10}$
11	−2.2	4.84	$= \sqrt{5.16}$	11	121	
13	−.2	.04	$= 2.27$	13	169	$= \frac{22.7}{10}$
11	−2.2	4.84		11	121	$= 2.27$
11	−2.2	4.84		11	121	
$\sum$ 132		51.60		$\sum$ 132	1794	

column scores are squared and added ($\sum X^2$). With these two values, the formula is applied. The *SD* is again 2.27.

An explanation relative to the symbol used to represent the standard deviation should be made. As can be seen, σ has been used for this purpose. In some statistics books, σ is reserved for a parameter standard deviation and s is used for a sample mean. The distinction between a parameter and a sample will be made in Chapter 10.

Grouped Data

The formula for calculating the standard deviation from grouped data by the short method—that is, calculating it from an assumed mean in a frequency table rather than from the actual mean—is:

$$\sigma = i\sqrt{\frac{\sum fd^2}{N} - \left(\frac{\sum fd}{N}\right)^2} \tag{8.4}$$

As explained when the calculation of the mean from grouped data by the short method was presented in Chapter 7, the use of an assumed mean (AM) requires a correction (C). The correction was developed as follows:

$$C = c \times i$$

$$c = \frac{\sum fd}{N}$$

$$\therefore C = \left(\frac{\sum fd}{N}\right) i$$

In the standard deviation formula, the correction before multiplying by size of the interval (c) is used. Multiplication by the interval (i) does not take place until after square root is taken.

It will readily be seen from the formula and from Table 7, where the standard deviation is computed, that the only computation that is new at this point is $\sum fd^2$. The steps to be followed in finding SD are as follows:

1. Calculate the fd column, as previously described in the presentation of the mean in Table 2.

2. Add another column, fd^2, which is calculated by multiplying each figure in column d by the corresponding figure in column fd. It should be noted that only d is squared. Thus: $d \times fd = fd^2$. Add this column serially, since all the signs are positive (multiplying two negatives produces a positive); this will be $\sum fd^2$. In this problem: $\sum fd^2 = 342$. In the formula, this sum is divided by N; the quotient is 5.10.

3. Compute the correction required when computations are made from an assumed mean. In this instance: $(\sum fd/N)^2 = .01$.

4. Substitute in the formula and complete the computations. The SD for the skeletal ages of the 67 13-year-old boys is 11.30 months.

Table 7

Calculation of Measures of Variability from Data Grouped into a Frequency Table
(Data from Table 2)

Step intervals Scores in months	f	d	fd	fd^2
180–184	1	6	6	36
175–179	1	5	5	25
170–174	2	4	8	32
165–169	6	3	18	54
160–164	7	2	14	28
155–159	11	1	11 (+62)	11
150–154	14	0	0	
145–149	8	−1	−8	8
140–144	7	−2	−14	28
135–139	7	−3	−21	63
130–134	2	−4	−8	32
125–129	1	−5	−5 (−56)	25
	$N = 67$		+6	342

Quartile deviation

$$Q = \frac{Q_3 - Q_1}{2}$$

$Q_3 = 159.68$ (Table 5)
$Q_1 = 144.32$ (Table 5)

$$Q = \frac{159.68 - 144.32}{2}$$

$$= \frac{15.36}{2}$$

$= 7.68$ months

Standard deviation

$$\sigma = i\sqrt{\frac{\Sigma fd^2}{N} - \left(\frac{\Sigma fd}{N}\right)^2}$$

$$\frac{\Sigma fd^2}{N} = \frac{342}{67} = 5.10$$

$$\left(\frac{\Sigma fd}{N}\right)^2 = \left(\frac{6}{67}\right)^2 = (.09)^2 = .01$$

$$= 5\sqrt{5.10 - .01}$$
$$= 5 \times 2.26$$
$= 11.30$ months

Probable error

$PE = .6745\sigma$ or $.6745 \times 11.30 = 7.62$ months

Sheppard's Correction

When considering the assumptions made when various statistics are calculated from a frequency table, a grouping error was indicated when midpoints were used to represent the scores in the intervals. This error is a tendency for scores in the intervals to crowd a bit toward the center of the distribution. Although the grouping error does not influence the mean, it does affect the standard deviation. A correction for this tendency, known as

Sheppard's correction, can be made if desired. The formula is:

$$\sigma_c = \sqrt{\sigma^2 - \frac{i^2}{12}} \tag{8.5}$$

in which i is the size of the interval and 12 is a constant. Substituting in the formula for the SD of the 67 skeletal ages:

$$\sigma_c = \sqrt{11.30^2 - \frac{5^2}{12}} = 11.21 \text{ months}$$

Sheppard's correction provides a close approximation to the SD, which would be obtained from ungrouped scores. However, it is usually disregarded in most statistical applications. Guilford[1] has suggested that when the size of a class interval, i, is equal to $.49\sigma$, Sheppard's correction amounts to only about 1 per cent. Such an error can be tolerated unless very precise calculations are wanted.

PROBABLE ERROR

Probable error as a measure of variability is little used today. However, it does appear frequently in early reports of scientific studies in education and psychology. Therefore, an understanding of it is necessary for those who search the literature of an earlier day.

Probable error indicates the spread of the middle 50 per cent of the scores taken from the mean. As can be seen, both PE and Q describe a middle 50 per cent relationship. However, PE relates to the mean, and Q relates to the median as the measures of central tendency. In a normal distribution, all comparable measures are the same—that is, the mean and median and the probable error and quartile deviation.

Probable error is derived from the standard deviation, rather than the first and third quartiles as for the quartile deviation. The formula is:

$$PE = .6745\sigma \tag{8.6}$$

The PE for the 67 skeletal ages is 7.62 months; the computation is shown in Table 7.

[1] J. P. Guilford, *Fundamental Statistics in Psychology and Education*, (4th ed.) (New York: McGraw-Hill Book Company, 1965), p. 85.

USES OF VARIABILITY MEASURES

Variability measures, of course, continue to describe data such as test scores representing human performances. As pointed out at the start of this chapter, central tendency alone is inadequate, as it accounts only for typical performance and does not indicate the internal arrangement or dispersion of the scores. Both central tendency and variability indicators are needed in describing such performances.

Variability measures also provide a common unit for specifying the distance from central tendency to any individual score or point on the scale of scores. For example, a score of 15 points above the mean is meaningless. However, if 15 points is 1.5σ above the mean, the performance becomes understandable.

Measures of variability can be used as "yardsticks" on the scale of scores, regardless of differences in distribution ranges. Given the following, for example:

$$\text{Height: } M = 65 \text{ inches}; \quad \sigma = 2 \text{ inches}$$

$$\text{Weight: } M = 135 \text{ pounds}; \quad \sigma = 15 \text{ pounds}$$

An individual whose height is 67 inches (2 inches above the mean for height) and whose weight is 150 pounds (15 pounds above the mean for weight) is 1σ above the mean on both tests. Thus, his positions on the scale for both tests are the same.

In considering the uses of the various measures of variability, ease and quickness of computation are in the following order: range, quartile deviation, mean deviation, standard deviation, and probable error. When the reliability of the measures is compared, the first three elements are reversed, although standard deviation and probable error are the same. Thus, standard deviations from repeated random samples cluster closer together than do other variability measures. As will be explained later, quartile deviations from repeated samples range about 25 per cent more than do standard deviations. Specific uses of the variability measures follow.

Range

In random sampling, the range is subject to the greatest fluctuation as compared with the other measures of variability. As a consequence, it is the most unreliable of these measures; only two scores determine it, the lowest and the highest. An extreme score at either end will distort this variability indicator. For example, for two groups of 100 subjects each, 98 subjects in both groups may have scores between 75 and 125, a range of 50.

But, if Group *A* had an extreme score of 140, while Group *B* did not, the Group *A* range would be 65. The one extreme score in this illustration carries far too much weight in describing variability of the scores in Group *A* than 1 score in 100 should.

However, the range does have an important use when a knowledge of the total spread of scores is wanted. An illustration of this use of the range appears later in this chapter. In physical education and athletics, extreme scores are frequently of great interest and even appear in the news media: the tall and the short basketball player, the heavy football lineman, the speedy back, the young girl world champion swimmer, and the like.

Quartile Deviation

According to the definition given, the quartile deviation is used to indicate variability when the median is the measure of central tendency. Both of these measures are obtained by counting scores. Therefore, both have comparable characteristics, which accounts for their close association in descriptive statistics.

The quartile deviation is uninfluenced by the upper and lower 25 per cent of the scores. These scores may be located anywhere below the first quartile and above the third quartile without affecting the amount. Thus, a fault of the range is avoided by cutting off the extremes in the distribution. Inasmuch as one-half of the distribution is cut off at the two ends combined, great importance is placed on the center mass of scores when the quartile deviation is used to describe the variability of a distribution of scores.

Other situations in which the median is the appropriate measure of central tendency were given in Chapter 7. Without repeating them here, they also apply to the quartile deviation.

Standard Deviation

By definition given, the standard deviation is used as the measure of variability when the mean is the measure of central tendency. Both these measures are obtained from the actual distance of scores in the distribution rather than from their order. So, both have common characteristics, which is the reason for their close association in describing the performance of a group. Whenever the mean is the appropriate indicator of central tendency, as presented in Chapter 7, the standard deviation is appropriate to describe variability.

The standard deviation is utilized when coefficients of correlation and other statistics are to be computed. It is the only measure of variability encountered in advanced statistics. The standard deviation is also used extensively in the construction of various test scales, as presented in the next chapter.

COEFFICIENT OF VARIATION

When the variability of two groups is to be compared, a direct comparison of standard deviations is appropriate only when the means are essentially the same. Each standard deviation is computed from a specific mean; if two means are appreciably different, the respective standard deviations are computed from different points. Consider the following questions: Are college men more variable in weight than college women? How does the variability of the same group compare on a 10-minute and on a 20-minute test?

Further, the variability of the same group on unlike tests may be wanted: Are college men more variable in weight than in height? Are high school girls more variable in the standing broad jump than in the 50-yard dash?

In all these instances, the *absolute* variability can be obtained by computing the standard deviations. For example, the same group may have standard deviations of 2 inches for height and 15 pounds for weight. A comparison of the two standard deviations, however, would be meaningless. It is still not clear as to which is more variable—height or weight.

An indication of *relative* variability—variability relative to central tendency—is needed. The coefficient of variation (V) provides such an indicator. This coefficient may be used with either standard deviation and mean or quartile deviation and median. The respective formulas are:

$$V = \frac{100\sigma}{M} \tag{8.7}$$

$$V = \frac{100Q}{Mdn} \tag{8.8}$$

For the 67 skeletal ages of 13-year-old boys, the mean was 152.45 months, and the standard deviation was 11.30 months. The coefficient of variation is:

$$V = \frac{100 \times 11.30}{152.45} = 7.41$$

Use of the coefficient of variation is based upon the supposition that a true zero point exists. For most of the traits that the physical education scientist measures, this assumption is met. For example, consider body weight and standing height: A person's scores on these tests are always distances from zero, or no weight or height; there is no such thing as less than nothing on these measures.

However, if a measure such as temperature is considered, a common zero point does not exist. True, zero temperature does occur as measured, but where it is measured depends upon which scale is used, centigrade or Fahrenheit. And less than zero is possible. When positive and negative values exist on any test, the mean could be zero—so, V would also be zero.

The true zero point may be unknown in educational and psychological tests. Some mental tests, especially the "homemade" variety, are not scored in equal units; and distance from zero is obscure. Garrett[2] illustrates the latter point with the following example: A vocabulary test is given to a group of school children with the following results: $M = 25$; $\sigma = 5$; $V = 20$. By adding 10 easy questions that all children answer correctly, the mean score increases by 10 to 35, but σ remains the same; consequently, V equals 14. The lesson to be learned from this illustration is that one may not know how many easy questions that all children can answer are inadvertently included in a written test; and this number may vary from test to test. In this situation, the location of a true zero point is unknown.

The coefficient of variation is not considered an especially valid measure by which to compare the relative reliability of two or more distributions. No reliability statistic[3] is available for it; as a consequence, the significance of the difference between more than one V cannot be tested. However, V is useful to compare the relative variability of groups on the same test administered under different conditions, such as motivated and unmotivated. Typically, V is used in reporting growth data for the same test administered to children of opposite sexes and at different ages or to the same children as they mature.

RESEARCH USES OF VARIABILITY MEASURES

Two illustrations of the use of variability measures in research will be presented here. These uses are related: (1) to the equating of groups for experimentation or for study in other ways; and (2) to the presentation of growth data.

---

[2] Henry E. Garrett, *Statistics in Psychology and Education*, (6th ed.) (New York: David McKay Co., Inc., 1966), p. 59.

[3] Reliability statistics are presented in Chapter 10.

Equating Groups

In experimental research, it may be desirable to equate two or more groups on the basis of test scores. This is usually done by a process of matching—that is, of placing individuals with like scores (approximately) in separate groups. When the matching process is completed, the similarity of the groups should be shown statistically in so far as the test scores are concerned. This similarity is usually indicated by giving the mean and the standard deviation of the test scores for each group. If these are nearly alike, equation is accepted. Thus, it is demonstrated that not only are the central values the same but that the spread of scores in the different groups is also comparable.

To illustrate this procedure, the equating of groups by Jarman,[4] also reported by Clarke and Jarman,[5] in a study of the scholastic achievement of boys 9, 12, and 15 years of age as related to five strength and growth measures is cited. The strength and growth measures were Rogers' Strength Index, Rogers' Physical Fitness Index, Rogers' Arm Strength Score, McCloy's Classification Index, and Wetzel's Developmental Level. For each strength and growth measure at each age, two groups of 20 boys were formed in the following manner Two subjects were selected at a time; these subjects had intelligence quotients (IQ) as nearly equal as possible, but one had a high score and the other had a low score on a given growth variable. Thus, in each instance, high and low scoring groups on the strength and growth measures were established with the groups having comparable IQ's.

Table 8

Intelligence Quotient Means and Standard Deviations for Nine-Year-Old Boys in Five Equated Groups

Test Groups	IQ Means			IQ Standard Deviations		
	High group	Low group	Diff.	High group	Low group	Diff.
Strength Index	106.52	106.53	.01	8.15	9.50	1.35
Physical Fitness Index	107.50	108.00	.50	7.25	7.50	.25
Arm Strength Score	105.75	105.50	.25	9.45	8.83	.62
Classification Index	108.75	109.25	.50	8.85	8.60	.25
Development Level	109.00	109.50	.50	9.00	9.00	.00

---

[4] Boyd O. Jarman, "Academic Achievement of Boys Nine, Twelve, and Fifteen Years of Age as Related to Various Strength and Growth Measures," microcard Master's Thesis, University of Oregon, 1959.

[5] H. Harrison Clarke and Boyd O. Jarman, "Scholastic Achievement of Boys 9, 12, and 15 Years of Age as Related to Various Strength and Growth Measures," *Research Quarterly*, 32, No. 2 (May 1961), 155.

The equating process was repeated 15 times, once at each of the three ages for each of the five experimental variables. To show the degree the groups were equated by IQ's, the means and standard deviations for each equational operation were computed. In Table 8, the results of the equations for the 9-year-old boys are presented. The differences between the IQ means ranged from .01 to .50 IQ points; the differences between the standard deviations varied from .00 to 1.35 IQ points. Although tests of significance for the differences between the means and standard deviations are not given here, such differences were found to be slight.

Growth Study Results

Growth studies encompass a diversity of detectable and measurable changes in size, shape, and function that occur in living organisms with the passing of time; and the degree of individual differences is defined by measures of variability. Common statistics utilized are mean, standard deviation, coefficient of variation, and range.

In the Medford Boys' Growth Study, Wickens,[6] also reported by Clarke and Wickens,[7] presented maturity, structural, muscular strength, and motor ability growth curves of boys 9 through 15 years of age. Cross-sectional samples of 40 boys at each age served as subjects. Table 9 presents results from this study for skeletal age; tests were given within two months of each boy's birthday.

Table 9

Skeletal Age (Months): Central Tendency and Variability of Boys Nine to Fifteen Years of Age

Chronological age					
Years	Months	Mean	Standard deviation	Coefficient variation	Range
9	108	106.1	11.6	10.9	51
10	120	114.4	11.8	10.3	48
11	132	131.8	13.2	10.0	54
12	144	146.3	12.1	8.3	52
13	156	160.5	12.5	7.8	62
14	168	173.6	11.2	6.5	42
15	180	184.3	7.7	4.2	32

[6] J. Stuart Wickens, "Maturity, Structural, Muscular Strength, and Motor Ability Growth Curves of Boys Nine to Fifteen Years of Age," microcard Doctoral Dissertation, University of Oregon, 1958.

[7] H. Harrison Clarke and J. Stuart Wickens, "Maturity, Structural, Strength, and Motor Ability Growth Curves of Boys 9 to 15 Years of Age," *Research Quarterly*, 33, No. 1 (March 1962), 26.

A number of observations may be made from this table, among which are the following:

1. In a normal population, chronological age and skeletal age would be expected to coincide. However, for the Medford boys, the 10-year-olds were 5.6 months retarded; and the 15-, 13-, and 14-year-old boys were advanced by 4.3, 4.5, and 5.6 months, respectively.

2. The standard deviations did not change appreciably between ages 9 and 14 years inclusive; for these years, the largest standard deviation was 13.2 months at 11 years of age and the smallest was 11.2 months at 14 years of age, a difference of 1.97 months.

3. The coefficients of variation clustered between 10.0 and 10.9 for ages 9, 10, and 11 years. Beginning at age 12 years, the size of this coefficient steadily declined until it reached 4.2 months at 15 years of age.

4. The greatest range of scores was 62 months (five years, two months) at 13 years of age. All but the oldest two ages had ranges that equaled or exceeded 48 months, or four years.

5. The lower variability at age 15 years was thought at first to be due to a truncation effect of some of the boys reaching full maturity at this age. However, subsequent testing revealed as great a variability at 15 years as at the other ages. As a consequence, this occurrence must be considered a sampling circumstance.

SUMMARY

In this chapter, the computation, characteristics, and research uses of the following measures of variability were presented: range, quartile deviation, mean deviation, standard deviation, and probable error. Measures of variability further described test data by indicating the spread of scores within the distribution, usually from a measure of central tendency: the quartile deviation with the median, the mean deviation with either mean or median, and the standard deviation and probable error with the mean. The coefficient of variation was considered as a measure of variability relative to its appropriate measure of central tendency.

CHAPTER 9

The Normal Curve

An understanding of the normal probability curve is essential for the student of research. Upon it is based an understanding of reliability, that important phase of statistics dealing with the interpretation of statistical results. It is only through measures of reliability that the true value of such obtained measures as means, standard deviations, and coefficients of correlation can be understood and that tests of significance can be made.

The normal probability curve is also known as the normal curve, bell-shaped curve, curve of error, and Gaussian curve. Here, its designation will be limited simply to normal curve. The normal curve is bilaterally symmetrical with a high concentration of scores in the center and a sloping off toward the ends. The frequency polygon drawn from the frequency distribution of the 67 skeletal ages of 13-year-old boys (Figure 2) resembles the normal curve. As is typical of small samples, irregularities usually appear largely due to sampling error. However, it may be guessed that this curve does not depart significantly from the normal probability curve; whether or not this guess is tenable will be tested in the next chapter. Such curves are typical of many sample distributions based upon physical, mental, and psychological test scores.

PRINCIPLE OF THE NORMAL CURVE

The principle of the normal curve is based upon the probable occurrence of an event when the probability depends upon chance: when each event has an equal chance of occurring. Thus, the occurrence of the event must be equally likely and must be mutually independent. By "mutually independent" is meant that one event has no effect on any other event. To illustrate: If a coin is flipped to determine heads or tails, each flip is unaffected—is independent—of flips made before and after; the chances remain 1 out of 2 each time that heads will fall.

The customary way of introducing the statistics of probability is to refer to various games of chance such as tossing coins, rolling dice, or drawing cards. In each instance, there is a specified event, and this event can occur in more than one way. A tossed coin has 2 possibilities, a head or a tail; a die has 6 possible results; and drawing from a playing deck of cards permits 52 different outcomes. As can be seen, the chance occurrences of the events vary. However, all can be expressed as *probability ratios* with the number of times a given event can occur as the numerator and the total number of outcomes possible as the denominator. Thus, the probability ratios for the above examples are: $\frac{1}{2}$, one chance in two to toss a head; $\frac{1}{6}$, one chance in six to roll a given number on a die, say a 5; $\frac{1}{52}$, to draw a given card, such as the ace of spades.

As shown in flipping a coin, the chances are even, or one in two, that it will come down heads, and there is the same probability that it will come down tails. These probabilities add to 1.00, or certainty of occurrence: $\frac{1}{2} + \frac{1}{2} = 1.00$. If two coins are flipped, there are four possibilities, as follows:

a	*b*	*a*	*b*	*a*	*b*	*a*	*b*
H	*H*	*H*	*T*	*T*	*H*	*T*	*T*

Thus, the chances of both coins falling heads is one in four; 1 head and 1 tail, 1 chance in 2; and of both tails, 1 chance in 4. The ratios are: $\frac{1}{4} + \frac{1}{2} + \frac{1}{4} = 1.00$. If this process were to be carried still further, it will be found that there is 1 chance in 8 of getting all heads when 3 coins are flipped, and 1 chance in 1024 when 10 coins are tossed.

The same ratio of chance probabilities in flipping coins is found in the binomial expansion theorem. To illustrate the above examples:

$$\text{2 coins: } (H + T)^2 = H^2 + 2HT + T^2$$

$$\text{3 coins: } (H + T)^3 = H^3 + 3H^2T + 3HT^2 + T^3$$

$$\text{10 coins: } (H + T)^{10} = H^{10} + 10H^9T + 45H^8T^2 + 120H^7T^3 + 210H^6T^4 + 252H^5T^5 + 210H^4T^6 + 120H^3T^7 + 45H^2T^8 + 10HT^9 + T^{10}$$

The normal distribution closely resembles the binomial distribution. With limited binomial expansion, even to $(H + T)^{10}$, the plotted graph would show a series of distinct bars, each bar erected at one of the number of heads and tails. When an infinitely large number of coins is tossed, these bars merge provided that the width of the graph is unchanged. Then, the normal and binomial graphs become as one. Generally speaking, then, the two curves can be considered identical. A smoothed polygon representing the chance possibilities when 10 coins are tossed is shown in Figure 7.

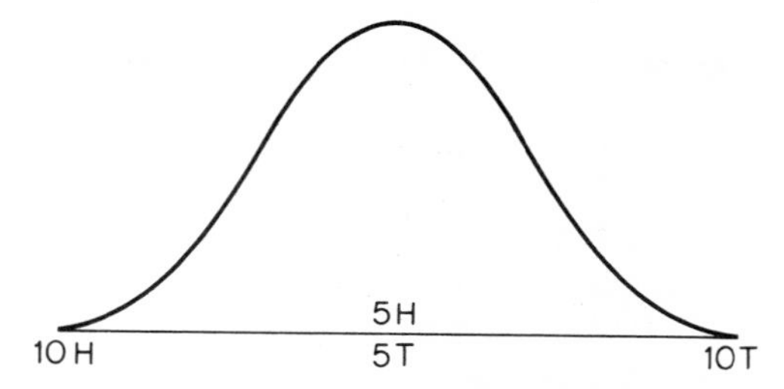

Figure 7. Theoretical Curve for Coin Tossing

This theory of normal distribution as applied to the chance occurrence of heads and tails in coin tossing is also applied to the chance occurrence of human characteristics. Heredity, environment, and training are the factors that influence the amount of any human attribute: biological, anthropometrical, motor, psychological and sociological. These factors are very much a matter of chance, and the scores of these various factors will cluster about the middle and will be distributed in much the same way as in coin tossing.

The occurrence of the normal curve, however, whether it be in coin tossing or in the presence of human traits, depends upon two very important factors:

1. The occurrence of the event must depend upon *chance*. If skill in coin tossing, which influences the results, is present, the requisite of chance is not satisfied; the results are biased and a normal distribution will not result. The same situation prevails when loaded dice are rolled. Also, the strength of athletes could not be used to represent the general run of students, as this particular group is a select one physically—selection thereby not depending upon chance occurrence.

2. A *large number* of observations must be made. An even distribution of heads and tails would not be expected from only a few tosses; with a small number of flips, runs of heads would not be compensated by opposite runs of tails, or vice versa, over many trials. But, with a large number of trials, the distribution would begin to take on a normal aspect. The same rule applies to human traits. For example, a teacher would not be justified in grading on a normal curve if the class were small, and, so, she would have only a few observations upon which to base her grades. It would be possible for the entire class to be exceptionally good, exceptionally poor, or quite a normal group.

Actually, the normal curve is a mathematical model—a theoretical curve as utilized in statistics. It should not be considered as an actual and exact curve found in physical, motor, and psychological assessments. However, this model describes the distribution of human traits so well that its properties can be used to make inferences and predictions about them.

PROPERTIES OF THE NORMAL CURVE

Although the normal curve is bilaterally symmetrical, not all symmetrical curves are normal, as will be demonstrated later in this chapter. Actually, there is only one normal curve as conceived as a mathematical model. The binomial expansion explanation above gives definiteness to the description of the normal curve. In addition, this curve has a general equation that constructs it mathematically. With this formula, the height of any ordinate can be determined for a given N, M, and σ. A description of this process will not be included here inasmuch as it has little use in educational and psychological research.

Other characteristics of the normal curve are: (1) It is asymptotic to the base line—extends out at each end indefinitely without touching the base line. (2) The points of inflection—where the curve changes direction—are each one standard deviation from the ordinate at the mean. (3) The height of an ordinate at any given standard deviation distance from the mean ordinate is an exact proportion of the height of the mean ordinate. Thus, the area under the curve included between the mean ordinate and an ordinate at any given standard deviation from the mean will be an exact proportion of the total area under the curve.

Statistical Relationships

Measures of central tendency and variability have definite statistical relationships to the normal curve, as follows:

Central tendency. In the normal curve, the mean, the median, and the mode are all exactly in the center of the distribution and hence are numerically equal. This must be true, as it has been shown that the normal curve is perfectly bilaterally symmetrical; as a consequence, all the measures must fall in the exact middle of the curve.

Measures of variability. In the normal curve, the measures of variability include certain constant fractional amounts of the total area of the curve. The relationships between the various measures of variability are as follows:

$$PE \text{ (and } Q) = .6745\sigma = .8453AD$$

$$AD = 1.1829PE \text{ (and } Q) = .7979\sigma$$

$$\sigma = 1.4826PE \text{ (and } Q) = 1.2533AD$$

It will be noted that PE and Q are the same in a normal curve. Actually, the PE and Q for the 67 skeletal ages of 13-year-old boys, used so far to illustrate statistical calculations, are nearly the same; as computed in Chapter 8, the *PE* is 7.62 months, and the *Q* is 7.65 months.

If σ, which indicates the spread of the middle 68.26 per cent of the scores, is laid off in plus and minus distances from the mean on the base line of a normal curve, it will, for practical purposes, take up the middle one-third of the base line; actually two σ's are present, one on each side of the mean. Thus, as shown in Figure 8, 6 σ's encompass nearly the complete distribution;

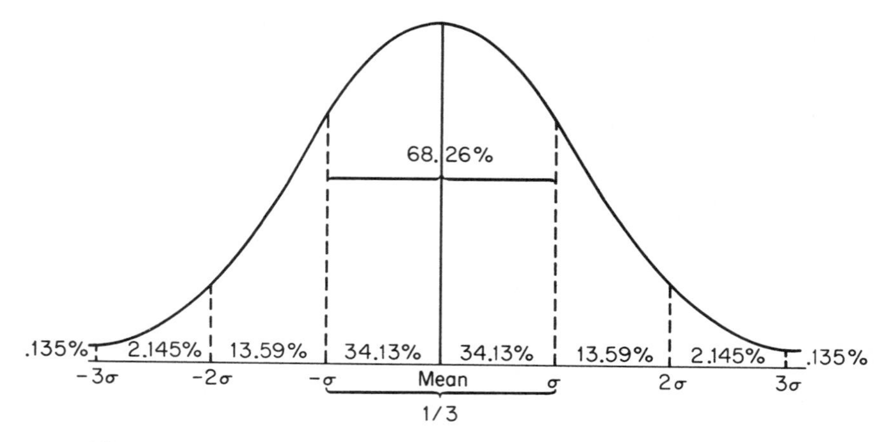

Figure 8. Properties of the Normal Curve in Terms of Standard Deviation

within the limits of 6 standard deviations lie 99.73 per cent of the scores, as will be seen next.

Proportionate Areas

A most important factor related to the normal curve is the division of the curve into percentage areas. Knowing the mean and the standard deviation and knowing that the distribution is normal, the percentage of scores falling between the mean and any given standard deviation distance above or below the mean can be obtained from a standard table. Table 10 shows the fractional parts of the total area under the normal curve that correspond to distances on the base line and successive points from the mean in standard deviation units.

To illustrate the use of Table 10, go down the left margin, x/σ to 1.0; the next column headed .00 indicates 1.00σ from the mean. The percentage is 34.13; doubling this amount, $\pm\,\sigma = 68.26$. This is where the percentage spread for standard deviation, the middle 68.26 per cent from the mean, came from in the definition for standard deviation. The percentages for other sigma distances from the mean may also be read from the table. Thus: $2\sigma = 47.72$, or 95.44 for $\pm\,2\sigma$; $3\sigma = 49.865$, or 99.73 for $\pm\,3\sigma$. To use the

Table 10

Percentage Parts of the Total Area under the Normal Probability Curve Corresponding to Distances on the Base Line between the Mean and Successive Points from the Mean in Units of Standard Deviation[a]

Example: Between the mean and a point 1.57 sigma is found 44.18 per cent of the entire area under the curve.

(x/σ)	*.00*	*.01*	*.02*	*.03*	*.04*	*.05*	*.06*	*.07*	*.08*	*.09*
.0	.00	.40	.80	1.20	1.60	1.99	2.39	2.79	3.19	3.59
.1	3.98	4.38	4.78	5.17	5.57	5.96	6.36	6.75	7.14	7.53
.2	7.93	8.32	8.71	9.10	9.48	9.87	10.26	10.64	11.03	11.41
.3	11.79	12.17	12.55	12.93	13.31	13.68	14.06	14.43	14.80	15.17
.4	15.54	15.91	16.28	16.64	17.00	17.36	17.72	18.08	18.44	18.79
.5	19.15	19.50	19.85	20.19	20.54	20.88	21.23	21.57	21.90	22.24
.6	22.57	22.91	23.24	23.57	23.89	24.22	24.54	24.86	25.17	25.49
.7	25.80	26.11	26.42	26.73	27.04	27.34	27.64	27.94	28.23	28.52
.8	28.81	29.10	29.39	29.67	29.95	30.23	30.51	30.78	31.06	31.33
.9	31.59	31.86	32.12	32.38	32.64	32.90	33.15	33.40	33.65	33.89
1.0	34.13	34.38	34.61	34.85	35.08	35.31	35.54	35.77	35.99	36.21
1.1	36.43	36.65	36.86	37.08	37.29	37.49	37.70	37.90	38.10	38.30
1.2	38.49	38.69	38.88	39.07	39.25	39.44	39.62	39.80	39.97	40.15
1.3	40.32	40.49	40.66	40.82	40.99	41.15	41.31	41.47	41.62	41.77
1.4	41.92	42.07	42.22	42.36	42.51	42.65	42.79	42.92	43.06	43.19
1.5	43.32	43.45	43.57	43.70	43.83	43.94	44.06	44.18	44.29	44.41
1.6	44.52	44.63	44.74	44.84	44.95	45.05	45.15	45.25	45.35	45.45
1.7	45.54	45.64	45.73	45.82	45.91	45.99	46.08	46.16	46.25	46.33
1.8	46.41	46.49	46.56	46.64	46.71	46.78	46.86	46.93	46.99	47.06
1.9	47.13	47.19	47.26	47.32	47.38	47.44	47.50	47.56	47.61	47.67
2.0	47.72	47.78	47.83	47.88	47.93	47.98	48.03	48.08	48.12	48.17
2.1	48.21	48.26	48.30	48.34	48.38	48.42	48.46	48.50	48.54	48.57
2.2	48.61	48.64	48.68	48.71	48.75	48.78	48.81	48.84	48.87	48.90
2.3	48.93	48.96	48.98	49.01	49.04	49.06	49.09	49.11	49.13	49.16
2.4	49.18	49.20	49.22	49.25	49.27	49.29	49.31	49.32	49.34	49.36
2.5	49.38	49.40	49.41	49.43	49.45	49.46	49.48	49.49	49.51	49.52
2.6	49.53	49.55	49.56	49.57	49.59	49.60	49.61	49.62	49.63	49.64
2.7	49.65	49.66	49.67	49.68	49.69	49.70	49.71	49.72	49.73	49.74
2.8	49.74	49.75	49.76	49.77	49.77	49.78	49.79	49.79	49.80	49.81
2.9	49.81	49.82	49.82	49.83	49.84	49.84	49.85	49.85	49.86	49.86
3.0	49.865									
3.1	49.903									
3.2	49.93129									
3.3	49.95166									
3.4	49.96631									
3.5	49.97674									
3.6	49.98409									
3.7	49.98922									
3.8	49.99277									
3.9	49.99519									

[a] An adaptation from Karl Pearson, *Tables for Statisticians and Biometricians* (Cambridge: Cambridge University Press, 1924).

body of the table: $1.47\sigma = 42.92$ per cent; go down left margin to 1.4 and over to column .07.

DIVERGENCE FROM NORMALITY

Most physical, mental, and psychological traits are distributed normally in nature. Thus, test data obtained by educators and psychologists usually result in a normal curve, provided a sufficiently large number of subjects is tested, and a representative sample of the total population is obtained. This phenomenon is so well established that it is seldom challenged. However, there are traits that are not normally distributed. Further, some distributions obtained may deviate from normality for various reasons even though the trait may be normal in the total population.

Some illustrations of traits that do not distribute normally are: The incidence of infectious diseases is greater during childhood than during middle and later years; the opposite is true for degenerative diseases. The curve of forgetting shows greatest decrease during a short time after learning. Learning curves may exhibit plateaus.

Illustrations of divergence from normality for test data obtained from testing traits normally distributed in nature are: (1) The test utilized to measure the trait is too hard or too easy, thus creating concentrations of scores at the lower and upper ends of the distribution, respectively. (2) The utilization of a biased, or nonrepresentative, sample could result in a skewed distribution; an illustration of such a biased sample would be to obtain strength test scores from athletes. (3) Tests from a small, homogeneous group would be likely to result in a narrow, peaked distribution, whereas a large, heterogeneous group would be likely to produce a broad, flat distribution. Rolling loaded dice would also result in a non-normal distribution, as would coin tossing if a biased coin were used or the tosser could apply skill to this performance.

Because of the value and utility of the normal curve, it may be desirable to test a given distribution for normality. There are two general methods that may be applied; these are the inspectional and chi-square tests. The *inspectional test* consists of superimposing a frequency polygon for the distribution on a theoretically calculated normal curve for the mean and standard deviation of obtained data. This method will not be described here, since no statistical test is available to determine the significance of any departures from the normal curve. In the *chi-square test*, the actual frequencies in each interval of an obtained frequency table are compared with the theoretical frequencies needed to yield a normal curve. A test of significance for chi-square is possible to determine the significance of deviations from normality. This test, however, does not indicate the ways by which a given distribution departs from normality.

In addition to the general determination of normality, other tests are available for specific phases of normality. The most common of these are *skewness* and *kurtosis*. These measures continue to describe a given frequency distribution, as it is possible to have differently shaped curves with the same means and standard deviations. In considering these indicators of divergence from normality, the question of whether such departures are significant must be raised. Methods of testing such significance will be presented in Chapter 10.

Skewness

As explained above, the normal curve is bilaterally symmetrical with the concentration of scores in the center and identical slopes to the upper and lower ends. When the concentration of scores is above or below the center, the distribution is *skewed.* Skewness may be either positive or negative; the direction is designated after the "tail" rather than the "hump" of the curve. Thus, in *positive* skewness, the concentration of scores is below the center, and it tails off toward the right; in *negative* skewness, the opposite is true.

In the normal curve, the three measures of central tendency coincide; these measures differ in a skewed distribution. Obviously, the mode—the high point in the curve—must be to the right or left of center depending on whether the hump is to the right or left. The mean will be lower than the median in negative skewness and higher than the median in positive skewness. Thus, the mean is pulled toward the tail of the distribution, where scores farther away from the center occur; as shown in Chapter 7, the mean is affected by extreme scores, and the median is not. In fact, one means of indicating skewness is to determine the amount of separation of the mean and median relative to the standard deviation of the distribution. This method, however, will not be considered here, since a test of its significance is not available.

A useful formula for determining skewness is based upon the location of the median (P_{50}) between the 10th and 90th percentiles. If the median is exactly between these percentiles, no skewness is present by this method. If the median is nearer the 10th percentile, the hump of the curve is toward the low end, so skewness is positive in direction; negative skewness is indicated when the median is nearer the 90th percentile. The formula is:

$$Sk = \frac{P_{90} + P_{10}}{2} - P_{50} \tag{9.1}$$

The percentiles for the 67 skeletal ages of 13-year-old boys used to illustrate statistical computations so far in this book were computed in Table 5. Substituting these values in the formula:

$$\begin{aligned} Sk &= \frac{167.25 + 137.14}{2} - 152.54 \\ &= 152.20 - 152.54 \\ &= -.34 \end{aligned}$$

Thus, the skewness indicated is negative by $-.34$ months. The median is closer to P_{90} than to P_{10}. Whether or not the amount of $-.34$ months is a significant departure from normality remains to be seen; a test of significance will be presented later.

This method of determining skewness is not the strongest measure. However, for most problems in physical education, recreation, and health, it is considered adequate, as only rough approximations of skewness are needed. When more precise indices of skewness are desired, computation based on the moments of the distribution should be utilized.[1]

Kurtosis

Kurtosis refers to the height of the curve. The curve may be bilaterally symmetrical but still be a height different from the normal curve. Three terms designate the general height of a curve, as follows: *mesokurtic*, comparable to the normal curve; *leptokurtic*, higher or more peaked than the normal curve; and *platykurtic*, lower or flatter than the normal curve. Thus, a symmetrical, nonskewed curve may have the same mean as a normal curve distribution, but the standard deviations would differ: smaller for the leptokurtic and larger for the platykurtic distribution.

The formula for kurtosis is based on the ratio of scores between the middle 50 and middle 80 per cent of the distribution. A Ku of .263 is the ratio for the normal curve. A smaller ratio indicates a leptokurtic tendency; a larger ratio indicates a platykurtic trend. The formula is:

$$Ku = \frac{Q}{P_{90} - P_{10}} \tag{9.2}$$

The skeletal ages of the 13-year-old boys will illustrate this computation. The values for P_{90} and P_{10} are given above in the skewness problem. Q is 7.65 months, as calculated in Table 7. Substituting in the formula:

$$Ku = \frac{7.65}{167.25 - 137.14} = .254$$

Thus, the distribution of skeletal ages has a leptokurtic tendency, as Ku is smaller than the .263 necessary for a mesokurtic, or normal, distribution. The amount of leptokurtic trend is: $.254 - .263 = -.009$. It should be noted that calculated kurtosis is not interpreted as a deviation from zero but from .263.

As for the skewness measure given above, this method of determining kurtosis is not a strong one, but it does have usefulness in obtaining a rough

---

[1] Quinn McNemar, *Psychological Statistics* (3rd ed.) (New York: John Wiley & Sons, Inc., 1962), p. 25.

approximation. Computation based on the moments of the distribution should be employed if a more exact result is wanted.[2]

PROBLEMS BASED ON THE NORMAL CURVE

If the assumption that a given distribution conforms reasonably well to the normal curve is tenable, a number of problems can be solved from its mean and standard deviation by utilizing the percentage properties of the curve (Table 10). Although there may be too few cases in the skeletal age distribution of 13-year-old boys to warrant this assumption, nevertheless, this distribution will be used to illustrate several such computations that may be made. The mean of the distribution is 152.45 months (Table 2) and the standard deviation is 11.30 months (Table 7).

1. What percentage of scores is above 166 months? A score of 166.0 months is 13.55 months above the mean: $166.0 - 152.45 = 13.55$. This figure by itself has little meaning until its standard deviation distance is determined: $(13.55/11.30) = 1.20\sigma$. The percentage of scores between the mean and 1.20σ is 38.49, as found from Table 10. As 50 per cent of the cases fall above the mean in a normal distribution, the percentage that remains is: $50.00 - 38.49 = 11.51$. Thus, 11.51 per cent of the scores fall above 166.0 months.

If the problem had been to find the percentage of scores below 166.0 months, 38.49 would have been added to the 50 per cent below the mean. The answer is: 88.49 per cent.

2. What percentage of scores falls between 140 and 166 months? The percentage of scores between the mean and 166 months was obtained in the first problem as 38.49 per cent, and this percentage was above the mean. The percentage of scores between the mean and 140 months must next be determined:

Score distance: $140 - 152.45 = -12.45$ (below the mean)

Standard deviation distance: $(-12.45/11.30) = -1.10\sigma$

Percentage (Table 10): $-1.10\sigma = -36.43$

To obtain the percentage between the two scores when the scores are on opposite sides of the mean, the percentages are added: $36.43 + 38.49 = 74.92$ per cent. Therefore, in a normal curve, 74.92 per cent of the scores falls between 140 and 160 months. If the two scores had been on the same side of

[2] *Ibid.*, p. 26.

the mean, then the procedure would have been to subtract the higher from the lower percentage to obtain the answer.

3. What score limits of the distribution contain the middle 50 per cent? The computational process described above must now be reversed. For the middle 50 per cent of the scores, 25 per cent will be on either side of the mean in a normal curve. Entering the body of Table 10 with 25.00, the closest standard deviation is .67 ($.67\sigma = 24.86\%$; $.68\sigma = 25.17\%$). This standard deviation distance is multiplied by the standard deviation to obtain the score distance from the mean: $.67\sigma \times 11.30$ months $= 7.57$ months. This amount is then subtracted from and added to the mean to obtain the score limits for the middle 50 per cent:

$$152.45 - 7.57 = 144.88 \text{ months}$$

$$152.45 + 7.57 = 160.02 \text{ months}$$

4. What percentage of students would receive grades of A, B, C, D, and F, if grading were based on the normal curve? Frequently, the expression "grading on a normal curve" has been heard. A strict application of this practice will be explained here. In the question, five grades—A, B, C, D, and F—are to be utilized. These grades will be spread over six standard deviations ($\pm 3\sigma$ from mean); from Table 10, the total percentage is 99.73 (2×49.865), so the sigmas at the extremes will be open-ended. Consequently, each grade will occupy: $6\sigma \div 5$ grades $= 1.2\sigma$.

As there are an uneven number of grades, the center grade, C, occupies the middle 1.2σ of the normal curve, with $.6\sigma$ on each side of the mean. In Table 10, $.6\sigma = 22.57$ per cent. Doubling this amount for the two sides, 45 per cent receive a C grade.

The B grade occupies the normal curve from $.6\sigma$ to 1.8σ ($.6\sigma + 1.2\sigma = 1.8\sigma$). The percentage in Table 10 from the mean to 1.8σ is 46.41. Subtracting the percentage above the mean allotted to the C grade ($46.41\% - 22.57\%$), approximately 24 per cent receive a B grade. The same percentage receive a D grade. Thus: $-.6\sigma + (-1.2\sigma) = -1.8\sigma$. The remaining percentages to 50 per cent at each end of the normal curve are given A and F grades, or 3.5 per cent.

Thus, strict grading on the normal curve results in the following: F, 3.5 per cent; D, 24 per cent; C, 45 per cent; B, 24 per cent; and A, 3.5 per cent.

SCORING SCALES

Percentiles were presented in Chapter 7 as a means of scaling test scores to make them meaningful so that a person's performance in relation to others is known. For example, a score recorded at the 30th percentile is immediately understood as better than 30 per cent and as poorer than 70 per cent of those having taken the test. It was shown, however, that the percentile scale favors mediocrity in performance, as the percentiles bunch together in the middle of the distribution—68 per cent within $\pm\sigma$ from the mean in a normal curve. Inequalities in scale values are also prevalent, especially marked at the tails of the distribution.

In order to avoid shortcomings of the percentile scale, a number of scoring scales based on the properties of the normal curve have been proposed and are in general use. These scales differ mostly in divisions made of the base line of the normal curve. The construction of several of these scales is presented below. The data utilized, again, are from the 67 skeletal ages of 13-year-old boys: $M = 152.45$ months; $\sigma = 11.30$ months.

Z Scale

The Z scale consists of standard deviation distances of scores from the mean. Consequently, the mean has a Z score of 0; those scores above the mean have plus scale values and those scores below the mean have negative scale values. The formula for computing Z scores is:

$$Z = \frac{X - M}{\sigma} \tag{9.3}$$

To illustrate the use of this formula, given a boy's skeletal age of 165 months:

$$Z = \frac{165 - 152.45}{11.30} = \frac{12.55}{11.30} = 1.11$$

Also, given a skeletal age of 147 months:

$$Z = \frac{147 - 152.45}{11.30} = \frac{-5.45}{11.30} = -.48$$

As observed, a Z score of 0 equals the mean of the distribution; the scale has both positive and negative designations, and the Z's are small decimal fractions. The other normal-curve scales convert the M and σ into distributions in which all scores are positive and reasonably easy to handle. There are several arrangements for them.

T Scale

The concept of the T scale was originated by William A. McCall[3] in the construction of a series of elementary school reading tests. Zero in the T scale is located 5σ below the mean, with 100 at 5σ above the mean. The unit for the scale, or one "T" is $.1\sigma$ of the distribution. The mean T score, therefore, is 50; each 10 points above and below this point represent one standard deviation. Thus, the percentile equivalents of T scores of 40 and 60 are respectively 16 and 84 in a normal curve, inasmuch as 34 per cent lies 1σ from the mean.

By mean and standard deviation. When the data are normally distributed, the T scale may be satisfactorily constructed from the mean and standard deviation. The process followed is to enter the mean as T_{50}; then add $.1\sigma$ for each T above the mean and subtract $.1\sigma$ for each T below the mean. To illustrate: For the 67 skeletal ages of 13-year-old boys, the mean was 152.45 months and the standard deviation was 11.30 months.

$$.1\sigma = .1\ (11.30) = 1.13 \text{ months}$$

Subtracting and adding 1.13 months for each T above and below the mean, we obtain the following results:

M and above		*M* and below	
T_{50}	152.45	T_{50}	152.45
T_{51}	153.58	T_{49}	151.32
T_{52}	154.71	T_{48}	150.19

and so on to the ends of the distribution. Each decile point on the T scale will be 1σ farther from the mean. Thus, by subtracting and adding 11.30 months from the mean of 152.45 months:

M and above		*M* and below	
T_{50}	152.45	T_{50}	152.45
T_{60}	163.75	T_{40}	141.15
T_{70}	175.05	T_{30}	129.85
T_{80}	186.35	T_{20}	118.55

In Chapter 7, when the frequency table for these data was constructed, the low score was 128 months, and the high score was 182 months. It will be observed in the above explanation that T_{20} and T_{80} exceeded these extreme

[3] William A. McCall, *Measurement* (New York: The Macmillan Company, 1939), Ch. 22.

scores. However, this situation is typical of the *T* scale, since scores beyond $\pm 3\sigma$ are rare in a normal distribution. The situation here is further aggravated by the small number of scores (67) upon which to construct the *T* scale.

On the credit side, this method of constructing the *T* scale has advantages: The scale is simple to construct once the mean and standard deviation are known; irregularities within the distribution are ignored, thus are smoothed out; all scores in the distribution are awarded scale values when gaps exist in the original data, as in the illustration (i.e., all scores from 125 to 182 months are not found); and the scale may be extended to provide for extreme scores if desired.

By percentage amounts. As indicated, the construction of the *T* scale from the mean and standard deviation is proper when the data upon which the scale is based are normal. However, when the test data are not symmetrical, the method is not appropriate. When data are significantly skewed, the *T* scale should be constructed by normalizing standard scores. This normalizing process is accomplished by using percentage amounts from the mean for standard deviation equivalents. For example, 34.13 per cent above the mean is the percentage equivalent of 1σ in a normal curve; thus, the *T* score is 60, whether or not the distance is exactly 1σ.

Construction of the *T* scale by percentage amounts can be accomplished from the individual scores arranged in order of a frequency table with an interval of 1. However, this process will be explained here utilizing the

Table 11

Calculation of *T* Scores by Percentage Amounts Method
(Data from Table 1)

(1) Skeletal age Months Intervals	(2) f	(3) *cum f*	(4) *cum f* below score + $\frac{1}{2}f$ for given score	(5) Column 4 in per cents	(6) *T* Scores	(7) *T* Score Values: Midpoints
180–184	1	67	66.5	99.75	78	182
175–179	1	66	65.5	98.25	71	177
170–174	2	65	64.0	96.00	68	172
165–169	6	63	60.0	90.00	63	167
160–164	7	57	53.5	80.25	59	162
155–159	11	50	44.5	66.75	54	157
150–154	14	39	31.0	46.50	49	152
145–149	8	24	21.0	31.50	45	147
140–144	7	17	13.5	20.25	42	142
135–139	7	10	6.5	9.75	37	137
130–134	2	3	2.0	3.00	31	132
125–129	1	1	.5	.75	26	127
	$N = 67$					

frequency table constructed in Table 1 for the skeletal ages of the 67 boys 13 years of age. As shown in Table 11, the following steps are necessary:

1. Construct a frequency table from the individual scores in the usual manner; the step intervals and frequencies from Table 1 appear in columns 1 and 2.

2. Cumulative frequencies are given in column 3. The frequencies in column 2 are added cumulatively from the bottom, as was done in constructing the cumulative frequency curve in Table 5.

3. In column 4, add the *cum f* below each interval to $\frac{1}{2}$ the scores in the interval. For example, take the interval, 140–144: Add the 10 scores below the interval (*cum f*) to one-half the scores in the interval ($\frac{1}{2}$ of $7 = 3.5$); $10 + 3.5 = 13.5$. A second illustration for interval, 165–169: 57 scores from the *cum f* column added to $\frac{1}{2}$ of 6, the scores in the interval; $57 + 3 = 60$.

4. Column 4 is changed to percentages in column 5. To do this, first obtain a percentage rate—the percentage value of a single score. In this problem, the rate is: $\frac{1}{67} = 1.5$ (1.49 is slightly more accurate). This rate is multiplied by each *cum f* in column 4. For example, again take the interval 140–144: The column 4 amount is 13.5; $13.5 \times 1.5 = 20.25$.

5. The *T* score for the column 5 percentages may be read directly from Table 12 and listed in column 6. To illustrate with the 160–164 interval: The column 5 value is 80.25; entering the per cent of the Table 12, the nearest *T* score is 59.

6. As developed from a frequency table with intervals greater than 1, the *T* score values are the midpoints of the various intervals; these are given in column 7. Thus, 147 months, midpoint of the interval 145–149, has a *T* score of 45.

7. In constructing a *T* scale, however, *T* scores for all scale values within the distribution should be provided; therefore, interpolations should be performed. An easy method for completing such interpolations based upon an algebraic equation follows, illustrating with a value of 170 months.

172	68
170	X
167	63

(Brackets: 5 spanning 172–167; 3 spanning 170–167; 3 on the right.)

$$3:5::X:5$$

$$\frac{3}{5} = \frac{X}{5}, \quad \text{or} \quad \frac{3 \times 5}{5} = X$$

$$X = \frac{15}{5} = 3.0$$

$$63 + 3.0 = 66.0$$

For the data in this problem, the *T* scales by both methods coincide quite well. For example, the values at T_{60} by the two methods are 164 months by the mean standard deviation process and 163 months by the percentage amounts procedure. These results would be expected from data that are as bilaterally symmetrical as those in this problem; no appreciable skewness is

Table 12

Percentage *T*-Score Equivalents

The per cents refer to the percentage of the total frequency below a given score $+\frac{1}{2}$ of the frequency on that score. *T* scores are read directly from the given percentages.*

Per cent	*T* score	Per cent	*T* score
.0032	10	53.98	51
.0048	11	57.93	52
.007	12	61.79	53
.011	13	65.54	54
.016	14	69.15	55
.023	15	72.57	56
.034	16	75.80	57
.048	17	78.81	58
.069	18	81.59	59
.097	19	84.13	60
.13	20	86.43	61
.19	21	88.49	62
.26	22	90.32	63
.35	23	91.92	64
.47	24	93.32	65
.62	25	94.52	66
.82	26	95.54	67
1.07	27	96.41	68
1.39	28	97.13	69
1.79	29	97.72	70
2.28	30	98.21	71
2.87	31	98.61	72
3.59	32	98.93	73
4.46	33	99.18	74
5.48	34	99.38	75
6.68	35	99.53	76
8.08	36	99.65	77
9.68	37	99.74	78
11.51	38	99.81	79
13.57	39	99.865	80
15.87	40	99.903	81
18.41	41	99.931	82
21.19	42	99.952	83
24.20	43	99.966	84
27.43	44	99.977	85
30.85	45	99.984	86
34.46	46	99.9890	87
38.21	47	99.9928	88
42.07	48	99.9952	89
46.02	49	99.9968	90
50.00	50		

* *T* scores under 10 or above 90 differ slightly so are not included here.

present. If the data had been significantly skewed, however, larger differences between the scales by the two methods would have occurred.

Although the T scale is the most commonly used of the standard-score scales, a common fault of the scale is that its ends are never or seldom utilized. As shown before (Table 10), 99.73 per cent of the scores in a normal distribution fall between $\pm 3\sigma$; T_{20} and T_{80} are at these points. Table 12 also demonstrates this fact; T scores on this table extend only between 10 and 90. T scores under 10 and above 90 differ so slightly in percentage amounts that they cannot be read as two-place numbers. As a consequence of this characteristic of the T scale, other scales have been proposed based upon standard scores but placing 0 and 100 on the scales nearer to the mean in order to utilize all the scale. Some of these scales will be considered below.

6-Sigma Scale

A 6-sigma scale has been utilized by a number of investigators in physical education measurement. Zero for this scale is located 3 sigmas below the mean, and 100 is 3 sigmas above the mean. The scale may be constructed by the same two methods as for the T scale. These procedures are explained below, again utilizing the 67 skeletal ages of boys 13 years of age.

By mean and standard deviation. The steps in constructing the 6-sigma scale are as follows:

1. Locate the zero scale value. The zero scale value is three sigmas below the mean. Multiplying the σ of 11.30 months by 3 and subtracting from the mean:

$$11.30 \text{ months} \times 3 = 33.90 \text{ months}$$

$$152.45 \text{ months} - 33.90 \text{ months} = 118.55 \text{ months}$$

Thus, the 6-sigma scale value of zero is 118.55 months.

2. Determine the rate of increase for each scale value. The 6-sigma scale of 100 points is spread over 6 sigmas, $\pm 3\sigma$ from M. The distance, then, is: 6×11.30 months $= 67.80$ months. Each scale point will be $\frac{1}{100}$ of this distance, or $(67.80/100) = .68$ months.

3. Assign scale values. Starting with the zero value of 118.55 months, add .68 months for each point on the scale. For each decile position on the scale, this amount is $.68 \times 10 = 6.80$ months. The assignment of scale values for each decile position is shown in Table 13. In the actual construction of a 6-sigma scale, of course, values for all scale points would be given. The decision of whether or not to use fractions in the scale depends on the range. For a large range, fractions would not be used; for a small range, they would be used.

By percentage amounts. Without a special table, as prepared for the *T* scale, the construction of the 6-sigma scale by use of percentage amounts when the data are significantly skewed is more complicated; so it will not be described in detail here. The process requires the use of Table 10. From this table, percentages of scores for the sigma equivalents of the scale values, 0 to 100, must be determined; the values on the scale are then derived in terms of percentages from the mean rather than from standard deviation distances.

Table 13

Calculation of 6-Sigma Scale by Mean Standard Deviation Process in Deciles

Mean = 152.45 Months
Standard Deviation = 11.30 Months
Decile Scale Value = 6.80 Months

6-σ Position	Calculation	6-σ Decile table	
		6-σ Scale	Score
0	118.55		
10	118.55 + 6.80 = 125.35	100	186.6
20	125.35 + 6.80 = 132.15	90	179.6
30	132.15 + 6.80 = 138.95	80	173.0
40	138.95 + 6.80 = 145.75	70	166.2
50	145.75 + 6.80 = 152.55*	60	159.4
60	152.55 + 6.80 = 159.35	50	152.6
70	159.35 + 6.80 = 166.15	40	145.8
80	166.15 + 6.80 = 172.95	30	139.0
90	172.95 + 6.80 = 179.75	20	132.2
100	179.75 + 6.80 = 186.55	10	125.4
		0	118.6

* Difference between this amount and the computed mean is due to rounding off of rate of increase.

Neilson, Cozens, and associates solved the problem of skewness in a simple way when they encountered significant skewness in constructing a large number of 6-sigma achievement scales in physical education activities. They estimated the size of the standard deviation above the mean and below the mean. These estimates were obtained by dividing by three the range of scores above the mean and the range of scores below the mean. The quotients thus obtained were used in place of the standard deviation values; scales on either side of the mean had different values as reflected by the two "standard deviation equivalents." The 6-sigma scales were constructed by the mean standard deviation method.[4]

[4] One reference among several is: Frederick W. Cozens and N. P. Neilson, *Achievement Scales in Physical Education Activities for Boys and Girls in Elementary and Junior High Schools* (New York: A. S. Barnes & Company, Inc., 1934), p. 169.

Other Standard-Score Scales

A fourth type of scoring table based upon standard deviation distances is the Hull scale, which extends $3\frac{1}{2}$ sigmas either side of the mean. It goes beyond the somewhat narrow limits of the 6-sigma scale, but it does not leave the ends of the scale so generally unused as does the T scale. As a result, it has considerable merit for wider use as a scale.

The stanine is a fifth scoring scale based upon the properties of the normal curve. In this instance, a 9-point scale is used. The standard deviation distances for points on the scale are: 1, below -1.75; 2, between -1.75 and -1.25; 3, between -1.25 and $-.75$; 4, between $-.75$ and $-.25$; 5, between $-.25$ and $+.25$; 6, between $+.25$ and $+.75$; 7, between $+.75$ and $+1.25$; 8, between $+1.25$ and $+1.75$; 9, above $+1.75$.

The standard-score scale for the Graduate Record Examination is a variation of the T scale: The mean equals 500 instead of 50; the standard deviation for scale points is 100 instead of 10; and the scale extends only to three standard deviations instead of five. Thus, GRE scores of 200 and 800 are respectively three sigmas below and above the GRE mean of 500.

Comparison of Various Scales

Figure 9 is presented to compare the various scoring scales as related to the normal curve. The percentile scale is the only one that does not divide the base line into equal segments. As was discussed in Chapter 7, the percentile scale bunches in the middle, as that is where the bulk of the scores are located; 68.26 per cent are within $\pm 1\sigma$ of the mean, which represents about one-third of the range of scores. The test-score increments between percentiles is not constant but varies, especially toward the tails of the distribution.

The decision as to which scale, other than the percentile, the investigator will use is largely pragmatic—the scale that best fits his data or that he likes the best after evaluating their characteristics. Selection of the T scale will mean under normal circumstances that the parts of the scale below 20 and above 80 will be seldom utilized, as these points are located $\pm 3\sigma$ from the mean. Psychologically, too, T_{20} does not seem too low, but it is; and T_{80} does not seem too high, but it is exceptional. However, this scale can be extended by the mean standard deviation construction method to $\pm 5\sigma$ if desired in order to accommodate extreme scores.

With the 6-sigma scale, the entire scale from 0 to 100 will be utilized. However, occasional scores may fall beyond these points. This is not a serious matter, as the number that do so will be very small if normal probability prevails.

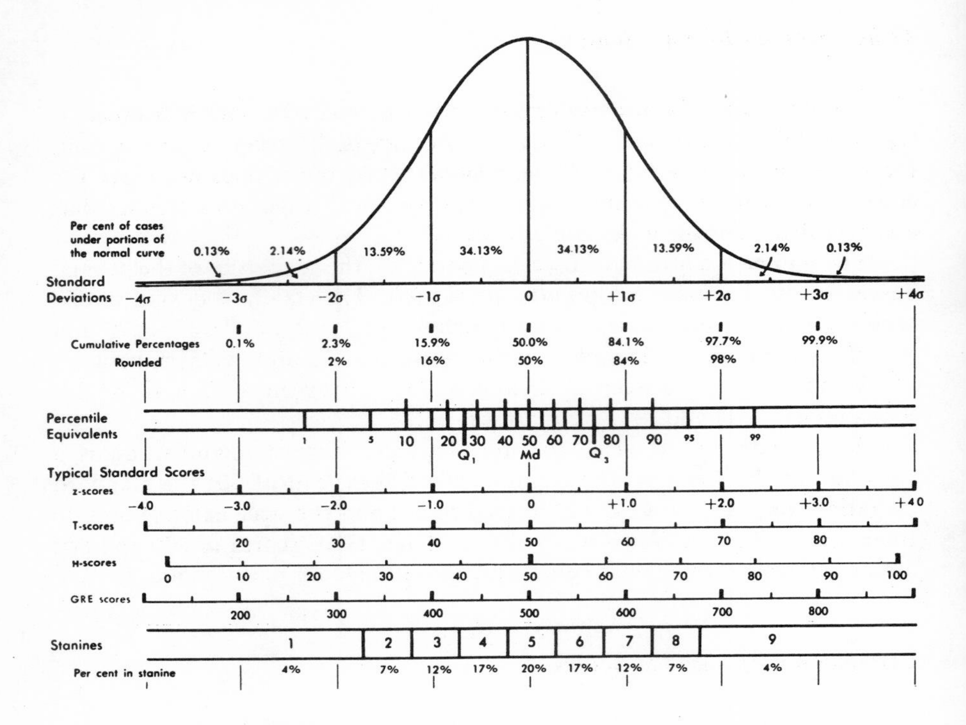

Figure 9. The Normal Curve and Various Scales

The Hull scale, which extends to $\pm 3.5\sigma$, may be considered a compromise between the *T* scale and the 6-sigma scale, and the occurrence of an extreme score falling outside the scale is more remote than for the 6-sigma scale. However, an exceptional score can fall outside this scale. In constructing Hull scales for Medford Boys' Growth Study data, a check was run on the number of scores that were sufficiently extreme as to extend above 100 points and below 1 point in the distribution. In one study, a total of 412 boys were tested at six ages, 9 to 14 years inclusive, with eight anthropometric tests; thus, for the eight scales, 3,296 entries were made (412 boys $\times$ 8 scales $=$ 3,296). For all scales, only seven entries (.02%) were above 100, and only one entry was below 1.[5]

[5] Charles J. Becker, "The Construction of Maturity and Anthropometric Test Norms for Boys Nine Through Fourteen Years of Age," microcard Master's Thesis, University of Oregon, 1960.

SUMMARY

The normal probability curve was presented in this chapter as representing the typical distribution of many physical, motor, psychological, and mental traits as found generally in nature. This curve was likened to the curve obtained from binomial expansion in algebra. The characteristics of this curve as related to the mean and standard deviation were developed and deviations from normality in terms of skewness and kurtosis were examined. Several problems utilizing normal curve proportions were solved. Scoring tables based on standard deviation distances were presented, including the *T* scale, 6-sigma scale, Hull scale, and stanines.

CHAPTER 10

Reliability and Tests of Significance

In Chapter 7, two types of statistics were indicated: descriptive statistics and statistics of inference. So far in this book, only the descriptive form has been presented. In this chapter, statistics of inference will be explained. This form of statistics is vital for statistical interpretations and for the application of tests of significance.

MEANING OF RELIABILITY

In research, the actual or true measure of any quality in a total population is seldom, if ever, obtained. For example, in the development of norms, it is impractical, if not impossible, to test all individuals in the population for which the test is intended. Fortunately, such a practice is unnecessary; a sample, when properly drawn, closely resembles all individuals in the population.

The term *population* means all individuals in a defined group. A statistic, such as the mean or standard deviation, computed from all individuals in a population for a given variable is known as a *parameter*. Population parameters are seldom, if ever, computed, especially when populations are extensive; rather, samples are drawn from large populations and sample statistics are computed from which corresponding parameters are inferred. Population parameters for the mean and standard deviation are symbolized by $\bar{M}$ and $\bar{\sigma}$, each with a bar over it; the symbols for samples will remain herein as M and σ, without the bar.[1]

A population is designated in terms of the research problem, as is the specific variable or trait under investigation. To illustrate: If the investigator were to study the weights of 12-year-old boys in the state of Oregon, then all 12-year-old boys in the state of Oregon constitute the population. Thus, in the illustration, in order to determine the parameter mean weight of 12-year-old boys in Oregon, all boys of this age in the state must be tested. To do so, however, would place a great and unnecessary hardship on the investigator. However, a sample, a small group, can be drawn from this population. It is

[1] In some statistics books, M and σ are reserved for parameter mean and standard deviation and $\bar{X}$ and S for sample mean and standard deviation.

the usual procedure to depend upon sampling and to assume that the sample represents the whole, which it does within definable limits to be considered later.

Sampling is a common practice in society today, being employed in such diverse fields as business, politics, science, agriculture, medicine, psychology, education, and recreation. The various opinion polls are examples. Around the time of national elections, these polls predict from samples how the American public will vote. Such samples actually are minute compared with the millions of citizens who actually cast ballots; yet, they are surprisingly close in anticipating election results. When one buys a packet of seeds to plant, the germination rate is given. How does the nurseryman know this rate? Certainly, those particular seeds had not been planted to make the determination. Rather, a sample had been drawn from the huge number of seeds from which those in the packet came. Much useful information can be inferred from observation secured from a few experimental animals, a handful of corn, a small section of human tissue, a pin-prick of blood, or a group of school children.

The United States Government hires thousands of men and women to gather and compile and draw conclusions from statistical facts that help keep the nation functioning. Eliminate from any government department, or any business, those who specialize in sampling data, and management is soon in trouble. The gathering and classifying of basic facts from samples provide the foundation for logical, inductive reasoning. From these samples, general truths are inferred.

After a sample is obtained, a measure of reliability can be applied to any statistic computed from it, say the mean. The reliability measure indicates by inference how near the sample corresponds to the parameter mean—the unknown mean of the entire population. Thus, the reliability of the mean provides the limits within which a sample mean approximates the corresponding parameter mean. What is true for the reliability of the mean is equally true for other statistics computed from a sample. Consequently, statistical methods are available for determining the reliability of the mean, median, standard deviation, skewness, percentage, coefficient of correlation, and so forth.

SAMPLING

Processes

If the inferences concerning facts or characteristics of a population obtained from a sample are to be valid, obviously the sample must be adequately representative of the population. By the very nature of sampling, complete agreement between sample and population will not be achieved, except by coincidence. However, great uniformity between the two does result when a proper sampling process is applied. Yet, a sampling error does occur; the nature and amount of this sampling error will receive attention later in this chapter.

Sampling is representative, or random as it is frequently called, when each person in the population from which the sample is obtained has an equal chance of being chosen. Further, the selection of any one individual is independent of the selection of any other. Examples are a well-conducted lottery, the drawing of selective service numbers, coin tossing, dice throwing, and other operations that permit the "laws of chance" to operate freely.

Random samples may be drawn in various ways. A good method is by use of a table of random numbers; in such a table, the numbers have been scrambled by lottery procedure. As an illustration of this method, Kirchner and Glines[2] used a table of random numbers to establish samples of elementary school boys and girls for the purpose of normative surveying of the muscular fitness of children in Eugene, Oregon. From a total of approximately 6,000 elementary school chlidren at the time, they wanted 1,200 to test—100 boys and 100 girls in each of the 6 elementary school grades. First, they determined the number of children in each school so that a proportionate number in the sample could be taken. Then, they numbered the children in each grade; the specific boys and girls to be tested were identified as those whose numbers were drawn from a table of random numbers. Thus, chance was operational in the selection of children for testing; each child in the Eugene elementary schools had an equal chance of being chosen. The results obtained from testing this sample were proposed as indicative of the muscular fitness status of all Eugene elementary school children.

Samples, of course, can be biased. Bias occurs when the members of a sample are selected in a manner that favors one result over another. For example, a random sample of college athletes may be drawn; generalization from this sample to the characteristics of athletes could be properly made. But, if generalizations to all college students were made, the sample would be considered biased, for if physical and motor traits were being studied, the athletes would be a select group.

An unfortunate example of biased sampling was the *Literary Digest* public-opinion poll during the 1936 Presidential campaign. In an earlier campaign, it was observed that a sample drawn from telephone directories and automobile registration lists revealed the way people voted. This

---

[2] Glenn Kirchner and Don Glines, "Comparative Analysis of Eugene, Oregon, Elementary School Children Using the Kraus-Weber Test of Minimum Muscular Fitness," *Research Quarterly*, 30, No. 1 (March 1959), 75.

sampling procedure was used in 1936, in the midst of the great depression, with devastating results. It so happened that the individuals who had telephones and owned automobiles that year voted for the candidate who lost, Alfred Landon. Landon was predicted by the poll to win the election, but Franklin D. Roosevelt defeated him in a landslide, carrying 46 of the 48 states.

The investigator should be alert to the possibility of biased sampling. Conditions should be controlled to prevent this occurrence or, if uncontrolled, to discover their effects. When bias is known or suspected, a more detailed than usual description of the sample should be made, and generalizations from the results should be restricted to the nature of the sample. For example, in pack-carrying studies,[3] the subjects were mostly male college students majoring in physical education. Anticipating that a bias had been introduced by using physical education majors, the sample was further described in terms of the heights, weights, Strength and Physical Fitness Indices, and somatotypes of the subjects.

Sampling Theory

The statistics of sampling are of utmost importance to research in education and psychology. In most, if not all, scientific studies, the investigator will use a sample and will wish to infer from his results to the total population from which the sample was taken. He will not be content with a statement that the findings are limited only to the particular subjects tested.

An understanding of the elementary principles of sampling may be gained from an illustration. The account of the muscular fitness survey of Eugene elementary school children mentioned above will be extended for this purpose. As indicated, 1,200 boys and girls composed a random sample from a population of over 6,000 children. The investigators found that 38.1 per cent of the sample failed one or more of the Kraus-Weber tests. This sample percentage may *not* be accepted unconditionally but should be considered only as an *approximation* of the true value of the population. In other words, the true failure percentage of all elementary school boys and girls may well be some other value than that of the sample percentage. However, since the sample was part of the population, the deviation from this totality is in small amounts, and since the members of the sample were drawn at random, chance will dictate the amount of the sampling error for the percentage obtained from samples of a given size. What is said here about

---

[3] H. Harrison Clarke, Clayton T. Shay, and Donald K. Mathews, "Strength Decrements from Carrying Various Army Packs on Military Marches," *Research Quarterly*, 26, No. 3 (October 1955), 253.

the percentage of failures on the Kraus-Weber test can be repeated for other statistics, such as the mean and standard deviation.

Statistical methods are available that provide a definitive statement of the fidelity with which a sample represents its population. Such statements are made in terms of normal probability; the inferences made are related to the characteristics of the normal curve. The reason this can be done is that the distribution of means from repeated samples of the same size from the same population corresponds to a normal curve. Theoretically, the correspondence is identical; in practice, nonsignificant deviations would be found between an exact normal curve and an actual distribution of means obtained from repeated samples of a given population.

To illustrate this effect, one of the authors had members of his statistics classes twice toss 7 coins 50 times; these combined tosses provided one series of 100 times tossed. The mean number of heads was computed for each of the 50 and 100 tosses. These 50 and 100 trials constituted samples from an infinite number of tosses that could be made. The means of these tosses provided sample means that could be incorporated into a distribution of sample means. The distributions of sample means for the 50 and 100 tosses formed appear in Table 14.

The distributions of coin-tossing means resemble the normal curve;

Table 14

Distributions of Sample Means from Coin Tossing
Mean Number of Heads from 50 and 100 Tosses

	Frequencies	
Mean intervals	50 Tosses	100 Tosses
4.00–4.07	2	
3.92–3.99	3	
3.84–3.91	5	2
3.76–3.83	14	4
3.68–3.75	16	8
3.60–3.67	26	10
3.52–3.59	24	12
3.44–3.51	27	16
3.36–3.43	17	13
3.28–3.35	14	8
3.20–3.27	3	6
3.12–3.19	6	1
3.04–3.11	2	
2.96–3.03	1	
N	160	80
M	3.53	3.51
σ	.20	.16

the concentration of means in the center and the tailing off toward the ends are obvious. With 8 possibilities for heads (0 to 7 inclusive) for the 7 coins, the middle—or theoretical—mean is 3.50. The coin-tossing means for the two distributions are close to this theoretical mean, 3.53 for the 50 tosses and 3.51 for the 100 tosses. The overall number of tosses was 8,000. According to the tabulations, if a single sample had been drawn, the mean would most likely be around 3.50. For the 50 tosses, the chances of drawing a sample with a mean between 2.96 and 3.03 is only 1 in 160, as only one of the 160 means fell in that interval; for 100 tosses, no chance is indicated that the sample mean would fall that low.

The distribution of sample means was more extensive for the tosses of 50 than for the tosses of 100. In Table 14, the upper and lower two intervals do not have sample means for the tosses of 100. This situation is further reflected in the standard deviations of the two distributions. The standard deviation of .20 for the 50 tosses is 25 per cent greater than the standard deviation of .16 for the 100 tosses. These results are typical and illustrate a sampling truth: The larger the samples taken from the same population, the closer together are the repeated sample means.

The standard deviation of a distribution of sample means, of course, is not the same as the standard deviation of a single sample. In the former instance, the standard deviation will be several times smaller, depending on the size of the samples. The standard deviation of a distribution of sample means reflects its sampling error; the smaller the standard deviation, the smaller is the error. The term *sampling error* does not intimate that a mistake has been made in sampling. Rather, it refers to the amount of difference that would logically be expected between samples as a consequence of the fact that they were independently drawn from a large population and so will naturally differ from each other.

In research, the investigator will not draw repeated samples in order to establish his sampling error. Instead, he will draw one sample and relate it to the population mean by use of a statistic known as the *standard error*. The standard error of the mean of a given random sample is comparable to the standard deviation of a distribution of sample means of the same size as the given sample. The reference to the population mean will be made by inference that applies normal probability concepts. Inference will be necessary because investigators seldom, if ever, know their population means, as all subjects in the population are not tested. This situation is unlike the coin-tossing illustration where a theoretical "population mean" exists.

The above comments about the sampling error of the mean can be applied for other statistics. Thus, comparable results would occur if distributions of other sample statistics were obtained. Standard error formulas to indicate sampling reliability are available for the standard deviation, percentages, coefficients of correlation, and other statistics of use to the investigator.

STANDARD ERROR OF LARGE SAMPLES

The *standard error* is the principle reliability measure in current use. In the statistics and research of 30 years ago, another such measure, the *probable error*,[4] was also in common use. Thus, the scientific literature of this earlier time contains frequent reference to probable error. However, in this book, attention will be given to standard error only.

Factors Affecting Reliability

Three major factors affect the reliability of a statistic or, to express it differently, show how nearly a sample statistic approximates the same statistic for the total population. These three factors are presented below, using the mean as the statistic for purposes of illustration.

Representativeness of the sample. This factor does not need further explanation here, as it has been stressed in some detail that if the investigator wishes to infer from the results of his sample to the population from which it was drawn—and he invariably does—the sample must be random, or representative. As has been shown, normal probability is definitely lacking if the factor of selection or bias enters into the process.

Size of sample. The second factor that influences the reliability of the mean is the number of subjects contained in the sample. It can be readily demonstrated that a sample mean may be changed by the addition of one new subject to the sample and that this new subject will affect the mean much more when it is based on a few scores than when a large number is involved. For example, the addition of one extreme score to a sample of 10 subjects will cause a greater change in the mean than the addition of a similar score to a sample of 1,000 subjects, as the score counts for less in the larger group ($\frac{1}{10}$ as contrasted with $\frac{1}{1000}$).

Further, the reliability of the mean increases not in direct proportion to the number of subjects upon which it is based but in proportion to the square root of the number. Thus, the reliability of the mean obtained from 50 subjects is not twice that from 25; 100 cases would be needed to obtain twice the reliability. To illustrate:

$$\sqrt{25} = 5; \qquad \sqrt{100} = 10$$

Variability. The third factor that affects the reliability of a statistic is the variability of the sample. The more variable the distribution, the

[4] Not to be confused with probable error presented as a measure of variability in Chapter 8.

farther scores can be from the mean. The farther scores are removed from the mean, the greater will be the fluctuation of scores that affect the sample mean. This phenomenon can also be noted by the effect of extreme scores on a sample mean. To illustrate: An extreme weight of 225 pounds will have a greater effect on a sample mean of 150 pounds than will an extreme height of 76 inches on a sample mean of 65 inches.

It should be pointed out that the factor of variability is entirely dependent upon the nature of the variable being considered. For example, the variability of weight is much greater than the variability of height for any given sample. This is an unavoidable situation, since heights simply do not vary to the same extent as weights. For the investigator to control variability would be either to change the nature of his sample or to introduce unwarranted bias into it.

Thus, the reliability of the mean, or of any other statistic, depends first upon the representativeness of the sample itself. When this condition has been met, the other two factors—the number of subjects and the variability of the distribution—can be accounted for in a formula.

Standard Error of the Mean

The reliability of the mean is directly proportional to the standard deviation of the population and inversely proportional to the square root of the size of the sample. The standard deviation of the population is not known; therefore, the standard deviation of the sample is used. This practice is satisfactory when samples are large; when samples are small, adjustments must be made, as explained later. At this point, a large sample is assumed. Thus, the standard error of the mean is:

$$\sigma_M = \frac{\sigma}{\sqrt{N}} \tag{10.1}$$

Taking skeletal age data in months from Tables 2 and 7: $M = 152.45$; $\sigma = 11.30$; $N = 67$. Substituting in the formula:

$$\sigma_M = \frac{11.30}{\sqrt{67}} = \frac{11.30}{8.19} = 1.38$$

It will be noted in the standard error of the mean that the larger the number of cases and the smaller the deviation of the scores, or the greater the reliability of the sample mean, the less will be this measure. This fact was further demonstrated in Table 14, when the distribution of sample means for 100 coin tosses varied less than for 50 coin tosses.

As indicated earlier, the σ_M can be thought of as the σ of a distribution of sample means of the same size as the given sample. Not knowing the population mean but knowing the standard error of the sample mean, inferences can be made relative to the probable location of the population mean in relation to the sample mean. The chances of the population mean being close to the sample mean are much greater than that of being farther away. The validity of this assumption was demonstrated in the coin-tossing experiment when the distribution of sample means resembled a normal curve.

Therefore, using the sample mean and its standard error and applying normal probability proportions from Table 10, the inference can be made that the chances are 68.26 in 100 that the population mean is within one standard error either side of the sample mean. The 68.26 proportion is taken from the table in the same manner that standard deviation percentages were obtained in the preceding chapter. This same process can be extended to $\pm 3\sigma_M$.

Utilizing the skeletal age data, the following definitive statements may be made relative to the reliability of the sample of 67 12-year-old boys:

1. Chances are 68.26 in 100 that the population mean lies between 151.07 and 153.83 months: 152.45 ± 1.38.

2. Chances are 95.44 in 100 that the population mean lies between 149.69 and 155.21 months: $152.45 \pm 2 \times 1.38$.

3. Chances are 99.73 in 100 that the population mean lies between 148.31 and 156.59 months: $152.45 \pm 3 \times 1.38$.

If the investigator feels that the amount of the standard error is too large and wishes to obtain a smaller amount, his only recourse is to increase the size of the sample. As already indicated, the effect of sample size on reliability is in proportion to the square root of the number. This situation can be demonstrated with the following illustration of samples of 25 and 100, in which the standard deviation has been maintained as a constant, although in practice it would be expected to change somewhat with the addition of new cases to the sample:

$$\sigma_M = \frac{\sigma}{\sqrt{N}} = \frac{10}{\sqrt{25}} = 2.0$$

$$= \frac{10}{\sqrt{100}} = 1.0$$

Thus, the standard error for a sample of 25 is twice as large as for a sample of 100 subjects; the reliability of the 100 sample has twice the reliability of the 25 sample.

This question is frequently asked: "How large a sample do I need?" There is no satisfactory answer to this question, except in terms of the amount of a predetermined standard error. Knowing the standard deviation and the standard error desired, the number of subjects needed can be computed. In the above problem, if the standard error wanted were around 1.0 and the standard deviation were 10, the sample size would need to be 100.

Levels of Confidence

In considering the probable location of the population mean from the sample mean, the concept of levels of confidence has been developed. Two such levels of confidence have come into common use. The two levels are the .05 and .01, also stated as 5 per cent and 1 per cent. Other levels of confidence may be used if desired by the investigator, such as the .10, .02, and .001. This presentation will be limited to the .05 and .01 levels.

A level of confidence indicates the chances that the population mean falls outside the limits expressed. Thus, for the .05 level, the chances are 5 in 100 that the population mean is beyond the expressed limits and 95 in 100 that it is between. These limits are located in the following manner: The middle 95 per cent of the normal probability curve is involved, or 47.5 per cent either side of the mean; entering the body of Table 10, 47.5 per cent is $1.96\sigma_M$ from the mean. Therefore, the chances are 95 in 100 that the population mean lies between the sample mean and $\pm 1.96\sigma_M$; this middle 95 per cent is known as the *confidence interval.* And, the chances are 5 in 100 that the population mean lies beyond the sample mean by $\pm 1.96\sigma_M$. To illustrate with the skeletal age problem:

$$M \pm 1.96\sigma_M$$

$$152.45 \pm 1.96 \times 1.38$$

$$152.45 \pm 2.70$$

By level of confidence, the chances are 5 in 100 that the population mean lies beyond the limits of 149.75 and 155.15 months; there are $2\frac{1}{2}$ chances that it lies below 149.75 and $2\frac{1}{2}$ chances that it lies above 155.15 months.

At the .01 level of confidence, the chances are 1 in 100 that the population mean lies outside the limits expressed. These limits are located in the same manner as before, except for the .01 level. The middle 99 per cent of the normal probability curve is involved; from Table 10, $\pm 2.58\sigma_M$ will encompass 49.5 per cent. Again illustrating with the skeletal age problem:

$$M \pm 2.58\sigma_M$$

$$152.45 \pm 2.58 \times 1.38$$

$$152.45 \pm 3.56$$

Thus, the chances are 1 in 100 that the population mean lies beyond the limits of 148.89 and 156.01 months; there is one chance in 200 that it is below 148.89 and one chance in 200 that it is above 156.01.

Other Statistics

Standard errors are also available for other statistics presented so far. The formulas differ, but interpretation remains the same as for the mean. Each statistic is obtained from a sample; the purpose is to infer from it to the population statistic. Inferences can be made by application of normal probability, since the distribution of a given statistic from repeated samples resembles a normal curve, as was true for the mean.

Median. The standard error of the median may be computed from either the standard or quartile deviations as the measure of variability. The formulas are:

$$\sigma_{Mdn} = \frac{1.25\sigma}{\sqrt{N}} \tag{10.2}$$

$$\sigma_{Mdn} = \frac{1.86Q}{\sqrt{N}} \tag{10.3}$$

The formula with Q (10.3) is the preferred one when the median is the appropriate measure of central tendency; for a normal distribution, either formula is satisfactory. Applying this formula to the skeletal age sample of 67 12-year-old boys ($Q = 7.65$ months):

$$\sigma_{Mdn} = \frac{1.86Q}{\sqrt{N}} = \frac{1.86 \times 7.65}{\sqrt{67}} = 1.74 \text{ months}$$

The standard error of the median is approximately 25 per cent greater than the standard error of the mean. For this problem, the standard error of the mean, as computed above, was 1.38 months; the difference between the two standard errors (1.74 − 1.38) is .36, which is 25 per cent higher. This demonstrates that the reliability of the mean is greater—is less subject to sampling fluctuations—than the median.

Since its sampling error is greater, a larger sample is needed when the median is the measure of central tendency to produce a standard error of the same size as when the mean represents central tendency. In order to reduce the standard error of the median to the same magnitude as the mean, 57 per cent more subjects are needed in the sample. To illustrate with the skeletal age problem: For the N of 67, a 57 per cent increase in sample size equals 105.

Using 105 in the formula and maintaining the same Q as before:

$$\sigma_{Mdn} = \frac{1.86Q}{\sqrt{N}} = \frac{1.86 \times 7.65}{\sqrt{105}} = 1.39 \text{ months}$$

It is, therefore, poor research economy to use the median instead of the mean if the reason is ease of computation. The median should only be used as central tendency when the mean is inappropriate because of extreme scores, skewness, and the like, as discussed in Chapter 7.

Standard deviation. Two formulas are available for computing the standard error of the standard deviation, as follows:

$$\sigma_\sigma = \frac{\sigma}{\sqrt{2N}} \tag{10.4}$$

$$\sigma_\sigma = \frac{.71\sigma}{\sqrt{N}} \tag{10.5}$$

Applying formula 10.4 to the skeletal age sample ($\sigma = 11.30$ months):

$$\sigma_\sigma = \frac{\sigma}{\sqrt{2N}} = \frac{11.30}{\sqrt{2 \times 67}} = .98 \text{ months}$$

As for the other statistics considered, the standard deviation of 11.30 months was obtained from a sample; and, again, the purpose is to infer from the sample standard deviation to the parameter standard deviation. Levels of confidence can be applied in the same manner as before. Thus, at the .05 level, the chances are 5 in 100 that the population standard deviation lies outside the limits expressed by:

$$11{:}30 \pm 1.96 \times .98 \text{ months}$$

or, below 9.38 or above 13.22 months.

Quartile deviation. The standard error of the quartile deviation may be obtained from either of the following formulas:

$$\sigma_Q = \frac{.79\sigma}{\sqrt{N}} \tag{10.6}$$

$$\sigma_Q = \frac{1.17Q}{\sqrt{N}} \tag{10.7}$$

The formula with Q is the preferred one when the median and quartile deviation are the appropriate measures of central tendency and variability; for a normal distribution, either method is satisfactory. Applying formula 10.7 to the skeletal age data ($Q = 7.65$ months):

$$\sigma_Q = \frac{1.17Q}{\sqrt{N}} = \frac{1.17 \times 7.65}{\sqrt{62}} = 1.10 \text{ months}$$

As for the median compared to the mean, the sampling error of the quartile deviation is greater as contrasted with the standard deviation. The usual levels of confidence can be applied to the sample quartile deviation of 7.65 months by use of its standard error of 1.10 months.

Percentage. Research problems may be involved in the percentage of a given sample that manifests certain characteristics or that reveals different attitudes toward problems in education. The reliability of a percentage can be determined through its standard error. The formula is:

$$\sigma_P = \sqrt{\frac{PQ}{N}} \tag{10.8}$$

in which:

P = percentage occurrence
$Q = 100 - P$

To illustrate the use of this formula, an example will be given. Borcher[5] interviewed a sample of 202 men and women drawn from the registration lists of 40,324 voters in four Willamette Valley, Oregon, communities in order to determine their opinions toward physical education. As one phase of the study, each respondent indicated the five physical education activities in schools they considered most important for young people. For secondary schools, swimming was checked by the largest number; the percentage was 71.8. The question should now be asked: How well does the sample of 202 reflect the opinions of the population of 40,324? Applying the standard error formula and interpreting:

$$\sigma_P = \sqrt{\frac{PQ}{N}} = \sqrt{\frac{(71.8)(28.2)}{202}} = 3.2$$

To interpret at the .05 level in the usual way: The chances are 95 in 100 that the population percentage lies inside the limits and 5 in 100 that it lies outside

[5] Bill Borcher, "An Analysis of Public Opinion in Regard to Physical Education," microcard Doctoral Dissertation, University of Oregon, 1964.

the limits expressed by

$$71.8\% \pm 1.96 \times 3.2$$

or the limits of 65.5 and 78.1 per cent. The .01 and other levels of confidence, of course, may be used.

STANDARD ERROR OF SMALL SAMPLES

The preceding presentations of the normal probability curve in Chapter 9 and of reliability so far in this chapter assume large samples. As was shown, a normal probability distribution occurs when many chance observations are made, either in coin tossing or in drawing random subjects from a huge population. Further, a distribution of sample means will resemble the normal curve only when a large number of samples have been drawn. For example, in the coin-tossing experiment, the distribution of 160 means from tossing 7 coins 50 times approaches, but is not precisely, a normal curve. A small number of sample tosses would have produced an erratic and ill-defined distribution. With small samples, various deviations from the reliability theory for large samples discussed above occur. A discussion of these deviations and the statistical adjustments for them are considered here.

Effect of Standard Deviation

With a small sample, the standard deviation will underestimate (that is, be smaller than) the standard deviation of the population from which it is drawn. Extreme deviations in the population are rare and so are likely to be missed in small samples; the total range of scores is more and more curtailed as samples reduce in size. This fact reduces the amounts of the standard deviations as compared with this deviation for a large sample. The range covered by samples[6] are approximately as follows:

Sample size	Range
10	$\pm 2.0\sigma$
50	$\pm 2.5\sigma$
200	$\pm 3.0\sigma$
1000	$\pm 3.5\sigma$

Because of this situation, a change in the formula for standard deviation should be made for small samples so as to increase its amount. This change

[6] Henry E. Garrett, *Statistics in Psychology and Education* (6th ed.) (New York: David McKay Company, Inc., 1966), p. 208.

is made by using $N - 1$ in the formula rather than N. Instead of the symbol σ, s is utilized to designate the standard deviation of a small sample. Thus, the formula is:

$$s = \sqrt{\frac{\sum x^2}{N - 1}} \tag{10.9}$$

The standard error for the mean becomes:

$$\sigma_M = \frac{s}{\sqrt{N}} \tag{10.10}$$

The use of s instead of σ is suggested when N is 30 or less. Any larger number would have little effect on the computation and is generally disregarded.

Degrees of Freedom

In the formula for s, a new statistical concept known as degrees of freedom (*df*) was employed; reference is made to $N - 1$. Degrees of freedom refer to the scores that are free to move in the computation of a given statistic. The degrees of freedom vary for some statistics. However, when computing a single statistic from a single distribution *df* equal $N - 1$.

To explain degrees of freedom by use of the mean, a single statistic from a single distribution demonstrates: All scores are free to move except 1, hence $N - 1$. Take the five scores of 10, 9, 8, 7, and 6, the mean of which is 8. All scores but the last one can be different, that is, free to move; the last one, however, makes the final determination of the mean. In the illustration, any last number other than 6 would have produced a different mean.

Distribution of t

A phenomenon of distributions of sample means is that a normal curve results only when a large number of samples are drawn. Under this circumstance, the use of the normal probability table (Table 10) is appropriate. In its use above, the standard error distances from the mean at the .05 and .01 levels of confidence were determined as 1.96 and 2.58. However, these are *not* the proper distances when samples are small.

When samples are small, distributions of sample means lie mostly under the normal curve, except that the tails or ends of the curves are higher than the corresponding parts of the normal curve; the smaller the samples, the higher this will be. As the levels of confidence involve the tails of the distribution, adjustments of standard error distances are necessary for the various levels of confidence. Such adjustments are done by use of a statistic known as a t.

A t is a standard error distance from the mean. In the earlier discussion, two t's have actually been used. These are: At the .05 level, $t = 1.96$; at the .01 level, $t = 2.58$. For small samples, a larger t is necessary for the same level of confidence depending upon the degrees of freedom; such t's are found in Table 15.

In Table 15, df's appear in the left-hand column; the other columns give the t's for the four levels of confidence—.10, .05, .02, and .01—identified as probability (P) at the heads of the columns. The t's in Table 15 at the .05 and .01 levels for df's of infinity and 1,000 are 1.96 and 2.58, the same t's obtained from Table 10. However, for the rest of the table, the t's increase in magnitude as the df's decrease in amount. For the sample of 67 skeletal ages of 12-year-old boys: $df = N - 1 = 67 - 1 = 66$. Entering Table 15 with 70 df, the nearest df on the table, the t's at the .05 and .01 levels are 2.00 and 2.65, respectively. These t's should be used in indicating the reliability of the mean rather than the former t's of 1.96 and 2.58. Thus, for the mean of 152.45 months and the σ_M of 1.38 months at the .05 level: $M = 152.45 \pm 2.00 \times 1.38$. The differences between the t's for a large sample and the sample of 67 boys is small. However, such is not the case for df of 10, where the t's are 2.23 and 3.17 at the two levels of confidence.

Other Statistics

The adjustments indicated for interpreting the reliability of a mean obtained from a small sample apply to such other statistics as the median, quartile deviation, standard deviation, and percentage when they are likewise obtained from small samples. The degrees of freedom for these statistics are the same as for the mean: $df = N - 1$.

DIFFERENCES BETWEEN MEANS

A most important point, which deals with the significance of a difference between statistics, has now been reached. From what has been explained before, the means of two or more random samples drawn from the same large population will be expected to vary from each other because of sampling error, that is, due to the act of obtaining random samples. Thus, a difference found between two such means may not be a real difference at all. For example, say the same strength test is given to random samples of 10-year-old

Table 15

Table of t for Levels of Significance

Degrees of freedom	Probability (P) .10	.05	.02	.01
1	t = 6.34	t = 12.71	t = 31.82	t = 63.66
2	2.92	4.30	6.96	9.92
3	2.35	3.18	4.54	5.84
4	2.13	2.78	3.75	4.60
5	2.02	2.57	3.36	4.03
6	1.94	2.45	3.14	3.71
7	1.90	2.36	3.00	3.50
8	1.86	2.31	2.90	3.36
9	1.83	2.26	2.82	3.25
10	1.81	2.23	2.76	3.17
11	1.80	2.20	2.72	3.11
12	1.78	2.18	2.68	3.06
13	1.77	2.16	2.65	3.01
14	1.76	2.14	2.62	2.98
15	1.75	2.13	2.60	2.95
16	1.75	2.12	2.58	2.92
17	1.74	2.11	2.57	2.90
18	1.73	2.10	2.55	2.88
19	1.73	2.09	2.54	2.86
20	1.72	2.09	2.53	2.84
21	1.72	2.08	2.52	2.83
22	1.72	2.07	2.51	2.82
23	1.71	2.07	2.50	2.81
24	1.71	2.06	2.49	2.80
25	1.71	2.06	2.48	2.79
26	1.71	2.06	2.48	2.78
27	1.70	2.05	2.47	2.77
28	1.70	2.05	2.47	2.76
29	1.70	2.04	2.46	2.76
30	1.70	2.04	2.46	2.75
35	1.69	2.03	2.44	2.72
40	1.68	2.02	2.42	2.71
45	1.68	2.02	2.41	2.69
50	1.68	2.01	2.40	2.68
60	1.67	2.00	2.39	2.66
70	1.67	2.00	2.38	2.65
80	1.66	1.99	2.38	2.64
90	1.66	1.99	2.37	2.63
100	1.66	1.98	2.36	2.63
125	1.66	1.98	2.36	2.62
150	1.66	1.98	2.35	2.61
200	1.65	1.97	2.35	2.60
300	1.65	1.97	2.34	2.59
400	1.65	1.97	2.34	2.59
500	1.65	1.96	2.33	2.59
1000	1.65	1.96	2.33	2.58
∞	1.65	1.96	2.33	2.58

boys in two neighboring communities. Assume that the mean strength score in Community *A* is 110 pounds and in Community *B* is 115 pounds; the difference between the means is 5 pounds. May this difference be attributed to the chance error arising from the random selection of the sample members, or is it evidence of a real superiority in strength for the 10-year-old boys in Community *B*? A test of the significance between these means is needed.

Null Hypothesis

The null hypothesis is a *statistical* hypothesis to the effect that no real difference exists between the means of two samples—that any difference found may be attributed to sampling error. This form of hypothesis should not be confused with an experimental hypothesis, which has been reached by critical evaluation. The null hypothesis is merely a convenient way to express a statistical concept.

The null hypothesis is stated for the purpose of testing; it is either accepted or rejected. To accept the hypothesis is to conclude that a given difference between means may be due to sampling error; at least, under the conditions of the study, no other conclusion is tenable. To reject the null hypothesis is to conclude that a difference between means of the magnitude obtained cannot be attributed to sampling error—that a real or definite difference exists.

The null hypothesis is accepted or rejected at a level of significance. Levels of significance are comparable to the levels of confidence discussed above. For this purpose, however, level of significance is the proper terminology. The common significance levels are the .05 and .01, as explained earlier.

Another common way of expressing the significance of a difference between means is merely to state that the difference is or is not significant at the level of significance accepted. To state that a difference between means is not significant is the same as accepting the null hypothesis; to state that a difference is significant is synonomous with rejecting the null hypothesis.

Uncorrelated Data

When two samples are independently drawn, they are uncorrelated; the means computed from the samples are known as uncorrelated means. Only the standard errors of the two sample means are considered in computing a standard error of the difference between these means (σ_{DM}). The formula is:

$$\sigma_{DM} = \sqrt{\sigma_{M_1}^2 + \sigma_{M_2}^2} \qquad (10.11)$$

If the standard errors of the two means are not needed in the problem, σ_{DM} can be computed from the standard deviations of the two samples. Thus:

$$\sigma_{DM} = \sqrt{\frac{\sigma_1^2}{N_1} + \frac{\sigma_2^2}{N_2}} \qquad (10.12)$$

To illustrate with a study by Whittle[7] who compared two samples of 81 12-year-old boys each: The boys in one sample had participated for three years in a "good" elementary school physical education program; the boys in the other sample had had no physical education or had participated in a "poor" program. The Rogers' Physical Fitness Index (PFI) was one of the tests utilized in making comparisons between the samples. The PFI means in the good and poor programs were 120.79 and 103.02, respectively; the difference between the means was 17.77. The questions now arise: May this difference be attributed to sampling errors? Or, is there a real difference due to participation in physical education?

Utilizing formula 10.11:

$$\sigma_{M_1} = 2.21; \qquad \sigma_{M_2} = 2.25$$

$$\begin{aligned}\sigma_{DM} &= \sqrt{\sigma_{M_1}^2 + \sigma_{M_2}^2} \\ &= \sqrt{2.21^2 + 2.25^2} = \sqrt{9.94} = 3.15\end{aligned}$$

Thus, $DM = 17.77 \pm 3.15$. The application of the null to these results is illustrated at the .01 level of significance in Figure 10. The chances are 50–50 that a difference between the means due to sampling error would favor the poor program. The chances are 68.26 in 100 (Table 10) that a difference as great as 3.15, the σ_{DM}, could favor either group by sampling error. To extend the chance occurrences to the .01 level of significance, the standard error obtained for the difference between means is multiplied by the t for this level:

$$\sigma_{DM} \times t = 3.15 \times 2.58 = 8.13$$

Thus, a difference between means as great as 8.13 could occur by chance at the .01 level of significance. To state it differently: There is only 1 chance in 100 that a difference between the means as great as 8.13 could occur by sampling procedure. Inasmuch as the difference between means, 17.77, exceeds this amount, the null hypothesis is rejected at this significance level.

---

[7] H. Douglas Whittle, "Effects of Elementary School Physical Education upon Some Aspects of Physical, Motor, and Personality Development of Boys Twelve Years of Age," microcard Doctoral Dissertation, University of Oregon, 1956.

The null hypothesis may be applied at other levels of significance in the same manner by utilizing appropriate *t*'s.

A simpler way of applying tests of significance to the differences between means, and the one generally utilized, is by use of the *t* ratio.[8] The *t* ratio is

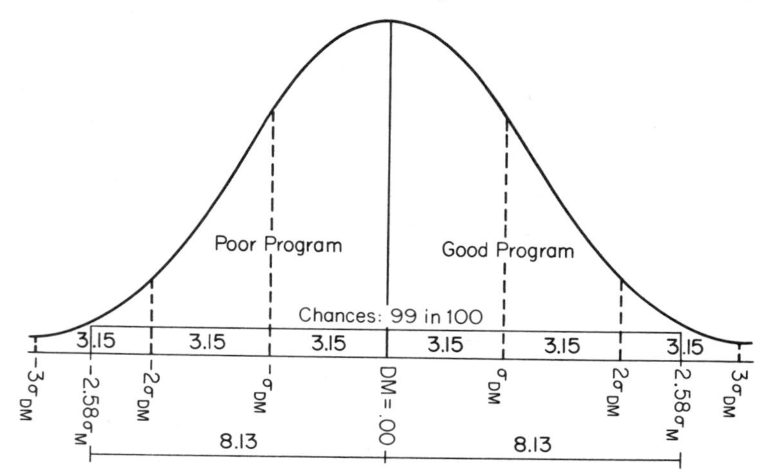

Figure 10. Application of Null Hypothesis: Difference Between Means. Physical Fitness Indices

the ratio of the difference between means and the standard error of the difference. For the problem under consideration:

$$t = \frac{DM}{\sigma_{DM}} = \frac{17.77}{3.15} = 5.69$$

The *t* ratio necessary for a given level of significance is obtained from Table 15. For uncorrelated groups, the *N*'s are combined and 1 degree of freedom is lost for each mean. Therefore, the *df* necessary for entering the table are:

$$df = N_1 + N_2 - 2$$

$$81 + 81 - 2 = 160$$

Entering Table 15 with *df* of 160, the *t* ratio necessary at the .01 level of significance is 2.61. Inasmuch as the *t* ratio obtained in this study was 5.69, much greater than 2.61, the investigator rejected the null hypothesis above the stated level.

---

[8] The term, critical ratio (*CR*), is used for large samples; the *t* ratio applies to small samples. In this text, the *t* ratio will be utilized throughout.

The t ratios for other levels of significance and for other df's may also be obtained from the table. For example, a t ratio of 2.09 is necessary for significance at the .05 level for df 20.

Correlated Data

In the preceding section, the difference between the means of uncorrelated groups was considered; two samples were independently drawn. In this section, the difference between correlated means will be presented. Here, only one sample is independently drawn from the population; the data for the second mean are obtained in some manner that produces a correlation with the sample randomly drawn.

There are various ways by which correlated means may be obtained. A common occurrence is found in the one-group experiment. Typically, two means are computed from the same sample: a pretest mean before and a post-test mean after application of an experimental factor. Another such situation is encountered when two equivalent groups are formed through an equating process (such as indicated in Chapter 9). Here, one sample is randomly drawn; the subjects in the other group are paired with the individuals in the random sample on the basis of a factor or factors significant to the experiment in order to control it or them by experimental design.

The statistical treatment of the difference between correlated means differs from the treatment for uncorrelated means in the formula used to compute the standard error. The formula for correlated means is:

$$\sigma_{DM} = \sqrt{\sigma^2_{M_1} + \sigma^2_{M_2} - 2r_{12}\sigma_{M_1}\sigma_{M_2}} \qquad (10.13)$$

The r in the formula designates a coefficient of correlation. The meaning, computation, and interpretation of r will be explained in the next chapter.

To illustrate: Kurimoto[9] longitudinally studied the growth changes of the same boys fifteen through eighteen years of age on many maturity, body size, physique type, strength, and motor measures. Most of his tests naturally improve with age during these years. However, the Physical Fitness Index does not, as it is derived from norms based on age and weight. Therefore, the test could be used to determine age changes that result from developmental activity. The means of 66 boys at 15 and 16 years of age were 113.17 and 117.21, respectively; the difference between the means was 4.04, showing an increase at the older age. The standard errors of the means were 2.48

---

[9] Etsuo Kurimoto, "Longitudinal Analysis of Maturity, Structural, Strength, and Motor Development of Boys Fifteen Through Eighteen Years of Age," microcard Doctoral Dissertation, University of Oregon, 1963.

at 15 years and 2.63 at 16 years; the interage correlation was .73. Utilizing formula 10.13:

$$\sigma_{DM} = \sqrt{\sigma^2_{M_1} + \sigma^2_{M_2} - 2r\sigma_{M_1}\sigma_{M_2}}$$
$$= \sqrt{2.48^2 + 2.63^2 - 2(.73)(2.48)(2.63)}$$
$$= \sqrt{12.95 - 9.65} = 1.52$$

A t ratio is computed:

$$t = \frac{DM}{\sigma_{DM}} = \frac{4.04}{1.52} = 2.66$$

The degrees of freedom for the difference between correlated means: $N - 1$, or $66 - 1 = 65$. Entering Table 15 with 65 *df*, t's of 2.00 and 2.66 are necessary at the .05 and .01 levels of significance, respectively. In this problem, the t ratio exactly equals the 2.66 for significance at the .01 level.

An alternative method, the differences method, may be used to test the significance of a difference between correlated means without the necessity of computing a correlation coefficient. This method is usually perferred when the number of subjects is small. The computational process consists of obtaining the difference between each pair of scores, the standard deviation of the differences, the standard error of the differences mean, and a t ratio.

To illustrate: The same 15 boys were tested on bar pushups (pushups from one end of parallel bars) at the ages of 13 and 14 years. The question to be answered: Did the mean number of pushups increase significantly over the one-year period? The test results and computations are shown in Table 16. The procedures are as follows:

1. The numbers of bar pushups for each boy are listed in pairs in the first two columns of the table.

2. The differences between these scores are given in column 3; in each instance, the 13-year-old score is subtracted from the 14-year-old score. The sum of this difference column is 30; divided by the N of 15, the mean of the differences is 2.0. This difference, of course, is the same as the difference between the means obtained from averaging columns 1 and 2.

3. In order to obtain the standard deviation of the differences columns x and x^2 are needed. For the x column, each of the differences in the third column is subtracted from the differences mean (2.0). A computational check on this column is possible by adding the scores; the sum should be zero. In the final column, the values in the fourth column are squared and added ($\sum = 62$).

4. The standard deviation formula for small samples (s) is logically used in this problem because of the small N (formula 10.2). This computation is shown in the lower part of the table.

Table 16

Computation of Mean Differences for Correlated Groups
Bar Pushups for Boys 13 and 14 Years of Age

Ages		Differences		
13 Years	14 Years	(14–13)	x	x^2
2	4	2	0	0
4	7	3	1	1
3	7	4	2	4
1	2	1	−1	1
4	5	1	−1	1
8	11	3	1	1
5	9	4	2	4
6	9	3	1	1
7	4	−3	−5	25
5	7	2	0	0
7	10	3	1	1
8	11	3	1	1
5	5	0	−2	4
3	2	−1	−3	9
5	10	5	3	9
73	103	$\frac{30}{15} = 2.0$		62
M 4.87	6.87			

$$D_M = 2.0$$

$$s = \sqrt{\frac{\Sigma x^2}{N-1}} = \sqrt{\frac{62}{15-1}} = 2.10$$

$$\sigma_{DM} = \frac{s}{\sqrt{N}} = \frac{2.10}{3.88} = .54$$

$$t = \frac{2.0}{.54} = 3.70$$

With 14 *df* (15 − 1), a *t* ratio of 2.98 is needed for a significant difference between these correlated means at the .01 level. Therefore, the null hypothesis is rejected at this level, since the *t* ratio obtained for this problem was 3.70.

When equivalent, or equated, groups are utilized, the correlation in the formula is computed from the scores of the paired subjects. These paired scores would be placed opposite each other in columns 1 and 2 if the differences method were used.

The formula for the difference between correlated means should always be used when appropriate; in fact, consideration should be given to the use of equating procedures when forming experimental groups for the advantage gained by a smaller σ_{DM}. If the pairing of scores produces an r of .75, the reduction of σ_{DM} is approximately one-half, which, as explained earlier, is equal to quadrupling the number of subjects as compared to random samples. To demonstrate: $\sigma_{M_1} = 3$; $\sigma_{M_2} = 4$; $r = .75$

Uncorrelated:
$$\sigma_{DM} = \sqrt{\sigma^2_{M_1} + \sigma^2_{M_2}}$$
$$= \sqrt{3^2 + 4^2} = 5.0$$

Correlated:
$$\sigma_{DM} = \sqrt{\sigma^2_{M_1} + \sigma^2_{M_2} - 2r\sigma_{M_1}\sigma_{M_2}}$$
$$= \sqrt{3^2 + 4^2 - 2(.75)(3)(4)} = 2.6$$

Matched Groups

For equivalent groups, two groups are formed by equating individuals on the basis of a crucial test, as indicated above and described in Chapter 9. Thus, the number of subjects in each group is identical, and the means and standard deviations will be comparable.

When it is not feasible to equate groups, an alternate method is to form the two groups by obtaining matching means and standard deviations. In this instance, the N's may or may not be the same, and the order of the scores is not regulated as in pairing. For this method, the formula for standard error of the mean is:

$$\sigma_{DM} = \sqrt{(\sigma^2_{M_1} + \sigma^2_{M_2})(1 - r^2_{12})} \qquad (10.14)$$

The r_{12} in the formula is the correlation between the matching variable and the experimental variable when these are not the same. If the two variables are the same, the reliability (test-retest) coefficient (r_{xx}) is used; however, in this case, the r is not squared.

Comparison with Norm

An occasion may arise when the investigator wishes to compare a mean obtained from a sample with a mean representing a norm for a large population. For example, in the study by Whittle mentioned above, 81 12-year-old boys, who had participated for three years in a "good" physical education program, had a mean Physical Fitness Index of 120.79. Is this mean significantly higher than the PFI mean of 100 from the large sample?

With a standard deviation of 19.89, the standard error of the mean is computed: $\sigma/\sqrt{N} = 19.89/\sqrt{81} = 2.21$. The difference between the means is 20.79 (120.79 − 100). A t ratio is obtained: $20.79/2.21 = 9.41$. This t ratio is so large that reference to Table 15 is not necessary, although the investigator may still wish to know that a t ratio of 2.64 meets the requirement for significance at the .01 level. Thus, these boys were far superior to the mean performance expected from the population from which the norms were obtained.

However, the mean PFI for the 81 boys in the "poor" physical education program in Whittle's study was much lower, 103.2—only 3.2 above the norm of 100. With a standard deviation of 20.25, the computations are:

$$\sigma_M = \frac{\sigma}{\sqrt{N}} = \frac{20.25}{\sqrt{81}} = 2.25$$

$$t = \frac{3.2}{2.25} = 1.42$$

Entering Table 15 with 80 *df*, a *t* ratio of 2.02 is needed in order to reject the null hypothesis at the .05 level. Thus, the results of this testing are within allowable limits from the norm.

Choice of Significance Levels

At an earlier time, although not then so known, a *t* ratio of 3.00 was generally required to justify acceptance of significance; in present terminology, this is equivalent to the .003 level. As has been explained, other levels of significance are utilized by investigators today, especially the .05 and the .01. Consequently, a determination of which level of significance to adopt must be made.

In deciding on the significance level, it should be stressed that acceptance of the null hypothesis does not prove that no difference between means exists. Rather, in the given problem, for the number of subjects especially, the difference in the total population could be zero, and the amount obtained could be attributed to sampling error. Further, if the null hypothesis is rejected, say at the .05 level, there are still 5 chances in 100 that the difference between means could be due to sampling error.

The investigator, therefore, is faced with a balancing of risks at which level to accept or reject the null hypothesis. As can be seen, two distinct types of errors are possible in making this decision—known and defined, as follows:

Type I: *rejecting the null hypothesis when in fact it is true.*

Type II: *accepting the null hypothesis when in fact it is false.*

At the .05 level, there are 5 chances in 100 of being wrong in the rejecting null hypothesis when it is true (Type I error); at the .01 level, there is only 1 chance in 100 of being wrong. As the level of significance is decreased the chances of making a Type II error are increased; the chances of making a Type I error are decreased as the level of significance is increased.

In the adoption of levels of significance, various practices have been followed. Strict statisticians maintain that the decision should be made as part of the experimental design, before the data are collected and analyzed. Some investigators have utilized both the .05 and .01 levels coincidentally, a process that permits reference to either level in accordance with the magnitude of the differences obtained between means. McNemar[10] suggests a flexible plan of accepting the null hypothesis at the .10 level, rejecting it at the .01 level, and reserving judgment in between. A practical-type consideration of the level to adopt is to use higher levels (.01 and .001) when the application of the research results necessitates expensive equipment or extensive curricular reorganization and to use lower levels (.10 and .05) when the adoption of new practices are simple and uninvolved.

Two- and One-Tailed Tests

In the presentation of tests of significance so far, the assumption has been made that chance differences between sample means could favor either group equally. For example: If the same strength test were given to two random samples from the same population, there is no reason to believe that the results would favor one group over the other. Still, a difference between means would be expected by sampling error; however, the chances of a higher mean for either sample are equal. The test of significance applied is a two-tailed test. The two-tailed test only has been considered to this point, and it is the common one employed in research. The tables utilized thus far are also constructed for two-tailed tests. At the .05 level, for example, one-half of this amount (.025 or 2.5%) is placed at either end of the normal curve of sampling probability.

In some experiments, the scientific hypothesis being tested is concerned with the results obtained in one direction only. In such situations, all chances of a significant difference between means are at one end of the normal curve of sampling reliability; thus, a one-tailed test is appropriate. Instances where one-tailed tests are proper follow.

1. When a difference, if it exists at all, must necessarily be in one direction. For example, if a skill is taught, teaching and practice do not make children worse in performing the skill; they may not get better, but, if anything happens, they should improve. Another example can be taken from studies of muscle fatigue from exercise. Fatiguing exercise interferes with the

---

[10] Quinn McNemar, *Psychological Statistics* (3rd ed.) (New York: John Wiley & Sons, Inc., 1962), p. 69.

contractile power of muscles (as one chins the bar, it becomes harder and harder as he continues until it is no longer possible). In both illustrations, the differences move in one direction only: in the former, to improve performance; in the latter, to hinder it.

2. When results in the opposite direction to the one predicted are not to be used to decide upon a course of action that is different from the course of action if no difference is found. In this instance, the experimenter is only interested in results in one direction. Examples are intimated by the following questions: Is a new type of gymnasium shoe better than one now on the market? Are boys stronger than girls? In these situations, the investigator is not concerned with which product is better or which sex is stronger (two-tailed tests), but, rather, whether one is better or stronger than the other (one-tailed tests). Some danger exists here of the researcher taking advantage of smaller differences between means as being significant by stating experimental hypotheses only in order to produce one-tailed tests.

The statistical procedure in applying a one-tailed test is to use the t ratios in the .10 column of Table 15 for the .05 level and the t ratios in the .02 column for the .01 level. When the .10 level of the table is utilized, one-half this amount (.05) is at each end of the normal curve of sampling probability; for the .02 level, also, one-half the amount (.01) is at each end. These amounts are correct for one-tailed tests.

DIFFERENCES BETWEEN OTHER STATISTICS

In presenting tests of significance above, attention has been confined to the difference between means. The same approach is made for the differences between other statistics. The standard error and the t ratio for a given statistic are computed; Table 15 is utilized to determine the t ratio needed for the various levels of significance; the degrees of freedom are the same as for the difference between means. The only change is in the formulas used, so, what has been said before for the difference between means can be repeated for each of the other statistics. The differences between statistics considered so far in this text will be explained here.

Medians

When the proper measure of central tendency is the median, the formula for computing the standard error of the difference between uncorrelated medians is:

$$\sigma_{DMdn} = \sqrt{\sigma^2_{Mdn_1} + \sigma^2_{Mdn2}} \qquad (10.15)$$

A t ratio is obtained:

$$t = \frac{DMdn}{\sigma_{DMdn}}$$

When medians are correlated, the computation of r does not meet basic assumptions for correlation and so cannot be accurately determined.

Standard Deviations

When N is reasonably large, say 30 and above, the standard errors for uncorrelated and correlated standard deviations can be obtained from the following formulas:

Uncorrelated: $$\sigma_{D\sigma} = \sqrt{\sigma^2_{\sigma 1} + \sigma^2_{\sigma 2}} \qquad (10.16)$$

Correlated: $$\sigma_{D\sigma} = \sqrt{\sigma^2_{\sigma 1} + \sigma^2_{\sigma 2} - 2r\sigma_{\sigma 1}\sigma_{\sigma 2}} \qquad (10.17)$$

A t ratio is obtained:

$$t = \frac{D\sigma}{\sigma_{D\sigma}}$$

When samples are small and uncorrelated, the t ratio is inappropriate for testing the difference between standard deviations. The reason is that a distribution of standard deviations from repeated samples of the same population is skewed rather than normal. In this situation, an F test should be applied. The F test will not be presented here.

Percentages

The significance of the differences between percentages for uncorrelated and correlated samples can be determined through use of the appropriate formula for the standard error of the difference. The formulas are:

Uncorrelated: $$\sigma_{DP} = \sqrt{\sigma^2_{P_1} + \sigma^2_{P_2}} \qquad (10.18)$$

or: $$= \sqrt{PQ\left(\frac{1}{N_1} + \frac{1}{N_2}\right)} \qquad (10.19)$$

Correlated: $$\sigma_{DP} = \sqrt{\sigma^2_{P_1} + \sigma^2_{P_2} - 2r\sigma_{P_1}\sigma_{P_2}} \qquad (10.20)$$

In the formulas, P_1 and P_2 represent the percentages being tested for significance; their computations are made by use of formula 10.8. A t ratio is obtained:

$$t = \frac{DP}{\sigma_{DP}}$$

In Borcher's study mentioned earlier in this chapter, a sample of 202 Willamette Valley, Oregon, voters were asked if they favored a physical education requirement in the elementary schools of the state. Of this number, 23 had completed only two years of high school, and 24 had had only a grade school education. The favorable responses of these voters were 92 per cent for the two-year high school (P_1) group and 63 per cent for the grade school (P_2) group. The question to be resolved: Is this difference of 29 per cent (DP) between these groups significant? The statistical computations are as follows:

$$\sigma_{P_1} = \sqrt{\frac{PQ}{N-1}} = \sqrt{\frac{(92)(8)}{23-1}} = 5.79$$

$$\sigma_{P_2} = \sqrt{\frac{PQ}{N-1}} = \sqrt{\frac{(63)(37)}{24-1}} = 10.06$$

$$\sigma_{DP} = \sqrt{\sigma_{P_1}^2 + \sigma_{P_2}^2} = \sqrt{5.79^2 + 10.06^2} = 11.56$$

$$t = \frac{DP}{\sigma_{DP}} = \frac{29.0}{11.56} = 2.51$$

$$df = N_1 + N_2 - 2 = 23 + 24 - 2 = 45$$

Entering Table 15 with 45 df, t ratios of 2.02 and 2.41 are needed for significance at the .05 and .02 levels, respectively. The t ratio of 2.51 in Borcher's study was sufficiently high to reject the null hypothesis at the .02 level. He was able to conclude, therefore, that the differences in the voters' education were an influential factor in their acceptance of physical education at the elementary school level.

Skewness

In Chapter 9, skewness was presented as a form of deviation from a normal probability distribution; the process of computing skewness was explained. After skewness is computed, a test of significance is necessary in order to determine if any amount of skewness obtained can be attributed to sampling error. In order to make this test of significance, the standard error of skewness and a t ratio are needed. The formulas will be given in the example to follow.

In the Medford Boys' Growth Study, 112 boys 12 years of age were given bar pushups (pushups from one end of parallel bars). Skewness was found to be 2.49. The standard error of skewness and t ratio were:

$$\sigma_{Sk} = \frac{.5185D}{\sqrt{N}} \tag{10.21}$$

in which $D = P_{90} - P_{10}$. In this problem, these percentiles were: $P_{90} =$ 11.26 times; $P_{10} = .90$ times. Substituting in the formula:

$$\sigma_{Sk} = \frac{.5185(11.26 - .90)}{\sqrt{112}} = .51$$

$$t = \frac{Sk}{\sigma_{Sk}} = \frac{2.49}{.51} = 4.88$$

Entering Table 15 with $df = N - 1$, or $112 - 1 = 111$, a t ratio of 2.63 indicates significant skewness at the .01 level. With a t ratio of 4.88 for these 12-year-old boys on the bar pushups test, the null hypothesis is rejected beyond this level. It is most unlikely that this amount of skewness could have occurred by sampling error.

Kurtosis

Kurtosis, as related to the height of a given distribution curve, was presented in Chapter 9. When a curve is mesokurtic, it corresponds to the height of a normal curve; in this case, kurtosis equals .263. If kurtosis is less than .263, the distribution is leptokurtic; if greater than .263, it is platykurtic. However, a deviation from normal for a given sample needs to be tested for significance in the usual manner.

Kurtosis was computed for the bar pushup performances of the 112 12-year-old boys in the skewness problem above. $Ku = .239$, which is lower than .263: $.239 - .263 = -.024$, a leptokurtic distribution. The standard error of kurtosis is:

$$\sigma_{Ku} = \frac{.28}{\sqrt{N}} \tag{10.22}$$

For this problem:

$$\sigma_{Ku} = \frac{.28}{\sqrt{112}} = .026$$

$$t = \frac{Ku}{\sigma_{Ku}} = \frac{-.024}{.026} = -.96$$

Entering Table 15 with $df = N - 1$, or $112 - 1 = 111$, a t ratio of 1.98 indicates significance at the .05 level. As the t ratio for the bar pushup distribution does not reach this amount, the null hypothesis is accepted.

CONDITIONS FOR USE OF STANDARD ERROR FORMULAS

The application of sampling statistics depends upon certain conditions of sampling. If these are not satisfied, standard errors may give incorrect impressions. After making this assertion, it must also be said that the investigator can hardly draw any conclusions from his research without such errors. However, in planning studies, the conditions for proper use of standard errors should be understood and recognized. The consideration of such basic conditions follows.

1. As developed in this chapter, standard error inferences may be made relative to the location of the population mean from a sample mean by application of normal probability. Justification for this practice emanates from the fact that a distribution of sample means of the same size resembles a normal curve. Even when samples exhibit skewness, the means of repeated samples will tend to be normally distributed, especially if N is large. What is said about the distribution of sample means applies equally well to repeated samples for other statistics.

2. In using standard error, the sample should be randomly obtained so that chance operates, thus permitting application of normal probability. Situations that tend to interfere with randomness of selection will produce improper standard errors, leading to inaccurate and misleading conclusions. Some such situations lead to standard errors that are too small to describe the actual distribution of sample means, and others lead to standard errors that are too large; these would result in overconfidence and underconfidence, respectively, in the reliability of a sample mean.

3. Random sampling implies independence of observation. If certain restricting conditions tie subjects together, observations are not independent. This situation may occur when samples are obtained from subgroups of the population.

4. When sample sizes are small, the null hypothesis is apt to be accepted too often for the reason that a difference between means must be sizable before it is rejected. On the other hand, if a real difference is so small that its statistical demonstration requires very large samples that run into the thousands, its practical or scientific importance may be questioned.

ANALYSIS OF VARIANCE[11]

Analysis of variance is an extension of the significance of differences between means. The t ratio is proper when the significance of the difference between the means of two independent samples is tested. However, it is not appropriate when more than two means are compared, each with all others. When more than two groups are involved, the means are no longer completely independent, as each sample serves more than once in the significance tests. Analysis of variance compensates for this situation and is the proper test of significance to use under this circumstance.

In analysis of variance, an F ratio is obtained. As for t ratios, F ratios indicate whether or not differences between means are significant. If an F test is insignificant at a given level, the null hypothesis is automatically accepted for the differences between all sets of paired means; thus, the differences present can be attributed to sampling error at the level chosen. If the F ratio is significant, the null hypothesis is rejected. However, it does not indicate which of several differences between paired means are significant, other than for the pair with the greatest difference.

A number of proposals have been made for making *post hoc* comparisons between paired means following significant F tests. Winer[12] contrasted the power of five such methods. He concluded that: The Scheffe method has the greatest power and is most conservative with respect to Type I error; the Tukey honestly significant difference method is also a stringent test of significance; the Duncan multiple range, the Newman-Keuls, and the Tukey least significant difference methods are the least powerful tests.

SUMMARY

Statistical reliability was explained as being based on the phenomenon that the distribution of given statistics obtained from a large number of

---

[11] For one way and two-way analysis of variance, see: H. Harrrison Clarke and David H. Clarke, *Advanced Statistics* (Eugene, Oregon: H. H. Clarke, 2561 Pioneer Pike, 1969), Ch. I.

[12] B. J. Winer, *Statistical Principles in Experimental Design* (New York: McGraw-Hill Book Company, 1962), p. 88.

random samples drawn from the same large population takes on the shape of a normal curve; and the standard deviation of this distribution of the sample statistic is comparable to the standard error of the statistic for a single sample. As a consequence, the limits within which the population statistic is located can be inferred by application of the principle of normal probability. Standard error formulas were applied to the mean, median, percentage, quartile deviation, and standard deviation. The means of applying statistical reliability to large and small samples were explained. The .05 and .01 levels of confidence were applied based on the distribution of t.

Tests of significance and the null hypothesis were applied at the .05 and .01 levels to the differences between means, medians, percentages, quartile deviations, and standard deviations for both uncorrelated and correlated statistics, and to the presence of skewness and kurtosis deviations from the normal curve. The selection of levels of significance as related to Type I and Type II errors was discussed. The appropriateness and application on two-tailed and one-tailed tests were presented.

CHAPTER 11

Product-Moment Correlation

Up to this point in presenting statistics, only one variable has been treated at a time. This chapter considers the degree of relationship between two variables, that is, correlation. There are various methods of computing correlation, but the method most commonly used is the *product-moment* method, which is signified by the symbol r, also known as Pearson-r, after its originator. This method is appropriate when data are linear (to be explained later), as is the case for the bulk of research data analyzed in health and physical education.

No single statistic has provided so many possibilities for discovery in health and physical education as has correlation; scientific progress depends upon finding the correlations of human traits. If the correlation is high enough, one trait can be predicted from another. When excellence of performance is desired, whether it be academic or athletic, the identification of traits significantly related to such performance is vital if improvement is to be effected.

MEANING OF CORRELATION

Correlation simply refers to the relationship existing between pairs of measures. Usually, each pair of measures is obtained from the same individual. Thus, if the heights and weights of 100 boys are to be correlated, the heights and weights of these boys are used, and the heights and weights must be kept in pairs. Although not so frequent a practice, measures of the same trait from two individuals who have been paired on some basis are correlated; examples are correlating personality traits of husbands and wives or equated pairs in an equivalent group experiment.

The coefficient of correlation is a single figure that indicates the extent to which traits are related: to indicate the extent that variations in one trait go with variations in another. A different way of expressing this meaning is the closeness with which traits together vary from their respective means. The range of possible magnitude of correlations extends from +1.00 through .00 to −1.00, all divisions of the scale being used such as .903, .137, −.356, and so forth. The sign does not have mathematical meaning, but, rather, it indicates the direction of the correlation—the plus sign for a positive correlation and the minus sign for a negative correlation.

A +1.00 indicates a perfect positive correlation: A large amount of one variable is found with a large amount of the other; a small amount of one with a small amount of the other; and these are in direct proportion throughout the ranges of their distribution. An illustration of a +1.00 correlation is of that between the circumference of a circle and its diameter; this relationship is always *pi* (3.1416) regardless of the size of the circle. A −1.00 is just as significant a correlation as is a +1.00, but the proportions are in reverse: A large amount of one variable is found with a small amount of the other. An illustration of a −1.00 correlation is of that between the circumference of a wheel and the number of times it revolves for a given distance: the larger the wheel, the fewer times it revolves.

In some instances, especially in physical education, negative correlations have positive connotations. This is true when a high score on one of the traits represents a good performance whereas a low score on the other trait is best. An example is the correlation between distance in the long jump and time for the 50-yard dash. In computing correlations, the magnitude of the scores rather than their value is considered.

For a .00 correlation, no relationship exists: An individual with a high score in one variable may appear anywhere on the scale for the opposite variable. With high positive and negative correlations, one can predict with considerable accuracy an individual's score in one variable by merely knowing his score in the other. With zero or near-zero correlations, such prediction would be worthless—in fact, would be entirely a matter of guessing.

To explain the meaning of the term *product-moment*: "Moment" is the sum of the deviations of scores from their mean raised to some power and divided by N; "product-moment" is when pairs of deviations in x and y are multiplied, summed, and divided by N. In correlation, x and y have the same meaning, except x represents one of the variables, and y represents the other. Thus: $x = X - Mx$; $y = Y - My$. Correlation in this chapter is confined to the product-moment method. This method will be applied to both grouped and ungrouped data.

COMPUTATION OF UNGROUPED DATA

There are many variations of the formula for computing product-moment correlations from ungrouped data, all of which yield the same answer. The basic formula from which the others are derived is:

$$r_{xy} = \frac{\sum xy}{N\sigma x\sigma y} \tag{11.1}$$

in which:

r_{xy} = correlation between variables X and Y

x and y = $X - Mx$; $Y - My$

$\sum xy$ = sum of products of x and y deviations

σx and σy = standard deviations of the X and Y distributions

This formula illustrates the definition of correlation given earlier as the "closeness with which traits together vary from their respective means." Inasmuch as the magnitude of the traits may differ, the variances from the means are relative to the amounts of the standard deviations.

Only one correlational method for ungrouped data will be described here. The one chosen can be applied directly to the raw scores (original measurements) rather than relating each score to its mean (formula 11.1). This method is especially convenient if the number of subjects is small. A further advantage is that the formula can be simply programmed for electronic computer operation. The formula may appear formidable but is actually easy to apply.

$$r_{xy} = \frac{N\sum XY - (\sum X)(\sum Y)}{\sqrt{[N\sum X^2 - (\sum X)^2][N\sum Y^2 - (\sum Y)^2]}} \tag{11.2}$$

where X and Y are the raw scores for the two variables.

The computation of a coefficient of correlation using formula 11.2 is shown in Table 17. The data are the heights and weights of 15 boys 15 years of age. These boys were tested within two months of their birthdays so that they would not vary in chronological age by more than four months. The steps in making the computations are:

1. Enter X and Y scores by pairs in columns 1 and 2.
2. Square X and Y scores, columns 3 and 4.
3. Obtain the XY products ($X \times Y$), column 5.
4. Apply formula 11.2 as shown in the table.

Table 17

Computation of a Product-Moment Correlation by the Raw Data Method
Data: Heights and Weights of 15-Year-Old Boys

Height X	Weight Y	X^2	Y^2	XY
62.2	135	3,869	18,225	8,397
70.0	129	4,900	16,641	9,030
67.6	164	4,570	26,896	11,086
61.9	104	3,832	10,816	6,438
67.9	138	4,610	19,044	9,370
67.0	193	4,489	37,249	12,931
64.3	112	4,135	12,544	7,202
67.5	152	4,556	23,104	10,260
66.1	114	4,369	12,996	7,535
67.2	121	4,516	14,641	8,131
70.9	149	5,027	22,201	10,564
67.8	158	4,597	24,964	10,712
64.9	119	4,202	14,161	7,723
67.0	138	4,489	19,044	9,246
66.3	116	4,397	13,456	7,691
Σ 998.6	2,042	66,557	285,982	136,316

$$r_{xy} = \frac{N \sum XY - (\sum X)(\sum Y)}{\sqrt{[N \sum X^2 - (\sum X)^2][N \sum Y^2 - (\sum Y)^2]}}$$

$$= \frac{(15)(136{,}316) - (998.6)(2{,}042)}{\sqrt{[(15)(66{,}557) - (998.6)^2][(15)(285{,}982) - (2{,}042)^2]}}$$

$$= \frac{5{,}611}{\sqrt{[1{,}134][119{,}966]}}$$

$$= \frac{5{,}611}{11{,}666}$$

$$= .48$$

COMPUTATION OF GROUPED DATA

When N is moderate or large, the computation of a coefficient of correlation by the grouped-data method is convenient. In this process, a scattergram is prepared, which has the additional advantage of graphing the correlation. Thus, the investigator can see the pattern of the relationship, which is not possible from the correlational methods with raw data.

The procedures for calculating a product-moment coefficient of correlation by the scattergram (grouped-data) method may best be described by showing the actual computations involved. To illustrate this method, the skeletal ages and standing heights of 100 13-year-old boys will be used; each boy was tested within 2 months of his birthday. These scores are listed in Table 18. The problem is to determine the correlation between the skeletal

Table 18

Pairs of Scores for Correlation Problem
Skeletal Age Versus Standing Height

SA	*Ht*	*SA*	*Ht*	*SA*	*Ht*	*SA*	*Ht*	*SA*	*Ht*
149	58	162	64	154	59	162	59	160	64
150	59	146	64	134	58	162	65	164	64
157	64	149	59	135	55	148	60	161	63
153	64	144	59	156	64	156	59	154	66
182^{H}	65	164	64	161	67	153	60	150	57
136	56	135	54	151	62	132	56	151	60
168	62	147	60	154	62	169	61	164	67
173	62	158	61	136	60	136	56	133	57
144	60	155	58	156	61	140	61	169	63
158	60	130	52	154	58	157	60	154	61
144	60	148	60	135	59	173	61	149	59
147	59	154	58	154	62	151	60	148	57
168	66	168	69^{H}	162	61	171	67	146	62
163	63	140	60	156	60	138	61	156	63
144	59	171	64	154	59	154	61	149	64
155	61	151	56	171	65	167	64	166	64
158	60	140	57	169	67	158	64	154	56
172	67	154	62	176	64	159	63	149	61
170	62	149	58	156	60	166	68	178	65
168	63	135	51^{L}	154	62	157	60	158	63

SA = Skeletal age in months
Ht = Standing height in inches
H = High score
L = Low score

ages and the standing heights of the 13-year-old boys. The steps, illustrated in Figure 11, follow on page 226.

1. Construct a scattergram by preparing a double-entry table as follows:
(a) Decide upon the step intervals to be used for each variable. This is done in the same manner described in Chapter 7 for setting up a frequency table. Care should be taken to obtain approximately the same number of intervals for each variable; the size of the intervals will not be the same unless the ranges of the two variables are comparable. In the illustration, the interval sizes are 2 inches for standing height and 5 months for skeletal age; the number of intervals are 10 and 11, respectively.
(b) List the intervals for one variable on the left (*Y* variable) and the other variable at the top (*X* variable). For the *Y* variable (skeletal age), the intervals run from high at the top to low at the bottom, in the accepted manner for frequency tables, and for the *X* variable (standing height), from low at the left to high at the right. (Actually, there is no mathematical reason for this procedure, but it is common practice.)
(c) Starting with the first pair of scores in the tabulation, 149 for skeletal age and 58 for standing height, make a tally in the proper square. The

X – Variable: Standing Height (

Y – Variable: Skeletal Age

	50-51	52-53	54-55	56-57	58-59	60-61	62-63	64-65	66-67	68-69	f_y	d_y	fd_y	fd^2_y	$x'y'$ −	$x'y'$ +
180-184								I 10 / 10			1	5	5	25		10
175-179								II 16 / 8			2	4	8	32		16
170-174						I	II 6 / 3	II 12 / 6	II 18 / 9		7	3	21	63		36
165-69						I	III 6 / 2	II 8 / 4	II 12 / 6	II 16* / 8	10	2	20	40		42
160-164					I -1 / -1	I	II 2 / 1	卌 10 / 2	II 6 / 3		11	1	11	11	1	18
155-159					II	卌 IIII	III	III			17	0	65			
150-154				III 6 / 2	卌 5 / 1	卌	卌 -5 / -1	I -2 / -2	I -3 / -3		20	-1	-20	20	10	11
145-149				I 4 / 4	卌 10 / 2	IIII	I -2 / -2	II -8 / -4			13	-2	-26	52	10	14
140-144				I 6 / 6	II 6 / 3	IIII					7	-3	-21	63		12
135-139	I 20 / 20		II 24 / 12	II 16 / 8	I 4 / 4	II					8	-4	-32	128		64
130 134		I 20 / 20		II 20 / 10	I 5 / 5						4	-5	-20	100		45
f_x	1	1	2	9	17	27	16	18	7	2	100		-119 65 -54	534	-21	268 -21 247
d_x	-5	-4	-3	-2	-1	0	1	2	3	4						
fd_x	-5	-4	-6	-18	-17	-50	16	36	21	8	81 -50 31					
fd^2_x	25	16	18	36	17		16	72	63	32	295					

$$c_y = \frac{\sum fd_y}{N} = \frac{-54}{100} = -.54$$

$$c_x = \frac{\sum fd_x}{N} = \frac{31}{100} = .31$$

$$\sigma'_y = \sqrt{\frac{\sum fd^2_y}{N} - c^2_y} = \sqrt{\frac{534}{100} - (-.54)^2} = 2.247$$

$$\sigma'_x = \sqrt{\frac{\sum fd^2_x}{N} - c^2_x} = \sqrt{\frac{295}{100} - .31^2} = 1.689$$

$$r = \frac{\frac{\sum x'y'}{N} - c_x c_y}{\sigma'_x \sigma'_y}$$

$$= \frac{\frac{247}{100} - (-.54)(.31)}{(2.247)(1.689)}$$

$$= \frac{2.47 - (-.167)}{3.795}$$

$$= \frac{2.637}{3.795}$$

$$= .695$$

$$M_y = AM_y + (c_y \times i)$$

$$= 157.0 + (-.54 \times 5) = 154.30$$

$$\sigma_y = \sigma'_y \times i = 2.25 \times 5 = 11.25$$

$$M_x = AM_x + (c_x \times i) =$$

$$= 60.5 + (.31 \times 2) = 61.12$$

$$\sigma_x = \sigma'_x \times i = 1.69 \times 2 = 3.38$$

Figure 11. Calculation of the Coefficient of Correlation by Product-Moment Method Utilizing a Scattergram

proper square is where intervals 145–149 and 58–59 meet on the scattergram; as can be seen, eventually 5 pairs of scores fall in this square. Continue until all 100 pairs of scores are entered. The tallies are placed across the top of the various squares.
(d) Complete the scattergram with frequency columns by counting the scores tallied in rows and columns: fy at the right for skeletal age and fx at the bottom for standing height. In effect, two frequency tables now exist with the scattergram intervening; the intervals are on left side and top and the frequencies are at right side and bottom, respectively.

2. Select as assumed mean (AM) for each variable the midpoint of an interval approximately in the middle of each distribution. Rule off with heavy lines the squares in the row and column in which these assumed means lie as shown in the table: 155–159 for the Y variable and 60–61 for the X variable. Then compute c and σ' for each variable; these procedures were described earlier in the computations of the mean and standard deviation and are shown at the right side of the table. In making these computations the following columns are necessarily adjacent to the scattergram: fy, dy, fdy, and fd^2y at the right side, and fx, dx, fdx, and fd^2x at the bottom. In the computations of r from the scattergram, the size of the step interval is not considered; the amounts of variance of the two variables were compressed into approximately the same space in constructing the scattergram by differences in the size of the intervals (2 and 5 in this problem). So far in calculating r, with the exception of construction of the scattergram, no new statistical work has been required.

3. The next step in the problem is to compute $\sum x'y'$. This computation is made by multiplying the deviation of the scores from one assumed mean by the deviation from the other, in terms of deviation units (that is, without considering the size of the interval). This procedure is explained as follows:
(a) The lines representing the two assumed means divide the scattergram into four quadrants: upper right, upper left, lower right, lower left. Scores in the upper right quadrant are above both assumed means, so the values for both variables are plus; this quadrant, therefore, is a positive quadrant since plus times plus equals plus. Scores in the lower left quadrant are below both assumed means, so the values for both variables are negative; this quadrant, then, is also positive since negative times negative equals plus. In the upper left and lower right quadrants, the values are above one assumed mean but below the other; consequently, the values in these quadrants are negative since plus times minus equals minus.
(b) Each of the squares containing frequencies on the scattergram is given a value indicating its interval deviation from the two AM's. This value is determined by multiplying the interval deviation from one AM by the interval deviation from the other AM. On the scattergram, these values appear in the lower right corners of each square. For example, take the square with 2

frequencies formed by the step intervals 165–169 and 68–69 (an asterisk appears in the upper right corner). This square deviates +2 from *AMy* and +4 from *AMx*; thus: $2 \times 4 = 8$. The values of all squares are determined in like manner.

(c) As there are more scores in some squares than in others, this fact must now be taken into account. To do so, the frequencies in each square are multiplied by the square value just determined. Thus, for the illustration above (square with the asterisk), $2 \times 8 = 16$. These values appear in the centers of the squares throughout the scattergram.

(d) When the products of all the squares have been computed, with due regard for plus and minus signs, the entries for the $x'y'$ column can be made. Add the products for each step interval of the Y variable, placing the sum of the positive values in the column under the plus sign, and the sum of the negative values in the column under the negative sign. The algebraic sum of this column, then, is the difference between positive and negative values, 247 for this problem. This procedure may be duplicated for the X variable columns to check the work; the two answers should agree.

4. Compute the coefficient of correlation, r, by means of the formula:

$$r = \frac{\dfrac{\sum x'y'}{N} - cxcy}{\sigma'_x \sigma'_y} \tag{11.3}$$

This computation is shown in Figure 12: $r = .695$.

In the lower right corner of Figure 12, calculations of the means and standard deviations for the two variables are made. As seen, most of the necessary computations for these statistics had been made in the correlation computation.

INTERPRETATION OF PRODUCT-MOMENT CORRELATION

In the presentation of sampling reliability, the explanation was made in considerable detail that the distribution of means of repeated samples of the same size drawn from the same population (as well as other statistics) takes on the form of a normal distribution. The whole concept of statistical reliability was then based on this assumption of normality. In a distribution of sample r's, however, normality exists only when the population r is .00 and the sample size is large. With a high population correlation, say of .80, the distribution of sample r's is negatively skewed (positively skewed if $-.80$) and leptokurtic; Figure 12 illustrates this situation. As a consequence of this

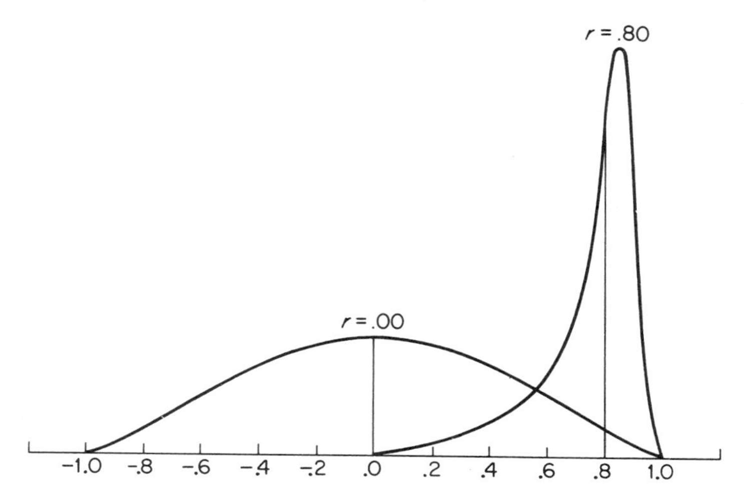

Figure 12. Distribution of Sample r's around Population r's of .0 and .8

fact, a special problem exists in applying tests of significance, in determining the probable limits of the true relationships, and in making other correlational applications. Several of these situations will be considered below.

Significance

Invariably, the investigator will want to know if any obtained r is significant, that is, whether or not an obtained coefficient can be attributed to sampling error. A standard error of a coefficient of correlation (σ_r) may be computed and a t ratio obtained.

$$\sigma_r = \frac{1 - r^2}{\sqrt{N}} \qquad t = \frac{r}{\sigma_r} \tag{11.4}$$

However, this formula is based on the assumption that the sampling distribution of r is normal. Thus, to use the formula when the population r is substantial violates the validity of reliability statistics.

When only the significance of the correlation is wanted, the null hypothesis can be applied. In this case, the null hypothesis states that the population r is in fact zero, and any correlation obtained is due to sampling error. In applying the null hypothesis, the amount of correlation necessary to reject at a given level of significance is determined. In doing so, the standard error for $r = .00$ is first computed. If $r = .00$, formula 11.4 becomes:

$$\sigma_{r_{.00}} = \frac{1}{\sqrt{N}} \tag{11.5}$$

($N - 2$ should be used in the denominator when N is small, 30 and below.) This amount is multiplied by the appropriate t for the df of the problem. Inasmuch as two variables are involved in a product-moment correlation, one df is lost for each variable; therefore, $df = N - 2$. This t is multiplied by $\sigma_{r_{.00}}$.

An example will clarify this process. For the correlation between skeletal age and standing height, r is .695 and N is 100. Utilizing formula 11.5:

$$\sigma_{r_{.00}} = \frac{1}{\sqrt{N}} = \frac{1}{\sqrt{100}} = .10$$

Entering Table 15 with $df = N - 2$, or $100 - 2 = 98$, $t = 2.63$ at the .01 level. Then:

$$\sigma_{r_{.00}} \times t = .10 \times 2.63 = .263$$

Thus, a correlation as high as .263 should occur only 1 in 100 times by sampling error. Inasmuch as the r of .695 is much higher than .263, the null hypothesis can be rejected with assurance.

The above process was explained in detail in order to demonstrate the meaning and application of the null hypothesis to a coefficient of correlation. However, a simple way is available to obtain the r's needed to reject the null hypothesis at the .05 and .01 levels. In Table 19 the r's are given for all degrees of freedom.

For the illustrated problem, enter this table with df of 98. By interpolation between df's of 90 and 100, the r's necessary to reject the null hypothesis at the .05 and .01 levels are .197 and .259. These r's are not quite the same as for the computational method above, where the r at the .01 was .263. The differences are in rounding off; the table is considered the more accurate.

An examination of the r's in Table 19 shows the great importance of sample size in the significance of correlation coefficients. With df of 10, a correlation of .708 is necessary for significance at this level; and, for df of 1,000, the significant r is .081. Therefore, descriptions of correlation coefficients as being high or low are meaningless without reference to the correlation needed for the number of subjects upon which the correlation is based.

Table 19

Correlation Coefficients at the .05 and .01 Levels of Significance

Degrees of freedom ($N-2$)	.05	.01	Degrees of freedom ($N-2$)	.05	.01
1	.997	1.000	24	.388	.496
2	.950	.990	25	.381	.487
3	.878	.959	26	.374	.478
4	.811	.917	27	.367	.470
5	.754	.874	28	.361	.463
6	.707	.834	29	.355	.456
7	.666	.798	30	.349	.449
8	.632	.765	35	.325	.418
9	.602	.735	40	.304	.393
10	.576	.708	45	.288	.372
11	.553	.684	50	.273	.354
12	.532	.661	60	.250	.325
13	.514	.641	70	.232	.302
14	.497	.623	80	.217	.283
15	.482	.606	90	.205	.267
16	.468	.590	100	.195	.254
17	.456	.575	125	.174	.228
18	.444	.561	150	.159	.208
19	.433	.549	200	.138	.181
20	.423	.537	300	.113	.148
21	.413	.526	400	.098	.128
22	.404	.515	500	.088	.115
23	.396	.505	1,000	.062	.081

Fisher's z Coefficient

As explained above, the sampling distribution of r is not normal except when the population r is .00; and, when r is high, the sampling distribution is skewed and leptokurtic. Thus, the standard error of r is invalidated. Yet, the investigator frequently wishes to make statistical inferences from high correlations.

R. A. Fisher developed a useful and accurate technique for handling sampling errors for high values of r, although it can be used with low r's as well. The technique consists of converting the obtained r into a Fisher z coefficient equivalent. The distribution of sample z's is nearly normally distributed, so it is safe to apply to a standard error of z in the same manner as for the mean and other statistics previously considered. The sampling distribution of z's is shown in Figure 13; compare this sampling distribution representing r's with the sampling distribution of r's in Figure 13.[1]

[1] R. A. Fisher, *Statistical Methods for Research Workers* (10th ed.) (London: Oliver and Boyd, 1946), p. 200.

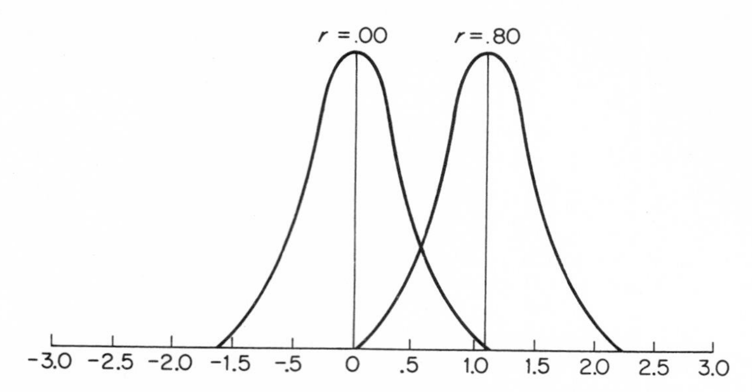

Figure 13. Distribution of Sample *z*-Coefficient Equivalents of Population *r*'s of .00 and .80

The mathematical convergence of *r* to *z* requires logarithmic computations. However, a direct convergence table is available and appears in Table 20. The *z* coefficient equivalent of the *r* of .695 in the illustrated problem is .86, when interpolated. Situations in which the Fisher *z* coefficient is utilized follow.

Table 20

Conversion of Product-Moment Correlation to Fisher's *z* Coefficient Equivalent*

r	*z*	*r*	*z*	*r*	*z*	*r*	*z*	*r*	*z*	*r*	*z*
.25	.26	.40	.42	.55	.62	.70	.87	.85	1.26	.950	1.83
.26	.27	.41	.44	.56	.63	.71	.89	.86	1.29	.955	1.89
.27	.28	.42	.45	.57	.65	.72	.91	.87	1.33	.960	1.95
.28	.29	.43	.46	.58	.66	.73	.93	.88	1.38	.965	2.01
.29	.30	.44	.47	.59	.68	.74	.95	.89	1.42	.970	2.09
.30	.31	.45	.48	.60	.69	.75	.97	.90	1.47	.975	2.18
.31	.32	.46	.50	.61	.71	.76	1.00	.905	1.50	.980	2.30
.32	.33	.47	.51	.62	.73	.77	1.02	.910	1.53	.985	2.44
.33	.34	.48	.52	.63	.74	.78	1.05	.915	1.56	.990	2.65
.34	.35	.49	.54	.64	.76	.79	1.07	.920	1.59	.995	2.99
.35	.37	.50	.55	.65	.78	.80	1.10	.925	1.62		
.36	.38	.51	.56	.66	.79	.81	1.13	.930	1.66		
.37	.39	.52	.58	.67	.81	.82	1.16	.935	1.70		
.38	.40	.53	.59	.68	.83	.83	1.19	.940	1.74		
.39	.41	.54	.60	.69	.85	.84	1.22	.945	1.78		

* *r*'s under .25 may be taken as equivalent to *z*'s.

Reliability limits. Levels of confidence can be applied to correlation coefficients through z coefficients. A standard error of z is needed (σ_z):

$$\sigma_z = \frac{1}{\sqrt{N - 3}} \tag{11.6}$$

In this instance, $df = N - 3$. Two degrees of freedom are lost for the two variables in the correlation and one is lost for the conversion from r to z.

In the illustrated problem: $r = .695$; $z = .860$; $N = 100$. Applying formula 11.6:

$$\sigma_z = \frac{1}{\sqrt{N - 3}} = \frac{1}{\sqrt{100 - 3}} = .102$$

Entering Table 15, the t at the .05 level for df of 97 is 1.98. Thus:

$$\sigma_z \times t = .102 \times 1.98 = .202$$

Adding and subtracting this amount from the z of .860:

$$.860 + .202 = 1.062$$

$$.860 - .202 = .658$$

Returning to Table 20, the r's for these z's are determined; the amounts are .580 and .785. Interpreting, the chances are 95 in 100 that the population r lies between .580 and .785, and 5 in 100 that it lies below or above these limits.

The reliability limits for the .01 level of confidence can be determined in the same manner as for the .05 level by substituting the t of 2.63 for the 1.98 at the .05 level, as shown in Table 15.

Difference between uncorrelated *r*'s. The investigator may encounter a situation where he wishes to determine the significance between two coefficients of correlation. When the coefficients are uncorrelated (i.e., the correlations are from independent random samples), the difference between z coefficient equivalents of the r's is tested for significance by application of the t ratio. A standard error of the difference between z's (σ_{Dz}) is needed. The formula is:

$$\sigma_{Dz} = \sqrt{\frac{1}{N - 3} + \frac{1}{N - 3}} \tag{11.7}$$

An illustration will explain the procedure for making this test of significance. In a study by Carter,[2] the body weights and upper arm girths were correlated separately for 120 junior high school and 120 upper elementary school boys; the r's were .89 and .79, respectively. If these correlations are to be compared, the possibility that the difference of .10 correlational points may be due to sampling errors must be determined. In other words, should the null hypothesis be accepted or rejected? The procedures for testing the null hypothesis in this problem follow.

1. Determine the difference between z coefficient equivalents for the two r's; the equivalents are obtained from Table 20.

School levels	r	z
Junior High School	.89	1.42
Upper Elementary School	.79	1.07
D_z		.35

2. Compute the standard error of the difference between z's by use of formula 11.7 and the t ratio:

$$\sigma_{Dz} = \sqrt{\frac{1}{N-3} + \frac{1}{N-3}} = \sqrt{\frac{1}{120-3} + \frac{1}{120-3}} = .134$$

$$t = \frac{D_z}{\sigma_{Dz}} = \frac{.35}{.134} = 2.68$$

3. Enter Table 15 with $df = N_1 + N_2 - 6$, or $120 + 120 - 6 = 234$. A t ratio of 2.60 is needed for significance at the .01 level. Inasmuch as the t ratio obtained for this problem was 2.68, the null hypothesis is rejected at this level. Thus, there is only 1 chance in 100 that the correlation difference of .10 between body weight-arm girth correlations of the junior high and elementary school boys could have occurred as a consequence of random sampling.

Averaging correlations. On occasion, the investigator may have several r's that he wishes to combine. One example is when correlations are computed for the same two variables for several samples from the same population. Another example is when the correlations have been obtained from samples drawn at successive years. Of course, a new correlation could be computed from the raw data for all samples. However, a much simpler way is to average the correlations.

---

[2] Gavin H. Carter, "Reconstruction of the Rogers Strength and Physical Fitness Indices for Upper Elementary, Junior High, and Senior High School Boys," microcard Doctoral Dissertation, University of Oregon, 1957.

If the sample r's are about the same value and are not large, a simple arithmetic average is satisfactory. However, if the r's differ considerably in size and are large, the Fisher z coefficient equivalents should be averaged, inasmuch as the value of correlation coefficients does not vary along a linear scale. If N differs for the various samples, a weighted mean should be computed, using df $(N - 3)$ rather than N in the computations. The hypothetical correlations given below will serve to illustrate this process; Table 20 is used to obtain the z coefficients.

r	z	N	$(N - 3)$	Weighted $z(N - 3)$
.74	.95	78	75	71.25
.82	1.16	103	100	116.00
.60	.69	63	60	41.40
			235	228.65

$$M_z = \frac{228.65}{235} = .97$$

Returning to Table 20, the r for the z of .97 is .75. Had the r's been averaged directly, using $df = N - 2$, the weighted r is .738.

Actually, the difference between averaging r's and z equivalents is not great unless the differences in r's are considerable. However, when such is the case, a serious question can be raised as to whether or not r's that differ greatly come from the same population by random sampling.

Difference Between Correlated r's

A situation encountered occasionally is when the investigator wants to determine the significance of the difference between two correlated r's. A correlated situation occurs when two variables X_2 and X_3 are correlated with the same third variable X_1 utilizing the same subjects. Thus, there are two correlations, r_{12} and r_{13}, and the significance of their difference is to be tested. An illustration of this situation is when several test items are correlated against some performance criterion of, say, academic achievement or athletic ability.

For this kind of problem, Hotelling[3] developed a t ratio. The Hotelling

[3] Harold Hotelling, "The Selection of Variates for Use in Prediction, with Some Comments on the General Problem of Nuisance Parameters," *Annals of Mathematical Statistics*, II (1940), 271.

formula is:

$$t_{d_r} = (r_{12} - r_{13})\sqrt{\frac{(N-3)(1+r_{23})}{2(1 - r_{23}^2 - r_{12}^2 - r_{13}^2 + 2r_{23}r_{12}r_{13})}} \tag{11.8}$$

FACTORS AFFECTING CORRELATION

The major assumption that must be met when using the product-moment method of correlation is that the data are linear. By linear is meant that the plotted pairs of scores, as in the scattergram in Figure 12, are best represented by a straight line. If the correlation in Figure 12 had been +1.00, all pairs of scores would have fallen on a straight line from the lower left to the upper right corner of the scattergram. If the correlation had been −1.00, the straight line would have been from the upper left to the lower right corner. When correlations are less than ±1.00, which is almost always the case, the drift of scores across the scattergram should be linear.

The product-moment correlation follows a straight line only. Therefore, if the pairs of scores show a definite curve of some sort, a curvilinear relationship may be present. The presence of curvilinearity should be tested for significance. If present, the product-moment method should not be used; the proper method is the correlation ratio, or *eta*. The r will always be too low in designating the relationship when applied to curvilinear data.

At one time, an assumption for use of the product-moment correlation was that the data for the two variables were normally distributed. This assumption is no longer valid, unless the nonnormality of the data causes a curvilinear relationship. This may happen when one or both distributions are markedly skewed. In this event, the curvilinearity can be avoided by T scaling the two distributions, utilizing the normalizing process, and correlating the T scale equivalents. If the data are still curvilinear, then use *eta* as the correlational method. Otherwise, the forms of distributions may vary, so long as they are reasonably symmetrical and unimodal.

Errors of measurement, if accidental or random, distribute normally; they are "hit or miss" in their effects. Such random errors reduce the size of correlations. Two completely inaccurate tests, where chance determines the score, will produce a zero correlation. The same situation does not prevail for systematic errors, where the errors are in one direction. An illustration of systematic errors would be the use of an improperly calibrated testing instrument.

Another factor affecting the magnitude of product-moment correlations is the range of scores for the variables. A narrow range tends to reduce r, as slight changes anywhere in a distribution result in much greater variations in distribution positions. It becomes almost essential to pin point testing when the range of scores is small without introducing considerable random testing error into the correlation.

PREDICTION VALUE OF CORRELATION

The real importance of r is not in terms of its magnitude per se but in terms of its predictive value. The predictive value of r increases in a curvilinear manner from .00 to 1.00. Thus, whereas an r of .80 is twice an r of .40 in magnitude, its predictive value is more than twice as great. A number of statistical procedures have been proposed to reveal the predictive value of the correlation coefficient. Three ways by which this value can be expressed are the coefficient of alienation, the coefficient of forecasting efficiency, and coefficient of determination. All these coefficients are based on r^2.

Coefficient of alienation. The coefficient of alienation (k) is the absence of predictive value between two variables. The formula is:

$$k = \sqrt{1 - r^2} \tag{11.9}$$

For the correlation of .695 between the skeletal ages and the heights of the 13-year-old boys:

$$k = \sqrt{1 - .695^2} = .72$$

Thus, the absence of predictive value for a correlation of .695 is .72. The larger the coefficient of alienation the less is its predictive value. When $r =$ .99, $k = .14$. It is not until $r = 1.00$ that $k = .00$.

Coefficient of forecasting efficiency. The coefficient of forecasting efficiency (E), also known as the predictive index (PI), expresses the presence of predictive value. The formula is:

$$E = 1 - \sqrt{1 - r^2} \qquad (\text{or, } E = 1 - k) \tag{11.10}$$

For the skeletal age-height correlation of .695:

$$E = 1 - \sqrt{1 - .695^2} = .28$$

This coefficient may be interpreted as per cent of predictive value better than a "best guess" ($E \times 100$). In the illustration, the prediction of skeletal age from height for 13-year-old boys is 28 per cent better than guessing.

When $r = 1.00$, $E = 1.00$, or 100 per cent predictive accuracy;

when $r = .00$, $E = .00$, or no predictive accuracy.

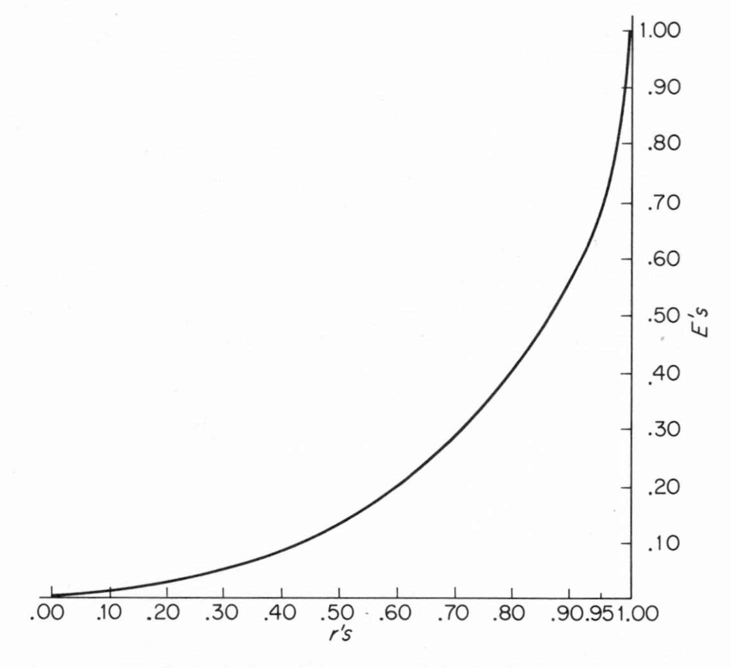

Figure 14. Predictive Value of r in Terms of the Coefficient of Forecasting Efficiency (E)

As indicated earlier, the predictive value of r increases in a curvilinear manner. This curvilinearity may be shown by plotting the coefficients of forecasting efficiency, as shown in Figure 14. As demonstrated in the graph and as computed by E, an r of .80 has five times the predictive value of an r of .40:

$$E = 1 - \sqrt{1 - .80^2} = .40$$

$$E = 1 - \sqrt{1 - .40^2} = .08$$

The E of .40 is five times greater than the E of .08.

Coefficient of determination. The coefficient of determination (d) is simply:

$$d = r^2 \tag{11.11}$$

When multiplied by 100, this coefficient gives the percentage of variance in Y that is associated with, determined by, or accounted for by variance in X.

For the skeletal age-height correlation of .695:

$$d = .695^2 = .48$$

Thus, 48 per cent of the variance in Y is accounted for by the variance in X (or vice versa, as this relationship is reversible). To account for one-half the variance of any set of measurements, the r between variables would have to be .707.

OTHER CORRELATIONAL METHODS[4]

Various methods of computing correlations have been devised, many of these for special conditions. Several of the more commonly used ones are mentioned below.

Multiple correlation. The coefficient of multiple correlation indicates the degree to which values of one variable correlate with the values of two or more other variables. For example, how well does broad jumping ability correlate with sprinting ability and leg strength?

Partial correlation. The coefficient of partial correlation determines the net relationships between two variables when the influence of one or more other factors is excluded. For example, how well do weight and strength correlate when skeletal age is held constant?

Rank-difference method. The rank-difference method, designated as *rho*, is designed to correlate two variables when the scores are arranged as ranks. For example, if football players were ranked according to their tackling and blocking abilities, these two traits could be correlated by this method.

Biserial correlation. This correlation method is used when one variable is in a continuum and the other is a dichotomy (classified into two categories). This method was utilized by McCurdy and Larson when they correlated the results of their "Organic Efficiency Test" with a criterion consisting of two groups, infirmary patients and varsity swimmers.

Tetrachoric correlation. This method is used when both variables are dichotomies.

Contingency coefficient. The contingency coefficient is used when both variables are classified into the same number of categories from two or more.

---

[4] For presentation of these methods, see: H. Harrison Clarke and David H. Clarke, *Advanced Statistics* (Eugene, Oregon: H. H. Clarke, 2561 Pioneer Pike, 1969).

SUMMARY

The product-moment method of correlation applied to both ungrouped and grouped data was presented in this chapter. The significance of a correlation coefficient by application of the null hypothesis was considered. The use of the Fisher z coefficient with high coefficients was demonstrated for determining reliability limits, for averaging correlations, and for testing the difference between correlations for significance. The predictive value of correlation coefficients was demonstrated by use of the coefficient of alienation, the coefficient of forecasting efficiency (predictive index), and the coefficient of determination.

PART IV

LABORATORY RESEARCH

Laboratory resources may be in a formally established laboratory, or they may be a gymnasium, athletic field, track, or swimming pool when utilized for conducting scientific investigations. Such scientific studies involve the adoption of a study design with appropriate hypotheses, the use of proper tests to measure the essential elements under investigation, and the appropriate statistical analyses of these data.

The first chapter in Part IV, Chapter 12, presents "Laboratory and Experimental Research." The methods presented are common to the various types of studies considered in subsequent chapters. This practice was adopted in order to avoid unnecessary duplication of methodology; cross references to this chapter should suffice. The other chapters are devoted to five broad investigative areas, as follows: Chapter 13, Physiology of Exercise; Chapter 14, Motor Learning; Chapter 15, Psychological Studies; Chapter 16, Kinesiological Research; and Chapter 17, Growth and Development.

CHAPTER 12

Laboratory and Experimental Research

Most research in physical education has taken place in what may be defined as a research laboratory and has employed the experimental method. A number of reasons may be given to account for this trend, but chief among them is the growing availability of appropriate facilities and needed equipment. More and more research laboratories are being developed in physical education, staffed by competent personnel, and equipped with sensitive and precise instruments. This development fosters larger graduate programs; therefore, more doctoral candidates obtain their degrees to continue the general trend. Subsequently, these doctorates engage in their own research pursuits or sponsor their own research programs and thereby uncover more problems that stimulate greater interest on the part of still more candidates, all of which contributes to further productivity. Consequently, the upward research spiral has favored the sciences in physical education rather than the arts or humanities.

Such an assessment does not imply that this is desirable, for it should be clear that all forms of research are endorsed, provided they are done properly. The experimental method has certain inherent guarantees that, once followed, give assurance that the outcome will be dependable. If care is taken in developing a problem and carrying it out, the end result may permit the formulation of generalizations—a situation that is ultimately appealing to an investigator.

A number of experimental methods may be employed in research; the acceptability of any one will depend entirely on the experiment to be conducted. There are advantages and disadvantages of each, and the student of research must be reasonably knowledgeable in all the more common ones so as to know when they are to be used. Failure to use the proper experimental design can render the results invalid. This chapter will deal with such factors as well as general considerations that concern instrumentation, precision of testing, tester competency, and the establishment of a research laboratory.

EXPERIMENTAL METHODS

The primary responsibility of the investigator is to adopt the appropriate experimental methodology before proceeding with data collection. The essence of the experimental method is to attempt to control all the essential factors except one variable, which is manipulated in such a manner that the effect of its operation can be determined and measured. Thus, if a single factor is to be studied, and it is determined later that either of two factors could account for the measured change, serious doubt may be cast on the validity of the research. It is incumbent that the investigator assess correctly those factors that must be controlled and then control them in his study.

The simple research designs will be discussed primarily in this chapter, with brief reference to more sophisticated plans. However, this text is not intended primarily for the advanced researcher; some of the advanced techniques would not be germane to the majority of students and others interested in research methodology. In most instances, the advanced techniques require advanced knowledge of statistics, particularly in the area of complex analysis of variance, which is also beyond the scope of this book. Therefore, the basic elements of methodology will be emphasized with the aim of providing a clear understanding of elements that permeate the majority of research problems.

Main Effects vs Control

The definition of the experimental method emphasizes the control of all essential factors. Frequently, a misunderstanding exists of what is entailed when one attempts to control experimental variables. Actually, the term is a misnomer, because operationally one seldom controls variable factors; rather, one measures their basic properties to determine the directional change that would be expected under normal conditions. In experiments dealing with human performance, it is sometimes essential to know the normal reactions of subjects tested under conditions identical to those of the experimental group. Therefore, one variable is allowed to operate in the experimental group but not in the control group; if the two groups eventually differ, the investigator should be able to claim that the difference was due to the main effects involved.

Deciding which factors must be controlled is sometimes difficult, especially for the neophyte who is relatively unfamiliar with the literature. It is easy to confuse those things that result in better precision of testing, such as the reduction of error and standardizing of procedure, with the need for a control group. These matters will be discussed subsequently, where it will be pointed out that *all* testing must adhere to certain procedures that insure accuracy; however, the use of a control group as such may be necessary in certain instances where other factors (e.g., maturation, learning, conditioning, etc.) could account for changes in the experimental variable under question. If it can be shown that no change will normally occur, this may obviate the necessity for a control group.

Having made these rather general statements, the discussion that follows will be more specific. These procedures are merely a means to an end; the problem is formulated first, and then the appropriate experimental design is selected to provide the best means of solving the problem. Then the proper statistical treatment is provided. Occasionally, an investigator becomes so enamored of the manipulative procedures that he tries to design a study around the experimental method (or statistical test). Frequently, such results seem contrived and may not be as satisfactory as a simple straightforward approach. On the other hand, a knowledge of the more advanced techniques makes such a choice possible and, at least, acquaints the researcher with some of the assumptions that are required for their use.

Simple Experimental Designs

The simple experimental designs are so called because they are relatively uncomplicated and lead to problem solution in a direct manner. One or the other of the techniques described below is employed in much of published research in physical education and, therefore, can be considered potentially more functional for the beginner researcher.

1. Single group design. The single group design involves one group of subjects in the following manner: They are first given an initial test, the experimental factor is applied, and the final test follows. This is particularly well-adapted to studies of physical conditioning, where changes in physical fitness are known not to occur unless systematic exercise is given.

The strength of this design is that it does not require the equation or rotation of groups, and it is particularly well-adapted to classroom use. The weaknesses that may be encountered begin with the lack of a control group, but this is a deficiency only if a control group is needed and cannot be considered a blanket indictment. However, if the changes that result from conditioning can be attributed in part to maturation—the subjects grew larger, became more mature, and consequently stronger, and so on—then the full impact of the main effects cannot be ascertained. This is true, similarly, if learning of the criterion variables can be said to exist; it could then be argued that the full effects of the conditioning program are unknown because of the ameliorating influence of this factor.

A primary aim of the experimental study is to rule out chance as a factor for differences in performance. Thus, the investigator is concerned with assuring himself that the main effects are not due to some extraneous factor. In a training study, for example, if the initial mean a_1 is improved to a final mean a_2, and the difference, $a_2 - a_1$, is statistically significant, it is imperative that the investigator be able to say with confidence that the difference was due to the conditioning activity imposed and not to such factors as maturation or learning. A number of ways of handling this situation in the planning stages may be cited, as follows: (1) employing subjects who will not be physically maturing during the experiment; (2) selecting those variables that are not particularly susceptible to learning, such as strength measures, physiological traits, and so on; and (3) if in doubt, utilizing a control group selected from the same population, but not permitting them to participate in the training program.

An example of the one group experiment is a study by Davis,[1] in which a group of subjects were conditioned for five weeks to middle distance swimming. They were measured before and after the program on a number of muscular strength, endurance, and cardiovascular variables. Of interest was the finding that the amount of strength decrement from the first and last 200-yard swim at maximal speed was the same, even though the mean time decreased by 23.7 seconds during the training period. Apparently, the subjects swam faster for the same degree of muscular fatigue.

A variation of the single group design is the reverse design in which an initial test is given, and factor *A* is applied. Then the subjects are retested, and factor *B* is applied, to be followed by the final test. Unless the cumulative effect of factors *A* and *B* are sought, this design would seem to have little advantage to offer. Fewer subjects are required, to be sure, but there are a number of weaknesses that make this design particularly susceptible to artifact. For example, in learning studies, gains may be greater as a result of factor *A*, since the typical curve of learning shows more rapid acceleration in earlier stages of practice plus the additional possibility of plateaus occurring. The practice effect of taking a series of measurements may be more pronounced for factor *B* than for factor *A*, which would cause spuriously large differences. Related to this is the possibility of a carry-over of attitude or method of attack by the subject from one experimental task to another, which in fatigue or endurance studies may result in learning to endure pain or discomfort. Differential maturation and other factors may also impinge upon the acceptability of this method of experimental design.

---

[1] Jack F. Davis, "Effects of Training and Conditioning for Middle Distance Swimming upon Measures of Cardiovascular Condition, General Physical Fitness, Gross Strength Motor Fitness, and Strength of Involved Muscles," microcard Doctoral Dissertation, University of Oregon, 1955.

2. Repeated measures design. A variation of the single group design is the repeated measures design, in which all subjects in a group receive all treatments. If several experimental treatments are to be investigated, it may be desirable for all subjects to be exposed to each treatment; this process serves to control intersubject variability, which is sometimes a problem when different subjects are employed. In fact, the subject serves as his own control in this design. Such a design is not normally utilized in situations that involve physical conditioning or learning, for example, because a basic assumption is that each subject must be susceptible to the main effects. Once conditioning or learning has occurred, it is not possible to return to the previous level for another treatment.

It should be pointed out that some performance variables themselves contain a rather large amount of learning, but as long as the learning per se is not examined, other ways of ameliorating the mitigating influence of this factor may be applied. For example, one method is to give a sufficient number of trials of the criterion task to all subjects at the outset of the experiment in a deliberate attempt to cause learning to occur at an approximately equal extent. How many trails will be needed in order for learning to occur should be determined by preliminary investigation during the preparatory experimental stages. This point should be given very careful consideration if novel or unfamiliar tasks are to be employed, because, as shown in Chapter 14, large amounts of learning may occur that, if not anticipated, could cause difficulties with data analysis and interpretation.

The small amount of learning (or conditioning) that may occur during the experiment can be tolerated by rotating the order of treatment administration—employing a randomized order—or by a systematic method, such as a Latin square arrangement, which will be discussed later in this chapter. The intent is to balance the effect of individual differences and the progressive influence that the same order of experimental treatment might have on the results.

The repeated measures design is illustrated in a study of the effect of muscular tension on reaction time.[2] Forty-one subjects were given a simple reaction time measure that consisted of responding to an auditory signal and giving a maximal contraction of the handgripping muscles. However, each test was preceded by a preparatory submaximal muscular contraction, amounting to 0 (control condition), 10, 15, 20, 25, and 30 kg. Each subject undertook all conditions, but the order of testing was balanced to offset possible learning of the task. Reaction time did improve significantly, but the differences were entirely between control and 10 kg pretension, both of which were slower than all other conditions. Thus, the concept that

[2] David H. Clarke, "Effect of Preliminary Muscular Tension on Reaction Latency," *Research Quarterly*, 39, No. 1 (March 1968), 60.

increased muscular tension, in the form of preparatory set, resulted in faster reaction time was supported.

3. Random group design. A common experimental procedure is to employ a random group design consisting of two or more groups of different subjects (independent groups). In this manner, several experimental treatments may be administered, randomly assigned to the various groups; if a control group is needed, one group may be used for this purpose. In its simplest form, the subjects, assigned randomly to groups *A* and *B*, would be given a preliminary test. Group *A* would undergo the experimental treatment; group *B* would serve as a control so would not receive the treatment; both groups would be retested on the criterion task at the conclusion of the treatment period. When more than one treatment is desired, other groups would be added.

The advantages of employing a random group design are similar to the repeated measures design; that is, the difficulties of the single group experiment may be avoided. A control group may be used, and a number of treatment groups may be included so that the simultaneous observation of several factors may be made. In contrast to the repeated measures design, the subjects are tested only once; therefore, the total number of subjects will be larger.

In the random group experiment, it is logical to expect that the groups selected will have different means, due to the sampling process.[3] The differences in initial means may affect the corresponding differences in final means. Analysis of covariance is a statistic that may be used in analyzing the results of such a study, as final means adjusted for differences between initial means are tested for significance.

A study employing this technique[4] divided 62 college men into two groups: One group was given ten weeks of weight training exercises; the other remained inactive in order to serve as a control group. At the outset of the experiment, all subjects were measured for arm strength, effective arm mass, and speed in a lateral adductive arm movement. The experimental group improved significantly in speed, strength, and strength/mass ratio, whereas the control group declined. However, individual differences in the amount of change in the strength/mass ratio correlated low but significantly with individual changes in maximal speed of movement.

4. Related group design. Very closely allied to the previous experimental method is the related group design. Sometimes called the equated group, or parallel group, design. This procedure involves dividing a sample into two or more groups, primarily on the basis of some initial trait, so

---

[3] See Chapter 10.

[4] David H. Clarke and Franklin M. Henry, "Neuromotor Specificity and Increased Speed from Strength Development," *Research Quarterly*, 32, No. 3 (October 1961), 315.

that the groups are equated (as described in Chapter 9). The equating may be done by pairing and then randomly assigning the pairs to groups or by simply adjusting various groups so that both means and standard deviations are equivalent. Thus, the groups are formed, the treatment administered to the experimental group—perhaps while the control group does nothing—and then the post test is administered to all groups.

For some experiments, experimental and control groups need not be equal on the initial test; the control group may be wanted simply to assure that a practice effect, or some other influence, did not cause a significant change from initial to final test; thus, only a finding of no difference is required.[5] Equating on the basis of some initial factor may not assure equal vulnerability to change; randomizing subjects, rather than equating, offers this assurance.

To illustrate the equated group design: Two groups of male subjects were equated by Brumbach[6] on the basis of serum cholesterol, a physical fitness test, deviations from normal weight, and chronological age in order to study the effect of exercise on serum cholesterol. One group, designated control, participated in no organized physical activity for ten weeks; the experimental group engaged in a formal exercise program consisting of vigorous exercise, running, and weight lifting. The exercise group improved more in physical fitness than the control group, but the difference between the means in final serum cholesterol was not significant.

Complex Experimental Designs

A wide variety of experimental designs is available for a multitude of situations found in research. Some of these are particularly adapted to problems in education, medicine, and agriculture; and, lately, they are being employed in physical education. They are very useful in specific instances, although many of them will be seen only rarely. An account of a number of experimental and quasi-experimental designs will be found in the text by Good.[7]

As research becomes more inclusive, as more variables are brought to bear on a problem, advantage may be taken of a situation by means of the design of the experiment. Thus, the use of complex experimental designs has developed in popularity. Actually, the term *complex* may be misleading, as there may be nothing particularly difficult in the design except the fact

[5] *Ibid.*, 322–23.

[6] Wayne B. Brumbach, "Changes in Serum Cholesterol Levels of Male College Students Who Participated in a Special Exercise Program," *Research Quarterly*, 32, No. 2 (May 1961), 147.

[7] Carter V. Good, *Introduction to Eductional Research*, 2nd ed. (New York: Appleton-Century-Crofts, 1963), Ch. 8.

that it is more involved. The simple designs are primarily concerned with the effects of a single experimental variable whereby groups are differentiated on the basis of just one factor. The complex designs, on the other hand, permit examination of the separate influences of two or more independent variables in order to obtain an estimate of their interaction—the combined effect of their influence over and above the effect of each factor taken separately.

These designs are not routine methods to be applied indiscriminately by a beginner researcher unless he is willing to undertake advanced study, particularly in statistics. Bearing in mind that the experimental protocol is dictated by the problem, the student may find that he is organizing an experiment that will require a complex design for successful completion. Reducing the scope of the study would be one method of coping with a complex experimental design. For further description, the discussion by Winer[8] will prove helpful.

Factorial designs. The factorial designs permit simultaneous examination of the effects of two or more experimental variables, as well as their interaction. Thus, the term 2 × 2 indicates that 2 variations each of 2 factors are being investigated; 2 × 2 × 2 would indicate that 2 variations each of 3 factors are examined. In an example of the latter design, Hanson, Clarke,

Table 21

Scheme of Experimental Factors for Treatment Groups in 2 × 2 × 2 Factorial Design

	Sedentary		Spontaneous	
Light	Nonstroke	Stroke	Nonstroke	Stroke
Dark	Nonstroke	Stroke	Nonstroke	Stroke

and Kelley[9] studied the effects of three sets of factors on the ability of the laboratory rat to run on a motor-driven belt treadmill: running in light areas vs running in dark areas; a comparison of those housed in spontaneous cages vs those in sedentary cages; and post-trial stroking versus nonstroking. Table 21 illustrates the arrangement of experimental factors, with an equal number of subjects assigned randomly to each of the eight cells (2 × 2 × 2 = 8).

---

[8] B. J. Winer, *Statistical Principles in Experimental Design* (New York: McGraw-Hill Book Company, 1962).

[9] Dale Hanson, David Clarke, and David Kelley, "Effect of Selected Treatments Upon the Treadmill Running Success of Male Rats," *Research Quarterly*, 40, No. 1 (March 1969).

Relationship Studies

A perusal of the literature in health and physical education will reveal many studies designed to examine the relationships among variables. The relationship study is not experimental, but it does require that at least two different measures be obtained on the same subjects. Thus, the process represents a single group design. Relationship studies are typically based upon zero-order, partial, and multiple correlations.

Any significant relationship may have importance for the investigator. However, the ultimate goal for such studies is the ability to predict a criterion measure from one or more test variables. If the correlation coefficient is sufficiently high to warrant, regression equations provide the means for making such predictions.[10]

Comparative Studies

The comparison of two or more traits for various identifiable groups is another prevalent type of study. More specifically, a comparison of the difference between two or more means is involved, in which usually the factor causing the difference has been isolated and is known. The typical analysis of results may require computing a t ratio (two means) or an F ratio by analysis of variance (more than two means).[11]

CONTROL OF EXPERIMENTAL FACTORS

In this chapter it has been pointed out that the investigator must do everything in his power to control the experimental factors, and the need for a control group was indicated for certain research designs. In addition, other methods are at the disposal of the experimenter to make his testing more precise, to reduce the error that is inevitably involved in testing human subjects, and to make the data collection as rigorous as possible. Problems of instrumentation will be discussed subsequently, but, first, a number of other matters are to be mentioned.

Subjects

In experimental research in health and physical education, the investigator will use mostly human subjects and to a lesser extent small animals such

---

[10] See Chapter 11 for statistical applications.

[11] See Chapter 10.

as laboratory rats, as discussed in Chapter 13. Too often the choice of subjects is made carelessly, considering availability without serious thought to the type needed. Frequently, samples have consisted of students enrolled in college or university classes, high school students, varsity athletes, and the like simply because they were conveniently available for testing. This statement is not intended to criticize the use of such subjects categorically, for in many experiments they are entirely satisfactory. However, selection of a sample should be made on considerations other than just convenience. The following matters are pertinent to this discussion:

1. Randomization. The concept of population samples and reliability are discussed in Chapter 10, so only brief mention of this aspect will be made here. The point to be stressed is that a sample, to be representative of the population from which it is drawn, must be obtained at random; further, each individual in the population should have an equal chance of being chosen. This process permits application of the principles of normal probability. When sampling procedures violate the assumptions of normality, then the sample may be biased. In a practical way, the investigator should exert care in obtaining his subjects in regard to both type and number; for example, if adult males are desired, then they should be of the same sex, old enough to be considered adult, and restricted somewhat in range of age. The selection of actual subjects to form the same population may be accomplished by using a table of random numbers.[12]

2. Age. In some studies, the age of the subjects need only be specified in broad categories, such as junior high school girls or adult men; in other situations, a strict control of age is necessary. The control of age is especially important in growth studies where the variables are affected by age. Thus, a single age may be restricted to testing the subjects within a few days to a month or more from their birthdays. On the other end of the scale, the study of the aging process may mean that subjects must be recruited from the ranks of the elderly. Whether or not old men or women can be tested on vigorous physical activities is a question of their health; thus, the sample at these ages may indeed be biased, as those who are infirm will not be available, so the sample will reflect only healthy adults. In determining procedures, subjects of widely divergent ages should not be mixed when the research calls for homogeneity.

3. Sex. The traditional approach to physical education research is to restrict each study to one of the sexes. Definite differences between the sexes exist in such measures as physique type, body size, strength, and motor

---

[12] R. A. Fisher and F. Yates, *Statistical Tables for Biological, Agricultural, and Medical Research* (5th ed.) (New York: Hafner Publishing Co., 1957).

ability. As a consequence, the sexes should not be combined in the same sample.

4. Physical ability. The research design that seeks to understand the nature of human performance should use subjects randomly selected from the population, as outlined above. When a sample is thus drawn, it will inevitably include those individuals of high and low physical ability; the majority will be centered about the middle of the distribution, according to the dictates of normal probability. A bias may be introduced should the investigator select as subjects either those of extremely low or extremely high physical ability. The best random sample would span the range, avoiding too much concentration at the extremes, either intentionally or unintentionally. The danger of using all athletes or physical education majors should be clear, except in such instances where they are the subject of the investigation (e.g., athletes versus nonathletes, etc.). On the other hand, some studies require subjects who possess unique physical attributes that make their use in experiments imperative. For example, the analysis of the pole vault, springboard dive, and others can only be accomplished with subjects who are skilled in such activities.

5. Motivation and interest. Experimental control will also extend to subject motivation and interest. All subjects may not be equally interested in the experiment nor motivated to participate wholly, yet, in most situations, they are usually willing to follow directions and do their best. Experienced researchers know the frustration that occurs when subjects refuse or are unable to give a maximum effort when one is called for or when they continually miss appointments. Still, some subjects may be lost from a study for one reason or another, so frequently the investigator will find that his sample size has shrunk during the course of the study. The repeated measures design in which the subjects must return to the laboratory several times is particularly frustrating, especially toward the end of the experiment when subject loss is most serious.

One technique that helps to assure adequate interest and motivation is to recruit subjects from a population known to the investigator. Although this practice may violate the assumptions of randomization, certain kinds of experiments demand excessive time and energy, and one simply must have the full cooperation of the individuals serving as subjects. Anything less than total cooperation may result in the collection of inconsistent and unreliable data.

Methodology

The manner of handling the various details of experiments is extremely important to the success of the research; many of these details can be foreseen by careful preparation before data collection. As will be emphasized repeatedly in the chapters to follow, the haphazard rush into the mainstream of testing frequently results in inadequate and inappropriate data collection. Some experiments are difficult to perform, some require rather technical background, and most require considerable precision. The detailed discussion of many of these aspects will be considered when the appropriate subject matter is considered. Several general factors related to methodology that bear on the control of experimental protocol will be discussed here.

1. Randomization. Not only should the subjects be selected randomly and assigned to treatment groups by random means, but the order with which the various treatments are given should also be arranged so that the order will not affect results. Especially important in repeated measures designs, a randomizing helps hold constant any learning or conditioning that may occur or other factors that could have a cumulative effect on the outcome.

For example, in a single group experiment, the subjects carried army packs of different types and amounts on 7.5 mile military marches; muscular fatigue from marching and carrying the packs was studied.[13] Over a period of several such marches, the strength and motor fitness of the subjects improved significantly. Thus, the subjects were in much better condition for pack carrying on the final march than on the first. Consequently, less muscular fatigue from carrying the final packs could be logically expected as a consequence of the conditioning; the real differences due to the main effects studied (muscular fatigue from pack carrying) are obscured. Although conditioning from repeated marches cannot be avoided, the effect of such conditioning can be equalized by distributing it evenly over the various carries. This distribution can be accomplished by a Latin-square arrangement.[14] One such Latin-square is as follows:

	Order of Treatments			
Groups I	*A*	*B*	*C*	*D*
II	*B*	*A*	*D*	*C*
III	*C*	*D*	*B*	*A*
IV	*D*	*C*	*A*	*B*

By way of explanation, suppose that four packs are to be carried by 24 subjects, each subject carrying each pack on a different march. Placement of the subjects into four groups of 6 each (I, II, III, IV) gives the sequence in which they are to proceed during the experiment. Therefore, subjects in

[13] H. Harrison Clarke, Clayton T. Shay, and Donald K. Mathews, "Strength Decrements from Carrying Various Army Packs on Military Marches," *Research Quarterly*, **26**, No. 3 (October 1955), 253.

[14] See Fisher and Yates, *op. cit.*, for a series of Latin-square arrangements.

group III, for example, would carry packs *C*, *D*, *B*, *A* in that order for the four marches.

2. Statistical control. Occasionally, in experimental research, factors may occlude the true findings, which either could not be controlled or were not taken into account during the planning phase of the study. The use of age of the subjects is a pertinent example of the distortion of a correlational analysis that could result if subjects of varying ages during the period of rapid growth were combined in the same sample. The correlation between two strength tests would be higher than would be true if homogeneous ages were employed. Because maturation results in an increase in size and muscle tissue, this results in greater strength, which tends to inflate the real correlation. The way to cope with such a situation is to use partial correlation whereby the effect of such tertiary factors may be statistically partialled out of the correlation.

Investigator

Investigators must possess the technical qualifications to handle the detailed phases of data collection. The necessary qualifications are dependent upon the type of experiment conducted and so are specific. On the other hand, some things are more general in nature, which tend to permeate a number of experimental designs and seek to add some control to the gathering of data.

1. Personal characteristics of the investigator. The fact that so much of experimental research involves the direct contact by the investigator with his subjects prompts this brief discussion of the personal characteristics of the investigator. Obviously, if volunteer subjects are employed and if they receive no remuneration for their efforts, the researcher is asking them to devote time and energy to his work. The extent to which he makes them welcome and treats them considerately during the arduous periods will largely determine how well they perform. It is something of an art to drive subjects, sometimes to exhausting efforts, and yet at the same time not antagonize them. The zeal, enthusiasm, and personality of the investigator are essential characteristics for ensuring full subject cooperation. Moreover, when the testing phase may last several weeks, it is also difficult for the investigator to maintain proper decorum and still be pleasant and interested after many hours of repetitious and technical work. In order to counteract any such situations, the systematic rotation of testing sequence (Latin-square) may be desirable in order to prevent him from exerting undue influences on one group and not on the others.

2. Hawthorne effect. A number of years ago reports emerged from the study of factory workers in General Electric Company's Hawthorne plant, where conditions that should have reduced productivity were imposed. However, this did not occur, but productivity did not result from the physical conditions. The reason was attributed to group solidarity that accompanied the special attention these workers received. Apparently, this attention resulted in the development of an informal social cohesiveness among the worker subjects, which increased their motivation; as a consequence, productivity actually increased. As suggested by Hanson,[15] the manner of dealing with experimental subjects over a period of time may develop the same type of esprit de corps on the part of those in the group that alone may enhance performance. On the other hand, control subjects who are tested before and after the experimental period and who are not seen during the interim time would not be expected to exhibit this trait. The investigator should be alert to the presence of this phenomenon.

INSTRUMENTATION

Scientific research carries the impression that a formal laboratory is required; in many disciplines, this is correct. In physical education, however, a number of settings may be employed, including a formal laboratory to be sure but it should not be so limited; the playing field, track, gymnasium, pool, or other facility may be just as functional for the needs of many experiments.

Regardless of locale, however, the need is apparent for kinds of instruments that are specific to the research anticipated. Such instruments will be considered in succeeding chapters that deal with study areas available to physical education. In discussing instrumentation here, attention is given to the individual who uses instruments. A differentiation is made between what the instrument *can* do and what the operator is *able* to do when testing human subjects.

Precision

A major concern of the investigator in deciding on the feasibility of a study is whether or not the measurement tools are available. If not, either the study will need to be abandoned or proper instruments must first be designed and constructed. However, the availability of an instrument is not enough, as the investigator must be qualified to use it properly; he must be able to use it with *precision*. Just how precise must the measurement be to secure valid data? This has been a perplexing problem with investigators; at first, many have been inclined to say "as precise as possible." However,

---

[15] Dale L. Hanson, "Influence of the Hawthorne Effect Upon Physical Education Research," *Research Quarterly*, 38, No. 4 (December 1967), 723.

this is not true; the decision must be based upon logical and statistical grounds and upon matters related to systematic or variable error that can be tolerated.

Instruments are available in the various fields of science and technology to measure factors with the most extreme precision; occasionally physical educators bemoan the fact that strength must be measured with dynamometers and tensiometers, which do not have such great precision. Yet, it may be shown in the statistical analysis, for example, that little difference occurs between a manuometer that can be read to $\frac{1}{10}$ kg than for one that can be read to $\frac{1}{100}$ kg, assuming that the typical range of grip strength values in a sample of individuals is 30 kg. In other words, the addition of greater accuracy might make the investigator feel better, but the resultant gain would be trivial as related to the study's results.

The back and leg dynamometer is a cruder instrument than the manuometer, as the typical scale values are given in increments of 10 pounds. Still, this instrument is very useful in obtaining leg lift measures where the range is likely to be 1,000 pounds and more. Much the same argument may be used when employing timers to test human performance. Reaction time and speed of movement studies have widely employed electric chronoscopes that measure to .01 sec. Actually then, times may be read to the nearest .001 sec, which obviates the necessity for more precise methods, since simple reaction time may average approximately .17 sec, with the range of values somewhere between, say, .12 and .22 sec. On the other hand, a simple stop watch may be adequate for the timing of a short running event where the precision is to .1 sec over a range of several seconds. In longer runs, such as 300 and 400 yards, testing in full seconds may be adequate for some uses in physical education research.

1. Systematic error. Error may be classified in two ways, as far as this discussion is concerned; these are systematic error and variable error. For systematic error, *true* scores may not be absolutely essential to the purposes of the investigation, so long as the error involved affects all scores in the same way. However, it is best to reduce systematic error as much as possible. Calibration of testing instruments is one way of taking care of this problem; the investigator should make such calibrations at the beginning of the experiment and as often as may be necessary during the period of data collection. Manufacturer's specifications that accompany an instrument, even dial faces, have been improperly applied or are out of alignment. Thus, all sensitive items of equipment should be compared with known standards, and a conversion chart should be prepared that can be used during testing. If this proves cumbersome, it may be permissible to use some other scheme and apply a *standard* correction later to means and standard deviations. This will not be acceptable if the error is not systematic, and it underlines the necessity for determining the instrumental precision by actual calibration.

Moreover, if the instrument changes its characteristics during the course of the experiment, a corresponding lack of accuracy will result; unfortunately, such a change may go undetected.

Other sources of systematic error may be reduced by carefully standardizing all the pertinent aspects of testing, such as subject position, placement of straps, electronics, and other devices and keeping motivation, temperature, and fatigue constant so that the response of the subject is not influenced by tertiary factors.

2. Variable error. No matter how much care is taken to ensure that the instruments are calibrated and the testing procedures standardized, a certain amount of error is inherent in the testing process. It is nearly impossible to avoid some error, especially where human effort is involved. Yet, the investigator must do all in his power to reduce it to a minimum. Practice in reading instruments and interpolating between divisions will enable greater consistency and a reduction in reading error.

An important discussion of errors in measurement is presented by Henry and others[16] who point out that variable errors are random, varying irregularly and unsystematically, and are presumably uncorrelated. Moreover, the removal of several small errors will affect the total error by only a small amount: "the elimination of any variable error no larger than a third of the total error is ordinarily a waste of time." On the other hand, large errors may disturb the data collection, so every effort must be made to reduce them through greater testing precision.

Before any investigator collects test data for a study, he should practice the tests under authoritative supervision and should demonstrate his testing competency. Testing competency may be demonstrated by obtaining test-retest objectivity coefficients that are equal to those reported for the test. The test should be given independently by the trainee and a competent tester to the same subjects. This process should be continued until the correlation between the two testers is satisfactory. For example, the objectivity coefficients of the various cable-tension strength tests exceed .90. Until the neophyte tester achieves this goal, he should not collect test scores for scientific studies.

Reliability

Reliability will be discussed here, as it is closely allied to instrumental procedures, although the focus of attention is on the subject rather than on

[16] Franklin M. Henry, *et al.*, "Errors in Measurement," in *Research Methods Applied to Health, Physical Education and Recreation* (Washington, D.C.: American Association for Health, Physical Education and Recreation, 1952), Ch. 19.

the test. An additional source of error is present when the performance of human subjects is measured. Such error is available in two forms, as trial-to-trial variability (intraindividual difference variance) and as subject-to-subject variability (interindividual difference variance), both of which are ordinarily large when compared with the error variance discussed above.

In computational terms, Henry[17] has expressed the test-retest reliability coefficient as the "true score" variance divided by the total variance. The "true" measure of individual differences is said to be the interindividual difference variance (σ_t^2), and the total variance consists of the sum of interindividual difference variance (σ_t^2), intraindividual difference variance (σ_i^2), and variable errors of measurement (σ_e^2). The calculation of the reliability coefficient will decline in proportion to the intraindividual difference and variable error variance. If the latter is small, as should be the case, it may have but slight influence on the magnitude of the correlation, thus, the reliability may well be related to the consistency from trial-to-trial of the subjects' performance. On the other hand, systematic errors, provided they affect all scores to the same proportion, will have no affect at all. In order to enhance test-retest reliability, one method is to increase the replications, which will increase reliability in direct proportion to the square root of the number of trials.[18]

ESTABLISHING THE RESEARCH LABORATORY

Many large universities that offer programs for advanced degrees in health and physical education have well-established research laboratories, some of which rival the best in the life sciences on their respective campuses. Others are less well-equipped but are nevertheless quite serviceable. The discussion here is not directed toward these institutions, as they have committed themselves to the dictum that a research laboratory is a vital and essential part of faculty research and graduate study. However, not all students studying research methods will be destined for employment in such institutions, nor will they be advising graduate student research right away; yet, they may feel the need for establishing programs of their own and eventually inaugurating graduate study. For these reasons, the ensuing discussion will be directed to the establishment of a research laboratory.

A persistent lament heard from individuals teaching in small colleges, community colleges, public schools, and in some universities is that they do not have a research laboratory and therefore—it follows—they cannot do

---

[17] Franklin M. Henry, "Reliability, Measurement Error, and Intra-Individual Difference," *Research Quarterly*, 30, No. 1 (March 1959), 21.

[18] See Chapter 10 for a discussion of reliability and the determination of the standard error of the mean.

research. Nothing is farther from the truth, for in fact, a formal and well-equipped laboratory is not of itself the most important factor in the pursuit of scholarly problems. Obviously, there will be some things that will be extremely difficult to accomplish without a certain type of facility, but this is more of a problem of selection and feasibility of investigations to be made. Problems can be selected for which little special equipment is needed. In such a situation, it will be necessary to start slowly and gradually increase in complexity as more money and facilities become available. The emphasis is correctly placed on getting started.

It is deplorable how few graduate students think of themselves as researchers or who lack confidence that they can make a contribution to the field as scientists. Somehow, many feel that research is up to someone else with more qualified experience. It is understandable how master's degree candidates who are experiencing graduate study for the first time might not be imbued with the desire to do research, but it is inconceivable that this would happen with doctoral candidates. Perhaps the difficulty is in the mistaken impression that teaching and research are separate entities and that when a person desires a teaching career it is at the exclusion of a research career. Obviously, such is not the case; for example, in health and physical education, almost every member of the Research Council of AAHPER is also a teacher or professor. As outlined in earlier chapters, it is the unshakable belief of the authors that the most effective teacher—even of activities—is one who continually engages in some research and is conversant with the research conducted in his area of endeavor.

Inaugurating the Laboratory

A research laboratory is any room that is available to conduct experiments; the basic prerequisite is that it permits one to obtain valid data. Thus, a gymnasium, pool, track, or supply room might be acceptable, depending on the problem to be investigated. Equipment may be locked up with other supply items and equipment of the health and physical education programs. The room may be used for other classes when not used as a laboratory; or vice versa, a room may be used for a laboratory during periods of the day when it is not in use for classes, intramurals, or varsity athletics. Researchers have been known to collect data in their offices or in the shower room (where an ample supply of water is available) and even to transport equipment from school to school to test boys and girls in corners of gymnasiums, on auditorium stages, and elsewhere. The major consideration is that the data must be obtained accurately; frequently, this may be done without the use of a formal suite of rooms labeled "laboratory."

The experience of many in research when no laboratory as such was available has been to utilize whatever facilities that may be at hand, to be satisfied with any progress that can be made, and to maintain steady productivity. When the individual can demonstrate that he has a sustained desire and ability to develop a problem and carry it through to completion, this demonstration constitutes a powerful argument when requesting additional equipment or facilities.

One of the prime times for inaugurating the research laboratory is at the time of new construction, when a new health and physical education facility is being planned. The inclusion of space for a research laboratory is a wise investment for the future, because at this time the room may be adequately fitted with proper electrical outlets, hot water, shielded for electrical interference, equipped with gas and vacuum lines, and so forth. Provisions may also be made for building in equipment, such as treadmills, environmental chambers, observation rooms, and the like; such items would be much more difficult to obtain at a later time. Frequently, approval for construction of a new building carries with it the purchase of needed equipment. Thus, this is an ideal time to obtain the essential equipment for research, as a new and functional research laboratory is instantly available.

Finances

The manner of financing a research laboratory in physical education should be essentially the same as in other departments of the university, that is, through the departmental budget. The basic facility and primary operating equipment should be planned over a period of time and supported in a manner similar to other departmental items. Included as the laboratory staff are research laboratory assistants, technicians, and custodians.

The tendency today is to obtain funds from extramural sources in the form of research grants, which, of course, is an excellent way of supporting specific research projects that sometimes last for several years. The investigator should bear in mind that grants such as these must be actively sought, correctly proposed, accurately written up, and submitted to the appropriate agency. Upon approval and funding, it is incumbent for the researcher to carry the project through to completion, including the submission of whatever written reports are required.

The appropriation of outside funds for research is very intriguing. However, the researcher may also find that intramural grants are available from his own institution. Although these may not be as large financially, at least they may provide basic equipment for modest projects; known sometimes as "starter grants," their purpose for faculty members is to provide a stimulus for inaugurating a research program. The intent is to let other sources take over once the investigator has made an initial thrust. In a similar manner, such grants are often available to graduate students, particularly doctoral candidates, to assist in the completion of the thesis requirement as well as for other aspects of the research program. The student should investigate these sources on his campus.

The inauguration of a research laboratory in most places will be supported by individual departments and will more than likely begin inauspiciously with a modest budget. The ultimate quality of the research is not dependent as much upon great financial support as it is on the ability of the personnel. Given properly prepared investigators, important contributions to science may be made on a low budget and modest facilities.

Suggestions for a Comprehensive Laboratory

Standard plans for a research laboratory in physical education are not available, just as there can be no standard research program. Similarities from one institution to another will be noted because there are some functions that seem to be universally accepted; even though the physical proportions of rooms differ, the utilitarian aspects are quite similar. In fact, there are some aspects of laboratory work in physical education that would resemble functions in other fields of study. For example, biochemical analysis must hold to the same rigorous standards wherever carried out. Thus, the growth of laboratories proceeds first of all from the needs of the investigators who will be using them. Except in the instance where a new facility is being planned, it is essential that the laboratory be sufficiently functional to handle the collection and analysis of data of those problems most likely to be pursued. Second, expansion should accommodate those future needs—both real and proposed—that will arise as a result of faculty growth and graduate student expansion. Little is gained in spending funds that are needed for other things on a fully equipped biochemical laboratory if the technical personnel are not available.

The main ingredients that are required in a comprehensive research laboratory parallel the subject matter in physical education as set forth in succeeding chapters and dictated by types of problems anticipated. It would be inappropriate to predict specific needs at the start, so the facility requirements may be stated rather generally, with brief notes concerning broad categories of use. One room, of course, may be available for multiple uses; the sizes will vary, and the general architectural layout must be determined according to criteria associated with local requirements. The following facilities should receive consideration in developing a research laboratory.

1. Biochemical laboratory. The inclusion of such a facility as a laboratory for chemical analysis of blood, gas, tissues, and so forth, will depend upon the personnel available to support such an enterprise. An affirmative answer will mean that considerable planning is necessary for its construction. Consideration must be given to sinks and counter tops that are resistant to corrosion, gas lines, vacuum lines, hooded ovens, cabinets, and a refrigerator. Centrifuges, autoclaves, and other items of equipment, plus the array of chemicals, glassware, and other items are needed to support biochemical analyses. This facility adds considerable sophistication to research, and it provides for an ideal teaching station for advanced experimental research. But sophisticated personnel are also needed to operate it.

2. *Cardiovascular laboratory.* The collection of data on problems in exercise physiology must take place away from the biochemical laboratory, although in planning the two may be adjacent. Depending upon whether or not chemical work is to be done, the collection of gas for analysis will require certain techniques and analyses, so the cardiovascular laboratory should require such things as environmental chambers, treadmills, recorders, and sufficient electrical outlets.

3. *Animal laboratory.* A trend noted today in exercise physiology is the development of research with small animals, usually the laboratory rat. A room set aside for such purposes should be planned in terms of the intended use, especially with regard to the number of animals to be housed at any one time and the type of devices for exercising them. In construction, consideration should be given to temperature control, automatic light control so as to rotate periods of light and darkness, and deodorization. This laboratory will require a supply of water and will need sinks and counter space as well as a dissection table and other accessories. At the same time, thought should be given to adequate disposal of wastes as well as to sterilizing cages and water bottles.

4. *Kinesiology laboratory.* The study of problems requiring motion analysis may require a slightly higher ceiling than rooms for other research, so this should be investigated and weighed against the probable extra cost involved in construction. If at all possible, thought should be given to the question of cinematography, the placement of overhead cameras, and lights for indoor filming. In addition, it may be necessary to screen the room or part of the room for use with electromyographic equipment.

5. *Photography laboratory.* More than just a dark room, the modern photography laboratory offers facilities for developing film, enlarging of prints, both in black and white and in color, analyzing motion analysis film and meeting the general requirements necessary for high speed photography. This laboratory should be located adjacent to the kinesiology laboratory.

6. *Motor learning laboratory.* The basic requirement for the majority of motor learning studies is to provide an area that is quiet and relatively free

of traffic—where subjects can concentrate on tasks and not be disturbed. The amount of room needed will depend upon the nature of the experimentation to be undertaken.

7. General testing room. A number of research projects of a general nature will simply require a room where testing may be done; in some instances, the gymnasium, the playing field, or the pool may be utilized. Such facilities would be needed for tests of motor fitness, motor performance, strength, anthropometry, ergometry, and circulatory-respiratory functions.

8. Faculty research facilities. Thought should be given to providing space for faculty members to do their research, either in terms of a separate laboratory or a space within the main laboratory. Perhaps a small cubicle could house specific equipment, including a desk or work table, in which the faculty member could establish a working area outside his main office. Such resources may be important in encouraging faculty participation in research problems.

9. Shop. One of the most important adjuncts to any experimental laboratory is a shop where repairs of equipment may be made or new equipment may be fashioned. Much of the apparatus used in research cannot be purchased commercially, so the necessity for including a shop, equipped with the necessary power tools and all the supportive paraphernalia, should not be underestimated. Sending items away for repairs or contracting for each new apparatus needed is not only time-consuming but also quite expensive. Even better is the provision of a trained mechanical or electrical engineer who will maintain the shop and help plan and solve the problems of equipment raised by the investigator.

10. Offices. The well-equipped modern research laboratory should be planned with office space adjoining so that proper supervision is provided. Enough space should be included for both faculty and graduate research assistants.

11. Computer laboratory. No research facility is complete without a computer laboratory with a sufficient number of calculators to handle peak traffic in data analysis and to support courses in statistics. The area selected for this purpose may be a rather small room, in comparison to some of the others in the laboratory, but thought should be given to adequate lighting and soundproofing.

A list of common items of research laboratory equipment is not provided here. However, a Committee in Research Laboratory Equipment is maintained by the Research Council, AAHPER. Periodically, this committee issues a list of such equipment with names and addresses of the distributors. For several years, J. Grove Wolf, University of Wisconsin, has chaired this committee.

SUMMARY

The largest proportion of research in physical education involves the experimental method, which makes use of a laboratory environment. Knowledge of the various forms of methodology is important because it assists the investigator in organizing and carrying out his research. One of the most important aspects of this problem concerns an understanding of the use of adequate experimental controls; it is essential to know when to use a control group so that the magnitude of the main effects can be known.

Among the simple experimental designs, the following have been emphasized: the single group design, the repeated measures design, the random group design, and the related group design. The majority of experiments in the past have employed some form of these methods, although more complex designs, such as the factorial designs, are becoming popular with advanced students.

The researcher must be acquainted with various means of controlling experimental factors, in addition to selection of the proper design. Subjects themselves constitute an essential part of research; matters pertaining to their randomization and selection according to age, sex, and physical ability are crucial to success in the experiment as well as to the maintaining of motivation and interest of the participants. Beyond these factors are considerations of rotation of treatments and other means of exerting statistical control.

A major concern of the investigator is the selection of proper instruments, whether or not the testing takes place in the formal confines of a research laboratory. Questions of validity help decide the precision that is required for the measurement of selected variables; it is possible to be overly precise in some cases and yet not sufficiently exact in others. Each problem must be decided on its own merits, and each will involve considerations of systematic and variable errors. The question of error may also involve a subject's repeated response to a test as well as the variance between subjects, all of which concern reliability.

Establishing a research laboratory is a growing function of higher education, although it usually remains for the larger universities to develop the comprehensive facility. The size does not reflect necessarily negatively on the quality of the research, for very important work has grown from rather meager beginnings. When developing a laboratory, a number of considerations must be made relative to the needs and the projected type of research to be undertaken.

SELECTED REFERENCES

Donnelly, Richard J., "Laboratory Research in Physical Education," *Research Quarterly*, 31, No. 2 (May 1960), 232.

Fisher, R., and F. Yates, *Statistical Tables for Biological, Agricultural, and Medical Research*. New York: Hafner Publishing Co., 1957.

Good, Carter V., *Introduction to Educational Research* (2nd ed.), New York: Appleton-Century-Crofts, 1963.

Henry, Franklin M., "Reliability, Measurement Error, and Intra-Individual Difference," *Research Quarterly*, 30, No. 1 (March 1959), 21.

Henry, Franklin M., *et al.*, "Errors in Measurement," in *Research Methods Applied to Health, Physical Education and Recreation* (1st ed.), Washington, D.C.: American Association for Health, Physical Education and Recreation, 1952.

Hunsicker, Paul, "A Survey of Laboratory Facilities in College Physical Education Departments," *Research Quarterly*, 21, No. 4 (December 1950), 420.

Morehouse, Laurence E., and Eugene R. O'Connell, "A Plan for Gradually Equipping a Physical Education Research Laboratory," *Journal of Health, Physical Education and Recreation*, 29, No. 9 (December 1958), 28.

Winer, B. J., *Statistical Principles in Experimental Design*. New York: McGraw-Hill Book Company, 1962.

CHAPTER 13

Physiology of Exercise

The study of exercise and its physiology forms a sizable portion of the research activity in physical education. The methods employed are generally experimental, and the techniques are usually scientific. A wide variety of procedures is available for the solution of problems; others are being refined and continually developed to fit the multitude of special requirements dictated by current needs. The development of a specific instrument that will adequately assess the characteristics of some physiological variable may involve the coordinated efforts of professor and student for numerous hours. These requirements cannot be anticipated here, as science is changing and moving much too rapidly; any concerted effort to look into the future would be immediately doomed to failure as being at once inept and ultimately nearsighted. To claim an increased reliance upon automatic and electronic devices is begging the issue. Almost any scientific field can see such evidences, but the larger question is the use to which such devices will be put, that is, the specific problems to be solved. It would seem that before exercise physiologists can deal with problems of work on the moon, they must first solve them on earth.

A clear differentiation of research does not exist between what is considered to be physiology and what is exercise physiology. As outlined briefly in Chapter 1, the physiological factors that relate to movement, including immediate (exercise) and long-term (training) aspects would typify the field of physiology of exercise. Although the bulk of past research has emphasized human performance, increasingly greater attention has been given to animal studies, notably those employing rats. At any rate, the methods and techniques needed require the same degree of care and precision for physiologist or physical educator, and certain variables appear common to both. In presenting material for this chapter some of the most common techniques are given. No single volume could contain a complete documentation of all tests considered as physiology of exercise, nor could each be completely documented. A compromise is in order for both considerations. Thus, the techniques that have been selected offer some solution to recurring problems; the references given are selective and, in many cases, offer further sources of pertinent material.

MUSCULAR STRENGTH

One of the oldest and most basic techniques to be used for research in physical education is the assessment of muscular strength. Various devices have been used, including spring scales, dynamometers, strain gauges, myometers, and tensiometers. Many combinations exist, such as the electronic myodynagraph[1] and the California hand ergograph,[2] but all serve a primary purpose: to obtain a measure of maximum strength. Perhaps the simplest and most widely used is the cable tensiometer. This instrument is small and compact and has the advantage of being extremely versatile; adequate documentation and current description of 38 strength tests are described by Clarke and Clarke.[3]

The current concern has been less with developing new devices than with understanding the characteristics of muscular contraction and relating strength to other variables. Actually, strength is becoming thought of as less an entity unto itself as the end result of the excitation-contraction coupling sequence that requires the activation of motor units. Although under conscious control of the will, volitional contraction involves coordination by higher nervous centers; thus, the strength in action can be seen as an expression of neuromotor coordination and helps explain the lack of correlation between measured muscular strength and the speed of limb movement.[4] Such tasks are highly specific.

Although the inherent properties and characteristics of the contractile elements of muscle are the primary responsibility of the biochemist and physiologist, the *in vivo* investigation of the contraction characteristics, while the muscle-tendon-joint complex remains intact, is the responsibility of the physical educator. Attempts at the quantitative assessment of the uptake and release of muscular tension have revealed the mathematical parameters to be quite distinctive and reproducible from one sample to another;

---

[1] Willis C. Beasley, "Instrumentation and Equipment for Quantitative Clinical Muscle Testing," *Archives of Physical Medicine and Rehabilitation*, 37, No. 10 (October 1956), 604.

[2] George Q. Rich, "Muscular Fatigue Curves of Boys and Girls," *Research Quarterly*, 31, No. 3 (October 1960), 485.

[3] H. Harrison Clarke and David H. Clarke, *Developmental and Adapted Physical Education* (Englewood Cliffs, N.J.: Prentice-Hall, Inc., 1963), pp. 73–96.

[4] F. M. Henry and J. D. Whitley, "Relationships Between Individual Differences in Strength, Speed, and Mass in an Arm Movement," *Research Quarterly*, 31, No. 1 (March 1960), 24.

these attempts have been helpful in comparing the effects of fatigue[5] and temperature[6] on the contraction.

Essentially, one needs to have available a device for exerting force and at the same time recording the tension on fast moving paper. Many ways of doing so are available, which will be discussed subsequently, but the recorder must have a minimum paper speed of 150 mm per sec in order to spread out the contraction that has a half-time of approximately .08 sec. The half-time of release is faster (.04 sec), and analysis at this paper speed becomes very difficult. Once the record has been obtained, serial measures are made at intervals of convenience for adequate analysis and interpretation. These must be rather frequent as the literature indicates the curve form to be fast-changing and to contain multiple components. The details of curve fitting will be discussed subsequently.

A search of the literature very quickly reveals the extensive manner in which strength measurements have been used in research studies. In its usual sense, this has meant maximal strength, and measures have ordinarily been isometric in nature. The trend seems further established that to assess the quantity of muscular strength of an individual, multiple tests must be given. This has been true for the construction of tests[7] and for their application.[8] For a presentation of the results of a large number of such efforts, the reader is directed to a recent monograph on the subject.[9]

MUSCULAR FATIGUE/ENDURANCE

Instrumentation

The systematic repetitive contraction of muscles is known to produce fatigue, and since the early work of Mosso,[10] it has been a prime target for

---

[5] Joseph Royce, "Force-Time Characteristics of the Exertion and Release of Hand Grip Strength Under Normal and Fatigued Conditions," *Research Quarterly*, 33, No. 3 (October 1962), 444.

[6] David H. Clarke and Joseph Royce, "Rate of Muscle Tension Development and Release under Extreme Temperatures," *Int. Z. angew. Physiol. einschl. Arbeitsphysiol.*, 19 (1962), 330.

[7] H. Harrison Clarke and Theodore G. Schopf, "Construction of a Muscular Strength Test for Boys in Grades Four, Five, and Six," *Research Quarterly*, 33, No. 4 (December 1962), 515.

[8] H. Harrison Clarke and Kay H. Petersen, "Contrast of Maturational, Structural, and Strength Characteristics of Athletes and Nonathletes 10 to 15 Years of Age," *Research Quarterly*, 32, No. 2 (May 1961), 163.

[9] H. Harrison Clarke, *Muscular Strength and Endurance in Man* (Englewood Cliffs, N.J.: Prentice-Hall, Inc., 1966), Ch. 6.

[10] Angelo Mosso, *Fatigue*, trans. M. and W. B. Drummond (New York: G. P. Putnam's Sons, 1906).

research. Whether or not one is concerned with the reduction in strength, called fatigue, or its reciprocal, endurance, a desire to understand muscular behavior under a variety of experimental conditions has been evident. The most obvious muscle groups studied have been those of the arm and shoulder because of the ease of management and the amount of flexibility. However, the differences in muscle position about the joints make direct comparisons of performance difficult; this situation has resulted in the usual practice of employing a single muscle group for all comparisons. Apparently, rather pronounced differences in work production exist in various sites about the body so that eventually all should be studied.

The basic requirement for investigating muscular fatigue is to possess an instrument that will permit the detailed quantification of repetitive effort. In the past, two types of devices have been prominent in the literature. First

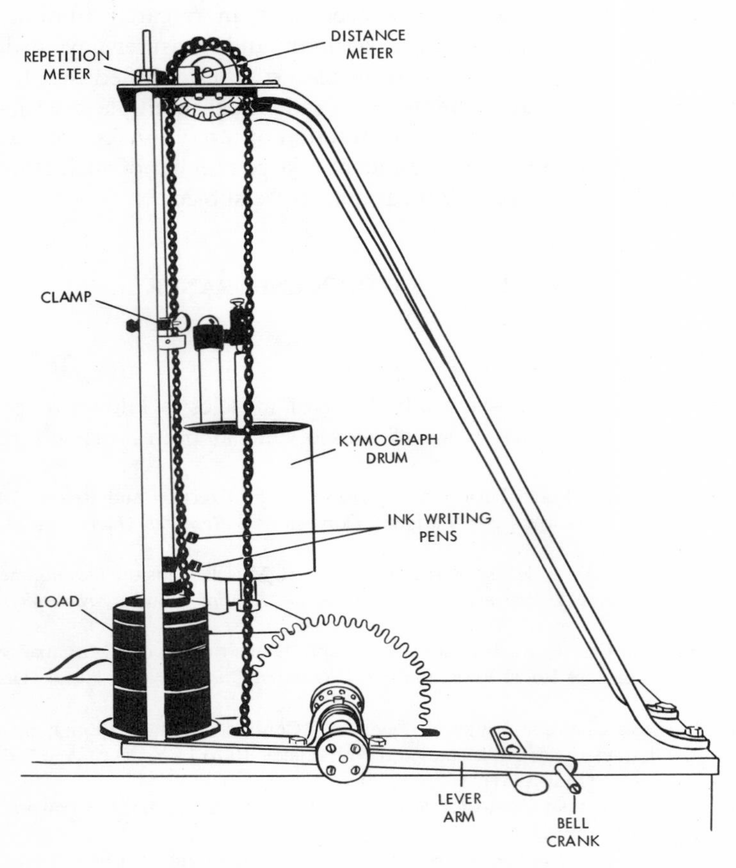

Figure 15. Kelso-Hellebrandt Ergograph

are the Kelso-Hellebrandt ergographs designed for finger and wrist, radioulnar, elbow and shoulder, thumb, and grip. These ergographs are weight loaded, since weights must be placed on a carriage for the subject to raise and lower, usually according to a fixed rhythm and often at a percentage of the subject's maximal strength. The details concerning load and cadence were established by carefully controlled experimentation over a number of years, as were the conditions associated with optimum work output.[11] An illustration of the Kelso-Hellebrandt elbow-shoulder ergograph appears in Figure 15.

The second device is the California spring loaded ergograph used in studies of muscular fatigue of the hand-gripping muscles.[12] Employing an adjustable Smedley hand dynamometer, a mechanical connection is made to an ink-writing pen attached to a writing table and paper drive unit driven by a high speed monodrum (see Figure 16). Thus, changes in muscular tension

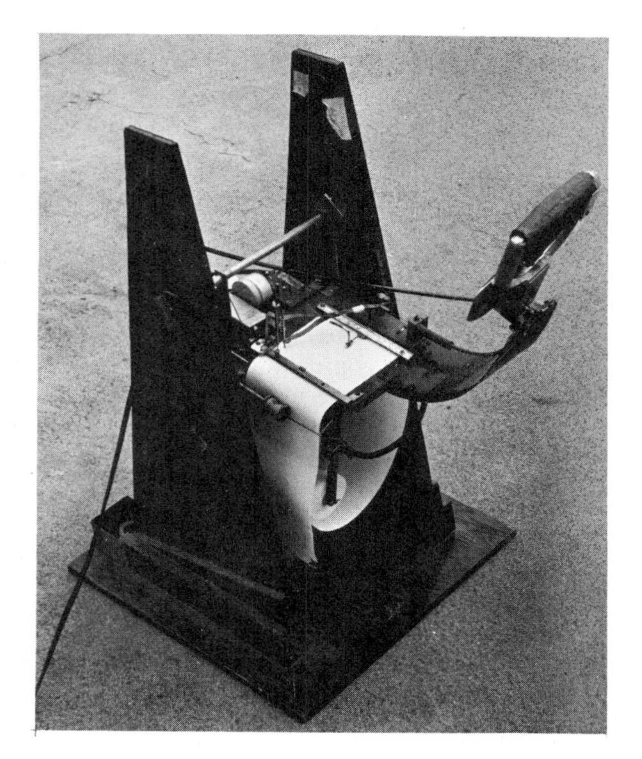

Figure 16. California Spring-Loaded Hand Ergograph

---

[11] Clarke, *op. cit.*, Chs. 3, 4.

[12] Rich, *op. cit.*

are transmitted directly to the recording paper by virtue of the change in hand movement, according to an 8-to-1 ratio. Calibration with known weights permits an accurate assessment of strength at any time by direct measurement of the fatigue record. In all instances, the force of exertion is given by continuous recording so that the contraction-by-contraction progress of fatigue can be obtained for isotonic exercise; for isometric fatigue, the force at any time can be measured by extrapolation from the beginning of exercise, provided that the paper speed is known.

A variety of other devices exists, ranging from force transducers[13] to strain gauges.[14] One currently in use is the Maryland dynograph, consisting of a load cell and recorder. The load cell[15] translates changes in force into changes in voltage, the sensitive element of which is bound by special strain gauges. These form a balanced Wheatstone bridge so that changes in force on the cell will change the resistance of the gauges and thus produce a change in the output voltage, which is subsequently amplified and monitored by a recorder.[16] The advantage gained by this system is its versatility; the assembly can be adapted to nearly any muscle group desired, whether strong or weak. A special hand-grip device permits measurement of the hand and forearm flexors; standard straps, similar to those used in cable-tension strength tests, may be employed for other limb attachments. The load cell is not rigidly anchored, because tortional movements will cause spurious recordings; rather, it must be held at right angles to the limb and in direct series with any attachments. The position on the extremity of the strap or the angle of pull of the joint are matters of choice, although the optimum angles for strength application are known.[17]

The two basic exercise patterns employing spring loaded ergography have been isotonic and isometric contractions. The recording of all repetitions beginning with initial maximum to final strength allows the sampling of strength at appropriate intervals on the fatigue record. This arrangement permits a detailed mathematical analysis of fatigue[18,19] and recovery.[20]

[13] P. A. Merton, "Voluntary Strength and Fatigue," *Journal of Physiology*, 123, No. 3 (1954), 553.

[14] A. R. Lind, "Muscle Fatigue and Recovery from Fatigue Induced by Sustained Contractions," *Journal of Physiology*, 147, No. 1 (1959), 162.

[15] Suggested source: Type U–1 Load Cell, Baldwin-Lima-Hamilton Corp., Waltham, Mass.

[16] Suggested source: Type RS Dynograph, Beckman Instruments, Inc., Schiller Park, Ill.

[17] Clarke, *op. cit.*, Ch. 2.

[18] Joel E. Grose, "Depression of Muscle Fatigue Curves by Heat and Cold," *Research Quarterly*, 29, No. 1 (March 1958), 19.

[19] Joseph Royce, "Isometric Fatigue Curves in Human Muscle with Normal and Occluded Circulation," *Research Quarterly*, 29, No. 2 (May 1958), 204.

[20] David H. Clarke, "Strength Recovery from Static and Dynamic Muscular Fatigue," *Research Quarterly*, 33, No. 3 (October 1962), 349.

They were found to progress toward their asymptote in an exponential manner under control of a rate constant. In other words, the progress of fatigue and its recovery are nonlinear. Knowledge of the various components that describe these curves has permitted a greater understanding of the underlying physiology that is taking place. For example, the time characteristics of blood flow in isometric contraction appear far different from those in isotonic activity. The extent of these differences can be seen more clearly by appropriate mathematical analysis.

The following section is thus presented to acquaint the reader with the technical aspects of curve analysis as applied to the single component equation found in dynamic exercise; more complicated curve forms require additional steps. Consultation with a reference such as Riggs[21] will help by adding necessary background information and providing models for further use.

Exponential Curve Analysis

The exponential theory, as applied to dynamic muscular fatigue, operates under the assumption that a certain fraction of the available energy stores are used up by each contraction, considering only the work of the muscle over and above that of the steady state. Thus, a decrease in work output in any given contraction will always be a constant proportion of the contraction that was immediately preceding rather than a constant value. For example, if the first contraction involved 50 kg of force and there were a 10 per cent reduction of each contraction, the second would be 45 kg, the third 40.5 kg, the fourth 36.45 kg, and so forth. In terms of units of time, the mathematical expression describing the force y at any time t would be

$$y_t = a_0 e^{-kt} + c$$

where a_0 is the amount of the first contraction above the asymptote c, e is the Naperian log base, and k is the rate constant. The numerical value of k is computed from the relationship $k = 0.693/t_{1/2}$ where $t_{1/2}$ represents the amount of time required for fatigue to progress from the initial force to one-half the amount of that force, considering only the amount of work above the asymptote. The value 0.693 derives from the fact that $e^{-0.693} = 1/2$. It should be noted that $t_{1/10}$ is frequently utilized; in this case $e^{-2.303} = 1/10$ and $k = 2.303/t_{1/10}$.

---

[21] Douglas S. Riggs, *The Mathematical Approach to Physiological Problems* (Baltimore: Williams & Wilkins, 1963), Ch. 6.

The following sequence may be employed to obtain the mathematical values, with the specific aim to determine the rate constant k:

1. Plot the measured strength means for each of the experimental points on regular coordinate graph paper with force on the ordinate and time on the abscissa.

2. Estimate the asymptote (c) by visual inspection. This is not necessarily final strength or the fatigue level, as an asymptote is a line that approaches a steady state but never reaches it even though extended to infinity.

3. Subtract the value of the asymptote from each of the experimental points.

4. Plot these residual values on semilogarithmic paper (two cycle paper will probably suffice).

5. Fit a straight line by eye to the points thus plotted. An exponential curve, when plotted on a semilogarithmic graph, yields a straight line; when this line accounts for all the points, it is a single component curve. When it fits only the latter points, and the early ones depart either positively or negatively, it suggests additional components and further analysis.

6. When the points in the latter portion of the curve fail to conform to a straight line, it may be necessary to revise the estimate of the asymptote and repeat steps 3 and 4. For example, if the points tend to fall away, lowering the asymptote will tend to bring them up; conversely, if the values rise above the line, raising the estimate of the asymptote will lower them. Because of the nature of semilogarithmic graphs, the early values are influenced by this technique less than the latter ones. It is an excellent practice to try several asymptotes to make certain that the best one is finally selected.

7. The intercept with the force at time zero is read as a_0, and represents the amount of fatigable strength at the outset of the experiment.

8. The amount of time required to drop from a_0 to one-half its value—$t_{1/2}$—is read from the graph.

9. The constant k is then computed by the half-time procedure as $0.693/t_{1/2}$.

10. In order to construct the smooth curve, the data obtained from the semilogarithmic analysis is calculated by reading the straight line intercept at each measurement point and by adding the constant value of c.

11. Each of these calculated values is plotted on coordinate graph paper as a smooth curve. The experimental points are then superimposed on the mathematical curve. When a proper analysis has been performed, and the curve follows the exponential law, the experimental values should fall closely on or near the mathematical curve.

Studies in Muscular Fatigue

The research involving muscular fatigue has extended over several decades. The student of exercise physiology may find the research studies selected here to be helpful as examples of studies dealing with the variables under discussion; a serious review of the literature must be undertaken in order to comprehend fully the vast range of data available.

In 1958, Clarke *et al.*,[22] utilized the Kelso-Hellebrandt ergograph to determine the conditions for optimum work output in muscles controlling elbow flexion, shoulder flexion, and grip ergography. They administered 25 different combinations of load and cadence to male subjects using a random group design (see Chapter 12); each session was limited to two minutes, and the ergographic lever arm kept constant at 8 inches. In some instances, a clear advantage was not demonstrated for one condition over another in cumulative work done. However, for elbow flexion ergography, the best combination was a load of $\frac{1}{4}$ proportion of elbow flexion strength and a cadence of 76. For shoulder flexion, the combination was $\frac{3}{4}$ proportion of strength and a cadence of 84; for grip ergography, $\frac{1}{2}$ proportion and a cadence of 76.

An illustration of spring loaded ergography employing an isometric condition in a repeated measures design was presented by Royce,[23] who examined fatigue curves of the forearm muscles. The subjects were given two exercise bouts, the first of which they held as a maximum static contraction for 90 sec. The second test was the same as the first, except that the circulation was occluded by a pressure cuff inflated about the upper arm at the outset of the exercise. To the point where the exerted force became less than approximately 60 per cent, no difference was found between the two curves; the nonoccluded force leveled off, whereas the occluded condition continued to diminish. Royce hypothesized that the muscular tension was sufficient to cause occlusion of blood flow during the first 50 sec; thus, there was a critical point where the internal muscle pressure just balanced systolic blood pressure. The entire curve was described by a mathematical equation of four components derived from the physiological factors involved.

A similar static exercise, but lasting two minutes, was given by Clarke and Stelmach.[24] However, for 10 min before and after exercise, the subjects immersed their arms in water of 46°C and 10°C; a control condition was administered in which no temperature change was induced. Following exercise, recovery of strength was examined at 1-min intervals. It was found that heat caused a decrease in initial strength, final strength, and total work but fatigable work remained unchanged. On the other hand, cold decreased

---

[22] H. Harrison Clarke, Everett A. Irish, Garland A. Trzynka, and William Popowich, "Conditions for Optimum Work Output in Elbow Flexion, Shoulder Flexion, and Grip Ergography," *Archives of Physical Medicine and Rehabilitation*, 39, No. 8 (August 1958), 475.

[23] Royce, *op. cit.*

[24] David H. Clarke and George E. Stelmach, "Muscular Fatigue and Recovery Curve Parameters at Various Temperatures," *Research Quarterly*, 37, No. 4 (December 1966), 468.

initial strength and fatigable work and increased final strength, while the total work done was the same as the controlled condition. Recovery of strength was more rapid for heat; cold had a retarding influence. Both exercise and recovery curves were described mathematically by exponential equations.

PERIPHERAL BLOOD FLOW

Instrumentation

The variation in volume of muscle resulting from exercise has been of interest since the seventeenth century. It was not until later that experiments indicated that the postexercise volume change was not due to enlargement of the muscle tissue per se but resulted from other factors. Supposedly, the hyperemia that follows exercise reflects increased blood flow, although the contraction of muscles results in temporary circulatory embarrassment.[25] Thus, interest has been focused on the postexercise circulation changes. These changes can be assessed in two ways: by measuring volume and by measuring flow.

The instrument utilized for this purpose is the plethysmograph. A large proportion of the literature reflects its use in conjunction with the arm and hand, although it has been used successfully with the leg.[26] Changes in volume may be measured with a volume plethysmograph and changes in blood flow with a venous occlusion plethysmograph. Of the two procedures, the volume measure is most straightforward. The essence of this technique is to place the limb into a water-filled or air-filled cylinder and monitor the volume change by the amount of displacement, as illustrated in Figure 17. The measurement may be made rather accurately if an outlet is provided at the base of the cylinder at an angle along the side of the water jacket. The scores obtained may be made in convenient units (usually millimeters) if a scale is placed behind the pipette. When necessary, this may be calibrated in terms of actual volume, although for statistical purposes little advantage is gained by this procedure. If a base line is established under control or resting conditions, the amount of volume change resulting from exercise, for example, is the difference between the initial and final levels. To ensure

---

[25] B. C. Abbott and R. J. Baskin, "Volume Changes in Frog Muscle During Contraction," *Journal of Physiology*, 161 (1962), 379.

[26] Don Lehmkuhl and C. J. Imig, "Measurement of Maximal Blood Flow Following a Standardized Fatiguing Exercise for Evaluation of the Functional Capacity of the Peripheral Circulation," *American Journal of Physical Medicine*, 40, No. 4 (August 1961), 146.

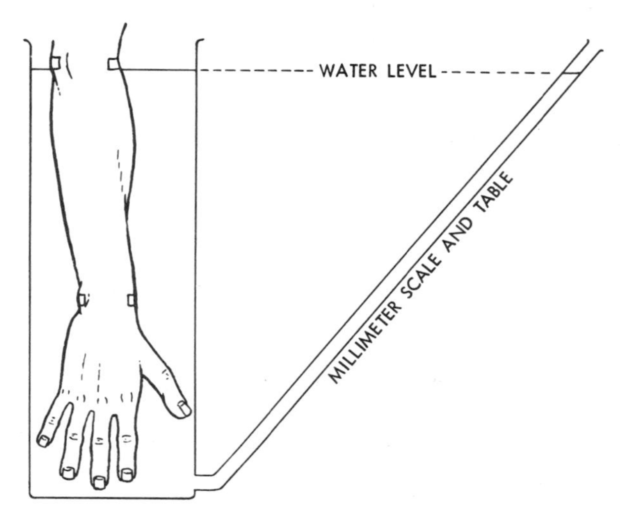

Figure 17. Arm Volume Plethysmograph

sufficient accuracy, especially if reimmersions are to be made, marks with flesh pencil or tape are essential as an aid to standardizing the procedure.

When an air plethysmograph is employed, every care must be taken to ensure a complete air seal at the points of insertion of the extremity. Once again a connection is made with the plethysmograph and the recording device, usually through a connecting tube, which is attached to a tambour and writing unit that, in turn, mechanically moves a pen against a kymograph. The kymograph paper may be smoked or the pen may be ink fed; at any rate, the expansion of the limb is transmitted via air column to the recording stylus.

The measurement of blood flow employs the venous occlusion plethysmograph, which contains the essential ingredients of the air volume plethysmograph. In order to measure the quantity of flow, a blood pressure cuff is placed about the extremity proximal to the plethysmograph and inflated to a pressure sufficient to occlude the venous flow but not the arterial flow (40 mm Hg is sufficient). In this manner, the blood continues to enter the extremity from the systemic circulation, but it cannot leave. Thus, the volume change can be monitored as the limb swells. Calibration can be made by introducing known air samples and measuring the displacement.

Various other methods are available for recording the volume changes besides the mechanical method utilizing tambour and pen. The increased use of biomedical instrumentation may permit the coupling of this phenomenon with other measures on the same recording. This may be accomplished with the use of a pressure transducer where the change in air pressure is detected and converted to an electrical signal and then magnified and reproduced on recording paper. This is costly for the single operation, but when multiple factors are to be studied, the additional cost for plethysmography is not great.

Studies in Blood Flow

From the studies involving assessment of peripheral blood flow, several are presented here to give an indication of the breadth of research. Bauer and Imig[27] employed the venous occlusion plethysmography to measure volume blood flow through the forearm before and after isometric and isotonic hand-grip exercises. The strength endurance index (SEI) was determined as the maximum force that could be maintained for 1 min; the subjects were given $\frac{1}{4}$ SEI and $\frac{1}{2}$ SEI, each maintained for 1 and 2 min. In the case of rhythmic exercise, the cadence varied from 30 to 60 contractions per min. The maximum levels of blood flow were similar following related intensities and duration of sustained and rhythmic exercise. The blood flow returned to normal more rapidly after isometric contractions than after isotonic exercise, and a proportionality existed between work done during exercise and maximum blood flow. Thus, the greater duration of blood flow following rhythmic exercise may mean that this is a better index of the functional status of the peripheral vascular bed.

A series of experiments were reported by Rohter and Hyman,[28] in which digital pulse and blood flow were measured while subjects performed various contractions on a hand dynamometer. Pressure of the hand against the dynamometer obliterated the digital pulse at approximately 25 per cent of maximum contraction and occluded the blood flow at 45 per cent. Apparently, the dynamometer compressed the superficial palmar arch artery first and then occluded the deep palmar arch artery. Inasmuch as maximum hand grip did not cause a measurable reduction in radial pulse wave, the point of occlusion was considered to be at some point distal to the muscles of the forearm. During strong contraction of the biceps, the radial pulse wave remained undiminished, which would indicate that occlusion during these conditions must occur immediately distal to the elbow, probably where the artery passes under the fascia of the biceps near its point of insertion.

---

[27] Adelia C. Bauer and C. J. Imig, "Blood Flow Through the Human Forearm Following Different Types, Intensities, and Durations of Exercise," *American Journal of Physical Medicine*, 38, No. 2 (April 1959), 48.

[28] Frank D. Rohter and Chester Hyman, "Blood Flow in Arm and Finger During Muscle Contraction and Joint Position Changes," *Journal of Applied Physiology*, 17, No. 5 (September 1962), 819.

Wilmore and Horvath[29] investigated the postexercise recovery patterns of blood flow following maximal exercise when the circulation to lower limbs was either unrestricted or restricted during the exercise period. The subjects were given an exhaustive maximal bicycle ergometer ride at 1500 kgm per min while the circulation was either unrestricted or the circulation to the lower limbs was arrested during the exercise. Blood flow was measured by venous occlusion plethysmography and heart rate by electrocardiogram. The occlusion of the lower extremities reduced the normal working capacity from $\frac{1}{3}$ to $\frac{1}{6}$, although the maximum heart rates were the same. Heart rate recovery was faster after the shorter exercise condition where circulatory occlusion was present than after the longer exercise with intact circulation. The blood flow recovery curves were the same after both conditions of exercise and exhibited the characteristics of a two-component exponential equation. This suggested the occurrence of primary and secondary phases associated with reactive hyperemia and the blood flow debt.

WORK

The heart of exercise physiology is the production of work; for research purposes, the work must be measurable, or at least the task must be standardized in some way. Many activities may involve work, but such things as cadence and distance traveled render most exercises useless for controlled experimental study. Thus, the selection of an exercise modality must be carefully considered in light of the objectives of the study. For example, if the task is isometric, a rather heavy load will be given with the subject in either a standing[30] or a supine[31] position, and the load can be very specifically administered. However, if it is isotonic, as in most cases it will be, a selection of exercise modalities can be made among several standardized procedures. The decision to employ the treadmill, bicycle ergometer, or step-bench will depend upon a number of factors, cost and availability being among them, but other matters also weigh heavily, as will be discussed.

Treadmill

One of the most widely used techniques for exercise physiology research is the treadmill. Treadmills come in all sizes and shapes, some portable and

[29] Jack H. Wilmore and Steven M. Horvath, "Alterations in Peripheral Blood Flow Consequent to Maximal Exercise," *American Heart Journal*, 66, No. 3 (September 1963), 353.

[30] David H. Clarke, "Energy Cost of Isometric Exercise," *Research Quarterly*, 31, No. 1 (March 1960), 3.

[31] Joseph Royce, "Oxygen Intake Curves Reflecting Circulatory Factors in Static Work," *Int. Z. angew. Physiol. einschl. Arbeitsphysiol.*, 19 (1962), 222.

others installed permanently in the laboratory floor. The specifications may vary, but, in general, two variables should be provided—speed and inclination. The treadmill should have the capability of varying speed between 0–16 mph and inclination between 0–20 per cent, thus providing a range of work loads that should meet the needs of most research designs. The grade is based on the incline that would result from the elevation of 100 horizontal feet; therefore, 1 per cent grade would be the rise of the belt equivalent to a 1 foot vertical elevation taken at a distance of 100 horizontal feet.

The treadmill has the advantages of ease of running or walking and of positioning so as to obtain various cardiopulmonary measures, although running does impart some disturbing bodily motion. Variations in belt speed and grade can be standardized for the necessary application. One difficulty is in standardizing the work done, as this amount varies directly with body weight. Maintaining constant belt speed and grade does not hold constant the work accomplished; equating body weight and treadmill speed are difficult and not at all practical.

Another problem encountered, especially when all-out runs to exhaustion are made, is maintenance of pace. Any slackening of speed by the subject will result in his delivery to the rear of the treadmill, which will in all probability terminate the exercise. If the criterion is a run to exhaustion, pace maintenance is especially difficult to control; this problem is not present in submaximal exercises or in experiments dealing with maximal oxygen intake.[32]

Bicycle Ergometer

Another widely used device for work studies is the bicycle ergometer. In its simplest form, this ergometer is a stationary bicycle with one wheel adapted so that a belt can be passed around and attached to a spring balance. In a closed loop design,[33] the work load can be changed while in motion simply by increasing the tension on the belt, which in turn is monitored on the scale. The addition of lead strips to the wheel gives the proper inertia for smooth operation. The ergometer can be calibrated for work load by determining the distance the rim of the wheel is moved by one pedal revolution; this amount times the product of resistance and cadence (per min) gives the total work accomplished in foot-pounds or kilogram-meters per min. The usual procedure is to employ a constant pedal rate (50–60 revolutions per min); only the resistance is varied.

---

[32] Henry L. Taylor, Elsworth Buskirk, and Austin Henschel, "Maximal Oxygen Intake as an Objective Measure of Cardio-Respiratory Performance," *Journal of Applied Physiology*, 8, No. 1 (July 1955), 73.

[33] Joseph Royce and Franklin Henry, "Two Inexpensive Bicycle Ergometers," *Research Quarterly*, 34, No. 1 (March 1963), 111.

A more sophisticated design is the electric-brake bicycle ergometer, although the results of testing are not necessarily better with the more elaborate instrument. The resistance is provided by increasing the field current through an electromagnetic brake, which is monitored by a power output meter. This meter is calibrated to determine friction losses and power output over the usable speeds and loads to be employed by comparing the results with the known power input of an electric motor.[34]

The bicycle ergometer has certain advantages as a tool for research. First, it is rather small and compact, and most of the friction belt types are portable, although the electric-brake bicycle ergometer tends to be larger, heavier, and thus less mobile. Because it is stationary and because the subject remains seated, electrodes and gas collection equipment can be attached conveniently, with less danger of bodily movements interfering with data collection and of leaks occurring around respiratory apparatus. The most important advantage, however, is the ability to set and maintain a constant work load for all subjects. Body weight does not become a variable in work load determinations, so the investigator may study the individual differences in performance of a standard task. The load or cadence may be reduced, although here there are certain questions related to efficiency that should be studied.[35] However, with a mechanical revolution counter, the actual number of revolutions can be recorded, so that slight deviations in rhythm can be accounted for. It has been claimed that difficulty is experienced in learning to ride the bicycle and that practice sessions are needed; the same can be said for other exercise tasks. However, once the subject has adjusted to the proper pedal rate, little difficulty is ordinarily found.

Step-Bench

Probably the most inexpensive and simplest device for work is the step-bench. The reader is undoubtedly aware of physical fitness tests utilizing this technique so that further description is unnecessary. The height of the bench and cadence may vary, depending upon the objectives of the study and perhaps the age and sex of the subjects. The work load varies once again with body weight, and the movement of the subject makes instrumentation very difficult, although many of the problems may be overcome successfully with care. At any rate it can be used for a number of tasks requiring sustained effort or involvement of large muscle groups.

---

[34] A. Holmgren and K. H. Mattsson, "A New Ergometer with Constant Work Load at Varying Pedalling Rate," *Scandinavian Journal of Clinical and Laboratory Investigation*, 6, No. 2 (1954), 137.

[35] Sylvia Dickinson, "The Efficiency of Bicycle-Pedalling, as Affected by Speed and Load," *Journal of Physiology*, 67, No. 3 (June 1929), 242.

ENERGY COST

Possibly one of the most important laboratory skills for research in physical education is the measurement of energy expenditure. This process permeates much of the literature of exercise physiology. Modern laboratories today usually have available one or more of the instruments necessary to perform gas analysis; thus, the student who is interested in exercise physiology should learn to use these instruments. This is also true of the doctoral student who plans to teach in this area and who anticipates thesis advisement of graduate students.

The basic concepts concerning energy expenditure should already be known from undergraduate courses in exercise physiology. The student should understand the difference between direct and indirect calorimetry in measuring the amount of heat produced by the body as a result of muscular work. The direct measurement of heat requires rather expensive equipment and rigorous laboratory protocol, including the body calorimeter, which is a chamber especially equipped for measuring the heat given off by the body. The high cost and limited application to experiments involving exercise means that direct calorimetry is seldom used.

On the other hand, indirect calorimetry is the common method employed in energy cost studies. Calculation of energy expenditure is made on the basis of oxygen consumed and carbon dioxide produced, which in turn may be converted to Calories (kilocalories) if desired. More often, one is interested in oxygen utilization in liters per minute, rather than in Calories, because the design of the experiment so often involves comparisons of one level of exercise to another or the influence of mitigating environmental or other factors on the energy cost. Assuming that comparable conditions are to be imposed on the subjects in the experiment, this process has been found acceptable. Two methods of indirect calorimetry are employed: the closed-circuit method and the open-circuit method.

Closed-Circuit Method

The closed-circuit method employs a wet spirometer, similar in design to that of Benedict,[36] in which a gas, oxygen, is introduced into the spirometer. The subject is connected to the gas by means of a mouthpiece and hoses controlled by one-way valves so that he inhales the oxygen and exhales back into the system. The expired air passes through a cannister of soda lime, where the carbon dioxide is absorbed and the oxygen is readmitted

---

[36] Francis G. Benedict, "A Portable Respiration Apparatus for Clinical Use," *Boston Medical and Surgical Journal*, 178, No. 20 (May 16, 1918), 667.

to the spirometer. Thus, the cylinder will rise and fall with each breath but will slowly become depleted as the body utilizes the oxygen for metabolic needs. Equipment manufactured for the purpose of measuring basal metabolic rate contains an ink-writing unit with kymograph so that a recording of the respiration may be obtained. Oxygen utilization is ordinarily inferred from the steepness of slope of the respiratory line, which, in steady state conditions, will be linear. An adequate estimation of resting metabolism can be obtained in 6 to 10 min. All measures must be corrected to standard temperature and pressure dry (*STPD*), in accordance with established procedures.

Basal metabolism is important for clinical applications, where the preparation of the subject is carefully standardized, and the metabolism is expressed in Calories/hour/square meter of body surface. However, in exercise studies, the need is far more apparent for resting rate rather than basal rate; for this reason, the resting condition may be supine, sitting, or even standing, depending upon the experimental design. The closed-circuit apparatus may be used for these; but difficulty is often experienced in the exercise task, as extensive subject movement sometimes makes measurement very difficult. In fact, there may be a real restriction in the use of the closed circuit device for exercise studies, as data are available that reflect a contamination of the source gas by carbon dioxide.[37] Apparently, this is the result of the ineffectiveness in commerical spirometers to absorb carbon dioxide; thus, the contamination is a function of flow rate.

Open-Circuit Method

The preferred manner of obtaining data on energy cost is by means of the open-circuit method. This method is ordinarily more accurate, and it is not influenced by variations in respiratory rate nor the depth of respiration, as is the closed-circuit method. The classic procedure here is to breathe in atmospheric air—which has known percentages of oxygen, carbon dioxide, nitrogen, and so forth—and exhale into a collection receptacle, usually a Douglas bag. The mouthpiece utilized is a three-way, high-velocity valve, permitting unobstructed inhalation of room air and exhalation into the collection assembly. Usually, several Douglas bags will be used, as the resting, exercise, and recovery samples may be collected separately. For this, a four-way or five-way valve must be used so that the exhaled air can be directed to the appropriate bag without loss of time or inappropriate mixing of the various gases.

The total volume of expired air is determined by passing the quantity

[37] Benjamin Ricci, *Physiological Basis of Human Performance* (Philadelphia: Lea & Febiger, 1967), pp. 163–64.

of gas from each bag through a dry gas meter. Thus, if the total volume of expired gas is known, and also the percentage composition of the inspired air, the oxygen requirement will be calculated as the difference between the percentage inspired and percentage expired air. Corrections must be made for standard conditions of temperature and pressure.

The manner of analyzing the expired air in the open-circuit method provides some choice, but two methods are most frequently employed in research laboratories; both of these methods extract small gas samples from each of the collection bags and subject them to standardized analysis. The two procedures employ the Haldane[38] and the Scholander[39] apparatus; both require very careful techniques under exacting laboratory specifications. The experimenter who wishes to employ these methods must plan to spend sufficient time in the laboratory to perfect the procedures needed to obtain valid data; slight errors in these micromethods can result in large discrepancies. In addition to the basic references cited, the reader is directed to Consolazio, Johnson, and Pecora[40] for additional specific information on equipment and procedures to be employed.

Presently, a growing reliance is evident on still another procedure for obtaining O_2 and CO_2 from expired air, which bypasses the traditional and laborious devices just described. This procedure is the continuous recording method whereby the expired air is drawn through oxygen[41] and carbon dioxide[42] analyzers by a vacuum pump. The method has the advantages of simplicity of use and provides a continual monitoring of the changes in expired air, with apparently no serious loss of accuracy (and which may be coupled to a recorder for direct write-out). Calibration with known gases and comparisons with the Haldane or Scholander analyzers are routine matters to ascertain the acceptability of the analysis.

Computations

The calculations required to complete the analysis of oxygen utilization are based upon obtaining the percentage of the gas in the sample introduced

---

[38] J. S. Haldane and J. G. Priestley, *Respiration* (New York: Oxford University Press, Inc., 1935).

[39] P. F. Scholander, "Analyzer for Accurate Estimation of Respiratory Gases in One-Half Cubic Centimeter Samples," *Journal of Biological Chemistry*, 167, No. 1 (January 1947), 235.

[40] C. Frank Consolazio, Robert E. Johnson, and Louis J. Pecora, *Physiological Measurements of Metabolic Functions in Man* (New York: McGraw-Hill Book Company, 1963), Ch. 2.

[41] Suggested source: Model C-2 or E-2 Oxygen Analyzers, Beckman Instruments, Inc., Schiller Park, Ill.

[42] Suggested source: Model LB-1 Carbon Dioxide Analyzer, Beckman Instruments, Inc., Schiller Park, Ill.

to the Haldane or Scholander analyzers. This percentage applies to all volumes, but they in turn must be corrected for temperature and pressure according to the following formula:

$$Vex = \frac{273}{273 + t} \times \frac{P}{760} \times Vm$$

where

Vex = vol of expired air at standard conditions (0°C and 760 mm Hg)

t = room temperature in degrees centigrade

P = barometric pressure in mm Hg − vapor pressure at room temperature

Vm = measured vol of expired air

The computations given below are made for determination of O_2 requirement of any measured sample. The procedures are repeated for all collection bags; thus, data may be obtained for rest, exercise, and recovery separately.

1. Vol of O_2 inspired $= \frac{20.93}{100} \times \frac{\%N_2 \text{ in expired air}}{79.04} \times Vex$ (note that 20.93 and 79.04 represent per cent O_2 and N_2 in room air).
2. Vol of O_2 expired $= \frac{\%O_2 \text{ in expired air}}{100} \times Vex$
3. Vol of O_2 consumed = Vol of O_2 inspired − vol of O_2 expired.

When this has been done for each collection bag, the additional computations can then be made.

4. Resting rate = resting vol of O_2 consumed ÷ length of collection in min.
5. Net O_2 consumed = vol of O_2 consumed − the resting rate × the length of collection of each bag.
6. Net O_2 income per min = net O_2 consumed during exercise ÷ length of collection during exercise.
7. Oxygen debt = net O_2 consumed during recovery.
8. O_2 requirement per min = net O_2 income (amount, not rate) plus the oxygen debt ÷ length of work period in min.

Respiratory Quotient

Many instances occur in which the CO_2 production associated with exercise must be known. For example, through knowledge of the respiratory quotient (*RQ*), or respiratory exchange ratio (*R*), meaningful information may be obtained concerning the role of various foods in supplying the fuel for metabolism. Although certain restrictions of interpretation of the *RQ* in exercise studies are present, the computation may be needed. *RQ* is given as the ratio of the quantity of carbon dioxide produced to oxygen consumed; thus the following computational steps should be followed to obtain the volume of CO_2 and *RQ*:

1. $\text{Vol of } CO_2 \text{ produced} = \dfrac{\%CO_2 \text{ in expired air} - .04}{100} \times Vex$ (note that .04 represents per cent CO_2 in room air).

2. $RQ = \dfrac{\text{vol } CO_2 \text{ produced}}{\text{vol } O_2 \text{ consumed}}$

Mechanical Efficiency

In exercise physiology, the extent of human efficiency by relating the mechanical work performed to the energy cost of that work may be studied. If the work load is held constant, a reduction in energy cost will result in greater efficiency; applications may be made to a variety of physiological situations involving diet[43] or optimum conditions for work output.[44] Mechanical efficiency may be calculated as follows:

1. $O_2 \text{ equivalent of the work} = \dfrac{\text{work done in fp}}{15{,}575}$ (note that 15,575 is the foot-pound equivalent of a liter of oxygen, assuming the excess metabolism of work requires carbohydrate as its fuel).

2. $\text{Net Mechanical Efficiency} = \dfrac{O_2 \text{ equivalent of the work}}{\text{net } O_2 \text{ requirement (liters)}} \times 100$

3. $\text{Gross Mechanical Efficiency} = \dfrac{O_2 \text{ equivalent of the work}}{\text{net } O_2 \text{ requirement} + \text{resting } O_2 \text{ during work (liters)}} \times 100$

CARDIOVASCULAR VARIABLES

Several other cardiovascular variables are commonly studied by exercise physiologists as part of their research design, some of which are rather

---

[43] August Krogh and Johannes Lindhard, "The Relative Value of Fat and Carbohydrate as Sources of Muscular Energy," *Biochemical Journal*, 14, No. 3–4 (July 1920), 290.

[44] Nils Rönnholm, Martti J. Karvonen, and Veikko O. Lapinleimu, "Mechanical Efficiency of Rhythmic and Paced Work of Lifting," *Journal of Applied Physiology*, 17, No. 5 (September 1962), 768.

advanced techniques whereas others are rather pedestrian. The more technical procedures require additional laboratory training or perhaps the use of clinical technicians so that no errors are made and sterile conditions are maintained when blood is taken. A growing tendency is found today in the larger laboratories to employ personnel whose function is to assist in the collection of such data. They are also responsible for the chemical assays, as they can be trained in the various biochemical techniques required for such studies.

There was a time when the researcher himself was expected to possess the expertise necessary to gather and treat all his experimental data. But, more and more, the tendency is to employ others for many of the more tedious and complicated laboratory processes, thus freeing the investigator of considerable time that can be spent in enlarging the project; frequently, too, the research problem can be more comprehensive. The same can be said for the use of computers in the reduction and statistical analysis of the resultant data from such multivariate studies; the repetitious and detailed treatment of the data may be accomplished in a fraction of the time and, one hopes, more accurately. Thus, the team approach used today has permitted far more sophisticated research designs than ever before.

Heart Rate

Nothing new or startling is involved in the simple determination of heart rate, as this is a time-honored and long-standing physiological parameter, among the most early of measured variables. The reason, of course, is the absolute simplicity involved in monitoring the pulse: No equipment is needed and very little training is required. As used in early physical fitness tests,[45] the emphasis was placed on the recovery of the heart following a given exercise task and was based on the assumption that the individual with the best physical fitness was the one whose pulse would recover most rapidly. More recently,[46] the suggestion has been made that the heart rate during exercise should be studied—that this phenomenon more adequately reflects the circulatory system in its response to the stress of exercise.

The tendency today is to monitor heart rate by the use of electrodes and recorder rather than to depend upon a manual method, because of the greater chance for error when counting in the latter instance. This is particularly true during exercise, when subject movement and muscular contraction may

---

[45] Lucien Brouha, "The Step Test: A Simple Method of Measuring Physical Fitness for Muscular Work in Young Men," *Research Quarterly*, 14, No. 1 (March 1943), 31.

[46] P.-O. Astrand, "Human Fitness with Special Reference to Sex and Age," *Physiological Reviews*, 36, No. 3 (July 1956), 325.

interfere with detection of the pulse beat. An error introduced as a consequence will probably go undetected; if 10-, 15-, or 20-sec counts are taken, with conversion to minute rate, an error of one beat per measured interval will cause the heart rate to be off from 3 to 6 beats per min. This amount of error is intolerable in research applications, so the more sophisticated techniques have grown in favor.

Any number of electrocardiographic systems that give very acceptable recordings are available to the research worker. Further, telemetry may be employed in gathering such data so that the subject may be freed of electrode-recorder leads and can be at some distance from the receiver and still monitor his heart rate. Telemetry is becoming popular, as field use is possible where large-scale physical activity is involved in the exercise regimen. Care must be taken, however, that unwanted muscle action potentials do not interfere with the recording during exercise. Trial and error electrode placement will help alleviate this problem.

Blood Pressure

Reliable blood pressure determinations must still be obtained in humans by the usual procedure involving the sphygmomanometer and stethoscope for studies in exercise physiology. The manual method is often difficult to do successfully for the novice, so he should plan on sufficient practice to ensure adequate results. Even so, the dangers of variations exist in auditory acuity and in interpretation of the sound levels, as well as in the occurrence of other variables related to individual differences, strength of the heart beat and factors related to equipment. Resting blood pressure may be given on various read-out devices, but movement artifacts are pronounced during exercise. Therefore, great care and sufficient amplification are needed for successful recording.

Brachial Pulse Wave

The integrity of the cardiovascular system may also be obtained by means of an additional technique, that of measuring the brachial pulse wave. In addition to blood pressure determinations in the resting condition, a number of other variables associated with dynamics of cardiac function that reflect cardiovascular status may be obtained. The instrument utilized for these purposes is the heartometer;[47] techniques for using this instrument have been studied extensively by Cureton.[48] In essence, the heartometer employs a

[47] Manufactured by Cameron Heartometer Corporation, 6449 N. Newark Avenue, Chicago, Ill.

[48] Thomas Kirk Cureton, *Physical Fitness Appraisal and Guidance* (St. Louis: C. V. Mosby Company, 1947), Ch. 8.

standard blood pressure cuff around the upper arm to pick up the pulse beat as it is amplified and transmitted to a sensitive bellows. In turn, the bellows is attached to a series of levers that move a writing arm on a circular graph. A description of the instrument and the method of operation, in addition to other considerations, is presented by Blevins and Cureton.[49] The diagram of a normal pulse wave is presented in Figure 18; the variables that may be obtained are described below:

1. Systolic amplitude. The systolic pulse wave amplitude (*AB*) represents the magnitude of the left ventricular contraction.

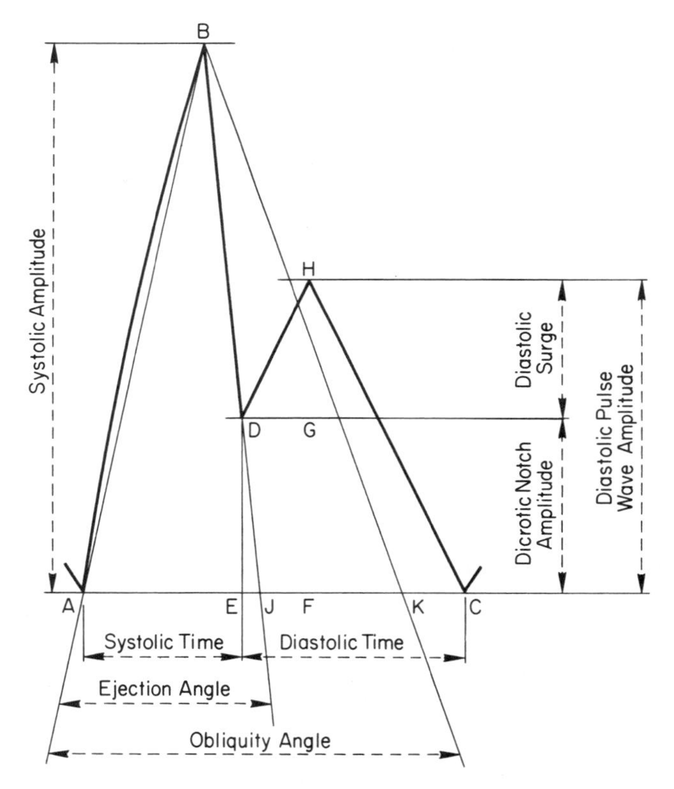

Figure 18. Diagram of Brachial Pulse Wave (Blevins and Cureton, *op. cit.*, p. 114. Reproduced by permission of the Cameron Heartometer Corp., *The American Corrective Therapy Journal*, and the authors.)

---

[49] J. W. Blevins and T. K. Cureton, "The Cameron Heartometer in Industrial Medicine," *Journal of the Association for Physical and Mental Rehabilitation*, 21, No. 4 (July–August 1967), 112. Used by permission of the Cameron Heartometer Corp., *The American Corrective Therapy Journal*, and the authors.

2. Dicrotic notch amplitude. Upon completion of the systolic contraction, a back pressure occurs that closes the aortic valves at the dicrotic notch, giving the dicrotic notch amplitude (*DE*). The ratio *DE/AB* is called the fatigue ratio, which may represent a loss of cardiovascular tone.

3. Diastolic surge. The closing of the aortic valves transmits a recoil back along the arterial tree, resulting in a diastolic surge (*GH*), which represents the elasticity and tone of the arterial tissue.

4. Diastolic amplitude. The diastolic pulse wave amplitude (*FH*) occurs after closing of the semilunar valves, which is the total of the dicrotic notch amplitude and the diastolic surge. Thus, the diastolic wave (*DHC*) represents the resting phase of the heart. In terms of duration, the systolic time (*AE*) is the working phase of the heart; the diastolic time (*EC*) is the resting phase.

5. Total. The area under the curve (*ABDHCA*) represents the total volume of blood being pumped with each stroke.

6. Other. Additional variables may be obtained from the brachial pulse wave, such as the angle of obliquity, the ratio of rest to work, and so forth; these may be of interest in evaluating cardiovascular status.

Cardiac Output

Considerable interest has been evident in the assessment of cardiac output, going back to the early work by Fick in 1870, who employed a direct cardiac puncture. Although one infers blood flow from the heart rate, the amount of blood volume cannot be known from this measure alone, so it has been important to devise a technique whereby the cardiac output could be determined. Such a technique was provided by Cournand[50] by which a catheter is threaded through the basilic vein into the right side of the heart to the pulmonary artery; mixed venous blood samples are taken. Arterial puncture provides arterial blood samples; the oxygen utilization can be obtained by the Douglas bag technique. Cardiac output in ml/min is then calculated by the following formula:

$$\text{Cardiac output} = \frac{O_2 \text{ requirement (ml/min)}}{\text{arterio-venous } O_2 \text{ difference (ml/ml)}}$$

The difficulty inherent in this procedure is apparent: The heart catheterization is not routinely possible, except under the most rigidly controlled

[50] Andre Cournand, "Measurement of the Cardiac Output in Man Using the Right Heart Catheterization," *Federation Proceedings*, 4, No. 2 (June 1945), 207.

situations; therefore, its use in exercise physiology is questionable. However, these problems have been surmounted in recent research,[51] where an indwelling catheter proceeding from the femoral vein into the right side of the heart was utilized during a bicycle ergometer experiment.

More feasible are the indirect measures whereby a foreign gas, notably acetylene, is used to obtain the A-V O_2 difference or some of the more popular dye dilution techniques.[52] Recently, radioisotopes have been substituted for dyes, and the cardiac output has been measured by use of external detectors.[53] Perhaps more practical for studies in physical education is a photoelectric device called an oximeter, which can continuously measure the O_2 saturation of arterial blood and can be used for obtaining mixed venous blood determinations.[54,55] This method has the obvious advantage of avoiding the necessity for puncturing blood vessels.

Blood Gas Determinations

When blood gas measures must be obtained, the typical researcher in physical education may need to obtain assistance in securing the blood samples and in using the measurement apparatus. These procedures cannot be considered routine for exercise physiology laboratories. However, as the research becomes more sophisticated and as more research funds become available, they will undoubtedly come into greater use. When such equipment can be obtained and used, the research design may be considerably enhanced or, at least, permit the delineation of a far greater number of studies than otherwise would be possible.

The basic instrument utilized for blood gas measures is the Van Slyke-Neill manometric apparatus,[56] or, more recently, the Roughton-Scholander

---

[51] J. Stenberg, P. O. Astrand, B. Ekblom, J. Royce, and B. Saltin, "Hemodynamic Response to Work with Different Muscle Groups, Sitting and Supine," *Journal of Applied Physiology*, 22, No. 1 (Januray 1967), 61.

[52] Erling Asmussen and Marius Nielsen, "The Cardiac Output in Rest and Work Determined Simultaneously by the Acetylene and the Dye Injection Methods," *Acta Physiologica Scandinavica*, 27, No. 2–3 (1952), 217.

[53] Hideo Ueda, Iwao Ito, and Masahiro Iio, "External Measurement of Cardiac Output Using Radioisotopes by Means of a Digital Data Readout Device," *American Journal of Medical Electronics*, 2, No. 3 (July–September 1963), 229.

[54] Nils J. Nilsson, "Oximetry" *Physiological Reviews*. 40, No. 1 (January 1960), 1.

[55] W. Sleator, J. O. Elam, W. N. Elam, and H. L. White, "Oximetric Determinations of Cardiac Output Responses to Light Exercise," *Journal of Applied Physiology*, 3, No. 11 (May 1951), 649.

[56] Donald D. Van Slyke and James M. Neill, "The Determination of Gases in Blood and Other Solutions by Vacuum Extraction and Manometric Measurement," *Journal of Biological Chemistry*, 61, No. 2 (September 1924), 523.

syringe pipette.[57,58] Other devices are currently available. For additional information, the reader is directed to descriptions provided by Consolazio, Johnson, and Pecora.[59]

Blood Lactate and Pyruvate

Because of the importance of anaerobic mechanisms in controlling exercise metabolism, the study of various other constituents of the blood, particularly blood lactate and pyruvate, has become necessary. Blood lactate determinations may be made according to the methods of Barker and Summerson[60] and Strom;[61] blood pyruvate may be performed by the procedures of Friedemann and Haugen[62] and Asmussen.[63] For details of these and other procedures, Peters and Van Slyke[64] and Wasserman, Burton, and Van Kessel[65] will be helpful references.

Cardiovascular Studies

Oxygen Debt. The vast literature dealing with cardiovascular dynamics reveals interest in numerous topics. One that has intrigued investigators for a number of years has been the description of oxygen debt and more specifically the identification of the lactic and alactic portions. For example, the early work of Margaria, Edwards, and Dill[66] presented pertinent data on this

---

[57] F. J. W. Roughton and P. F. Scholander, "Micro Gasometric Estimation of the Blood Gases: I. Oxygen," *Journal of Biological Chemistry*, 148, No. 3 (June 1943), 541.

[58] P. F. Scholander and F. J. W. Roughton, "Micro Gasometric Estimation of the Blood Gases: IV. Carbon Dioxide," *Journal of Biological Chemistry*, 148, No. 3 (June 1943), 573.

[59] Consolazio, Johnson, and Pecora, *op. cit.*, Ch. 4.

[60] S. B. Barker and William H. Summerson, "The Calorimetric Determination of Lactic Acid in Biological Material," *Journal of Biological Chemistry*, 138, No. 2 (April 1941), 535.

[61] Gunnar Ström, "The Influence of Anoxia on Lactate Utilization in Man after Prolonged Muscular Work," *Acta Physiologica Scandinavica*, 17, No. 4 (1949), 440.

[62] Theodore E. Friedemann and Gladys E. Haugen, "Pyruvic Acid: II. The Determination of Keto Acids in Blood and Urine," *Journal of Biological Chemistry*, 147, No. 2 (February 1943), 415.

[63] Erling Asmussen, "Pyruvate and Lactate Content of the Blood During and After Muscular Work," *Acta Physiologica Scandinavica*, 20, No. 2–3 (1950), 125.

[64] John P. Peters and Donald D. Van Slyke, *Quantitative Clinical Chemistry, Vol. II, Methods* (Baltimore: The Williams & Wilkins Co., 1932).

[65] K. Wasserman, G. G. Burton, and A. L. Van Kessel, "The Excess Lactate Concept and the Oxygen Debt of Exercise," *Journal of Applied Physiology*, 20, No. 6 (November 1965), 1299.

[66] R. Margaria, H. T. Edwards, and D. B. Dill, "The Possible Mechanisms of Contracting and Paying the Oxygen Debt and the Role of Lactic Acid in Muscular Contraction," *American Journal of Physiology*, 106, No. 3 (December 1933), 689.

problem in the form of lactic acid concentration in the blood as a function of the amount of oxygen debt after exercises of varying intensity. No extra lactic acid was found in light exercise, even though an oxygen debt occurred; at the heavier work loads, the lactic acid increased as a function of exercise intensity. The alactacid debt exhibited a logarithmic decrement, as did the lactacid debt, but the speed of payment was 30 times faster. The half-time value for the alactacid debt was 30 sec, as compared to 15 min for the lactic debt.

The lactic and alactic oxygen debts examined by Henry and DeMoor[67] in a repeated measures design (Chapter 12) involved continuous closed circuit oxygen consumption records at rest, during 6 min of bicycle ergometer exercise and 25 min of recovery. The work loads were so adjusted that each subject gave net O_2 requirements ranging from 0.21 to 2.11 l/min. Additional data were obtained on O_2 uptake and debt payoff at 6 min of exercise at 680 kgm/min. The debt payoff curve was exponential, controlled by a two component equation, and identified with the reduction of alactic and lactic acid incurred during exercise. When the workload increased, the alactic component remained essentially unchanged, but the lactic component not only became more prominent but became progressively slower.

Subsequently, doubt was cast upon the presence of an alactic debt by Huckabee,[68,69] who found that lactate (called excess lactate by the author) occurred at all levels of exercise intensity and that it paralleled the development of other oxygen debt. Knuttgen[70] reopened the question by examining the oxygen debt, pyruvate, lactate, and excess lactate following 20 min of ergometer exercise at loads of 300, 700, 1100, and 1600 kgm/min. The last work period continued for only 5.75 min, as it represented the subject's limit of endurance. The increases in excess lactate and total lactate were very slight at the two lower intensity bouts, but when a critical level of work of approximately 1.5 l/min oxygen uptake with 1.5 l debt occurred, a rapid rise in oxygen debt resulted, which was accompanied by corresponding increases in total lactate as well as excess lactate. Thus, these results supported the concept that an alactacid oxygen debt was present at the lower work intensities, but as the exercise became more severe a lactacid debt emerged.

---

[67] Franklin M. Henry and Janice C. DeMoor, "Lactic and Alactic Oxygen Consumption in Moderate Exercise of Graded Intensity," *Journal of Applied Physiology*, 8, No. 6 (May 1956), 608.

[68] William E. Huckabee, "Relationships of Pyruvate and Lactate During Anaerobic Metabolism: I. Effect of Infusion of Pyruvate or Glucose and of Hyperventilation," *Journal of Clinical Investigation*, 37, No. 2 (February 1958), 244.

[69] William E. Huckabee, "Relationships of Pyruvate and Lactate During Anaerobic Metabolism: II. Exercise and Formation of O_2-Debt." *Journal of Clinical Investigation* 37, No. 2 (February 1958), 255.

[70] Howard G. Knuttgen, "Oxygen Debt, Lactate, Pyruvate, and Excess Lactate After Muscular Work," *Journal of Applied Physiology*, 17, No. 4 (July 1962), 639.

Aerobic capacity. One of the important theoretical considerations in exercise physiology has been the determination of aerobic capacity and the prediction of this value from submaximal work. The relationship through the moderate exercise range between oxygen intake and work load is linear; the production of oxidizable substrate is dependent upon the rate of working so that up to a point a direct proportion between the two occurs. Eventually, the factors that contribute to increased oxygen uptake will come to equilibrium, as the anaerobic processes will become more prominent. This result is illustrated in data presented by Astrand[71] for male and female subjects over a variety of work loads and oxygen intake values; the blood lactate values that were obtained during exercise served to indicate the reliance upon anaerobic reserves.

The reader may be interested in procedures relative to obtaining maximal oxygen intake; several sources are available. Taylor, Buskirk, and Henschel[72] examined two methods in adult males, one involving treadmill speed and the other treadmill grade. In the first method, the treadmill grade was set at zero, and the subjects ran for 3 min on successive days at progressively increasing speeds. In the second method, the speed was held constant and the grade increased by 2½ per cent. The technique employed was to continue the incremental adjustments until the oxygen intake reached a plateau, in which two successive oxygen intake values did not differ by more than 150 cc/min or 2.1 cc/kg of body weight/min. Raising the grade with speed constant (7 mph) was the most satisfactory method of obtaining a maximal oxygen intake.

Thus, the maximal oxygen intake as an objective measure of cardiorespiratory fitness has achieved a prominent place in the literature; it is not surprising to note that attempts have been made to estimate this value without actually measuring the oxygen consumption. Astrand[73] reasoned that since the heart rate adjustment to exercise paralleled the oxygen intake, an estimate of the aerobic capacity from the value of exercise heart rate alone might be possible during submaximal exercise. As a result, a nomogram was developed by Astrand and Ryhming[74] for the purpose of estimating maximal oxygen intake from the pulse rate obtained from a single work bout involving

---

[71] Per-Olaf Astrand, *Experimental Studies of Physical Working Capacity in Relation to Sex and Age* (Copenhagen: Ejnar Munksgaard, 1952), Chs. 3, 9.

[72] Henry L. Taylor, Elsworth Buskirk, and Austin Henschel, "Maximal Oxygen Intake as an Objective Measure of Cardio-Respiratory Performance," *Journal of Applied Physiology*, 8, No. 1 (July 1955), 73.

[73] P.-O. Astrand, "Human Physical Fitness with Special Reference to Sex and Age," *Physiological Reviews*, 36, No. 3 (July 1956), 307.

[74] P.-O. Astrand and Irma Ryhming, "A Nomogram for Calculation of Aerobic Capacity (Physical Fitness) from Pulse Rate During Submaximal Work," *Journal of Applied Physiology*, 7, No. 2 (September 1954), 218.

a step-bench, a bicycle erometer exercise, or running on the treadmill. In this regard the reader should note the limitations of this method of prediction.[75] For a discussion of other such submaximal tests, the discussion by Wyndham[76] may be consulted.

Training. Robinson and Harmon[77] sought to determine the effects on the lactic acid mechanism in work and its relationships to other constituents of the blood. For this purpose, a single group experiment involved 9 non-athletes of varied physical fitness who went through a conditioning program for 6 months, during which time observations were made at varying intervals. These tests were performed on a treadmill during a walk, a moderate run, and a run to exhaustion. No change in basal HbO_2 capacity, plasma protein, blood lactic acid, blood sugar, alkaline reserve, or alveolar CO_2 tension resulted, but an increase in the capacity to accumulate lactic acid during anaerobic work occurred. At the same time, a corresponding reduction in alkaline reserve and alveolar P_{CO_2} took place.

In 1942, Knehr, Dill, and Neufeld[78] studied 14 subjects following a 6-month program of running. They were tested at rest and while working at two grades of treadmill running, one submaximal and the other maximal. The training resulted in a decrease in resting heart rate and a slight increase in plasma chloride; no significant changes were found in resting alveolar P_{CO_2}, alkaline reserve, metabolic rate, hemoglobin, or the formed elements of the blood, blood pressure, and respiratory rate and volume. The reduction in oxygen intake during grade walking reflected an increase in efficiency over the period of training, whereas the increased oxygen intake and larger debt during maximal work indicated increased aerobic capacity and greater utilization of anaerobic energy reserves. This was accompanied by an increased tolerance for lactate.

Concentrating on the resting cardiovascular system, Henry[79] examined the influence of training on 18 male subjects over a season of competitive athletics. In addition, 15 subjects served as controls (random group design) and did not engage in formal conditioning. Training did not change peripheral resistance, but it did increase arterial elasticity and stroke volume

---

[75] Loring B. Rowell, Henry L. Taylor, and Yang Wang, "Limitations to Prediction of Maximal Oxygen Intake," *Journal of Applied Physiology*, 19, No. 5 (September 1964) 919.

[76] C. H. Wyndham, "Submaximal Tests for Estimating Maximum Oxygen Intake," *Canadian Medical Association Journal*, 96, No. 12 (March 25, 1967), 736.

[77] S. Robinson and P. M. Harmon, "The Lactic Acid Mechanism and Certain Properties of the Blood in Relation to Training," *American Journal of Physiology*, 32, No. 3 (April 1941), 757.

[78] C. A. Knehr, D. B. Dill, and William Neufeld, "Training and Its Effects on Man at Rest and at Work," *American Journal of Physiology*, 136 (March 1942), 148.

[79] Franklin M. Henry, "Influence of Athletic Training on the Resting Cardiovascular System," *Research Quarterly*, 25, No. 1 (March 1954), 28.

along with a decrease in heart rate. Brachial pulse wave sphygmograms, particularly the systolic wave amplitude, were significantly different for the athletes over the controls, but they changed very little as a result of training. It was concluded that the change in resting heart rate was a useful test of cardiovascular conditioning.

BODY COMPOSITION

The study of the physical and chemical aspects of the body has led to a variety of techniques designed to estimate its physical composition. The concept that a body displaces an amount of water equal to its own volume was passed down by Archimedes as long ago as the third century B.C. Even though the possibilities for estimating body composition were suggested earlier, it was not until Behnke[80] perfected a technique for ascertaining the body composition of adult males that the procedure began to gain wide acceptance. Early work by Rathbun and Pace[81] and a later review by Keys and Brozek[82] centered attention on the possibilities of the estimation of various components of the body, most notably the lean and fat contents. Inasmuch as the technique for measuring body density by immersing the body in water is a very simple one, it has become a rather important procedure to be used in research laboratories. The initial materials include a tank for water, a harness for suspension, and a scale for obtaining submerged weights. In addition, apparatus for measuring residual lung volume is needed.

As described by Siri,[83] the weight of the body in air is compared to its weight in water when totally submerged. Thus, a means must be found whereby the body can be fully immersed in water and weighed in this position. A tank of some sort will suffice; successful attempts have been made in measuring subjects suspended both vertically and horizontally. The vertical position is easier because it is a more natural one, and subject movement can be controlled more effectively. A harness is employed to lower the subject underwater directly beneath the scale. The horizontal position is probably

---

[80] A. R. Behnke, B. G. Feen, and W. C. Welham, "The Specific Gravity of Healthy Men. Body Weight ÷ Volume as an Index of Obesity," *Journal of the American Medical Association*, 118, No. 7 (February 14, 1942), 495.

[81] Edith N. Rathbun and Nello Pace, "Studies on Body Composition: I. The Determination of Total Body Fat by Means of the Body Specific Gravity," *Journal of Biological Chemistry*, 158, No. 3 (May 1945), 667.

[82] Ancel Keys and Josef Brozek, "Body Fat in Adult Man," *Physiological Reviews* 33, No. 3 (July 1953), 245.

[83] William E. Siri, "The Gross Composition of the Body," *Advances in Biological and Medical Physics*, 4 (1956), 239.

more difficult to control, but experience has shown it to be entirely satisfactory when certain controls are incorporated. One control technique is to use a rectangular frame with nylon webbing as a stretcher on which the subject reclines. The size depends upon the dimensions of the water tank; in any event, oscillating movements can be reduced by applying bumper guards to the sides of the frame. The entire assembly can then be attached to the scale which in turn can be damped to avoid excessive indicator movement.

The prime requisite is to obtain the underwater weight of the subject when completely submerged in water. In order to do so, he must exhale completely before the weight is read on the scale. Extra lead weight may be necessary to hold the subject down; this weight, plus the weight of any harness, must later be subtracted. However, this process does not account for the buoyant effect of gas in the gastrointestinal tract or for residual lung volume, both of which may affect the estimate of specific gravity. The former condition may be reduced by being weighed in the morning in the post-absorptive state, and the latter may be measured directly.[84] In the event that residual lung volume cannot be determined experimentally, an estimate (1500 cc for young men and 1300 cc for women, for example) may be obtained. The resulting error can be considered small[85] so the disturbance for later statistical use is minimal.

The following computational procedures may be employed in determining body density. As indicated, residual air in the lungs is estimated, and corrections are made for the harness weight and for water density:

1. Weight in air (lbs)
2. Weight immersed in water, full exhalation
3. Weight of the harness in water
4. Underwater weight (item 2 − item 3)
5. Estimated volume of residual air in lungs (cc)
6. Weight of water displaced by residual lung volume (item 5 ÷ 454, the weight equivalent of this volume in lbs)
7. Water density at temperature of the water used
8. Correction for residual air and density (item 6 × item 7)
9. Net weight in water (item 4 + item 8)

$$\text{Body density} = \frac{\text{body weight in air}}{\text{body weight in air} - \text{net weight in water}}$$

[84] Behnke, *op. cit.*

[85] J. Brozek and A. Keys, "The Evaluation of Leanness-Fatness in Man: Norms and Interrelationships," *British Journal of Nutrition*, 5, No. 2 (1951), 194.

When related to the reference body which has 14 per cent fat, the following formula may be used:[86]

$$\text{Per cent body fat} = 100\,(4.201/\text{density} - 3.813)$$

Based upon the above determinations, other constituents of body composition can be calculated. The weight of the fat component can be assessed from knowledge of the percentage of fat; in a similar manner, the lean body weight is the residual, that is, nonessential fat, or the body weight less the body fat weight. Other combinations are possible, and further readings will elicit additional parameters of interest on this topic.[87,88,89]

Other techniques for assessing body composition have proven successful to researchers. The estimation of nutritional status by means of fat fold measures have been used repeatedly and can be considered very useful in certain kinds of studies. The technique is to sample the thickness of the skinfold at various sites on the body and then to predict the body density, or specific gravity. From this, per cent fat and lean body mass can be obtained. Although more advanced and rather sophisticated techniques are available in the literature and have been employed by physiologists and others interested in these problems, it is doubtful that they will be available routinely to physical education research laboratories. At any rate, the more important question may be to discover if function relates to structure. Stated in another way, to what extent does knowledge of the constituents of the body enable one to predict performance ability? For the thoughtful student, this should point to some rather intriguing problems.

ANIMAL RESEARCH

Research in exercise physiology with the use of small animals is becoming more and more popular. The obvious advantage gained lies in the fact that the lives of the subjects can be rigidly controlled in such important aspects as diet and exercise, which is more difficult or even impossible in humans. The analysis of far more variables is also possible where dissection and examination of a wide variety of tissues and organs may be accomplished at the end of the experiment. Thus, the use of animals extends the research

---

[86] Keys and Brozek (July 1953), *op. cit.*

[87] Josef Brozek and Austin Henschel, *Techniques for Measuring Body Composition.* Washington, D.C.: National Academy of Sciences, National Research Council, 1961.

[88] Josef Brozek, ed., "Body Composition, Part I," *Annals of the New York Academy of Sciences*, 110 (September 1963), 1.

[89] Josef Brozek, ed., "Body Composition, Part II," *Annals of the New York Academy of Sciences*, 110 (September 1963), 425.

possibilities into areas that would be impossible otherwise. The obvious drawback concerns the direct applicability that such studies would have on human performance; there is no guarantee that what happens with animals would occur in the same way in human studies. As the life cycle of most laboratory animals is considerably shorter than humans, the design may be telescoped in such a way as to follow changes from birth to maturity.

The usual laboratory animal in physical education has been the male albino rat, to which the following discussion will be limited. They may be purchased commercially of the same age and strain, thus assuring control of these two variables. These animals are typically assigned randomly to the experimental or control groups at the outset of the experiment; a color coding system may be established, and the tails of the animals marked appropriately so that they may be instantly identified to avoid any error of repeated treatment at a later time. A matching mark should appear on the cage to facilitate this process.

Two types of cages for rats are in general use today: those that are sedentary and those that permit spontaneous exercise. The sedentary cage is small and rectangular, permitting movement but no exercise; the activity cage is accompanied by an exercise wheel, to which the animal has access. A mechanical revolution counter attached to the cage can be set to record the number of wheel revolutions in either direction, and it may be read at intervals throughout the experiment. A method for studying the intensity of exercise per bout or the total per hour is also possible.[90]

Laboratory Care

When one undertakes an animal study, he accepts responsibility for their care and feeding throughout the experiment. This must be done carefully and conscientiously on a regular basis, for neglect here can result in the loss of subjects. The diet may be one of the variables to be studied, and if so, it must be rigidly followed, with caloric accounting taken of new food added plus any leftover food measured. Otherwise, it is expected that the rats will be fed *ad libitum* from a stock diet. Specific information about the diet may be obtained from a local distributor. Water bottles should also be provided and kept full; these bottles should always be sterilized.

The animal laboratory should be isolated from the rest of the laboratory in order to assure that the animals will not be disturbed or contaminated. Thus, normal spontaneous activity will be permitted. A control over light in the laboratory is necessary so that alternating periods of light and darkness

---

[90] Dale Hanson, Wayne Van Huss, and Gundars Strautneik, "Effects of Forced Exercise Upon the Amount and Intensity of the Spontaneous Activity of Young Rats," *Research Quarterly*, 37, No. 2 (May 1966), 221.

are maintained; rats are known to be more active during dark hours and to sleep during light. Normal care also requires disposal of excrement on a regular basis. Other routine problems involve proper temperature, air circulation, deodorizing, and general laboratory cleanliness. As a general rule, as few people as possible should have contact with the animals; and if the investigator himself has a cold or other infection, he should wear a hospital face mask to avoid possible contamination.

Exercise

The manner of exercise becomes very important in animal studies, as the primary reason for using animals is usually to study the effects of activity on certain parameters. Whereas humans can be given explicit instructions and encouraged to follow a set routine, rats are not always cooperative when it comes to an exercise routine. In fact, experienced researchers spend hours in devising appropriate means to control this variable, and even then can seldom state the extent of the physical or metabolic work accomplished

The two procedures most often employed are running and swimming. Running on an improvised treadmill in small compartments can be accomplished very readily with certain rats. Others, however, either cannot or will not run; they are even willing to undergo rather painful stimuli rather than to adapt to the exercise routine. Various forms of inducement may be offered to the animal to force him to run, including electric shock, but the results have not always been favorable. In fact, the stress that is involved in forced exercise may confound the true results that are investigated.[91] Recently, success has been obtained with a short strong blast of compressed air that is not physically traumatic but that serves to keep the rat forward in his running compartment.[92] Other variables, such as running in light or dark areas, the use of such rewards as stroking, or even housing in spontaneous activity cages have, at best, produced only a modest improvement.[93] For an inexpensive variable speed treadmill, the design of Brannon, Kelley, and Tomik[94] should be of interest.

Swimming has gained wide acceptance as an exercise medium, as it

---

[91] Henry J. Montoye, Richard Nelson, Perry Johnson, and Ross Macnab, "Effects of Exercise on Swimming Endurance and Organ Weight in Mature Rats," *Research Quarterly* 31, No. 3 (October 1960), 474.

[92] David L. Kelley, University of Maryland, personal communication.

[93] Dale Hanson, David Clarke, and David Kelley, "Effect of Selected Treatments Upon the Treadmill Running Success of Male Rats," *Research Quarterly*, 40, No. 1 (March 1969).

[94] Frances J. Brannon, David L. Kelley, and William J. Tomik, "A Small Animal Motor-Driven Treadmill," *Research Quarterly*, 39, No. 2 (May 1968), 402.

provides the built-in incentive that the rat will swim out of sheer self preservation. The typical procedure is to fill a container to such a depth that the animals can neither touch the bottom with their feet nor prop themselves on their tails. Then they will perform a vertical treading motion until exhausted. Great care must be exercised, of course, that they do not drown; the briefest inattention may result in just such an accident. In order to maintain negative buoyancy, a weight may be attached to the tail, amounting from 2 to 6 per cent of body weight. The animals may be placed in individual compartments or swim together. The water should be kept at body temperature and the animals dried before returning them to their cages.

SUGGESTED PROBLEMS

The area of exercise physiology is so broad that the identification of appropriate topics is bound only by the limits of the imagination. Based upon a thorough review of the literature, the student will discover a number of worthy topics. Additional answers may well come to such questions as the following:

1. Although training studies have been undertaken in the past, they have frequently involved subjects already in a state of moderate conditioning. What is the training pattern among physiological variables for the sedentary? How long do the effects of training persist?
2. What is the extent of physiological sex differences at various ages?
3. What are the environmental effects upon various performance criteria, including the effects of temperature, altitude, deep diving, and others?
4. What is the relationship between physiological variables and performance such as learning?
5. What is the extent of individual differences among various physiological parameters?
6. What is the physiological cost of varied physical activities? Can comparative values be established based on intensity of play?
7. In the area of adapted physical education, what is the energy cost of performance for those with handicapping conditions?

SUMMARY

The study of the underlying mechanisms that permit physical performance is known as exercise physiology and includes factors that relate to the immediate and long-term aspects of activity. While primarily concerned with human performance, increasing effort is being placed on animal studies, especially when it is essential to control such variables as diet and activity or when certain types of blood and tissue analyses are employed.

The range of research possibilities is wide; with the advent of more sophisticated instrumentation, the field is growing considerably. Where formerly a simple dynamometer was employed to measure strength, a host of techniques are presently available, some electronically coupled to standard laboratory recorders that permit the investigation of muscular strength, endurance relationships, and other characteristics of muscular contraction.

A number of devices for measurement of work are widely employed in research laboratories, but the bicycle ergometer and treadmill are most popular. Both permit certain types of standardization, and both may be used to study the energy cost of activity. The usual procedure in this design is to collect expired air and submit small samples to some gas analysis apparatus where the percentages of the gases may be precisely determined. Increasing attention is being given to methods of recording continuously expired air, thus providing additional information concerning the time factor associated with oxygen uptake and debt payoff.

Other cardiovascular variables, such as heart rate, blood pressure, cardiac output, and various blood gas determinations, are receiving wide attention in exercise physiology laboratories, as indicators of physical fitness and as a means for aiding in the assessment of performance. Heart rate in particular has been employed for years for this purpose. Recent dictum proposes that greater reliance be placed on exercise heart rate than recovery heart rate, as it more adequately reflects circulatory response to the stress of exercise.

Assessing the various components of the body has involved a knowledge of body composition. The methods used for the process are rapidly becoming more accessible to researchers in physical education who are raising questions related to structure and function. The technique of densitometry can be applied to these problems, as well as other procedures designed to study relative portions of body fat and lean tissue.

SELECTED REFERENCES

Astrand, P.-O., "Human Physical Fitness with Special Reference to Sex and Age," *Physiological Reviews*, 36, No. 3 (July 1956), 325.

Brozek, Josef, ed., "Body Composition, Part I," *Annals of the New York Academy of Sciences*, 110 (September 1963), 1.

———, "Body Composition, Part II," *Annals of the New York Academy of Sciences*, 110 (September 1963), 425.

Brozek, Josef, and Austin Henschel, *Techniques for Measuring Body Composition*. Washington, D.C.: National Academy of Sciences, National Research Council, 1961.

Clarke, H. Harrison, *Muscular Strength and Endurance in Man*. Englewood Cliffs, N.J.: Prentice-Hall, Inc., 1966.

Clarke, H. Harrison, and David H. Clarke, *Developmental and Adapted Physical Education.* Englewood Cliffs, N.J.: Prentice-Hall, Inc., 1963.

Consolazio, C. Frank, Robert E. Johnson, and Louis J. Pecora, *Physiological Measurements of Metabolic Functions in Man.* New York: McGraw-Hill Book Company, 1963.

Haldane, J. S., and J. G. Priestley, *Respiration.* New York: Oxford University Press, 1935.

Keys, Ancel, and Josef Brozek, "Body Fat in Adult Man," *Physiological Reviews*, 33, No. 3 (July 1953), 245.

Peters, John P., and Donald D. Van Slyke, *Quantitative Clinical Chemistry, Vol. II, Methods.* Baltimore: The Williams & Wilkins Co., 1932.

Riggs, Douglas S., *The Mathematical Approach to Physiological Problems.* Baltimore: The Williams & Wilkins Co., 1963.

Royce, Joseph, and Franklin Henry, "Two Inexpensive Bicycle Ergometers," *Research Quarterly*, 34, No. 1 (March 1963), 111.

Scholander, P. F., "Analyzer for Accurate Estimation of Respiratory Gases in One-Half Cubic Centimeter Samples," *Journal of Biological Chemistry*, 167, No. 1 (January 1947), 235.

Taylor, Henry, L., Elsworth Buskirk, and Austin Henschel, "Maximal Oxygen Intake as an Objective Measure of Cardio-Respiratory Performance," *Journal of Applied Physiology*, 8, No. 1 (July 1955), 73.

Van Slyke, Donald D., and James M. Neill, "The Determination of Gases in Blood and Other Solutions by Vacuum Extraction and Manometric Measurement," *Journal of Biological Chemistry*, 61, No. 2 (September 1924), 523.

Wasserman, K., G. G. Burton, and A. L. Van Kessel, "The Excess Lactate Concept and the Oxygen Debt of Exercise," *Journal of Applied Physiology*, 20, No. 6 (November 1965), 1299.

CHAPTER 14

Motor Learning

The area of psychology of sport that deals with learning and its related topics is usually termed motor learning. It is apparent from a perusal of the psychological literature that the primary interest of psychologists is in learning per se and only incidentally in the motor aspects of performance. Thus, there has developed a growing and maturing concern for an understanding of the motor performance capabilities of individuals involved in large scale muscular and coordinative acts. Although the line is not clearly drawn between what would be considered psychology and what would be physical education, there seems a greater concern in physical education for what may be termed gross motor activity than for fine motor ability. Large overlapping inevitably occurs, but this merely serves to strengthen both fields.

In contrast to the field of exercise physiology, where instrumentation is far more standardized, the motor learning specialist quite often must rely upon his own ingenuity for the development of suitable instruments or tests. Basic devices, such as timers, counters, pursuit rotors, and rather widely used tests of learning, such as star tracing or mirror tracing devices, can be purchased commercially, along with other types of equipment used in psychology. However, the tasks involving learning that are used so widely in physical education seem to be of two types—those that are self-testing and require very little or no accessory equipment and those for which the device has been fashioned by the investigator for a particular task.

When it comes to studying motor learning, the usual sports and games so commonly taught in activity classes are notoriously poor as learning modalities in research. Aside from the obvious difficulty of obtaining adequate measures from trial to trial is the more serious concern that the individual is so practiced in the event that he has in fact learned it. It is well-known that the greatest learning takes place in the early phases, and later in practice the gains are small; thus, common skills almost invariably find the individual with enough sophistication so that relatively little learning occurs. What is needed then is a novel skill, one in which the subject is naive and which can be expected not to have been practiced before. Sometimes old skills may be so modified as to meet this criterion, but more often some new task must be found. Even then, there is no guarantee that it will be suitable for learning, because its level of difficulty may be such that the subject grasps it right away or it is so difficult that extremely high trial-to-trial variability makes it unstable. The proper combination of factors seems to be a blending of the degree of difficulty and the ability of the subject to master the skill so that the trial-by-trial performances reflect a refinement of the task in a measureable manner. Some of these tasks will be discussed in this chapter, the aim being to study their applicability and their use in various other matters connected with performance psychology.

LEARNING TASKS

The decision to present selected motor learning tasks at the outset is prompted by the utilitarian purpose that once described their function can be used in later discussion. No attempt will be made to be exhaustive; rather, the tests most commonly used in physical education will be presented. The specialist in the field of motor learning will be aware of others, and the reader may acquire sufficient insight so as to develop other tests that can be used to study learning. As pointed out above, the modification of known skills has proven useful and quite often permits the use of available equipment and space. Indeed, one of the most intriguing aspects of this type of study is the simplicity with which it can be accomplished and, in most cases, at a fraction of the cost of equipment generally employed, as contrasted, for example, with physiology of exercise and other experimental research. This may or may not be an important consideration, but it has given solace to those researchers operating on a limited budget.

Stabilometer

The stabilometer has been used in studies of motor learning and motor performance, sometimes as a measure of balance,[1] but more recently it has been utilized in the study of motor learning itself. The instrument is actually nothing more than a horizontally pivoted board upon which the subject stands, the center of rotation being above the level of the feet so that the task is to try and maintain balance. This is done through the use of a selected number of trials; the technique is to measure the number of deviations, which may be called errors, so that in successive trials the subject reduces his error

---

[1] H. Hugh Mumby, "Kinesthetic Acuity and Balance Related to Wrestling Ability," *Research Quarterly*, 24, No. 3 (October 1953), 327.

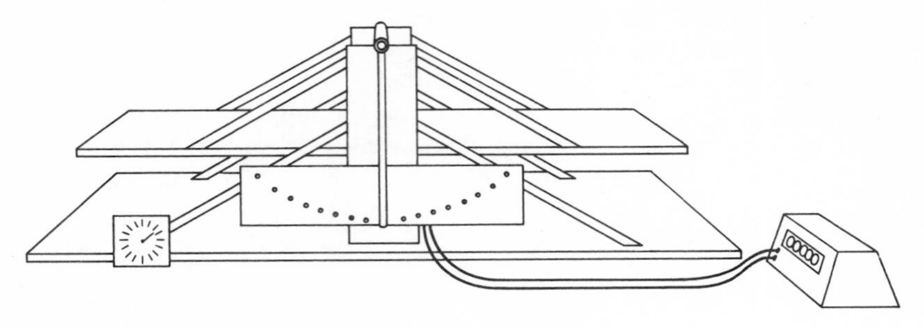

Figure 19. Stabilometer

of movement. A stabilometer currently in use is shown in Figure 19 and has been described by Bachman[2] as follows:

> Motion of the board was measured by a work adder. Any movement was transmitted by a 1.5 in. lever arm which was mounted on the axle. A waxed string which was fastened to the lever arm passed over the groove of a pulley 3.63 in. in net diameter that was independently pivoted, the spring being held taut by a coil spring exerting 150 gr tension. The pulley carried a flat disc 6 inch in diameter and $\frac{1}{8}$ inch thick, with a milled or knurled edge. A pawl rested against this edge, permitting easy rotation in one direction, but preventing any movement in the opposite direction. (In the latter case, the string slipped in the pulley groove.) The disc carried a calibrated dial which was scaled in 100 arbitrary units. Each scale unit represented 12 degrees of back and forth platform tilting. Microswitches were fastened under each end of the tilting board and wired in series with an electric clock so that no time was registered during such periods as the subject had the board completely out of balance and against the baseboard and could thereby rest without movement. This provision insured that each 30-sec trial represented that much net time of actual balancing effort.

Another way to handle the measurement of work done is to attach to the platform an electrical counting device, which is activated by the movement of an arm that mirrors the tilting of the platform. Copper electrical contacts can be so arranged as to activate a Veedor-Root counting device at selected intervals.

Each trial is usually 30 sec in duration, followed by 30 sec of rest, with 10 trials being used for the learning period. When this procedure is followed, the resultant learning curve obeys mathematical laws of the exponential

[2] John C. Bachman, "Specificity vs Generality in Learning and Performing Two Large Muscle Motor Tasks," *Research Quarterly*, 32, No. 1 (March 1961), 5. Used by permission of the author and AAHPER.

form.[3] Examples of stabilometer learning curves are available in a further study by Bachman.[4]

Ladder Climb

Bachman[5] has also provided another task, original with him, consisting of a free-standing ladder upon which the subject climbs. The apparatus, described as two parallel ladders connected by a common side, is 14 inches wide with the following specifications, as given by Bachman:

> The rungs (made of 1 in. dowling, 5 in. apart) were staggered in the two sections so that the distance from the bottom of the ladder to rung number 16 (the top) was 40 inches. A vertical extension was adjusted for each subject in such a manner that its top rung could just be grasped by his upward extended hand. Climbing was done near the middle of a 5 feet by 10 feet mat to lessen fear of injury in case of a fall. Tennis shoes were worn . . . to prevent, as much as possible, slipping off the ladder rungs. In the starting position, the ladder was held by the subject directly in front of him with the toes of both feet placed on the bottom crosspiece. It was required that climbing be done one step at a time.

In a manner similar to the stabilometer, the ladder climb is administered in 30 sec periods interspersed by 30 sec of rest. The task is to climb as high as possible before losing balance and then to reclimb once again, repeating as often as is necessary during each trial. The total accumulation of steps taken is utilized as the score for each testing period, and 10 trials constitute the performance. Examination of the learning curve[6] reflects a similar mathematical model as the stabilometer performance, that is, it follows the exponential law. However, as the ladder climb involves a progressive accumulation of scores, whereas the stabilometer results in a reduction, the learning curve goes upward rather than downward. There is also the addition of an extra component to the ladder climb early in performance that has been attributed to familiarity with the equipment.

Rho Test

The so-called rho test, the name coined because the path of movement circumscribes the lower case Greek letter rho, which has been reflected and

---

[3] For a description of exponential curve analysis, see Chapter 13.

[4] John C. Bachman, "Motor Learning and Performance as Related to Age and Sex in Two Measures of Balance Coordination," *Research Quarterly*, 32, No. 2 (May 1961), 123.

[5] Bachman (March 1961), *op. cit.*

[6] Bachman (May 1961), *op. cit.*, p. 128.

inverted, has been used in motor performance investigations for several years. Originally used by Mendryk[7] in the study of reaction and movement times, it was found to be a convenient device for lengthening the prescribed movement. It has subsequently proven to be an effective test for the determination of learning.[8]

The following description may be helpful in visualizing the apparatus and task, as adapted from Mendryk. A horizontal 4-inch hand lever is fastened to a bearing placed on a panel, $7\frac{1}{2} \times 13$ inches, at a distance of four inches to the right of a reaction key. The operating handle on this lever is a roller .64 inches high and .38 inches in diameter, held lightly between the thumb and the first two fingers. At the start, the lever is placed so that the handle is over the reaction key, holding it in the down position. At the signal, the subject moves the lever clockwise through one complete circle, and the lever abruptly stops when it strikes a rubber-covered peg mounted just in front of the reaction key. The subject's hand, however, continues in motion forward to the target, which is a piece of lightweight celluloid, $2 \times 3 \times .035$ inches, hinged so as to project vertically when in the ready position. The slightest touch of the finger tip against it is sufficient to cause it to flip down to the horizontal position flush with the main panel. Thus, the movement encompasses 36 inches, 25 in a circular motion and 11 directed forward. Appropriate chronoscopes may be installed to obtain both reaction time (*RT*) and movement time (*MT*).

In a typical application, the following testing sequence would be employed: The signal to start activates one timer; the subject's initial circular movement stops this clock (and hence gives the *RT*) and at the same time starts the second chronoscope. At the completion of the circular and linear phases, the second clock stops as soon as the celluloid target is touched (and thus gives the *MT*). Various combinations of these variables may be measured simply by adjusting the circuitry, although care must be taken to ensure that reaction time is not included as part of the performance score.

Data presented by Alderman[9] show that approximately a 38 per cent gain in performance occurs when 64 trials are given, spaced by 15-sec intervals.

Pursuit Rotor

Another technique for studying motor learning is provided by use of a pursuit rotor. Originally designed by Koerth,[10] the currently available

[7] Stephen Mendryk, "Reaction Time, Movement Time, and Task Specificity Relationships at Ages 12, 22, and 48 Years," *Research Quarterly*, 31, No. 2 (May 1960), 156.

[8] Richard B. Alderman, "Influence of Local Fatigue on Speed and Accuracy in Motor Learning," *Research Quarterly*, 36, No. 2 (May 1965), 131.

[9] *Ibid.*

[10] Wilhelmine Koerth, "Pursuit Apparatus: Eye-Hand Coordination," *Psychological Monographs*, 31, No. 1 (1922), 288.

instruments would seem to vary only in minor detail. The description given by Alderman[11] is representative of the pursuit rotors commonly in use:

> The subject grasped a stylus handle equipped with a rigid extension attached to his forearm by means of a strap. This served to eliminate finger and wrist action. The stylus proper (a metal rod 5-inches long, with the usual $\frac{1}{2}$-in. vertical bend at the $\frac{1}{8}$-in. diameter tip) was hinged horizontally to the handle. In response to an oral command and the initiation of turntable rotation (78 rpm), the subject pursued the target with the tip of the stylus. The target was a silver disc, 1-in. in diameter, the center of which was 4 inches from the center of the turntable and flush with the surface of the turntable. The subject's task was to maintain stylus-tip contact with the target disc as much as possible during each 15-sec trial. The amount of stylus-tip contact time per trial was recorded by a $\frac{1}{100}$-sec electric chronoscope. Each subject received a 10-sec rest between trials and each test day consisted of 60 trials.

Thus, as is noted for the rho test, a rather large number of trials is needed to secure the best estimate of performance and to allow the appropriate learning to occur. The amount of learning is substantial when the test is administered as described; in fact, Alderman found a 440 per cent gain in performance. It should be noted, perhaps, that the pursuit rotor may be obtained commercially.[12]

Juggling

The task of juggling is quite different from the ones mentioned so far, primarily in the method of scoring and thus in assessing performance. Obviously, the scoring of trials would not be the same, and thus no learning curves, as such, are available. However, it can be considered a motor task, and it is likely that few individuals have had prior experience or practice that would invalidate their inclusion as subjects.

As suggested by Knapp and Dixon,[13] the task consists of juggling three balls to the extent that one ball must be in the air at all times; if two balls touch a hand simultaneously, the count must be discontinued. The criterion for learning is to make 100 consecutive catches; scoring is based upon the cumulative number of minutes of practice until the criterion is met. Learning thus becomes a matter of reaching a fixed goal with considerable variability among individual capabilities. In fact, it has been necessary to eliminate

---

[11] Alderman, *op. cit.*, p. 133. Used by permission of the author and AAHPER.

[12] Suggested source: Lafayette Instrument Company, Lafayette, Indiana 47902.

[13] Clyde G. Knapp and W. Robert Dixon, "Learning to Juggle: I. A Study to Determine the Effect of Two Different Distributions of Practice on Learning Efficiency," *Research Quarterly*, 21, No. 3 (October 1950), 331.

subjects simply because they failed to learn the task, even after extended practice.[14]

Ball Toss

A number of skills involving throwing are available in a variety of physical activities, some of which involve speed whereas others require accuracy. When throwing at a wall target, there may be elements of both. Whether or not these can be successful learning media is questionable, since throwing per se is a skill that most subjects have practiced. Thus, better performers exhibit higher scores and perhaps less variability, but they may not exhibit real learning. The use of an accuracy throw, as given by a ball toss seems to offer better possibilities, particularly if the task is a novel one. Attempts have been made to modify a known task,[15] and still others have taken a standard ball and have modified the skill. For instance, Egstrom, Logan, and Wallis[16] tossed a ball over a crossbar and onto a target consisting of three concentric circles ranging from 7 inches in diameter to 35 inches. Scoring was accomplished by assigning values of 5, 3, and 1 to the target areas.

More recently, Ambo[17] modified the ball toss task so that a continuous scoring method could be employed. In order to do this, a circular board four feet in diameter was placed on the floor at an angle of 34 degrees. In the center, a steel metric tape was secured so that it could rotate 360 degrees, thus permitting a rapid measure of each trial. In order to facilitate the scoring, the target face was chalked, and the ball was dampened with water so that a clear impression was made on the board. The distance from the target center to the center of the mark was used as the measure of accuracy. To control the trajectory, a bar—placed 3 feet 11 inches from the subject and 8 feet from the target—was adjusted to 6 inches above each subject's standing height. In this particular investigation, it was deemed advisable to standardize the throwing motion so that only the movement of elbow extension and wrist flexion was possible. To do this, an adjustable platform was employed upon which the subject rested his upper arm at shoulder height; a strap helped to

---

[14] Clyde G. Knapp, W. Robert Dixon, and Murney Lazier, "Learning to Juggle: III. A Study of Performance by Two Different Age Groups," *Research Quarterly*, 29, No. 1 (March 1958), 32.

[15] Robert N. Singer, "Massed and Distributed Practice Effects on the Acquisition and Retention of a Novel Basketball Skill," *Research Quarterly*, 36, No. 1 (March 1965), 68.

[16] Glen H. Egstrom, Gene A. Logan, and Earl L. Wallis, "Acquisition of Throwing Skill Involving Projectiles of Varying Weights," *Research Quarterly*, 31, No. 3 (October 1960), 420.

[17] Dennis M. Ambo, "Individual Differences in Various Structural and Strength Measures of the Hand and Forearm and their Relation to Accuracy of Performance," unpublished Master's Thesis, University of Maryland, 1966.

stabilize this position. A soccer ball was used, and each subject was given 50 trials.

A rather sizable learning occurred from this task. For 70 subjects, the improvement in accuracy amounted to approximately 50 per cent over the first 7 trials; a steady state occurred after trial 35. The progress of learning was curvilinear, occurring rapidly at first and slower during later stages.

Mirror Tracing

As developed by Snoddy,[18] this task consists of tracing the path of a 6-sided star while looking in a mirror (see Figure 20). Essentially, the device

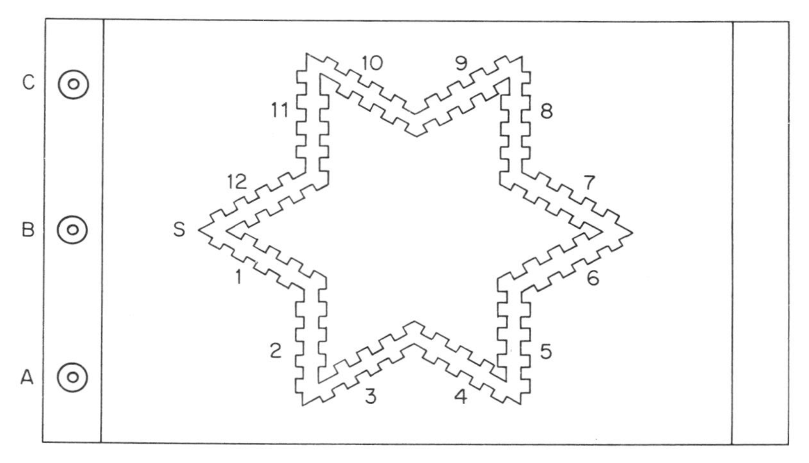

Figure 20. Mirror-Tracing Star Test (Reproduced by permission of the American Psychological Association. Originally published by the *Journal of Applied Psychology*.)

is a sheet of brass, from which a star-shaped path $\frac{1}{4}$-inch wide has been cut. This is then mounted upon a heavy glass plate. Rather than using a smooth-sided figure, the star is cut in an indented manner, as illustrated, to facilitate the learning, presumably by supplying feedback of information concerning errors. At any rate, it tends to force the subject out into the path. A soft copper stylus is used; an electrical connection is made between the brass plate, the stylus, and a counter so that each contact with the edge of the star is

[18] George S. Snoddy, "Learning and Stability: A Psychological Analysis of a Case of Motor Learning with Clinical Applications," *Journal of Applied Psychology*, 10, No. 1 (1926), 1.

counted mechanically. The usual procedure is to obscure the hand and star from direct vision but to observe it by means of a mirror image. The subject begins at *S* and proceeds in the direction indicated, each trial separated by 10 sec. The usual learning curves result from 20 circuits.

Ring-Peg Test

Lambert[19] devised a ring-peg test to study motor learning; the test apparatus consists of a peg board on which are placed two identical patterns of pegs situated in opposition to each other. The subject can view directly the near pattern. The far pattern is obscured by a plywood panel but can be seen through a mirror that is attached to the end of the peg board, as shown in Figure 21. Thus, the subject moves washers from the near, visual side, to

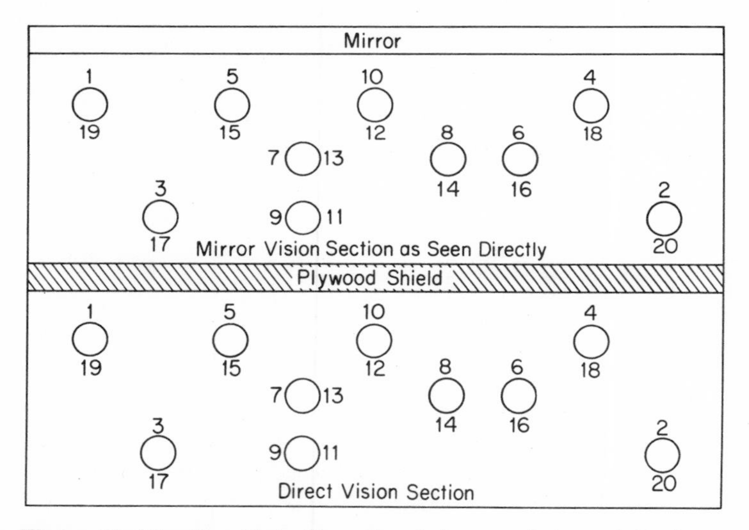

Figure 21. Ring-Peg Test (Reproduced by permission of Professor Philip Lambert, Director, Instructional Research Laboratory, University of Wisconsin, and AAHPER.)

corresponding pegs on the far, mirrored side. This is done in the sequence as given until two washers from each peg are distributed to the opposite side. In order to control the alternating hand sequence, the subject begins by depressing with both index fingers a key that turns off a light. The investigator then starts a stop watch that serves as the signal to begin, and the subject

[19] Philip Lambert, "Practice Effect of Non-Dominant vs. Dominant Musculature in Acquiring Two-Handed Skill," *Research Quarterly*, 22, No. 1 (March 1951), 50.

proceeds with his left hand to peg one. He completes the task, returns his hand to the key, goes to peg two with his right hand, and thus alternates throughout the board until a total of 20 washers has been placed on the far side. The watch is stopped with the positioning of the 20th washer, thus constituting the first trial.

The decision to use one hand or two depends upon the experimental circumstances, as does the total number of trials. Examination of the performance curves reveals considerable learning, even beyond 40 trials.

Maze

A maze can be developed for use by humans as well as by animals for the purpose of studying learning. Two such attempts were made by Cratty.[20] One maze was a small stylus pattern adapted from Cook;[21] the other was a large maze, identical in pattern to the small one (see Figure 22) but through

Figure 22. Cratty's Maze Pathway (Bryant J. Cratty, "Recency Versus Primacy in a Complex Motor Task," *Research Quarterly*, 34, March, 1963. Reproduced by permission of Dr. Bryant Cratty and AAHPER.)

which the subjects could walk. Cratty gave the following description of the small maze:

> The pathway of the small maze was drilled, routed, and smoothed until it became $\frac{1}{2}$ in. wide. The masonite containing the pattern was then mounted on a second piece of plywood so that a clearance between the two surfaces

[20] Bryant J. Cratty, "Comparison of Learning a Fine Motor Task with Learning a Similar Gross Motor Task, Using Kinesthetic Cues," *Research Quarterly*, 33, No. 2 (May 1962), 212. Used by permission of the author and AAHPER.

[21] T. W. Cook, "Studies in Cross-Education: III. Kinesthetic Learning of an Irregular Pattern," *Journal of Experimental Psychology*, 17, No. 5 (October 1934), 749.

resulted, which allowed the lip of the stylus to pass freely. The stylus was lathe-turned with a handle 6 in. long and 1 in. in diameter; a tip was turned to $\frac{1}{8}$ in. diameter and made $\frac{3}{4}$ in. long. The tip of the stylus was threaded and a washer 1 in. in diameter was attached so that the stylus would fit into the maze pathway and slide through without binding. The small maze was then attached to a table for stability and placed in a quiet room. The maze was covered until the subject's stylus was placed in the pathway's starting point.

The large maze was increased 30 times in length and 96 times in width, but the original pattern was retained. The subject made contact with the pathway through the volar surface of his hand against $\frac{3}{8}$-inch plastic tubing that was glued to wooden supports at a height of 30 inches from the ground and placed two feet apart. Neither maze contained blind alleys. The task is to traverse each maze as quickly as possible while blindfolded. Times are recorded with a stopwatch to the nearest $\frac{1}{10}$ sec with 12 trials constituting the learning period. Both tasks yield large amounts of learning.

Summary

In summary, tasks that have been developed for the study of motor learning have been presented. Before serious study may be undertaken in this field, an acquaintance with the tests that have been devised to produce measurable learning is necessary. It should be pointed out that other tasks are needed, so thought should be given to this end in the future.

The remaining portion of the chapter will be devoted to a discussion of some of the more current research concepts that have been the concern of investigators in physical education. In so doing, specific references will be selected to illustrate the methodological approach undertaken with a brief note of the findings. The selections are made not with the intention of reviewing the literature nor of emphasizing only a limited point of view but of offering examples that may serve to underscore the research technique.

DOCTRINE OF SPECIFICITY

One of the more mature developments in the field of motor performance has been the identification of the extreme specificity among tasks of motor ability. In spite of early evidence to the contrary,[22] physical education has typically thought of coordination as being a general trait; one was either coordinated or uncoordinated. If he could be considered an athlete, for

[22] Harold G. Seashore, "Some Relationships of Fine and Gross Motor Abilities," *Research Quarterly*, 13, No. 3 (October 1942), 259.

instance, this would be seen to carry over automatically from one motor task to another; nearly everyone can envision examples of such a person. Reference to the development of general motor abilities tests was supposed to measure the degree of generality in the performance of physical tasks. The difficulty was, however, that few persons evaluated the extent of the relationship of individual differences among large neuromotor coordination abilities. The establishment of the doctrine of specificity can be attributed to Henry,[23] who largely conceived the theoretical framework and then stimulated the experimental testing of hypotheses. The considerable advancement of the theory has provided insight into motor performance and human capabilities.

Reaction Time vs Movement Time

When reaction time and movement time have been examined, it has been typical to find a low (usually nonsignificant) correlation between them. This has resulted from tests of both arm and leg tasks.[24] Apparently, individual differences in reaction time are not related to individual differences in movement time—ability to move fast is in no way dependent upon the ability to react fast. These are separate coordinations involving excitation on the one hand and contraction of muscles on the other.

Strength and Speed

Perhaps the larger question concerns the contraction of muscle per se and those factors governing the physical limits of action. In an important paper on this subject, Henry and Whitley[25] theorized that since the force (F) that would move a limb mass (m) a distance (d) in a time (t) could be given by the equation $F = 2md/t^2$, the result would be a measure of strength in action. Thus, the correlation of interest would be between measured muscular strength and force estimated from the formula. Using a horizontal adductive arm movement, it was found that the correlation was nonsignificant. Apparently, individual differences in isometric strength do not predict strength in action as given by maximal speed of movement. In other words, there is a maximum amount of specificity in such tasks, both being controlled by separate neuromotor coordination pathways of the central nervous system. Far from being an isolated finding, such results persist from sample to sample and from one

---

[23] Franklin M. Henry, "Specificity vs Generality in Learning Motor Skills," *Proceedings of the College Physical Education Association*, 61 (1958), 126.

[24] Leon E. Smith, "Reaction Time and Movement Time in Four Large Muscle Movements," *Research Quarterly*, 32, No. 1 (March 1961), 88.

[25] F. M. Henry and J. D. Whitley, "Relationships between Individual Differences in Strength, Speed, and Mass in an Arm Movement," *Research Quarterly*, 31, No. 1 (March 1960), 24.

study to another. In fact, when subjects are trained with weights to effect a change in strength, the correlation between changes in strength and changes in speed is still low.[26]

Memory Drum Theory

As a consequence of the experimental observations and with respect to the neuroanatomy involved, Henry proposed a memory drum theory to explain the occurrence of planned and purposeful movement.[27] Learned acts of skill, developed as a result of practice over varying periods of time, are stored in the unconscious motor memory so that at a later time they may be tapped and brought forth in response to some stimulus. Analagous to computer program concepts, the appropriate act is programmed in some form of motor "memory drum" that will call into play appropriate coordinations when given the proper cues. Thus, an experiment was designed to test the hypothesis that the reaction time would be longer when the response movement was more complex than would be the case when the response was simple. This, indeed, was the case; undoubtedly, the more choices that are to be made in movement the more time that is required to program properly the events to follow.

Specificity vs Generality

It is essential to the interpretation of the literature in this area that the reader be acquainted with the mathematical and statistical use of the terms specificity and generality. As commonly employed, the relationship of individual differences in one task to those in another task is given by the correlation coefficient (r), provided that the influence of error variance (unreliability) is removed by the correction for attenuation. In order to assess the obtained correlation, two avenues are available: One is the test of significance, and the other is the test for specificity and generality. In the former instance, one may simply refer to a table of correlations at the appropriate degrees of freedom ($N - 2$) and either accept or reject the hypothesis that the two variables are related (or not related). In other words, this permits the investigator to determine if the correlation is essentially zero or not. It should be pointed out that since a correlation does not have to be particularly large to be significant, it does not help very much in deciding the larger issue.

[26] David H. Clarke and Franklin M. Henry, "Neuromotor Specificity and Increased Speed from Strength Development," *Research Quarterly*, 32, No. 3 (October 1961), 315.

[27] Franklin M. Henry and Donald E. Rogers, "Increased Response Latency for Complicated Movements and a 'Memory Drum' Theory of Neuromotor Reactions," *Research Quarterly*, 31, No. 3 (October 1960), 448.

The other procedure—that of determining the specificity or generality—is dependent upon the assessment of individual difference variance that is common between two tasks. This is done by calculating r^2; when multiplied by 100 it gives the per cent of generality. On the other hand, the amount of individual difference variance not common between two tasks is given by the squared coefficient of alienation k^2, which is defined as $1 - r^2$. Thus, $k^2 \times 100$ is the per cent of specificity. The interpretive decision that may be made will depend upon the relative balance of the two factors; as related to the question of motor ability, it could be argued that greater specificity than generality exists if k^2 is greater than r^2. It should be clear, therefore, that a correlation of $r = .71$ would be a rough dividing line between these two concepts. (See Chapter 11 for a further development of these statistical concepts.)

DISTRIBUTION OF PRACTICE

The manner in which learning takes place has been a study of interest for a number of years. The question relates to the length of time between bouts of practice and the distributions of practice schedules required to learn some act, either mental or physical. Aside from the practical value that it will yield information as to the most effective approach to the teaching of physical activities, it also may give basic information on the way people learn motor acts. Actually, the data available seem to divide themselves into the dichotomous functions of massed vs distributed practice. Although these are relative terms and must be described for each experimental situation, the main question is whether or not individuals learn more effectively when trials are given with only brief intertrial rest intervals or when they are spaced by varying periods of time.

Before such a study may be undertaken, however, the investigator must have a task that provides learning, as indicated earlier in this chapter. In fact, the typical learning curves seem to be based upon massed practice, that is, the rest interval between each trial is of very short duration, usually long enough for the investigator to record the data from the previous trial and to reset timers, counters, and the like for the next trial. Whether or not the same amount of learning could be achieved with fewer practice sessions set at differing intervals is an intriguing one in the study of motor learning.

It is felt that spaced practice periods are more effective than massed periods of practice for both verbal and motor learning,[28] although Ryan[29]

[28] Joseph B. Oxendine, "Effect of Progressively Changing Practice Schedules on the Learning of a Motor Skill," *Research Quarterly*, 36, No. 3 (October 1965), 307.

[29] E. Dean Ryan, "Prerest and Postrest Performance on the Stabilometer as a Function of Distribution of Practice," *Research Quarterly*, 36, No. 2 (May 1965), 197.

points out that this may depend upon the nature of the task itself. For example, some tasks, such as performance on the stabilometer, can be called "self-paced" tasks, in which the performer is allotted a certain amount of time for each trial; what the performer does during the time of practice depends upon his reactions to the skill and, of course, his ability to learn the skill. The time between trials can be lengthened, as well as the duration of the trial itself. However, when practice was distributed by spacing 10, 20, 30, and 40 sec rest between trials, no effect on stabilometer performance was noted. When learning to juggle, 5 min practice time per day was more effective than 15 min,[30] and when a novel basketball skill was employed, the subjects that rested 24 hours between sets of trials learned the skill more rapidly than did the subjects that participated in massed practice to 5 min of interpolated rest.[31]

RETENTION

The next matter involves the retention of motor performance. This has also been of interest to investigators who have asked the question of how long skills can be retained once they have been learned. It has been a commonplace observation that certain skills are retained for rather extended periods of time, sometimes even years. Skills learned in childhood, such as swimming, skiing, skating, bicycling, and others, are apparently learned so well that in later adult life they can be brought forth with reasonably good accuracy. Obviously, the amount of excellence will be impaired, but apparently the skill can be relearned rather quickly to the previous level. The characteristics of this learning are matters of prime concern to investigators in the field of motor performance.

It would be naive to suggest that the problem should be studied longitudinally for years, as suggested in the previous example, since the time element would render the topic useless to most investigators. Thus, the concern has been to employ a motor learning task, apply a series of trials, and then permit rest periods to ensue, followed by more trials on the criterion task. The extent of retention, or its reciprocal, forgetting, may be dependent on the type of skill learned. For example, in a study employing a random group design, (Chapter 12), Ryan[32] found the retention, when given 3, 5, 7,

---

[30] Clyde G. Knapp, W. Robert Dixon, and Murney Lazier, "Learning to Juggle: III. A Study of Performance by Two Different Age Groups," *Research Quarterly*, 29, No. 1 (March 1958), 32.

[31] Robert N. Singer, "Massed and Distributed Practice Effects on the Acquisition and Retention of a Novel Basketball Skill," *Research Quarterly*, 36, No. 1 (March 1965), 68.

[32] E. Dean Ryan, "Retention of Stabilometer and Pursuit Rotor Skills," *Research Quarterly*, 33, No. 4 (December 1962), 593.

and 21 days after the original learning trials, to be greater for the pursuit rotor than for the stabilometer skills in the early retention trails, but they actually appeared to gain in ability (called reminiscence) for the pursuit rotor.

Apparently, the loss in ability was not related to the length of rest, a finding that prompted additional work with the stabilometer.[33] The subjects in this random group experiment were retested at intervals of 3 months, 6 months, and 12 months in order to study not only the amount of retention but also the pattern of relearning. All three groups lost considerable proficiency, ranging from 50 to 81 per cent; the subjects with the longest interval retained the least ability. In fact, the 12-month rest period apparently impaired the relearning phase, as this group failed to recover their performance to the extent of the other groups.

REMINISCENCE

Very closely allied to problems of practice distribution and retention is the question of reminiscence. Reminiscence may be described as the increase in performance that may occur following the cessation of practice. As pointed out above in the study by Ryan, such reminiscence occurred in the condition of retention for the pursuit motor skill; however, it is not always present, as attested to by studies employing the stabilometer and the ladder.[34]

A number of attempts have been made to explain the occurrence of reminiscence; the reader will find the review by Fox and Young [35] helpful in dealing with this phenomenon. A single theory that would broadly apply to studies in the motor learning field does not seem feasible at this time, inasmuch as so little is known of the neurology involved in learning. The intangible variable would seem to be the element of time in the standardization of what can be called a nonpractice interval. In serial learning trials, very short rest periods are employed; the trial-by-trial improvement in performance is not referred to as reminiscence, but when the rest interval is extended, the term may apply.

Perhaps it is the potentiality for change that is vital, and the interpolation of rest must come before all of the learning has taken place. Inasmuch as learning curves tend to be exponential, the closer one gets to the asymptote, the less change in performance can be expected. Thus, a period of rest given

---

[33] E. Dean Ryan, "Retention of Stabilometer Performance over Extended Periods of Time," *Research Quarterly*, 36, No. 1 (March 1965), 46.

[34] Judith L. Meyers, "Retention of Balance Coordination Learning as Influenced by Extended Lay-Offs," *Research Quarterly*, 38, No. 1 (March 1967), 72.

[35] Margaret G. Fox and Vera P. Young, "Effect of Reminiscence on Learning Selected Badminton Skills," *Research Quarterly*, 33, No. 3 (October 1962), 386.

late in learning will result more in forgetting, whereas that given earlier would be more apt to exhibit reminiscence. Whether or not this will occur is a matter for experimentation.

TRANSFER

One of the most prevalent constructs in education today is the anticipation that things learned will carry over to practical endeavors—that the underlying elements present in one situation will be available for application in another. In other words, there are basic elements that can be expected to exhibit transfer. It should be pointed out that much of this is undocumented; its acceptance must remain tentative until more evidence becomes available. Isolating the causative factors of this learning process is difficult and will probably be done in very carefully controlled situations.

Similar strong feelings exist in physical education that elements in motor skills may be transferred. This is implied by the emphasis upon the so-called elements in general motor fitness that has persisted for so long. If one is able to accept the doctrine of specificity, however, it is difficult to imagine that a high degree of transfer occurs in the area of neuromotor coordinations, except where there are like elements. Even then, there is controversy as to whether or not teaching progression should always be from simple to complex or whether mastery of the more complex is equally justified, thus obviating the necessity for presenting the simple skills. This is especially intriguing if the complex activity includes the simple skills.

By way of illustration, in 1962, Cratty[36] employed the practice of learning of a small maze to determine if this facilitated learning of a large maze. One group of subjects was given practice on a stylus maze that was identical to the large maze, while another group practiced on one that was a reversal of the large maze, and still another group practiced on a stylus maze completely unrelated to the large maze. A control group received no stylus maze practice, thus completing the random group design. Apparently, practice on the similar pattern resulted in improved large maze scores, illustrating the positive transfer effects of such practice. Negative transfer also occurs, as shown by the retarding effect on learning from practice of the reverse pattern stylus maze.

Later, Rivenes[37] experimented with the possibility of multiple-task transfer whereby subjects learning several skills would be examined for transfer effects. He devised an apparatus resembling a modified shuffleboard.

---

[36] Bryant J. Cratty, "Transfer of Small-Pattern Practice to Large-Pattern Learning," *Research Quarterly*, 33, No. 4 (December 1962), 523.

[37] Richard S. Rivenes, "Multiple-Task Transfer Effects in Perceptual-Motor Learning," *Research Quarterly*, 38, No. 3 (October 1967), 485.

The subject stood with his back to the apparatus and received his visual cues from a mirror; the nonpreferred hand was used in performing the skill. Target distances were graded into degrees of difficulty; three were shorter than the transfer task, and three were longer. The practice sequence provided various multiple- and single-task conditions. Apparently, the multiple-task practice of relatively easy tasks facilitated transfer, although with the more difficult tasks, single-task practice would appear to be most effective in causing transfer.

MENTAL PRACTICE

Motor acts, to be learned, must first be conceived, usually a visual process that involves certain cognitive processes of the higher nervous centers. Physical education teachers have long known that this cognition is enhanced by demonstrating the skill to be learned, usually after a brief description. The more complicated the skill the more explanation and demonstration that is required; along the same lines, the more advanced the performer the less rehearsal is needed. Novel skills, such as those usually used in the study of motor learning, probably obtain needed feedback from the performance itself, although the subject may anticipate the task to varying degrees, depending upon his previous experience and ability.

Aside from these considerations is the question here of the role of mental practice per se on the ability to learn motor skills. It is a rather commonplace observation among individuals that they can conjure up the mental image of a skill, and thus, in a sense, rehearse it prior to the actual performance. This type of kinesthetic organization must draw upon some sort of mental proprioception to guide later response. The question is not whether mental practice is effective but how effective it is and under what circumstances can it be expected to operate. The reader is directed to two excellent reviews on this subject by Richardson.[38,39]

By way of illustration, Smith and Harrison[40] utilized the experimental approach with an eye-hand coordination task. They employed a three-hole punchboard that counted the number of hits made by the subject with a metal stylus; stress was given to speed and accuracy of movement. Five

---

[38] Alan Richardson, "Mental Practice: A Review and Discussion, Part I," *Research Quarterly*, 38, No. 1 (March 1967), 95.

[39] Alan Richardson, "Mental Practice: A Review and Discussion, Part II," *Research Quarterly*, 38, No. 2 (May 1967), 263.

[40] Leon E. Smith and John S. Harrison, "Comparison of the Effects of Visual, Motor, Mental, and Guided Practice upon Speed and Accuracy of Performing a Simple Eye-Hand Coordination Task," *Research Quarterly*, 33, No. 2 (May 1962), 299.

groups were used with learning situations assigned as follows: first, interpolated motor practice; second, visual practice; third, reversed-visual practice; fourth, mental practice; and fifth, guided practice. An additional control group that received no practice was included; only the initial and final tests given all subjects were administered. The results showed that mental practice and visual practice improved performance significantly by achieving more correct hits and fewer errors in the criterion task.

Such studies have also been attempted using total body performance. In fact, Jones[41] employed a gymnastic skill, the hock-swing upstart, selected because it could be scored on a pass-fail basis, thus making subjective estimates unnecessary. The mental practice was carried out in two forms, both given before the subjects were permitted to practice the skill. One group of subjects was given directed mental practice, during which the experimenter controlled most of the mental practice by reading instructions aloud; the second group recieved essentially undirected mental practice. After 6 successive sessions, the criterion task was administered for the first time. It was found that the group given undirected mental practice achieved a significantly greater skill in the performance.

TIMING

The ability to time movements is an important ingredient in the performance of physical activities. It is notably lacking in early childhood; as a youngster grows older, he makes rapid improvements so that he can catch, kick, or hit a ball with some implement. Each of these skills, and a host of others, requires the individual to mentally plot the path of some moving object and then to intercept its flight at some optimal point. Learning to do this successfully may indeed occupy an individual's attention and require continual practice for years, as attested to by the degree of excellence required by contemporary athletes.

The common feature of most of these tasks is to anticipate the arrival of some object and then to plan ahead so that it may be anticipated at the correct moment. This is generally referred to as coincidence-anticipation. The illustration as explained by Slater-Hammel[42] is pertinent:

> As a means of illustrating the nature of coincidence-anticipation, let it be supposed that a subject (*S*) is given the simple task of moving his hand off a

[41] John Gerald Jones, "Motor Learning Without Demonstration of Physical Practice, Under Two Conditions of Mental Practice," *Research Quarterly*, 36, No. 3 (October 1965), 270.

[42] A. T. Slater-Hammel, "Reliability, Accuracy, and Refractoriness of a Transit Reaction," *Research Quarterly*, 31, No. 2 (May 1960), 217. Used by permission of the author and AAHPER.

signal key at the instant a moving marker passes across a fixed marker. In performance of this task there are two possible procedures available to *S*. First, *S* may take exact coincidence of the markers to be the stimulus for his response, and second, *S* may attempt to make his response simultaneous with coincidence using coincidence-anticipation; under this operating rule the inevitable delays in human sensory-response systems will enter, and *S*'s response will always be one reaction time late. If the second procedure is followed, *S* may be said to be using coincidence-anticipation, and it is only by anticipating coincidence of the markers that *S* can possibly avoid being late.

Thus a variety of experimental situations could be devised to study timing control. Grose[43] elected to study movements of the finger, arm, and whole body in response to a moving target. His target was a pointer that moved along a track at a rate of 4.15 feet per sec; the three tasks were to intercept the moving pointer by pressing a contact plate with the hand, by moving the arm, or by stepping forward two steps and kicking a target. The individuals in all three tasks tended toward early estimates of coincidence. Apparently, coincidence timing exhibits greater task specificity rather than generality; also of interest was the finding that individual differences in reaction time were not related to coincidence timing ability.

In order to study the problem associated with simultaneous timing of arms and legs, Norrie[44] developed a target board that contained a series of two-inch diameter metal discs, accompanied by appropriate microswitches that activated marking pens. The tasks were a series of simultaneous movements involving various combinations of hand and foot actions to be performed as quickly as possible, each requiring contact with certain discs on the target board. For the more complicated tasks, starting time differences and contact time differences were significantly longer than for the simpler tasks. There also seemed to be rather considerable generality between the time measures.

A number of recent studies concerned with tracking have linked subject response with proprioceptive feedback.[45,46] Additional references on these and related topics can be found in Adams[47] and Schmidt.[48]

---

[43] Joel E. Grose, "Timing Control and Finger, Arm, and Whole Body Movements," *Research Quarterly*, 38, No. 1 (March 1967), 10.

[44] Mary Lou Norrie, "Timing of Two Simultaneous Movements of Arms and Legs," *Research Quarterly*, 35, No. 4 (December 1964), 511.

[45] Jack A. Adams and Lyle R. Creamer, "Proprioception Variables as Determiners of Anticipatory Timing Behavior," *Human Factors*, 4 (August 1962), 217.

[46] M. J. Ellis, R. A. Schmidt, and M. G. Wade, "Proprioception Variables as Determinants of Lapsed Time Estimation," *Ergonomics*, 11, No. 6 (November 1968), 577.

[47] Jack A. Adams, "Motor Skills," *Annual Review of Psychology*, 15 (1964), 181.

[48] Richard A. Schmidt, "Anticipation and Timing in Motor Performance," *Psychological Bulletin*, 70, No. 6 (1968), 631.

KINESTHESIS

An area of special concern to those interested in the experimental psychology of performance has been that of kinesthesis. Essentially, this involves the perception of movement, the sensation of position, or the control of motor performance. It is a developmental phenomenon that is mostly lacking or undeveloped in infancy and quite often well-developed in the adult. Babies and young children are typically uncoordinated in their responses and have poor balance. As they grow during childhood, they become better at proprioceptive adjustments and develop the awareness of spatial relationships, both with their own bodies and in relation to their external environment. It is largely held that the introduction of physical skills in childhood will lead to enhanced adult ability, although the evidence for this may be fragmentary. Observation would have it, though, that youngsters in their preadolescent years may achieve rather high levels of skill in certain types of athletics. Presumably, this is a result of large amounts of practice.

Whether or not there is any such single entity as "kinesthetic sense" is questionable, and just how proprioceptive feedback is utilized by the individual is not clearly understood. However, it is reasonable to indicate that certain adjustments can be made, but the extent of the performer's awareness of them is not always clear. His muscular adaptation to changing external stimuli is often reflexive and many times involves just a monosynaptic relay in the central nervous system for adjustment of muscular tension. At any rate, this ability must be marked by a high degree of individual differences, judging by the range of performance capabilities exhibited by the general population.

Physiologically, the proprioceptors that are of importance to muscular function include: the muscle spindles, which monitor muscle length; the Golgi tendon organs, which monitor muscular tension; the pacinian corpuscles in joints and articular cartilages, which monitor joint and limb position in space; and a series of free nerve endings present in muscles, tendons, ligaments, and joints, whose function in kinesthesis may be a result of muscular tension. The vestibular receptors of the inner ear are also extremely important in balance control, especially in those activities involved in tumbling, diving, and the like.

Because kinesthesis is such a general term, a rather large number of tasks have been used in research to represent its function. The reasoning seems to be that if kinesthesis means muscular control, then administration of a test involving body or limb position or muscular adaptation would seem to suffice as a measure of kinesthesis. The description of a substantial number of these tasks can be found in studies by Wiebe[49] and Scott.[50] It is interesting to note, however, that the findings in both studies reflected a lack of relationship among the various tests used. In other words, the low correlations obtained would indicate a small amount of generality and thus would support the doctrine of specificity of motor performance. It would seem then, that there may actually be no such single entity as kinesthesis but rather that it is made up of a large number of specific items.

The relationship of kinesthesis to other performance abilities has also resulted in rather low correlation. Roloff[51] correlated a battery of tests, including balance stick, arm raising, weight shifting, and arm circling, against the Scott motor ability test. The resulting coefficient of .42 is low, although it is both significant and positive. Witte[52] gave 7- to 9-year-old boys and girls the four kinesthetic tests of forward arm raising with the preferred and nonpreferred arms and sideward arm raising with the preferred and nonpreferred arms. The correlation with certain ball handling measures was .28, indicating that no real relationship existed between these two functions.

In order to study the effectiveness of feedback of visual information on kinesthetic learning, Morford[53] employed a modification of the apparatus designed by Henry[54] to study the dynamic muscular response to changing external tensions. One group received practice while given kinesthetic information only, and the two other groups were given varying amounts of supplementary visual cues (random group design). It was found that the feedback of visual information facilitated subsequent kinesthetic performance.

The question of perceptual recall of visual tactual information has been of recent interest to investigators, and it seemingly represents a growing interest in such phenomena for the future. For example, Cratty and Hutton[55] sought to determine if a configural aftereffect was produced when subjects traversed, while blindfolded, curved and straight pathways. It was concluded that this was indeed possible. This concern has been extended to the field of

---

[49] Vernon R. Wiebe, "A Study of Tests of Kinesthesis," *Research Quarterly*, 25, No. 2 (May 1954), 222.

[50] M. Gladys Scott, "Measurement of Kinesthesis," *Research Quarterly*, 26, No. 3 (October 1955), 324.

[51] Louise L. Roloff, "Kinesthesis in Relation to the Learning of Selected Motor Skills," *Research Quarterly*, 24, No. 2 (May 1953), 210.

[52] Fae Witte, "Relation of Kinesthetic Perception to a Selected Motor Skill for Elementary School Children," *Research Quarterly*, 33, No. 3.(October 1962), 476.

[53] W. R. Morford, "The Value of Supplementary Visual Information During Practice on Dynamic Kinesthetic Learning," *Research Quarterly*, 37, No. 3 (October 1966), 393.

[54] Franklin M. Henry, "Dynamic Kinesthetic Perception and Adjustment," *Research Quarterly*, 24, No. 2 (May 1953), 176.

[55] Bryant J. Cratty and Robert S. Hutton, "Figural Aftereffects Resulting from Gross Action Patterns," *Research Quarterly*, 35, No. 2 (May 1964), 116.

muscular performance where the immediate effects of various overloads on contraction have been studied. Nelson and Nofsinger[56] gave overload trials ranging from 15 to 45 per cent of maximal strength and then tested the speed of movement of the elbow flexor muscles. Although no actual change in performance was noted, the subjects experienced a kinesthetic illusion of greater speed.

BALANCE

It is not intended to separate the skill of balance from kinesthesis, but it deserves special mention. Ordinarily, balance is included in the variables of the kinesthetics researcher, as the fine adjustments made by muscles in maintaining balance are primary ingredients of many skills. It is perhaps most obvious in the host of gymnastic skills available, notably those performed in other than the standing position, but balance—however one defines it—is also essential in most other skills. A difference between standing balance and dynamically changing balance may be argued; perhaps, the latter may best be described by such terms as agility, speed, form, and so forth, although this may merely serve to emphasize the complexity of kinesthetic phenomena. There remains the additional concept that balance is reflected in how well a person is able to balance an implement.

It should be fairly obvious at this point that a single entity called balance may be elusive. Thus, one may find a number of test items that one way or another incorporate some form of balance. As has been true with motor ability tests in general, a lack of correlation between items of balance has been reported, suggesting high specificity. However, factor analysis has identified factors in motor ability that seem to emphasize traits of balance.[57]

A rather different approach was taken by Estep[58] in employing a device known as an ataxiameter to measure static equilibrium. Essentially, this instrument monitors body sway by summing the movements away from a stationary standing position. Two groups of subjects were selected, one that was rated high and the other that was rated low in motor ability. The difference between these groups in static equilibrium was significantly in favor of the better ability group. Using the stabilometer and ladder climb

---

[56] Richard C. Nelson and Michael R. Nofsinger, "Effect of Overload on Speed of Elbow Flexion and the Associated Aftereffects," *Research Quarterly*, 36, No. 2 (May 1965), 174.

[57] Frances Z. Cumbee, Margaret Meyer, and Gerald Peterson, "Factorial Analysis of Motor Coordination Variables for Third and Fourth Grade Girls," *Research Quarterly* 28, No. 2 (May 1957), 100.

[58] Dorothy P. Estep, "Relationship of Static Equilibrium to Ability in Motor Activities," *Research Quarterly*, 28, No. 1 (March 1957), 5.

tasks, Bachman[59] found that the rate of learning a balancing task was not influenced by age or sex over the developmental years of 6 to 26.

SUGGESTED PROBLEMS

In addition to the investigation of the numerous topics listed in this chapter, several questions remain that are of interest in the study of motor learning and motor performance.

1. New learning tasks are needed, especially those that require large muscle involvement. What are the characteristics of those individuals who learn rapidly as compared with those who learn slowly?
2. Is there a substantial relationship between motor learning and other forms of learning, for example, verbal?
3. What degrees of consistency exist in the trial-by-trial performance of a motor learning task?
4. Does learning change with increasing age? Are the characteristics of retention dependent upon the growth processes?
5. Based upon electromyographic data, can the pattern of skilled behavior be described?
6. What environmental or other mitigating influences alter the rate of learning? Can learning be facilitated?

SUMMARY

Motor learning involves the repeated practice of some act that leads to improved performance. The dividing line between what may be called motor learning and what is learning per se, such as verbal or other cognitive processes, is not always clear, nor is it fully understood just what factors operate to bring about learning in the first place. What is known is that learning of motor acts will occur with practice only if the task itself is novel to the performer; the usual skills taught in physical education are inappropriate for studies in motor learning because of subject familiarity.

The tests of motor learning apparently are few in number, if one differentiates between learning on the one hand and performance on the other. Many performance tests exist, but whether or not they result in learning depends upon what happens when a series of trials is given. The typical learning curve reflects rapid gains at first, gradually tapering off as a steady state

---

[59] John C. Bachman, "Motor Learning and Performance as Related to Age and Sex in Two Measures of Balance Coordination," *Research Quarterly*, 32, No. 2 (May 1961), 123.

is approached. The number of trials required will be determined by the type of task and the subjects employed, data that are available for several learning tests.

Psychomotor performance is seen to involve several rather clearly defined areas for which research opportunities exist. For example, the distribution of practice relates to the length and concentration of practice schedules, ordinarily with the intention to seek the arrangement that gives optimum learning. Ultimately, this involves the additional question of retention of performance, which examines the degree of impairment resulting from various periods of rest. This may even involve measurement of relearning following retraining.

Important corollary concepts of interest to the researcher include reminiscence and mental practice. Reminiscence is the increased performance that occurs in some tasks following the cessation of practice, whereas mental practice is the nonperformance rehearsal of a skill that leads to enhanced ability. The conditions under which these operate is vital to a full understanding of this field. This is also true of the transfer of one task to another. How much of what is learned in one task is transferred to another may very well depend upon how similar are the elements in both.

The study of timing control, tracking, and anticipation of movement are receiving attention in current research, as the understanding of such concepts would seem of vital importance. So many activities performed by individuals require fine adjustments to coordinate motion successfully; in some, the subject himself may be approaching a stationary object, and in others an object may be moving while the subject remains stationary. At any rate, the ability to understand one's position in space, to control muscle function, may be described as kinesthesis, and a rather substantial number of tests have been employed at one time or another to assess its function. How these matters relate to balance, motor skills, and proprioception has been the subject of some investigation.

SELECTED REFERENCES

Adams, Jack A., "Human Tracking Behavior," *Psychological Bulletin*, 58, No. 1 (January 1961), 55.

———, "Motor Skills," *Annual Review of Psychology*, 15 (1964), 181.

Bilodeau, Edward A., ed., *Acquisition of Skill*. New York: Academic Press, 1966.

———, and Ina McD. Bilodeau, "Motor-Skills Learning," *Annual Review of Psychology*, 12 (1961), 243.

Cratty, Bryant J., *Movement Behavior and Motor Learning*. Philadelphia: Lea & Febiger, 1964.

Fleishman, Edwin A., and James F. Parker, "Factors in the Retention and Relearning of Perceptual-Motor Skill," *Journal of Experimental Psychology*, 64, No. 3 (September 1962), 215.

Fox, Margaret G., and Vera P. Young, "Effect of Reminiscence on Learning Selected Badminton Skills," *Research Quarterly*, 33, No. 3 (October 1962), 386.

Gagne, Robert M., and Edwin A. Fleishman, *Psychology and Human Performance*. New York: Holt, Rinehart & Winston, Inc., 1959.

Henry, Franklin M., "Specificity vs Generality in Learning Motor Skills," *Proceedings of the College Physical Education Association*, 61 (1958), 126.

Hill, Winfred F., *Learning: A Survey of Psychological Interpretations*. San Francisco: Chandler Publishing Company ,1963.

Howard, I. P., and W. B. Templeton, *Human Spacial Orientation*. New York: John Wiley & Sons, Inc., 1966.

Jahnke, John C., and Carl P. Duncan, "Reminiscence and Forgetting in Motor Learning After Extended Rest Intervals," *Journal of Experimental Psychology*, 52, No. 5 (November 1956), 273.

Richardson, Alan, "Mental Practice: A Review and Discussion, Part I," *Research Quarterly* 38, No. 1 (March 1967), 95.

———, "Mental Practice: A Review and Discussion, Part II," *Research Quarterly*, 38, No. 2 (May 1967), 263.

Schmidt, Richard A., "Anticipation and Timing in Motor Performance," *Psychological Bulletin*, 70, No. 6 (1968), 631.

Scott, M. Gladys, "Measurement of Kinesthesis," *Research Quarterly*, 26, No. 3 (October 1955), 324.

Singer, Robert N., "Massed and Distributed Practice Effects on the Acquisition and Retention of a Novel Basketball Skill," *Research Quarterly*, 36, No. 1 (March 1965), 68.

Smith, Karl U., and William M. Smith, *Perception and Motion*. Philadelphia: W. B. Saunders Company, 1962.

CHAPTER 15

Psychological Studies

Psychological studies that apply to research in physical education will be treated separately from those that involve motor learning, although both may be considered aspects of psychology. The discipline of psychology is subdivided into a variety of supporting areas; the research involving physical performance variables reflects this categorization. The differentiation is appropriate, since the type of problem studied and methodology are not the same.

The research problem undertaken in psychological studies is not apt to be designed in quite the straightforward manner as those found in motor learning, because the instruments generally employed are not as precise. For example, where learning may be judged almost exactly by improvement in performance as measured to a fraction of a second, personality or social adjustment must be estimated somewhat less objectively. Moreover, some psychological tests require special training that puts their use beyond the reach of individuals who are not adequately prepared in the subject matter.

The fact that there are certain difficulties and limitations in some types of psychological research should serve to stimulate a greater desire for excellence. A constant search for new techniques and better refinements of old ones is needed; such will not occur unless interest is shown in really studying various types of psychological problems. Mental and emotional characteristics are complex; human drives and motives are deep-seated; and social and psychological traits are difficult to define. Yet, human overt behavior is determined by underlying forces: the need to be accepted by one's peer group, the drive toward greater personal success, and the decisions that are made on hundreds of questions during one's lifetime. All these forces serve to indicate the need for careful examination of the many topics that are presented in this connection.

The physical educator becomes interested in psychological studies because of the belief that personality plays a role in the selection of and participation in physical activities and sports and that somehow the involvement in physical education contributes to personal and social adjustment. At any rate, the development of personality and the achievement of desirable social values have been objectives of physical education since early leaders led the profession away from the formalized type of program that emphasized gymnastics, calisthenics, and marching.

The psychological tools available frequently provide only an indirect method of bringing data to bear on this subject, and so the analysis that is made is often tentative. In fact, the finding that athletes are different from nonathletes may not mean that athletics *causes* enhanced personality characteristics. It may be just as tenable to conclude that athletics attracts the more well-adjusted individuals in society (or perhaps rejects maladjusted persons). This statement is not intended to cast doubt on current research but to urge pursuance of the more difficult problem of causation.

In some instances, rather direct methods of dealing with psychological problems are available. For example, use of sociometric questionnaires, teachers' ratings, differential motive-incentive conditions, and others provide useful technical tools for the researcher. Many of these techniques will be discussed in this chapter, together with selected research studies that are intended to serve as a stimulus for more careful examination of current topics.

PERSONAL AND SOCIAL ADJUSTMENT

Research in the area of personal and social adjustment has been largely neglected by investigators in physical education; most experiments undertaken by psychologists and sociologists have not studied these factors as related to physical measures. Early indications that a relationship between the two existed came from Tryon,[1] who studied children's opinions of each other and concluded that the 12-year-old boy who lacks skill and has a distaste for organized games is ridiculed and shunned by the group. At this age, activity of any sort is preferred to inactivity, and skill, leadership, and daring in games are among the most prized physical attributes. At 15 years of age, the pattern has not changed much; prestige is still largely related to physical skill. Bower[2] studied adolescent boys and drew similar conclusions: physical ability is important for popularity; strength is important since it underlies favorable traits such as physical ability and the functional traits of aggressiveness and leadership.

---

[1] Carolyn M. Tryon, "Evaluations of Adolescent Personality by Adolescents," *Monographs of the Society for Research in Child Development*, 4, No. 4 (1939), 1.

[2] Philip A. Bower, "The Relation of Physical, Mental, and Personality Factors to Popularity in Adolescent Boys," microcard Doctoral Dissertation, University of California at Berkeley, 1941.

A number of investigations have related personal and social adjustment and group status to leadership qualities and the establishment of friendships. Alexandra[3] obtained data on leadership in adolescence and compared them to personality adjustment. She found that "leaders" were significantly better adjusted than "nonleaders." Marks[4] studied the interests, leadership, and sociometric status of 730 adolescents; he described the acceptable adolescent as being sociable, involved with people, and relatively impulsive. In a sociometric study of children's friendships, Potashin[5] indicated that sociological factors were of little significance in determining friendships, although they were of slightly greater importance than physical or intellectual similarity. A child who is one of a pair of friends is usually well-accepted by the rest of his classmates, whereas a child who is not a friend is not so well-accepted. From a study of personal and social adjustment and friendships, Singer[6] noted that group impression of an individual is developed in the early school years. He concluded that marked success in friendship status did not mean that an individual was free of personality difficulties.

Research in the area of sociometric status has largely dealt with personality and social behavior. Bedoian[7] studied socially overaccepted and socially underaccepted pupils in terms of their mental health. He concluded that those who possessed superior sociometric status also had better mental health than pupils who were ignored, unwanted, and disliked by their peers. Bonney[8] identified the following traits as being most important in differentiating between popular and unpopular children from the standpoint of general social acceptance: leadership, enthusiasm, activity in recitation, friendliness, appearance, frequent laughter, and ease with adults. Those traits that proved to have the least value were: quietness, attention-getting, bossiness, fighting, activity in games, sense of humor, and older friends. In studying elementary school children, Greenblatt[9] found little or no relationship between a child's

---

[3] Sister M. Alexandra, "Personality Adjustment and Leadership," *Education*, 66, No. 9 (May 1946), 584.

[4] J. B. Marks, "Interests, Leadership and Sociometric Status Among Adolescents," *Sociometry*, 17, No. 4 (November 1954), 340.

[5] Reva Potashin, "A Sociometric Study of Children's Friendships." *Sociometry*, 9, No. 1 (February 1946), 48.

[6] Arthur Singer, "Certain Aspects of Personality and Their Relation to Certain Group Modes, and Constancy of Friendship Choices," *Journal of Educational Research*, 45, No. 1 (September 1951), 33.

[7] Vagharsh H. Bedoian, "Mental Health Analysis of Socially Over-Accepted, Socially Under-Accepted, Overage and Underage Pupils in the Sixth Grade," *Journal of Educational Psychology*, 44, No. 6 (October 1953), 366.

[8] Merl E. Bonney, "Personality Traits of Socially Successful and Socially Unsuccessful Children," *Journal of Educational Psychology*, 34, No. 7 (November 1943), 449.

[9] E. L. Greenblatt, "Relationship of Mental Health and Social Status," *Journal of Educational Research*, 44, No. 3 (November 1950), 193.

sociometric standing or his mental health status and his mental age or his deviation from grade level expectancy, but he did indicate that individual pupils tended to choose other individual pupils with similar mental health or sociometric scores.

Precedent for the study of personal and social adjustment and various physical factors, as well as the examination of other psychological attributes, has been established. The pursuance of research in this area should be made with care and precision; the tools selected should yield the most useful data. In many cases, instruments already available will be employed, although the indiscriminate use of tests previously designed for other purposes is apt to lead to disappointment and may not answer the questions raised in the research design. The development of new procedures and techniques are needed in some areas of psychological research; in others, more concern should be given to their validity. Encouragement should be given to new and original procedures and to the ingenuity of thought in dealing with psychological problems.

GENERAL PERSONALITY TECHNIQUES

Projective Techniques

The individual's overt response to a situation is made up of a number of factors, some of which he is undoubtedly aware and some that are deep-seated and perhaps hidden in the depths of his unconscious memory. Drives and motives are complex, and the single response to a single stimulus may be conditioned to a considerable extent by tertiary considerations. At any rate, the assessment of the basic elements of personality may be approached in a number of ways, the most difficult of which is through use of projective techniques.

Projective techniques were developed originally to help assess psychological disorders, and they have since gained increasing acceptance as tools for the estimation of various degrees of normal personality. The tendency in research is to create as objective a situation as possible (questions are answered that can be scored numerically, etc.), but projective devices are relatively unstructured, so the response of the subject must be interpreted very carefully. The individual's perception of things or events will be conditioned by his basic drives and then projected to the external test situation, whether it be an interpretation of ink blots or the description of events portrayed in a picture. Regardless of the method employed, the investigator should be prepared to study these matters very carefully under proper guidance of trained evaluators. A number of hours of advanced work in psychology will be necessary before adequate data interpretation can be made. The following tests are currently in use and are suggested:

1. Rorschach (Ink Blot) Test[10]
2. Thematic Apperception Test[11]
3. Sentence Completion Test[12]
4. House-Tree-Person Test[13]
5. Rosenzweig Picture-Frustration (P-F) Study[14]

Inventory Techniques

The most widely used method of obtaining data on a variety of psychological characteristics is by means of inventory or questionnaire. In this manner, subjects answer a host of questions designed to bring out the basic elements of personality, mental health, and the like. The advantages gained over the projective techniques are the simplicity of testing and ease of scoring. Thus, several subjects may be tested simultaneously, as long as the proper testing decorum is maintained, the environment is quiet and conducive to proper introspection, and some confidence is imparted by the test administrator. The subject must be assured that results will be kept in the strictest confidence, that the best answer in any situation must be given honestly, and that there are no right or wrong answers (unless otherwise specified by the test). The data are certain to be invalidated by improper testing conditions that would permit talking or moving about or would encourage frivolous responses. Similarly, if the proper instructions are not given, or if the respondents are not assured that the data will be used statistically rather than personally, the subjects may choose to mask their true feelings, giving what they think is wanted rather than what actually may be their true choices.

The indiscriminant use of inventory techniques is one of the principle criticisms in psychological research. If a test fails to measure the traits it purports to measure, or if improper application is made in research, no amount

---

[10] Samuel J. Beck, Anne G. Beck, Eugene E. Levitt, and Herman B. Molish, *Rorschach's Test: I. Basic Processes* (New York: Grune & Stratton, 1961).

[11] Leopold Bellak and Eileen Ort, "Thematic Apperception Test and Other Perceptive Methods," in Daniel Brower and Lawrence E. Abt, ed., *Progress in Clinical Psychology*, Vol. I (New York: Grune & Stratton, 1952), Ch. 9.

[12] James Quinter Holsopple and Florence R. Miale, *Sentence Completion: A Projective Method for the Study of Personality* (Springfield, Ill.: Charles C. Thomas, Publisher, 1954).

[13] John N. Buck, "The H-T-P Test," *Journal of Clinical Psychology*, 4, No. 2 (April 1948), 151; "The H-T-P Technique: A Qualitative and Quantitative Scoring Manual," *Journal of Clinical Psychology*, 4, No. 4 (October 1948), 317.

[14] Saul Rosenzweig, "The Picture-Association Method and its Application in a Study of Reactions to Frustration," *Journal of Personality*, 14, No. 1 (September 1945), 3.

of care in testing can save the data. For example, a test designed solely for use with neuropsychiatric patients or for individual counselling purposes may not be appropriate for examining large groups where statistical procedures are employed and where the population may contain no subjects classified as mentally ill. The essential consideration here should be to evaluate every test carefully to assure its applicability for the problem selected and then to employ the most favorable testing protocol. The reader will find a discussion of testing procedures by Cronbach[15] helpful in preparing for this type of research.

Selected tests available for use are briefly described below. The specific needs of the research problem will dictate which ones are applicable. The usual procedure is for the subject to respond to a number of questions on a yes-no or true-false basis, and the responses are scored with a key provided with the test manual. The answer sheet may be submitted to automatic scoring, so this process should be investigated and the appropriate procedures applied. No attempt has been made to be encyclopedic but rather to point up a few tests that seem to be more widely used and perhaps more applicable to problems in physical education. The various Mental Measurements Yearbooks[16] will prove helpful in securing additional material appropriate to such research, as well as critical reviews concerning test acceptability.

Mental health analysis. The Mental Health Analysis[17] has been divided into two sections, with five categories in each. Section I is designed to measure the presence of *mental health liabilities:* behavioral immaturity, emotional instability, feelings of inadequacy, physical defects, and nervous manifestations. Section II purports to measure *mental health assets*: close personal relationships, interpersonal skills, social participation, satisfying work and recreation, and adequate outlook and goals.

The reliability of the Mental Health Analysis was determined by applying the Richardson-Kudor correlation formula to 1,960 cases; a correlation of .95 was obtained for the total score. Validity of the instrument was obtained through a study of the literature in the field and a delineation of the most important mental health concepts.

California Psychological Inventory. The California Psychological Inventory[18] is a 480-item true-false questionnaire designed to test nonpathological subjects 13 years of age and above. The 18 scales of the inventory were

---

[15] Lee J. Cronbach, *Essentials of Psychological Testing* (2nd ed.) (New York: Harper & Row, Publishers, 1960).

[16] Oscar Krisen Buros, ed., *The Sixth Mental Measurements Yearbook* (Highland Park, N.J.: The Gryphon Press, 1965). Other Yearbooks were published in 1938, 1940, 1948, 1953, and 1959.

[17] Louis P. Thorpe, Willis M. Clark, and Ernest W. Tiegs, *Manual of Directions: Mental Health Analysis* (Los Angeles: California Test Bureau).

[18] Harrison G. Gough, *California Psychological Inventory* (Palo Alto, Calif.: Consulting Psychologists Press, Inc., 1956).

identified as the following: dominance, capacity for status, sociability, social presence, self-acceptance, sense of well-being, responsibility, socialization, self-control, tolerance, good impression, communality, conformance, achievement via independence, intellectual efficiency, psychological-mindedness, flexibility, and femininity. These scales have been cross-validated and are based on the test responses of individuals considered to exhibit various kinds of effective behavior. Norms have been constructed from data gathered on over 13,000 cases spread geographically over 30 states.

Cattell's Sixteen Personality Factor Questionnaire. The factors in Cattell's Sixteen Personality Factor Questionnaire[19] for college students are as follows:

A *Cyclothymia:* good natured, easygoing, ready to cooperate, attentive to people, softhearted, kindly, trustful.

B *General Intelligence:* intellectual, cultured.

C *Ego Strength:* calm, emotionally mature and stable, realistic about life, absence of neurotic fatigue, placid.

E *Ascendance:* assertive, hard, stern, self-assured, independent-minded, solemn, unconventional, attention-getting.

F *Surgency:* talkative, cheerful, serene, happy go-lucky, frank, expressive, quick and alert.

G *Character:* persevering, determined, responsible, conscientious.

H *Parmia:* adventurous, responsive, friendly, impulsive and frivolous, carefree.

I *Premia:* demanding, impatient, attention-seeking, anxious.

L *Protension:* jealous, suspicious, brooding, tyrannical, irritable.

M *Autia:* unconventional, self-absorbed, imaginative, creative.

N *Shrewdness:* socially alert, calculating mind, aloof, emotionally disciplined, ambitious, expedient.

O *Guilt Proneness:* worrying, anxious, sensitive, depressed, strong sense of duty, moody.

Q_1 *Radicalism:* well-informed, more inclined to experiment than to moralize, leading and persuading people, breaking custom and tradition.

Q_2 *Self-Sufficiency:* resourceful, extroverted, dissatisfied with group integration.

Q_3 *Self-Sentiment Formation:* controlled, exacting will power.

Q_4 *Ergic Tension:* tense, excitable, irritable, in turmoil.

---

[19] Raymond B. Cattell and Glen F. Stice, *Handbook for the Sixteen Personality Factor Questionnaire* (Champaigne, Ill.: Institute for Personality and Ability Testing, 1957).

Bernreuter Personality Inventory. The Bernreuter Personality Inventory[20] contains 125 questions designed for high school and college students and adults, adapted largely from Laird's C_2 Test of Introversion-Extroversion, Allport's A-S Reaction Study, Thurstone's Neurotic Inventory, and Bernreuter's Self-Sufficiency Test. The 6 traits are as follows: neurotic tendency, self-sufficiency, introversion-extroversion, dominance-submission, sociability, and confidence.

Bell Adjustment Inventory. The revised student form of the Bell Adjustment Inventory[21] measures personal and social adjustment in the following 6 categories: home adjustment, health adjustment, submissiveness, emotionality, hostility, and masculinity-femininity. High scores indicate an unsatisfactory adjustment, whereas low scores denote a satisfactory adjustment. The reliability of the 200 statement inventory is reported to be satisfactory (.80 or above). An adult form is also available that includes an additional scale for occupational adjustment but does not contain the hostility and masculinity-femininity scales.

Washburne's Social Adjustment Inventory. Washburne's Social Adjustment Inventory[22] is designed to determine the degree of social and emotional adjustment for all ages above the eighth grade. This inventory consists of 123 items designed to give a separate measure of development in each of several traits and a combined score that purports to measure adjustment in all the traits combined. The test was validated by examining item discrimination when given to such groups as prisoners, maladjusted high school pupils, average pupils, and well-adjusted pupils. The validity coefficient is .90; and the coefficient of reliability is .92. The test contains 6 subtests, an essay-type subtest of social and emotional adjustment, and a subtest of truthfulness or accuracy. The subtests are as follows:

1. *Truthfulness:* relative freedom from deliberate or unintentional inaccuracies in answering questions.
2. *Happiness:* contentment; sense of well-being.
3. *Alienation:* sense of social membership; psychological security and emotional stability in social situations.
4. *Sympathy:* sensitive, empathic, nonnegative responsiveness to people.
5. *Purpose:* sense of long-range purpose.

---

[20] Palo Alto, California: Consulting Psychologists Press, Inc.

[21] Hugh M. Bell, *Bell Adjustment Inventory*, Revised 1962 Student Form (Palo Alto, Calif.: Consulting Psychologists Press, Inc., 1962).

[22] John N. Washburne, *Social Adjustment Inventory* (New York: Harcourt, Brace & World, Inc., 1940).

6. *Impulse-judgment:* ability to judge well between conflicting impulses so that remote but greater advantages are chosen over immediate but obviously lesser satisfactions.

7. *Control:* sense of self-control and self-regulation.

8. *Wishes:* development of values related to the broad realities of the individual's life circumstances.

Minnesota Multiphasic Personality Inventory. One of the most widely used tests of personality over the years, since first presented in 1943, is the Minnesota Multiphasic Personality Inventory.[23] Developed for administration to individuals over 16 years of age, the MMPI provides 14 scores, as follows: hypochondriasis, depression, hysteria, psychopathic deviate, masculinity and femininity, paranoia, psychathenia, schizophrenia, hypomania, social, question, lie, validity, and test-taking attitude.

California Test of Personality. Employed primarily as a test of personal and social adjustment, the California Test of Personality[24] provides for the evaluation of children in kindergarten and extends to the adult form. The 15 scores include the following: self-reliance, sense of personal worth, sense of personal freedom, feeling of belonging, withdrawing tendencies, nervous symptoms, total personal adjustment, social standards, social skills, antisocial tendencies, family relations, school relations or occupational relations, community relations, total social adjustment, and total adjustment.

The Guilford-Martin Inventory of Factors GAMIN. The Guilford-Martin Inventory[25] is available for grades 9–16 and for adults, and provides the following five scores: general activity, ascendance-submission, masculinity-femininity, inferiority feelings, and nervousness.

Relationship Studies

The literature relative to personal and social adjustment and various physical factors seems characterized by its diversity. A wide variety of social and psychological instruments has been employed, many of the inventory type and some using projective techniques. In addition, the physical and motor variables have varied, depending in part upon the intention of the

---

[23] Starke R. Hathaway and J. Charnley McKinley, *Minnesota Multiphasic Personality Inventory*, Revised Form (New York: Psychological Corporation, 1951).

[24] Louis P. Thorpe, Willis W. Clark, and Ernest W. Tiegs, *California Test of Personality*, Revised Form (Los Angeles: California Test Bureau, 1953).

[25] J. P. Guilford and H. G. Martin, *The Guilford-Martin Inventory of Factors GAMIN-*Abridged Edition (Beverly Hills, Calif.: Sheridan Supply Co., 1948).

study in question, which makes generalization difficult. A few of these studies will be given in this section with the hope that it will stimulate further research.

Physique. To determine the relationship between body build and social traits and play activities, Bartell[26] administered the Washburne Social Adjustment Inventory, the California Test of Personality, and the Bell Adjustment Inventory as social adjustment devices, and Van Dalen's Play Inventory as a measure of play activity to 697 high school boys. A tendency was found for those subjects with medium builds to be better adjusted socially than either the obese or slender subjects.

Hanley[27] tested the hypothesis that certain sociometrically derived reputation traits as measured by Sheldon's Temperament Scale for junior high school boys would correlate significantly with components of their mature somatotypes. He found that the traits "good-at-games" and "active-in-games" correlated .48 and .45, respectively, with mesomorphy.

Jones and Bayley[28] studied the physical maturity of adolescents as related to behavior. Social behavior ratings were made by staff members of subjects as observed in free play; their scores on a Reputation Test were decided by classmates. The results indicated that the early-maturing boys were more likely to get and maintain prestige associated with athletics.

Physical activities. In a study to determine if higher athletic skills were associated with better social or personal adjustment in high school boys, Biddulph[29] administered the California Test of Personality and a sociometric device together with ratings obtained from four different teachers. Two groups, one of high athletic achievement and one of low athletic achievement, were compared. Students ranking high in athletic achievement demonstrated a significantly higher degree of personal and social adjustment than did students ranking low in athletic achievement.

In an investigation of the psychological characteristics of athletes and nonparticipants at three educational levels, Schendel[30] administered the

---

[26] Joseph A. Bartell, "A Comparison Between Body Build and Body Size with Respect to Certain Sociophysical Factors Among High School Boys," microcard Doctoral Dissertation, University of Pittsburgh, 1952.

[27] Charles Hanley, "Physique and Reputation of Junior High School Boys," *Child Development*, 22, No. 4 (December 1951), 247.

[28] Mary Cover Jones and Nancy Bayley, "Physical Maturing Among Boys as Related to Behavior," *Journal of Educational Psychology*, 41, No. 3 (March 1950), 129.

[29] Lowell G. Biddulph, "Athletic Achievement and the Personal and Social Adjustment of High School Boys," *Research Quarterly*, 25, No. 1 (March 1954), 1.

[30] Jack Schendel, "Psychological Differences Between Athletes and Nonparticipants in Athletics at Three Educational Levels," *Research Quarterly*, 36, No. 1 (March 1965), 52.

California Psychological Inventory to 334 subjects in junior high school, senior high school, and college. Significant differences were found between the means of 8 of the scales for the athletes and nonparticipants in the ninth grade, on 4 scales of twelfth graders, and on 9 scales of the subjects in college. Nearly all significant differences were in favor of the athletes; on the other hand, few differences in psychological characteristics were found between athletes rated as substitutes, regular players, or outstanding performers.

In an effort to determine group differences in attitudes and dispositions of personality between weight lifters and nonweight lifters, Thune[31] administered a personality inventory adapted from Nelson's Questionnaire, Henry's Interest and Attitude Inventory, and several standard personality inventories. He obtained significant differences between weightlifters and the control group in all categories: present health, self-confidence, and the trait "manly individualistic." He also observed that basically the weight lifters were shy and lacked self-confidence.

Husman[32] administered several projective techniques, including the Rosenzweig Picture Frustration Study, a portion of the Thematic Apperception Test, and a sentence completion test, to study aggression of boxers, wrestlers, and cross-country runners. These tests were given before the season, before and after an athletic contest, and at the end of the season. The data indicated that boxers were significantly less aggressive and less extrapunitive, and they tended to be more intrapunitive than other subjects tested. Husman concluded that boxing and wrestling did not attract aggressive personalities.

By use of the House-Tree-Person test of personality, Johnson and Hutton[33] studied the personalities of 8 college wrestlers before a wrestling season, 4 to 5 hours before the first intercollegiate match of the season, and the morning after the first match. A decrease in functioning intelligence and an increase in aggressive feelings and neurotic symptoms were evident in the before-match situation. A general return to the preseason personality level by the following morning occurred.

In analyzing the personality profiles of 5 collegiate football teams, Kroll and Petersen[34] employed Cattell's Sixteen Personality Factor Questionnaire,

---

[31] John B. Thune, "Personality of Weightlifters," *Research Quarterly*, 20, No. 3 (October 1949), 296.

[32] Burris F. Husman, "Aggression in Boxers and Wrestlers as Measured by Projective Techniques," *Research Quarterly*, 26, No. 4 (December 1955), 421.

[33] Warren R. Johnson and Daniel C. Hutton, "Effects of a Combative Sport Upon Personality Dynamics as Measured by a Projective Test," *Research Quarterly*, 26, No. 1 (March 1955), 49.

[34] Walter Kroll and Kay H. Petersen, "Personality Profiles of Collegiate Football Teams," *Research Quarterly*, 36, No. 4 (December 1965), 433.

securing data on several categories of winning and losing teams. The statistical technique involved a multiple-discriminant analysis and a maximum-likelihood classification method. Results indicated significant discrimination among the five teams, the largest contributors to the first discriminant function being factors *B* (intelligence), *H* (timid vs bold), *O* (confident vs worrying), and Q_3 (casual vs controlled). The percentage of correct classifications was 82, when predicted on the basis of winning and losing categories. Later, Kroll[35] employed the Cattell test in studying 94 wrestlers made up of Olympic participants, excellent college wrestlers, and those of average or below average ability. Discriminant function analysis did not establish any profile differences among the three groups, although the wrestlers were significantly more tough-minded, self-reliant, and masculine (factor I) than the average college student.

Physical and motor ability. Jones[36] reported that among boys competitive athletic skills are primary sources of social esteem in the period preceding maturity. He attributed this partly to the high premium that adolescents placed upon athletic proficiency, but also because strength and other aspects of physical ability were closely related to such favorable traits as activity, aggressiveness, and leadership. After studying the physical ability of 78 elementary school boys, as related to measurements of reputation and personality adjustment, he made the following observations: Boys superior in strength at the end of adolescence showed a tendency to be tall, heavy, mesomorphic, early maturing, proficient in athletics, high in popularity and social prestige, and well-adjusted; biological fitness and social acceptance may be due largely to the tendency to accord a high value to physical superiority.

Rarick and McKee[37] utilized the case-study technique to discover personal characteristics and environmental factors that were common to 10 children of high motor proficiency and 10 children of low motor proficiency, as determined by Seils's battery of motor skills. They concluded that children in the superior motor performance group tended to be active, popular, calm, resourceful, attentive, and cooperative; whereas, children exhibiting low motor performance more frequently showed negative personality traits and were more often shy, retiring, and tense.

---

[35] Walter Kroll, "Sixteen Personality Factor Profiles of Collegiate Wrestlers," *Research Quarterly*, 38, No. 1 (March 1967), 49.

[36] Harold E. Jones, "Physical Ability as a Factor in Social Adjustment in Adolescence," *Journal of Educational Research*, 40, No. 4 (December 1946), 287.

[37] G. Lawrence Rarick and R. McKee, "A Study of Twenty Third-Grade Children Exhibiting Extreme Levels of Achievement on Tests of Motor Proficiency," *Research Quarterly*, 20, No. 2 (May 1949), 142.

In studying success in college, Weber[38] investigated the relationship between physical fitness as measured by the Iowa Physical Efficiency Profile and by the academic grades and the relationship between physical fitness and personality as measured by the Minnesota Multiphasic Personality Inventory. He found no significant relationship between physical fitness and personality, and he concluded that the physically fit subjects had no more stable traits of personality than did the physically unfit. Also employing the Minnesota Multiphasic Personality Inventory, France[39] studied the relationships between tests of physical performance and selected traits of personality of college men. A battery of three physical achievement tests (agility run, pullups, hop-step-and-jump) was selected as an index of performance. No significant relationship was found between these motor and personality traits.

The relationship between physical fitness—as measured by the AAHPER Youth Fitness Test—and personality—as assessed by Allport's A-S Reaction Study, Cattell's Sixteen Personality Factor Questionnaire, and the Kudor Preference Record-Form C—was studied by Tillman.[40] Those in the upper 15 per cent of 386 high school boys on the fitness test were significantly more ascendant than those in the lower 15 per cent, were also more surgent on Cattell's factor *F*, exhibited greater social dependence on Q_2, and showed less tension on factor Q_4. Very few changes in personality were found following a 9-month physical fitness program.

Conclusion

The results of the various studies that have employed inventory techniques are frequently contradictory and many times are not sufficiently definitive for the type of problem to be solved. The data tend to support the hypothesis that desirable traits of personality are associated with physical prowess, but so often that result has been based more upon elimination of chance factors than upon the appearance of real differences or high relationships. For example, a correlation may be significantly different from zero, yet the amount of individual difference variance in common between the two traits may not be very high if the correlation is fairly low.[41] One of the

---

[38] Robert John Weber, "Relationship of Physical Fitness to Success in College and to Personality," *Research Quarterly*, 24, No. 4 (December 1953), 471.

[39] Wellman Lyle France, "A Study of Relationships Between Tests of Physical Performance and Various Traits of Personality," microcard Doctoral Dissertation, Purdue University, 1953.

[40] Kenneth Tillman, "Relationship Between Physical Fitness and Selected Personality Traits," *Research Quarterly*, 36, No. 4 (December 1965), 483.

[41] See Chapter 11.

causes of such a situation may be low reliability on one or both variables, which would tend to lower the correlation coefficient. The alternative explanation is that the relationship may not be very substantial under the best of conditions. When personality is assessed from the stated responses to items proposed in questionnaire form, one may have to accept a certain loss of rigor.

PEER STATUS

Support is mounting for the concept that peer evaluation of an individual may be a better indicator of his group behavior and may reveal more about his inner drives than the inventory technique. The rating given by one's peers concerning social acceptance may well provide greater insight into a subject's effective relationships with people than can be ascertained by more devious means. Perhaps the compromise is between types of data obtained; peer status and mental health, for example, certainly are two separate entities. The choice of instruments must match the problem, but the selection of a research study itself must also be approached realistically. Little is gained by using invalid tools no matter how urgent is the research.

Instruments

Cowell Personal Distance Ballot Social distance scales have been used in education to evaluate the closeness of personal relationships. In physical education, the Cowell Personal Distance Ballot,[42] shown in Figure 23, was developed to represent boys' attitudes toward accepting boys. Thus, the ballot is prepared by listing the names of all classmates, or other acquaintances, to be evaluated; each boy answers the ballot by checking on the 7-point scale how near to his family he would like to have each of the listed individuals. A Personal Distance Score is derived by adding the total *weighted* scores given the subject by the class or group and dividing by the total number of respondents. A low score is a desirable score in this instance.

Sociometric questionnaire. The use of the sociometric technique has not been employed extensively as a measure of social adjustment in physical education. The systematic investigation of group structure and the position of the individual had its chief origin in the work of Moreno,[43] first published in

---

[42] Charles C. Cowell, "Validating an Index of Social Adjustment for High School Use," *Research Quarterly*, 29, No. 1 (March 1958), 7. (Available through Tri-State Offset Co., 817 Main Street, Cincinnati, Ohio.)

[43] J. L. Moreno, *Who Shall Survive?* (New York: The Beacon Press, 1934).

Medford Boys' Growth Study

What To Do	I would be willing to accept him:						
If you had full power to treat each student on this list as you feel, just how would you consider him? How near would you like to have him to your family? Check each student in *one* column as to your feeling toward him. Circle your own name.	Into my family as a brother 1	As a very close "pal" or "chum" 2	As a member of my "gang" or club 3	On my street as a "nextdoor neighbor" 4	Into my class at school 5	Into my school 6	Into my city 7
1. Breedlove, William							
2. Gordon, James							
3. Kurovsky, Dennis							
4. Landis, David							
5. Mann, Robert							
6. Pierce, Ronald							
7. Swanson, Gary							
8. Wright, Larry							
9. Etc.							
10.							

Figure 23. Cowell Personal Distance Ballot

1934. He defined sociometry as "the mathematical study of psychological properties of populations."

The sociometric test consists of asking an individual to choose his associates for any group of which he is, or might become, a member. For example, the individuals within a group might be asked to choose from the group those members whom they wish to have with them in the formation of some new group, whether it be one of recreation, work, or study.[44] When Moreno first introduced this technique, it was no more than a tentative, qualitative, and rough outline. The results were diagrammed with individuals being represented as triangles or circles with respect to sex and the lines drawn from one to another representing choices. As the number of persons thereon increased, these sociograms became extremely complex and resistent to analysis. Furthermore, at the time of the original study, no specific rules for the construction of the sociogram were available, so they could be composed in many diverse ways.

Soon after the appearance of Moreno's basic work, attention was given to methodology in sociometric research. Moreno and Jennings[45] were responsible for early work in this area, studying deviations from chance expectancy; their paper was notable for the stimulus it provided. Lemann and Solomon[46] investigated certain group characteristics by means of data obtained from sociometric tests and rating scales, using as subjects the members of three small dormitories at a girls' college. Emphasis was placed on methodology and the improvement of sociometric techniques; a method of determining status groups was developed, which took into account both choices and rejections and which yielded meaningful and workable divisions into high, middle, and low status groups. Those subjects who were "highly noticed" by others were more likely to be noticed unfavorably than favorably—that is, they were more likely to have low status than high status. Those who were "very unnoticed" by the group were more likely to be liked than disliked.

Bonney[47] studied the choices between the sexes in a classroom situation as evidenced by sociometric analysis. The acceptance of interpersonal attitudes that existed among sex groups seemed much more likely to be due to such factors as the socio-economic home background, the extent to which

---

[44] Edward Gottheil, "Sociometric Technique and Experimental Method in Social Psychology," *Journal of Social Psychology*, 35 (February 1952), 9.

[45] J. L. Moreno and H. H. Jennings, "Statistics on Social Configurations," *Sociometry*, 1, No. 3–4 (January-April 1938), 342.

[46] Thomas B. Lemann and Richard L. Solomon, "Group Characteristics as Revealed in Sociometric Patterns and Personality Ratings," *Sociometry*, 15, No. 1–2 (February-May 1952), 7.

[47] Merl E. Bonney, "Choosing Between the Sexes on a Sociometric Measurement," *Journal of Social Psychology*, 39 (February 1954), 99.

boys and girls had enjoyed pleasant associations in groups and to which teachers and other adults had encouraged or minimized differences by direct and indirect teaching, rather than due to inherent differences in the various stages of sex development.

In analyzing teachers' judgments of sociometric status, Gronlund[48] studied 632 boys and 626 girls in the sixth grade. He felt that the correlation coefficients representing the generality of the accuracy of teachers' sociometric perceptions probably underestimated the amount of generality present. The variations among teachers in their opportunity to observe choice behavior tended to reduce the extent of generality. However, despite this, the correlation coefficients representing generality of the teachers' judgments accuracy were all found to be statistically significant. He therefore concluded that the accuracy of teachers' sociometric perceptions had generality over sociometric criteria.

A sociometric questionnaire was developed and utilized in the Medford Boys' Growth Study[49] in which each boy was asked to list as many other boys in his homeroom as he wanted in each of the following five categories:[50]

Friends: List your good boy friends and boys you would like for friends.

Movies: List the boys you would like to go to the movies with.

Sports: List the boys you would like to play sports with.

Homework: List the boys you would like to study homework with.

Party: List the boys you would like to invite to a birthday party.

The manner of scoring the questionnaire is relatively simple. For example, if unlimited choices are given, as noted above, two possibilities may be employed: (1) itemizing the number of times each subject is chosen by other boys; and (2) itemizing the number of different boys each subject has chosen from those in his group. In this manner, two different numerical values are available for each subject; in the event different numbers of subjects are involved, the percentage of choices may be utilized. It may also be permissible to restrict to three the number of choices that may be made and

---

[48] Norman E. Gronlund, "Generality of Teachers' Sociometric Perceptions: Relative Judgment Accuracy on Several Sociometric Criteria," *Journal of Educational Psychology*, 47, No. 1 (January 1956), 25.

[49] See Chapter 17.

[50] H. Harrison Clarke and David H. Clarke, "Social Status and Mental Health of Boys as Related to Their Maturity, Structural, and Strength Characteristics," *Research Quarterly*, 32, No. 3 (October 1961), 326.

to include a negative question such as to list those individuals with whom they do not wish to associate. Breck[51] found two methods of scoring sociometric questionnaires to be particularly valuable: (1) tabulating only expressions of choice, assigning one point to each expression; and (2) tabulating expressions of choice and deducting expressions of rejection, assigning one point for each acceptance and subtracting one point for each rejection.

Social Adjustment and Various Physical Measures

The interrelationships of the five categories of the Medford sociometric questionnaire were studied by Devine[52] for boys at 9 and 11 years of age. The intercorrelations at 9 years were relatively low ranging from .62 to .75; thus, each category contributed some unique element to peer-status assessment. At 11 years of age, the boys chosen as friends were also generally chosen in the party, movies, and sports categories ($r = .91$ to .97); the lowest correlations were with the homework category ($r = .59$ to .76). Thus, at this age, the sociometric questionnaire could well be limited to two categories—friends and homework.

Clarke and Greene[53] administered the following five personal-social tests to the same 78 boys 10 years of age: sociometric questionnaire, friends and homework categories only; Cowell Personal Distance Ballot, a second peer-status instrument; Cowell Social Behavior Trend Index, based on the ratings of teachers; level of aspiration test, as noted below; and SRA Junior Inventory, in which each boy answered questions about himself. The highest intercorrelations among these instruments were: .73 between friends and homework categories on the sociometric questionnaire, −.74 between the friends category and Cowell Personal Distance Ballot (a low score on the ballot is desirable), and −.52 between the homework category and Cowell's ballot. All these instruments correlated low with various physical tests; the highest correlation was −.30 between the friends category and degree of ectomorphy; with mesomorphy, the correlation was .22.

---

[51] Sabina J. Breck, "A Sociometric Measurement of Status in Physical Education Classes," *Research Quarterly*, 21, No. 2 (May 1950), 75.

[52] Barry M. Devine, "Analysis of Responses on a Sociometric Questionnaire and the Re-examination of Structural and Strength Relationships for Nine- and Eleven-Year-Old Boys," microcard Master's Thesis, University of Oregon, 1960.

[53] H. Harrison Clarke and Walter H. Greene, "Relationships Between Personal-Social Measures Applied to 10-Year-Old Boys," *Research Quarterly*, 34, No. 3 (October 1963), 288.

Later, Greene[54] longitudinally related peer status to the maturity, physique, structural, strength, and motor ability characteristics of the same boys from 7 to 12 years of age. The highest multiple correlation obtained was .485 between the sports category at 12 years of age and standing broad jump, mesomorphy, Physical Fitness Index, and cable-tension strength average. Mean differences in favor of high sociometric groups (boys highly chosen at least three of four years) were found for the standing broad jump, cable-tension strength average, mesomorphy, Physical Fitness Index, and 60-yard shuttle run; in some instances, high endomorphy means were found with low sociometric groups.

BEHAVIOR RATING

Another approach to social and psychological evaluation may be made through various types of behavior ratings. This would imply knowledge of the subject by the evaluator, so its use by teachers has proven successful in assessing pupil behavior. If the instrument is carefully prepared and if the method of rating is clear, it should prove useful as an adjunct in understanding the status of the subject in a social environment. The main limitation that should be kept in mind is that the adult tends to assign rather different values to certain behavior than might the peer group or the individual himself. For example, a student who finds himself in conflict with the adult value system may receive wide acceptance within his group, a fact that might lead to reinforcement of his own behavior. The fact that this may occur at different ages and for different reasons makes the study of social and psychological problems all the more intriguing; it might well serve to stimulate research concerning the role that sports and games might play in this process.

The usual precautions must be taken in the use of behavior rating scales as in other subjective measures where an individual must make decisions that are not always clear and obvious and where precision may be lacking. If the investigator himself is not performing the rating but must rely upon others who are acquainted with the subjects, he must carefully instruct them on the meaning of questions and the applicability of the rating categories. Inasmuch as the data may be pooled from several raters, the need for standardization of use is acute. This is eased somewhat if several persons can judge the same subject, providing each rater has an adequate opportunity for observation.

---

[54] Walter H. Greene, "Peer Status and Level of Aspiration of Boys as Related to Their Maturity, Physique, Structural, Strength, and Motor Ability Characteristics," microcard Doctoral Dissertation, University of Oregon, 1964.

A precaution that should be mentioned concerns the "halo effect" where the rater tends to give high ratings in every category to pupils he likes and, conversely, tends to rate all traits very low for those individuals whom he does not like. One must strive to be as objective as possible in this regard and not permit deficiencies of a subject in one category to influence decisions in all categories. That such a condition may exist is shown by Grant,[55] who found high positive intercorrelations between items in a rating scale. On the other hand, if the items themselves do not discriminate among traits of behavior, such a finding might be expected. Langlie[56] found that sex differences in ratings exist, as both men and women teachers tend to rate girls as superior to boys, even though test records do not verify this trend.

Blanchard scale. Blanchard[57] employed 85 trait actions, had them evaluated by 16 physical education teachers, and selected the 45 that received the highest ratings. From this group, 24 were finally selected for the behavior frequency rating scale shown in Figure 24. The reliability of this battery is .71, and the intercorrelation of one trait action with the rest of the items in its category is .93.

Cowell Social Behavior Trend Index. Cowell[58] developed 12 pairs of behavior "trends" representing good and poor adjustments after studying factors that differentiate junior high school boys who tend to participate wholeheartedly in physical education and those who tend to participate reluctantly. From a factor analysis, 10 of the pairs of positive and negative behavior trends were retained as common factors underlying good and poor adjustment. Forms A and B, representing positive and negative scales, appear in Figure 25. Cowell recommended that three teachers rate each pupil on both forms at different times; a pupil's social adjustment score is the combined total of the ratings of the three teachers. Thus, a socially well-adjusted pupil would get a high positive score, a socially maladjusted pupil would receive a high negative score. These raw scores can be transposed to percentile values from scales presented by Cowell and Schwehn.[59]

---

[55] Donald L. Grant, "An Exploratory Study of the Halo Effect in Rating," microcard Doctoral Dissertation, Ohio State University, 1952.

[56] T. A. Langlie, "Personality Ratings: I. Reliability of Teachers' Ratings," *Journal of Genetic Psychology*, 50 (1937), 339.

[57] B. E. Blanchard, "A Behavior Frequency Rating Scale for the Measurement of Character and Personality in Physical Education Classroom Situations," *Research Quarterly*, 7, No. 2 (May 1936), 56.

[58] Cowell, *op. cit.*

[59] Charles C. Cowell and Hilda M. Schwehn, *Modern Principles and Methods in High School Physical Education* (Boston: Allyn and Bacon, Inc., 1958), pp. 305–8.

Name:...*Grade:*..................*Age:*..............*Date:*.............
School:...*Name of Rater:*..

Behavior Rating Scale

Personal Information	Frequency of Observation						
	No Opportunity to Observe	Never	Seldom	Fairly Often	Frequently	Extremely Often	Score
Leadership							
1. Popular with classmates		1	2	3	4	5	
2. Seeks responsibility in the classroom		1	2	3	4	5	
3. Shows intellectual leadership in the classroom		1	2	3	4	5	
Positive Active Qualities							
4. Quits on tasks requiring perseverance		5	4	3	2	1	
5. Exhibits aggressiveness in his relationship with others		1	2	3	4	5	
6 Shows initiative in assuming responsibility in unfamiliar situations		1	2	3	4	5	
7. Is alert to new opportunities		1	2	3	4	5	
Positive Mental Qualities							
8. Shows keenness of mind		1	2	3	4	5	
9. Volunteers ideas		1	2	3	4	5	
Self-Control							
10. Grumbles over decisions of classmates.........		5	4	3	2	1	
11. Takes a justified criticism by teacher or classmate without showing anger or pouting		1	2	3	4	5	
Co-operation							
12. Is loyal to his group		1	2	3	4	5	
13. Discharges his group responsibilities well		1	2	3	4	5	
14. Is co-operative in his attitude toward his teacher		1	2	3	4	5	
Social Action Standards							
15. Makes loud-mouthed criticism and comments		5	4	3	2	1	
16. Respects the rights of others		1	2	3	4	5	
Ethical Social Qualities							
17. Cheats		5	4	3	2	1	
18. Is truthful		1	2	3	4	5	
Qualities of Efficiency							
19. Seems satisfied to "get by" with tasks assigned...		5	4	3	2	1	
20. Is dependable and trustworthy.................		1	2	3	4	5	
21. Has good study habits.......................		1	2	3	4	5	
Sociability							
22. Is liked by others		1	2	3	4	5	
23. Makes a friendly approach to others in the group		1	2	3	4	5	
24. Is friendly		1	2	3	4	5	

Figure 24. Blanchard's Behavior Rating Scale

Cowell Social Behavior Trend Index (Form A)

Date:__________ Grade:_____
School:__________ Age:_____
Describer:__________

Last Name First Name

INSTRUCTIONS:—Think carefully of the student's behavior in group situations and check *each behavior trend* according to its degree of descriptiveness.

Behavior Trends	Descriptive of the Student			
	Markedly (+3)	Somewhat (+2)	Only Slightly (+1)	Not at All (0)
1. Enters heartily and with enjoyment into the spirit of social intercourse				
2. Frank; talkative and sociable, does not stand on ceremony				
3. Self-confident and self-reliant, tends to take success for granted, strong initiative, prefers to lead				
4. Quick and decisive in movement, pronounced or excessive energy output				
5. Prefers group activities, work or play; not satisfied with individual projects				
6. Adaptable to new situations, makes adjustment readily, welcomes change				
7. Is self-composed, seldom shows signs of embarrassment				
8. Tends to elation of spirits, seldom gloomy or moody				
9. Seeks a broad range of friendships, not selective or exclusive in games and the like				
10. Hearty and cordial, even to strangers, forms acquaintanceships very easily				

Cowell Social Behavior Trend Index (Form B)

Date:__________ Grade:_____
School:__________ Age:_____
Describer:__________

Last Name First Name

INSTRUCTIONS:—Think carefully of the student's behavior in group situations and check *each behavior trend* according to its degree of descriptiveness.

Behavior Trends	Descriptive of the Student			
	Markedly (−3)	Somewhat (−2)	Only Slightly (−1)	Not at All (−0)
1. Somewhat prudish, awkward, easily embarrassed in his social contacts				
2. Secretive, seclusive, not inclined to talk unless spoken to				
3. Lacking in self-confidence and initiative, a follower				
4. Slow in movement, deliberative or perhaps indecisive. Energy output moderate or deficient				
5. Prefers to work and play alone, tends to avoid group activities				
6. Shrinks from making new adjustments, prefers the habitual to the stress of reorganization required by the new				
7. Is self-conscious, easily embarrassed, timid or "bashfull"				
8. Tends to depression, frequently gloomy or moody				
9. Shows preference for a narrow range of intimate friends and tends to exclude others from his association				
10. Reserved and distant except to intimate friends, does not form acquaintanceships readily				

Figure 25. Cowell Social Behavior Trend Index

SELF-IMAGE

A growing interest has developed in recent years over the concept of self-image. The concern is that an individual's impression of himself may reflect various personality factors or be related to his performance capabilities. There have been a few such studies in physical education, some of which have used inventory techniques and some that have used a more direct approach. For a discussion of body-image and the self-concept, the reader is directed to Fisher and Cleveland.[60]

Instruments

Body Cathexis Test. One technique of assessing an individual's attitude toward his body is through use of a Body Cathexis Test. As developed by Secord and Jourard,[61] a 46-word questionnaire was employed consisting of a wide variety of terms describing the various parts of the body and their functions. The subject was instructed to indicate on a five-point scale whether or not he had strong positive feelings (1), strong negative feelings (5), or was more moderately disposed (2, 3, 4). A quantitative score could be obtained by summing the values for each item. Thus, a subject with a high score was not as satisfied with his body as one with a low score.

Body Rating Scale. The Body Rating Scale was developed originally as a Semantic Differential Test by Osgood *et al.*,[62] who provided the subject with a word stem (my body is) and then gave a series of bipolar adjectives that could be rated on a 7-point scale (e.g., masculine 1–2–3–4–5–6–7 non-masculine). The sum of the values for each response constituted a score for this test; a low score indicated that the subject favorably perceived his body.

Adjective Check List. The Adjective Check List for college students[63] consists of 300 adjectives commonly used to describe attributes of a person, and it may be employed by an individual to rate himself or to be rated by others. Twenty-four scales and indices are available for use with this instrument.

---

[60] Seymour Fisher and Sidney E. Cleveland, *Body Image and Personality* (Princeton, N.J.: D. Van Nostrand Company, Inc., 1958).

[61] Paul F. Secord and Sidney M. Jourard, "The Appraisal of Body-Cathexis: Body-Cathexis and the Self," *Journal of Consulting Psychology*, 17, No. 5 (October 1953), 343.

[62] Charles E. Osgood *et al.*, *The Measurement of Meaning* (Urbana: University of Illinois Press, 1957).

[63] Harrison G. Gough and Alfred B. Heilbrun, *The Adjective Check List Manual* (Palo Alto, Calif.: Consulting Psychologists Press, Inc., 1965).

In 1960, an adjective checklist was developed by Davidson and Long[64] to determine a child's self-perception. Fifty different adjectives were selected for this checklist on the basis that they were often used as traits to describe children, such as afraid, noisy, forgetful, friendly, and so forth. An early form of the Davidson-Lang Adjective Check List has been employed in the Medford Boys' Growth Study and is illustrated in Figure 26.

Name: ______________________________ Date: ______________________
School: _____________________________ Grade: _____________________

Directions: These are words that are often used to describe children. Please check the ones that apply to you.

______Afraid	______A Good Pupil	______Polite
______Bad	______A Good Sport	______Quiet
______Bossy	______A Hard Worker	______Selfish
______A Brat	______Helpful	______Silly
______A Bully	______Honest	______A Show Off
______Careless	______Kind	______A Sissy
______Cheerful	______Lazy	______A Sloppy Worker
______Clean	______A Leader	______A Smart Aleck
______Clever	______Not Eager To Learn	______A Sore Loser
______Clumsy	______Loving	______Smart
______A Copy Cat	______Mean	______Stupid
______A Crybaby	______Neat	______A Time Waster
______Dependable	______Nervous	______A Trouble Maker
______Fair	______Noisy	______Unhappy
______Forgetful	______Not Alert	______Not Eager To Study
______Friendly	______Outstanding	______Willing
______Generous	______A Pest	

Figure 26. Davidson Adjective Check List

Self-Image and Physical Ability

The use of tests of self-image are beginning to be employed in physical education to study the relationship between what an individual thinks of himself and what his ability is in physical tasks. For example, Sloan[65] gave the Body Cathexis Test and the Body Rating Scale to a group of college men and selected two groups, one scoring low (the desired direction) and one scoring high. These groups were given the following physical performance tests: medicine ball put, wall pass, zig-zag run, standing broad jump, and 60-yard dash. Based upon an analysis of the difference between the means of these

[64] Helen H. Davidson and Gerhard Long, "Children's Perceptions of Their Teachers' Feelings Toward Them Related to Self-Perception, School Achievement and Behavior," *Journal of Experimental Education*, 29, No. 2 (December 1960), 107.

[65] William W. Sloan, "A Study of the Relationship Between Certain Objective Measures of Body-Image and Performance on a Selected Test of Motor Abilities," unpublished Master's Thesis, University of Maryland, 1963.

two groups in physical ability, he concluded that an individual possessing a positive body-image would be more likely to have a higher level of motor ability than his counterpart who had a negative attitude toward his body. On the other hand, Leahy[66] found low correlations (.08 to −.22) between the Body Cathexis Test and the Body Rating Scale and the gross motor task of stabilometer balancing in college men.

Reynolds[67] formed groups of 13-year-old boys who checked and who did not check each of the 50 adjectives on the Davidson Adjective Check List; the differences between the means on 16 physical and motor tests for the groups thus formed were tested for significance. The adjectives showing greatest differentiation in descending order were: cry-baby, stupid, bossy, leader, mean, nervous, and sissy. For example, those boys who marked the word cry-baby were significantly weaker in arm strength and cable-tension strength and scored significantly lower in pullups, Physical Fitness Index, and the standing broad jump than did those who did not check this adjective.

An interesting technique was devised by Broekhoff[68] to assess the body-image of boys. At 16 years of age, the subjects were asked to identify their own physique from a series of somatotype photographs (faces obscured) in the following sequence: (1) Each selected a "look alike" physique from pictures of 16-year-old boys, ranging from the extreme endomorphic physique through mesomorphic somatotypes and midtypes to the extreme ectomorphic physique. (2) Each did the same for a similar series of photographs of 13-year-old boys. (3) From both series, they selected their "ideal" body type. (4) From a third series of photographs, each tried to identify his own picture at 13 years of age. Even though they failed to recognize their own somatotype pictures, they nevertheless selected body builds closely resembling their actual body type. Moreover, these boys appeared to have a definite image of an ideal physique; the great majority selected a well-balanced mesomorphic physique as the ideal body type.

LEVEL OF ASPIRATION

A technique of personality evaluation that has proven fairly successful involves an assessment of level of aspiration. Essentially this is a technique

---

[66] Robert F. Leahy, "A Study of the Relationship Between Certain Objective Measures of Body-Image and a Measure of Motor Performance on the Stabilometer," unpublished Master's Thesis, University of Maryland, 1966.

[67] Robert M. Reynolds, "Responses on the Davidson Adjective Check List as Related to Maturity, Physical, and Mental Characteristics of Thirteen-Year-Old Boys," microcard Doctoral Dissertation, University of Oregon, 1965.

[68] Jan Broekhoff, "Relationships Between Physical, Socio-psychological, and Mental Characteristics of Thirteen-Year-Old Boys," microcard Doctoral Dissertation, University of Oregon, 1965.

whereby the subject performs some task—either mental or physical—and then reveals the score he would attain if he could have a second trial. It represents to some extent an objective judgment of probable future performance, the individual differences in aspiration level in an experimental situation being readily measured and sufficiently generalized to appear in dissimilar tasks. Thus, the possibility is presented for enhancing the understanding of human drives and motivation.

From empirical observation, people evaluate themselves for future performance in different ways. Under specific situations, individuals react in one of three possible ways: They feel that they can perform better than previously; they feel they can do as well; or they feel they will not do as well. Asking such a question following tests of speed printing, spatial relations, and accuracy of quoit throwing, Frank[69] obtained aspiration scores by subtracting from the average of individual levels of aspiration the median of the performance that preceded each of them. The ratio between the level of aspiration and the level of performance remained constant, irrespective of the test being employed, and thereby represented a stable element of the personality.

In 1938, Gardner[70] measured the level of aspiration of 32 college men following the administration of four tasks: card sorting, digit-symbol substitution, a multiple choice test of opposites, and a complicated activity consisting of cancellation performed while counting backward by threes. After each trial, a score was reported to the subject; he was then asked to set his aspiration level for the next trial. Reliabilities of the measures ranged from .76 to .98, most of them being above .90. Intercorrelations between tasks for these measures ranged from .42 to .69 when corrected for attenuation. However, in studying individual differences in aspiration level and ratings on 8 personality variables of high school boys, Gardner[71] obtained low and, for the most part, insignificant correlations, which would indicate that the level of aspiration represents a specific trait of personality.

In general, experiments involving level of aspiration have used mental rather than physical tasks, since the technique originated in psychology. An early study in physical education was conducted by Smith,[72] who studied the influence of athletic success and failure on the level of aspiration of the

---

[69] Jerome D. Frank, "Individual Differences in Certain Aspects of the Level of Aspiration," *American Journal of Psychology*, 47, No. 1 (January 1935), 119.

[70] John W. Gardner, "Individual Differences in Aspiration Level in a Standard Sequence of Objective Success and Failure Situations," *Psychological Bulletin*, 35, No. 8 (October 1938), 521.

[71] John W. Gardner, "The Relation of Certain Personality Variables to Level of Aspiration," *Psychological Bulletin*, 36, No. 6 (June 1939), 540.

[72] Carnie H. Smith, "Influence of Athletic Success and Failure on the Level of Aspiration," *Research Quarterly*, 20, No. 2 (May 1949), 196.

participants. Members of a freshman football team were interviewed prior to each game and were asked to indicate quantitatively their immediate aspiration level—the number of minutes they thought they would play in that game—and their ultimate aspiration—the number of minutes they thought they would play in some game before the season ended. Among the findings were the following: a tendency for successful players to raise their levels of aspiration and for failing players to lower their levels; a trend for players to escape from failure-producing situations after having experienced failures; a tendency for players with somewhat higher levels of aspiration to maintain some hopes of success; and a trend for players with highest aspiration levels to experience success repeatedly even though they raised their goals.

A level of aspiration test based upon maximum grip strength has been utilized in the Medford Boys' Growth Study. The following protocol was followed:

1. After instructing the subject in grip testing technique, his grip strength is taken (*P*–1). He is then informed of his score.
2. The subject is asked to estimate what score he believes he can attain on a second grip strength effort. This score is recorded as his first aspiration score (*A*–1).
3. A second grip strength test is administered and recorded (*P*–2), and the subject is informed of this score.
4. Steps 2 and 3 are repeated to obtain a second aspiration score (*A*–2) and a third grip strength measure (*P*–3).

Two useful level of aspiration scores available are:

1. *First aspiration discrepancy* (*AD*–1): the difference between *P*–1 and *A*–1.
2. *Second aspiration discrepancy* (*AD*–2): the difference between *P*–2 and *A*–2.

Clarke and Clarke[73] administered such a test to 98 9-year-old boys and formed three groups comprised of those with the highest postive scores on *AD*–1 and *AD–2*, those with zero discrepancies (*P*–1 and *A*–1 being the same), and those with the greatest negative scores. It was found that the boys in a high *AD*–1 group had a significantly greater Physical Fitness Index mean than did boys in zero and low *AD*–1 groups. Where high and zero groups were compared, the high group was significantly superior in the following five additional tests: standing height, body weight, McCloy's Classification Index, McCloy's arm strength score, and Strength Index. Apparently, the

---

[73] H. Harrison Clarke and David H. Clarke, "Relationship Between Level of Aspiration and Selected Physical Factors of Boys Aged Nine Years," *Research Quarterly*, 32, No. 1 (March 1961), 12.

9-year-old boy who strives to attain higher goals is physically superior in size and strength to others his own age who are not willing to risk the chance of failure and who thereby choose the aspiration level that seems to ensure at least some measure of continued success.

On the other hand, Clarke and Stratton[74] found the second aspiration discrepancy (*AD*–2) to be the most representative of the various performances, aspirations, and discrepancies studied. It correlated relatively well with performance discrepancy, aspiration discrepancy, and grip strength performance scores. This discrepancy measure differentiated best between the three basic groups—high-positive, low-positive to low-negative, and high-negative—formed on the basis of magnitude and direction of aspirations to achieve grip strength scores.

Subsequently, Stratton[75] studied the reliability of level of aspiration scores and their relationship to measures of the growth and development of 11-year-old boys. The reliability coefficients with the tests taken one week apart ranged from .44 to .68; the most reliable measure was the difference between the second grip strength test and the second aspiration (*AD*–2). Other findings related to this form of level of aspiration testing were: No age effect was found; previous annual experience in grip strength testing did not affect level of aspiration testing of 9-year-old boys; experience in level of aspiration and grip strength tended to cause 11-year-old boys to be more consistent in setting their grip strength levels and the setting of aspirations closer to their actual abilities. Among the relationships found with level of aspiration measures were: A significant difference was obtained between high and low first aspiration discrepancy (*AD*–1) means on the Dreese-Mooney Interest Inventory; the high average magnitude of discrepancy and average variability of discrepancy groups had significantly higher standing broad jump means than did the low groups; the high average variability of discrepancy group had a higher grip strength mean than did the low group.

Greene[76] longitudinally related peer status and level of aspiration measures to the maturity, physique, structural, strength, and motor ability characteristics of the same boys from 7 to 12 years of age. The highest multiple correlation obtained was .485 between the sports category at 12 years of age and the standing broad jump, mesomorphy, Physical Fitness Index, and

---

[74] H. Harrison Clarke and Stephen T. Stratton, "A Level of Aspiration Test Based on the Grip Strength Efforts of Nine-Year-Old Boys," *Child Development*, 33, No. 4 (December 1962), 897.

[75] Stephen T. Stratton, "The Reliability of Level of Aspiration Scores and Their Relationship to Measures of the Growth and Development of Eleven-Year-Old Boys," microcard Doctoral Dissertation, University of Oregon, 1964.

[76] Walter H. Greene, "Peer Status and Level of Aspiration of Boys as Related to Their Maturity, Physique, Structural, Strength, and Motor Ability Characteristics," microcard Doctoral Dissertation, University of Oregon, 1964.

cable-tension strength average. Mean differences in favor of high sociometric groups (boys highly chosen at least three of four years) were found for the standing broad jump, cable-tension strength average, mesomorphy, Physical Fitness Index, and 60-yard shuttle run; in some instances, high endomorphy means were found with low sociometric groups. Based on the level of aspiration, such tests as the following differentiated between high and low groups: body weight, upper arm girth, cable-tension strength average, Wetzel physique channel, standing height, mesomorphy, ectomorphy, and standing broad jump.

MOTIVATION

The student of psychology will be aware of the numerous theories that explain personality and will identify many of the causative factors that underlie behavior. The study of these basic drives and interrelated aspects of psychology is best left to the psychologist, although it does form the substructure for the discipline in physical education that seeks to answer questions presented by physical performance. At this point, it is the physical educator's responsibility to develop and expand the literature in the psychology of sport so as to gain a greater understanding of the factors associated with movement and physical capabilities.

One such major aspect may be called motivation, although human drives and motives are so pervasive that great injustice may be done by separating them from other topics mentioned previously. The motivation theories of Freud, Hull, Hebb, Maslow, and others may be regarded as essential sources in the study of personality; the presentation by Cofer and Johnson[77] will prove helpful in understanding the theoretical aspects of personality dynamics.

Action Motivation

The discussion of motivation here will be restricted to those studies, usually experimental in design, that seek to alter performance by manipulating certain psychological factors. In other words, circumstances exist that may enhance or perhaps interfere with overt action; and, although the usual emphasis is to seek ways of causing improvement, examination of those factors that inhibit behavior may be just as valid. At any rate, anyone who has tested subjects on physical tasks is aware of the problem posed by motivation; the instructions usually adopted suggest that all subjects be given the

---

[77] Charles N. Cofer and Warren R. Johnson, "Personality Dynamics in Relation to Exercise and Sports," in Warren R. Johnson, ed., *Science and Medicine of Exercise and Sports* (New York: Harper & Row, Publishers, 1960), Ch. 28.

same degree of motivation, so this factor is at least held constant. This practice does not guarantee that all subjects will be motivated equally, however, because there may well be wide individual differences in such a trait: some subjects are normally aggressive when it comes to performance of physical tasks and others seem more reticent. The conditions that pertain in such situations should prove provocative to the investigator.

Available information suggests that the selection of a criterion task may be crucial in carrying out experimentation in motivation. Two studies, both involving peripheral muscle activity, illustrate the differences that are involved when a single strength test is employed as contrasted with a series of repetitive endurance efforts. An example of the former is given by Ryan,[78] who administered a grip strength test to 80 male subjects and followed one week later with a second test. However, on the second test, the subjects were divided into four independent groups. Each group was given a different motive-incentive condition, as follows: The control group received the same instructions as on the first test, to squeeze the dynamometer as hard as possible; the second group was given verbal encouragement during the test to try to exceed their first score (although they had no knowledge of the results); group three did have knowledge of the previous attempt and was told to watch the dynamometer dial and try to exceed this score; group four had an electrode attached to the opposite wrist and was told that if they fell short of their first effort they would receive a severe electric shock. The results indicated that no differences in performance existed between the four motive-incentive conditions.

The results of this study are in contrast to those of Nelson,[79] whose subjects were subjected to exhaustion exercise on an elbow-flexion ergograph. Ten motivational situations arranged in a random group design were applied, as follows:

1. *Normal Instructions:* The subjects were instructed to exercise as long as possible.

2. *Verbal Encouragement:* The investigator gave continual verbal encouragement during the exercise bout.

3. *Individual Competition:* Two subjects were asked to compete against each other to attain the highest endurance score.

---

[78] E. Dean Ryan, "Effect of Differential Motive-Incentive Conditions on Physical Performance," *Research Quarterly*, 32, No. 1 (March 1961), 83.

[79] Jack K. Nelson, "An Analysis of the Effects of Applying Various Motivational Situations to College Men Subjected to a Stressful Physical Performance," microcard Doctoral Dissertation, University of Oregon, 1962; in H. Harrison Clarke, *Muscular Strength and Endurance in Man* (Englewood Cliffs, N.J.: Prentice-Hall, Inc., 1966), pp. 101–9.

4. *Group Competition:* The subjects were encouraged to determine their fitness by being shown a scale that purported to show ergographic performances of college men.

5. *Obtainable Goal:* Each subject was directed to exercise for a total of 40 repetitions, a goal that was obtainable.

6. *Observer's Presence:* After the exercise began, an official-looking observer walked in and observed the exercise with apparent interest.

7. *Instructor Interest:* The subject's class instructor urged him to do as well as possible and to report his score after testing.

8. *Ego Involvement:* In a casual manner, before exercise was started, each subject was told that junior high school pupils had averaged 62 repetitions and that senior high school students had averaged more than 70 repetitions. The investigator made it clear that the subject was expected to do better, even though these norms were fictitious and extremely high.

9. *Air Force Space Program:* The subjects were told that they were part of the Air Force space program that was determining standards for future astronauts.

10. *Competition with Russian Students:* The subjects were told that they were participating in a nation-wide program to compare performances of American and Russian students.

The analysis, based on the total work accomplished, resulted in the identification of three motivational groups. The low group consisted of those subjects given normal instructions, verbal encouragement, and instructor interest; the moderate group was composed of those given an obtainable goal, observer's presence, group competition, and competition with the Russians; and the high group consisted of ego involvement, Air Froce space program, and individual competition. Thus, it was demonstrated that applying different motivations did affect the performances of college men in stressful physical performance involving exercise to the point of volitional exhaustion.

Hypnosis

Special mention should be made of the technique of hypnosis. Although hypnosis is not a research procedure available to everyone, some pertinent studies have been made utilizing hypnosis and posthypnotic suggestion in connection with certain physical performance variables. By the very nature of the method, it should be clear that rather extensive training should be undertaken prior to experimentation. Used indiscriminately, rather severe repercussions and possible mental health hazards may result, so employment by novices should be discouraged. A student desiring to use hypnosis should obtain assistance from competent professional sources.

The discussion of hypnosis in connection with motivational studies is not intended to imply that this is the only use to which it may be put. There have been a number of studies merely designed to investigate the effects of hypnosis on a variety of bodily functions and other factors, including exercise.[80] However, several reports in physical education are notable for the emphasis placed on large-muscle performance. In one of these, Johnson, Massey, and Kramer[81] investigated the effect of posthypnotic suggestion on all-out rides for 100 revolutions on a loaded bicycle ergometer. Ten subjects were selected on the basis of their ability to learn to enter a trance quickly and to carry out posthypnotic suggestions. They were placed under a trance before each of two rides, but before one of these they were given the suggestion that they would be unusually strong and resistent to fatigue. The difference between the means of the two criterion exercises was not significant. Later, Massey, Johnson, and Kramer[82] employed hypnosis to control the psychological variable so often present in warm-up studies. Utilizing the ergometer task described above, 15 subjects were given warm-up exercises involving generalized activity and no warm-up for the task; however, prior to both conditions they were placed in a deep hypnotic state so that there was no conscious awareness of this period of time. Upon arousal they were tested on the all-out ergometer ride. Once again, no statistically significant differences were found.

SUGGESTED PROBLEMS

The researcher interested in personality dynamics and psychological traits in general may wish to probe the following questions:

1. Can the tests of personality presently in use be improved or new ones constructed? Is it possible to identify personality through physical behavior?
2. In what ways can motivation be determined? Can a physiological basis be used to predict motivational change?
3. What are the individual and group patterns of changes in personality with age?
4. What factors determine academic achievement in school?
5. What are the characteristics of subjects in the extreme categories of personality? What cultural factors play a role in personality development?

---

[80] Cofer and Johnson, *op. cit.*, pp. 552–54.

[81] Warren R. Johnson, Benjamin H. Massey, and George F. Kramer, "Effect of Posthypnotic Suggestions on All-Out Effort of Short Duration," *Research Quarterly*, 31, No. 2 (May 1960), 142.

[82] Benjamin H. Massey, Warren R. Johnson, and George F. Kramer, "Effect of Warm-Up Exercise upon Muscular Performance Using Hypnosis to Control the Psychological Variable," *Research Quarterly*, 32, No. 1 (March 1961), 63.

6. Does the pattern of social acceptance change with age and physical ability? Is there a change in individual social acceptance as boys and girls change physically or develop athletic skills?

SUMMARY

A variety of research procedures involving psychological problems is available. The main purpose of this chapter was to stimulate study of that aspect of psychology concerned with personal and social adjustment as related to physical performance, as well as to encourage the development of related topics.

The measurement of psychological characteristics ordinarily is not accomplished in the objective manner that marks the majority of research procedures in physical education, because psychological variables are more elusive and sometimes difficult to define clearly. Internal drives and motives are often unclear to the individual himself, so the methods of obtaining adequate data are complex and perhaps indirect. The use of projective techniques provides an example of the difficulty experienced by the novice; they should not be attempted without sufficient training and experience in this type of evaluation.

Inventory techniques are characterized in general by their ease of application and scoring but are marked in many cases by questionable validity. Ample precedence is evident for their use in psychological studies, and their relevance to physical performance seems logical. The proper selection of tests along with extreme care taken in their administration are essential ingredients for success in this type of research.

The evaluation of peer status appears to be more direct, especially when ratings are made by acquaintances. The sociometric questionnaire has been employed as a measure of social adjustment with apparent success for a number of years, and in one form or another it asks subjects to list individuals with whom they would like to be associated. Thus, social acceptance and rejection may be evaluated. Closely related to this technique are the various behavior rating scales used by trained observers.

The area of self-image and self-concept is receiving some attention due to the feeling that an individual's body concept may reflect his physical ability. This is reinforced by the various studies involving level of aspiration and other attempts at the measurement of motivation.

SELECTED REFERENCES

Allen, R. M., *Personality Assessment Procedures: Psychometric, Projective, and Other Procedures*. New York: Harper & Row, Publishers, 1958.

Buros, Oscar Krisen, ed., *The Fifth Mental Measurements Yearbook*. Highland Park N.J.: The Gryphon Press, 1959.

Clarke, H. Harrison, *Application of Measurement to Health and Physical Education*, 4th ed. Englewood Cliffs, N.J.: Prentice-Hall, Inc., 1967.

Cronbach, Lee J., *Essentials of Psychological Testing* (2nd ed.), New York: Harper & Row, Publishers, 1960.

Ferguson, L. W., *Personality Measurement*. New York: McGraw-Hill Book Company, 1952.

Fisher, Seymour, and Sidney E. Cleveland, *Body Image and Personality*. Princeton, N.J.: D. Van Nostrand Company, Inc., 1958.

Johnson, Warren R., ed., *Science and Medicine of Exercise and Sports*. New York: Harper & Row, Publishers, 1960, Chs. 28, 29.

Moreno, J. L., *Who Shall Survive?* New York: The Beacon Press, 1934.

CHAPTER 16

Kinesiological Research

An area of research in physical education that has been developed largely as a direct result of the efforts of scholars within the field is that of kinesiology. The term has been coined to represent the study of human movement, which would seem to describe much of the research in physical education; however, kinesiology as the subject field can be more rigorously defined.

As constituted here, kinesiological research will deal largely with the anatomical and mechanical analysis of performance, both in terms of local muscular action and gross body movement. No attempt is made to resolve all the questions raised by such a designation, for the analysis of performance might take directions other than that of purely kinesiological. For example, take the choreographer's terminology in describing movements in the dance or the historical researcher's description of ancient rites. Certain arbitrary decisions must be made, and the types of research considered to be kinesiological here may be something quite different in other frames of reference.

Two points of view seem evident from the current instructional efforts in the teaching of kinesiology. One can be described as anatomical, in which movement is depicted in terms of muscle action with strong emphasis placed upon the description of actions through muscle origin and insertion. The second approach, often superimposed upon the first, is the description of action in terms of known physical laws. Thus, the appropriate laws of motion, mechanical principles, and the like are brought to bear to give the fullest possible understanding of human movement. It is pointless to argue the merits of either approach, except perhaps to indicate that the tendency today is to utilize the most appropriate means to gain the fullest possible analysis of performance.

The modern kinesiologist employs the camera, the electromyograph, the goniometer, and any other device that will yield information on the way people move. This is not to suggest that the researcher is limited in any way; considerable overlapping will be inevitable, particularly between kinesiology and physiology of exercise. The electromyograph is widely used to study the functional state of muscles and yields information on muscle excitation, a matter of concern in physiology. It also tells the kinesiologist about the patterning of muscle action and helps him to decide about questions related to movement sequence. As will be described later such overlapping serves to underlie the difficulty in designating specific areas of research in physical education.

Although the trends in kinesiology reflect greater concentration on mechanical and cinematographical analysis, this does not mean that developments no longer take place in the field of anatomy. Perhaps the research is less voluminous, but nonetheless there is a concern that differences among individuals may exist in so-called muscle origin and insertion, which in turn may account for differences in performance. Thus, anatomical structure may bear upon mechanical analysis, a fact well-known to the comparative anatomist,[1] although not so well-documented for various human males and females. This situation, coupled with an increasing attention to the relative contributions made by separate muscles within a well-defined group, offers an intriguing area for study in physical education.

ELECTROMYOGRAPHY EQUIPMENT AND USE

A motor unit is composed of the nerve cell, its motor nerve, and the muscle fibers that it innervates. When an impulse from the spinal cord travels down the nerve fiber and is propagated beyond the myoneural junction, all the muscle fibers of the motor unit contract simultaneously, which action is accompanied by an electrical potential that can be detected, amplified, and recorded. The number of motor units in a muscle may run into the thousands, and the number of muscle fibers per motor unit will vary, probably from a very few to several hundred, depending upon the muscle selected. It has been difficult to assess adequately the number of fibers in a unit because of the overlapping of motor units (one motor neuron may innervate fibers belonging to several motor units), as well as the presence of intrafusal fibers (see Chapter 14).

The elements associated with the propagation of the nerve impulse result in a change in electrical potential of the muscle membrane. This is known as the action potential, and the record obtained of this activity is known as the electromyogram. A wave of negative electricity accompanies

---

[1] Milton Hildebrand, "Motions of the Running Cheetah and Horse," *Journal of Mammalogy*, 40, No. 4 (November 1959), 481.

the contraction of a single muscle fiber; two electrodes placed in close proximity to each other along the fiber will monitor this wave in quick succession. The well-known diphasic spike (Fig. 27) results, in which the initial peak signaling the passage of the wave under the first electrode and the opposite peak marking the passage of the wave under the second electrode. In order to understand the use of electromyography in kinesiological research, acquaintance with some of the problems associated with obtaining an acceptable recording is first necessary.

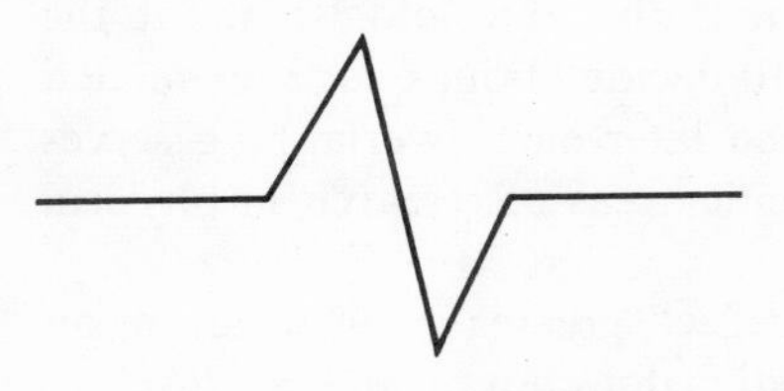

Figure 27. Diphasic Spike

Electrodes

Electrodes may be of two general types: needle electrodes or skin electrodes. The criteria for selecting one or the other depends upon the function that is to be assessed. The value of the former is that it provides a means of recording the action potential produced by a single motor unit or by even a single muscle fiber.[2] It consists of an ordinary stainless steel hypodermic needle with an insulated wire inserted into the lumen so that it is flush with its bevel. Thus, the needle becomes one electrode and the wire the other; because they are so close to each other, they may reach the same motor unit. This is known as a coaxial needle electrode, and it will produce a diphasic spike. The advantage gained by using this type of electrode stems from the fact that more specific motor unit activity may be assessed, a function of vital importance in medicine where information on lower motor neuron lesions, muscular atrophies, and so on can be of diagnostic and prognostic value. Among the disadvantages of such a study in physical education is the problem associated with needle insertion, involving important considerations of subject acceptance and asepsis.

Employment of surface electrodes is probably much more feasible and, in the long run, may prove more desirable from the standpoint of the information needed. Where large muscles are to be investigated, the additive recording of a large number of motor units may be desirable, especially when they are to be monitored over a period of, say, a few seconds of contraction time. Skin electrodes consist of small, metal (e.g., silver) discs that are placed

---

[2] Gerald G. Hirschberg and Arthur S. Abramson, "Clinical Electromyography," *Archives of Physical Medicine*, 31, No. 9 (September 1950), 576.

over the belly of the muscle to be monitored, usually separated by a distance of 1 mm to 1 inch or more, depending upon the size of the muscle to be monitored; the smaller the muscle, the smaller and more closely spaced will be the electrodes.[3] The site selected may straddle the motor point, although it is not essential to do this in all cases, since muscle excursion is certain to alter this relationship during contraction. Nevertheless, the location of various motor points may be accomplished by electrical stimulation or by reference to standard positions, such as those designated by Walthard and Tchicaloff;[4] although the precise anatomical site of each motor point varies slightly among subjects, the relative position follows a fairly fixed pattern.

The electrodes are secured in place by some sort of adhesive so that they do not shift in position nor disturb the conductance from the skin. Electrolyte gel is ordinarily used to promote the contact between electrodes and skin. The biopotential skin electrodes and adhesive collars designed by the Spinco Division of Beckman Instruments, Inc., have proven satisfactory for use in *EMG* research. These contain an electrolyte reservoir space between the electrode space and a silver/silver chloride pellet inside the electrode. Thus, when electrolyte gel is squeezed into the reservoir holes, a closed connection is formed between skin and pellet. Disposable adhesive collars form a hermetic seal to hold the entire assembly in position on the subject so that it will be impervious to movement and perspiration and consequently insure a stable baseline on the recording throughout the testing sequence.

Once again, the question of number of electrodes arises. For each muscle group investigated, it would be possible to use a single electrode, but the monopolar recording is more likely to pick up unwanted current from other muscles than the bipolar electrodes. The choice may then be to use two surface electrodes placed across the belly of the muscle. This will ensure a restricted field of sensitivity, a condition highly desirable in this type of research. In addition, a third (indifferent) electrode will be required to be placed at some remote site on the body, which will serve to reduce interference (such as the cardiac potential).

A source of additional resistance to current flow is found in the skin itself where layers of metabolizing and nonmetabolizing cells offer obstacles to the conduction of electricity, so there must be some attention given to the skin preparation prior to electrode placement. In general, it has been found satisfactory to shave off all hair, sand the skin lightly with fine sandpaper to remove the layer of horny and dead cells, clean with alcohol, and apply

---

[3] A. L. O'Connell and E. B. Gardner, "The Use of Electromyography in Kinesiological Research," *Research Quarterly*, 34, No. 2 (May 1963), 166.

[4] Karl M. Walthard and Michel Tchicaloff, "Motor Points," in *Electrodiagnosis and Electromyography* (2nd ed.), ed. Sidney Licht (New Haven: Elizabeth Licht, Publisher, 1961), Ch. 6.

electrode paste. To test the skin resistance, an ohmmeter can be employed after the electrodes have been secured in place. Although the amount of impedance that can be tolerated may vary with the equipment used, it is generally advisable to reduce it to 10,000 ohms or even 5,000 ohms if possible. If intolerable resistance is noted, reapplication of electrodes will help reduce it to acceptable limits. A discussion of these and other problems associated with electromyographic research will be found in a report by Davis.[5]

Recording

A variety of devices are available for detecting and reproducing the electromyogram for research and other applications, ranging from single channel to multiple channel recorders. The number of channels required will depend upon the number of muscle groups tested—hence, the number of electrode sets. Some of the 8 channel recorders, for example, offer tremendous versatility for most needs of the investigator in a wide variety of applications. Perhaps in the future one could envision a greater requirement than this, but it is difficult to see how more than 8 sets of muscles would be tested simultaneously.

At any rate, the investment in multiple-channel recording equipment for a laboratory can reap important dividends in the versatility that it provides, because, for a fraction of the initial cost, other physiological parameters may be included by purchasing additional coupling devices. These needs will be dictated by the experimental design. Actually, only one channel may be required and be entirely adequate for a host of research investigations. This may illustrate the thin dividing line between studies of a kinesiological nature and those oriented more physiologically or medically. Whereas the kinesiologist may need to know the relative interaction between muscle groups during a movement, the physiologist may be more interested in the quality of the electromyographic response. This will be illustrated subsequently.

Among the devices useful to demonstrate the action current that accompanies the contraction are the loud speaker and the oscilloscope. The simplest is the loud speaker, which has its greatest value as a diagnostic medical adjunct. A physician trained in its use can interpret the character of the sound and relate it to the appropriate abnormality. This sound may even be put on magnetic tape for subsequent evaluation. Its use for physical education research cannot be encouraged, however, for obvious reasons. On the other

---

[5] John F. Davis, "Manual of Surface Electromyography," *WADC Technical Report, 59–184*, Wright-Patterson Air Force Base, Ohio, Wright Air Development Center (December 1959).

hand, the cathode ray oscilloscope offers the possibility for the most accurate method of obtaining the necessary record. Its advantages over the direct-writing method are that it does not have to overcome the inertia of a pen, and it will provide much greater fidelity of response. A camera may be employed to photograph the tracing on the screen.

Beyond this, however, there is ordinarily an operational requirement that some sort of write-out device be available in more convenient form so that the investigator can obtain immediately a record of the electrical activity. Several such systems may be incorporated to meet this demand, depending once again upon the experimental requirements. One of these has been described by de Vries[6] who sought a device that would have extremely high sensitivity and would thus detect the low level motor unit activity in resting muscle with the use of surface electrodes. As a result, an *EMG* monitor was designed that possessed a precision of $\pm 0.01\ \mu v$ at the 10-μv level and $\pm 0.05\ \mu v$ at the 1.0-μv level. A voltage gain amplifier feeds a voltage controlled oscillator, the frequency output of which is related linearly to the integral of the muscle action potential and is counted as pulses by an electronic counter. The count registered per unit time is related to the mean *EMG* voltage according to the equation:

$$\mu v \text{ root mean square } (RMS) = \frac{\text{counter reading (total pulses)}}{\text{integration period (sec)}}$$

Thus, a testing sequence may be followed during active contraction so that during one interval (e.g., 1 sec) the muscle action potentials are counted, and during a second interval they are read. This can be alternated for the period of time selected.

Monitoring the integrator with an oscilloscope for artifacts due to 60 cps interference, the electrocardiogram, or other factors, is also appropriate; it is often necessary to enclose the subject in a room shielded by copper or bronze screening. de Vries feels bipolar electrodes do not discriminate changes in *EMG* activity for his reserach as well as unipolar leads and therefore uses a single vacuum cup electrode and ground. For a further description of these and other factors, an additional reference[7] will prove helpful.

Another method to be mentioned here is the usual pen-writing system that results in a permanent, written record of the *EMG*. This is quite satisfactory when surface electrodes are employed, and the record obtained may be

---

[6] Herbert A. de Vries, "Quantitative Electromyographic Investigation of the Spasm Theory of Muscle Pain," *American Journal of Physical Medicine*, 45, No. 3 (June 1966), 119.

[7] Herbert A. de Vries, "Muscle Tonus in Postural Muscles," *American Journal of Physical Medicine*, 44, No. 6 (December 1965), 275.

analyzed later according to the procedures established by the investigator. Equipment available for such purposes should be selected with care, and the manufacturer's specifications should be followed very closely. As indicated earlier, the problem that arises is to amplify a small signal from the muscle to such an extent that there is an appropriate pen deflection. This requires precision, fidelity, and compatibility of the various components if the resultant record is to be meaningful. Fortunately, the further possibility remains that the action potentials may be integrated electronically so that the tremendous difficulty in measuring manually the individual amplitudes of a large number of muscle action potential spikes can be alleviated. Although the task of measuring records will not be eliminated, the investigator should carefully explore the question of providing an automatic means of measuring the so-called "area under the curve" by instrumental integration; this method averages such factors as number, amplitude, and duration of the action potentials. The reader will find Basmajian[8] helpful in dealing with various types of recorders.

Measurement

After the problems associated with instrumentation, electrode placement, and testing procedure have been solved, the last question has to do with measurement of the record. It cannot be emphasized too strongly that this is meaningless if the greatest care has not been taken in obtaining the data in the first place. Nothing can be done with the record if there have been errors introduced at some earlier point, so the researcher should plan his design to control all essential factors and then provide time to practice with the equipment. If multiple-channel operation is anticipated, this will compound the difficulties and may require greater care and longer practice. Experience suggests that the investigator will need assistance in using the equipment and helping the subject; hopefully, a laboratory technician who understands the electronic and practical aspects of electromyography will be available.

Thus, with careful planning, the kind of record to be obtained will be known. In fact, a clear decision should be made in advance on the manner of measuring the records in order to coordinate it with the testing procedure. Literally, yards and yards of *EMG* tracings may be obtained in the course of an experiment, but probably only certain portions are crucial. Again, this will depend upon the experimental design, but testing should not begin until these problems have been solved.

In general, some sort of sampling procedure is used to obtain the estimate of *EMG* activity, and this may well be obtained by proper timing. For example, it may be sufficient to measure the middle 3 sec of a 5-sec contraction

[8] J. V. Basmajian, *Muscles Alive* (Baltimore: The Williams & Wilkins Co., 1962), Ch. 1.

or to sample at intervals during a sustained contraction or even to monitor the activity through a range of isotonic movement. It should be clear that the basic element is time, and there must be a way of coordinating the subject and record. If these are not standardized, confusion and error may result, especially later on when the investigator is working on the data and finds he has no point of reference. Two devices on the electromyograph may be helpful in this task: a time marker and an event marker. The time marker, given in standard intervals (e.g., sec), gives a visual indication of testing duration; and the event marker, operated by the tester, can be used to indicate special matters of interest (e.g., subject activity).

The method of measuring the record itself will require some thought. For the nonintegrated *EMG*, it may be possible to overlay an appropriate scale, calibrated according to the settings on the gain control, and to read the amplitude of the pen deflections, converting them into microvolts if necessary. However, if an integrated electromyogram is obtained, several investigators have employed a planimeter. Essentially, this process involves running the planimeter from point to point along the wave form created by the pen deflections and returning to the starting point. The resultant "area under the curve" may be converted to some appropriate unit or may remain in arbitrary values. No further accuracy is obtained by converting to some standard value, so investigators commonly express their result as an *EMG* unit.[9]

ELECTROMYOGRAPHICAL STUDIES

Once the practical matters have been settled successfully, the investigator is ready to begin his experimental work. The type of problem selected may take a number of directions, the review of literature in electromyography being quite voluminous. It should be stressed that the *EMG* technique itself is important only to the extent that it contributes to solution of a problem, that it exists as a means to achieve some goal—in this case, the fullest possible understanding of some aspect of human behavior. In order to assist in appreciating this concept, a sampling of research will be presented to illustrate the range of subject matter that exists in this field.

Muscle Function

Familiarity with the many studies performed by physiologists who have attempted to understand the action of the motor unit as well as factors

[9] H. J. Ralston, "Uses and Limitations of Electromyography in the Quantitative Study of Skeletal Muscle Function," *American Journal of Orthodontics*, 47, No. 7 (July 1961), 521.

associated with the so-called small motor nerve system gives an indication of the extent that electromyographic research may be carried. For example, Buchthal, Guld, and Rosenfalck[10] employed two multielectrodes to chart the territory of a motor unit in human biceps muscles. These electrodes were inserted at right angles to each other; 12 leads, each 1.5 mm long, were placed at distances of .5 mm along their length. The first multielectrode was so inserted that the maximum action potential magnitude was recorded on leads 5 to 7; the second was inserted as close as possible to the first and turned so as to obtain maximum amplitude of the potentials. The action potentials were found to belong to the same motor unit if their time relationships were identical, irrespective of the frequency of discharge. Thus, it was determined that the action potentials of a motor unit spread over an area approximately circular in shape, the average territory determined to be 4 to 6 mm. Of interest, also, was the finding that as many as 6 different motor units intermingled, and 3 motor units overlapped completely.

Much of the research devoted to the action of the muscle spindles has come from the study of various mammalian muscles (frog and cat, particularly) where such experimentation is more feasible. Illustrative of this approach is the investigation by Hunt and Kuffler[11] who used adult cats, preparing the hind limb in a rigidly isometric system so that the contractile force could be measured. The nerve leading to the muscle under study was available both for stimulation and for action potential recording. Of interest here was the finding that during maximal muscle contraction the sensory discharge from the muscle spindles (gamma afferent fibers) ceased. In other words, the spindles did not participate in tension development. The reference by Hunt and Perl[12] will be helpful in pursuing these matters further.

Relation of EMG *to Tension*

One of the most pressing issues has been the relationship between the electrical activity created during contraction and the tension produced. At first glance, one might assume that the two would be equivalent; but it must be remembered that the events associated with excitation on the one hand and contraction on the other are sequential, actually representing two distinct phenomena. There is no question that they are closely tied together, but the question remains as to whether or not they are actually equivalent.

---

[10] Fritz Buchthal, Christian Guld, and Poul Rosenfalck, "Multielectrode Study of the Territory of a Motor Unit," *Acta Physiologica Scandinavica*, 39, No. 1 (1957), 83.

[11] Carlton C. Hunt and Stephen W. Kuffler, "Further Study of Efferent Small-Nerve Fibres to Mammalian Muscle Spindles: Multiple Spindle Innervation and Activity During Contraction," *Journal of Physiology*, 113, No. 2–3 (April 1951), 283.

[12] C. C. Hunt and E. R. Perl, "Spinal Reflex Mechanisms Concerned with Skeletal Muscle," *Physiological Reviews*, 40, No. 3 (July 1960), 538.

In 1952, Inman and others[13] investigated the integrated *EMG* during an isometric contraction of the biceps of a cineplastic amputee whose muscle had been freed from its insertion and connected directly to a dynamometer. It was noted that the two factors, *EMG* and tension, paralleled each other. The same results were obtained in normal subjects in isometric contractions of the elbow flexors and ankle dorsi flexors, irrespective of the type of electrodes (skin, wire, or needle) employed, as long as care was taken that the muscle length did not change during contraction. However, this relationship failed to exist when the muscle was allowed to vary in length.

During that same year, Lippold[14] studied the integrated activity of the gastrocnemius-soleus muscles in 30 human subjects during a series of isometric contractions. When the data from 10 experiments were plotted according to a line of best fit, a linear relationship was found. Moreover, when the experimental values were correlated with the expected value obtained by fitting, the relationship was quite high ($r = .93$ to .99). The author noted considerable variation among the regression lines, however, which would indicate that some caution should be exhibited in interpretation of the correlations.

Extending the concept to the relation between the action potential of a muscle and its tension under conditions of constant velocity and constant tension, Bigland and Lippold[15] tested five young adult males and females. A special dynamometer was constructed to permit isotonic contractions of the calf muscles in plantar flexion so that the subject could control the velocity of contraction. Integrated action potentials were recorded by using surface suction electrodes. It was found that at constant velocity of either shortening or lengthening, the electrical activity was directly proportional to the tension, although the amount of electrical activity was less during lengthening. At constant tension, the electrical activity increased in a linear manner with velocity of shortening but seemed almost independent of speed during lengthening. The correlation of the observed points to the straight line during the condition of constant velocity of shortening was .93. It was of interest to note, also, that Bigland and Lippold compared the results of surface electrodes and needle electrodes and obtained essentially the same results. More recently, deJong and Freund[16] studied the amplitude of the action potential

---

[13] Verne T. Inman *et al.*, "Relation of Human Electromyogram to Muscular Tension," *Electroencephalography and Clinical Neurophysiology*, 4, No. 2 (May 1952), 187.

[14] O. C. J. Lippold, "The Relation Between Integrated Action Potentials in a Human Muscle and Its Isometric Tension," *Journal of Physiology*, 117, No. 4 (August 1952), 492.

[15] Brenda Bigland and O. C. J. Lippold, "The Relation Between Force, Velocity and Integrated Electrical Activity in Human Muscles," *Journal of Physiology*, 123, No. 1 (January 1954), 214.

[16] Rudolph H. deJong and Felix G. Freund, "Relation Between Electromyogram and Isometric Twitch Tension in Human Muscle," *Archives of Physical Medicine and Rehabilitation*, 48, No. 10 (October 1967), 539.

and isometric twitch tension of the adductor pollicis brevis muscle when given graded electrical stimulation. When the data were plotted for 15 subjects, a linear relationship between *EMG* and tension occurred; the correlation was .693.

The electromyograph has also been used to study the changes within muscle that occur with fatigue. As indicated in Chapter 13, the operational definition of fatigue is the observable impairment in performance. What happens is subject to conjecture unless some way is found to monitor motor unit activity. Thus, Edwards and Lippold[17] studied the action potentials in human calf muscles that held a continuous isometric contraction at 25 per cent of maximum for a period of 4 min. Electromyographic recordings were made for 5 sec every 10 sec of contraction. When compared with the slope of the line for normal tension vs *EMG*, a linear relationship was found, but the slope of the regression line was different. In fact, more electrical activity was required to maintain a given tension in the fatigued state. This was related to the recruitment of motor units required to compensate for the decrease in force of contraction in the fatigued muscle fibers.

Pattern of Movement

Beyond the functional details of the neuromuscular apparatus lies another important use of electromyography—that of motion analysis. Various ways of studying this problem are available; others will be discussed later in this chapter. However, the *EMG* possesses an important advantage in ability to reflect rather precisely in time the interplay of the musculature participating in a movement. Although the physical educator seems more prone to examine the so-called large motor sports skills, it should be pointed out that some of the more basic actions remain to be thoroughly researched. This is not to decry the interest in movement analysis but to indicate that a host of varied research topics are available.

Inman, Saunders, and Abbott[18] provided some of the first electromyographic results of movement analysis. They studied muscles of the shoulder joint, depicting the pattern of individual response throughout a range of motion and revealing the angle at which the action potentials was greatest. Emphasis was placed on interrelated patterns of behavior; the statement that there is no such thing as a prime mover, at least as ordinarily understood, will prove thought provoking to the reader of this study.

---

[17] R. G. Edwards and O. C. J. Lippold, "The Relation Between Force and Integrated Electrical Activity in Fatigued Muscle," *Journal of Physiology*, 132, No. 3 (June 1956), 677.

[18] Verne T. Inman, J. B. deC. M. Saunders, and Leroy C. Abbott, "Observations on the Function of the Shoulder Joint," *Journal of Bone and Joint Surgery*, 26, No. 1 (January 1944), 1.

Although the muscular action of the elbow joint tends to be taken for granted, since the joint is ginglymus and permits only flexion and extension, the action of the various muscles has received limited study. In 1957, Basmajian and Latif[19] evaluated the role of both heads of the biceps, the brachialis, and the brachioradialis in flexion, extension, pronation, and supination at the elbow joint. Bipolar concentric needle electrodes were employed in a wide variety of movements and positions, both freely moving and with a 2-pound load. Aside from the detail of muscle function provided, a lack of unanimity of action was noted; this finding should prove of interest to investigators in physical education who have found a great deal of specificity in a range of physical activities of the body as a whole. Such findings as that the biceps does not act as a chief flexor of the elbow when the forearm is pronated, even with a 2-pound load, and does not supinate the forearm when the elbow is extended unless strongly resisted also provide very basic kinesiologic data.

Also of interest to this discussion is the analysis of movements of the thumb. It has long been recognized that the active movements of the thumb are important, so much so that it is considered a major disability when its function has been lost. Ebskov and Long[20] described a method whereby fine wire electrodes were inserted into extrinsic and intrinsic thumb muscles, and, at the same time, the movement was electrically monitored by a specially designed goniometer (called a Hexitron). Thus, it was possible to delineate very carefully the muscular functioning of various movements of the unloaded or loaded thumb by recording all tracings simultaneously. The reader will find a discussion of the question of computer data processing relevant, especially when greater electronic sophistication provides so much data that reduction by hand becomes exceedingly time consuming.

A number of studies have been undertaken to examine normal and pathological walking, both by physicians and others who have been concerned with basic gait patterns. For instance, in physical medicine, the proper development of prosthetic devices had to wait for research to be completed on the normal walking process. Then it became possible to make comparisons with ambulatory patterns while wearing the prosthesis. One such study by Sheffield, Gersten, and Mastellone[21] examined 12 muscles of the foot in 10 adult male subjects during walking. They employed both surface and needle

---

[19] J. V. Basmajian and A. Latif, "Integrated Actions and Functions of the Chief Flexors of the Elbow," *Journal of Bone and Joint Surgery*, 39–A, No. 5 (October 1957), 1106.

[20] Bent Ebskov and Charles Long, "A Method of Electromyographic Kinesiology of the Thumb," *Archives of Physical Medicine and Rehabilitation*, 48, No. 2 (February 1967), 78.

[21] Fred J. Sheffield, Jerome W. Gersten, and Aniello F. Mastellone, "Electromyographic Study of the Muscles of the Foot in Normal Walking," *American Journal of Physical Medicine*, 35, No. 4 (August 1956), 223.

EMG electrodes and placed three small microswitches in a specially adapted shoe. This latter procedure permitted the investigators to know precisely the time sequence of foot movement; such information as heel strike, metatarsal strike, toe strike, and so forth was transmitted to the recorder, and the *EMG* evaluation of gait pattern was then synchronized with the foot movements. The details of muscle function from such an analysis revealed the precise interplay of action of agonist and antagonist in human walking.

In summary, although the concept of electromyography is not new, the availability of more versatile and flexible equipment has placed this type of research within the investigatory capabilities of more laboratories than ever before. No longer is it necessary to build homemade equipment or fashion electronic devices to cope with these problems, nor is it essential that one know of all the circuitry that enters into their construction. In the same manner that one carefully chooses a high fidelity audio system, the investigator must know enough to make the proper choices and then study the literature to thoroughly understand the specifications and capabilities called for by his research design. Consultation with manufacturers representatives, electronic engineers, and examination of basic references[22] will also assist in successfully conducting electromyographic research.

CINEMATOGRAPHIC EQUIPMENT AND USE

The art of photographing human movement known as cinematography is widely employed in kinesiology as a means of recording the events associated with muscular action. In the larger context, it provides a pictorial record of events that occur so rapidly that careful analysis is impossible by observation alone. The human eye is a notoriously poor recorder; accounts of the same action by several observers frequently result in discrepancies. However, with the use of special photographic equipment, a record can be obtained of the movement that can be used later for detailed analysis. Properly done, motion pictures provide data that will yield to lengthy analysis; in fact, they may be so extensive that a major difficulty is to delimit the problem to manageable proportions. The filming of the action is probably the least time consuming part of cinematography; more time will be required to handle the host of details surrounding such things as selection of equipment, calibration of camera, setting up the proper experimental protocol, and analyzing the data.

Equipment Requirements

The actual selection of a problem usually rests with the interests of the experimenter. Judging by past research, one would strongly suspect that the analysis of sports skills has depended upon the type of sport engaged in by

[22] E. E. Suckling, *Bioelectricity* (New York: McGraw-Hill Book Company, 1961).

the researcher himself, which would seem logical considering his insight into the activity; in addition to greater motivation, there is the added knowledge gained by participation. This is certainly no prerequisite, and the study of sports skills is by no means the only use of cinematography, although it does form the bulk of published research in physical education. In reality, almost anything that needs to be timed may be a subject for these techniques if the proper type of camera is used and especially if it is not feasible to employ other timing devices. For example, the timing of running events, arm or leg movement, and such things as reaction time will be more successfully determined by the use of standard timing clocks plus appropriate microswitches that can be operated mechanically. These devices have the added feature of simplicity of testing, ease of recording, and reduced cost.

A difficulty of cinematographic research is the expense of providing the equipment, including the purchase and development of film; if the camera is operating at high speed, film will be moved at a rather rapid rate. Consider the footage required in a simple speed of movement task if a rather large number of subjects are to be given several trials; then calculate the amount of time that will be required to determine the factor of speed once the film has been developed. It will be found that both time and cost mount quickly. However, as problems become more complex, more sophisticated equipment must be employed. For example, in a study of limb movement by Henry,[23] electric chronoscopes were required to measure the time during successive 15-degree intervals over a horizontal arc of approximately 120 degrees. It would seem that if considerable additional data were needed, it would probably be necessary to photograph the movement at high film speed.

Aside from the factor of timing is the matter of providing information about other parameters of interest to the researcher. Obviously, photography itself is just a means to an end; the resultant film is meaningless until the appropriate analysis has been completed. Inasmuch as the basic element in any sequence is time (i.e., the number of elapsed frames at known speed of film), other factors may be calculated, such as velocity, acceleration, force, distance, power, and so on, according to known mechanical principles.[24] In the case of body or implement motion, knowledge of mass may also be essential, but ordinarily this information can be made quickly available and usually remains constant throughout any single sequence. These principles were employed in an early study to determine mechanical expenditure of energy during running.[25]

---

[23] Franklin M. Henry and Donald E. Rogers, "Increased Response Latency for Complicated Movements and a 'Memory Drum' Theory of Neuromotor Reaction," *Research Quarterly*, 31, No. 3 (October 1960), 448.

[24] John W. Bunn, *Scientific Principles of Coaching* (Englewood Cliffs, N.J.: Prentice-Hall, Inc., 1960).

[25] W. O. Fenn, "Mechanical Energy Expenditure in Sprint Running as Measured by Moving Pictures," *American Journal of Physiology*, 90, No. 2 (October 1929), 343.

Forming the central core of investigations in this field is the descriptive analysis of skilled movements. It is considered essential by many kinesiologists that a rather complete "library" of documented research studies describing in detail the pattern of sports skills be developed. Inasmuch as physical education deals with movement, the argument is brought forth that fully effective teaching is hampered until as much is known about as wide a variety of skills as possible. Many of the textbooks in kinesiology are incomplete because of a lack of technical data, and so often descriptions of movements are empirical, fragmentary, and devoid of theoretical insight. Moreover, comparative data are lacking on the differences between skilled and unskilled performers, and the decision on what is proper "form" is often made on inconclusive evidence.

These and other matters fall within the purview of the cinematographer and make continued emphasis on such research techniques essential. In carrying out the basic responsibilities, several types of problems will be encountered and must be solved before a study may be undertaken. Some of these will be discussed.

Selection of Equipment

Ample consideration should be given to the purchase of proper cinematographic equipment, including cameras and accessories, stroboscopic equipment, floodlights, various tripods, and so on. The expenditure of money for high quality material will pay important dividends in the quality of the research produced and will also tend to serve for a long time without difficulty or loss of precision. Also, inferior quality may cause a premature lack of accuracy and render the equipment useless for research at an early date.

At the same time, thought should be given to the manner in which film is to be processed with consideration of the possibility of providing a dark room and equipment for developing film. Such facilities give greater flexibility to the investigator, who may wish to experiment with different procedures of developing his film as well as to work out problems associated with various camera settings and lighting techniques. Nothing is more exasperating than waiting several days for commercial processing to be completed only to find that the film is either too light or too dark for use.

The usual requirements for cinematographic research in the past have been to employ two cameras, one placed in front of the subject and one facing his side. Therefore, a two-dimensional view may be obtained, and analysis of movement in two planes can be accomplished. Although this will be discussed more fully subsequently, a growing need is evident to consider three-dimensional photography;[26] thus, three cameras will be needed, the third to be placed directly overhead. In so doing, the three cardinal planes can be viewed simultaneously and all portions of the movement accounted for.

Two considerations for human movement studies through cinematography involve film size and shutter speed; to satisfy these needs, the choice may be 16 mm film with the camera capable of operating at 64 to 128 frames per sec. Once again, this will be dictated by the design of the experiment, but a deviation from this standard should be thought out carefully. For example, film readers are designed primarily for this film size, and if the camera is actually operating at, say, 64 frames per sec, the time per frame is of the order of .0156 sec, usually sufficient to detect the significant aspects of movement. Although generally spring driven, it is possible to expand operations to electronically driven cameras capable of moving film at a rate of thousands of frames per sec.[27]

The additional equipment needed will include tripods and floodlights, especially if filming indoors, and other accessories dictated by the requirements of the research. These items, as well as the type and quantity of film, can be obtained at the usual photographic stores or perhaps through an outlet on campus, such as the audio-visual department. Perhaps even more important to the novice is the possibility that technical help may be obtained from these sources in the form of advice on a host of operational problems that can arise during the study. Arrangements may also be made to rent or borrow cameras if they are not already available.

Calibration of Cameras

Aside from the problems associated with obtaining the proper equipment are those involved with understanding and standardizing their operation. Most notably, the cameras must be calibrated so that their speed is known precisely; even though they may be advertized at 64 frames per sec, this does not guarantee that they are actually going at exactly that rate. The investigator is solely responsible for checking camera speed at the time of filming so that he can make the correct conversions of his data.

The usual spring-driven camera may be calibrated in one of two ways. The first is least expensive and consists of photographing an object (usually a ball) falling from a known height. Thus, the time t may be calculated according to the formula:

$$s = \tfrac{1}{2}gt^2$$

---

[26] James [*sic.* Jerome] Noss, "Control of Photographic Perspective in Motion Analysis," *Journal of Health, Physical Education and Recreation*, 38, No. 7 (September 1967), 81.

[27] Red Lake Laboratories, Santa Clara, California 95051.

where s is the distance, and g is the constant acceleration of gravity (32.2 feet/sec^2). The amount of film elapsing during the time of fall can be converted to frames per sec. One of the difficulties in this technique is in making the correct decision as to ball contact, which can occur between frames; therefore, it may be necessary to repeat the procedure several times and take an average value.

The second method consists of photographing the sweep hand of a clock (e.g., a hundredth second timer) and then counting the number of frames elapsing between seconds. This may be repeated for several seconds merely by permitting the camera to run, and it is much more accurate than the ball-drop technique. It may also permit the calculation of lag at the beginning of the film as the camera begins its operation and may help decide upon differences in film movement at varying spring tensions. An interesting method is described by Blievernicht[28] of synchronizing various film views in triaxial cinematography by using a timing device visible to all cameras.

Experimental Protocol

The experimental methodology is dependent upon the nature of the research design, but certain problems should be anticipated. Decisions to film outdoors may depend upon the indoor space available, say, for a large scale activity common to certain sports skills, and thus the environmental conditions of lightness-darkness are subject to wide variation. Placement of cameras must be made carefully so as to obtain optimum light. Indoors, the use of flood lights or a "sun gun" must be studied with the ultimate aim to reduce shadows to a minimum. It is sometimes difficult to differentiate the precise outline of a subject if he seems to blend into the background, which becomes even more difficult when the subject is moving. Once again, these problems can be alleviated by careful study and practice before the actual filming begins and by seeking professional advice if difficulty persists.

The background of the subject is quite important, as may be surmised, since much of the evaluation depends upon a clearly defined image. When photographing outdoors, there is less opportunity to choose the background than indoors; but, even so, good and poor outdoor backgrounds may be found. Essentially, one is desirous of obtaining a proper contrast so that the subject stands out well. If he blends into trees, buildings, or the like it may make analysis very difficult. This may even be a problem of proper camera setting—permitting too much light in the picture—or it may be the type of overcast day that gives poor contrast. These situations can be standardized indoors much more effectively, but the difficulty then comes in some

---

[28] David L. Blievernicht, "A Multidimensional Timing Device for Cinematography," *Research Quarterly*, 38, No. 1 (March 1967), 146.

restrictions of the activities to be filmed, as space is much more restrictive indoors in ordinary research laboratories.

One of the most important considerations for later analysis is to place some sort of grid at the average subject position from the cameras to serve as a frame of reference for measurement of distance. A common standard for the grid is 1 foot—that is, a marker sectioned in 1-foot segments (along with various subdivisions as needed) is placed in the photographic field so that the investigator may be able to calculate a distance multiplier by dividing the projected distance by the known distance. It should be pointed out that if the subject is moving away from this standard, it will not be accurate; this is especially true when several cameras are employed.

The ultimate decision to use more than one camera in cinematographic research is the result of a desire to secure a more complete analysis of the activity in question if possible. Therefore, if the motion takes place in planes other than that which is perpendicular to one camera, then another will be required. In this manner, the simultaneous recording of movement in two planes may be obtained, each of the two cameras situated perpendicularly to a different plane of the body. In actual practice, these two cameras are usually placed so that one photographs the side view and the other the front view. The decision as to whether or not this is sufficient will depend upon whether or not the action actually takes place in just two planes; if the answer is negative, then it may be essential to employ a third camera (placed overhead in this instance). This will permit the description of rotary movements that are so prevalent in human mechanics.

Inasmuch as the analysis of the data will involve the measurement of body angles, Noss[29] makes a special plea for triaxial photography to correct the distortion that is produced in any angle when the angle of incidence is varied. In fact, any angle may be seen to vary in a photograph from 0° to 180°, depending upon the angle of incidence. For this reason, triaxial analysis is especially valuable where the mean angle obtained from the three cameras will equal the true value of the subject angle. By way of illustration, suppose in Figure 28 that the subject angle is actually 45° but is so arranged in the photographic field that the cameras record angles of 27°, 36°, and 72°, none of which is correct. The average of the three (45°), however, is the true angle, and is obtained only by triaxial perspective.

An additional problem created by subject movement in the photographic field is parallax (see Figure 29). With the camera placed at *F*, camera-to-subject is a distance *b*; if the subject moves to *X* or *Z*, the distance becomes *a* or *c*, respectively. Because of the greater distance, the calibration of the subject in position *Y* is no longer applicable at the other positions at *x* and *z*. This situation may be relieved in part by lengthening the

---

[29] Noss, *op. cit.*

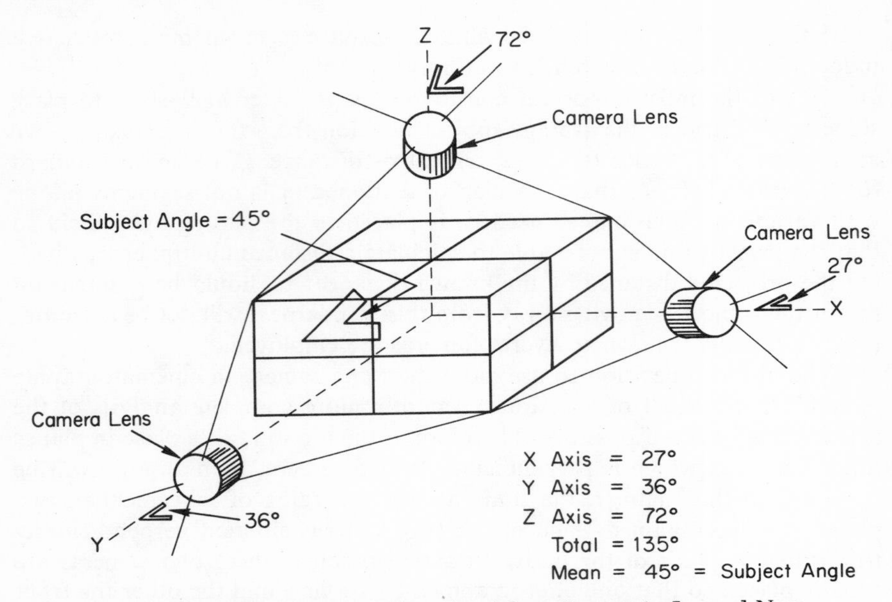

Figure 28. Tri-Axial Analysis (Reprinted from James [*sic.* Jerome] Noss, "Control of Photographic Perspective in Motion Analysis," *Journal of Health, Physical Education and Recreation*, 38, No. 7 (September, 1967, 81.) Used by permission of the author and AAHPER.

subject-to-camera distance, but the danger of this practice may be in sacrificing detail. The practice of "panning," employed in the usual motion pictures, would alter the photographic field entirely.

In order to synchronize the action, it is necessary to do something that will be observed simultaneously by all cameras. A usual practice has been to fire a flash bulb at the beginning of each sequence so that later analysis may be coordinated properly.

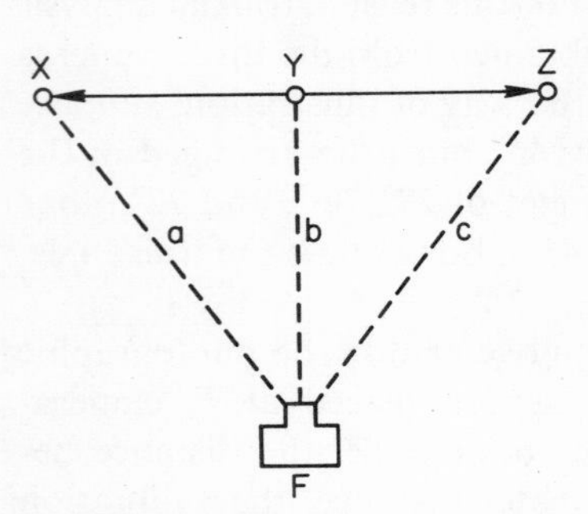

Figure 29. Parallax

Preparation of the subject should also receive careful attention. If the analysis is to include changes of limb position, changes of body angles, and so on, a clear differentiation of specific body parts in the film must be made. One way of doing so is to place contrasting markings (perhaps in the form of black tape) on selected bony prominences. In order to be effective, clothing should not obscure the limbs; placing marks over loosely fitting clothing is certain to result in errors of measurement.

The question of sample size in cinematographic research is pertinent, as is true with other types of studies. Ordinarily, the decision will be based upon feasibility, since the investigator must balance such factors as time and cost with sampling reliability. Inasmuch as the analysis of data may be quite time consuming and the production costs of filming rather high, the tendency is to employ very few subjects. In fact, many investigators have used expert performers of the skill, electing to film several sequences of the same act rather than photograph several different subjects whose ability may not be reflective of "optimum" performance. The highly skilled athlete is characterized by low intertrial variability, so the chances are enhanced that the actions will be more representative, at least for him. The question of studying individual differences through cinematography has not been resolved adequately, but it has permitted the basic analysis of skills with some comparisons between the highly skilled and poorly skilled performers.

Analysis of Data

Once the photographing has been done and the film developed, the analysis of data may proceed according to the investigator's plan. There may be two important contributions to be made in the analysis: the overall description of the skill and the detailed presentation of the technical patterns of motion. In either event, a decision must be made as to which frames of film are to be selected for measurement. To make this determination, the film will be viewed through a projector in order to get an impression of the usable sequences and to make a choice for additional analysis.

The next step is to employ a film reader (e.g., Recordak Model 310 A),[30] overlay standard graph paper, and plot, frame by frame, the change in the selected body parts. The decision as to exactly which frames need be examined will depend upon how rapidly movement is occurring. Obviously, human motion tends to flow from one body part to another, so sequential analysis is very important; in fact, such may be an extremely vital part of the description. Further questions of velocities, accelerations, angular changes, and so forth will be answered for each body part selected provided that the factors of time and distance are known. As indicated earlier, these problems should be anticipated and solved in the preparatory experimental phases. It also serves to emphasize the need for a fixed standard of measurement in the photographic field, for this permits the accurate alignment of the film in the film reader from one frame to the next.

Motion analysis utilizing these methods is laborious and time consuming; at first glance the problems may seem insurmountable to the graduate student.

---

[30] Eastman Kodak Company, Rochester, New York.

However, it should be pointed out that, as is true with most research, a reasonable compromise may be reached regarding the amount of time required. Thus, the problem may be delimited to such an extent that it becomes entirely feasible at the master's degree level. In fact, relief is in sight if funds can be obtained to purchase automatic read-out equipment that can feed data into a paper tape printer or card punch for computer analysis.[31] Although this will not make careful photography obsolete, it will permit more rapid analysis of a wider variety of skills and should eventually provide a means for the study of individual differences on a larger scale.

CINEMATOGRAPHIC STUDIES

A number of cinematographic studies are available in the related literature. Unfortunately, not enough of them have been published in the research journals so that, if a review of literature is undertaken, the reader should exhaust sources of unpublished studies. For example, microcard publications and the various volumes of *Completed Research in Health, Physical Education and Recreation*[32] contain references to a number of theses and dissertations that will prove of interest. The ones selected here for inclusion are readily available and can be considered somewhat representative of research in this area; rather than try to exhaust the literature, these references serve to illustrate the range of investigations undertaken and they in turn may serve as guides for the future.

Walking. Some of the early work in cinematography was directed to the detailed study of walking in an attempt to understand the mechanical principles and to assess the muscular pattern involved in human locomotion. In 1939, Elftman[33] utilized an apparatus that measured the point of application of foot pressure but also assessed the magnitude of force in several components. In addition, the subject was photographed at the rate of 92 exposures per sec as he walked behind a rectangular grid. The positions of the hip, knee, and ankle were plotted from successive frames, and values were calculated at intervals of 0.02 sec. In this manner, it was possible to determine such things as reversed effective force (defined as ma, where m = mass and a = acceleration), torque, and the rate at which energy is transferred in the various components of the system. Apparently, the transfer of energy in the leg occurs when it is in the middle of its swing and again while the foot is on the ground.

---

[31] Vanguard Instrument Corporation, Melville, L.I., N.Y. 11746.

[32] See Chapter 3.

[33] Herbert Elftman, "Forces and Energy Changes in the Leg During Walking," *American Journal of Physiology*, 125, No. 2 (February 1939), 339.

The more recent impetus for the study of walking resulted from the treatment of orthopedic disabilities. For example, the rehabilitation of lower extremity amputees was speeded by the care, precision, and construction of prosthetic devices, but, in order to evaluate gait patterns, normal ambulation had to be defined. Such studies as that of Eberhart and Inman[34] reflect the sophistication in design of such experiments. Of interest here was obtaining triaxial views while employing only two cameras. This feat was accomplished by having the subject move across a glass walkway, beneath which, and inclined at an angle of 45°, was a mirror. Thus, one camera photographing the side view would also obtain the bottom view, while a second camera was placed at the end of the walkway to obtain the front view. In this case, the cameras were operated synchronously, using 35 mm film exposed at a rate of 48 frames per sec.

Another technique employed by the same investigators was called "interrupted lights," in which small ophthalmic electric bulbs (illuminated by a 3-volt battery carried by the subject) were attached at certain joint centers, and the subject walked in a darkened room in front of the open lens of a camera. This in turn was synchronously interrupted 30 times per sec. Thus, a sequence of selected points was traced on the same negative, and accurate determinations of velocity and acceleration were obtained. The reader will find descriptions of pin attachment to bone, high speed cinematography (400–700 frames per sec), X ray moving pictures, electromyographic, and force plate studies helpful in designing kinesiologic research.

Running. Although man's interest in running may be traced to earliest times, the traditional concern seems to have been with techniques to produce greater speed rather than understanding propulsion per se. With the latter aim in mind, Deshon and Nelson[35] studied the relationships between running velocity and factors associated with leg positions and stride length. Employing a 16 mm Bolex camera operating at 64 frames per sec (with 35 mm lens setting between f—4.0 and f—5.6 using Kodachrome Type II film), 19 subjects were filmed for precisely 100 frames (approximately 15 yards) after accelerating to maximum speed. Intercorrelations were computed for velocity, length of one full running cycle, the angle of leg at the touchdown, and the height of the leg lift. The correlations ranged from .31 to .71. In general, reliabilities were high, showing that runners maintained rather consistent styles from one cycle to the next.

---

[34] Howard D. Eberhart and Verne T. Inman, "An Evaluation of Experimental Procedures Used in a Fundamental Study of Human Locomotion," *Annals of the New York Academy of Sciences*, 51, Art. 7 (January 1951), 1123.

[35] Deane E. Deshon and Richard C. Nelson, "A Cinematographical Analysis of Sprint Running," *Research Quarterly*, 35, No. 4 (December 1964), 451.

Jumping. To gain insight into human jumping performance, Eckert[36] studied the standing broad jump of subjects 8, 10, and 12 years of age. They were photographed with a camera set at 64 frames per sec with data included of the distance jumped and the isometric strength of the hip, knee, and ankle extensor muscles. From a cinematographical analysis of the film, force (F) was calculated according to the formula:

$$F = \frac{m(v_1 - v_0)}{\Delta t_1}$$

where m is mass, v_0 the velocity at deepest knee flexion, v_1 the velocity of projection, and Δ_t, the elapsed time between deepest knee flexion and take-off. In general, the correlations between propulsive force, isometric strength, and distance jumped were quite low. However, the relationship was improved somewhat when the isometric strength of the hip extensors was correlated with the angular velocity of the hip joint.

Vaulting. Some interest has been shown in studying pole vaulting from a cinematographical point of view. Fletcher, Lewis, and Wilkie[37] obtained records on five skilled pole vaulters by photographing with a camera operating at 64 frames per sec at a distance of 100 feet. Calibration was established by placing bright metal stakes at 2-foot intervals from the uprights—the uprights themselves were marked off in feet. In order to establish trajectory, the center of gravity was estimated with the use of a manikin placed in the various body positions encountered. When plotted, the trajectory formed a smooth line, suggesting that the procedure employed was acceptable. The subjects approached the vault at velocities of 21–31 feet/sec, and were moving at a rate of 5–10 feet/sec at the top of their flight. The authors indicated that the vaulter stores kinetic energy during the approach and uses his pole to alter his direction and convert kinetic energy into potential energy. Apparently, a high initial speed is associated with a net loss of energy during the vault so that the better performers actually take-off at moderate speed and perform more work while riding the pole.

Prompted by the advent of the more flexible Fiberglas pole, Hay[38] studied various factors related to the magnitude and direction of force at take-off with particular emphasis on the bend of the pole. The subject was

[36] Helen M. Eckert, "Linear Relationships of Isometric Strength to Propulsive Force, Angular Velocity, and Angular Acceleration in the Standing Broad Jump," *Research Quarterly*, 35, No. 3 (October 1964), 298.

[37] J. G. Fletcher, H. E. Lewis, and D. R. Wilkie, "Human Power Output: The Mechanics of Pole Vaulting," *Ergonomics*, 3, No. 1 (January 1960), 30.

[38] James G. Hay, "Pole Vaulting: A Mechanical Analysis of Factors Influencing Pole-Bend," *Research Quarterly*, 38, No. 1 (March 1967), 34.

photographed from the side at 128 frames per sec and from the front at 24 frames per sec. The usual timer and distance markers were placed in the field of vision for calibration purposes; the subject performed 6 trials at each of 5 heights. Such variables as horizontal and vertical velocity, angle of take-off, hand spread, distance from top hand to take-off foot at the instant of leaving the ground, and pole-bend were intercorrelated and found to vary between .03 and .68. It was felt that horizontal velocity was principally responsible for pole-bend.

Swimming. Illustrative of the cinematographical studies in swimming is the investigation of the dolphin stroke by deVries,[39] who photographed two subjects through an observation window with a camera operating at 128 frames per sec. Comparisons between subjects were made for various distance, time, and velocity components of the stroke cycle.

MECHANICAL ANALYSIS OF MOVEMENT

As indicated, an important aim in kinesiological research is to obtain as full an understanding of movement capabilities as possible, and much of this information is gained through analysis by cinematography and by electromyography. Both techniques yield insight into the mechanical aspects of movement in such a manner that motion may be analyzed by known physical laws. However, such techniques, useful as they may be, are required only if certain special circumstances prevail. A considerable number of studies are available in the literature that required neither method but employed other means to study the mechanical principles of muscular action. For example, the provocative work of A. V. Hill,[40] performed largely on frog muscle, gave a very important impetus to physiologists and others interested in the dynamics of muscle contraction. His finding that the shape of the force-velocity curve was governed by the manner of energy release during shortening was verified by thermal measurements. In order to explain the slow rise in tension of muscle, he postulated a two-component system, one consisting of active contractile structures and the other of series elastic elements. Although a number of studies have been conducted in this area, they have quite largely employed excised animal muscle; however, they are in general agreement that the relation between force and velocity is curvilinear.

---

[39] Herbert A. deVries, "A Cinematographical Analysis of the Dolphin Swimming Stroke," *Research Quarterly*, 30, No. 4 (December 1959), 413.

[40] A. V. Hill, "The Heat of Shortening and the Dynamic Constants of Muscle," *Proceedings of the Royal Society of London*, Series B, 126, No. B 843 (October 1938), 136.

Extending the research to human intact performance is the logical step in progression, one of the first being that of Dern, Levene, and Blair,[41] who examined the relationship of force and velocity of elbow flexion. They developed an apparatus called an isotonic lever, which was designed to give constant force or torque to oppose the arm movement. In such a manner, a variety of tensions could be produced and voluntary maximal contraction studied. The curves contained three phases: an increasing initial segment, a period of constant torque, and a final period of decreasing tension. Apparently, the results were independent of sex, muscular strength, and training of the subject.

In a comprehensive study of the force and velocity of human elbow flexor muscles, Wilkie[42] found that the curve could be represented by Hill's equation:

$$(P + a)(v + b) = (P_0 + a)b$$

where P represents force of contraction, v the velocity of shortening, P_0 the isometric tension, with a and b constants. Subsequently, Hubbard[43] studied the difference in control of slow (complex) and fast (ballistic) movements to determine if there were a critical velocity separating them or if overlapping occurred. Acceleration and velocity of finger, wrist, and forearm were imparted to a kymograph, and action potentials were recorded electromyographically. In describing reciprocal ballistic motion, it was of interest to note the differentiation into phases of acceleration, momentum, and deceleration, as well as the discussion of the activity of agonists and antagonists.

Among the investigations of various sports skills, several have provided theoretical insight into the mechanical aspects of the activity. In 1951, Henry and Trafton[44] studied the exponential nature of the time-velocity curve of sprint running, as well as individual differences in the curve constants, according to the integral form of the equation of motion:

$$y = v\left(t + \frac{1}{k}e^{-kt} - \frac{1}{k}\right)$$

This says that the distance (y) obtained by the runner at any time (t) as he approaches a maximum velocity (v) is controlled by the velocity constant

---

[41] R. J. Dern, Jack M. Levene, and H. A. Blair, "Forces Exerted at Different Velocities in Human Arm Movements," *American Journal of Physiology*, 151, No. 2 (December 1947), 415.

[42] D. R. Wilkie, "The Relation Between Force and Velocity in Human Muscle," *Journal of Physiology*, 110, No. 3-4 (December 1949), 249.

[43] A. W. Hubbard, "The Upper Limits of Slow Movements and the Lower Limits of Ballistic Movements," microcard Doctoral Dissertation, University of Illinois, 1950.

[44] Franklin M. Henry and Irving R. Trafton, "The Velocity Curve of Sprint Running," *Research Quarterly*, 22, No. 4 (December 1951), 409.

(k) according to the exponential law (e is the Naperian log base). The runner ($N = 25$) broke an electric circuit by contacting a series of 10 light bamboo sticks spaced throughout a 50-yard course, set up in such a manner that they all recorded sequentially on the single pen of a chronograph. Confirmation of the distance covered by the average runner was obtained by means of the formula; further, reliable individual differences were found in the individual curve constants for velocity (v) and for the rate constant (k), although these two factors were found to be independent of each other. The reader will find an analysis of the force-time factors involved in the sprint start to be of concern to this discussion as well.[45]

In order to study water resistance and propulsion in crawl stroke swimming, Alley[46] constructed an apparatus that controlled velocity and permitted the measurement of drag, towing force, and the force required over and above the water resistance at a given velocity (called surplus-propulsive force), as well as the calculation of other variables. Essentially, this consisted of a motorized system that was connected to the swimmer and that at the same time kymographically recorded the forces exerted during a variety of kicking and stroking experiments. Among the findings was the note that the bow wave was important in limiting speed of swimming; also, when the swimmer was resisted by the apparatus (causing zero velocity), the effective-propulsive force of the whole stroke was approximately the same as for the arm stroke alone.

The mechanical principles were brought to bear by Heusner[47] in a study of the racing dive to determine optimum angles of take-off. He developed a mathematical equation to express such factors as diving time, glide, and the time to swim one length (25 yards); validation was by photographically recording the start and one length swim of 17 trained swimmers. The correlation between computed time and measured time was .975; the optimum angle of take-off was 13 degrees. Estimates were also made of the ability to swim if certain physical characteristics of body size were altered and when changes were made in some of the experimental variables. The reader will find the derivation of the formula helpful in understanding the mathematical concept as applied to this problem.

The study of human movement, then, can be seen to take on several important characteristics with a variety of procedures available to obtain reliable data so that they may be reduced to meaningful terms that can be expressed quantitatively. In the present instance, a range of studies that has

---

[45] Franklin M. Henry, "Force-Time Characteristics of the Spring Start," *Research Quarterly*, 23, No. 3 (October 1952), 301.

[46] Louis E. Alley, "An Analysis of Water Resistance and Propulsion in Swimming the Crawl Stroke," *Research Quarterly*, 23, No. 3 (October 1952), 253.

[47] William W. Heusner, "Theoretical Specifications for the Racing Dive: Optimum Angle of Take-Off," *Research Quarterly*, 30, No. 1 (March 1959), 25.

been discussed illustrates some of the ways in which a mechanical analysis may be pursued. Whether the intent is to examine rather discrete limb movements or whole body activities is irrelevant, provided that the problem is adequately designed and the proper procedures have been followed. The logical result, eventually, will be to amass sufficient information that completes descriptions of muscular activity; as seen from the kinesiological point of view, this is still a long way from fruition.

CENTER OF GRAVITY

One of the techniques frequently of concern to the researcher in kinesiology is the determination of center of gravity. As applied to problems of motion, plotting the flight of the center of gravity through space is often helpful in order that the proper arrangement of body parts can be made; although the center of gravity will follow a predetermined path—depending upon such factors as velocity and angle of take-off—the body may be performing certain coordinative movements. Since this is likely to be the central focus of the investigation, a complete analysis may require serial determinations of the path of the center of gravity.

Such matters as these would logically be dealt with in undergraduate courses in kinesiology, so discussion here will be limited. The treatment provided in Cooper and Glassow[48] will prove helpful to the investigator in this respect. One of the primary considerations to keep in mind is the transient nature of the center of gravity in other than stationary objects; since it is defined as the center of a mass, its position relative to body segments will vary as an individual moves. However, in a fixed part, the center of gravity will remain quite stationary, and in fact it may be located separately in various portions of the limbs and trunk.[49] One might even be quite successful in determining the exact center of the mass of the body in the standing position in the sagittal and frontal planes, but unless the experimental subject remains in this position, it will be of little value. Therefore, marking the subject with a piece of tape on some anatomical site and then plotting the path of this mark during the movement would not yield data of the true path of the center of gravity. It can readily be shown that the center of gravity of flexed segments of the body (e.g., knee flexion or trunk flexion) will even fall

---

[48] John M. Cooper and Ruth B. Glassow, *Kinesiology*, (2nd ed.) (St. Louis: The C. V. Mosby Company, 1968), Ch. 12.

[49] Wilfred Taylor Dempster, "Space Requirements of the Seated Operator," *WADC Technical Report, 55–159*, Wright-Patterson Air Force Base, Ohio, Wright Air Development Center (July 1955).

outside the body,[50] making it necessary to calculate this point in each new position. In practice, this may require that the investigator select certain frames of a cinematographical film and duplicate the positions in the laboratory.[51] For a detailed account of center of gravity determination, the student is directed to the work of Fenn.[52]

FLEXIBILITY AND JOINT MOTION

Flexibility has long been of concern to kinesiologists and anatomists in the study of joint and muscle capabilities, as well as to the teacher and coach who could envision advantages of increased flexibility to the performance of certain sports skills. Hurdlers and gymnasts, for example, require more joint range of motion in their activities than might be needed in other kinds of skills. The importance of flexibility as a factor in general performance is not clearly understood, although its inclusion in certain fitness test batteries is well-known. A discussion of a number of flexibility tests may be found in Clarke.[53]

With the advent of the electrogoniometer, as developed by Karpovich,[54] the position of joints can be monitored continuously during activity, and the patterns of motion can be studied in considerable detail. As described, the electrogoniometer consists of a small potentiometer of 0–10,000 ohms resistance placed directly over the center of rotation of the joint; the two arms of the potentiometer are positioned along the shafts of the articulating bones. Descriptions of the methods of calibration and techniques of testing when connected electronically to a recorder are helpful in gaining insight into this type of research. With the invention of the flexometer, too, Leighton[55] has provided a device for measuring the range of motion of most joints of the body.

---

[50] Marian Williams and Herbert R. Lissner, *Biomechanics of Human Motion* (Philadelphia: W. B. Saunders Company, 1962), pp. 46–56.

[51] William H. Groves, "Mechanical Analysis of Diving," *Research Quarterly*, 21, No. 2 (May 1950), 132.

[52] Wallace O. Fenn, "Work Against Gravity and Work Due to Velocity Changes in Running: Movements of the Center of Gravity Within the Body and Foot Pressure on the Ground," *American Journal of Physiology*, 93, No. 2 (June 1930), 433.

[53] H. Harrison Clarke, *Application of Measurement to Health and Physical Education* (4th ed.) (Englewood Cliffs, N.J.: Prentice-Hall, Inc., 1967), pp. 137–41.

[54] Peter V. Karpovich, Everett L. Herden, and Maxim M. Asa, "Electrogoniometric Study of Joints," *United States Armed Forces Medical Journal*, 11, No. 4 (April 1960), 424.

[55] Jack R. Leighton, "Flexibility Characteristics of Four Specialized Skill Groups of College Athletes," *Archives of Physical Medicine and Rehabilitation*, 38, No. 1 (January 1957), 24.

SUGGESTED PROBLEMS

The approach to problems of a kinesiological nature reflect a need for understanding equipment and procedures for obtaining meaningful data. Among the questions asked are the following:

1. What are the basic patterns for skilled movement in the currently employed physical activities, including, but not limited to, sports skills?
2. What is the difference between the highly skilled and the moderately skilled or the poorly skilled performer?
3. Are there anatomical differences between individuals that suggest functional advantages? Can high speed of limb movement, for example, reflect more favorable muscle-tendon-joint arrangements than those exhibiting slow speed?
4. What is the relationship between energy expended as calculated mechanically and that actually obtained by direct measurement?
5. Can the problems be solved for the ready use of cinematographical techniques so that adequate sampling procedures can be employed?

SUMMARY

Research in kinesiology is essentially designed to study the characteristics of human movement, both by means of a functional and a mechanical analysis of behavior patterns. Although a clear line of differentiation cannot be drawn between what may be technically physiology of exercise and what is considered kinesiology, the aim of the kinesiologist is seen to rely more on the appropriate physical laws of motion than on the underlying physiology to describe activity. Therefore, before research can be undertaken in this field, the individual must acquire the appropriate theoretical undergraduate preparation upon which will be superimposed graduate work in this area.

Electromyography is a major technical advancement that has permitted the detailed evaluation of the electrical activity associated with muscular contraction, thus providing information concerning the precise interplay of various skeletal muscles involved in specific movements. Electromyographic methods must be understood before application may be made to research. Associated problems seem to be centered around the choice and application of electrodes and the recording and measurement of signals detected during testing. Knowledge of the literature would involve not necessarily that of electromyography per se, but of specific research topics; the decision to solve them by *EMG* would be made only if this provided an adequate means to such an end. In the past, typical research has involved studies of muscle function, the relation of *EMG* to tension, and the examination of specific patterns of movement.

Cinematography is another major tool of the kinesiologist, as it provides a means of detecting movement that is not possible under ordinary visual circumstances. An activity filmed by high-speed camera can be analyzed frame by frame if necessary; the data can be employed to describe such factors of motion as velocity, acceleration, force, distance, and power. Analysis may be done for limbs and trunk separately or may be used to describe whole body activity; the result would be a complete analysis of movement. The investigator must deal with such problems as selection and calibration of equipment and the proper design and preparation of the experimental environment, all with the objective in mind of providing data that may be analyzed with the use of a film reader. Previous studies have dealt with topics ranging from walking and running to a host of activity skills.

The techniques of kinesiology research may take other forms than these, for the mechanical analysis of movement may be made simply by employing timers or other devices that serve to record muscle action or body activity. The decision will always be based upon the exigencies of experimental design rather than upon instrumentation. In other words, the researcher must use the most appropriate tools to solve the problem he has selected.

SELECTED REFERENCES

Basmajian, J. V., *Muscles Alive*. Baltimore: The Williams & Wilkins Co., 1962.

Bunn, John W., *Scientific Principles of Coaching*. Englewood Cliffs, N.J.: Prentice-Hall, Inc., 1960.

Clarke, H. Harrison, *Application of Measurement to Health and Physical Education* (4th ed.), Englewood Cliffs, N.J.: Prentice-Hall, Inc., 1967.

Cooper, John M., and Ruth B. Glassow, *Kinesiology* (2nd ed.), St. Louis: The C. V. Mosby Company, 1968.

Cureton, Thomas K., "Elementary Principles and Techniques of Cinematographic Analysis as Aids in Athletic Research," *Research Quarterly*, 10, No. 2 (May 1939), 3.

Davis, John F., "Manual of Surface Electromyography," *WADA Technical Report, 59–184*, Wright-Patterson Air Force Base, Ohio, Wright Air Development Center (December 1959).

Dewhurst, D. J., *Physical Instrumentation in Medicine and Biology*. New York: Pergamon Press, 1966.

Eberhart, Howard D., and Verne T. Inman, "An Evaluation of Experimental Procedures Used in a Fundamental Study of Human Locomotion," *Annals of the New York Academy of Sciences*, 51, Art. 7 (January 1951), 1123.

Hill, D. W., *Principles of Electronics in Medical Research*. London: Butterworth & Co. (Publishers), Ltd., 1965.

O'Connell, A. L., and E. B. Gardner, "The Use of Electromyography in Kinesiological Research," *Research Quarterly*, 34, No. 2 (May 1963), 166.

Rasch, Philip J., and Roger K. Burke, *Kinesiology and Applied Anatomy*. Philadelphia: Lea and Febiger, 1963.

Suckling, E. E., *Bioelectricity*. New York: McGraw-Hill Book Company, 1961.

Williams, Marian, and Herbert R. Lissner, *Biomechanics of Human Motion*. Philadelphia: W. B. Saunders Company, 1962.

CHAPTER 17

Growth and Development

HISTORICAL PERSPECTIVE

Man's interest in body structure and growth has a long history among scientific endeavors. Long before the establishment of functional research, ancient artisans demonstrated that matters of body size were important in a very practical way. Egyptian and Greek sculptors showed concern in the manner in which they emphasized relative proportions of limb and trunk, and in the way they highlighted the musculature. Scholars of history have noted that athletic prowess was depicted in ancient artifacts and relics. The impression left was not only of archeological value but served as a reminder of the interest in human physique as well.

Much later, the study of man through the anthropological observations of early naturalists and comparative anatomists fostered development of fields of study where body size was of vital concern. Knowledge of man and animal species depended in large part upon relative bone sizes and configurations. Although more advanced techniques helped decide evolutionary dates, the transition from archeological remains to descriptions of function was made partly on the basis of relative sizes.

From a practical standpoint, one may also look to those artisans who became concerned with the sizing of clothes and who also became vitally interested in human dimensions. Without yielding to the temptation to comment upon styles, it has always been necessary to account for relative body proportions in the clothing industry; such concerns as the ratio of trunk length to arm length, trunk length to leg length, and so on, have had to be understood.

The period 1650–1750 marks the time that anthropometry began to be employed intermittently as an investigative tool in the emerging science of human biology. Defined rather narrowly as the systematized measurement of the human body, anthropometry became a matter for serious study and the result was a substantial number of investigations spanning several decades. At the same time, a concern for the developmental aspects of human growth emerged to the extent of expanding upon the structural changes with age to include aspects of maturity. Thus, the examination of pubescence and interrelated topics has blended the structural and functional aspects of growth and development.

Primary emphasis in the past has been placed upon those physiological changes that have accompanied the onset of puberty and, of course, on the accompanying practical decision concerning the chronological age at which this will occur for boys and girls. Thus, a social factor is introduced that is recognized to have educational implications for curriculum development. This is notably true in physical education where separation of the sexes occurs at certain ages and where decisions relative to type of activity are made for boys and girls.

What makes a knowledge of growth and development so important is the necessity to make intelligent decisions about human characteristics as one grows older. Education is still plagued with "chronological confusion"; most of the really important decisions are made on the basis of a child's chronological age without respect to his maturity. The age of entering school is usually set by birth date, the curriculum presented by grade, and so forth. Only recently have educational dictums permitted classroom teachers the flexibility of dealing with students on the basis of their abilities. Such innovations as team teaching and flexible scheduling are helping to solve the problem raised by rigidity of the graded system.

Physical education is recognizing these difficulties and attempting to deal with them, although the support for inventive scheduling and classification is far less widespread. The irony is that actual physical danger may exist when students varying widely in size (regardless of the chronological age) compete against one another in games or athletics. The wise teacher discerns the potential danger and takes steps to equalize competition, but, in order to do this, he must carefully organize his classes. There is no question that this is difficult when class sizes are large and instructional help limited. The necessity for some equalization has been recognized in interscholastic athletics where sports such as boxing and wrestling utilize weight limitations and where schools compete in leagues based upon school population.

This chapter will not attempt to solve all the complex problems facing the physical education teacher, but implications drawn from many of the studies will undoubtedly be relevant in such a context. The characteristics of athletes vs nonathletes, for example, should be of interest to the developmental physical educator, as would be the cardiovascular effects of athletics to the individual interested in physiology of exercise. Once again, a clear differentiation between fields of study here cannot be made; many of the tasks in growth and development will be used elsewhere, but the intent will be somewhat different.

The inauguration of growth studies implies a longitudinal approach where the same subjects are followed over a period of a number of years. Obviously, the planning for this type of research is different than for a cross-sectional study, in which different subjects are obtained for each year under investigation. Sampling, of course, is a crucial factor in the latter design, for one makes the assumption that the subjects at each age are representative of that population. Whether or not they do describe the true growth process is not actually known in such an instance, although there are situations in which such assumptions may be valid. The uncertainty of the whole process suggests that the longitudinal approach is preferable.

GROWTH STUDIES

A number of extensive growth studies have been undertaken to study the long-term aspects of growth and development, which have provided extensive data, both on a cross-sectional and longitudinal basis for boys and girls. Although the early studies concentrated on physical growth patterns, other information related to social, psychological, and physical parameters was frequently included. Until recently, few of these growth studies concentrated on variables that could be considered crucial to physical education; as a result, extensive data concerning physical performances have been lacking. Considering the tremendous amount of work done, very little seems to have been done by physical educators.

Iowa Child Welfare Research Station

The Iowa Child Welfare Research Station was established in 1917 under the direction of Bird T. Baldwin[1] with the aim to study the development of children to their maximum. Employing large numbers of subjects from birth to maturity, data were collected on a variety of anthropometric variables, breathing capacity, and strengths of the muscles involving the grip, wrist, and elbow. Use was made of roentgenograms as criteria of anatomical age and of pubescent development as a measure of physiological age. Baldwin reported correlation coefficients between the measures of strength, weight, height, and lung capacity of the children at each age, finding them to be highest during early adolescence and lowest at seventeen years of age.

Brush Foundation

The Brush Foundation Study of Human Growth and Development was established in 1929 at Western Reserve University, Cleveland, Ohio, under

---

[1] Bird T. Baldwin, "The Physical Growth of Children from Birth to Maturity," *University of Iowa Studies in Child Welfare*, 1, No. 1 (June 1921), 1.

the direction of T. Wingate Todd.[2] The children were examined at 3, 6, 9, and 12 months of age, then at every 6 months through 5 years, and each year thereafter. In total, 25 anthropometrical measurements were made of a variety of body segments. X rays were taken of the hand, foot, elbow, knee hip, and shoulder on 575 boys and 484 girls.

Fels Research Institute

The Fels Research Institute was established in 1929 at Antioch College, Ohio, by Samuel S. Fels and directed by Lester W. Sontag[3] to study factors of structure, function, and behavior of children as related to their environment and heredity. Approximately 300 children and their families were studied longitudinally with data collected on body structure, growth, and health, utilizing the interdisciplinary approach through medicine, anthropology, psychology, genetics, biochemistry, biology, and psychophysiology. This project permitted description of average growth curves, including familial patterns, by comparing similarities between triplets, identical twins, siblings, and unrelated children. The determination of such physiological-biochemical measures as the excretion of sex hormones and other ketosteroids, blood enzyme levels, and other variables have helped understand the mechanics and significance of differences in the growth process.

Harvard University Growth Study

The Center for Research in Child Health and Development at Harvard University originated in 1930 under the directorship of Harold C. Stuart.[4] The center provided research facilities for the study of healthy children equivalent to those devoted to the study of sick children in order to gain greater familiarity with normal child development and preventive medicine. An attempt was made to explore all major aspects of development and such forces as bear upon the developmental progress of children. Several hundred boys and girls were employed as subjects; extensive seriatim examinations were obtained with some orthopedic and pediatric measures included, plus a host of anthropometric determinations. In addition, studies of mental

---

[2] Katherine Simmons, "The Brush Foundation Study of Child Growth and Development: II. Physical Growth and Development," *Monographs of the Society for Research in Child Development*, 9, No. 1 (1944), 1.

[3] Lester W. Sontag, "Biological and Medical Studies at the Samuel S. Fels Research Institute," *Child Development*, 17, No. 1-2 (March-June 1946), 81.

[4] Harold C. Stuart, "Studies from the Center for Research in Child Health and Development, School of Public Health, Harvard University," *Monographs of the Society for Research in Child Development*, 4, No. 1 (1939), 1.

development and personality were included to obtain as complete a picture of the growing child as possible. In 1956, when the original project was completed, 67 boys and 67 girls of the original sample were available for testing; their data covered the entire period from birth to 18 years of age.

Institute of Child Welfare, University of California

The Institute of Child Welfare, founded in 1927, conducted three separate long-term developmental investigations at the University of California at Berkeley under the direction of Harold E. Jones.[5] These investigations included the Berkeley Growth Study, the Child Guidance Study, and the Adolescent Growth Study. The Berkeley Growth Study initially enrolled some 30 boys and 30 girls at their birth and successfully followed about 20 of each sex to their maturity. Twenty-two physical measurements, photographs, hand-wrist X rays, and various psychometric data were obtained. The Child Guidance Study was essentially a psychological and sociological study. However, four physical strength measures were given: right and left grip strengths, push strength, and pull strength. In the Adolescent Growth Study, longitudinal data from extensive anthropometry, photographs, physiological measures, and dynamometric strength tests were collected from 70 boys and 75 girls annually from 9 to 17 years of age.

Medford, Oregon, Boys' Growth Study

The Medford Boys' Growth Study, probably the most recent of the longitudinal growth studies, was conducted from 1956 to 1968 by the Physical Education Research Laboratory, University of Oregon, in cooperation with the Medford, Oregon, public schools.[6] The purposes of this study follow:

1. To construct physical and motor growth curves and growth acceleration curves of boys 7 to 18 years of age for such factors as body structure, coordinated strength elements and batteries, strength of individual muscle groups, agility and speed, and muscular power.

2. To relate these physical and motor growth factors to chronological age, physiological maturity, physique type, nutritional status, socio-personal adjustment, interests, and scholastic aptitude and achievement.

---

[5] Harold E. Jones and Nancy Bayley, "The Berkeley Growth Study," *Child Development*, 12, No. 2 (June 1941), 167.

[6] H. Harrison Clarke, "Contributions and Implications of the Medford, Oregon, Boys' Growth Study" (4th ed.), unpublished paper, April 20, 1968.

3. To identify those physical and motor factors that are the most significant growth indicators, particularly as related to adolescence.

4. To contrast all traits in the study for boys who make and who do not make athletic teams competing in interschool competition; to make the same contrast for boys who score high and low in strength tests and batteries, agility and speed, and muscular power.

5. To revise and construct strength and other tests for boys of all ages; and to determine the interrelationships of the factors included in the study at various ages.

The total project was designed to permit three types of growth analyses: cross-sectional with 40 boys at each age from 9 to 15 years inclusive; longitudinal series with approximately 100 boys at each age 7, 9, 12, and 15 years, all followed to 18 years; and convergence at the end of 4 years, utilizing the boys in the longitudinal phase at overlapping years.

In all instances, the subjects were tested within two months of their birthdays, in order to assure reasonable homogeneity as related to chronological age. The test items included in the study are as follows:

1. *Maturity factors:* Chronological age, skeletal age, pubescent development.

2. *Physique type:* Somatotype components.

3. *Body size measures:* Body weight, standing and sitting heights, leg length, hip width, girths of upper arm, chest, abdominal, buttocks, thigh, and calf, lung capacity, Wetzel Grid, and skinfold measures over triceps, apex of scapula, lateral abdomen.

4. *Strength elements and batteries:* Grip strength, back lift, leg lift, arm strength tests, Rogers' Strength and Physical Fitness Indices, 11 cable-tension strength tests of muscle groups throughout the body.

5. *Motor tests:* 60-yard shuttle run, standing broad jump, and total body reaction and movement times.

6. *Scholastic aptitude and achievement:* Grade point average and the following tests depending on age and testing year: California Mental Maturity (Forms S and Secondary), Otis Quick-Scoring Gamma, Stanford Achievement (Elementary, Intermediate, and Advanced), Gates Reading (Primary and Advanced), Iowa Test of Educational Development.

7. *Psycho-personal adjustment:* The following tests depending on age and year: Sociometric Questionnaire, Cowell Personal Distance Scale, Cowell Social Behavior Trend, Adjective Check List, California Psychological Inventory, Mental Health Analysis, Level of Aspiration.

8. *Interests:* The following depending on age and testing year: Children's Interest Blank, Adjective Check List, Dreese and Mooney Interest Inventory, What I Like To Do, Kudor Preference Record (Forms D and Vocational), Garretson and Symonds Interest Form, Strong Vocational Interest Blank.

PROBLEMS PERTAINING TO GROWTH AND DEVELOPMENT

The common concept characterizing growth and development studies is that they are limited to the determination of changes in boys and girls as they grow up. Of course, this determination is a major function of such studies, but it need not nor should not be so limited. The questions below indicate the scope that is possible in this area of research as applied to physical education.

1. What are the shapes of mean growth curves and growth acceleration curves for various measures of such traits as body size, muscular strength, muscular endurance, and motor ability performances?

2. In what ways and to what extent do boys and girls differ in maturity, physique type, body size, strength, endurance, and motor ability elements? What significance have these differences for physical education?

3. What degrees of consistency exist for the various measures from age to age as children grow up?

4. What are the individual and group growth patterns of physical and motor traits for boys and girls who become athletes, honor-roll students, school drop-outs, leaders, delinquents, and the like?

5. What relationships exist between physical and motor traits and physiological maturity, physique type, nutritional status, socio-personal adjustment, socio-economic status, interests, and scholastic aptitude and achievement?

6. What are the significant age and sex differences found among the various growth and development parameters?

7. Based on skeletal age assessments made at an early age, what rate of growth change occurs for those boys and girls who are advanced as compared with those who are retarded in maturity?

8. What differences in growth patterns exist for children who demonstrate high strength or high motor ability at a young age as compared with those who score low on such measures?

Once oriented to growth and development research, the astute student will think of many other significant questions in need of answers. Further, all sorts of comparative and relationship studies can be conducted as indicated above as the purposes of the Medford Boys' Growth Study. Thus, growth studies can be and usually are much more than just a succession of means for various tests over a period of years, which indicate the changes taking place as children grow up. The next section will illustrate the richness of this research area with significant studies that have been conducted in this area.

GROWTH PATTERNS

A considerable amount of data has been amassed concerning the growth patterns of children and adolescents, the majority of which comes from longitudinal studies, some from birth to maturity. The early emphasis was placed upon serial measurement of physical dimensions, with the literature containing a wealth of information on size and structure. In some cases, other factors were studied in an attempt to obtain a more complete understanding of the growth process, but these are seen to be of secondary importance. More recently, however, it has become fashionable to relate structure to function so that a variety of performance variables have been included in the experimental design. The following review, although incomplete, will attempt to trace a pattern of activity through some of the pertinent literature in the field of growth and development.

Birth to Maturity

A report from the Brush Foundation by Simmons[7] presented anthropometric and skeletal age data from 999 children, ages 3 months to 17 years, selected primarily on the basis of their freedom from physical, mental, and nutritional handicaps and of their willingness to participate in a longitudinal study. Of particular interest were the 78 tables and 27 figures that were presented, accompanied by a brief discussion that emphasized sex and variability differences in development of various body segments. The analyses included a prediction of terminal stature, the interpretation of age-height-weight tables, and the relation of skeletal age to growth in stature and to menarchial age. In a study reported earlier, Simmons and Todd[8] found that sex differences in weight were significant at 3, 6, 9, 12, and 18 months and 2, 2½, 3, 12, and 13 years. For girls, the annual increment in stature decreased until the eleventh year when it rose; the boys began to increase in height beginning in their twelfth year. The use of age-height-weight tables in individual analysis was discouraged, and it was found that stature was superior to weight as a measure of growth.

Meredith[9] performed seriatim measurements on 1,243 boys, including

---

[7] Katherine Simmons, "The Brush Foundation Study of Child Growth and Development: II. Physical Growth and Development," *Monographs of the Society for Research in Child Development*, 9, No. 1 (1944), 1.

[8] Katherine Simmons and T. Wingate Todd, "Growth of Well Children: Analysis of Stature and Weight, 3 Months to 13 Years," *Growth*, 2, No. 2 (August 1938), 93.

[9] Howard V. Meredith, "The Rhythm of Physical Growth: A Study of Eighteen Anthropometric Measures on Iowa City Males Ranging in Age Between Birth and Eighteen Years," *University of Iowa Studies in Child Welfare*, 11, No. 3 (1935), 1.

such variables as stature; sitting height; various shoulder, chest, and hip diameters and circumferences; body weight; grip strength; breathing capacity; and several skin and subcutaneous tissue measures. Among the extensive data presented were means, standard deviations, coefficients of variation, and annual percentage increments. Logarithmic curves were fitted to the mean measurements of breathing capacity, maximum head breadth, thoracic circumference, weight, stature, and bicondylar diameter of the femur.

Shuttleworth[10] analyzed the growth curves for 9 physical dimensions, erupted teeth, and intelligence of 747 girls and 711 boys classified into 19 groups according to age of maximum growth. This point is believed to represent age of sexual maturity in both boys and girls and is highly reliable; it permits a very exact classification of individuals according to the timing of different phases of their growth patterns. Included in this monograph were 110 tables and 152 figures, permitting a number of generalizations concerning growth patterns from birth to maturity and the identification of several underlying factors governing the rate of growth.

In a comprehensive report, Krogman[11] presented appropriate growth data by means of tables, graphs, and figures, beginning with height-weight studies and including information on ethnic differences and extensive results concerning general body growth. In addition, studies were reported on bone growth and skeletal maturation with a concentration on pubertal development, the role of diet, and several other physiologic factors. Several functions for growth data were indicated, among which are the following: to establish standards of acceptable health and nutritional status, to assess acceptable growth progress, to provide a standard of comparability, and to study heredity.

Adolescence

The physiological changes that occur with puberty have been of interest to researchers in growth and development. For example, Dimock[12] studied 200 adolescent boys continuously for several years, providing data and interrelationships among various physiological, physical, personality, and social factors. Chronological age was found to be an unreliable index of pubescent status during the adolescent years. Regardless of age, the most

[10] Frank K. Shuttleworth, "The Physical and Mental Growth of Girls and Boys Age Six to Nineteen in Relation to Age at Maximum Growth," *Monographs of the Society for Research in Child Development*, 4, No. 3 (1939), 1.

[11] Wilton Marion Krogman, "The Physical Growth of Children: An Appraisal of Studies 1950–1955," *Monographs of the Society for Research in Child Development*, 20, No. 1 (1955), 1.

[12] Hedley S. Dimock, "A Research in Adolescence: I. Pubescence and Physical Growth," *Child Development*, 6, No. 3 (September 1935), 177.

rapid growth in height and weight came in the year when the individual made the transition from pubescence to postpubescence. During the period 12 to 16 years of age, boys increased rapidly in strength, as measured by Rogers' Strength Index, paralleling the most rapid gains in height and weight. A similar picture was found for motor ability and coordination. The data failed to support the common notion that rapid growth in height and weight leads to poor motor coordination and awkwardness.

Bayley[13] tested subjects at 6-month intervals beginning at 14 years of age and continuing until 18 years, obtaining X rays of the left hand and knee. Comparisons were made of means and standard deviations with available norms. A fairly good relationship existed within a group of adolescent children (90 boys and 87 girls) between skeletal maturation and growth in size.[14] The subjects were divided into early, average, and late maturing groups on the basis of skeletal development; a number of differences in anthropometric variables were found. For example, early maturing girls were relatively large, and late maturing girls were small before 13 years of age, but after this age the opposite was true.

When body build was determined by the bi-iliac width ÷ height, stem length ÷ height, and bi-iliac ÷ biacromial indices, very little relationship with rate of maturing could be found. Early maturing boys were relatively large at all ages, whereas late maturing boys were small between ages 11 to 16. When comparisons were made between skeletal maturation in boys and girls and rates of growth, a close relationship was observed, especially when growth was expressed as a percentage of a child's eventual mature size.[15] In individual cases where this did not hold true, chance factors were operating, although it is possible that illness and glandular dysfunction exerted a retarding influence on skeletal maturing and growth in size. When the curves of growth for both boys and girls were expressed as a percentage of mature size at successive skeletal ages, a remarkable similarity was found. It was felt that at a given skeletal age a child has achieved a certain proportion of his eventual adult size; this may be predicted fairly well if a child's present size and skeletal age are known.

The social and emotional development of 33 adolescents in relation to physical maturation at puberty was studied by More.[16] He reported that the

---

[13] Nancy Bayley, "Skeletal X Rays as Indicators of Maturity," *Journal of Consulting Psychology*, 4 (1940), 69.

[14] Nancy Bayley, "Size and Body Build of Adolescents in Relation to Rate of Skeletal Maturing," *Child Development*, 14, No. 2 (June 1943), 47.

[15] Nancy Bayley, "Skeletal Maturing in Adolescence as a Basis for Determining Percentage of Completed Growth," *Child Development*, 14, No. 1 (March 1943), 1.

[16] Douglas M. More, "Developmental Concordance and Discordance During Puberty and Early Adolescence," *Monographs of the Society for Research in Child Development*, 18, No. 1 (1953), 1.

advent of puberty in girls appeared to be a relatively abrupt phenomenon, requiring rather sudden emotional adjustments. Apparently, this occurrence was not nearly as crucial for boys, who may be less subject to external social pressures. At any rate, the socially successful girl was seen as the one who acted as if she were sexually mature, and this is enhanced if she matures earlier. It was surmised that in making the transition to adult status, the adolescent prepares for a new role by making several adjustments. The stimulus for this is a series of physiological changes that rapidly bring the body close to adult size with adult functions.

This adjustment is made more difficult by the establishment of an emotional life, which may or may not be altered during the adolescent period. Further, the social forces with which the individual interacts and the modes and expectations of the individual's peer group that provide a powerful stimulus for behavioral patterns increase the difficulties of this adjustment. All these factors must act in a social milieu in which a series of cultural, legal, and parental laws and mores operate to influence behavior. The successful integration of these factors is the major task that must be undertaken in adolescence.

Motor Performance and Growth

Many studies related to motor performance and growth involve forms of experimental design and include physiological, psychological, and other types of data. Overlapping of research should be expected, for the problems of age growth can be investigated in many ways. The problems of research in growth and development to be presented here will include those factors associated with the early years from birth to maturity where the major changes occur, and they will not involve the retrogressive alterations accompanying old age. The motor aspects of maturation are particularly relevant to this discussion since this subject is directly germane to research in health and physical education.

In 1940, Espenschade[17] reported the results of measuring gross motor performance of approximately 165 girls and boys who were tested over a span of three or four years beginning in the 8th grade. The subjects were enrolled in the adolescent phase of the Berkeley Growth Study so that it was possible to relate the physical traits to other growth criteria. The variables selected were 50-yard dash, standing broad jump, jump and reach, target throw, throw for distance, and the Brace Test. Although these measures are reliable, they were found inadequate for the determination of short-term

---

[17] Anna Espenschade, "Motor Performance in Adolescence Including the Study of Relationships with Measures of Physical Growth and Maturity," *Monographs of the Society for Research in Child Development*, 5, No. 1 (1940), 1.

changes in rate of growth during the adolescent period. Over the age range studied, growth in ability to perform motor acts appeared to reach its maximum at approximately 14 years of age in girls but continued through 17 years of age for boys. Sex differences appeared at all ages but were accentuated in older children. Correlations between motor performance of girls and all measures of physical growth and maturity were quite low and generally not significant, but for boys these correlations tended to be significantly related to measures of maturity. Correlations between motor performances of boys and anthropometric measures tended to decline with age. Measures of strength were substantially related to gross motor performance in boys but were only slightly related in girls. The subjects tended to retain a consistent ranking among their group in motor performance and to follow the growth trend; as they underwent rapid physical changes, so did their motor abilities.

Longitudinal data provided by Jones[18] included measures of right and left grips and push and pull strengths, each recorded semiannually from 11 years to 17.5 years of age; the subjects were 89 boys and 87 girls. Biological, social, and psychological factors were of primary concern in this growth study. When compared with such items of so-called "dynamic strength" as the dash, broad jump, jump and reach, and distance throw, static dynamometric strength was more closely related to biological growth. The premise here may be that strength itself is more nearly a growth variable than other types of motor performances that utilize the factor of neuromotor coordination to a greater extent.

Further, it was found that boys exhibited a positive relationship between strength and certain traits representing prestige and thus reflecting the role of physical proficiency in the adolescent value system—a factor much less important for girls. When such a trait is lacking in boys, the handicap must be overcome by strongly compensating personal traits in other areas. In describing the 10 boys highest in strength with the 10 lowest in strength, Jones found that the high group tended to be early maturing and to have high social prestige and satisfactory personal adjustment. On the other hand, the weak boys tended to be poorly adjusted, exhibiting either withdrawal symptoms or extroversion attention-seeking traits. Separation into early, average, and late maturers by means of X rays of hand and knee[19] resulted in the formation of other different strength groups.

Kurimoto[20] conducted the first longitudinal analysis of growth data from

---

[18] Harold E. Jones, *Motor Performance and Growth* (Berkeley: University of California Press, 1949).

[19] Harold E. Jones, "Skeletal Maturing as Related to Strength," *Child Development*, 17, No. 4 (December 1946), 173.

[20] Etsuo Kurimoto, "Longitudinal Analysis of Maturity, Structural, Strength, and Motor Developments of Boys Fifteen Through Eighteen Years of Age," microcard Doctoral Dissertation, University of Oregon, 1963.

the Medford Boys' Growth Study, annually examining 70 boys from 15 to 18 years of age. During this time, the structural, strength, and motor development increased on all tests; however, the amounts of increase became smaller with each yearly advance in age, as the subjects approached maturity. The somatotype components of the boys changed significantly from one age to another, the amount of mesomorphy increasing and the amount of ectomorphy decreasing. As shown in Table 22, the interage correlation coefficients ranged between .90 and .95 for skeletal age, whereas for structural

Table 22

Interage Correlations

	Skeletal age	Weight	Height	Mesomorphy	Leg lift	PFI
15 vs 16 years	.95	.87	.97	.91	.82	.77
16 vs 17 years	.95	.84	.98	.83	.67	.72
17 vs 18 years		.96	.99	.88	.77	.75
15 vs 17 years	.90	.92	.91	.81	.73	.76
16 vs 18 years		.81	.96	.86	.65	.72
15 vs 18 years		.86	.88	.82	.64	.62

measures they exceeded .80; for strength and motor ability tests, they were lower. When advanced and retarded maturity groups were formed at 15 years of age, the advanced subjects were larger and stronger than the retarded group. During the age period 15 to 17 years, the retarded group registered significantly greater mean gains on various tests than did the advanced maturity group. For skeletal age, weight, lung capacity, and leg lift strength, the significantly higher means of the advanced maturity groups at 15 years of age were maintained at 16 and 17 years of age.

Again, from the Medford study, the strength and motor development of boys was studied longitudinally from 7 through 12 years of age by Jordan.[21] A moderate degree of consistency was found over the 6-year period in push-ups, standing broad jump, 60-yard shuttle run, cable-tension strength average, Strength Index, and Physical Fitness Index. For these variables, the interage correlations ranged from .38 to .89; the highest such correlations were .69 to .89 for pushups, .54 to .83 for 60-yard shuttle run, and .45 to .81 for standing broad jump. The lowest interage correlations, generally, were for total-body reaction time, 10-foot run, and shoulder inward rotation strength. As the subjects advanced in age, their average performances increased on all tests. Comparisons of the strength and motor performance means for advanced and retarded maturity groups formed at 9 years of age

[21] David B. Jordan, "Longitudinal Analysis of Strength and Motor Development of Boys Ages Seven Through Twelve Years of Age," microcard Doctoral Dissertation, University of Oregon, 1966.

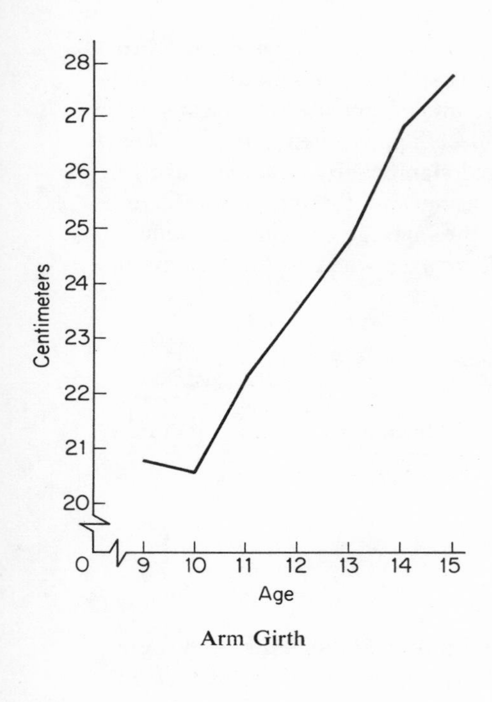

Arm Girth

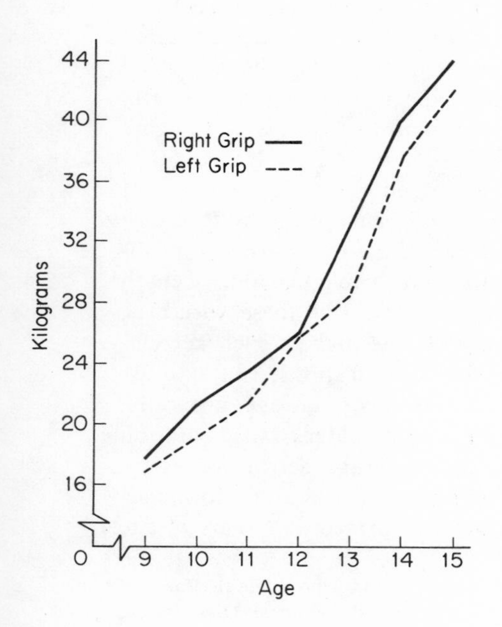

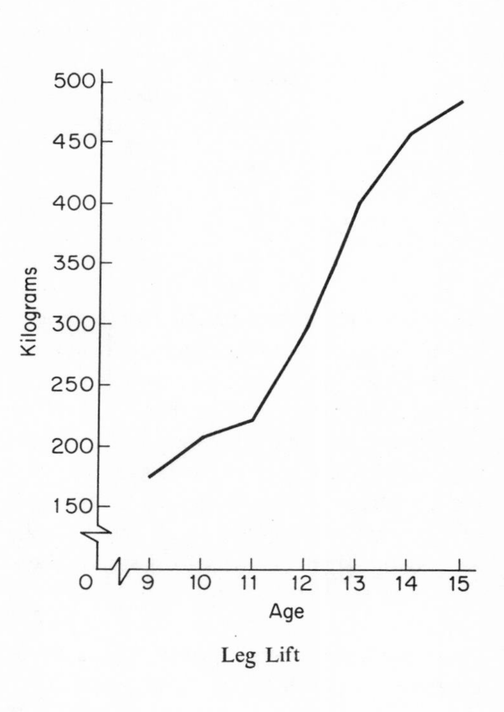

Leg Lift

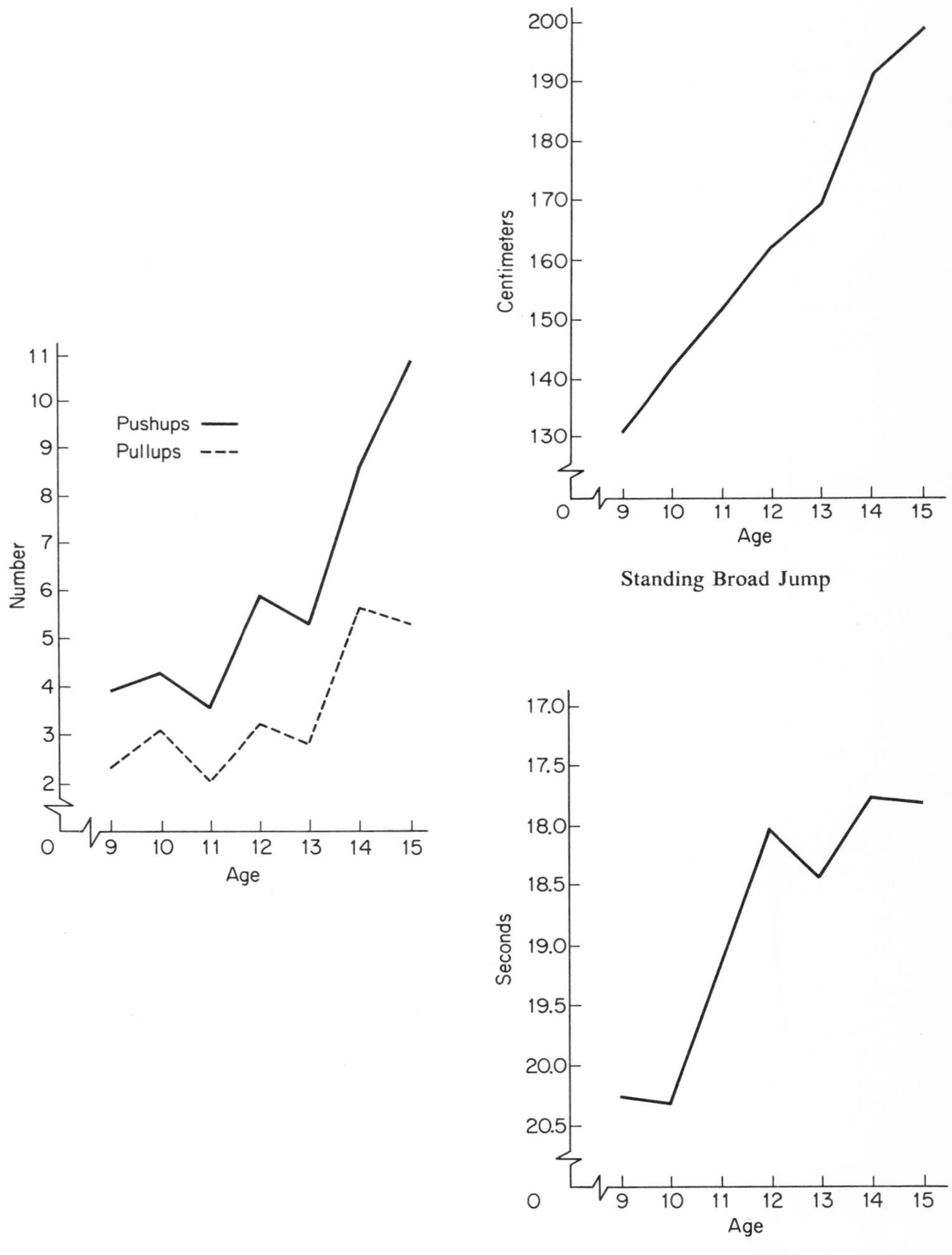

Figure 30. Growth Curves

revealed continuous significant differences until 12 years of age for the two gross strength batteries, Strength Index, and cable-tension strength average. For high and low cable-tension strength groups formed at 9 years of age, significant differences were obtained on other gross strength tests throughout the 4-year period. When growth patterns of high and low PFI groups formed at 9 years of age were compared, continuous significant differences were obtained for pushups and Strength Index over the 4-year period.

Sinclair[22] studied somatotype stability of boys 9 through 12 years of age and found, in contrast to Kurimoto[23] with older boys, that the average somatotype component did not differ significantly from age to age. However, numerous variations occurred in the somatotypes of individual boys. The mean ranges of the components for the four years were: endomorphy, 3.4 to 3.6; mesomorphy, 4.1 to 4.2; and ectomorphy, 2.8 to 3.2. For the components, the ranges of interage correlations were: endomorphy, .79 to .85; mesomorphy, .83 to .93; and ectomorphy, .85 to .89. The ranges of correlations between components were: .03 to .25 between endomorphy and mesomorphy; —.64 to —.69 between mesomorphy and ectomorphy; and —.64 and —.75 between endomorphy and ectomorphy. Zero-order correlations between somatotype components and measures of maturity, body size, muscular strength and endurance, and motor performances followed approximately the same pattern for the four years.

In studying growth curves on a cross-sectional basis, Clarke and Wickens[24] obtained data from 40 boys at each age from 9 to 15 years of age for 34 maturity, structural, strength, and motor ability tests. In addition, the variability of each test item at each age was studied. Figure 30 depicts the trend of several of the tests selected. It will be noted that considerable variation occurred from one variable to another as age increased.

Comments

Thus, it can be seen that the trend in growth studies in physical education is to move from the examination of structural factors to the addition of a variety of motor performance items. This would seem logical, as more emphasis is placed on developmental physical education. Although not stated explicitly, a growing interest in the study of individual differences is observed with less emphasis placed on average performances or trend and

---

[22] Gary D. Sinclair, "Stability of Physique Types of Boys Nine Through Twelve Years of Age," microcard Master's Thesis, University of Oregon, 1966.

[23] Kurimoto, *op. cit.*

[24] H. Harrison Clarke and J. Stuart Wickens, "Maturity, Structural, Strength, and Motor Ability Growth Curves of Boys 9 to 15 Years of Age," *Research Quarterly*, 33, No. 1 (March 1962), 26.

more concern with the variability at each age. For example, Clarke[25] reported skeletal age ranges of 5 to 7 years for boys of the same chronological ages tested within 2 months of their birthdays; the standard deviations for the various ages were between 12 and 13 months. The range in leg lift (tested on a dynamometer with use of a belt around the hips) was 930 pounds for 12-year-old boys; one boy was 4½ times stronger than another; the standard deviation was 169 pounds.

Questions that ask how early maturers differ from late maturers or how the strong compare with the weak seem sufficiently provocative to create research interest. If one needs to be reminded of the relevancy of such studies, he needs but to visit a local school and observe boys and girls in physical education and other classes to see the range of abilities of individuals who have the same chronological age. In order to make such study more meaningful, the following sections discuss pertinent techniques commonly associated with growth and development research together with selected relevant studies.

ANTHROPOMETRY

In its simplest form, anthropometry is the systematized measurement of the human body. In the original concept, it usually referred to linear dimensions of brain, skeleton, and other organs, but the concept is proposed here to broaden the scope of anthropometry and to include such variables as maturation, body physique, strength, and motor factors, even though they will be dealt with separately later in this chapter. In other words, total growth and development of an individual are reflected in ways other than pure size; the degree of skeletal maturation and strength development might also indicate structural components.

A difficulty faced by the researcher contemplating work in the field of anthropometry is that of site selection. As yet, no established test routine is available in anthropometry, so the choice is entirely dependent upon the wishes of the investigator. Not only are sites not specific, but the manner of obtaining the precise measures is still largely lacking in agreement. In practice, therefore, a description of testing techniques should be included in the body of the written paper or perhaps in an appendix.

Attempts have been made from time to time to reach some agreement concerning methods in the field of anthropometry. In fact, the first proposals were made at the congress of the German anthropological societies in 1874, and later in France and Russia.[26] At the 13th International Congress of Prehistoric Anthropology and Archeology held in Monaco in 1906, serious

---

[25] Clarke, *op. cit.*

[26] T. D. Stewart, ed., *Hrdlička's Practical Anthropometry* (4th ed.) (Philadelphia: The Wistar Institute of Anatomy and Biology, 1952), pp. 12–17.

consideration was given to this problem, resulting in the formation of an International Agreement on Anthropometry. This important work was continued by the British Association for the Advancement of Science and culminated with another agreement at the 14th Congress in 1912 at Geneva. As a result, certain general principles were established, many landmarks were descriptively located, and numerous body measurements were defined.

These efforts notwithstanding, it cannot be claimed today that uniformity exists in anthropometric testing. In order to reduce error as much as possible, measurement procedures must be defined precisely. For example, even though body weight seems a straightforward test, at least three important sources of error bear upon the measure for research purposes: (1) The first source concerns the amount and type of clothing worn by the subject. The use of nude weight would solve the problem. However, if this is found undesirable, a minimum of gymnasium clothing less shoes would probably be acceptable, especially when all subjects are dressed alike. (2) The second source concerns the accuracy required. If weight is to be recorded to the nearest half-pound, it should be made clear how to round off to the nearest half-pound. (3) The third source is proper scale calibration. It might be argued that a small systematic error in scale calibration in a cross-sectional study would affect all subjects in an equal manner and thus do no serious injustice to a statistical treatment of the data. However, even if one could rationalize this point of view, the acceptance of such error in longitudinal studies would be extremely hazardous, since all data must be directly comparable. Six months later, the scale may be out of balance even further. Thus, calibration must be accomplished on all instruments at each primary testing session.

Although the example of body weight has been used, it should be obvious that the same concepts are applicable to other anthropometric variables. Standardization of testing technique is essential in growth studies, as often different members of a testing team become involved from time to time. Assurance must be obtained that *exactly* the same procedures are employed at all times. This should require advanced testing of different subjects to insure adequate repeatability of measures; in such instances the correlation coefficient between two separate tests will help decide upon testing consistency, as described in Chapter 12.

The types of instruments that are required for anthropometric research are usually few in number and ordinarily quite simple. Height—both standing and sitting—is measured by a stadiometer or other devices; breadth measures are obtained by use of sliding wooden or metal calipers; circumference of limbs is taken by a cloth or steel tape; and skin folds are determined with fat calipers.

Inasmuch as the instruments themselves may remain constant, the selection of a site must be rigidly defined and then precisely measured. Clothing must not interfere in any of the anthropometric measures for obvious reasons. When dealing with girths where the tape must be placed around soft tissue, care must be taken to exert the same tension on the ends of the tape at each administration. Tapes with a built-in calibrated spring handle (Gulick handle) serve best for this testing, but hanging a constant weight from one end of the tape will also provide equal compressibility of soft tissue. Variables such as chest circumference will fluctuate slightly with the breathing cycle; it is often expedient to carefully estimate the midpoint between extremes of quiet inhalation and exhalation and use this figure. Fat folds are frequently difficult measurements for the novice tester, but once again care must be taken to administer the test properly without including muscle in the skinfold or deviating from the site as defined. Since many of these items are included in tests of nutritional status or as determiners of body composition, errors of testing may be compounded when introduced into regression formulas.

MATURITY

Beyond the concern for growth in size comes the interest in assessment of maturity, as this gives a more realistic picture of individual capacities. Anthropometric measures alone do not reveal sufficient information concerning maturation, so this trait should be studied separately. Performance in physical activities is influenced to a considerable extent by the degree of progress made toward full maturity by an individual. Certainly, this is a factor in athletics and, in fact, may be somewhat inversely related to chronological age; thus, the more mature are individuals for their age would seem to be an advantage at any given time in making varsity teams and playing regularly. This may even be extended to other educational endeavors.

Skeletal Age

The method of determining skeletal age most widely used is that of the hand-wrist X ray whereby each of some 30 bones and epiphyses are compared with standards, for example, those of Greulich and Pyle.[27] According to these authors, skeletal age provides an objective index of the progress an individual is making toward physical maturity and can be employed from

---

[27] William Walter Greulich and S. Idell Pyle, *Radiographic Atlas of Skeletal Development of the Hand and Wrist* (2nd ed.) (Stanford, California: Stanford University Press, 1959).

birth to maturity. In practice, the process consists of comparing the obtained X ray with those in the atlas in terms of degree of bone ossification, the contours of the ends and shafts of the bones, and the degree of fusion of the epiphyses. The average of all assessments is taken as the skeletal age, and it is usually given in months.

The main difficulties to be encountered in obtaining the hand-wrist X ray are related to equipment and safety precautions. If the investigator must rely upon commercial or medical facilities, the cost would probably be prohibitive and would make field testing very difficult. However, portable equipment may be obtained that can be set up quickly and used by trained operators; dark room facilities, if already available, would solve the problem of film development. X-ray development resources, especially if located on campus, as in the Student Health Center, might not be too great an expense if a large number of X rays could be processed at one time.

The other problem concerns the amount of radiation exposure and resultant health hazard that could exist if adequate precautions are not taken during the filming. Such things as restricting the focus of the cone of the X-ray machine, placing the hand to be filmed in a lead lined box, protecting the subject and operator with lead shields, and so on are important considerations; if used properly, slight and very minimal radiation well within tolerance limits results. An illustration of the X-ray unit utilized in the Medford Boys' Growth Study appears in Figure 31. The procedures followed to produce satisfactory roentgenographs are below.

1. Type of film exposure holder: no-screen cardboard holder for 8″ × 10″ X-ray film.

2. Focal distance: the lower edge of the aluminum cone placed a distance of 30 inches directly above the cardboard holder.

3. Amperage: 15 milliamperes.

4. Voltage: 110 kilovolts.

5. Exposure time: 1 sec.

Aside from these considerations, the process of film evaluation is quite time consuming. Reasoning that if the hand and wrist could be taken as indicative of growth of the whole skeleton, then it might be possible that fewer than 30 sites on the X ray would give an accurate assessment of the total. Considerable advantage would result if a reduction could be achieved without losing appreciably in the validity of the ratings. In order to test this hypothesis, Clarke and Hayman[28] tested 273 boys 9 through 15 years of age,

---

[28] H. Harrison Clarke and Noel R. Hayman, "Reduction of Bone Assessments Necessary for the Skeletal Age Determination of Boys," *Research Quarterly*, 33, No. 2 (May 1962), 202.

Figure 31. X-Ray Unit for Skeletal Age

intercorrelated the skeletal ages of the individual bones, and then correlated them with the total hand-wrist assessment. A multiple correlation of .9989 was obtained between the skeletal age of all bones and the following four bones located longitudinally in the center of the hand: the capitate, metacarpal III, proximal phalanx III, and middle phalanx III. The difference among the skeletal age means by assessment of the four bones was .15 month (about five days); the *t* ratio was .03.

In an analysis of 273 boys by Clarke and Harrison,[29] advanced, normal,

[29] H. Harrison Clarke and James C. E. Harrison, "Differences in Physical and Motor Traits Between Boys of Advanced, Normal, and Retarded Maturity," *Research Quarterly*, 33, No. 1 (March 1962), 13.

and retarded maturity groups (Figure 32) were formed based on skeletal age at 9, 12, and 15 years of age. The boys in these three groups at each age were contrasted for structural, strength, and muscular power characteristics. In all instances where the differences were significant, the more mature group had the highest mean. The most significant differences among the means were obtained at 15, 12, and 9 years of age, in that order. Without exception, the

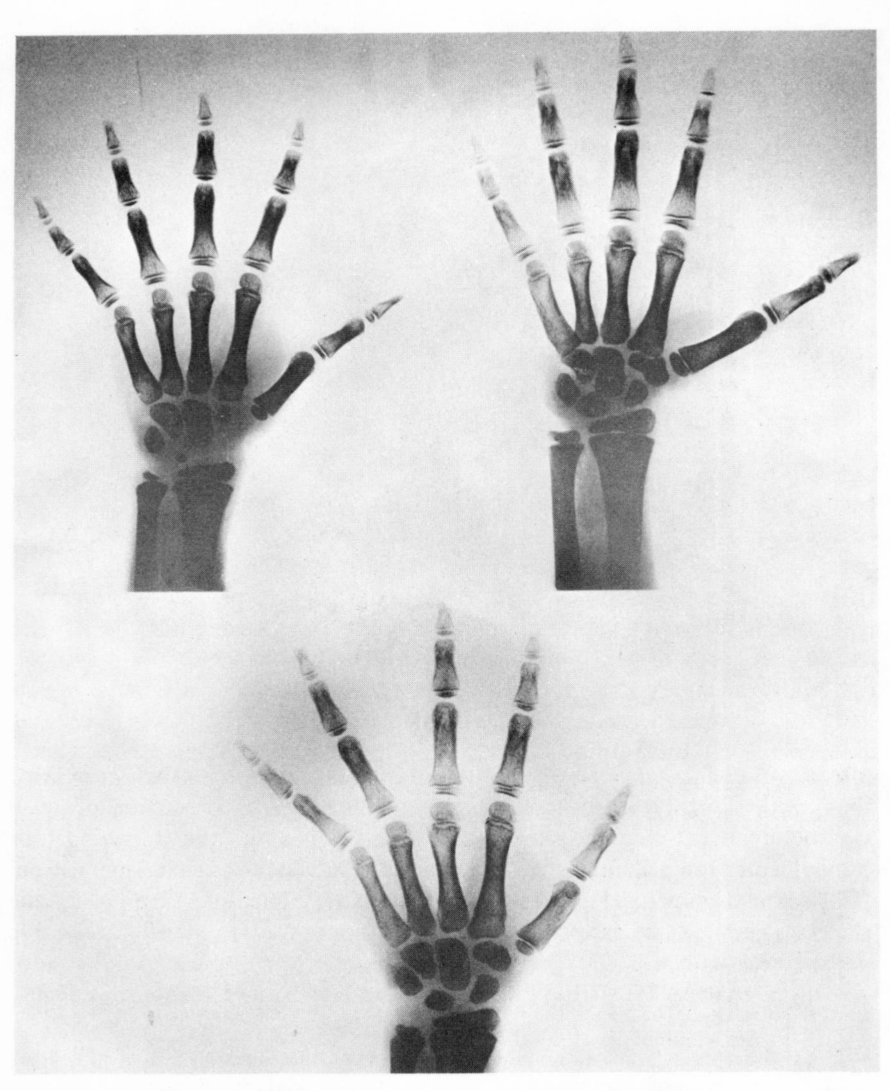

Figure 32. Skeletal Age: Hand-Wrist X-Rays (Three Boys)
(Upper left, *Retarded*; upper right, *Advanced*; bottom, *Normal*)

differences among all body weight means were significant. Other test variables in which the differences among the means were relatively high in significance were hip width, grip strength, sitting height, upper arm girth, and calf girth; in addition were the variables of chest girth, mean of 12 cable-tension strength tests, Strength Index, standing height, and elbow flexion strength.

When subjects were classified into various groups based upon athletic ability, Clarke and Petersen[30] found that outstanding athletes in upper elementary and junior high schools had significantly higher mean skeletal ages than did regular players, substitutes, and nonparticipants. In studying maturity relative to chronological age, the outstanding elementary school athletes only were found to be advanced.

Pubescent Assessment

An important adjunct to the study of maturity is the assessment of pubescent status. Puberty refers to that age when asexual life becomes sexual and the reproductive organs become functionally operative. It is considered to be a point in time dividing two periods: the prepubescent, which begins at birth, and the pubescent, which begins at the onset of puberty and continues until maturity. During this time, a number of physiological adjustments take place. For boys, the transition to the pubescent state is gradual, evident by the rapid growth of fine pubic hair, which becomes pigmented; eventually pubescence ends when the pubic hair becomes coarse and kinky. Other secondary sex characteristics also occur, such as a deepening of the voice and the increase in development of the genitalia, but these are less objective measures than pubic hair development for research purposes. For girls, the age of menarche is usually used as the index of pubescence, although the first appearance of pubic hair precedes menarche by a year or more.[31]

One of the earliest attempts to standardize a rating scheme of pubescent assessment was by Crampton,[32] who divided pubescence into three stages: the growth of fine pubic hair, the pigmentation of the hair, and the appearance of the kink or twist. Subsequently, a 5-point scale was devised by Greulich, *et al.*,[33] in such a manner that 1 = prepubescence, 2 = appearance of fine

---

[30] H. Harrison Clarke and Kay H. Petersen, "Contrast of Maturational, Structural, and Strength Characteristics of Athletes and Nonathletes 10 to 15 Years of Age," *Research Quarterly*, 32, No. 2 (May 1961), 163.

[31] Ernest H. Watson and George H. Lowrey, *Growth and Development of Children* (2nd ed.) (Chicago: The Year Book Publishers, Inc., 1952), p. 211.

[32] C. Ward Crampton, "Physiological Age—A Fundamental Principle," *American Physical Education Review*, 13, No. 3–6 (May-June 1908), reprinted in *Child Development*, 15, No. 1 (March 1944), 1.

[33] W. W. Greulich, *et al.*, "Somatic and Endocrine Studies of Puberal and Adolescent Boys," *Monographs of the Society for Research in Child Development*, 7, No. 3 (1942).

pubic hair, 3 = pigmentation, 4 = appearance of kinky or curly hair, and 5 = postpubescence with the development of the external sexual characteristics of adults.

These categories are useful in grouping the population under study but are only general approximations of physiological maturity. They do not indicate how long an individual has been in each stage, and the adolescent period, defined as the time between puberty and maturity, is short in comparison with the preadolescent and postadolescent periods. Thus, a person is classified as category 1 until he exhibits the first signs of puberty and is given 5 for any time after achieving maturity. During the interim time, however, these designations may prove very useful.

Clarke and Degutis[34] compared the skeletal ages and various physical and motor factors with the pubescent development of 10-, 13-, and 16-year-old boys. Physical maturation was differentiated by pubescent assessment most effectively at 13 years of age, although it was not so sensitive to maturational changes as was skeletal age. Although the distribution by pubescent assessment of 13-year-old boys disclosed some boys at this age in each of the 5 pubescent categories, most of them were equally distributed in pubescent groups 2 and 3, according to the classification of Greulich referred to above. At 10 years of age, nearly all boys were classified in group 1; at age 16 years, they appeared mostly in group 5 but with some in group 4. Considerable overlapping occurred in the skeletal age ranges of adjacent pubescent groups at each chronological age. With few exceptions, 13- and 16-year-old boys who were advanced in pubescent development for their respective ages had higher mean scores on body size, strength, and motor tests. At 16 years of age, a significantly greater percentage of ectomorphs were found in group 4 than in group 5, indicating retarded maturation.

PHYSIQUE TYPE

Body build has been a matter of interest to scholars in the field of growth and development for a long time, as efforts were made to categorize human performance and behavior. A variety of descriptive terms has been employed with varying degrees of success over the years; terms such as respiratory (asthmatic), cerebral (bookworm), plethoric (phlegmatic), phthisic (energetic), and so on, illustrate attempts made along these lines. In 1925, Kretschmer[35] suggested the terms *pyknic* to represent the fat body type, *athletic* to designate the muscular individual, and *asthenic* for the lean person.

[34] H. Harrison Clarke and Ernest W. Degutis, "Comparison of Skeletal Age and Various Physical and Motor Factors with the Pubescent Development of 10-, 13-, and 16-Year-Old Boys," *Research Quarterly*, 33, No. 3 (October 1962), 356.

[35] William H. Sheldon, S. S. Stevens, and W. B. Tucker, *The Varieties of Human Physique* (New York: Harper & Row, Publishers, 1940).

The most generally accepted description of physique type today is accorded Sheldon's designation of the somatotype,[36] in which the terms endomorph, mesomorph, and ectomorph are most widely known. These components are briefly described as: *endomorphy*, preponderance of soft roundness throughout the various regions of the body; *mesomorphy*, heavy, hard, and rectangular physique with rugged, massive muscles and large, prominent bones; *ectomorphy*, frail, delicate body structure with thin segments, anteroposteriorly.

The *Atlas* gives the progression of weight changes, as a series of norms or means, for each of the known somatotypes from 18 to 65 years of age, based upon a sample of 46,000 male subjects. Under this scheme, each somatotype component is rated on a scale from 1 to 7 with the higher number representing the degree that the component is found to exist in the subject. Thus, a three-number sequence is given, one for each component; the first numeral refers to endomorphy, and the last gives the amount of ectomorphy. For example, the greatest endomorphic somatotype would be given as 7–1–1, and the greatest ectomorphic dominance would be 1–1–7. As a result, Sheldon has described and illustrated 88 somatotypes. A further description of this process and various modifications may be found in a discussion by Clarke[37] along with several features of somatotype application.

Although no established norms for children are available as they are for men, their use in research has been well-established in the Medford Boys' Growth Study. One of the difficulties, however, has been to accept the 19 categories suggested by Sheldon, Stevens, and Tucker,[38] which tended to disperse the data too greatly when applied to a smaller sample of subjects. For this reason, Clarke, Irving, and Heath[39] classified 259 boys 9 to 15 years of age into the following five categories:

1. Endomorphs: endomorphic component of 5 and over; no other component above 4.

2. Mesomorphs: mesomorphic component of 5 and over; no other component above 4.

3. Ectomorphs: ectomorphic component of 5 and over; no other component above 4.

4. Endo-mesomorphs: mesomorphic component of 5 and over; endomorphy of 4 and above; ectomorphy below 4.

5. Midtypes: no component exceeding 4.

---

[36] William H. Sheldon, *Atlas of Men* (New York: Harper & Row, Publishers, 1954).

[37] H. Harrison Clarke, *Application of Measurement to Health and Physical Education* (4th ed.) (Englewood Cliffs, N.J.: Prentice-Hall, Inc., 1967), pp. 101–12.

[38] Sheldon, Stevens, and Tucker, *op. cit.*

[39] H. Harrison Clarke, Robert N. Irving, and Barbara Honeyman Heath, "Relation of Maturity, Structural, and Strength Measures to the Somatotypes of Boys 9 Through 15 Years of Age," *Research Quarterly*, 32, No. 4 (December 1961), 449.

These investigators found that endomorphs and endo-mesomorphs exceeded the other somatotype categories in the body bulk measures of body weight, Wetzel physique channel, upper arm girth, chest girth, and hip width; in general, the mesomorphs had higher means on these measures than did the ectomorphs and midtypes. Due to their excessive weight, the endomorphs were at a great disadvantage in performing pullups and pushups; their means for these tests were .06 and 2.1 times, respectively. The mesomorphs showed superiority over the other categories in Strength Index and Physical Fitness Index, as well as pullups and pushups. The ectomorphs and midtypes had higher Physical Fitness Index means than did the endomorphs and endo-mesomorphs.

Munroe[40] found that relationships between somatotype components and measures of body structure were markedly greater than corresponding zero-order correlations when contrasting structural measures were partialed out. For example, the correlation between endomorphy and weight was .71; with height held constant, the partial correlation was .86. Also, the correlation between ectomorphy and standing height was insignificant; with weight held constant, the partial rose to a high .926. These results demonstrate that the physique type is largely independent of body size; a mesomorph can be small or large, young or old. Both Munroe with 13-year-old boys and Sinclair[41] with boys at each age 9, 10, 11, and 12 years obtained multiple correlations between .887 and .964 between somatotype components and anthropometric measures. Multiple regression equations to predict the components at the several ages appear in their studies.

NUTRITIONAL STATUS

The physical educator's interest in nutrition and nutritional status has been well-established over the years, partly in connection with physical fitness and as a result of a concern for cosmetic values. The argument is advanced that proper posture and weight control are important adjuncts to be considered in activity programs. However, the interest in nutrition has important health overtones; the idea that obesity and cardiovascular disease are related is not new. Some problems in this regard may be solved with human subjects and others will employ animals; in both cases, however, the relationship between diet and physical performance is usually seen to be a physiological problem rather than one of growth and development.

---

[40] Richard A. Munroe, "Relationship Between Somatotype Components and Maturity, Structural, Strength, Musuclar Endurance, and Motor Ability Measures of Twelve-Year-Old Boys," microcard Doctoral Dissertation, University of Oregon, 1964.

[41] Sinclair, *op. cit.*

Unfortunately, this point of view would tend to ignore the supposition that the adult is a product of his childhood, that habits and patterns of activity or inactivity condition to a large extent the future behavior of the individual. If physical education is able to achieve its objectives, one would suppose that activity encouraged at the younger ages should somehow carry over to the mature years. Whether or not this is indeed the case may depend upon a host of factors, but it should underscore the desirability of studying nutritional patterns during childhood and adolescence, both with the aim to identify poor nutritional practices and to plot objectively developmental progress. A number of nutritional tests are available.[42]

Wetzel Grid

One of the widely used devices to assess nutritional status is the Wetzel Grid,[43] developed to study the individual differences in the growth of children and to provide a guide to adequate overall growth. The grid is arranged into physique channels based upon a child's age, height, and weight, which proceed from A_4 (obese) through M (average) to B_4 (thin). In addition, the subject's developmental level is given so that as growth occurs, his progress can be followed both with regard to direction and speed.

The relationships with various aspects of the Wetzel Grid for boys 9 to 15 years of age was studied by Weinberg.[44] A multiple correlation of .90 was obtained between the physique channels and upper arm girth, standing height, and body weight; this coefficient was increased to .96 with the addition of sitting height and leg length. Among the strength measures, only the Physical Fitness Index indicated a trend in body strength according to physique channels. The means of the borderline, fair, and good groups were significantly higher than the means of the stocky and obese groups. The developmental level correlated .98 with body weight. The highest correlations with the developmental ratio were .55 for calf girth, .51 for chest girth and for body weight, and .48 for upper arm girth.

Skinfolds

Skinfold thickness has long been a technique for estimating total body fat in humans and is considered useful for large scale testing. Lacking the

[42] H. Harrison Clarke, *Application of Measurement to Health and Physical Education*, *op. cit.*, Ch. 5.

[43] Normal C. Wetzel, *The Treatment of Growth Failure in Children* (Cleveland: NEA Service, Inc., 1948).

[44] Herbert A. Weinberg, "Structural, Strength, and Maturity Characteristics as Related to Aspects of the Wetzel Grid for Boys Nine Through Fifteen Years of Age," microcard Doctoral Dissertation, University of Oregon, 1964.

sophistication of other body composition procedures, such as the densitometric method outlined in Chapter 13, it has been useful as an index of nutritional status. Although much of the research utilizing these methods has been with adult males, their use with children has been encouraged.

The usual type of instrument employed is the skinfold caliper;[45] the sites selected are dependent upon the use to which the measures will be put. Care must be exercised in obtaining the skinfold to insure that identical procedures are followed for every subject. This technique involves locating the precise area, gathering the skin in one hand, and then applying the caliper with the other. The pressure that is recommended is 10 gr per square mm;[46] in testing, the calipers should come to rest for a few seconds as the soft tissues become slightly compressed. When grasping the skin, be sure not to include underlying muscle.

One of the most common techniques for determining per cent fat is by use of the formula developed by Keys and Brozek[47] for the reference body (see Chapter 13), which may be written:

$$\text{Per cent fat} = 100\,(4.201/\text{specific gravity} - 3.813)$$

The specific gravity in this instance may be obtained by use of the following calculations:

$$\text{Specific Gravity} = 1.1017 - (0.000282)(A) - (0.000736)(B) - (0.000883)(C)$$

where A, B, and C are the abdominal, chest, and arm skinfolds, respectively. Instructions for obtaining these skinfolds indicate right side measures at the following sites:

1. Abdominal skinfold: at the midaxillary line at waist level.

2. Chest skinfold: at the level of the xiphoid in the midaxillary line.

3. Arm skinfold: at the midposterior, midpoint between the tip of the acromion and the tip of the olecranon with the elbow in 90 degrees flexion and the arm hanging at the side.

Following the calculation of per cent fat, the total amount of fat may be determined as the appropriate percentage of body weight. The difference between fat weight and body weight is the lean body weight.

---

[45] Lange Skinfold Caliper, Cambridge Scientific Industries, Inc., 527 Poplar Street, Cambridge, Maryland 21613.

[46] Josef Brozek, ed., *Body Measurements and Human Physique* (Detroit: Wayne State University Press, 1956), p. 10.

[47] Ancel Keys and Josef Brozek, "Body Fat in Adult Man," *Physiological Reviews*, 33, No. 3 (July 1953), 245.

The fat may also be determined from X-ray photographs, although it may not be required since the correlation between X-ray measures of adipose tissue and skinfolds obtained by caliper ranges from .79 to .88.[48,49] The relationship of skinfold measures of 12-year-old boys to various maturity, physique, strength, muscular endurance, and motor ability characteristics was investigated by Geser.[50] When correlated with physique components, endomorphy had a high positive correlation of .824 with adipose tissue, while ectomorphy correlated negatively, −.657. The remainder of the correlations of adipose tissue with maturity, mesomorphy, strength, and motor measures were relatively low.

STRENGTH

Muscular strength has been of interest to researchers in physical education from the earliest times. The physiological aspects of strength have been prime targets of investigation, as muscular performance is a functional variable; the pattern of its activity is also of interest to the kinesiologist. The researcher in growth and development has yet another concern for strength, as an indicator of the growing process and its relationship to other motor performance variables.

The mean growth curves for right and left grips, leg lift, pushups and pullups, and Strength Index, as obtained by cross-sectional analysis,[51] are shown in Figure 30 (pp. 408–9). A relatively slow but consistent increase in mean grip strength occurred from 9 to 12 years of age, at which time it accelerated until 14 years of age, when it was followed by a slight deceleration. The pattern for leg lift was quite similar: a rather slow increase from 9 to 11 years of age, followed by a pronounced acceleration to 14 years of age, and then some deceleration at 15 years of age. The mean growth curves for pullups and pushups changed in a similar manner, although both were erratic. No real increase was apparent from 9 to 13 years of age except in pushups at 12 and 13 years of age; both variables accelerated after this period. The Strength Index curve resembled right and left grip, with a

---

[48] H. Harrison Clarke, L. Richard Geser, and Stanley B. Hunsdon, "Comparison of Upper Arm Measurements by Use of Roentgenogram and Anthropometric Techniques," *Research Quarterly*, 27, No. 4 (December 1956), 379.

[49] Stanley M. Garn and E. L. Gorman, "Comparison of Pinch-Caliper and Teleoroentgenogrammetric Measurements of Subcutaneous Fat," *Human Biology*, 28, No. 4 (December 1956), 407.

[50] Leo Richard Geser, "Skin Fold Measures of Twelve-Year-Old Boys as Related to Various Maturity, Physique, Strength, and Motor Measures," microcard Doctoral Dissertation, University of Oregon, 1965.

[51] Clarke and Wickens, *op. cit.*

moderate increase during 9 to 11 years of age with a rapid acceleration to 15 years of age.

Borms[52] investigated the relationship between selected maturity, physique, body size, and motor tests and gross and relative strength of boys 10, 13, and 16 years of age. The strength criteria utilized were Rogers' Strength Index and the average of 11 cable-tension strength tests as gross muscular strength measures and the Rogers' Physical Fitness Index as the relative muscular strength measure. Three strength groups, high, average, and low, were arranged for each of the three strength criteria at each of the three ages. It was found that, generally, the groups high in gross strength recorded significantly higher means than did the lower strength groups on maturity, body size measures, tests of motor ability elements, and mesomorphy. The low gross strength groups had significantly higher ectomorphy means. The high 10- and 13-year-olds on Strength Index and the cable-tension tests average recorded significantly higher mesomorphy and meso-endomorphy means, respectively. It was also found that, in terms of relative strength, the body size means of the low PFI groups were significantly higher than the means of the high groups. In most cases, the low PFI groups recorded significantly higher endomorphy means than did the high group. The high-low and average-low groups differed significantly on ectomorphy means, favoring the higher strength groups. At all ages, with one exception, the high PFI groups realized significantly higher means on motor ability tests.

MOTOR PERFORMANCE

Motor performance is a broad term, including a wide variety of physical tasks, such as running, jumping, throwing, and the like, and it extends to a number of athletic events, such as track and field and swimming. The development of such abilities through childhood to maturity should be of interest to those in physical education, as they have been to those studying other developmental traits.

By correlational analysis, Clarke and Degutis[53] studied the relationship between the standing broad jump and various maturity, structural, and strength measures of 12-year-old boys. The multiple correlations obtained were: (a) anthropometry: .41 with body weight, leg length, and lung capacity;

---

[52] Jan B. L. Borms, "Relationships Between Selected Maturity, Physique, Body Size, and Motor Factors and the Gross and Relative Strength of Ten-, Thirteen-, and Sixteen-Year-Old Boys," microcard Master's Thesis, University of Oregon, 1965.

[53] H. Harrison Clarke and Ernest W. Degutis, "Relationships Between Standing Broad Jump and Various Maturational, Anthropometric, and Strength Tests of 12-Year-Old Boys," *Research Quarterly*, 35, No. 3 (October 1964), 258.

(b) cable-tension strength: .52 with elbow flexion and hip extension; (c) combined variables: .69 with elbow flexion strength, body weight, hip extension strength, ankle plantar flexion strength, and leg length.

Flynn[54] studied various methods of scoring the standing broad jump performances of 12-year-old boys and obtained the following correlations (in parenthesis) and multiple correlations (*R*) with physical and motor traits:

R	SBJ scoring	Physical and motor tests
.917	Distance × weight	Weight (.84), Strength Index (.64), skin fold total (.44), abdominal girth (.63).
.908	Weight/distance	Abdominal girth (.87), Physical Fitness Index (−.44), skin fold total (.79)
.717	Leg length/distance	Physical Fitness Index (.50), leg length (.45), 10-foot run (.33), skin fold total (.44)
.690	Distance	Physical Fitness Index (.47), 10-foot run (−.42), sitting height (.22), skin fold total (−.33), cable-tension strength average (.35).

The relationship between maturity, physique type, structural, strength, and motor ability items and the 60-yard shuttle run performance of 14-year-old boys was examined by Radcliff.[55] Seventy-eight per cent of the correlations between the shuttle run and the experimental variables were significant at or beyond the .05 level. The highest correlation with the time element of the shuttle run was −.57 for standing broad jump. The highest coefficient of five multiple correlations computed with the 60-yard shuttle run was .65; the independent variables were standing broad jump, Physical Fitness Index, and total-body reaction time.

SUMMARY

Interest in growth and development has existed for a long time. The remains of ancient societies revealed that body size and physical dimension were understood and appreciated by sculptors and artisans. From accounts of athletic contests, it has become apparent that human physique and strength

[54] Kenneth W. Flynn, "Relationship Between Various Standing Broad Jump Measures and Strength, Speed, Body Size, and Physique Measures of Twelve-Year-Old Boys," unpublished Master's Thesis equivalent, University of Oregon, 1966.

[55] Robert A. Radcliff, "Relationships Between the Sixty-Yard Shuttle Run and Various Maturity, Physique, Structural, Strength, and Motor Characteristics of Fourteen-Year-Old Boys," microcard Master's Thesis, University of Oregon, 1965.

were important physical attributes. The 17th century saw the emergence of the field of anthropometry in the science of human biology.

A number of growth studies has been undertaken in the past to provide continuing data collection over several years. The major intent of most of these studies has been to obtain measures of physical dimensions of boys and girls during childhood and adolescence. Occasionally, variables of physical strength and motor ability were included, but the recent Medford, Oregon, Boys' Growth Study is probably the first major endeavor in physical education that emphasized the physical and motor growth patterns. Studying boys from 17 to 18 years of age, such factors as body structure, maturity, coordinated strength elements and batteries, agility, speed, and muscular power have been studied.

Anthropometry is the systematized measurement of the human body. No unanimity exists among researchers concerning the selection of sites or the method of obtaining data, but certain sources of error should be anticipated and every effort made to eliminate them. Such matters as interfering clothing, accuracy of measurement, and instrument calibration must be rigidly standardized if serial determinations are to be comparable from one examination to another.

Maturity measures give a different picture of the development of children than either chronological age or size factors taken separately. The skeletal age may be determined by taking the hand-wrist X ray and comparing the degree of ossification of the bones and epiphyses with known standards. Pubescent assessment, on the other hand, can be determined by evaluation of the onset of secondary sex characteristics and can be divided into various stages that categorize the population under study. Although less exact than skeletal age in differentiating growth, the pubescent assessment does reveal important information during the adolescent period.

The most widely used technique for determining physique type is the somatotype, in which the body is categorized into various degrees of endomorphy, mesomorphy, and ectomorphy. The performance capabilities of individuals, given certain body classifications, have been the subject of investigation, thus linking the important factors of body form and function.

Nutritional status may be evaluated in several ways, depending upon the outcomes desired. The Wetzel Grid was developed to study the individual differences in growth of children so that the level of development and the relative amounts of leanness and obesity could be evaluated. A direct method of calculating body fat is by means of skin folds whereby certain sites are selected and measured and the specific gravity is determined.

Growth and development are also assessed from measures of strength and motor performance. Growth curves of strength seem to follow the general trend of the organism as a whole, but these factors may depend upon whether they are gross measures or apportioned to body size.

SELECTED REFERENCES

Brozek, Josef, ed., *Body Measurements and Human Physique*. Detroit: Wayne State University Press, 1956.

Clarke, H. Harrison, *Application of Measurement to Health and Physical Education* (4th ed.), Englewood Cliffs, N.J.: Prentice-Hall, Inc., 1967.

Espenschade, Anna S., and Helen M. Eckert, *Motor Development*. Columbus, Ohio: Charles E. Merrill Books, Inc., 1968.

Greulich, William Walter, and S. Idell Pyle, *Radiographic Atlas of Skeletal Development of the Hand and Wrist* (2nd ed.), Stanford, California: Stanford University Press, 1959.

Stewart, T. D., ed., *Hrdlička's Practical Anthropometry*, 4th ed. Philadelphia: The Wistar Institute of Anatomy and Biology, 1952.

Sheldon, William H., *Atlas of Men*. New York: Harper & Row, Publishers, 1954.

Stoltz, H. R., and L. M. Stoltz, *Somatic Development of Adolescent Boys*. New York: The Macmillan Company, 1951.

Tanner, J. M., *Growth at Adolescence* (2nd ed.), Springfield, Ill.: Charles C Thomas, Publisher, 1962.

Watson, Ernest H., and George H. Lowrey, *Growth and Development of Children* (2nd ed.), Chicago: The Year Book Publishers, Inc., 1952.

Wetzel, Normal C., *The Treatment of Growth Failure in Children*. Cleveland: NEA Service, Inc., 1948.

PART V

THE RESEARCH REPORT

The final part of this book contains a single chapter, Preparation of the Research Report. This chapter is written primarily for the graduate student undertaking his first research writing. The main topics deal with the organization of the research thesis by sections and chapters, the use of written and oral sources, the construction and use of tables and graphs, forms for footnotes and bibliography, and publication based on the thesis.

CHAPTER 18

Preparation of the Research Report

The culmination of any research venture is the written report. The reader may wonder that such a statement need be made, for it is obvious that this is the next task once all research work has been done and the data have been analyzed. For the graduate student, the entire degree may hinge upon successful completion of the written thesis or dissertation, so this aspect is not only the last formal step but is the pivotal point of the whole program. However, for the sake of science, it should be stated that many scholars will not concede as evidence any data that have not been commmitted to writing and that have not stood the test of professional scrutiny. The fact that some will not accept in thesis form data that have not been published, and thereby have not been given editorial examination, is perhaps beside the point at the moment; however, the fact is that the research has not been completed until the final report is written.

The authors of this book contend that probably the most difficult part of the research program is writing the research report. It is not uncommon for even successful investigators to collect data, complete the analysis, and then let the written portion lapse, sometimes because of the pressure of time and other duties but often because it is difficult to cope with the many decisions that must be made for publication or perhaps even because the investigator has moved along to yet another project. Even so, the mark of a successful researcher is usually based upon the evaluations of published papers, not upon how busy he is collecting data.

No rules are available on writing skill, as the student will soon learn. The many books and other sources that can be found describing style and format of thesis writing will be helpful in deciding upon organizational matters, including lengthy discussion of the many ways of presenting footnotes and bibliographical entries, but none of these will tell the investigator how to write his thesis. The insistence upon rigidity and consistency of format, as valuable as it may be, is totally useless to one who must explore virgin territory in an attempt to bring order to chaos, to reduce statistical terms to meaningful statements, and to develop the underlying theoretical issues at stake. Such statements are not intended to leave the impression that no help is available to the writer, for there are things that can be mentioned that may shorten manuscript preparation time. Perhaps the best that can be said is no matter how difficult and time consuming the writing appears, it has seemed so to others before.

This chapter is written, therefore, primarily for the benefit of the graduate student undertaking his first research writing and not for the experienced investigator. Although each study is marked by individuality, nevertheless there are certain guidelines that, when followed, help to expedite the writing phase. Each institution, and sometimes departments or colleges within an institution, will have its own preferred form for thesis writing. In the larger universities, format guides are published and available to the student; these are helpful because they provide organizational consistency and thus relieve the author of the task of trying to guess on a number of what may be called minor details. Anything that will make the task easier is welcomed, and the author should immediately investigate such sources and follow them exactly. This should be done before the serious writing has started.

The primary suggestions given here are based upon writing the thesis, although consideration must also be given to the possibility of preparing the report for publication in some research journal. The graduate student should be alert to this possibility after finishing the thesis. In such instances, the journals themselves periodically publish their own guide to contributors, giving suggestions regarding such items as format, size, preparation of figures and tables, number of copies to be prepared, and where to send the manuscript.

ORGANIZATION OF THE THESIS REPORT

Quite obviously, the thesis report is organized into chapters, each of which serves a distinctive purpose. Preceding the chapters are certain "front" materials followed by other items of essential information. Institutions vary somewhat in detail as to how the various parts of the report should be handled but agree in general practice. Some appropriate suggestions pertaining to the overall thesis organization are given in this section.

Front Materials

Several items typically appear in the front of the thesis report; some may not be required at all institutions, and others may be optional with the student.

Vita. Some institutions require a vita as the first typed page in the thesis, inserted between a blank flyleaf and the title page. The vita includes such information about the investigator as the following, presented in outline form: (1) full name of the author and his place and date of birth; (2) undergraduate and graduate schools attended and degrees awarded with dates; (3) relevant professional experiences; (4) awards and honors received and professional offices held; (5) list of professional publications with complete bibliographical references.

Title Page. The institution where the thesis is written dictates the form of the title page. However, it is a single page containing the title of the thesis, the author's full name, and a statement indicating the college or university, name of the degree, and date the degree was awarded. An illustration of the latter statement is:

A THESIS

Presented to the School of Health, Physical Education, and Recreation
and the Graduate School of the University of Oregon
in partial fulfillment
of the requirements for the degree of
Master of Science
June 1968

The title of the study should be kept as short as possible consistent with a clear indication of the subject. Some words and phrases are redundant, such as "A Study of . . ." and "An Analysis of . . . ." The use of articles, such as "A" and "The," to precede the title are unnecessary: for example: not "A Comparative Study of . . ." but "Comparison of . . . ." Illustrations of some satisfactory titles are:

Muscular Strength Interrelationships Among Upper Elementary, Junior High, and Senior High School boys

Construction of a Motor Performance Test for Elementary School Girls

Longitudinal Analyses of Strength and Motor Development of Boys Seven Through Twelve Years of Age

Stability of Physique Types of Boys Nine Through Twelve Years of Age

Work Capacity of Altitude Acclimatized Men at Altitude and Sea Level

Approval page. Again, the institution at which the thesis is written specifies the form of the approval page. Typically, it is centered on a single sheet, immediately following the title page and bearing only the following:

APPROVED: (Signature of thesis adviser)
(Typed name of thesis adviser)

At some institutions, only the adviser of the thesis signs the approval sheet; at other colleges and universities, all members of the thesis (examining) committee sign.

Dedication. Dedication of the thesis is usually optional and is entirely a personal matter. However, many graduate students find use of the dedication an opportunity to recognize someone who has been a source of help and encouragement during the arduous period of study for the graduate degree. Subjects for dedications have been parents, wives or husbands, children, and others who may have given significant support to the student. The dedication should not be a eulogy but a simple designation, centered on a separate page, following the approval page.

Acknowledgements. Usually, the graduate student has had significant help from others in completing the thesis requirement. Certainly, such would be true for the thesis adviser and, possibly, members of his committee. Acknowledgements of this indebtedness on a separate page following the dedication is a thoughtful and gracious gesture on the part of the graduate student. Other sources of acknowledgments, when applicable, are: fellow graduate students who may have helped with testing or in other ways; subjects in toto if they participated repeatedly; administrators or teachers in schools where the study may have been conducted or testing accomplished; and sources of financial support. Acknowledgments should be simple and direct and not personal or effusive.

Table of contents. The table of contents should include chapter titles with major subheads and, possibly, minor subheads. Inasmuch as the thesis does not contain an index, the table of contents should be sufficiently detailed to help the reader locate readily any section in which he is interested. The chapter headings are usually typed in capital letters and their subdivisions in small letters, with the first letters of principal words capitalized. The relationship between main headings and subheads is shown by proper indentions. The page numbers should not be entered until the final typing is accomplished, as changes from the final draft may occur.

List of tables. When tables appear in the thesis, a list of them should be provided next. In each instance, the exact and complete title as it appears in the text should be given. The numbering of tables is usually by Arabic numerals, although Roman numerals are used at some institutions.

List of figures. In the event illustrations are employed in the thesis, they should also be listed separately with page numbers. As for tables, the titles should be given exactly as given in the body of the thesis. Usually, figures are numbered with Arabic numerals.

The Chapters

Although circumstances alter practice, most theses contain five chapters, as follows: Chapter I, Statement of the Problem; Chapter II, Review of Related Literature; Chapter III, Research Procedures; Chapter IV, Results of the Study; Chapter V, Summary and Conclusions. In studies that result in a short, concentrated report, certain of these chapters are combined; in others, where the results are very extensive and a logical division exists, more than one "results" chapter may be utilized. Assuming that there will be five chapters, the following contents are appropriate.

Statement of the problem. Although the formal statement of the problem may be delayed until later in the chapter, an indication of the nature of the problem should come early, preferably in the first paragraph. Thus, although the thesis title gives a sketchy indication, some elaboration is helpful to the reader at the outset in order to facilitate his understanding of the subsequent discussion.

As introductory to the problem statement, the investigator should orient the reader to the importance and need for the study. Some justification for undertaking the study should be provided. This statement should lead logically and smoothly into the statement itself.

The purpose of the study should be stated clearly and concisely. It must indicate exactly what the investigator intends to do, as he will be held rigidly to this intention after the study is completed; the entire study emanates from this statement. Details concerning the problem, its statement, delimitations, and hypotheses are considered in Chapter II. Definitions of terms may be included, but only those not generally understood or those that could be misinterpreted.

The following examples are given to illustrate statements of purposes of studies. In examining these statements, list the delimitations given and itemize the information still needed that should be clarified by the investigator.

1. To relate the personality traits of 16-year-old boys, as revealed by the individual adjectives on the Davidson Adjective Check List, to their maturity, physique type, body size, strength, and motor ability characteristics.

2. To determine the relationship between academic achievement and intelligence and the maturity, physique type, body size, muscular strength and endurance, and motor ability of the same boys 9 through 17 years of age.

3. To investigate the possibility of reducing the present laborious, time-consuming process of evaluating skeletal age by assessment of all bones and epiphyses of the wrist and hand for boys 9 through 15 years of age.

4. To contrast the maturational, structural, strength, and motor factors of elementary and junior high school boys with different levels of athletic ability disclosed in interscholastic competition.

5. To evaluate the physical and motor fitness of boys and girls in each grade, 4 through 12, in the Coos Bay, Oregon, School District.

6. To explore muscular strength interrelationships and to select by correlational methods the minimum number of cable-tension tests that reflect the total strength of various muscle groups of upper elementary, junior high, and senior high school girls.

Literature review. If only a limited literature exists relative to the problem, the review may be included in Chapter I. Otherwise, a separate chapter is indicated. A discussion of the literature search is contained in Chapter 3 of this text. The report of the literature should not be merely a chronological succession of abstracts of completed studies. Rather, it should be a synthesis of reports on a given related topic; there will usually be a succession of these syntheses.

Research procedures. The research procedures employed in the study should be explained in detail; the detail should be sufficient so that another investigator would be able to repeat the study precisely if desired. The nature of the study will dictate how these descriptions are made. The process varies for different kinds of studies, such as those involving the historical, philosophical, survey, or experimental method. But, in all instances, the types and sources of evidence utilized and the methods by which the evidence was evaluated must be presented.

Thus, for the historical study, the primary and secondary sources consulted and their evaluation by external and internal criticisms should be described. For a philosophical study, the hypotheses formed and the evidence employed to evaluate them should be stated. For surveys by questionnaire or interview, the construction of the inquiry forms, the selection of the individuals or institutions to be surveyed, the method of conducting the survey, and means of analyzing the replies should be presented.

In scientific studies, testing instruments are utilized, subjects are tested, and test data are analyzed statistically. For an experimental study, a single group may be used or two or more groups may be formed; for a relationship study, a criterion of some sort is usually employed and experimental variables are related to it; for comparative studies, specific groups are identified and evaluated with appropriate tests. In all instances, these procedures must be carefully described, including: the process of selecting subjects, descriptions of tests employed and their evaluation, the qualifications and training of testers, the application of the particular scientific method adopted, the experimental controls employed, and the statistical method applied in analyzing the data. Common formulas need not be given; unusual ones, however, might well be listed.

Any unique circumstances encountered in conducting the study should be described. Examples follow:

1. If the subjects are unusual in any way, additional descriptions of them may be desirable; consequently, generalizations made will be limited to such samples as described. To illustrate: One of the authors, while at Springfield College, used physical education majors in studies; therefore, the samples were not only indicated as random at that institution but percentile bar graphs were presented showing their height, weight, and Physical Fitness Index patterns, and three-dimensional shields showing their somatotype distributions were provided.

2. In longitudinal growth studies, subjects drop from the sample for various reasons, especially leaving the schools when parents move from the community. Whether or not this unavoidable attrition appreciably changes the sample is a moot question. In the Medford Boys' Growth Study, this effect was checked by comparing those who continued with and those who dropped from the original sample by comparisons with several representative tests.

3. If a pilot study was conducted, its description and results should be included.

4. Any method that was tried and abandoned and the reasons why it was inadequate or valueless should be stated.

5. If new apparatus and equipment or variations of old ones are employed, the validity and reliability of these tests should be established; detailed descriptions and drawings of them may frequently be indicated.

Research results. Usually, the research results are contained in a single chapter, although one or more additional chapters may be used if the situation warrants. Such additional chapters may be desirable when the results are especially extensive and fall into essentially discrete divisions. Seldom, however, is more than one chapter employed for this purpose.

Specific directions cannot be given for organizing this chapter because of the wide variety of studies and the kinds of data that exist. In an historical study, a narrative is told through a series of chronological and/or topical subjects. Philosophical reports center around hypotheses or principles with rational support from existing evidence and its critical appraisal. Survey results usually consist of appropriate tables and charts portraying the status of the conditions investigated. Experimental and relationship studies will focus upon tables and, possibly, graphs containing analyses of test data and the application of tests of significance.

The discussion in the results chapter must be presented systematically, which necessitates a logical flow of information. Generally, comparative findings should not be included in this chapter but should be reserved for the final chapter; straight reporting of results should be the purpose. When test data are utilized in studies, the raw scores may not be included, although some investigators preserve them for possible future reference by placing them at the end of the thesis in an appendix. Instead, tables and graphs will be employed to report the statistical analyses of the raw scores. The detailed information in such tables and graphs is not detailed in the text. Rather, the investigator presents the salient features of the results and interprets for the reader what the facts mean. This process may be quite simple when tables contain only several entries, but it may be very difficult when several hundred entries are made, as in an intercorrelational matrix with a large number of variables.

Summary and conclusions. The final chapter should give an overview of the study. Briefly, the purpose of the study, the methods employed, and the results should be summarized, and the conclusions should be stated and supported.

Table 23

Illustration of a Summarizing Table *t* Ratios Between Academic Performance Means

	Achievement tests			Grade point averages		
Experimental variables	9 yrs.	12 yrs.	15 yrs.	9 yrs.	12 yrs.	15 yrs.
Strength Index	3.00	.83	.13	5.69	1.53	1.10
Physical Fitness Index	2.31	.19	.03	.94	3.14	2.00
Rogers' Arm Strength Score	.76	.85	.33	1.94	1.21	2.19
McCloys' Classif. Index	2.06	1.17	1.86	1.84	.56	1.20
Wetzel Dev. Level	.83	1.07	2.22	1.67	1.27	.85

If extensive statistical analyses have been employed, tables that summarize the prominent features from several related tables presented in the results chapter will prove highly effective for this purpose. To illustrate: In a study by Jarman,[1] a series of high and low scoring groups of 20 boys each were formed separately on the basis of three strength and two growth measures at each age, 9, 12, and 15 years; each of the 15 pairs of high and low groups was equated by use of intelligence quotients. The differences among means on standard academic achievement tests and grade point averages were tested for significance by application of the *t* ratio. The numerous *t* ratios are shown in Table 23 in order to summarize these results in a single table. For these comparisons, a *t* ratio of 2.00 is significant at the .05 level. The essential results of the entire study can be seen readily from examination of this table.

Comparison of the results of the study should be made with those obtained by other investigators. Although a study rarely precisely duplicates another, nevertheless some bases for comparison may exist. For example, studies of the characteristics of athletes have been conducted by several

[1] Boyd O. Jarman, "Academic Achievement of Boys Nine, Twelve, and Fifteen Year, of Age as Related to Various Strength and Growth Measures," microcard Master's Thesis University of Oregon, 1959.

investigators; another study may use some of the same or similar variables or different ages or levels of athletic ability may be involved, and comparisons should be made. Further, the unique contribution of the investigation should be fitted into the body of knowledge in the study area.

In the conclusions, the purposes of the study as stated in Chapter I should be satisfied. What were the results in regard to the purposes to be achieved? If hypotheses had been stated, their tenability should now be indicated. If questions had been asked to define the scope of the study, they should be answered. Any shortcomings or deficiencies in the study should be noted. Any contradictions encountered should be resolved insofar as the evidence permits; speculation is permissible but only when so indicated. Frequently, suggestions for future studies may be desirable, although not mandatory.

Back Materials

Bibliography. A bibliography should be included, immediately following the last chapter of the research report. The bibliography should contain all references appearing in footnotes throughout the thesis but need not be so restricted. Any other materials particularly pertinent to the research may be included at the discretion of the investigator. However, loading a bibliography with irrelevant or insignificant references is contraindicated; it should contain only those references that the author found useful in the solution of the problem.

The bibliography should be alphabetized by authors' last names. If an author has more than one reference, they should be arranged alphabetically under his name by title. If he has published with others, his single references should be listed first; then joint publications should appear alphabetized by associate authors. If the bibliography is especially lengthy, some classification scheme may be desirable. Such schemes could be by topic or historical period or by type of publication, such as books, articles, theses, and the like.

Appendix. An appendix is not always utilized in the thesis report. However, one or more appendices may be useful when cumbersome or voluminous material not essential to understanding of the text needs to be recorded. Examples are: raw data from testing, questionnaires, test forms, descriptions of tests (especially when many are used), form letters, lists of cooperating individuals or institutions, daily exercise regimens, and the like. The appendix should not be a depository for miscellaneous or irrelevant materials; each entry should be justified as needed for an adequate understanding of the thesis.

Chapter Organization

Time spent at the start, before actual writing begins, in organizing the research report will be valuably spent. The first thing most thesis advisers look at is the sequential and orderly presentation of the material: whether or not it flows smoothly from item to item throughout. Any time duplication occurs, the researcher should examine its necessity; usually duplication can be avoided. However, occasional cross reference may be desirable, either by referring to material elsewhere in the report or by brief summarization as introductory to the presentation of new but relevant material.

The broad organization of the thesis by units and chapters was discussed in the preceding section. The use of headings and subheadings within each chapter will prove most beneficial in aiding the reader to follow the thesis presentation and will make easy the location of specific materials within the chapter. Headings may be designated as orders. This book employs a four-order system, which has proven successful and meets most organizational situations. These orders are:

First order: center heading
Second order: marginal heading
Third order: paragraph heading
Fourth order: numbered items under third-order headings

In this section of this chapter, the first-order heading is "Organization of the Thesis Report." The second-order headings are: "Front Materials," "The Chapters," "Back Materials," and "Chapter Organization." All but the last of the second-order headings have third-order headings; under "Back Materials," they are "Bibliography" and "Appendix."

A given order should not be employed unless two or more subheads of the order are desired. As can be seen in the above, the numbers in the various orders are: first order, one (but more will follow in this chapter); second-order, three; third order, eight, five, and two for the respective second-order headings; fourth order, not appearing in this chapter, but can be found elsewhere in this book.

The student inexperienced in thesis writing should examine recently completed studies at his institution, especially those in the field and allied to his own problem. A completed, acceptable report will provide the novice not only with an overview of an investigation properly put together but will give him many hints on how tricky problems he encounters may be resolved. The way tables and graphs are constructed, employed, and summarized will be particularly helpful, as will be the handling of hypotheses, the formulation of generalizations, and the drawing of supportable conclusions.

USE OF SOURCES

A matter of grave concern to the writer is the proper use of sources. No research report is complete without ample evidence that the sources of pertinent information have been examined. The great bulk of such material will appear as a review of the literature, but other sections of the thesis will contain various references appropriate to the study as well. The investigator bears the responsibility for making proper selections, and then he must see that they are cited correctly. The point cannot be stressed too strongly that each citation must be absolutely correct, both in terms of the footnote or bibliographical entry and in content. Failure to do so may well lead to loss of confidence on the part of the reader, who may feel that mistakes here could mean similar carelessness elsewhere in the study. The last thing a scientist wants is to engender the nagging doubt that perhaps he is not careful.

An author will make a number of decisions in presenting his material, chief among them being the selection of references. A discussion of the review of literature has been presented in Chapter 3 of this text, so it will be assumed that this task has been completed. The important thing now is to put it into writing. One of the important requisites is to give proper credit to sources utilized. This extends from the abstracting of appropriate results of various investigations to the use of ideas garnered from various authorities. Failure to do this is considered plagiarism and cannot be condoned.

No clear distinction can be given to help the writer make all decisions of this sort; certainly, the flagrant use of another's words and phraseology as one's own would constitute a breach of ethics. On the other hand, certain concepts of a scientific nature may be so well-established as to be considered in the public domain. If the author is speaking from his own general knowledge of his subject matter gained over a period of several years or is discussing theoretical matters that are not particularly controversial, no citation to a source may be required. However, in discussing new findings or rather poorly established theory, the author should give credit to the authors of such information. Little can be said for the practice of documenting facts by giving as reference undergraduate textbooks, unless it is considered essential to establish the premise that something is widely purported to be true. In such an instance the author may be preparing the way to suggest new findings or interpretations of a contradictory nature.

Thus, it is incumbent that the author give credit where credit is due, according to the procedures established for proper citation. One major point should be mentioned, however, which seems to cause much difficulty with beginning writers: when to quote and when not to quote. Differences of opinion may occur on this point, but the basic premise here is to avoid the use of quotations if at all possible. A far better technique is to paraphrase and cite the reference. If the author's words must be preserved, if the statement is so concise and technical that paraphrasing would destroy the full impact of what is being said, then it may be desirable to quote the text exactly, once again citing the reference. Such a practice should be followed judiciously and the passages selected with great care. Excessively long quotes are usually unnecessary in research, although the examination of sources in historical research may justify their greater use. Actually, reliance upon quotations is not evidence of high scholarship, for it serves as a crutch to the writer who rationalizes that since the original author said it so well, why change it. In most cases, such passages can be paraphrased to fit the context of the writer's discussion and many times far better than by direct quotation. Further, in reporting on the literature, materials from several sources may be synthesized in a single paragraph, which is superior writing to stringing out a series of quotes.

When short quotations, say three lines or less, are used, the passage should be included in the paragraph and enclosed in double quotation marks; a quotation within the quotation is identified by single quotation marks. Periods, commas, and question marks ending quotations are within the quotation marks; colons and semicolons at end of quotations are outside the quotation marks. Footnote reference numbers are outside the quotation marks, unless appearing with the author's name, when used.

Long quotations are set off from the text in a separate passage. They should be indented four typewriter spaces from the margin and single spaced. Quotation marks are omitted. The usual footnote reference is needed as for short quotations.

Quoting from oral sources, as from a speech or conversation, presents certain hazards, especially the accuracy of the quotation. A good policy in such instances is to submit the quotation to the author for approval of authenticity; actually, the same can be said when paraphrasing from a written source. The usual acknowledgements are necessary.

If the writer wishes to delete certain words, phrases, or portions of the original statement, he may do so by inserting ellipsis dots with a typewriter space between each (. . .). Conversely, when it is considered desirable to add to the original quotation in some way, the interpolation can be made within squared brackets [ ]; parentheses should not be used for this purpose, as they may appear in the original quote, so the differentiation between a quote and an interpolation would be obscure. When using either ellipses or interpolations, the burden of responsibility for such alterations is solely with the writer; he must not change the meaning or intent of the original statement.

Italicized words in a quotation, as elsewhere, are underlined. If the writer wishes to italicize words not italicized in the original, he may do so but must so indicate. Such an indication may be made in a footnote or in squared brackets immediately after the italicization, such as [italics not in original].

TABLES

Tables are frequently utilized in research reporting. In some reports, a large number of tables may be used, especially in comparative, relationship, growth, and survey studies. In experimental research, the number will usually be fewer; and they may not be employed at all in historical and philosophical studies. The novice researcher, therefore, should become familiar with the use of tables and their construction.

Construction

Various points in the construction of tables are as follows:

1. Emphasize only one significant fact in each table. Each table should present results as simply and concisely as possible.

2. Avoid crowded tables. If tables become too crowded, ways should be considered to make logical divisions of them or to arrange the material into more than one table.

3. Arrange tabulations in a logical manner. Space columns of figures so they may be easily read.

4. Construct the tables so that they may be read from right to left.

5. Although other arrangements are permissible, one acceptable way of ruling the table is as follows:

(a) Double horizontal line at the top, under the table title.
(b) Single horizontal line to separate the column headings from the table data.
(c) Single vertical lines to set off the main divisions of the table, although these may be omitted in simple tables. In some complex tables, vertical lines may also be used to mark off minor subdivisions.
(d) Omit vertical lines at both right and left margins.
(e) Use either a horizontal line or a double space after every fifth row of figures in a long table.
(f) Draw horizontal line at bottom of the table.

6. Align right-hand digits in columns of figures, except when decimal points are used. Decimal points must always be aligned.

7. Use superior letters ([a], [b], [c], etc.) to mark footnotes to a table, and place these notes directly beneath the table.

8. Label the table in sufficient detail so that it may be read and understood without supplementary explanation. Use a single phrase and avoid use of unnecessary words.

9. The table number and title should be at the top of the table. All letters in the title should be capitalized.

In the textual discussion, the writer should refer to the table by number; the relevancy of the salient information in the table should be explained. The table itself should appear after its mention in the text at the first convenient location. Generally, it should not interrupt a paragraph but should be placed after the paragraph on the same page if space permits; if space is not sufficient for the complete table, it should be located on the following page. If the table is wider than it is long, it may be placed broadside on the page if desired; this arrangement is preferable to using a second page.

Long tables of a page or more should occupy separate pages, starting at the top of the first one. Pages for a long table should be consecutive; the table title need not be repeated but merely indicated as *Table, continued*, giving the number. Pages of wide tables may be pasted together and folded in.

Illustrated Tables

Illustrations of actual tables utilized in research reports will be given. Many unique situations may be encountered, so the coverage by the illustrations is very limited. The student should study a number of research reports, expecially in the area of his own study, in order to gain some insight into ways by which various problems pertaining to tables have been resolved by others.

Simple table. Brose and Hanson[2] studied the effects of overload training on velocity and accuracy of throwing a regulation baseball for college men. As one phase of the investigation, correlations were computed to determine the relationship between successive test days for velocity and accuracy scores for both pre-training and post-training sessions. The table presented by these investigators has been adapted slightly and is shown in Table 24.

Table 24

Pre-Training and Post-Training Reliability for Velocity and Accuracy

Source	Pre-Training Velocity	Pre-Training Accuracy	Post-Training Velocity	Post-Training Accuracy
Day 1 vs 2	.98	.23	.94	.65
Day 2 vs 3	.94	.54	.93	.69
Day 3 vs 4	.92	.24	.92	.55

[2] Donald E. Brose and Dale L. Hanson, "Effects of Overload Training on Velocity and Accuracy of Throwing," *Research Quarterly*, 38, No. 4 (December 1967), 528.

As can be readily seen from the table, the correlations for the velocity rates were high, between .92 and .98. The correlations for accuracy were lower but especially low at the pre-training level.

Complex pattern. The handling of tables in an analysis of variance problem and subsequent tests of significance for paired means when a significant F ratio is obtained is fairly complex. Stafford[3] made single-age and longitudinal comparisons of the intelligence and academic achievement of elementary and junior high school athletes and nonparticipants. Athletes were judged by their coaches on their performances in interscholastic athletics, as follows: 3, outstanding athlete; 2, regular player; and 1, substitute. All other boys were designated as *NP*, nonparticipant; when individual sports were considered, boys who were athletes in other sports but not in the one under scrutiny were classified *NPA*. One phase of the study consisted of analysis of variance for Iowa Test of Educational Development means for 15-year-old track athletes in junior high school. The results of this analysis of variance not only for the composite score on the ITED but also for the means of the various parts of the test are shown in Table 25.

The F ratios for Reading in Social Studies, Composite Score, and Sources of Information were significant at the .05 level. Consequently, the Scheffe test to determine the significance between all pairs of means was made for

Table 25

Analysis of Variance for Iowa Test of Educational Development; Comparison of Fifteen-Year-Old Nonparticipants, Nonparticipating Athletes, and Track Athletes

ITED	Means				Mean Squares		F
	NP	*NPA*	1	2, 3	Within	Between	Ratio[a]
Basic social concepts	18.21	16.38	18.00	17.25	31.179	33.546	1.08
Background natural science	16.48	15.84	18.00	14.75	30.392	30.161	.99
Corr. and approp. expression	13.93	13.41	15.71	13.56	21.060	18.969	.90
Quantitative thinking	15.35	14.92	16.21	15.00	29.573	6.284	.21
Reading in social studies	15.06	12.35	18.22	10.82	37.354	130.549	3.50[b]
Reading in natural sciences	14.94	13.05	18.22	11.36	43.844	96.754	2.21
Literary materials	13.29	14.00	14.78	12.94	32.026	14.242	.45
General vocabulary	15.69	15.22	17.36	14.94	28.220	18.678	.66
Composite scores	16.04	12.95	19.33	12.09	32.558	137.411	4.22[b]
Sources of information	15.59	13.00	18.22	10.73	36.011	133.960	3.72[b]

[a] F ratio needed for significance at .05 level between 2.65 and 2.69 depending on degrees of freedom.

[b] Significant.

[3] Elba G. Stafford, "Single-Age and Longitudinal Comparisons of Intelligence and Academic Achievement of Elementary and Junior High School Athletes and Nonparticipants," microcard Doctoral Dissertation, University of Oregon, August 1968.

Table 26

Scheffe Test for ITED Composite Score; Comparison of Fifteen-Year-Old Nonparticipants, Nonparticipating Athletes, and Track Athletes

Means				Diff.	Confidence limits[a]	
NP	*NPA*	1	2, 3	means	Lower	Higher
16.04	12.95			3.09	.84	5.34[b]
16.04		19.33		−3.29	−6.55	−.03[b]
16.04			12.09	3.95	1.17	6.73[b]
	12.95	19.33		−6.38	−10.11	−2.65[b]
	12.95		12.09	.86	−2.12	3.84
		19.33	12.09	7.24	3.07	11.41[b]

[a] Confidence interval amount, 2.25 to 4.17 depending on degrees of freedom.

[b] Significant.

each of these tests. The results of this analysis for Composite Scores on the ITED are given in Table 26. As can be seen, the mean of the *NP*'s was significantly higher than the mean of the *NPA*'s and the 2-plus-3 athletes. The means of the 1-rated athletes were significantly superior to all other groups.

The major problem in the development of these tables was to reduce the essential analysis of variance and Scheffe test information to a minimal amount. If all available information had been included, many more tables would have been necessary: one for each analysis of variance and one for each Scheffe test. Actually, Stafford's dissertation contained 92 tables; had the above method not been used, the number of tables would have been well over 500.

FIGURES

The use of illustrations in research is widely endorsed and practiced extensively. There are occasions when the serial measurements of various functions can be presented more appropriately by a well-designed figure than by verbal description. In fact, this makes the presentation in the text much easier and clearer and conveys information to the reader more quickly. The researcher should anticipate the possibility of using graphical materials in the planning stage of the study and then prepare his data for use in this way when appropriate. Illustrations are most likely to appear in two places, namely, the methodology and results chapters. In the thesis, the former is likely to occur in Chapter 3 dealing with procedure, and the latter will be an integral part of Chapter 4 when presenting research results.

Purposes

Apparatus and techniques. The use of an illustration to show the apparatus, positioning of subject, and other technical matters pertaining to the conduct of the study can frequently be accomplished with a photograph far more effectively than by reliance upon verbal description. Such illustrations should be reserved for those techniques that are essential to a full understanding of the methodology and then only if they are rather unique. The simple and well-known procedures will not require this treatment, although it cannot be considered wrong to do so.

When taking photographs, careful attention should be given to all procedures essential to obtaining clear, accurate pictures. Lighting, background, arrangement of apparatus, and so forth are among the factors to be considered. When nothing of real value can actually be seen in the photograph, it may be better to abandon the effort; likewise, if poor background and unnecessary objects or equipment appear, it may obscure the details in such a way that the experimental procedure is lost. A suggestion in such an instance is to employ a line drawing based on the photograph where extraneous and distracting items can be eliminated. An illustration of such a drawing is contained in Figure 33 which shows the technique of administering the shoulder flexion strength test by cable-tension methods.

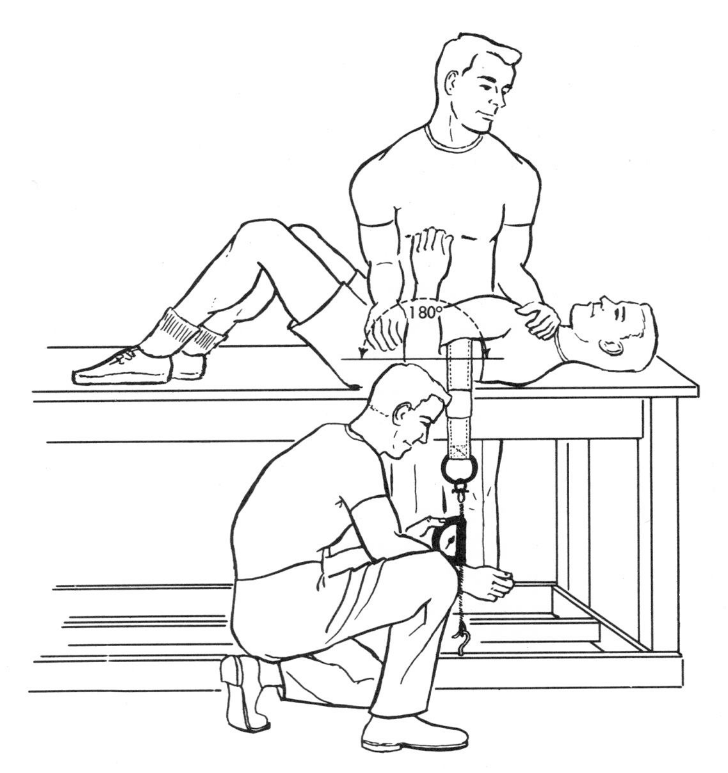

Figure 33. Shoulder Flexion Strength Test

Data presentation. The second major purpose for using illustrations in a thesis, the portrayal of results, is far more technical and requires much greater precision. The basic consideration in making effective graphs is to present the results in the simplest and most meaningful way in order to provide the greatest impact in the shortest space. This is accomplished by such things as utilizing a curve to represent a succession of values, by presenting several curves on one graph for comparative purposes, or by combining more than one variable on the same graph. The student may well examine a number of journals in the area of his study in order to gain some familiarity with and suggestions for constructing his own graphs. Some consideration of graphs is given in Chapter 7 of this text, as related to portraying a frequency distribution and cumulative frequencies and per cents. Many other types of graphs are available to the researcher, as he will note from his review of research literature.

Construction

Points to keep in mind in the logical construction of graphs to portray the results of research studies are as follows:

1. Select the type of graph that will best show the points to be emphasized.
2. Stress only one significant point in each graph.
3. Arrange the graph so that it may be read from left to right.
4. As a general rule, show the zero line on the graph. If the nature of the data is such that presentation of the zero line gives the graph a long drawn-out and unbalanced appearance, show the zero line and then place just above it on the scale two short wavy lines indicating a break in it.
5. Place the scale line at the left, except in especially wide graphs when it may be placed on both sides.
6. Distinguish clearly the line or lines of the graph from other rulings on the graph; other rulings should be kept at a minimum and only used when necessary for clarity.
7. Construct graphs that are pleasing in appearance, well-spaced and proportioned, and centered on the page.
8. Title the graph as clearly and completely as possible, using a single phrase and avoiding unnecessary words.
9. As a rule, place the title below the body of the graph.

Illustrations

The key to successful graphic presentation is to arrange the data in the most meaningful way, consolidating the values appropriately first and then arranging the ordinate and abscissa in an attempt to utilize the space as effectively as possible. The most successful figures are those that leave a minimum of unused area and are easily read. Obviously, this arrangement will depend upon the nature of the study and the type of data obtained; broad generalizations are difficult. The following suggestions, however, may prove helpful. As usual, the examples employed are selected simply to illustrate the principle rather than to serve as models of excellence.

1. It is incumbent that the investigator utilize the correct statistical treatment of the data, which has been mentioned repeatedly in this text. This trend is followed in graphic illustrations and is evidenced by the usual requirement of reducing plotted values to some measure of central tendency, notably the mean. When a number of subjects are employed, it is useless to consider the subject by subject response, since the serial mean response gives a much clearer picture. Questions of significance are answered separately as required.

2. Special mention should be made of the method of handling plotted data, especially serial determinations designed to illustrate progressive effects, such as would result from trials or successive measurements of a function over time. The tendency is to connect points on a dot-to-dot basis; this is an acceptable practice, especially when but a few points are involved. However, it may be more desirable to utilize a smooth curve in order to demonstrate linearity or curvilinearity. When each point is connected, the broken and erratic effect may confuse the analysis. A simple technique is to fit a line by visual inspection, a sort of least squares effect attempting to minimize error, and to seek an average of their positive and negative values. In the case of the exponential curve analysis discussed in Chapter 13, the smooth curve in Figure 34 is actually constructed mathematically, thereby taking on a specific value that is useful in making direct comparisons between conditions.

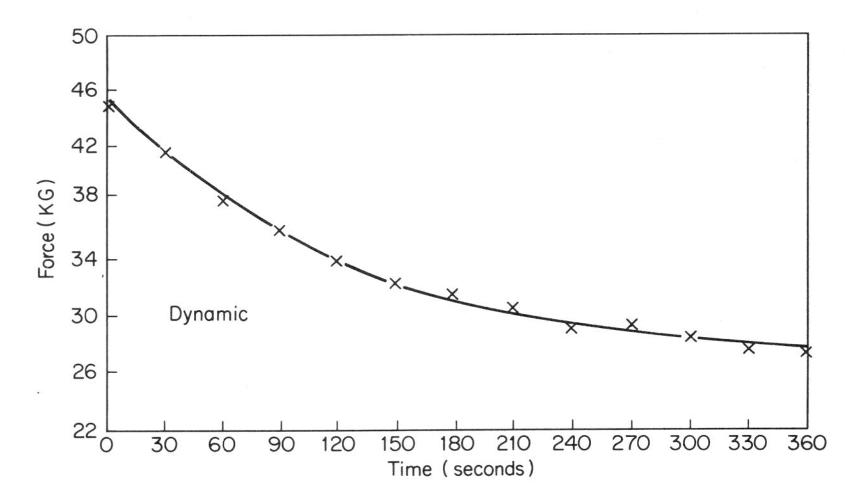

Figure 34. Single Curve Graph

3. Frequently, more than one set of data may be incorporated in a single illustration, thus saving space and making comparisons more meaningful than if presented separately. In this situation, at least one set of values must be in common between the different measures; this is ordinarily placed on the abscissa, although the reader will find examples of all sorts of combinations in the literature. The example in Figure 35 illustrates this principle.

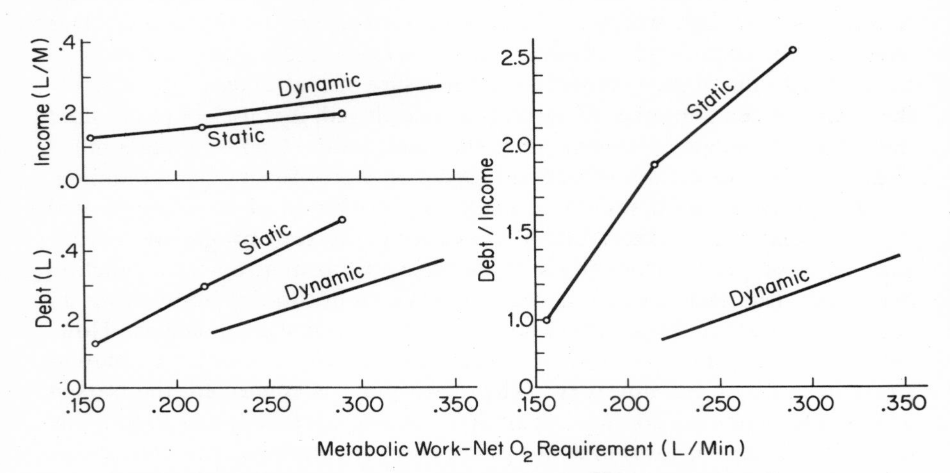

Figure 35. Multiple Curves Graph (David H. Clarke, "Energy Cost of Isometric Exercise," *Research Quarterly*, 31, No. 1 (March 1960), 3.)

4. Occasionally, available space can be utilized to amplify some particular aspect of the figure. These are called inserts and, properly proportioned, serve to add balance to the illustration (see Figure 36). Sometimes, this space is useful for presenting the legend or for recording portions of the data.

5. Finally, the author must make certain that the figure is clearly labeled, including the designation of units of measurement. They must coincide with tabular material, so if the data are a function of time, the use of minutes, seconds, and so forth must correspond in the illustration.

Art Work

When the author is unable to do his own finished art work, he must employ a professional or at least someone with skill and experience. In such a case, the work must be supervised carefully and detailed instructions provided concerning format, size of lines, lettering, and so on, since the artist

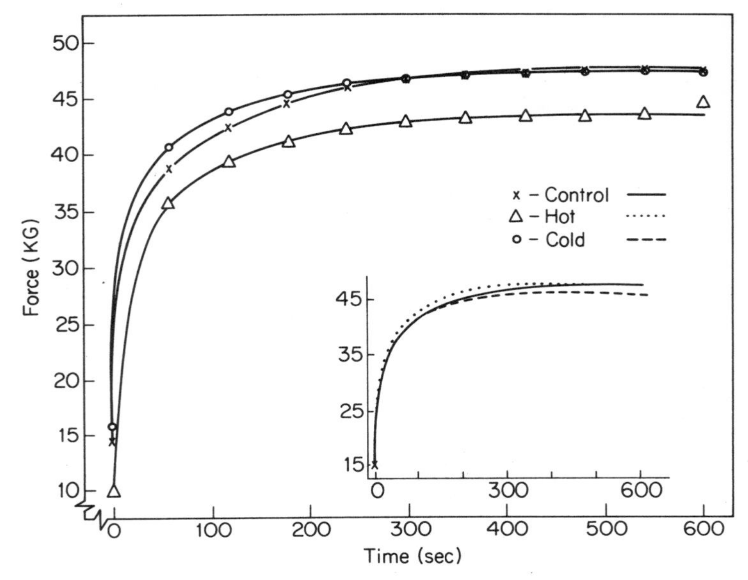

Figure 36. Graph with Insert (David H. Clarke and George E. Stelmach, "Muscular Fatigue and Recovery Curve Parameters at Various Temperatures," *Research Quarterly*, 37, No. 4 (December 1968), 468.)

will not understand the theoretical implications of the data. Therefore, a perfect copy must be provided. On the other hand, something can be said for the practice of the experimenter developing the ability to prepare his own graphs. Certainly, if he anticipates a career in which research plays a part, practice in drawing, inking, lettering, and preparing final copy of his work will not only save time and ensure accuracy but will cost less. In this respect, the use of lettering equipment, drafting tools, and the like can be mastered with practice, and the illustrative work will take on a professional appearance.

Most journals will accept a photograph or a multilith copy of the figure for reproduction, in which case the journal itself should be consulted for further specifications. At the same time, it may be desirable to have slides made for future use in lectures or in research presentations.

FOOTNOTES

The use of footnotes is inevitable in research writing. As a consequence, the investigator must acquire considerable facility in their formulation.

Purposes

The footnote may be used in the research report for a number of purposes, especially the following:

1. Source reference. Acknowledgements should be made to all sources utilized throughout the study, preferably by footnote reference. As in this book, footnote references are constantly made to articles, books, theses, and the like. Acknowledgements need to be made when the materials of others or when ideas uniquely developed by others are utilized. However, such references are not necessary when made to facts of general knowledge; the same situation prevails for statistical formulas commonly used, such as the mean, standard deviation, and coefficient of correlation. This purpose of footnotes is the most prevelant by far.

2. Amplify the discussion. On occasion, the writer may wish to add information relative to a point under consideration in the text but does not want to interrupt the thought under development; the footnote can be utilized for this purpose. Illustrations of this footnote use are: giving the distributor's name and address for an item of research equipment, listing the members of a committee, and adding an historical note. Footnotes of this type should be kept at a minimum, as usually things important enough to be said should be placed in the body of the report.

3. Cross reference. Where the author wishes to refer to materials appearing elsewhere in the report, a good way to do this is by footnote.

Footnote Procedures

Although institutions may differ in their requirements, the footnote usually appears at the bottom of the page where the citation is made. For reader convenience, this method is best since the reference is immediately available without seeking it elsewhere, such as at the end of the chapter. The following suggestions are made for the preparation of footnotes:

1. A raised Arabic numeral is placed in the text identifying the footnote. If the author's name is mentioned, the numeral can follow the name without spacing (e.g., Cureton[1]). If the author's name is not given in the text, the numeral may appear at the end of a paraphrase or quotation. The numeral may be placed after the key noun or major statement but not after a verb or a possessive pronoun.

2. Footnotes are separated from the text by a line $1\frac{1}{2}$ inches long from the left margin. This line should be one double space below the last line in the text; the footnote should start one double space below the line.

3. A footnote numeral precedes each footnote, corresponding with the one in the text. Again, it is a raised numeral (one-half typewriter space) with no spacing between it and the footnote.

4. Footnotes are single spaced in paragraph form; double spaced between footnotes.

5. Number footnotes consecutively from 1 throughout each chapter.

Footnote Form

A number of forms for footnotes have been developed. Manuals are available solely to present footnote and bibliographical procedures, as well as other matters involved in preparing research reports and other published materials, especially those by Campbell,[4] Turabian,[5] University of Chicago Press,[6] and U.S. Government Printing Office.[7] Some universities have form statements that graduate students must follow in preparing thesis reports. Journals and publishing houses also have form booklets; for example, the footnotes in this book follow the forms specified by its publisher, Prentice-Hall, Inc.[8]

Consequently, the graduate student in writing his thesis should adopt an acceptable form; once adopted, he should consistently follow it throughout the report. In making such a selection, he should first check any regulations established by the Graduate School at his institution. More often than not, such regulations are merely to use consistently any acceptable form. He may then consult the references given here, or he can adopt the practices given below.

Books. The order of items in a reference to a book is: author's name as it appears on the title page, with last name last; title of book and edition, if other than the first; city of publication; name of publisher; date of publication; chapter or page referred to. Illustrations of footnotes to books for various situations encountered follow.

1. Carl E. Willgoose, *Evaluation in Health Education and Physical Education* (New York: McGraw-Hill Book Company, 1961), p. 303.

2. Two or three authors: Anna S. Espenschade and Helen M. Eckert, *Motor Development* (Columbus, Ohio: Charles E. Merrill Books, Inc., 1967), pp. 181–86.

---

[4] W. G. Campbell, *Form and Style in Thesis Writing* (3rd ed.) (Boston: Houghton Mifflin Company, 1969).

[5] Kate L. Turabian, *A Manual for Writers of Term Papers, Theses, and Dissertations* (3rd ed.) (Chicago: University of Chicago Press, 1967).

[6] *A Manual of Style* (Chicago: University of Chicago Press, 1949).

[7] *U.S. Government Style Manual* (rev. ed.) (Washington, D.C.: U.S. Government Printing Office, 1959).

[8] *Author's Guide* (Englewood Cliffs, N.J.: Prentice-Hall, Inc., 1962).

3. More than three authors: Ruth Evans *et al.* [or, and others], *Physical Education for Elementary Schools* (New York: McGraw-Hill Book Company, 1958), Ch. 4.

4. No author given: *Author's Guide* (Englewood Cliffs, N.J.: Prentice-Hall, Inc., 1962), p. 76.

5. Edited book: Warren R. Johnson, ed., *Science and Medicine of Exercise and Sports* (New York: Harper & Row, Publishers, 1960), Ch. II.

6. Book editions: Henry E. Garrett, *Statistics in Psychology and Education* (6th ed.), (New York: David McKay Co., Inc., 1966), p. 461.

Articles, chapters, monographs series. The order of items in reference to an article in a journal is: author's name; title of article, title of journal; volume number; number of issue; date of publication; page number. Below are illustrations of footnotes not only to articles but to chapters in a book and to monographs in a series.

1. Article: Karl K. Klein, "The Deep Squat Exercise as Utilized in Weight Training for Athletics and Its Effects on the Ligaments of the Knee," *Journal of the Association for Physical and Mental Rehabilitation*, 15, No. 1 (January–February 1961), 6.

2. Chapter in Book: Celeste Ulrich, "Stress and Sports" in *Science and Medicine of Exercise and Sports*, Warren R. Johnson, ed. (New York: Harper & Row, Publishers, 1960), Ch. 13.

3. Monograph Series: Charles H. McCloy, *Appraising Physical Status: The Selection of Measurements*, University of Iowa Studies in Child Welfare, Vol. 12 (Iowa City: University of Iowa Press, 1936).

Unpublished materials. Footnotes for various kinds of unpublished materials are given below.

1. Thesis or Dissertation: Roger C. Wiley, "Single-Year and Longitudinal Comparisons of Maturity, Physique, Structural, Strength, and Motor Characteristics of Twelve-Year-Old Elementary School Athletes and Nonparticipants," Doctoral Dissertation, University of Oregon, 1963.[9]

2. Mimeographed: H. Harrison Clarke, "Contributions and Implications of the Medford, Oregon, Boys' Growth Study" (4th ed.), School of Health, Physical Education, and Recreation, University of Oregon, April 20, 1968. (Mimeographed)

---

[9] If the study has been microcarded, the word "*microcard*" may be placed before "Doctoral" in this reference; the same may be done for microfilmed publications if desired.

Abbreviations to Footnotes

A number of abbreviations are used in footnotes to reduce or eliminate the necessity for repeating the same reference when cited more than once. The full biographical reference should appear in the footnote when it is used for the first time in a chapter. Thereafter, one of the following may be substituted:

Ibid. is an abbreviation of *ibidem*, which means "in the same place." This abbreviation is used when succeeding consecutive citations made are to the same reference; no intervening references should occur. It may be used by itself if the reference is to the same page; if the reference is to a different page, the proper page must be added.

Op. cit. is an abbreviation of *opere citato*, which means "in the work cited." This abbreviation preceded by the author's last name, is used when other references intervene between different citations of the same reference. The citation should be to a different page, so the page number should be given.

Loc. cit. is an abbreviation for *loco citato*, which means "in the place cited." This abbreviation is used when citation is made to exact non-consecutive references.

In the following, these footnote abbreviations are illustrated in a variety of situations:

---

[1] C. H. McCloy and Norma D. Young, *Tests and Measurements in Physical Education* (3rd ed.) (New York: Appleton-Century-Crofts, 1954), p. 319.

[2] *Ibid.*

[3] *Ibid.*, pp. 218-25.

[4] Marie R. Liba, "Factor Analysis of Strength Variables," *Research Quarterly*, 38, No. 4 (December 1967), 649.

[5] McCloy and Young, *op. cit.*, p. 183.

[6] *Loc. cit.*

BIBLIOGRAPHY

As for footnotes, no universally accepted style for bibliographical entries exists. The style books mentioned above provide forms for this purpose. Minor differences exist between the forms for footnotes and bibliographical references. One such difference is that the surname is listed first. The entries are single spaced with double space between them. Each reference starts flush with the left-hand margin; subsequent lines are indented four spaces. If an author's name is repeated, an unbroken line 7 spaces in length is substituted.

Other differences will be seen in the following examples taken from those given above as footnotes:

Author's Guide. Englewood Cliffs, N.J.: Prentice-Hall, Inc., 1962.

Clarke, H. Harrison, "Contributions and Implications of the Medford, Oregon, Boys' Growth Study" (4th ed.), School of Health, Physical Education, and Recreation, University of Oregon, April 20, 1968. (Mimeographed)

Espenschade, Anna S., and Helen M. Eckert, *Motor Development*. Columbus, Ohio: Charles E. Merrill, Inc., 1967.

McCloy, Charles H., "Appraising Physical Status: The Selection of Measurements," *University of Iowa Studies in Child Welfare*, Vol. 12. Iowa City: University of Iowa Press, 1936.

Ulrich, Celeste, "Stress and Sports," in *Science and Medicine of Exercise and Sports*, Warren R. Johnson, ed. New York: Harper & Row, Publishers, 1960, Ch. 13.

Wiley, Roger C., "Single-Year and Longitudinal Comparisons of Maturity, Physique, Structural, Strength, and Motor Characteristics of Twelve-Year-Old Elementary School Athletes and Nonparticipants," microcard Doctoral Dissertation, University of Oregon, 1963.

THESIS REPRODUCTION

A number of choices are available to the student for duplicating his thesis. No longer is the time-honored practice of utilizing carbon copies the only acceptable procedure for supplying the number of copies required by the graduate schools. In fact, the least desirable form is the carbon copy, since some carbons may be indistinct, the quality of paper is usually of poorer and more fragile grade, and they are susceptible to smudging. The requirements established locally should be consulted to determine the number of copies needed as well as the acceptable methods of reproduction.

The most widely used alternate means of obtaining additional copies of the thesis are the multilith and Xerox processes. For these processes, the original copy of the manuscript is the only one that must be typed, as the remaining copies are made from it. Excellent reproductions on high quality paper will result, making all copies essentially originals. Usually, a number of extra copies may be obtained at a fraction of the original cost, which in turn may serve as working copies for future reference.

FOLLOW-UP WITH PUBLICATION

No discussion of research writing would be complete without suggesting that the investigator follow up his thesis or dissertation with a condensed paper submitted to a journal for publication. If the research is sound in the first place, then it is incumbent that the author make it more widely available so that others may have the benfit of the results. Such is the case whether or not it is a master's or a doctoral study; the decision must be made on scientific worth more than anything else. If the reader shares the belief that the primary means of supporting the body of knowledge of his discipline is through published research, then he must realize that the effort required to take this additional step is a vital one. Assuredly, the results of the thesis in his institutional library may even be microcarded or microfilmed and may be abstracted, but these are not considered the same as a publication. The impact of the research is much greater when the study has met the editorial standards of a scholarly journal

The writer should keep in mind that research journals do not publish theses, only articles; therefore, the thesis must be rewritten in article form. Ordinarily, this means extensive condensation, and in some cases whole portions of the original thesis may be omitted. The decision depends upon the nature of the study itself and the data that have been obtained.

The choice of the journal for submitting the manuscript depends on the type of study conducted. In the fields of health, physical education, and recreation, the *Research Quarterly* of the American Association for Health, Physical Education and Recreation is the most available one for most researchers, although a number of other journals might be equally acceptable. Perhaps it is a question of which audience would profit most from the data collected. A glance at the list of periodicals in Chapter 3 will disclose the many sources for publication that exist in physical education, health, recreation, and related disciplines. Other things being equal, such as publication lag, cost of publication, and so on, the *Research Quarterly* is presently the only research organ of the field that is broadly disseminated and widely read by the membership; as such, therefore, it is the logical preferred repository for the research article. When the best scientists within the field send their better research papers to this journal, the result will be a continuing upgrading of quality.

Format. The format to be employed for publication will depend upon the particular journal selected, as mentioned earlier. Some journals, and this is also true for the *Research Quarterly*, do not publish their "Guide to Contributors" in every issue but do so once in each volume (thus, once each year). The author should consult the latest statement as his format guide in order to avoid the possibility of rewriting to conform to a new format if one should have been adopted. In all instances, the directions should be followed precisely in order to facilitate reviewing and processing the manuscript.

In addition to the question of publication is the possibility of presenting the study at some scholarly meeting, perhaps at a state, district, or national

Research Section of the American Association for Health, Physical Education and Recreation. The experience gained from such a presentation is quite valuable and provides for further opportunity to condense a study. Ten to 15 minutes is typically allotted for each paper, so the author is forced to make some rather critical decisions as to the content to be included.

Authorship. A sensitive question in publishing research articles may involve authorship. In the traditional situation, an individual publishes the results of his investigation by himself; today, however, this practice has changed considerably. The tendency today is for multiple authorships to occur far more frequently than before, largely due to the natural result of group research activity. Therefore, group projects have sprung into existence, fostered by relatively easy access to funds. In such cases, it is highly legitimate for colleagues to work together on large problems of common interest.

The question may be raised concerning what the graduate student should do with the article that he wishes to publish resulting from his thesis or dissertation. He will note that the practice varies from one situation to another. The advice that he received on his thesis, sometimes amounting to considerable help from the stage of problem formulation to final writing, may result in his desire to co-author the article with his advisor. This is perfectly legitimate, as is the fact that he may be the sole author; in this latter instance, he should acknowledge both the institution and the advisor by means of a footnote reference.

An exception to the above rule is related to the problem created by funded research projects. In this situation, the professor inaugurates and actively directs a large research endeavor supported from a substantial grant received over a period of several years. The plan calls for a number of technicians to implement the gathering of data; typically, graduate students are involved and develop their graduate studies from the project. Such a situation is prevalent in many departments on campus and is a modern day departure from the typical procedure whereby each student on his own initiative goes through the formal steps of problem formulation, seeking a topic in a new area, constructing his equipment, testing his subjects, and so forth. The research experience gained from association with a large undertaking is sufficiently valid to receive widespread support. In such a situation, the project director must protect his grant; and, since the overall procedures and assembly were obtained from project funds, he will quite likely retain partial publication rights. Research papers that are an outgrowth of this project will, in all likelihood, be co-authored by the faculty member involved.

INDEX